KU-316-328

AA
EXPLORING
THE COMPLETE TOURING COMPANION
BRITAIN

(Previous page: Shoulder of Mutton Hill, Hampshire

First published 2000
Produced by AA Publishing

Reprinted 2003

Published by AA Publishing (a trading name of Automobile Association Developments Limited, whose registered office is Millstream, Maidenhead, Windsor, SL4 5GD; registered number 1878835)

Visit the AA Publishing website at www.theAA.com

ISBN 0 7495 2568 1 (Hardback)
ISBN 0 7495 3975 5 (Softback)

A01826

A CIP catalogue record for this book is available from the British Library.

The contents of this book are believed correct at the time of printing. Nevertheless, the publishers cannot be held responsible for any errors or omissions or for changes in the details given in this book or for the consequences of any reliance on the information provided by the same. This does not affect your statutory rights. We have tried to ensure accuracy in this book, but things do change and we would be grateful if readers would advise us of any inaccuracies they may encounter.

We have taken all reasonable steps to ensure that these outdoor activities are safe and achievable by persons with a realistic level of fitness. However, all outdoor activities involve a degree of risk and the publishers accept no responsibility for any injuries caused to readers whilst following these activities.

Please note that the illustrations in the book are of imaginary landscapes and do not depict actual scenes in Britain.

Colour separation by Chromagraphics, Singapore
Printed and bound by Oriental Press

CONTENTS

CENTRAL ENGLAND

NORTH ENGLAND

SCOTLAND

WALES

HOW TO USE THIS BOOK

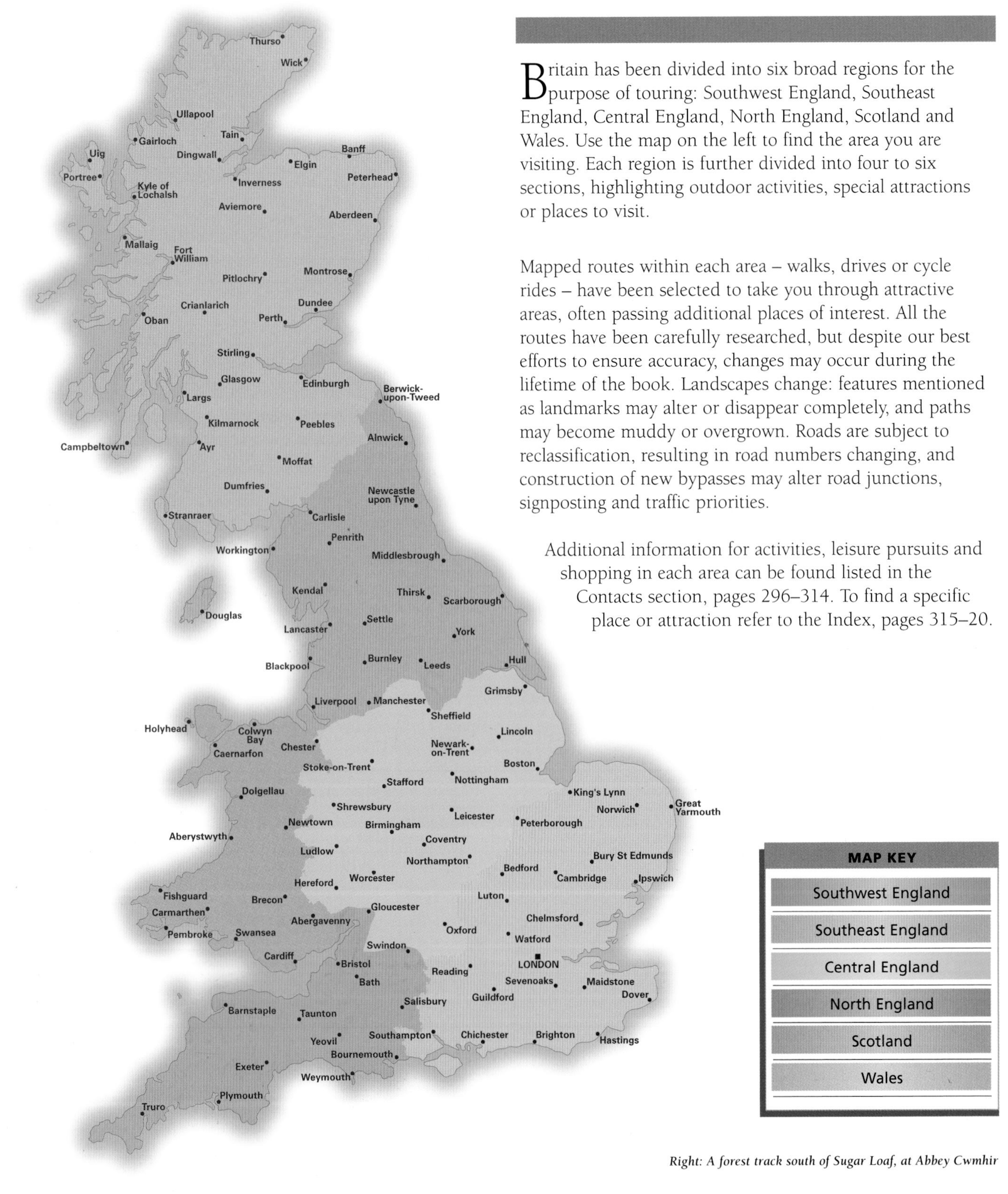

Britain has been divided into six broad regions for the purpose of touring: Southwest England, Southeast England, Central England, North England, Scotland and Wales. Use the map on the left to find the area you are visiting. Each region is further divided into four to six sections, highlighting outdoor activities, special attractions or places to visit.

Mapped routes within each area – walks, drives or cycle rides – have been selected to take you through attractive areas, often passing additional places of interest. All the routes have been carefully researched, but despite our best efforts to ensure accuracy, changes may occur during the lifetime of the book. Landscapes change: features mentioned as landmarks may alter or disappear completely, and paths may become muddy or overgrown. Roads are subject to reclassification, resulting in road numbers changing, and construction of new bypasses may alter road junctions, signposting and traffic priorities.

Additional information for activities, leisure pursuits and shopping in each area can be found listed in the Contacts section, pages 296–314. To find a specific place or attraction refer to the Index, pages 315–20.

Right: A forest track south of Sugar Loaf, at Abbey Cwmhir

INTRODUCTION

Choosing is the hard part. There's such a lot of Britain to see, and there are so many ways to see it. How about floating silently over the soft chalky downs of southern England in a hot-air balloon? Or chugging across the Yorkshire Moors in a handsome old steam locomotive? Maybe you fancy gliding along the serene canal waters that crisscross the country's heartlands? If all that sounds a bit too relaxed, you could always opt for a stiff hike in the Preseli Hills, or climb Ben Nevis, sail around the Isle of Wight, or cycle through the streets of Cambridge.

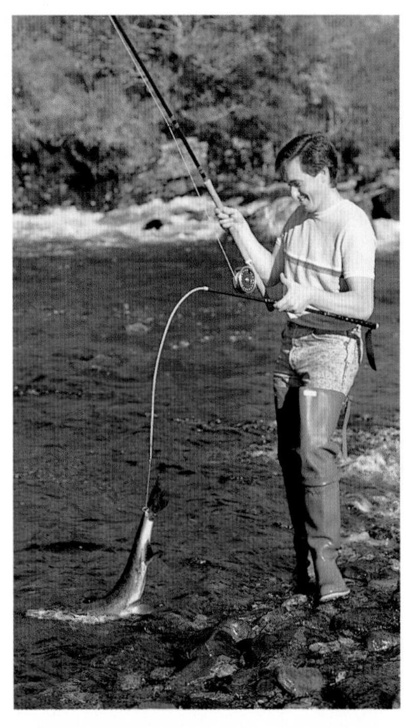

Britain's charms are no secret, and the activity holiday has a long tradition – even if it didn't always go under that name. The Romantics knew all about it: Wordsworth and Coleridge trudged many a mile to appreciate the glories of the Lake District. The Victorians flocked to the coastal resorts and inland spas on their new railways, to enjoy bracing salt-water dips, or health-giving mineral-water sips. In the 1930s the back-packing hiker and sturdy-legged cyclist were a familiar sight along the country lanes. Today, there are enough leisure options and inventive sports and activities, for all ages and abilities, to tempt even the most well-rooted couch potato – and they're all on the doorstep.

When you've decided what to do, there's the question of where to do it. Accessibility is rarely a problem: Britain is a small country, but it's packed with all manner of sights and scenery. Stick a pin on the map at random, and you're sure to find an area full of surprises. Chances are, within shouting distance there'll be swathes of beautiful, open countryside or magical forests and lakes; there'll be hidden corners of history, tranquil villages and ancient market towns; and there'll be magnificent stately homes, industrial monuments, gardens, watersports, outdoor museums, theme parks – not to mention the cities, with their galleries, theatres, shops and restaurants.

Every part of the country has its own special appeal. The West Country has lush, green hills, smugglers' bays and rocky sea-cliffs. In the southeast, London's breathless pace and world-famous landmarks are the main focus – but even

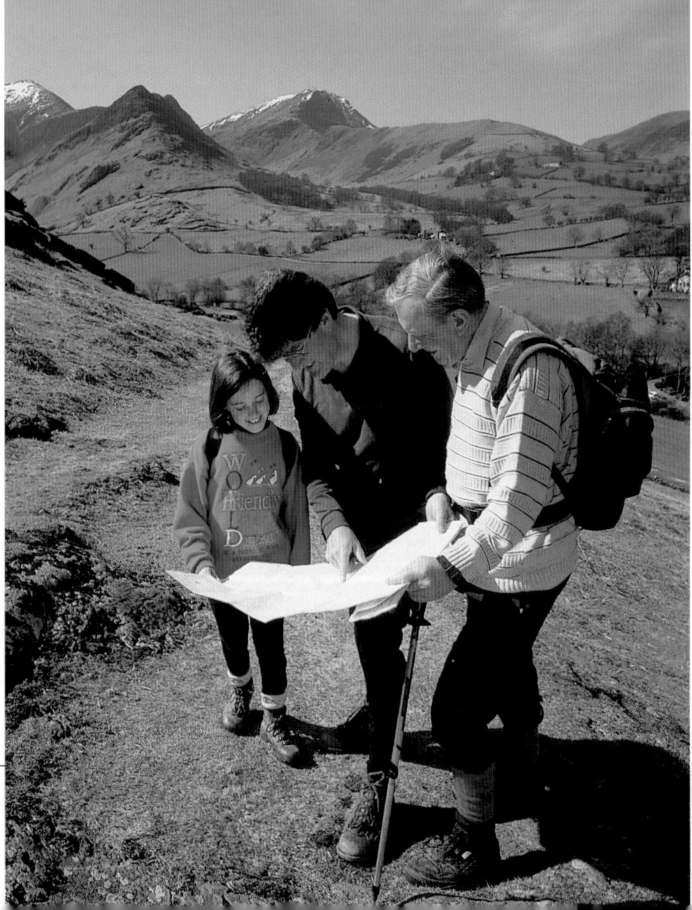

the capital's broad commuter belt has its own rural havens in the Sussex Downs and the wonderful orchards of the Weald of Kent. For a unique and evocative experience, roam the low marshlands and enjoy the wide skies and abundant bird life of the East Anglian shores. The great industrial cities of the Midlands and the North are hotbeds of culture and nightlife; and then there are the plunging valleys and isolated farms of Yorkshire; Northumberland's empty, majestic coast; the glowering Derbyshire peaks. Over the border in Scotland there's a whole new range of landscapes: Edinburgh's dignified terraces and medieval Old Town; the high-octane energy, monumental architecture and stunning art collections of Glasgow; the breathtaking spaces of the heather-covered Highlands; the romantic, lochside castles, and the remote, mystical peace of the offshore islands. To the west there's Wales, where you can travel in one day from the sheer waterfalls and craggy mountains of the north, through deserted hill country or along the lovely, sweeping coasts of Ceredigion and Pembrokeshire down to the busy, urban south.

Where do you start? That's where this book can help: by directing you to the best of Britain, the familiar and the unexpected; by suggesting some exciting, enlightening and even eccentric ways of making the most of it. This guide will show you not just where to go, but what you can do when you get there. For anyone who likes to get out and about, there are routes and tips ranging from scenic drives and gentle strolls to full-scale hikes and adventure sports. Whether you want to mess about on a barge, do a spot of fishing, take to the range on horseback or just head for the best shops for a little retail therapy, this guide aims to help you on your way.

There's so much out there, waiting to be explored. The choice is yours. What are you waiting for?

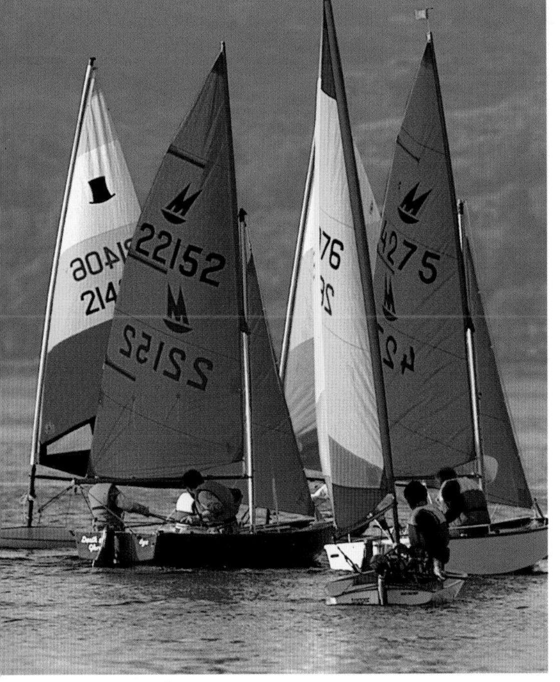

SOUTHWEST ENGLAND

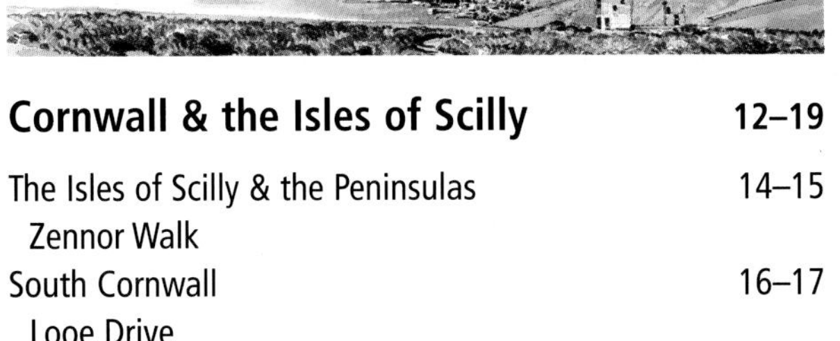

St Michael's Mount, Cornwall

CORNWALL & THE ISLES OF SCILLY

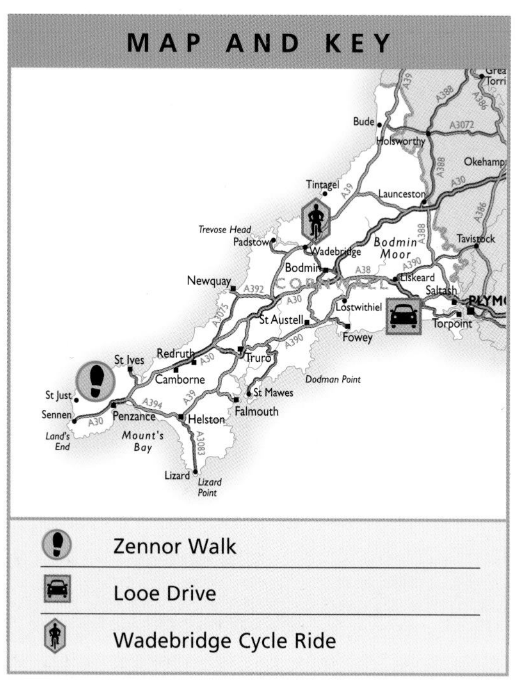

Cornwall's narrow peninsula leads westwards from the River Tamar to the rocky claw of Land's End and the Atlantic. Thirty miles (48km) across the sea to the southwest lie the fabled Isles of Scilly. A county of dramatic contrasts: the Isles of Scilly, Land's End and the North Cornish coast belong to the bracing Atlantic, while the Lizard Peninsula and South Cornwall have gentler, more intimate landscapes. The granite spine of central Cornwall runs from the old tin-mining district of Land's End to the lonely heights of Bodmin Moor, while on either side lies a secluded countryside dotted with tiny villages and a host of holiday attractions.

Helford
The tree-shrouded creeks of the Helford River and the narrow secluded lanes that surround it create a peaceful landscape that is a delightful contrast to the more bracing and rugged Cornish coast. Helford is where the Cornish spring comes early and where summer lingers.

BODMIN MOOR

Bodmin Moor is the granite heart of Cornwall where ancient rocks that have been sculpted by ice, wind and rain form jagged ridges and strange dramatic shapes. The moor is peppered with prehistoric stone circles and burial chambers and its great open spaces offer easy opportunities for walking and horse-riding.

PADSTOW

The historic fishing village of Padstow lies at the heart of the Camel Estuary. To either side of the estuary lie spectacular sections of the Cornish coast – Stepper Point on the south and Pentire Point and Rumps Point on the north.

ST MICHAEL'S MOUNT

Romantic St Michael's Mount has been a monastery and a prison in its day. This dramatic offshore island with its rugged cliffs, terraced rock gardens and traditional harbour is crowned by a fairy-tale castle and is reached across a granite causeway at low tide, or by ferry boat at high tide.

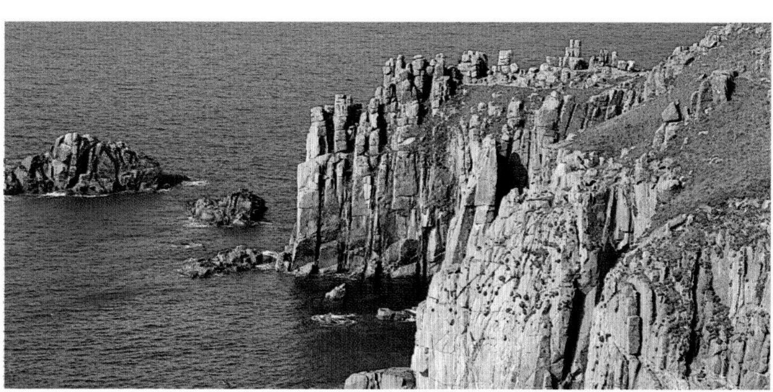

Land's End

The most westerly point in England will always attract visitors because of its spectacular granite cliffs towering above the restless Atlantic. There are numerous indoor attractions, but the natural beauty of Land's End is the main draw. Head off along the coast path, for a more exclusive 'Land's End Experience'.

The Eden Project

South Cornwall's Eden Project is a unique 'Global Garden' that re-creates the world's main plant habitats within huge dome-shaped conservatories called biomes. Here you will find thousands of the world's exotic species flourishing in their ideal environments that have been created on a spectacular scale.

Tresco, Isles of Scilly

Tresco is the most luxuriant of the Isles of Scilly. It has all the essential Scillonian attractions of golden sand and crystal clear sea, but is most famous for its beautiful Abbey Gardens, where exotic flowering plants grace the ruins of an ancient priory and where there is a unique museum of ships' figure-heads.

THE ISLES OF SCILLY & THE PENINSULAS

The Isles of Scilly have always been dependent on boats, and a fleet of powerful launches runs regularly between the five inhabited islands of St Mary's, St Agnes, St Martin's, Bryher and Tresco. No journey is more than a mile or two and by using the ferry system you get the best out of a stay on the islands. Scillonian boatmen will smooth your passage with good humour and entertaining chat. Take the chance of an evening trip on these same launches for bird-watching and seal-spotting round the dramatic Bishop Rock Lighthouse. You can even explore Scilly in a traditional sailing ship or enjoy some of the finest scuba-diving in Britain. And there's enough peaceful countryside on even the smallest island for the confirmed landlubber to enjoy walking, horse-riding or cycling.

The 'almost island' of the Land's End Peninsula seems like a bigger version of one of the Isles of Scilly. This is a world to quicken the heart – and the pace – with spectacular promontories such as Gurnard's Head and Logan Rock, and its moorland hills where inviting lanes and paths lead you off to some of the most inspiring and mysterious landscapes in Britain. It is a land of prehistoric stone circles and burial chambers matched by the gaunt ruins of Cornwall's famous tin-mining past. On the north coast is the resort of St Ives, the archetypal Cornish fishing village, where fishing still survives amidst conspicuous tourism. On the sunny south coast is

An artist captures Mousehole's picturesque harbour on canvas

PAINTERS' PALETTE

West Cornwall has always been famous for its artists and galleries.

Tate Gallery, St Ives – to see the work of leading 'modernist' painters, such as Peter Lanyon, Patrick Heron and Sir Terry Frost.

Penlee House Gallery – for the more traditional work of earlier artists in Penzance.

Newlyn Gallery – for new and exciting experimental art.

Painting schools – you can develop your own talents at one of several in the colourful towns of St Ives and Penzance, or just grab your sketchbook and head for old fishing villages such as Mousehole. Alternatively, stroll along the coastal footpath where you can create your own impressions.

The Isles of Scilly, off the Cornish coast, are blessed with a mild climate and golden sands. They are also an ideal place to take to the seas in search of seals and dolphins

Zennor Walk

WALK

Zennor & the Spectacular Coast Path

START/FINISH: Zennor, on B3306 between St Ives and St Just
DISTANCE: 5.5 miles (9km)
ASCENT: 800ft (244m); gradients are very steep in places on the coast path
TERRAIN: fields, farm tracks, coast path
PARKING: free car-park by the Old Chapel

Storm-tumbled cliffs, haunted by wheeling gulls, guard Penwith's wild and beautiful Atlantic shoreline. From the sleepy village of Zennor, this exhilarating, often windswept, ramble explores ancient fields dotted with granite farmsteads before traversing the Cornish coast's front line.

1 Turn left out of the car-park and head up the hill. Immediately after the 14th-century church, famous for a mermaid's carving on one of the pews and for an associated legend, turn right by some railings and take the footpath over fields. Cross numerous stiles to reach Tremedda Farm, one of several ancient, granite homesteads that hide in valleys or shelter behind gnarled, hardy hawthorns across this extensive patchwork of Stone-Age fields.

2 Cross the farm track via two stiles, continue across open fields to the hamlet of Tregerthen and cross another track. Follow the narrow, muddy track through thickets until it opens out to fields which lead to Wicca Farm.

3 Take the stile between the farmhouse and the barn, going straight through the farmyard and continuing along the road. Just after Boscubben Farm, turn left down the track to Treveal. At the hamlet take the right-hand fork at the footpath sign, where the track turns back on itself and leads down to a cattle grid.

4 Take the path signed River Cove down the wooded valley to the stream, where the path starts to rise and then descends to the coast. Veer left and follow the coast path, which eventually rises steeply to some prominent rocks at the summit of Mussel Point.

FLORAL BONANZA

The Lizard area is famous for its unique wild flowers, many of which are believed to have originated from southern Europe, when the Lizard area was joined to France by a marshy land bridge thousands of years ago.

Keen botanists will be in their element during May and June on places such as **Vellan Head** and **Rill Point** near Kynance Cove.

For lovers of garden plants there are outstanding subtropical gardens at **Glendurgan** and **Trebah** on the Helford River.

The cobbled backstreets of St Ives. The town is a popular haunt for surfers, sailors and artists

5 Continue round the point, pause to savour the breathtaking view west, then follow the path across the open, grassy hillside. After a prominent boulder on the right the path drops steeply into a small valley. Cross the stream on stepping stones to a stile.

6 Cross the stile and turn right, following the coast and descending slightly before ascending to a small point. The path then zigzags steeply down, almost to sea level. Continue along a flatter section for 875yds (800m), then bear inland and uphill steeply, over one stream and on to another. Look out for sea birds feeding at low tide on Gala Rocks, seals basking in Porthzennor Cove and, out to sea, squadrons of gannets diving for fish.

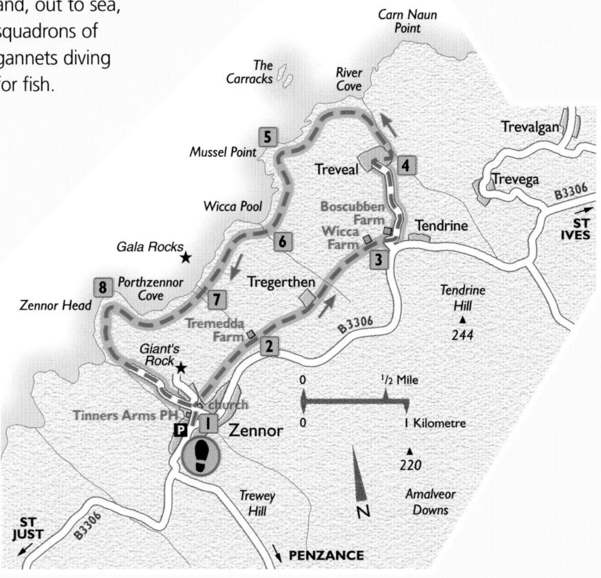

7 Continue at the same level to a waymark where the path drops to the right. Descend steeply and then begin a long ascent to a cluster of boulders at the summit of the point. Continue along a broad, grassy track to Zennor Head.

8 Head back inland, rising slightly, to a stile. Follow the narrow path for 50yds (46m), to where it meets the road above a white house. Take the road back to Zennor and the car-park.

Penzance at the heart of Mount's Bay, with its island castle of St Michael's Mount. The Land's End Peninsula is where Victorian painters were first captivated by the clear Atlantic light and by colourful fishing villages such as Mousehole and Newlyn. Artists have been putting Cornwall on canvas ever since. The peninsula has the ideal conditions for energetic adventure sports – sailing, surfing, body-boarding and rock-climbing – and for the gentler pastimes of walking, bird-watching, painting and sea-fishing.

The Lizard Peninsula is less well known than Land's End, yet its corrugated coastline of black cliffs and coves can seem even more dramatic at times. The Lizard's south coast is at its most beautiful at Kynance Cove and Mullion, where offshore islands of multicoloured serpentine rock echo to the calls of sea birds. Inland from the coast is the Lizard's main settlement, Helston, a pleasant market town famous for its Flora Day festival. Lizard Point is the most southerly point in England and the peninsula's mild climate makes it a paradise for botanists and bird-watchers. From here the coast turns sharply north, and then winds past the fishing villages of Cadgwith and Coverack to reach Helford River. This is where Cornwall becomes leafy and green and there are superb opportunities for walking, cycling and sailing. Beyond Helford lies the bustling port of Falmouth and the broad waters of the Fal Estuary.

ISLAND CIRCUIT

The 9-mile (14.5km) coastal footpath that encircles the main Scillonian island of **St Mary's** makes for an undemanding but delightful day walk. Use the OS Outdoor Leisure 25 map, although you can't miss the path. It stays close to the sea all the way and if you don't want to walk the whole distance, then you can always take a short cut along quiet inland lanes back to your starting point. Going clockwise from the island 'capital' of **Hugh Town** is the best way round.

GIG-RACING

Cornwall is the home of gig 'boat' racing. Gigs are long elegant vessels rowed by a crew of eight. They originated as pilot vessels in the Isles of Scilly, and elsewhere, where competing gigs raced each other to offer their services to passing cargo ships. From this old seagoing custom modern gig-racing developed.

Today, numerous Cornish villages have male and female gig teams and there are countless race meetings all round the coast. The islands are among the best places to watch gig-racing, especially from accompanying launches. You'll be expected to shout yourself hoarse supporting one or other crew!

FIVE FAVOURITE SURFING BEACHES

Widemouth Bay, Bude
A magnificent, mile-long (1.5km) beach on the exposed North Cornish coast.

Polzeath Great surfing at a beautiful spot near the mouth of the Camel River, with views out over the estuary and to Stepper Point beyond.

Fistral Beach, Newquay Surf City Host to regular events, including World Championships and only five minutes from the surfing shops and nightclubs of Newquay.

Perran Beach Two miles (3km) of beach with great waves and all the usual amenities at Perranporth.

Sennen Cove The first landfall for Atlantic swells. A magnificent beach with nearby cafés and a pub.

SOUTH CORNWALL

Sunny South Cornwall invites relaxation, but there's enough adventure and challenge here to tempt even the most devoted beach addict into action. The secluded and beautiful Roseland Peninsula at the mouth of Falmouth Bay is where it all starts. From here to the distant Rame Peninsula on the shores of Plymouth Sound lies one of the loveliest coastlines in Britain, a long meandering water margin that traces its intricate way in and out of tiny coves, past quiet beaches and fascinating towns and villages such as Fowey, Mevagissey and Looe. It is a coastline that is easily accessible, yet there is a rare sense of exclusiveness, because the outside world seems firmly shut out by a tangle of coastal hills, secluded valleys and shady woods.

You need curiosity and determination to explore this secretive coast – and stout walking boots. The coast path can be linked to other paths and tracks that ramble inland through deep woodland and quiet valleys and then somehow take you unexpectedly back to the coast. Fishing trips and cruises from the romantic harbours of Fowey, Polruan and Looe give views of the coastline from the sea. Away from the coast, the countryside of South Cornwall continues this

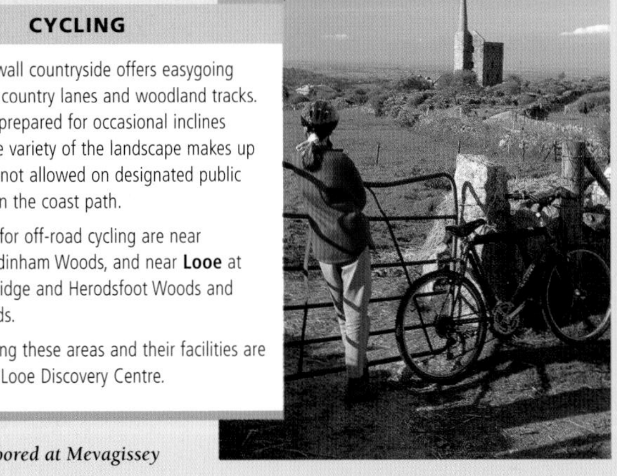

CYCLING

The South Cornwall countryside offers easygoing cycling on quiet country lanes and woodland tracks. You need to be prepared for occasional inclines however, but the variety of the landscape makes up for it. Cycling is not allowed on designated public footpaths and on the coast path.

The best places for off-road cycling are near **Bodmin** at Cardinham Woods, and near **Looe** at Duloe, Churchbridge and Herodsfoot Woods and Kilminorth Woods.

Leaflets describing these areas and their facilities are available at the Looe Discovery Centre.

Fishing boats moored at Mevagissey

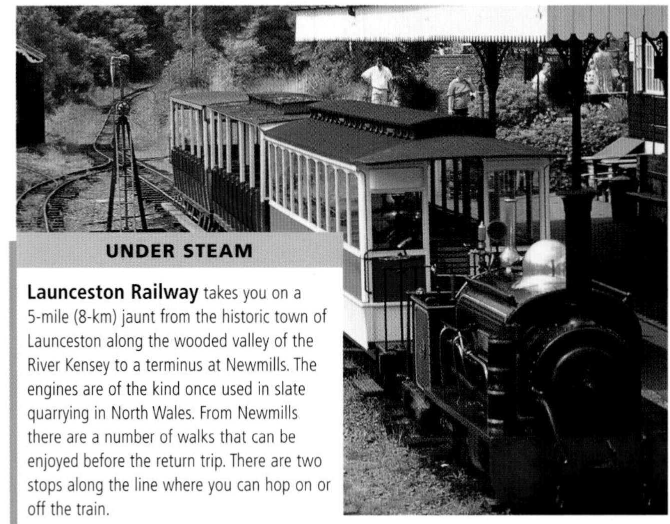

UNDER STEAM

Launceston Railway takes you on a 5-mile (8-km) jaunt from the historic town of Launceston along the wooded valley of the River Kensey to a terminus at Newmills. The engines are of the kind once used in slate quarrying in North Wales. From Newmills there are a number of walks that can be enjoyed before the return trip. There are two stops along the line where you can hop on or off the train.

Looe Drive

DRIVE

Riverside Villages & Coastal Resorts

START/FINISH: Looe. Located on A387 south of Liskeard

DISTANCE: 57 miles (91.5km)

Riverside villages offer unusual attractions in the form of displays of music, art and the American railroad. On the coast, cliffs shelter holiday resorts which are still busy fishing villages.

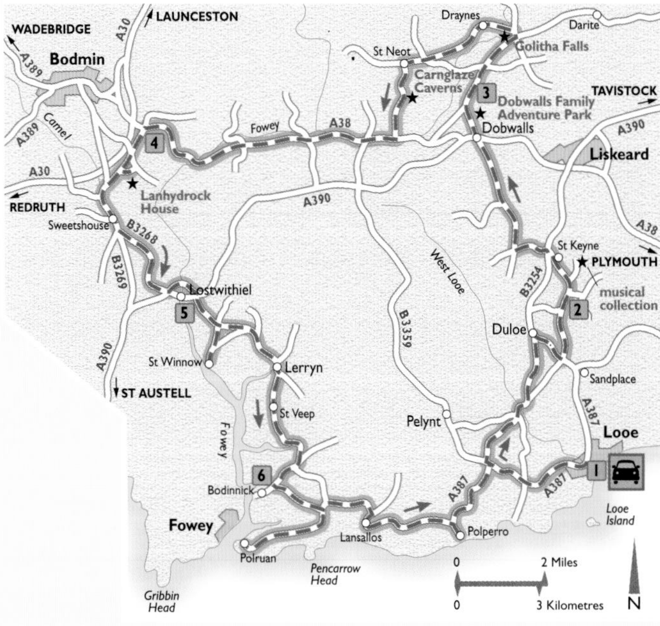

1 Take the A387 Polperro road, then turn right on the B3359 and right again to Duloe. The Looe River divides the seaside resort and fishing port into two towns, West Looe and East Looe. Summer holiday-makers throng the quays to watch the departure and return of the brightly coloured fishing boats, and visitors can wander the narrow, traffic-free streets that characterise the old part of East Looe. Turn right on to the

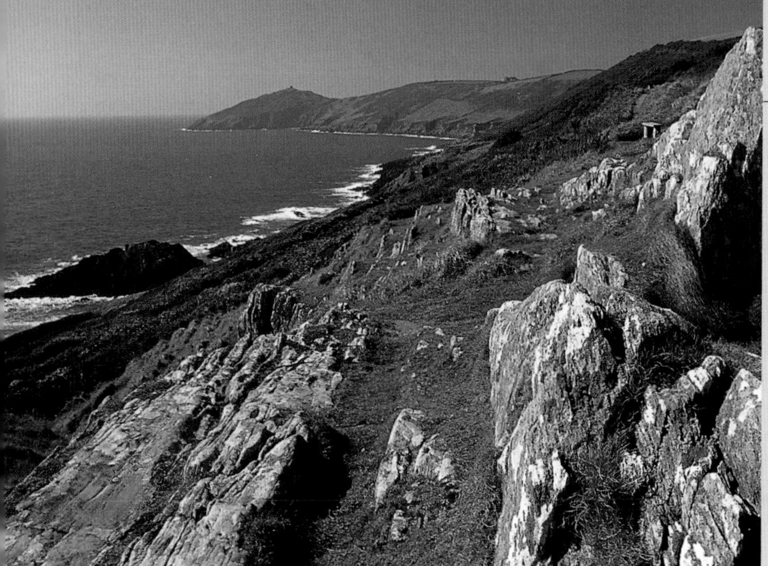

Rame Head peninsula seen in the distance from the dramatic coastline at Penlee Point

SEE CONTACTS SECTION FOR ADDITIONAL INFORMATION

B3254 to Sandplace. Turn left, then fork left over the railway. The road northwards from Sandplace to St Keyne runs alongside the single-track Liskeard to Looe railway line, perhaps the prettiest branch line in the West Country.

2 Follow the St Keyne signs, and turn left by the phone box. Then turn right at the T-junction. Near St Keyne station is the Paul Corin Musical Collection, one of Europe's finest collections of automatic musical instruments. Exhibits include fairground organs, player-pianos and a mighty Wurlitzer organ. North of the A38 near Dobwalls is the Dobwalls Family Adventure Park where miniature replicas of American locomotives draw passengers on two railroads through extensive parkland.

3 Turn right along Darite road, then left and follow signs to Draynes. Continue ahead to St Neot. Look out for the signed footpath to Golitha Falls (off the road to Draynes). From the car-park the trail runs through beech woods beside the Fowey river to the falls. St Neot is a large and attractive village noted for the stained glass in its 15th-century church. Take the road through Carnglaze, and turn right on to the A38. The majestic, 50-ft (15-m) high domed roofs of the slate caverns at Carnglaze bear testimony to the skill of the quarrymen who fashioned them. The most spectacular sight is an underground lake (guided tours).

4 Turn left to Lanhydrock House (NT). Only the gatehouse of 1651 and the north wing, with its 116-ft (35-m) long gallery survive of the original 17th-century building, which was largely destroyed by fire in 1881. The rest gives a vivid picture of life in Victorian times, complete with huge kitchen, dairy, bakehouse and servants' quarters. Turn left and left again on the B3268 to Lostwithiel.

5 Cross the bridge and follow signs to St Winnow. Return to the junction and turn right to Lerryn. The Church of St Winnow is romantically situated in a tiny peaceful village on the banks of the River Fowey. Note the old carved wagon roofs, several 16th-century carved bench ends and the 15th-century font. Turn right on Bodinnick road.

6 Turn left on the Polperro road. For Polruan turn right. Return and turn right to Lansallos, Polperro and Looe. Unspoilt Polruan has a regular passenger ferry service to Fowey on the other side of the river. One of the most attractive small beaches on this stretch of coast is reached by a 15-minute walk starting by the gate of Lansallos church. Strung along a narrow combe, Polperro's narrow streets lead down to a tiny harbour where the water laps against the walls of colour-washed cottages.

intimate theme. In the east of the region, tree-fringed creeks probe deep inland from Falmouth Estuary as far as the county capital of Truro, a busy shopping centre with an impressive late-Victorian cathedral and some of the finest preserved Georgian streets. East of Truro, a peaceful landscape of farms and tree-filled valleys rises gently from the coast to the strange 'Clay Country' of St Austell, a 'moonscape' of mini-alps and escarpments formed out of the waste of the china clay industry. Here you will find the breathtaking Eden Project, Cornwall's 'Global Garden'.

North from St Austell is the eastern section of Bodmin Moor, a treasure-house of prehistoric monuments, including stone circles and burial chambers, all matched by the remains of tin and copper mining and stone quarrying. At moorland reservoirs such as the nearby Sibleyback, there are opportunities for sailing, canoeing and windsurfing. For keen anglers, Sibleyback and Colliford Reservoirs have excellent trout fisheries, while the East and West Looe rivers can be fished for salmon. East of the moor the historic town of Launceston guards South Cornwall's border with Devon at another great fishing river, the Tamar.

For lovers of historic buildings, South Cornwall is a paradise. Antony House, near Torpoint on the banks of the Lynher River, is one of the finest Georgian houses in the West Country. Near Calstock, on the Tamar, is the well-preserved Elizabethan manor house of Cotehele, while Bodmin's magnificent Lanhydrock is a building that was re-created in its Tudor style after a destructive fire in the late 19th century. At Launceston and Restormel near Lostwithiel are dramatic Norman castles.

TOP FIVE HOUSES AND GARDENS

Trelissick (NT)

On the Fal estuary near Truro. The Palladian mansion is not open, but the park and gardens are the real attraction.

Lanhydrock (NT)

Near Bodmin. A 19th-century Tudor-style house set within rolling parkland and with magnolia and camellia gardens (right).

Mount Edgecumbe

On the south side of Plymouth Sound near Cawsand. A 16th-century mansion rebuilt in the late 20th century.

Antony House (NT)

Near Torpoint. Magnificent early 18th-century house in landscaped grounds.

Cotehele (NT)

Near Calstock. Well-preserved Tudor country house on the banks of the River Tamar.

LITERARY LANDSCAPE

Thomas Hardy

Follow in Hardy's footsteps from Boscastle along the wooded Valency Valley to the lovely, secluded church of St Juliot, where the writer met his first wife Emma.

John Betjeman

The Padstow area is rich with memories of Sir John Betjeman, who had a family home at Trebetherick on the Camel Estuary opposite Padstow, and who is buried in nearby St Enodoc's churchyard.

Winston Graham

The old tin-mining area around Perranporth and St Agnes was where Winston Graham lived and conceived his popular novels about life and tin mining in late 19th-century Cornwall. Winston Graham was the creator of the *Poldark Saga*.

NORTH CORNWALL

North Cornwall's Atlantic coast seems bigger and wilder than anywhere else in the county. Dark shattered cliffs rise for hundreds of feet from rocky shores at Bedruthan and Boscastle and at the great headlands of Pentire, Trevose and Tintagel. Yet the wildness of the north coast is tempered by the sandy beaches of Newquay and Perranporth and by the cheerful seaside towns of Bude, Padstow and St Agnes. Away from the coast, quiet lanes wander through a mellow countryside between villages and hamlets that seem untouched by time. Even farther inland lies the western edge of Bodmin Moor, a lonely wilderness where wind-sculpted slabs and pinnacles of silvery granite are scattered across the hills of Rough Tor and its neighbour Brown Willy. The latter may only be 1,377ft (420m) high, but it's the nearest thing Cornwall has to a 'mountain'. From rugged coast to granite ridges, you get the best of all worlds in North Cornwall.

A row of stone cottages at St Agnes

In the southwest of the region is St Agnes, a friendly unassuming coastal village that is surrounded by some of Cornwall's most intriguing tin-mining remains. Inland lie the old mining towns of Camborne and Redruth, hardly picturesque, but rich in industrial archaeology and home to the Cornwall School of Mines where there is an excellent geological museum. A few miles north of St Agnes, at Perranporth, is the first of North Cornwall's vast beaches, where acres of wave-rippled sand are exposed at low tide. Neighbouring Newquay is Britain's premier surfing venue where the magic mix of Atlantic swell and golden sand draws surfers from all over the world for top surfing competitions. Farther north, at the heart of the Camel

Golden beaches and the Atlantic swell have made Newquay Britain's surfing mecca

The wild and rocky shore at Bedruthan Steps, battered by wind and sea for centuries

Wadebridge Cycle Ride

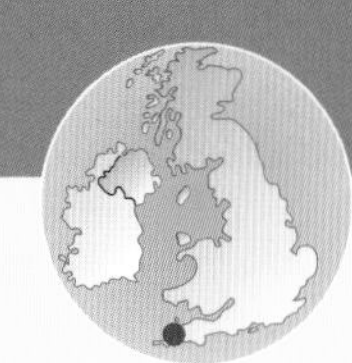

CYCLE RIDE

Wadebridge & the Camel Trail

START/FINISH: Wadebridge. A small town on the A39 between Bude and Truro, 7 miles (11.5km) northwest of Bodmin

DISTANCE: 24 miles (38.5km), with 11 miles (17.5km) off-road

TERRAIN/GRADIENT: gently undulating country lanes; level off-road section along the Camel Trail

PARKING: car-park on the link road between West Hill and Eddystone Road

Explore the undulating countryside and unspoiled villages between the north Cornish coast and the imposing flanks of Bodmin Moor. The route includes a delightfully level cycle along an 11-mile (17.5-km) section of the picturesque old Bodmin to Wadebridge railway – the Camel Trail. (The ride can be extended along the Camel Trail to Padstow.)

1 Turn right out of the car-park, then right again at the roundabout into Eddystone Road. On reaching the crossroads in the town centre, turn left and cross the medieval bridge over the River Camel, soon to bear left along the former A39. After nearly half a mile (800m) turn left on to the B3314, signed Rock. Proceed for 1 mile (1.5km) and cross the River Amble (traffic lights), with good views of the Camel Estuary and Padstow. In a further mile (1.5km) go over Gutt Bridge and turn immediately right to join a minor road, signed Chapel Amble.

2 Once in Chapel Amble continue for 1.5 miles (2.5km) passing the church on the left, just before the T-junction which is opposite Forge Gallery. Turn right, then left beyond The Maltsters Arms, and follow the road to a crossroads. Keep straight on, then shortly bear right for St Kew. In 547yds (500m) turn left, then almost immediately right. Take the second right turn (signed to St Kew Inn) after the school and head downhill into St Kew, passing the Donkey Sanctuary on the left. This delightful little village comprises a 15th-century stone-built inn, an elegant Georgian vicarage, a few houses and a splendid 15th-century church featuring some of the finest medieval glass in Cornwall. Pass the inn and take the second lane left, signed St Kew Highway. Keep right at a T-junction and shortly enter St Kew Highway, bearing right at The Red Lion to the A39.

GO FLY A KITE

You're never short of a stiff breeze on the North Cornish coast, which makes it the ideal place to harness the power of nature with a kite.

Polzeath Bay – power-kiting at the mouth of the Camel Estuary. One of the places the sport is well established. Power-kiting involves the flying of dynamically shaped kites that can be made to go through spectacular flight motions by skilled operators. It can be truly mesmerising and it doesn't take long to get the knack. Some of the most powerful kites can even lift you momentarily off the ground!

Watergate Bay, Newquay – here you can join kiting sessions run by the National Power Kite Training Centre and even have a go on a kite buggy, a lightweight cart that is pulled along flat tidal sands by kite power.

Estuary, is Padstow, Cornwall's culinary capital, home of the famous TV chef Rick Stein. North from Padstow, the rocky coast unwinds past Pentire Head and the tiny fishing villages of Port Isaac and Portquin to Tintagel Head and on to dramatic Boscastle, before the cliffs give way at Bude's 4-mile (6.5-km) sweep of golden sand near the border with Devon.

Tintagel is King Arthur Country, where the stupendous Tintagel Head is claimed to be the legendary Camelot. There is no evidence for this, but Tintagel has become the centre of an Arthurian 'industry' none the less. A visit to the headland is an experience in its own right, but turn north or south along the coastal footpath and you will find equally dramatic coastal features without the crowds, and without the Age of Chivalry. A mile or two inland from Tintagel is the 'biggest hole in Britain', the enormous Delabole slate quarry, 500ft (152m) deep and below the level of the Atlantic itself. You can peer into the depths from a special viewing platform if you want to.

ANTIQUES ADVENTURES

Cornwall's maritime history meant that the county was the repository of all sorts of exotic goods and chattels during the great days of sailing ships. Not everything brought in was legal, of course, and much of it ended up being drunk! If you are a dedicated antiques hunter you may come across some fascinating maritime items in the many antiques shops throughout North Cornwall. Enthusiasts can even enjoy a specialist holiday at **Mawgan Porth** near Newquay where they can learn about antique restoring and associated skills such as lace-making.

Breathtaking coastal footpaths at Tintagel, King Arthur's legendary Camelot

BEST FIVE FISHING VILLAGES IN CORNWALL

Cawsand and Longsand

Adjoining villages on the east-facing, sheltered anchorage of Cawsand Bay. Narrow streets hide plenty of good pubs.

Polperro

The archetype of the Cornish fishing village, with houses clinging to steep hillsides above a tiny harbour.

Cadgwith, The Lizard

Thatched cottages surround a shingle cove where lobster, crab and mackerel boats are beached.

Penberth Cove

Perfect hamlet with granite cottages above a steep slipway used by tiny, one-man operated boats.

Port Isaac

Slate-hung cottages rise in tiers above a small harbour with the narrowest streets imaginable.

DID YOU KNOW?

You need to be fit and gregarious to enjoy Padstow's Obby Oss. During this May Day festival the Oss – a great hooped mask, painted and plumed and representing a stylised horse – is paraded madly round the town by an operator hidden beneath its trailing black skirts. The Oss is led on by a 'Teazer' wielding a club, while bands play the same haunting May Day song from dawn to dusk. The Oss chases off men with its wooden 'snappers' and tries to drag women beneath its skirts, so beware! There are rival Blue and White Osses whose teams compete in making the most mayhem. Needless to say, the town's pubs do a roaring trade!

3 Turn right and continue along this busy road for half a mile (800m), to take the first turning left, signed St Mabyn. Steeply descend (beware of a sharp left-hand bend), cross the River Allen and climb steadily to St Mabyn. Go straight through the village, passing the church and St Mabyn Inn, and in 1.5 miles (2.5km) reach the Longstone crossroads at the B3266. Continue straight across, then in just over half a mile (800m) turn left and proceed to a T-junction in 1 mile (1.5km), turning right downhill to Poley's Bridge. Cross the bridge and bear right at a car-park to join the Camel Trail, an attractive walking and cycling route that follows the old Bodmin to Wadebridge railway line.

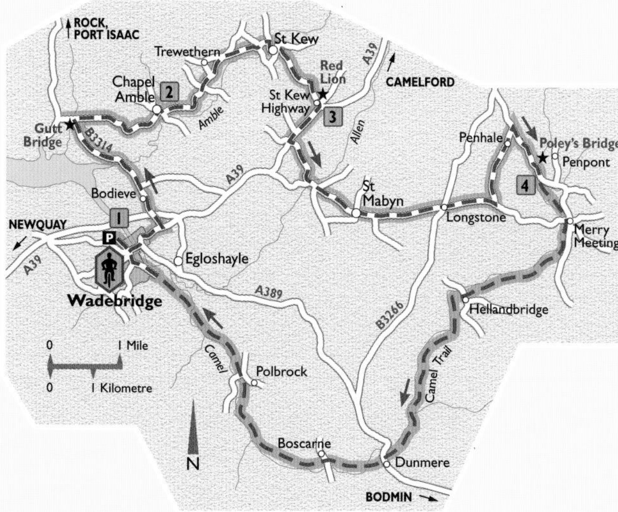

4 Remain on this level, well-surfaced track as it winds its way beside the fast-flowing River Camel. The dense woodland and river meadows of the Camel Valley provide a rich habitat for a diverse variety of wildlife, which is best appreciated from a relaxed cycle along the peaceful Camel Trail. Lookout for dipper and kingfisher, curlew and shelduck and, if you're lucky, you may spot the signs of otters. Also, remember that the trail is popular with walkers. Follow the Camel Trail signs for 11 miles (17.5km) back into Wadebridge, meeting traffic at Southern Way. Proceed along The Platt (cycle lane), then at the crossroads in the town centre, go straight on and return to the car-park.

DEVON & DARTMOOR

Devon seems to epitomise the picturesque heart of Olde England, all thatched cottages, clotted cream and cider, a county that is emphatically rural. Yet this famous farming county boasts a maritime tradition that goes back into the mists of time. Enjoy one of Britain's great wilderness areas, Dartmoor, charming villages such as Widdicombe and Buckland, the brash coastal resorts of Torbay, beautiful country towns such as Totnes, and the great cities of Plymouth and Exeter. Devon's mix of diverse landscapes, its wild moorland and peaceful woods, towering sea cliffs and sunny 'Riviera' coast, offers fascinating opportunities and activities.

TORBAY

Torbay is where Devon comes out to play on its Riviera Coast. Here the resort towns of Torquay and Paignton have merged into one long sweep of holiday development that reaches out towards Brixham. Sun, sea and sand, entertainment, shopping – this is tourism at its liveliest, and great fun because of it.

CLOVELLY

Clovelly is an unashamedly romantic and well-preserved 16th-century fishing village where colour-washed cottages and cobbled lanes cling to the steep North Devon cliffs above the tiny harbour. The village is extremely popular and can become very crowded at the height of the summer season.

Saltram House

Located near Plymouth is Saltram, an outstanding example of an 18th-century George II house, complete with its original contents. The state rooms are the work of Robert Adam and there are several paintings by Joshua Reynolds. The 18th-century gardens are a pleasure in themselves and include an orangery, a chapel and several follies.

Exeter Cathedral

Exeter's cathedral has two 12th-century towers framing its exquisitely carved West Front. The roof of the central aisle is an unbroken 300ft (91m) of Gothic vaulting, the longest of its kind in the world. The cathedral is surrounded by a grassy Cathedral Close, framed by handsome buildings and attractive shops.

MAP AND KEY

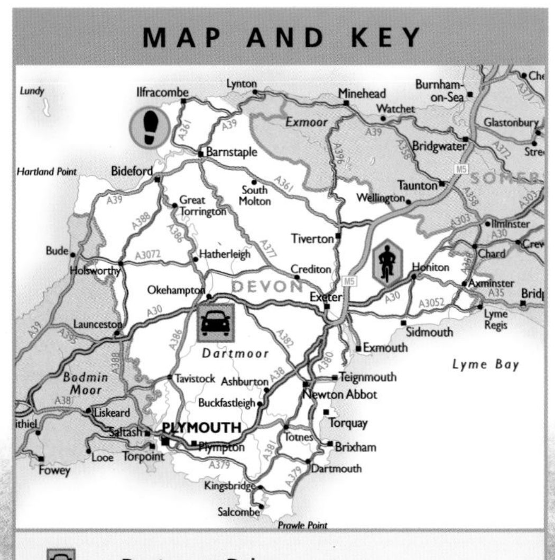

(car symbol)	Dartmoor Drive
(cyclist symbol)	Whimple Cycle Ride
(footprint symbol)	Woolacombe Walk

TOTNES

The ancient borough of Totnes has well-preserved Norman and Tudor features making it one of the West Country's most attractive towns. A Norman castle, a 15th-century church tower and the 16th-century High Street are the main attractions, but the town's position on the picturesque River Dart makes Totnes even more delightful.

DARTMOOR & THE ENGLISH RIVIERA

Dartmoor is one of England's most remarkable National Parks, a magnificent wilderness of 365sq miles (945sq km) at the heart of the well-cultivated West Country. At its highest point the moor rises to 2,000ft (609m). Dartmoor divides neatly into northern and southern sections. Northern Dartmoor matches parts of the Welsh Mountains and the Scottish Highlands for wildness. Here the lonely hills of Yes Tor, High Willhays and Hanginstone Hill rise up from a rolling expanse of dappled, windswept moorland. This is not for strolling; this is tough, but rewarding, walking country where weatherproof clothing and sturdy footwear are essential. On the western fringes lie the distinctive towns of Okehampton and Tavistock, while on the eastern edge is lovely Chagford and the remarkable stately home of Castle Drogo at Drewsteignton.

In its western section, Southern Dartmoor is every bit as extensive and remote as the northern moor, but it has no well-defined hilltops. Again, you need to be properly equipped; if you venture off the few moorland tracks you need to know how to use a map and compass. Southern Dartmoor runs from the village of

TOP CHALLENGING CLIMBING CRAGS

Screda Point, Hartland Quay

Dramatic, shark's tooth pinnacles up to 100ft (30m) high on the foreshore.

The Dewerstone, near Plymouth

A series of granite buttresses rising from the heavily wooded Plym Valley.

Haytor, near Bovey Tracey

Magnificent climbs on a granite tor 1,500ft (457m) above sea level. Great views but always windy.

Combshead Tor, near Burrator Reservoir

A jumble of boulders on the hillside above Narrator Brook, with plenty of gems.

The Old Redoubt, Berry Head, near Brixham

Wild climbing on one of the biggest and certainly the most awe-inspiring cliffs in Devon.

ROCK-CLIMBING

Dartmoor's granite tors, the great rounded bosses of rock that thrust out of the moor, are popular rock-climbing venues. Granite is popular amongst rock-climbers because of its solidity and its generous holds. This is a serious but immensely rewarding sport and the Dartmoor area is an ideal place to start before attempting the more challenging limestone sea cliffs of Torbay or the beetling slate cliffs of the North Devon Coast – if you should really get hooked!

THE DARTMOOR WAY

For the keen cyclist and walker, the Dartmoor Way provides a scenic 90-mile (140-km) route that passes close to some of Dartmoor's best historic buildings and visitor attractions. You can take several days to complete the trip and even make use of a helpful Baggage Forwarding Delivery service that leaves you unencumbered while cycling or walking between overnight destinations. There is a Dartmoor Way Pack with map and directions for the route and accommodation options, available at most local TICs.

Dartmoor Drive

DRIVE

Dartmoor & the Tamar Valley

START/FINISH: Okehampton. Located off the A30 between Exeter and Launceston

DISTANCE: 62 miles (100km)

Beginning from the ancient town of Okehampton, dominated by the impressive ruins of Okehampton Castle, this drive skirts the northwestern edge of Dartmoor before climbing on to its most spectacular, granite-dotted open moorland. The return journey is through the beautiful countryside of the Tamar Valley.

1 From the town centre take the B3260, signed Tavistock. In 3 miles (5km) cross a road bridge and turn right on to the A30, signed Launceston. Take the A386, signed Tavistock, and continue for 13 miles (21km), with fine views of Dartmoor on the left, to Tavistock. One of four stannary towns around the moor, Tavistock, though much older, is essentially a product of 19th-century prosperity.

2 Just before reaching the town centre, turn left on to the B3357, signed Princetown, crossing a bridge and turning left at a roundabout towards Princetown. The road soon climbs on to open moorland with huge outcrops of granite all around, including Cox Tor and Great Mis Tor on the left.

3 In 6.5 miles (10.5km) turn right, signed Princetown, and enter the town, with sombre views down over the prison to the left. In the centre of Princetown, at a T-junction, turn right on to the B3212 Yelverton road. In 6 miles (10km) reach a roundabout and take the first exit on to the A386, signed Plymouth.

4 In 200ft (61m) turn right, signed Crapstone and Buckland Monachorum. In 1 mile (1.5km) detour left to visit Buckland Abbey, a splendid former monastic foundation which was later the home of Sir Francis Drake. On the main route continue for a mile (1.5km) and turn left, signed Milton Combe and Bere Alston. In another half mile (800m) turn right for Bere Alston, descending through a delightful wooded valley to cross the River Tavy at a picturesque stone bridge, following signs for Bere Alston and Bere Ferrers. Ascend a 1-in-4 hill and in 1.5 miles (2.5km) turn right towards Gulworthy and Tavistock. In

Princetown and its gaunt prison, through wonderfully bleak 'Hound of the Baskervilles' country and then over sweeping moorland to the remote Erme Plains, location of prehistoric and medieval ruins. From Erme Plains the raw hills tumble down to the town of Ivybridge and the busy A38. On its eastern edge the rough, open country of the southern moor gives way to a greener landscape where the River Dart and the River Bovey wind through lushly wooded valleys and where great knuckles of granite, the dramatic Dartmoor Tors, protrude from grassy moorland at places such as Haytor and Foxtor.

CRUISING

The South Hams coast is punctuated by two major estuaries, at Dartmouth and Salcombe. You can take a river cruise inland through the serene and lovely Devon countryside from **Salcombe** to **Kingsbridge** or from **Dartmouth** as far as **Totnes**. You can even combine cruising with old-style rail travel by sailing up the River Dart and returning on the **Dart Valley Steam Railway**.

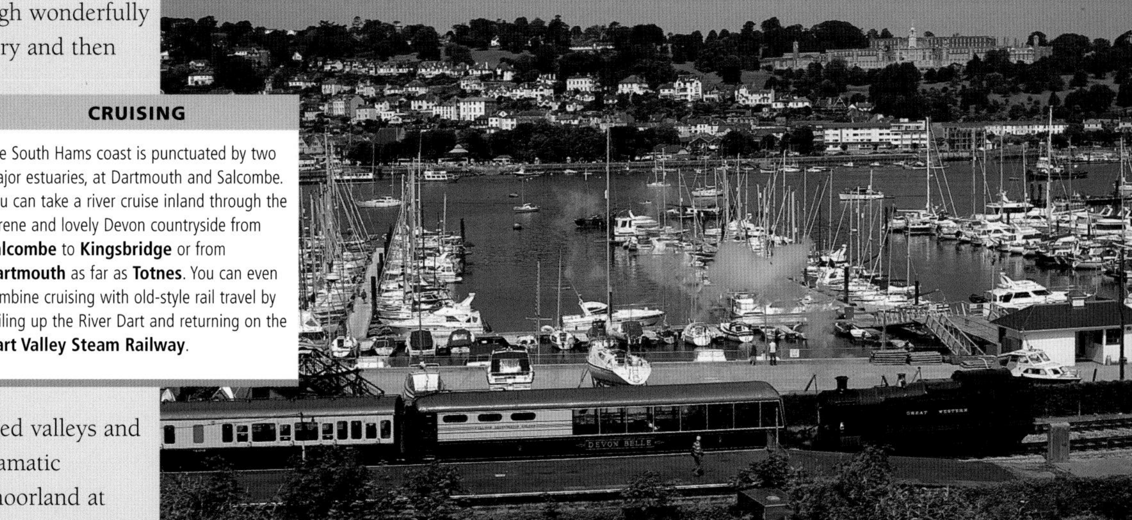

A view of Dartmouth from Kingswear

another 2.5 miles (4km) detour left for a mile (1.5km) to visit Morwellham Quay. This once thriving copper mine and port has been accurately renovated and restored to form a splendid open-air museum, staffed by craftsmen and other workers in period costume.

5 On the main route continue to the A390. Cross the main road and continue forward, signed Chipshop and Milton Abbot. In 5 miles (8km) cross the B3362, then in 1 mile (1.5km) turn right, signed Brentor. Keep straight on at the crossroads, signed Brentor, and in 1.5 miles (2.5km) reach the car-park for Brent Tor Church. Perched atop a high grassy mound with great rocks strewn all around, the church enjoys panoramic views on all sides.

6 Shortly after the church car-park turn left, signed Brentor and Lydford. In 3 miles (5km) pass the first entrance to Lydford Gorge on the left. This beautiful wooded gorge, owned by the National Trust, has a 3.5-mile (5.5-km) walk with a waterfall at one end and the spectacular Devil's Cauldron at the other. Continue into Lydford village, passing Lydford Castle, a great square stone keep which dates from 1195, then on reaching the A386, turn left, signed Okehampton. In 6 miles (9.5km) turn right on to the A30 and, in a mile (1.5km), turn left on to the B3260, signed Okehampton and return to the town centre.

South of Dartmoor lies a much mellower countryside. The resorts of Torquay, Brixham and Paignton – the collective Torbay – cling most tenaciously to the sun, sea and sand image of the official 'English Riviera'. This home-grown version of the French original is part of the much larger South Devon. The notional 'Riviera' coast extends south of Brixham to Start Point and Salcombe, behind which lies the deeply rural countryside of the South Hams.

Location has been kind to the area. Dartmoor absorbs the westerly wind and rain, and the east-facing coast soaks up the sun. Torquay and Paignton are the focus of easygoing holiday-making, but farther afield lies a fascinating coast and countryside dotted with peaceful hamlets and villages, and handsome towns such as Totnes, Kingsbridge, Salcombe and Dartmouth.

WHODUNIT?

One of Torbay's most famous residents was the crime novelist and playwright Agatha Christie. Dame Agatha, as she became, was born in Torquay and lived for many years in the area. Fans of the novelist and her enduring characters, which include Miss Marple and Hercule Poirot, can track down clues to how she developed her inimitable style. You can even spot locations that are described in her stories. Local TICs stock special publications that will direct you along a Christie 'trail' to enchanting villages such as Churston Ferrers, the ideal habitat for more than a few Miss Marples.

CANOEING

As a change from all that robust striding across the moors, try a canoe trip on one of Dartmoor's quieter rivers. Many of the moorland streams are internationally recognised for their extreme white-water canoeing so don't get carried away, literally; arrange canoeing through a recognised activities' centre. A more sedate option is a safe and easy drift in a hired canoe down the old Tavistock canal from the heart of the town. Just remember as you drift that you need to paddle all the way back, against the flow.

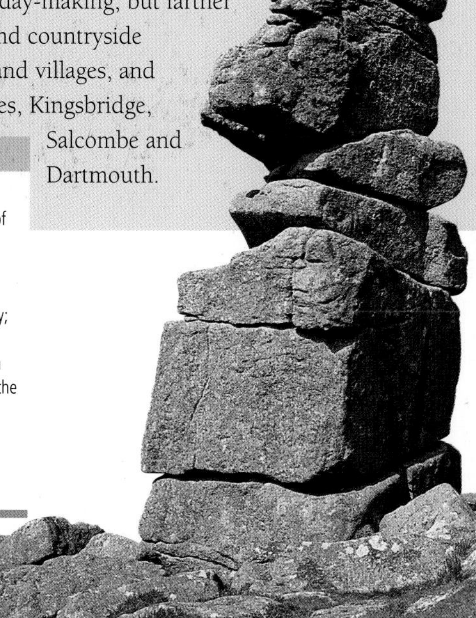

The Bowerman's Nose, on Dartmoor, near Lustleigh

EXETER & EAST DEVON

Exeter is an historic regional city with the easygoing atmosphere of a country town. You never feel overwhelmed by city life in Exeter and you never feel lost. All roads seem to lead eventually to the city's medieval cathedral at the centre of its grassy Cathedral Close, a pleasant open space that could pass for a village green. This is where locals and visitors alike come to relax and to enjoy the cathedral's dignified and reassuring presence. Taking a look at the cathedral area is a fascinating lesson in history and architecture. The Close is flanked on its south and east sides by the medieval Bishop's Palace and Deanery and by a section of the city's old Roman walls. The north side is lined with a fascinating mix of period buildings that include Francis Drake's favourite pub, the Ship Inn, and a timber-framed, Dutch-gabled building that once housed the 18th-century 'Mol's Coffee House'.

You can enjoy the best of Exeter without getting footsore. The city's major features are all contained within the old walls. The High Street is where you'll find the 14th-century guildhall with its glorious granite façade and ground-floor arcade. Inside the wainscoted hall, the city's silver and regalia are on display. Just off the north end of the High Street are Rougemont and Northernhay Gardens and one of the best-preserved sections of the old walls. Here you will find the Rougemont House Museum and the ruins of 12th-century Danes Castle. For underworld Exeter, don't miss a tour of the city's 13th-century water tunnels, which are now dry. Exeter's fortunes were built on the medieval wool trade and the city was once a major port connected by the 5-mile (8-km) long Exeter Ship Canal to the Exe Estuary at Topsham. Exeter's historic quay is now a marvellous shopping and leisure area of preserved buildings such as the 17th-century Customs House and Quay House, the latter now a fascinating interpretation centre.

FARM HOLIDAYS

Being down on the farm these days often means getting stuck in with the everyday work. Diversification has led to a number of farms in East Devon running working holidays. This doesn't mean you have to be up at dawn with the cock's crow, though it's often a magical time. You can get involved up to your armpits, just watch what's going on, or simply relax in comfortable farm accommodation in between enjoying a variety of other activities. It's the ideal holiday for youngsters, and farms that run working holidays cater specially for children.

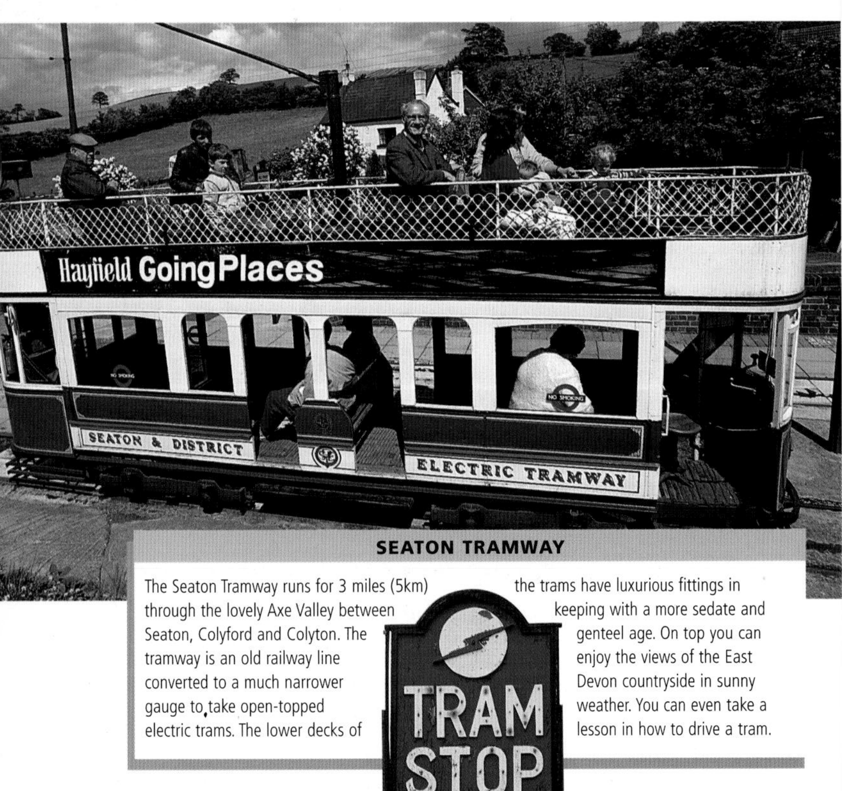

SEATON TRAMWAY

The Seaton Tramway runs for 3 miles (5km) through the lovely Axe Valley between Seaton, Colyford and Colyton. The tramway is an old railway line converted to a much narrower gauge to take open-topped electric trams. The lower decks of the trams have luxurious fittings in keeping with a more sedate and genteel age. On top you can enjoy the views of the East Devon countryside in sunny weather. You can even take a lesson in how to drive a tram.

Whimple Cycle Ride

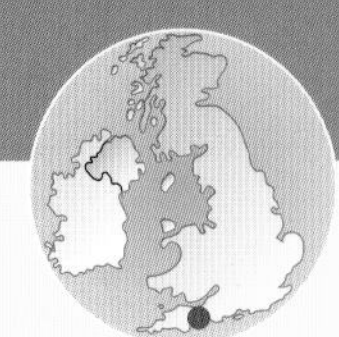

CYCLE RIDE

Orchards & Churches in Southeast Devon

START/FINISH: Whimple. Off the A30 7 miles (11km) east of Exeter. Whimple Station can be reached in 10 minutes from Exeter Central Station

DISTANCE: 18 miles (29km)

ROADS: mainly country lanes

PARKING: Webbers Close, Whimple or Whimple Station

This is a pleasant ride, with only a couple of uphill sections. It takes you through cider apple country and to several typical Devon villages with handsome churches and traditional inns.

1 The triangle of countryside through which this route winds its way is contained within the arms of the busy M5, A30 and A373 roads. The area is so detached from these traffic-laden corridors that you wonder what has happened to the rest of the world as you cycle blissfully along. From Whimple Station, go down Station Road and turn left at the junction. Pass the Thirsty Farmer Inn and at a mini-roundabout bear right, signed to Broadclyst. (If starting at Whimple car-park by Webbers Close, go along the passageway from the car-park, then through The Square, past the church and under the railway bridge to reach the mini-roundabout and turn left.) In a few yards, at the next mini-roundabout, keep straight on, then bear left, signed to Broadclyst, and pass several thatched cottages. At the next junction, keep left and continue for a level 3 miles (5km). At a crossroads (broken signpost) turn right, then bear off right along a narrow lane, signed Silverton.

2 Turn right at the next crossroads, signed Ashclyst Forest. There is quite a tough uphill climb for just over half a mile (800m) to the crown of the hill. Continue through the woods (good picnic areas) and follow the road round left, ignoring the right-hand junction. At a junction, signed Route 52 (part of the long-distance Buzzard Cycle Route), turn right and shortly reach a crossroads at Frogmore Farm. Go straight across, signed to Clyst Hydon. Climb steadily to White Down Copse, continue past Paradise Copse, heading downhill (don't take the first left), then keep straight on, signed to Clyst Hydon. These woods were once part of the Killerton Estate (now National Trust). The elegant 18th-century house

JUNGLE TREK

If you fancy a jungle trek in deepest Devon, then the 7-mile (11-km) coastal footpath along the deeply wooded coast between **Seaton** and **Lyme Regis** is for you.

Undercliff is an area of old landslip that is now bound together by dense woods of ash, beech, sycamore, oak and alder, all tangled up with dogwood, sloe, hawthorn and privet. Long twisting tendrils of traveller's joy hang like jungle creepers from the overarching canopy of branches. There are no distant views but there's plenty of wildlife, including scores of flowers and over 120 species of birds.

An OS Pathfinder 1316 map is useful, but the path is very clear and easy to follow. However, once you set out from either Seaton or Lyme Regis, there is only one escape inland and that's midway at Charton Bay.

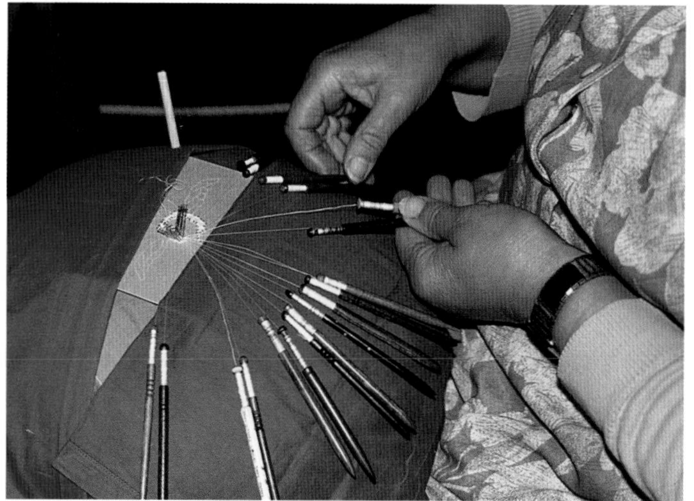

The tradition of lace-making can still be found at Honiton, renowned for this delicate art

EXETER SHOPPING

There is no shortage of top-quality shops in Exeter:

Guildhall Centre at Higher Market – located in Queen Street, the Higher Market was once a food market and its handsome neo-classical façade in Bath stone dates from 1834. It is now a modern shopping mall.

Princesshay – a pedestrianised shopping precinct that runs parallel to the High Street and has a range of shops.

The Quay – an excellent selection of antiques and craft shops. This was once the heart of Exeter's maritime life.

CITY TOURS

A great way of seeing the best of Exeter and learning all about the city's history is to join one of the Red Coat guided tours.

These last about 90 minutes, during which you are taken round by a knowledgeable and entertaining Red Coat guide.

The tours start from in front of the Royal Clarence Hotel in Cathedral Close. Details and times of the tours are available at local TICs.

and the 18 acres (7ha) of majestic gardens are located just to the west beyond the frantic M5. Relish the peace and quiet.

3 Climb for about 328yds (300m), then continue, bearing left at the next junction, to reach a junction just before Clyst Hydon. Turn left and in about a mile (1.5km), at a junction at Langford, on a left-hand bend, bear off right, passing a little red post box. Continue for 1.5 miles (2km) to reach a T-junction opposite St John the Baptist Church in Plymtree, which has some splendid fan-vaulting. Go right then follow

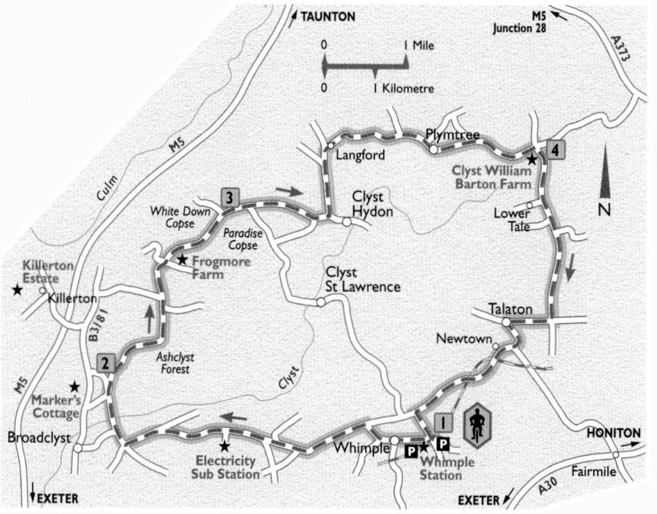

the road round left past the Blacksmith's Arms, which is next to a post office and general stores. Keep straight on and uphill, descend steeply, then climb uphill past Clyst William Barton Farm. At a T-junction turn right, signed Talaton.

4 Continue for nearly 2 miles (3km). At a crossroads turn right, signed to Talaton. The Church of St James in Talaton has a fine wagon roof and a medieval rood screen. At Talaton village shop and Talaton Inn, turn left, signed to Fairmile and Ottery St Mary. In 328yds (300m) go right, signed to Newtown and Whimple. Cross two bridges over the railway, then keep left at a junction and pass Whimple village sign. Climb steeply to a crossroads and turn right, signed Village Centre, to return to Whimple.

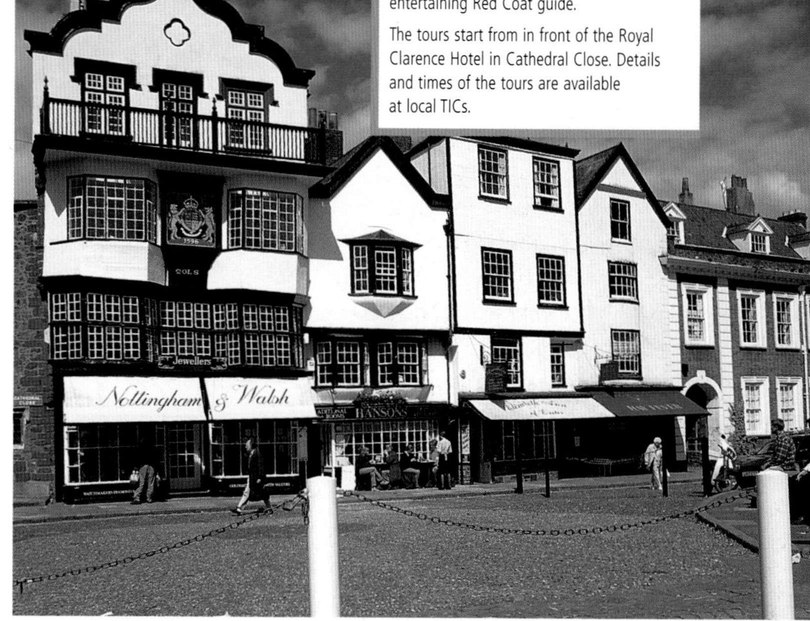

Handsome buildings and distinctive shops are found at Exeter's Cathedral Close

South of the city are the open spaces of the Exe Estuary, a bird-watchers' paradise. Exmouth, on the east side of the estuary, is Devon's oldest holiday resort. A few miles beyond Exmouth is Budleigh Salterton, with its great shingle beach. From Budleigh, the switchback coast rises and falls along a succession of red sandstone coastal hills and cliffs to reach the splendid seaside town of Sidmouth, with its long narrow promenade and its genteel legacy of Regency and Victorian buildings. Away from the coast, the area is classic rural Devon, a lush countryside of fertile farms with, at its heart, the towns of Honiton and Axminster. Honiton is famous for lace and Axminster for carpets, a reflection of the area's long association with the wool and textiles trade. With the traffic of the M5 out of sight and sound, the network of quiet lanes round delightful villages such as Ottery St Mary and Colyton are ideal for cycling and walking.

NORTHWEST DEVON

Northwest Devon combines tranquil countryside and dramatic coast in a particularly vivid way. It all starts at the great headland of Hartland Point, where slab-like cliffs rise from a foreshore of sea-polished rock. This is the coast of England at its most hostile, yet you cannot help being exhilarated by it all. In the great days of sail the lighthouse at Hartland was all that stood between tall ships and disaster, although it was often too late for vessels that finally lost the battle against wind and tide. North of Hartland, about 10 miles (16km) out to sea, lies the island of Lundy; its great cliffs of golden granite are a striking contrast to the dark slatey cliffs of the Devon coast.

Many of the vessels that came to grief on these cliffs were heading to and from Bristol, but others would have been bound for Bideford and Barnstaple on the estuaries of the rivers Taw and Torridge that drain into Bideford Bay to the north of Hartland Point. Few ships visit either town these days, but you can still catch the atmosphere of old seagoing ports at both of them. This is especially so at Bideford, where the long waterfront road of the Quay still looks straight on to the broad sweep of the Torridge, a view that is shared by a statue of the 19th-century novelist Charles Kingsley. Kingsley's novel *Westward Ho!* encapsulated England's stirring maritime history and has given rise to the only exclamatory place name in Britain, the resort of Westward Ho! on the coast near Bideford. At busy Barnstaple try to plan a visit on Tuesday or Friday when the old Victorian Pannier Market is in full swing beneath a glass roof and timber arches. Down by the town's riverside you'll find more

The old harbour at Ilfracombe, an ideal base for golfing, boating or fishing

LUNDY TRIP

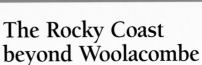

A day-trip to Lundy aboard the motor vessel *Oldenburg* is a great little adventure, provided you are a reasonable sailor. It is a delightful trip on fine summer days, and takes only a couple of hours, giving you time ashore to enjoy this remarkable island with its magnificent granite cliffs and its wealth of wildlife. The *Oldenburg* makes regular sailings from **Ilfracombe** and **Bideford** and calls in occasionally at **Clovelly**. Details of sailings can be obtained from local TICs.

The lighthouse at Lametry Bay

Woolacombe Walk

WALK

The Rocky Coast beyond Woolacombe

START/FINISH: Woolacombe. On the B3343, off the A361 south of Ilfracombe
DISTANCE: 6 miles (9.5km)
ASCENT/GRADIENT: 650ft (200m); short, gradual climbs
TERRAIN/PATHS: coastal grass and heathland, fields. Good paths
PARKING: either of the two car-parks by beach in Woolacombe village; can be busy in summer, but there is plenty of other parking

Spines of slate break through the quiet, heathy headlands away from bustling Woolacombe. This invigorating coastal ramble follows the South West Way around Morte Point and Bull Point, once the haunt of wreckers and rich in fauna and flora, before returning through peaceful inland valleys to the famous beach resort.

1 From either car-park turn left, following the South West Coast Path alongside the road to Mortehoe. It's possible to walk nearer to the sea in places but you must return to the road before the bend at the foot of the hill up to Mortehoe.

2 Follow the coast path signs to cut out the bend in the road and follow the road a short distance up the hill towards Mortehoe. About 300yds (273m) up the hill turn left. Follow the coast path signs for the next 3 miles (5km). Thrift, sea campion, kidney vetch and rock samphire grow on the cliffs. Amongst the grassy coastal downs grow patches of heath resplendently coloured with common gorse, ling and bell heather in late summer. This provides habitat for stonechats and warblers whilst buzzards and kestrels hover overhead. The path keeps close to the coast all around Morte Point, down into a little valley below Mortehoe and another behind the beach at Rockham and up to Bull Point lighthouse.

3 At the entrance to the lighthouse compound turn right up the tarmac drive. However, it's worth continuing on the coast path to the seat on the hillock above the lighthouse for the view along the coast to Ilfracombe and returning to the drive. The drive ascends 1 mile (1.5km) to the edge of the village at Mortehoe.

CRYSTAL GAZING

The North Devon town of **Great Torrington** is worth a visit for its wonderful position on a lofty hill above the River Torridge and for its historic buildings. But Torrington also boasts the **Dartington Crystal** factory where you can take a tour and browse the gift shop. As well as hundreds of Dartington crystal bowls, vases and decorative items, the huge shop also stocks other pottery and glassware. Round off a great shopping day by visiting the town on Thursday or Saturday morning when the Victorian Pannier Market is held.

maritime history in the colonnaded Queen Anne's Walk, built as a merchant's exchange in the 17th century and restored in 1986.

The shores of Bideford Bay have some of the finest beaches in the West Country. Saunton Sands on the north side of the Taw and Torridge estuaries extend for nearly 5 miles (8km). Beyond Saunton lies attractive Croyde Bay, overlooked on the north by the cliffs of Baggy Point. Woolacombe Bay to the north of the point has another superb stretch of beach. To the north of Woolacombe, the coast turns east and runs on to Victorian Ilfracombe, and then to Combe Martin where the high whalebacked coastal hills of Exmoor begin.

The countryside of Northwest Devon is a peaceful contrast to the area's dramatic coast. The twin rivers of the Taw and Torridge flow north from the edge of Dartmoor through what has become indelibly known as 'Tarka Country'. Over 70 years ago, the novelist Henry Williamson wrote his remarkable book, *Tarka the Otter*, in which he described the journey of an otter through the secluded countryside of the Taw and Torridge river valleys. Today, the 180-mile (289-km) Tarka Trail runs from the North Devon coast through Barnstaple and the Taw Valley to Dartmoor.

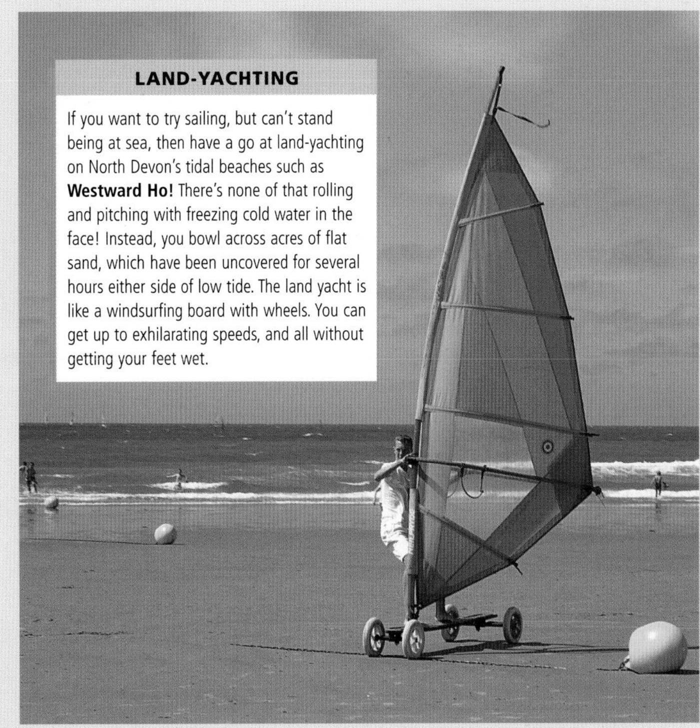

LAND-YACHTING

If you want to try sailing, but can't stand being at sea, then have a go at land-yachting on North Devon's tidal beaches such as **Westward Ho!** There's none of that rolling and pitching with freezing cold water in the face! Instead, you bowl across acres of flat sand, which have been uncovered for several hours either side of low tide. The land yacht is like a windsurfing board with wheels. You can get up to exhilarating speeds, and all without getting your feet wet.

SURFING

North Devon's beaches are ideal for learning how to surf or body-board. At **Woolacombe**, but especially at **Croyde Bay**, the Atlantic rollers come flying in to the flat golden sands **of the beaches**. Long-board surfing, like windsurfing, takes time to master, but it's worth it if you persevere. If 'stand-up' **surfing seems too** much to try, have a go at body-boarding where you lie flat or kneel on a much broader board. Top body-boarders fly through the air and execute spectacular manoeuvres through enormous waves, but beginners still get somewhere, without necessarily falling off!

4 Pass through the signed gateway at the end of the drive and take the second footpath signed to the left, passing through a thicket alongside a house. Take the stile into the field, carrying straight on across the middle of the field and coming out by a stile onto a bend in a tarmac drive. Keep right, going up the drive past the golf course and from the bend onto a road at the top.

5 Turn right down the road towards Mortehoe and take the first field gateway on the left. Keep straight ahead (bank on your right) and cross a stile onto a drive in a caravan site. Turn left, following the drive to a footpath by a stream. Cross the stream at the bottom and go up to the junction with a footpath. Bear right along the path and take the first turning left. Keep straight ahead between the caravans.

6 At the end of the caravan site drive, find a path descending through the trees and crossing the stream at the bottom. Ascend to the path junction and turn right and over a stile by a National Trust sign. The path descends the valley side for nearly a mile (1.5km). Just before the bottom there is a small gate at a sharp bend in the path. Take the gate and follow the road straight down to the coast road. Turn left to return to the start.

THE TARKA TRAIL

Walking – the 180-mile (289-km) Tarka Trail follows the valley of the River Taw through peaceful and lovely countryside. The trail is closely shadowed by a railway and you can combine rail travel with walking and cycling.

The Tarka Line railway – follows the Tarka Trail as far as Eggesford, before veering off to Exeter. On this North Devon section of the Tarka Trail, between Barnstaple and Eggesford, there are halts at Chapelton, Umberleigh, Portsmouth Arms and King's Nympton. There are car-parks at most of the halts, but space is limited.

Cycling – bikes can be hired at Barnstaple and Eggesford to cycle parts of the Tarka Trail, a good family route. For more experienced cyclists there's a tough off-road route through Eggesford Forest.

EXMOOR & THE SOMERSET LEVELS

NATIONAL PARK
EXMOOR

Exmoor and the Somerset Levels are a fascinating double act. Between them they occupy most of North Somerset from its Devon border to the Mendip Hills. Both are designated as 'moorland' but while Exmoor rises to 1,705ft (519m) at its highest point, the wetlands of the Somerset Levels never rise above 25ft (7m) and parts are even below sea-level. The sharp ridge of the wooded Polden Hills that intersect the Levels reaches a high point of only 300ft (90m). What they have in common is accessible and beautiful countryside, and peace and quiet in which to enjoy it. Their towns and villages such as Glastonbury and Dunster, Somerton and Exford are steeped in the history of the West Country.

SELWORTHY

The cream-coloured, thatched cottages of Selworthy village are almost too perfectly picturesque, but they are the epitome of Old Somerset. Built by Sir Thomas Acland in 1810 as retirement homes for workers of the Holnicote estate, the cottages are now in the care of the National Trust. The nearby 15th-century church has a very fine wagon roof.

Lorna Doone Country
R D Blackmore's 1869 novel Lorna Doone *has made the lovely Doone Valley one of the most romantic places in England. Against the valley's background of authentic medieval ruins and dramatic natural features, Blackmore grafted his tale of the robber clan, the Doones, and of the love story of Lorna and the honest yeoman Jan Ridd.*

Tarr Steps

The ancient stone causeway, or 'clapper bridge', known as Tarr Steps, spans the River Barle a mile (1.5km) or so downriver from Withypool at the heart of Southern Exmoor. The causeway is probably medieval in origin but has been repaired many times through the centuries. You can escape the frequent crowds by following a path upriver to Withypool.

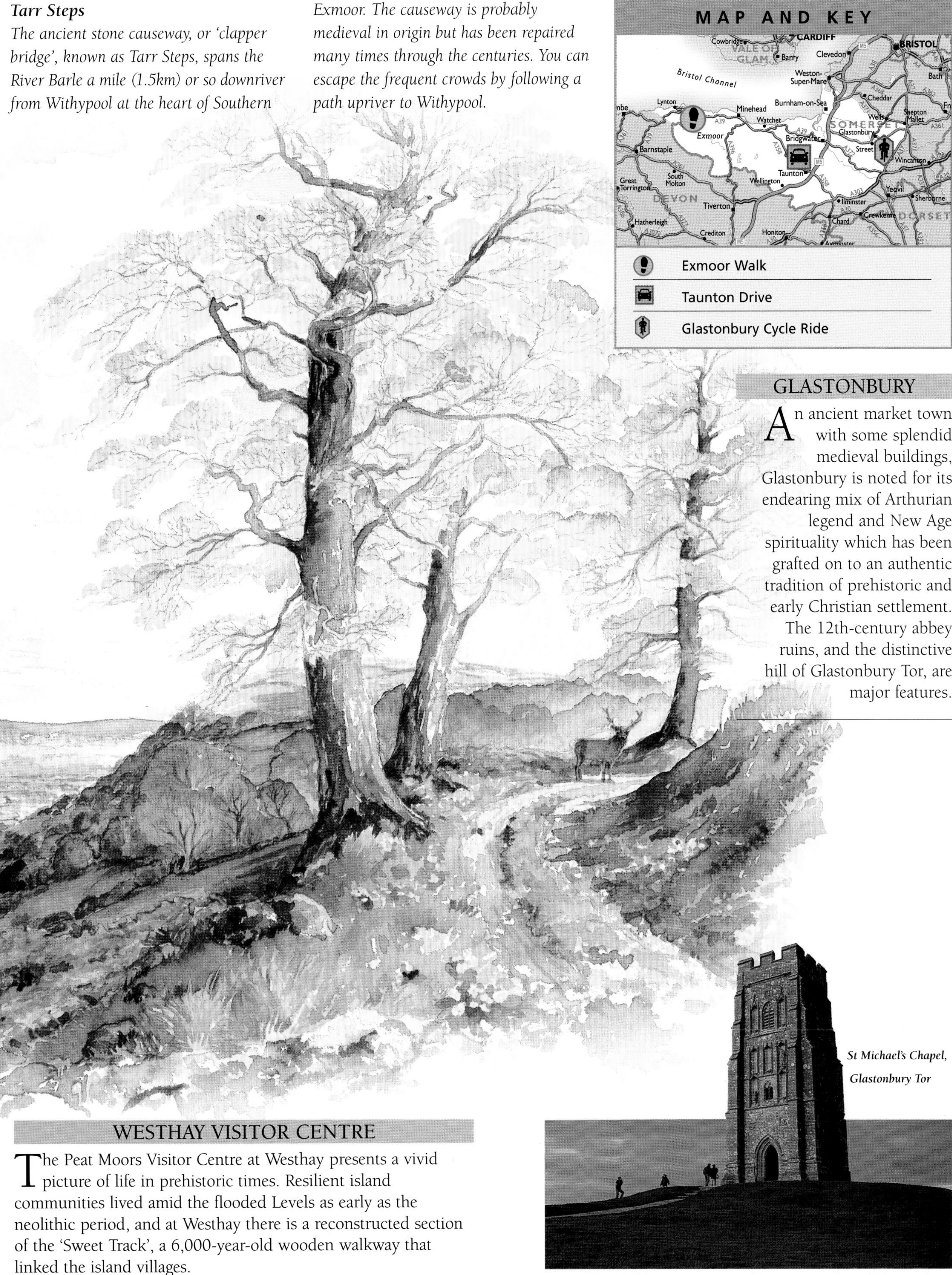

GLASTONBURY

An ancient market town with some splendid medieval buildings, Glastonbury is noted for its endearing mix of Arthurian legend and New Age spirituality which has been grafted on to an authentic tradition of prehistoric and early Christian settlement. The 12th-century abbey ruins, and the distinctive hill of Glastonbury Tor, are major features.

St Michael's Chapel, Glastonbury Tor

WESTHAY VISITOR CENTRE

The Peat Moors Visitor Centre at Westhay presents a vivid picture of life in prehistoric times. Resilient island communities lived amid the flooded Levels as early as the neolithic period, and at Westhay there is a reconstructed section of the 'Sweet Track', a 6,000-year-old wooden walkway that linked the island villages.

EXMOOR

Exmoor is a complex and beautiful mix of high moorland, wooded valleys, fertile farmland and smooth-browed coastal hills. The contrasts are dramatic. Windswept moors wash up against green pastures, twisted thorn trees stand next to clipped beech hedges, and roaring streams pour into gently meandering rivers. Most of the area lies within the Exmoor National Park, 265sq miles (686sq km) of countryside that is a working environment as well as a walkers' and horse-riders' paradise.

The Exmoor coast begins at Combe Martin in Devon, then runs east for 30 miles (48km) to Minehead, embracing such contrasting features as Lynton's rugged Valley of the Rocks and the leafy softness of Heddon's Mouth, Woody Bay and Culbone. Huge whalebacked headlands at Hangman Point and Foreland Point slope steeply down to a final plunge on to remote pebble beaches. Wooded valleys, called combes, slice down from the high moor carrying tumbling rivers, such as the Heddon and the East Lyn, to the sea. Coastal villages punctuate this lonely coast at Lynmouth and at Porlock where the high coastal hills are breached by the great

pebble beach at Porlock Bay, only to rise again at Hurlstone Point and North Hill, behind which shelter the thatched roofs of the beautiful villages of Allerford, Luccombe and Selworthy. Beyond North Hill, Exmoor's roller-coaster shoreline finally ends at Minehead and the low-lying coast of Bridgwater Bay.

Inland from all this coastal drama, high Exmoor lords it serenely over its rolling acres. Lacking Dartmoor's peppering of rocky crests, the wild moorland is more a smooth sea of

HORSE-RIDING

Exmoor is horse country in a big way. Stop for more than a minute or two in **Exford** and a string of glossy, elegant bays and greys will strut by on exercise. On the open moor look out for the pure-bred dun and bay Exmoor ponies, with their black tails and mealy muzzles. You can easily hire horses and ponies at several centres on the moor, and ambling across those sweeping hills on horseback is both a relaxing and an exhilarating experience.

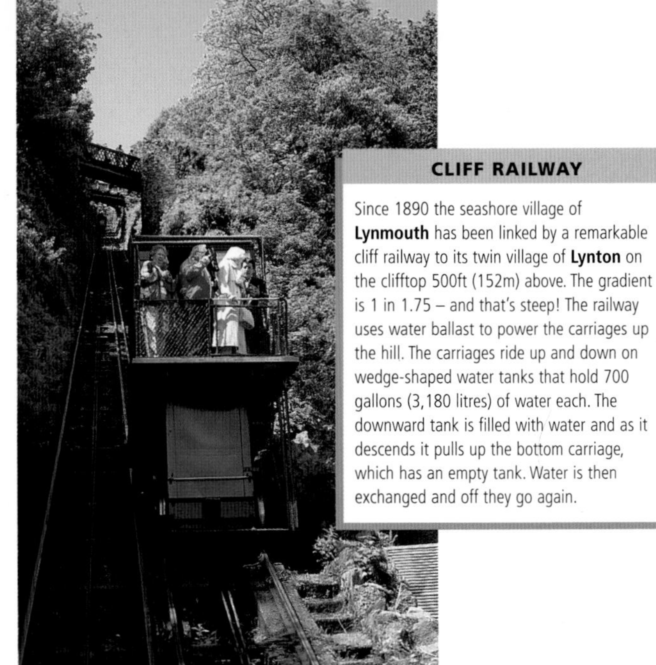

CLIFF RAILWAY

Since 1890 the seashore village of **Lynmouth** has been linked by a remarkable cliff railway to its twin village of **Lynton** on the clifftop 500ft (152m) above. The gradient is 1 in 1.75 – and that's steep! The railway uses water ballast to power the carriages up the hill. The carriages ride up and down on wedge-shaped water tanks that hold 700 gallons (3,180 litres) of water each. The downward tank is filled with water and as it descends it pulls up the bottom carriage, which has an empty tank. Water is then exchanged and off they go again.

Exmoor Walk

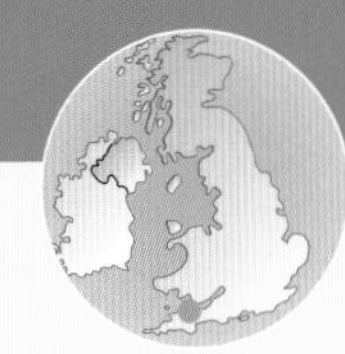

WALK

In Search of Lorna Doone on Exmoor

START/PARKING: National Park car-park and visitor centre at County Gate, 7 miles (11km) west of Porlock on A39

DISTANCE: 9 miles (14.5km)

ASCENT/GRADIENT: 920ft (280m); mostly easy gradients with short steep parts

TERRAIN/PATHS: valleys, fields, moor and heath; wide tracks and open moor; can be boggy

Track down the real places amid the hills and vales of Exmoor linked with a classic tale of adventure. R D Blackmore was inspired by local legends, real characters, places and events, in particular the tranquil, hidden combes. Most is fiction, so don't try to match the novel with reality.

1 Cross the road from the car-park entrance and take the bridleway along the heath, signed to Broomstreet Farm.

2 Turn right up the drive past Yenworthy Lodge. Cross the road, take the stile and follow a yellow waymarked path down to Oare. Skirt through trees around a farm at Oare House, a possible site for Plovers Barrows, home of the story's hero, Jan Ridd, then turn left onto a road, over a bridge and up to Oare church, which was the scene of the marriage between Jan and Lorna Doone, and subsequent dramatic events. Turn left, then take the gate to the left of the churchyard, signed to Larkbarrow. Follow the blue waymarks straight up over fields, keeping the field perimeter on your right.

3 At a bend leave the track and follow the Larkbarrow bridleway sign up over a field, bearing slightly right. Turn left through a gate and follow blue waymarks along the fence and banks for 1.5 miles (2.5km) to a waymark at the end of the straight line of the bank. Cross the middle of the field, bearing slightly left to a gate in the fence.

4 Go through the gate and keep straight upwards across the middle of the next field and over the top to a gate through a low bank on to the moor, still following Larkbarrow bridleway signs. Cross the moor straight ahead and bearing slightly left. Keep straight on, do not be misled by many tracks. In half a mile (800m) you should have rounded the head of a small combe and come to a gate in a bank with a bridleway sign.

DEER WATCHING

Exmoor has the only sizeable herd of wild red deer in Britain outside of the Scottish Highlands. There are about 700 to 800 deer on Exmoor, and there is a long-established tradition of deer-hunting with hounds. You are more likely to spot red deer where there are wooded areas, called coverts, rather than on open moorland. A good time and place to spot these magnificent and elegant creatures is just before dusk, near water, or where the open moor and wooded valley heads meet.

billowing hills from which long shallow combes carry gurgling rivers gently to the south and steeply to the north. Between Exmoor's broad-backed ridges the valleys have been transformed into fertile pastures that are protected by high beech hedges. It is this distinct contrast in landscape that makes Exmoor so appealing. You can head off into a wilderness of tawny moorland, around Dunkery Beacon, go Doone-hunting or deer-spotting around Oare and Malmsmead, or follow lonely paths to the source of the River Exe or to the bleak and solitary Hoar Oak Tree that marks the ancient boundary of the old royal hunting forest of Exmoor. For wildest Exmoor, make for the haunting, and reputedly haunted, Pinkworthy Pond, and the waterlogged expanse of the Chains above the lonely village of Simonsbath. To retreat into less wild country, follow the southern combes of the rivers Exe and Barle into deep woodland around the villages of Exford and Withypool, where Exmoor inns maintain a well-deserved reputation for good food and drink that can be enjoyed round roaring log fires on chilly autumn and winter evenings.

TOP FIVE VIEWS

The Valley of the Rocks, Lynmouth
Lorna Doone country. Impressive outcrops such as the Castle and Devil's Cheesewring.

Porlock Hill
Spectacular views of Porlock from the steep (1 in 4), hairpinned road that leads up to the hills of Exmoor.

Dunkery Beacon
Well worth the 20-minute walk to the 1,800-ft (550-m) summit for magnificent views of the Bristol Channel.

Hangley Cleave
On an unclassified road southwest of Simonsbath. Excellent all-round views.

Winsford Hill (NT)
On the B3223. There are Bronze Age barrows on the summit (1,398ft/426m) and fine views in every direction.

Pretty pastel cottages in the village of Porlock, which has a 17th-century weir

WALKER'S PARADISE

Exmoor is where you will find some of the best coastal and moorland walking in Britain within easy reach of each other.

South West Way coastal footpath starts – or ends – at Minehead and the course it takes along the Exmoor coast makes for invigorating walking.

The high moorland and its valleys also provide outstanding walking opportunities. The National Park Authority and the National Trust have designed a series of walks' leaflets that cover all the best areas of the moor and coast. There's no excuse; local TICs are awash with these excellent publications. One good option is:

The River Barle – walking down the banks from Simonsbath.

5 Through the gate, keep the bank on your left down to a track and gateway with a signpost. Turn right and follow the track signed to Doone Valley. The track passes through a small gate signed to Malmsmead, goes down to ford a stream, then up and down to a sturdy wooden bridge following a well-defined track. Turn right and follow the same side of the river for 3 miles (5km), all the way down to Malmsmead. The track crosses a plank bridge in the Doone settlement and goes uphill and right to Malmsmead. Cross a bridge by the water slide at Lank Combe, possibly the meeting place of Jan and Lorna, above which lies a hidden valley most like the Doone Valley of the novel, and, after Badgworthy Wood, pass the Blackmore Memorial.

6 Go through a gate and down the road to Malmsmead. Turn right at the road junction and cross the bridge by the ford. Continue up the road for 400yds (364m) and turn left down a bridleway to pass Parsonage Farm. Cross a bridge, turn right and continue up the steep hill to County Gate.

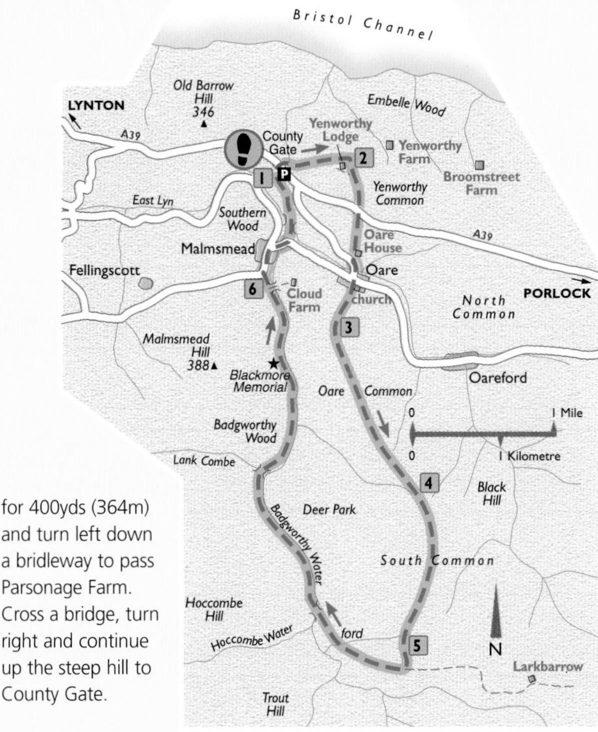

Walkers stop to rest and admire the view of Exmoor from Dunkery Beacon

THE QUANTOCKS & THE BLACKDOWN HILLS

When you climb on to the broad ridge of the Quantock Hills you feel that you have risen above it all. The ridge is only 12 miles (19km) long, yet it has the same sense of spaciousness and isolation as does Exmoor. The Quantocks run northwest to southeast between West Quantoxhead and the Vale of Taunton. To the west, across the Washford River lie the Brendon Hills and Exmoor; to the east the Somerset Levels. The crest of the Quantocks is a belt of rough moorland, a mix of heather and bracken, treeless except for the occasional wind-blasted hawthorn and pine. It undulates gently along its length, rising to a high point at Will's Neck, a mere 1,260ft (384m) in height yet a summit all the same. Other 'summits' have names to relish – Great Bear, Robin Upright, Black Ball, Dead Woman's Ditch.

The Quantocks are designated as being within an Area of Outstanding Natural Beauty and the National Trust owns much of the heath and woodland habitat. Walking is one of the best ways of exploring this wonderful area of hills with its rare mix of open heathland, woodland and farmed landscape. There are numerous waymarked paths and trails and the Ranger Service of the AONB organises guided walks with the added advantage of expert information. Along the base of the western slopes of the Quantocks lie delightful villages such as West Bagborough and Crowcombe. The gentler eastern slopes of the Hills are pierced by deeply wooded combes with tumbling lively streams. This is where the red deer of the Quantocks share the coverts with ponies and sheep. Where these eastern slopes spill on to the lower ground you'll discover the villages of Holford and Nether Stowey, home for several years to the great Romantic poets Wordsworth and Coleridge, and the places where they penned some of their greatest literary works. Perhaps it's something in the air of the Quantocks. Be inspired!

POETS' CORNER

Samuel Taylor Coleridge came to live at **Nether Stowey** on the northern flanks of the hills in 1796, to be joined a year later by William and Dorothy Wordsworth, who settled at **Alfoxton Park**, at nearby **Holford**. While living at Nether Stowey, Coleridge wrote 'The Rime of the Ancient Mariner' and is believed to have used the nearby port of Watchet as the opening location for this epic narrative. Here also, he wrote 'Kubla Khan', after a visit, some claim, to Wookey Hole, the great cavern 'measureless to man'.

ORIENTEERING

One way of really getting to grips with the landscape is to follow an orienteering course. Orienteering is carried out to a very high level in competition, but a number of permanent orienteering courses have been developed in the Southwest. At **Staple Hill** at the eastern end of the Blackdown Hills (OS map ref ST 246 159) there is a course that everyone can have a go at. You need to get hold of a special map pack giving details of the course, on sale at Taunton TIC.

A view across farmland of the Quantocks. The beauty of the area is best explored on foot

Taunton Drive

DRIVE

A Fenland Battlefield below the Breezy Quantocks

START/FINISH: Taunton. Just off M5 (J25) between Bridgwater and Exeter

DISTANCE: 71 miles (114km)

Memories of a rebellion are recalled on the battlefield of Sedgemoor, on the Somerset Levels near Bridgwater. Lanes then lead west through the wooded combes of the Quantocks to a largely unspoilt coastline, followed by a gentle drive through the Vale of Taunton back to Somerset's county town.

1 Take the Bristol road from the town centre, then turn left on to the A38 to Bridgwater, via North Petherton with its handsome 14th-century church and spacious green. Follow signs to Bristol (A38) through the town centre, then cross the river and follow signs to Glastonbury (A39).

2 Cross the M5 and turn immediately right to Chedzoy. Turn right at the T-junction, signed to Westonzoyland.

TOP FIVE CRAFT CENTRES

Muchelney Pottery, near Langport

Thatched pottery with wood-fired kiln, run by Bernard Leach's grandson, John.

Willow and Wetlands Visitor Centre, Stoke St Gregory

A traditional Somerset Levels industry.

Studio Art Glass, Moorlynch Vineyard

Hand-blown and finished glass created by Chris Rouse. The vineyard also offers wine tours and tasting, pottery and photography.

Original Forgery, Bampton

An old smithy on a family farm producing all sorts of ironwork.

Jano Clarke, Potter, Dunster

Ceramics for both domestic use and the collector.

The remains of ancient castle ramparts at Nether Stowey

Several miles south of the Quantocks, across Taunton Vale, lie the Blackdown Hills, half in Somerset, half in Devon and, as with the Quantocks, all within a designated Area of Outstanding Natural Beauty. The Blackdowns are bounded on the north by the M5. They are at their highest here in the north, although the Blackdown Hills AONB spreads as far south as the Honiton to Axminster road.

This is a secluded countryside of lovely hills and beech woods where there are miles of forest tracks to be enjoyed by walkers and horse-riders. On the western edge of the Blackdown escarpment, the towering Wellington Monument, memorial to the champion of Waterloo, dominates the town of Wellington and the Vale of Taunton. The Blackdown Hills are the kind of rare landscape that has a distinctive identity within the much larger rural area that surrounds it. Here you feel that you have entered another world, a little enclave of England that still manages to stand apart from the modern world.

IRON-AGE RAMPARTS

On the southern edge of the Blackdown Hills, close to the road between Cullompton and Honiton, stands **Hembury Iron-Age Hillfort**. This is one of the best examples of a fortified hilltop site in England.

The site has been excavated and traces were found of a much earlier neolithic, New Stone Age, causewayed camp, beneath the Iron-Age fortifications, which comprise sizeable earth ramparts. There is a great sense of antiquity here, at one of the earliest settlement sites in the West Country. A public footpath leads up from the road to the top of the hill.

3 In 2 miles (3km) turn left on to the A372, signed Langport, and proceed through Westonzoyland. After the Sedgemoor Inn, take the left fork and turn left into Liney Road. Follow the road until you reach the stone plinth opposite Bussex Farm House. Here, on the evening of 5 July 1685, the last battle on English soil took place when James II defeated the Duke of Monmouth. The battlefield is accessible by small tracks. To return to the A372 drive along Monmouth Road and turn right and drive back into Bridgwater, following signs to Minehead (A39).

4 Turn left, signed to Durleigh, and continue for 2 miles (3km). Turn left into Bishops Lydeard Road (just past West India pub) and proceed for 3.5 miles (5.5km) to Enmore. Turn right, signed to Spaxton and Barford Park. Pass Hawkridge Reservoir.

5 For Cockercombe turn left, following signs to Triscombe Stone. The road leads up the steep-sided combe through woodland to the top of the Quantock ridge. From the car-park there are magnificent views over the Vale of Taunton and, to the north, over the Bristol Channel to Wales. Once in Spaxton turn left and immediately right into Peartwater Road. Follow signs to Nether Stowey. Turn left off the A39 in 3 miles (5km), opposite a farm shop, into Nether Stowey. Here you'll find the cottage of the poet Samuel Taylor Coleridge (NT).

6 Turn left on to the A39 to Kilve. For Kilve Beach turn right after 4 miles (6.5km). In just over half a mile (800m) turn right for East Quantoxhead, with its village pond and partly Jacobean court house (1610). In 2.5 miles (4km) turn right on a minor road to Watchet.

7 Turn right on to the B3191, over the bridge, and along the coast. Turn left to Washford in 1.5 miles (2.5km), then turn right on to the A39 (for Cleeve Abbey turn immediately left into Abbey Road where there is also a cider farm). Turn left in just over half a mile (800m) and then right, signed Combe Country Park.

8 Continue ahead on the B3188 towards Wiveliscombe, passing Combe Sydenham Country Park at Monksilver with its handsome Elizabethan walled gardens, woodland walks and deer park.

9 Turn left on Milverton road. Just after the turning is a footpath leading to early 19th-century Willett's Folly Tower on your right, with views of the Quantocks. Turn left at the T-junction in half a mile (800m) and continue along the B3227 for 8 miles (13km) back to Taunton.

Part of a charming walk leading from Holford village

QUANTOCK WALKS

The compact nature of the Quantocks is what makes walking so pleasant here. There is a network of excellent paths and tracks throughout the area and it is easy to make circular walks of varying lengths, either up and over the Quantock ridge or along the broad back of the ridge itself. There are several car-parks.

Some of the best places to start a walk from are **Cothelstone Hill**, **Dead Woman's Ditch** or the **Triscombe Stone**.

You can walk the 11 miles (17km) of the ridge from **Lydeard Hill** car-park to **Staple Plain** car-park above **West Quantoxhead**.

There are several delightful walking routes from **Holford** village.

The OS Explorer 22 map, Quantock Hills and Bridgwater, is very useful for route-finding.

SEE CONTACTS SECTION FOR ADDITIONAL INFORMATION

THE SOMERSET LEVELS & THE POLDEN HILLS

On the Somerset Levels and moors, you will be walking on the bed of an ancient sea. The Levels lie just above the level of the sea and are nearest the coast; the moors lie farther inland and here you may even be technically 'under water', where parts of them lie below the present sea-level. Summer and winter alike, the area is often shrouded in an eerie mist, just like the sea. During prehistory, the area was a scattered archipelago of little island communities amid a glittering expanse of marshy water. Only when medieval farmers effectively 'plugged' the seashore at Bridgwater Bay with sea walls did exploitation of the Levels and moors begin. Natural drainage was supplied by the rivers Brue and Parrett, but man-made drainage ditches, known locally as rhynes, were excavated when the monastic estates of Wells and Glastonbury dominated rural life in the area. In the 18th century, enclosure of the Levels began in earnest with the installation of tidal sluices, straightening of river channels and the cutting of a network of rhynes and major drainage channels such as King's Sedgemoor Drain and the Huntspill 'River'.

Today the area is unrelentingly flat, except where isolated 'islands' of high ground, such as Burrow Mump, Dundon Hill and Turn Hill, rise like

BIKES ON THE LEVEL

For relaxed cycling you can't get more level than the Levels! This is cycling the old-fashioned way and you should consider using an equally old-fashioned upright bicycle to do the rounds. On summer evenings you'll see flocks of locals from nearby towns serenely coasting along the Levels to the many friendly pubs and inns. There are numerous cycling routes throughout the Levels and over the Polden Hills. Leaflets are available from local TICs.

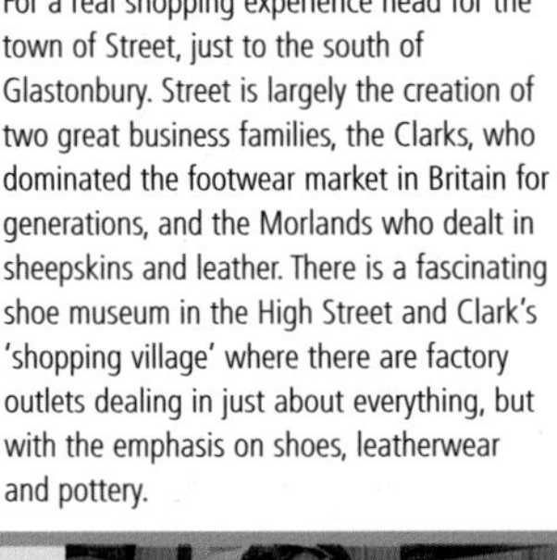

STREET AND FEET

For a real shopping experience head for the town of Street, just to the south of Glastonbury. Street is largely the creation of two great business families, the Clarks, who dominated the footwear market in Britain for generations, and the Morlands who dealt in sheepskins and leather. There is a fascinating shoe museum in the High Street and Clark's 'shopping village' where there are factory outlets dealing in just about everything, but with the emphasis on shoes, leatherwear and pottery.

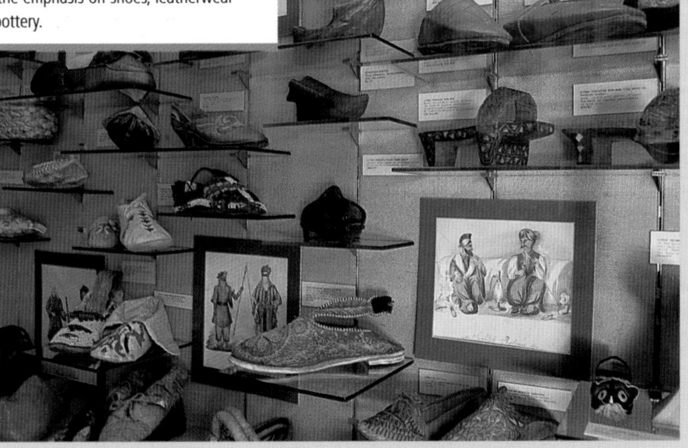

Vintage footware on display at Clark's shoe museum in Street

WILLOW WEAVING

The growing of willows has long been a rural industry in the Somerset Levels, especially around Athelney and Burrowbridge in the south. The willows are used for the weaving of baskets and the production of artists' charcoal. They are cut in the spring and there are several varieties with fascinating names such as Black Spaniard and Dicky Meadows. At the **Willows and Wetlands Visitor Centre** at **Stoke St Gregory** the processing of willows can be seen from planting to basket-making.

Glastonbury Cycle Ride

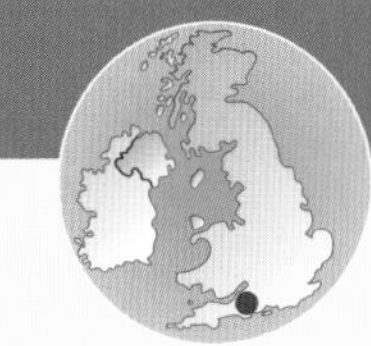

CYCLE RIDE

Glastonbury & the Somerset Levels

START/FINISH: Glastonbury. Located on the A39, 6 miles (9km) south of Wells

DISTANCE: 18 miles (29km)

GRADIENT: mainly flat with gentle climbs; one short steep climb

ROADS: country lanes (some quite narrow); a short stretch of busy A361

PARKING: plenty of pay-and-display car-parks in the town centre

A place of myth and legend, historic Glastonbury abounds in interesting places, in particular the impressive, ruined 12th-century abbey, and is the perfect start point for this gentle 3 to 4 hour ride. Almost traffic-free, it explores the narrow lanes that criss-cross the Levels, with plenty of opportunity for picnicking and enjoying the scenery and wildlife havens.

1 From Glastonbury, head up the High Street and turn right at the T-junction to join the A361, signed Shepton Mallet. Bear left at the mini-roundabout, keeping on the often busy A361 (take great care).

2 After 875 yds (800m), just beyond Well House Lane (leading to Glastonbury Tor and the remains of St Michael's Church), turn right into Cinnamon Lane. Take great care; this lane drops steeply and there can be loose gravel around. Take the first right, opposite an orchard on the left with great views of the Tor, and follow the canal for 1 mile (1.5km). When the road leaves the riverside continue for about another mile (1.5km).

3 At the end, turn left by the post box, then right, signed West Bradley. To visit West Pennard Court Barn Farm, turn left at the T-junction, signed to West Pennard, and continue for 547yds (500m) retrace your tracks back to the T-junction and go straight ahead, signed towards West Bradley. Follow the signs and the run of the road, heading for Parbrook. Pass West Bradley Orchards Fruit Farm, gently climb past the village church, then turn right towards Horn Blotton and Lydford.

4 Pass the Old School and climb the rise, turning right at the farm at the top, signed Baltonsborough. Enjoy the easy ride to Baltonsborough,

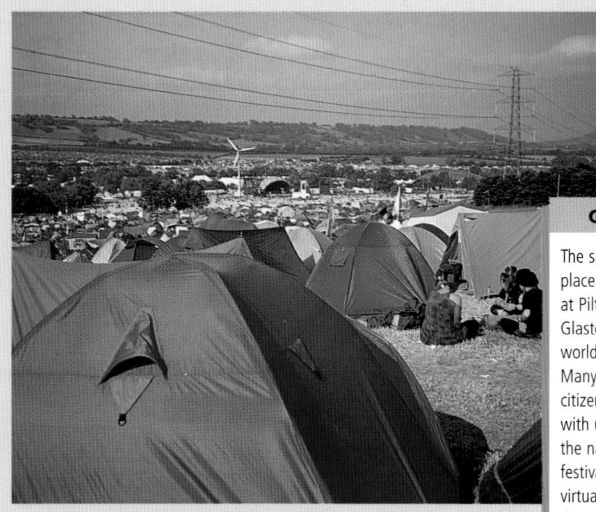

A sea of tents at Glastonbury Festival, Somerset's summer rock event

GLASTONBURY FESTIVAL

The spectacular Glastonbury Festival takes place each year on the farm of Michael Eavis at Pilton, several miles to the east of Glastonbury. This places the festival in a world far apart from Glastonbury proper. Many of Glastonbury's more restrained citizens are quick to point this out, perhaps with understandable exasperation at having the name of their historic town hijacked. The festival can either be sunny and superb, or a virtual mud-bath, but everyone enjoys themselves, whatever the weather!

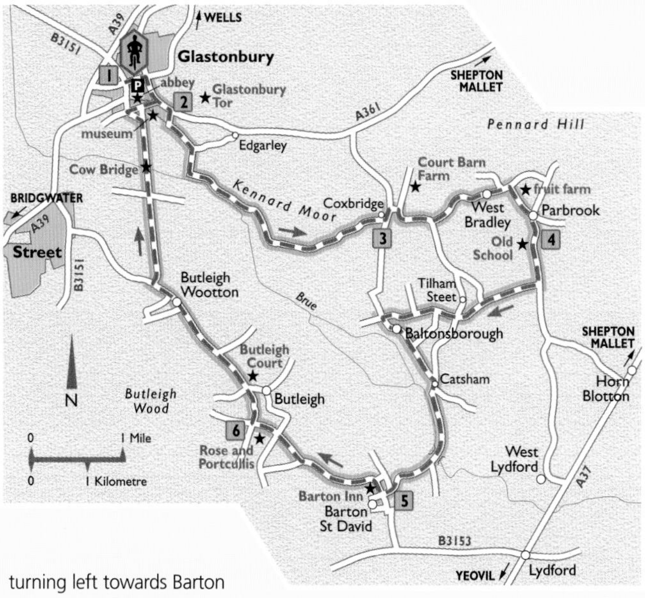

turning left towards Barton St David into Muchelney Road before the phone box, and follow the lane downhill. Bear left at the T-junction before crossing a tight hump-backed bridge to enter Barton St David.

5 At the slightly staggered crossroads (with the phone box opposite) turn right towards Butleigh. Pass the Barton Inn and the converted church, then continue out of the village. Drop down into Butleigh before tackling the ascent through the village to the Rose and Portcullis Inn at the top.

6 At the crossroads turn right into Sub Road towards Glastonbury. Go past Butleigh Court, a fine castellated building, then continue for 1.5 miles (2.5km) through Butleigh Wootton before turning right at the top of a rise, down across the levels back towards Glastonbury. Cross Cow Bridge, go through the '30' signs, and take the first right into Old Butleigh Road, up the steep ascent. Turn right at the top, passing the fascinating Somerset Rural Life Museum on the right, which is housed in a splendid tithe barn (Abbey Barn). Turn left at the mini-roundabout through the traffic-calming scheme, then left again back into Glastonbury High Street to the start point.

green mounds. This is walking country for the genuinely unhurried. Even the wooded Polden Hills at the central area of the Levels rise no higher than 300ft (90m). Once windmills lined the crest of the Poldens and today the drier ground of the hills supports arable farming. Walking on the natural 'balcony' of the Poldens gives unrivalled views over the Levels and moors, a chequerboard of green fields and meadows within a network of rhynes, their edges fringed by willows.

Glastonbury is the main settlement of the Levels. Once an islanded community in prehistory, modern Glastonbury is still 'afloat' with New Age and Old Age myth-making. Glastonbury Abbey saw one of the earliest examples of PR, when the impoverished 12th-century monks claimed to have found the bones of King Arthur and Queen Guinevere in the abbey grounds. The monks probably lived happily on the profits from the ensuing rush of pilgrims! Today Glastonbury is awash with modern pilgrims and alternative life-styles – you'll find some remarkable craft and New-Age shops here – although it remains a sedate market town steeped in history.

Even King Alfred showed up on the Levels. He took refuge from the Danes in 878 at the then island of Athelney Hill. Just north of Athelney is the splendidly named Westonzoyland. This was the scene for the last battle in England when the assembled forces of the Catholic James II defeated the rebel supporters of the Protestant Duke of Monmouth. The battle goes under the name Sedgemoor, Westonzoyland being too much of a mouthful, perhaps!

RIDING CAMELS AND LLAMAS

Never mind exotic destinations and desert safaris, you can enjoy your view of the Somerset Levels and coastal area from the back of a camel! The **Bridgwater Camel Company** runs camel-riding day treks, with accompanying llamas and Hereford steers carrying the picnic and barbecue gear. What the camels make of all that Levels water is anybody's guess!

WETLAND HABITAT

The Somerset Levels and moors make up the finest area of surviving wetland habitat in Britain and are internationally important as feeding sites for migratory birds. There are otters here, too, and the insect life is prolific, with rare dragonflies among the many fascinating species. Take a walk alongside the rhynes or down one of the wetland tracks, such as **London Drove** near Westhay. The western section of the **River Parrett Trail** is another fine walking route.

THE MENDIPS, BATH & BRISTOL

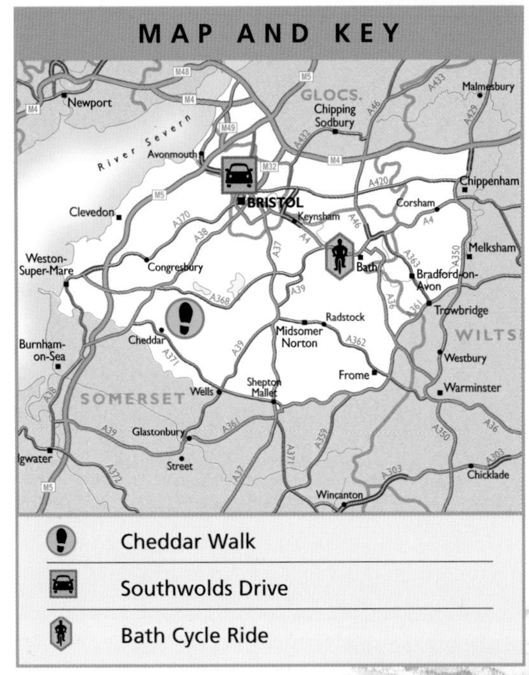

The West Country is at its busiest and most developed round Bristol and Bath, yet within easy reach of both these historic cities lie the peaceful Mendip Hills. Bristol is full of historic features and cultural adventure, the kind of city that rewards the dedicated urban explorer. In Bath you can find the spirit and style of the 18th century amid the city's outstanding Georgian

Bristol Cathedral
Bristol Cathedral is a powerful building that exudes medieval solidity. The early Norman chapter house survives and its interior features include some of the finest Norman design work to survive in England. The handsome gatehouse of the original Augustinian abbey that stood on the site adjoins the cathedral.

Bath's Royal Crescent
Royal Crescent is the most imposing of Bath's many Georgian features. The Crescent is composed of 30 terraced houses in an elegant and unbroken curve, the façade being decorated with 114 giant Ionic columns and other classical motifs. Near by, along Brock Street, is another of Bath's great architectural features, the Royal Circus.

architecture. On the Mendips you will go even farther back in time. The ancient landscape bears the marks of Roman lead-mining and the patterns of medieval farming, broken by the limestone gorges of Cheddar and Burrington where there are spectacular cliffs and caves. For a final contrast, the west coast towns preserve the architecture of Victorian Britain beside the sea.

CLEVEDON COURT

The National Trust's Clevedon Court is a well-preserved 14th-century manor house with a 12th-century tower and 13th-century great hall. The chapel is a delightful feature. Collections of Nailsea glass and traditional pottery are on display and there is also an 18th-century terraced garden with a fine collection of shrubs and rare plants.

Priddy
The village of Priddy stands at the heart of the high Mendips. Close by are impressive Bronze-Age circles and burial mounds. The popular Priddy Fair is held on the huge village green around 21 August each year, and is one of the great traditional country fairs of the West Country.

Cheddar Gorge
Towering limestone cliffs enclose the deep ravine of Cheddar Gorge, which slices dramatically through the gentle flanks of the Mendip Hills. The Gorge is over a mile (1.5km) long. At its southern end there are several cave systems that can be visited by joining a conducted tour.

WELLS

The smallest cathedral city in England, Wells crams a great deal of architectural splendour into its few acres. The west façade of Wells Cathedral is magnificent, a great stone screen which has nearly 300 statues. Near by is Vicar's Close, one of the best-preserved medieval streets in Europe.

THE MENDIP HILLS & CHEDDAR GORGE

The Mendip Hills were once a ridge-like island rising over the salty swamps and grassy mounds of ancient Somersaetas, the land of the summer herders. Today the Mendips remain island-like; their southern escarpment rises abruptly from the unrelenting flatness of the Somerset Levels. The Mendip ridge is 50 miles (80km) long, and from its western edge – the shapely Crook Peak above the roaring M5 – it sweeps southeast along a broad plateau. Its flanks are pierced by stupendous gorges, most famously at Cheddar where the limestone massif seems to have burst apart to expose towering cliffs on either side. East of Cheddar the broad back of the Mendips ridge descends gently towards the market town of Frome. This eastern section is far less hilly than the main bulk of the Mendips; no deep ravines slice into the landscape, and the land is more wooded. Here you will discover numerous delightful towns and villages, such as Frome itself, and the enchanting Mells with its wonderful medieval enclave and handsome church.

The Mendips are not lofty hills, but in the northwest they rise to their highest point at 1,066-ft (325-m) Beacon Batch, on Blackdown. The broad plateau of the Mendips, with its rolling farmland and areas of heath, seems satisfyingly remote, detached as it is from the busy plains that surround the hills. The roar of the M5 to the west and the hustle and bustle round Wells and Glastonbury to the south, are shut out by height and

TICKLE YOUR PALATE

The south-facing slopes of the Mendips, with their well-drained soil, are ideal for fruit growing. Strawberries have been a long-established Mendip favourite and the growing of grapes is now a significant industry. Excellent Somerset wines are now challenging the supremacy of the county's famous cider. Wine lovers can enjoy a relaxing tour of vineyards such as those at **Pilton**, **North Wootton**, **Whatley** and **Wraxall**. For cheese to complement the wine, visit the Cheddar Cheese Dairy in **Cheddar Gorge**, or Chewton Cheese Dairy at **Chewton Mendip** on the northern side of the Mendips. Ask at local TICs for further information.

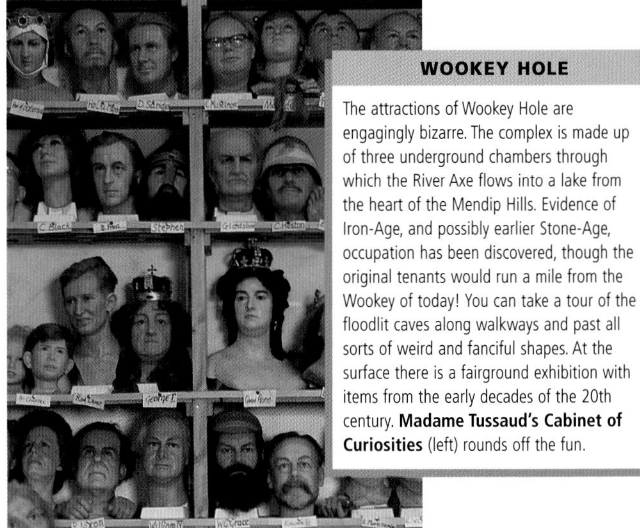

WOOKEY HOLE

The attractions of Wookey Hole are engagingly bizarre. The complex is made up of three underground chambers through which the River Axe flows into a lake from the heart of the Mendip Hills. Evidence of Iron-Age, and possibly earlier Stone-Age, occupation has been discovered, though the original tenants would run a mile from the Wookey of today! You can take a tour of the floodlit caves along walkways and past all sorts of weird and fanciful shapes. At the surface there is a fairground exhibition with items from the early decades of the 20th century. **Madame Tussaud's Cabinet of Curiosities** (left) rounds off the fun.

Cheddar Walk

WALK

The Other Sides to Cheddar Gorge

START/FINISH: Cheddar. Between Wells and Weston-Super-Mare on the A371

DISTANCE: 8 miles (13km)

ASCENT/GRADIENT: 990ft (300m); moderately steep gradients up and down edges of gorge; gradual elsewhere

PATHS: variable; paths around gorge slippery when wet

PARKING: pay-and-display car-park in Cliff Street, Cheddar, near a roundabout on B3135 at end of Cheddar Gorge

The remarkable plant life of this famous landmark is celebrated on a spectacular circuit from Cheddar. Explore several nature reserves, rich in lime-loving flora. Long, gradual climbs are rewarded with dramatic views of the gorge and beyond to the Welsh hills, Cotswolds and Exmoor.

1 From the car-park turn right towards the gorge. Cross the bridge and take the next road on the right, keeping uphill. Just before the brow of the hill turn left up behind the cottages. At the end of the lane follow the bridleway up to the left. Keep following the Gorge Walk waymarks along the edge of the gorge for 1.5 miles (2km). The path ascends to the top of a ridge and descends through woodland to the road at the head of the gorge. It was once thought that the gorge was one huge collapsed cave, but current theory considers that it was cut by a river swollen with meltwater from snow during the Ice Age. The greatest sheer drop is about 395ft (120m).

2 Cross the road and take the gate and track ahead into Black Rock reserve, one of several nature reserves on the walk. The gorge provides the only British habitat for the Cheddar pink and Cheddar bedstraw, plus another 17 nationally scarce plants and 29 resident species of butterfly. Follow the main track up the bottom of the valley for half a mile (800m). After the National Trust sign turn right over a wall and follow the waymarks up the bottom of the valley for another mile (1.5km).

3 At the road at the top turn right, then left along the waymarked path just before the causeway. Follow this to a junction with a track and turn right to the car-park. At the information board turn left and continue left along the track for about 330yds (300m). Turn left along

distance. Amid well-ploughed fields and heathland lie prehistoric burial mounds and ancient lead-workings that were exploited by the Romans. Near the village of Priddy are the Bronze-Age sites of Priddy Nine Barrows and Priddy Circles. The barrows are burial sites, but the purpose of the circles is still not fully understood. In the nearby Ebbor Gorge are caverns that were once occupied by Old Stone-Age hunters.

The main gorges of the Mendips – Cheddar, Ebbor and Burrington Combe – on the northern flanks of the hills, are riddled with the serpentine cave systems. Cheddar is the most famous of these great ravines. Its awesome walls rise sheer for over 1,000ft (304m). Cheddar village at the mouth of the gorge is heavily commercialised, but this does not detract from the natural splendour of the gorge itself. The underground scenery is every bit as dramatic as above ground. A short distance northeast of Cheddar is the historic town of Axbridge, with its charming medieval centre overlooked by a fine church and by the preserved King John's Hunting Lodge, a superb 15th-century timber-framed building. A mile or so south of the Mendips, and fed by the streams that have given it its famous name, is the delightful cathedral city of Wells.

SKI MENDIP

It snows on the Mendips most winters, but there's little chance it will be deep enough or that temperatures will be low enough for winter sports. You can enjoy winter sports at any time of the year, however, in the village of **Churchill**, at **High Action** dry-ski slope. The slope is 540ft (165m) long. There is snowboarding as well, and even a toboggan run. High Action runs horse-riding trips and organises archery, orienteering and other outdoor activities.

the waymarked path which crosses a dam and ascends to a road. Turn right along the road, then take the road ascending to the left.

4 At the masts bear left along a lane. Once on the heath it is worth a detour to Black Down summit, the highest point of the Mendips at 1,067ft (325m), for the views that take in the mountains of South Wales and the hills of the Forest of Dean, the Cotswolds, the Quantocks and Exmoor. From the gate at the end of the lane, bear left along the edge of the heath. At the bunker take the gate and follow the waymarked bridleway diagonally to the right and down across two fields. Then take the lane down to the road.

5 Turn right along the road and take the next turn to the left, down a farm drive. Keep right of Charterhouse

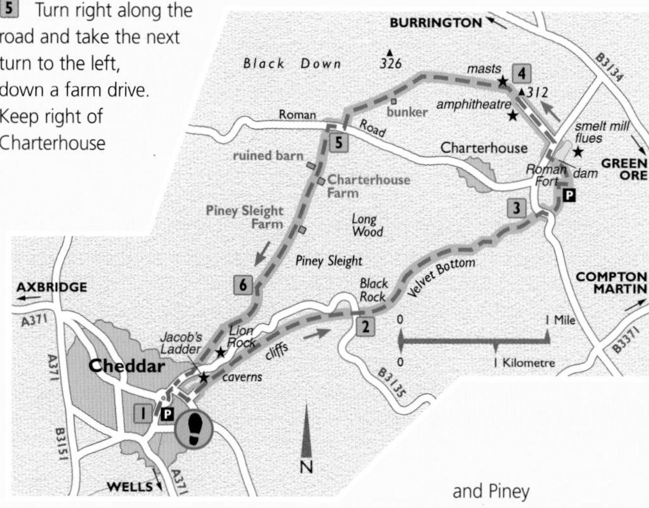

and Piney Sleight Farms, then follow the yellow waymarks ahead across fields, keeping close to the walls on your right.

6 Cross a stile from fields into a scrubby area. Bear left, then right, to pick up the Gorge Walk waymarks. Keep downhill with the gorge on your left. It is worth the detour down a steep flight of steps to a viewpoint. Returning, the path steepens to descend through woods to a track. Turn left down the track, then right and down the road through the gorge to return to the start.

ESCAPE ON FOOT

Walking on the Mendips, especially on the high ground of the hills, gives a real sense of escape, when you consider how busy the surrounding area is. There are several leaflets available at TICs that give details of short walks and circular routes.

West Mendip Way – a greater challenge at 30 miles (48km) from Wells to the coast at Uphill, south of Weston. The route can be done over three days and there is plenty of accommodation available along the way. The OS Explorers 141 and 153 maps cover the areas through which the route passes. Ask at TICs for West Mendip Way guidebooks.

A climber scales the heights of Cheddar Gorge, as an alternative to caving

CAVING

The rounded profile of the Mendips masks the honeycombed inner landscape of these limestone hills wherein massive caves, such as those at **Cheddar** and **Wookey**, are replicated in a huge network of smaller cave systems that riddle the ground. You can visit the large commercial caves in Cheddar Gorge and get muddy on more adventurous caving trips under close supervision.

The eerie Witch's Kitchen at Wookey Hole

BRISTOL & THE WEST COAST

Old Bristol was a major port. Its position so far from the sea may seem to deny this, but the River Avon was neatly tapped at Hotwells, on the west side of the city, to create the famous 'floating dock' – a long artificial channel where tidal water could be impounded at all stages of the tide. This allowed trading vessels to reach far inland and to stay afloat once there. Now, Bristol's docks lie down river, on the coast at Avonmouth, and the old floating dock has been transformed into a fashionable commercial and leisure district, the lively heart of modern Bristol. Here, at the watery cul-de sac of St Augustine's Reach you'll find the Watershed Media Centre, the At-Bristol attractions and the fashionable Arnolfini Arts Centre, some in converted warehouses.

Just east of St Augustine's Reach is College Green and the impressive buildings of Bristol Cathedral and crescent-shaped Council House. From the head of the Reach it is a short step along Corn Street to a cluster of fine old buildings. These include the Corn Exchange with its outside row of plinths, Bristol's famous 'Nails' on which merchants confirmed deals by 'paying on the nail'. Another arm of the dock is known as the Welsh Back, and is the quay where trading vessels and barges from Wales once off-loaded. Near by is the 17th-century timber building, the Landoger Trow, a popular pub, and opposite the Old Duke Inn, famous for its live jazz. Just north of the Welsh Back is the green open space of Castle Park, with the huge Broadmead shopping precinct beyond.

A few miles downriver from Bristol's urban bustle lies the great sweep of the Severn Estuary at Avonmouth, from where Bristol's 'West Coast' runs for 15 miles (24km) to the Victorian showpiece resort of Weston-Super-Mare. Avonmouth and Portishead are heavily industrialised, but you can still escape the industrial sprawl and, from Portishead Point, you can view the Welsh coast across the channel and watch the great ships glide in and out of the river's mouth.

Midway between Avonmouth and

BALLOONING

On summer evenings the blue skies above Bristol's **Durdham Downs** are often filled with brilliantly coloured hot-air balloons. The balloons come in all shapes and sizes, from soft-drink cans to bunches of carrots! You can sample what it's like to float serenely above Bristol and the River Avon and the Somerset countryside on balloon flights organised by a number of specialist companies in the Bristol area. Champagne is available, if you feel like rising even higher. One of the great delights of ballooning is that where you go is determined by the wind direction.

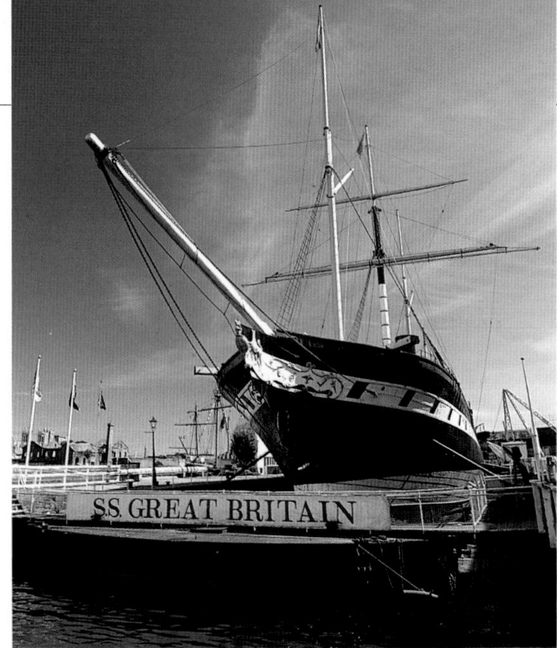

The SS Great Britain, *moored at Bristol's historic dockyards*

Southwolds Drive

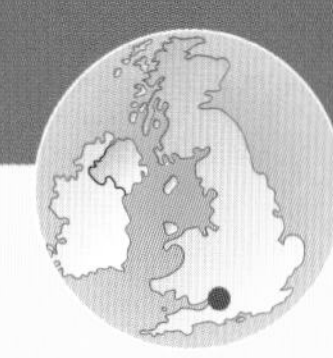

DRIVE

The Southwolds & the Vale of Berkeley

START/FINISH: Bristol. Between Bath and Avonmouth on the A4
DISTANCE: 63 miles (101km)

From the city of Bristol, rich in culture and history, this drive explores the steep escarpment of the Southwolds (southern Cotswolds) and the flatlands of the Severn Estuary, before returning to Bristol via the dramatic Avon Gorge.

1 Leave Bristol on the A4, following signs for the M32. At the St James Barton roundabout turn right and join the left lane for the M32. Join the M32 and exit at junction 2 to follow the B4469 towards Fishponds. At the mini-roundabout turn left (A432). Continue on the A432 to reach Fishponds, then at the Cross Hands branch right at the traffic lights, signed Chippenham (A420). Continue to reach Mangotsfield.

2 At the mini-roundabout turn left, then, at the church, turn right on to Cossham Street, then bear right at the mini-roundabout and proceed to Pucklechurch. Bear right, unclassified (signed Hinton) and in 200yds (183m) turn left, signed to Hinton. Continue through Hinton and turn left (A46) towards Stroud. At the M4 roundabout, take the second exit, straight across, then in 2 miles (3km) turn right at the traffic lights by Cross Hands Hotel (B4040), signed Malmesbury. Bear left at the signpost for Malmesbury at Acton Turville. At a T-junction turn left, signed to Badminton. Continue through Great and Little Badminton.

3 At the junction with the A46 continue straight across for Hawkesbury Upton. Pass the Hawkesbury Monument then bear right for Hillesley. Continue through Hillesley and then Alderley and in 1.5 miles (2km) bear left into Wotton-under-Edge. Follow signs for Dursley (B4060) to reach North Nibley and at the Black Horse turn left into The Street. At the church, bear right for Berkeley, descend and, on reaching the A38, turn left. In nearly half a mile (800m) turn right on to a minor road and at the following T-junction turn left (B4066). After 2 miles (3km) go forward and soon reach Berkeley which is noted for its castle. Near by is the Jenner Museum where the first smallpox vaccination was performed.

4 Turn left, signed Jenner Museum, and in 3 miles (5km) turn right, unclassified for Thornbury. Continue through Rockhampton and turn

WESTON-SUPER-MARE

A day in Weston is the ideal seaside experience, especially for families with young children. There's a safe, sandy beach and all the traditional fun and games from donkey rides to a Grand Pier with a huge, covered amusement centre. The **Sea Life Centre** has everything from shrimps to sharks and the **Tropicana Pleasure Beach** offers attractions from wave machines to giant slides. If it all gets too much for you, there's peaceful **Grove Park** near Royal Parade where you can unwind amid a riot of flowers. And there's plenty of evening action as well, from variety shows to clubbing and ballroom dancing, as well as the scores of pubs that stage live entertainment.

A horse-drawn beach attraction at Weston-Super-Mare

FIVE GOOD PUBS IN THE MENDIPS

Pony and Trap, Chew Magna Eighteenth-century pub with views over Chew Valleys.

Poachers Pocket, Chelynch Traditional 16th-century village pub with stone-flagged floors.

Bell, Leigh upon Mendip Comfortable and friendly 16th-century pub with garden.

Crown Inn, Churchill Unspoilt gem of a stone-built pub on the edge of the Mendip Hills. The Mendip Morris Men visit during the summer months.

Ring O'Bells, Compton Martin Old village pub with open fires and inglenook seats, large garden with swings and a slide, and a family room.

right (B4061). In 1 mile (1.5km) turn right into Church Road, to Thornbury Castle Hotel. Turn left past the church and keep left for Thornbury town centre. Turn right on to the B4061 (no sign) and continue through Thornbury. Soon turn right (B4461) towards Aust. In half a mile (800m) turn right again. At the junction roundabout with the M48, take the first exit A403 (Avonmouth).

5 Continue for 3 miles (5km) then turn left at the traffic lights (B4055) into Pilning and go forward, signed Bristol, through Easter Compton. Ascend to reach a roundabout and take the third exit A4018 (Bristol W), then at the third roundabout, take the third exit (signed Blaise Castle) along the B4057 (no sign) to Henbury. At the crossroads turn right then keep forward (one-way) to pass the road to Blaise Castle House on the left.

6 Continue on the B4057 for 2 miles (3km) then, at the traffic signals, turn right (A4162) into Sylvan Way, signed to Avonmouth. Shortly, turn left at the traffic lights (A4) for the City Centre. Continue on the A4 following signs for the City Centre. Enter Avon Gorge and pass beneath Brunel's suspension bridge at Clifton, to return to Bristol.

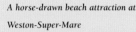

Weston is stylish Clevedon, where you will find the National Trust's Clevedon Court, a splendid 14th-century manor house. Clevedon itself is a charming mix of Regency and mainly Victorian buildings, a classic 19th-century resort that grew out of a small fishing village below a wooded hill. The town and its sea-front have survived with much of their period charm intact. Clevedon's pier, opened in 1869, collapsed in the 1970s but has been restored to its previous glory. South from Clevedon the coast becomes very flat where the Congresbury Yeo River reaches the muddy foreshore. Beyond lies Sand Bay, and Weston-Super-Mare, like Clevedon, once a tiny fishing village that was transformed by Victorian holiday-making and is now the largest town in North Somerset and a major West Country resort.

WATER WORLD

At the **West Country Water Park** you can try just about every kind of watersport on a specially manufactured lake. The Water Park is situated near the junction of the M4 and M5 motorways, just north of Bristol. You can sample windsurfing, jet skiing, water-skiing or more relaxed canoeing, dinghy sailing and rowing. You can even try surf-biking, an ingenious way of getting around on water. Special sessions are organised for youngsters and there's even clay pigeon shooting, if you really want to keep your feet dry!

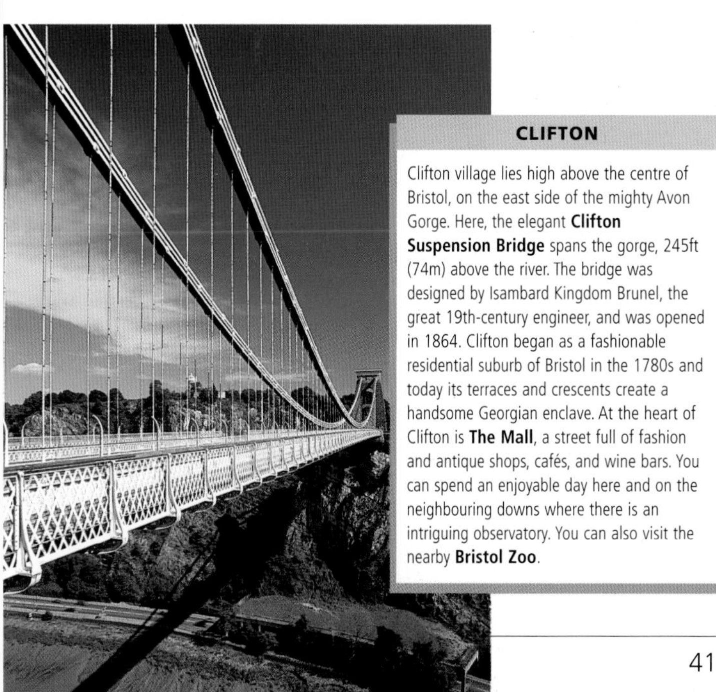

CLIFTON

Clifton village lies high above the centre of Bristol, on the east side of the mighty Avon Gorge. Here, the elegant **Clifton Suspension Bridge** spans the gorge, 245ft (74m) above the river. The bridge was designed by Isambard Kingdom Brunel, the great 19th-century engineer, and was opened in 1864. Clifton began as a fashionable residential suburb of Bristol in the 1780s and today its terraces and crescents create a handsome Georgian enclave. At the heart of Clifton is **The Mall**, a street full of fashion and antique shops, cafés, and wine bars. You can spend an enjoyable day here and on the neighbouring downs where there is an intriguing observatory. You can also visit the nearby **Bristol Zoo**.

BATH & THE AVON VALLEY

Bath is England's greatest architectural gem; its setting is the ultimate in picturesque – a landscape of dense, green hills beautifully deployed around a city of golden stone. From the north, the Somerset Cotswolds, the high bluffs of Lansdown, Bannerdown and Solsbury send down their streams to join the River Avon. Deeper waters than these created Bath and gave it the original Roman name *Aquae Sulis*. The hot springs, that once bubbled to the surface of an empty landscape, captivated the Roman colonisers, delighted to have found some form of Mediterranean warmth in a cold northern land. In modern Bath, 250,000 gallons (1,136,500 litres) of water still rise each day at 120°F (47°C). The preserved remains of 1st-century Roman baths, dedicated to the English deity Sulis and to the Roman goddess Minerva, survive in Stall Street. The remains comprise five baths and two pools with their underfloor heating systems, known as hypocausts, still intact.

Georgian Bath was a glorious expression of wealth, fashion and privilege. The greatest legacies of that time are the buildings and streets of this amazing city. Honey-coloured Bath stone gives a romantic hue to 18th-century classicism. Many of Bath's finest buildings and streets were the work of father and son architects, John Wood the Elder and John Wood the Younger. Wood the Younger carried through the vision of his father. Exquisite features such as Bath's Royal Circus and Royal Crescent are his works. Other wonderful Bath buildings include the King's Bath in Stall Street, alongside the even more famous Pump Room. In the King's Bath you can see the green viscous water of the spa pool where, before the fashionable decorum of the Georgian era, male and female bathers frolicked merrily together – sometimes 'unclothed', according to a delighted William Pepys. Although a less salubrious aspect was that the waters were also fetid. The Large Salon of the

SHOPPING AT ITS BEST

Antiques, crafts, paintings and the best bric-à-brac can all be found in Georgian Bath's numerous fascinating shopping outlets.

Bartlett Street for antiques.

Broad Street and **Walcot Street** for all manner of stylish craft and bric-à-brac shops.

Off **Brock Street**, between the Circus and the Royal Crescent, there are antiquarian and second-hand book shops.

Off **Queen Square** for fine galleries.

Pulteney Bridge, Bath's most unique shopping 'precinct', is two rows of shops on the bridge itself.

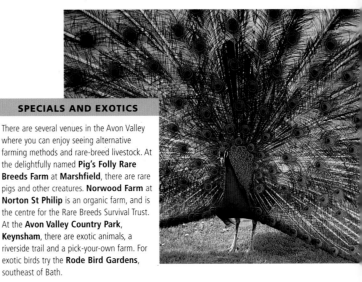

The ancient Roman baths, one of the attractions in the Georgian city of Bath

SPECIALS AND EXOTICS

There are several venues in the Avon Valley where you can enjoy seeing alternative farming methods and rare-breed livestock. At the delightfully named **Pig's Folly Rare Breeds Farm** at **Marshfield**, there are rare pigs and other creatures. **Norwood Farm** at **Norton St Philip** is an organic farm, and is the centre for the Rare Breeds Survival Trust. At the **Avon Valley Country Park**, **Keynsham**, there are exotic animals, a riverside trail and a pick-your-own farm. For exotic birds try the **Rode Bird Gardens**, southeast of Bath.

Bath Cycle Ride

CYCLE RIDE

The Bristol & Bath Railway Path

START/FINISH: Royal Crescent in Bath. The town is situated on the A4 southeast of Bristol

DISTANCE: 21 miles (34km)

GRADIENT: undulating with several climbs; level along cycle path

ROADS: stretches of A-road (great care); narrow country lanes with sharp bends

PARKING: on-street parking at the Victoria Park play area

Starting in the historic spa-town of Bath, this route makes use of the famous Bristol and Bath Railway Path. Constructed by the Bristol-based charity Sustrans, this was the first major urban cycle/pedestrian route in the country. The ride loops down through Keynsham and pretty villages, to return on the cycleway.

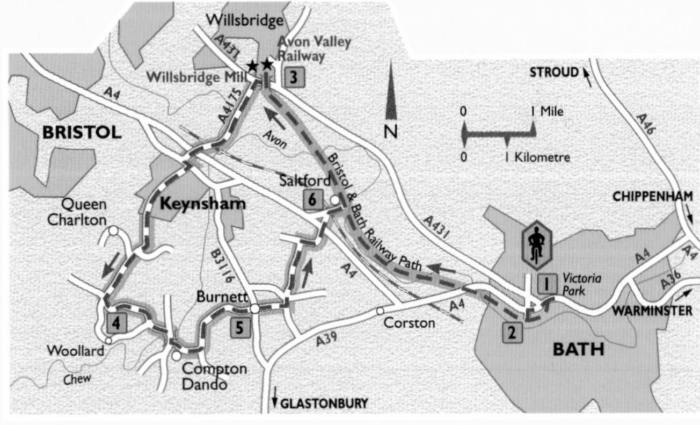

1 Head west from Victoria Park along the A4, towards Bristol. Beyond the traffic lights by the Total petrol station bear left into Locksbrook Road, signed Bristol and Bath Railway Path. Go through the industrial estate and across a mini-roundabout to reach the canal. Look out for a lock, a short way ahead on the left. Follow signs to the Bristol and Bath Railway Path on the left.

Pump Room is now an elegant tearoom, with a fountain at one end, a statue of Bath's great exemplar of manners and fashion, Beau Nash, at the other, and Bath water on tap, all to the accompaniment of classical music.

The River Avon slides quietly through Bath and under the Italianate Pulteney Bridge that links the heart of the city with the grandeur of the residential axis of Great Pulteney Street. Between Bath and Bristol, a distance of 11 miles (17km), the Avon is crowded on all sides by modern development and suburbia, yet the river retains its rural charm in places such as Saltford Lock before it is finally absorbed by busy Keynsham and then Bristol itself. It is to the east of Bath that the Avon Valley has its greatest rural charm, especially round Bradford-on-Avon, once a weaving town and today still enriched with its fine buildings in Bath stone. Between Bath and Bradford-on-Avon the Kennet and Avon Canal runs through the lovely Limpley Stoke Valley, along the famous Dundas Aqueduct beneath Conkwell Wood and on to Freshford, where the River Frome comes in from the south. Along this beautiful stretch of the Avon Valley, travel by boat is a must. Canalside pubs and tea gardens add to the relaxed pleasures of waterway life.

THE AMERICAN MUSEUM

Claverton Manor, just outside Bath, houses a remarkable American museum, a series of rooms with period furnishings showing how Americans lived in the 17th to 19th centuries. There are special exhibitions on quilts, Native Americans and religious groups such as the Shakers. There is an American arboretum in the gardens and you can enjoy tea and American cookies.

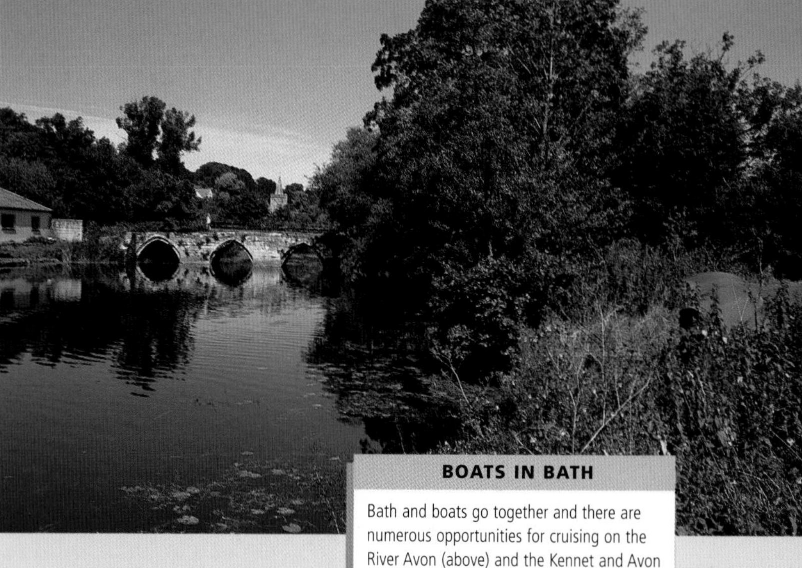

BOATS IN BATH

Bath and boats go together and there are numerous opportunities for cruising on the River Avon (above) and the Kennet and Avon Canal. The restored canal is ideal for combining boating with walking. You can go by boat one way and then stroll back along the old towpath, take a relaxed cruise on a classic narrow boat along the most picturesque sections of the canal, or an environmentally friendly electric boat.

You can also hire a rowing boat or punt for the ultimate in relaxing river boating. There are a number of cruise and hire companies; details are available from Bath TICs.

2 Enjoy a lazy, level ride for 5 miles (8km) along this traffic-free route to the Avon Valley Railway. At intervals along the cycle path, notice-boards give information about wildlife. At the Avon Valley Railway there are refreshment facilities, toilets and a wealth of railway memorabilia.

3 Leave the railway, head down the drive to the main road and turn sharp right under the old railway bridge. On reaching a roundabout, bear right if you wish to visit Willsbridge Mill; look out for a footpath on the right which takes you to the mill. It is the headquarters of the Avon Wildlife Trust, providing a nature oasis just within the bounds of Bristol, complete with exhibitions and nature trails. For the main route, bear left at the roundabout (signed Keynsham). Join the cycle path on the right of the road at The Brassmills pub and enter Keynsham, soon to pass the railway station to reach a roundabout by the Church of St John the Baptist. Turn left here, and first right into Charlton Road, signed Queen Charlton and Whitchurch. In 2 miles (3km) fork left towards Woollard then turn left at the unmarked crossroads (there is a bungalow on the opposite corner) into a small lane.

4 Continue towards Compton Dando – enjoy the descent, but do take care: gravel and a number of sharp corners must be negotiated before you finally drop down into Compton Dando. Turn right out of Peppershells Lane into the village. Bisected by the River Chew, it dates from medieval times and the church is well worth exploring. After crossing the bridge take the first turning left, signed Burnett. Climb Bathford Hill then in half a mile (800m) take the left fork, signed Avon Cycleway, dropping into the valley, and up the sharp rise on a narrow lane into Burnett.

5 Continue to the crossroads and cross the B3116 into Middlepiece Lane. Continue to a T-junction and turn left. Shortly, go straight over the crossroads, towards Saltford, and enjoy the freewheel downhill before eventually turning right, following the Avon Cycleway. At the end, turn right again into Manor Road, following the road to the main road. Take care crossing and go straight over into Beech Road. At the bottom turn right into the High Street and continue to The Bird in the Hand pub. Go down the side of the pub and just under the railway bridge turn right, which leads back on to the cycle path.

6 Turn towards Bath and retrace your route to the start of the cycle ride at Victoria Park.

BATH BUNS AND BISCUITS

The Bath Bun was made famous as the alleged creation of a 17th-century mythical character, Sally Lunn, who was said to live in Lilliput Alley, now North Parade Passage, at the heart of Old Bath. The recipe for the tea-cake was said to have been found in a cupboard in the cellar of 'Sally Lunn's' house. The French name for similar tea-cakes is *Sol et Lune*, reflecting the golden top and white underside of the bun and this suggests that Sally Lunn may be a corruption of the French original. Sally triumphs, however, and her supposed house is now the delightful Sally Lunn's Refreshment House and Museum.

Another famous Bath product is the Bath Oliver Biscuit. Created in the 1740s by Dr William Oliver, the first physician of the Bath General Hospital, it is a plain digestive biscuit that was prescribed as a healthy addition to taking the spa waters – probably to help mask the taste of Bath's elixir!

Sally Lunn's house and teashop

DORSET & SALISBURY PLAIN

Dorset's very name sounds as gentle as its smooth, green countryside of shallow river valleys and peaceful villages implies. This gentleness is maintained across the Dorset Downs, through Cranborne Chase and into neighbouring Wiltshire, where the River Nadder runs between the cathedral city of Salisbury and picturesque Sherborne. Beyond lies the vast openness of Salisbury Plain and the rolling hills of the 'White Horse' country of the Marlborough Downs. The Dorset coast is varied, embracing the sandstone of Golden Cap, the shingle beaches of Chesil and the limestone cliffs of Portland. Dorset's chief city is the popular resort of Bournemouth, vying with Dorchester and Shaftesbury and a host of pretty villages.

Stonehenge
At over 5,000 years old, Stonehenge is one of the world's most famous prehistoric sites, but it has become a victim of its fame and accessibility. Yet it is still a potent memorial to an ancient civilisation with which we have few tangible links.

LULWORTH COVE

One of the most remarkable of Dorset's coastal features is the symmetrical bay of Lulworth Cove. It has been formed by the sea's breaching of the harder limestone of the coast's outer cliff and then by its carving out of a circular basin through the softer inner core.

Corfe Castle

One of England's most romantic ruins, Corfe Castle dates from the 11th century and was a stronghold of King Alfred. The towers and ruined walls of the castle seem to grow out of the heathy ground of the hill upon which they stand. Below lies Corfe Village with its late medieval houses.

Milton Abbas

This charming village was built in the 1780s after the Earl of Shaftesbury demolished the original settlement because its proximity to his stately home offended him. There is some satisfaction in the knowledge that the village survived the earl.

Sherborne

Dorset's loveliest town has the county's finest church to add to its charms. Timber-framed façades line Sherborne's main street and the handsome buildings of the famous Sherborne School add to the town's attractiveness.

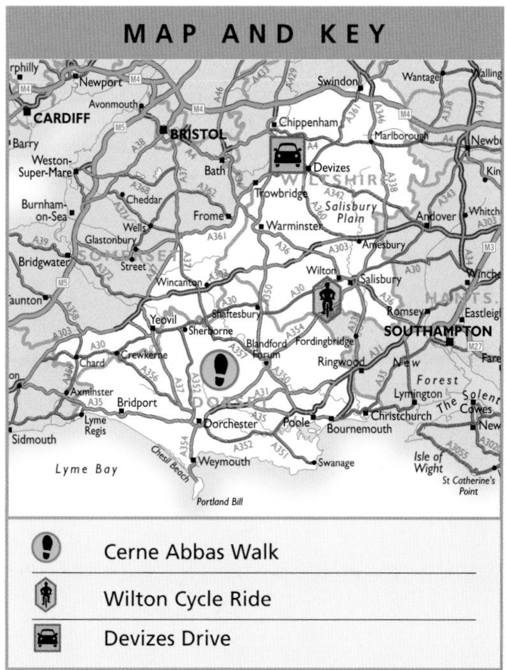

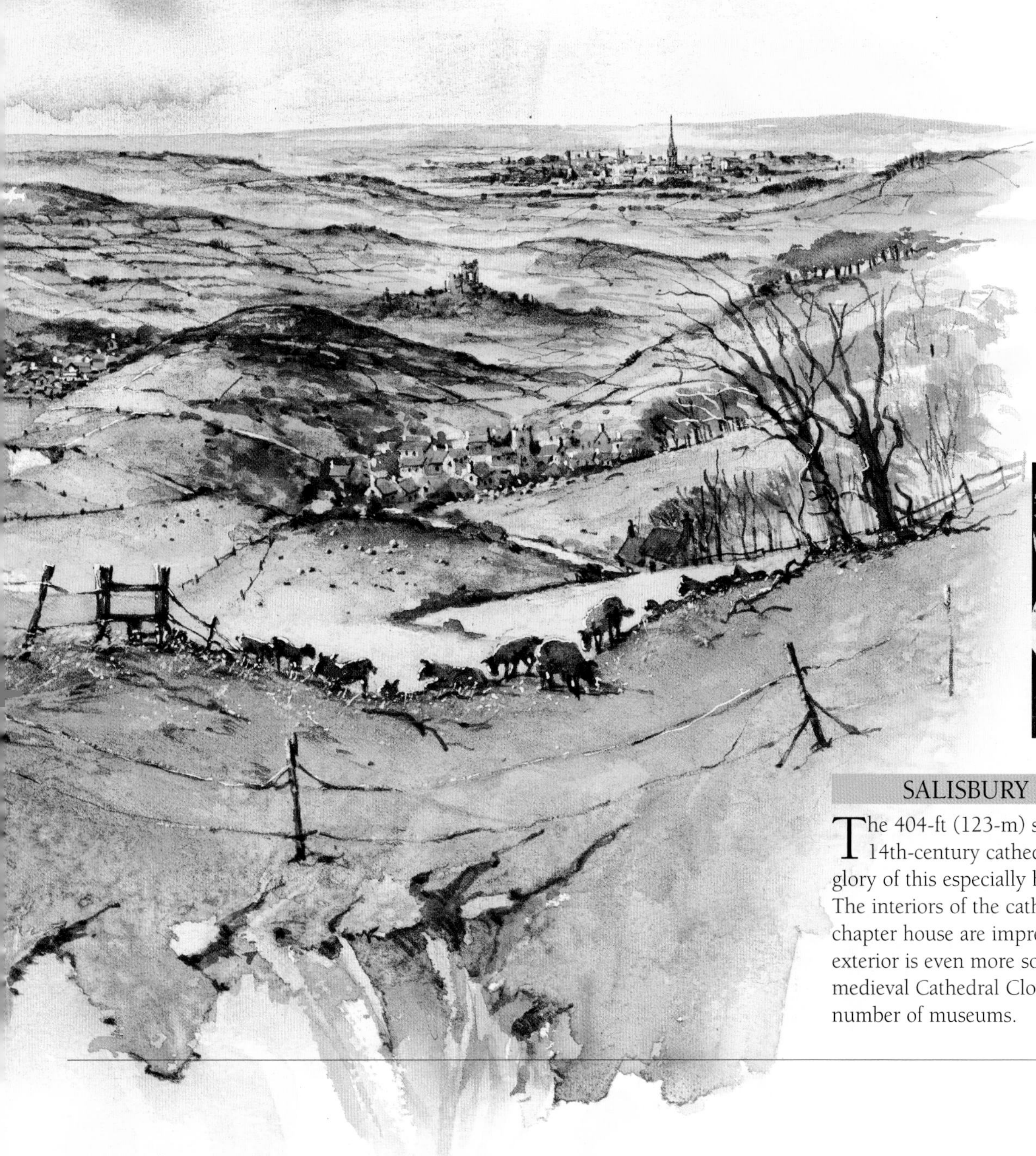

SALISBURY CATHEDRAL

The 404-ft (123-m) spire of Salisbury's 14th-century cathedral is the crowning glory of this especially harmonious building. The interiors of the cathedral, its cloisters and chapter house are impressive, but the splendid exterior is even more so, enhanced by the medieval Cathedral Close which houses a number of museums.

THE SOUTH COAST & BOURNEMOUTH

The Dorset coast begins at Lyme Regis and extends eastwards through a remarkable variety of coastal features. East of Lyme Bay the great orange-coloured cliff of Golden Cap lords it over the bay. There are still similarities to the hilly switchbacks of the Devon coast here, but soon the cliffs end, just beyond Burton Bradstock, where the remarkable 17-mile (27-km) long Chesil Beach introduces a very different coastal landscape. Land and sea merge at Chesil Beach. The great pebble ridge – the name Chesil derives from the Anglo Saxon for 'stone' – is only about 12yds (10m) high and, at the most, 200yds (180m) wide. Between Abbotsbury and Portland, the ridge impounds the brackish lake of the Fleet. Chesil Beach is a strange no man's land where the sense of space and distance is both exhilarating and unnerving. The rocky wedge of Portland Bill at its southeastern end is something of a relief, a recognisable chunk of 'dry land', with its chopped-off limestone cliffs and quarries of the Isle of Portland, and the friendly bustle of Weymouth and its sheltered bay beyond. Several miles east of Weymouth, limestone cliffs at their most beautiful and shapely begin to dominate the coast once more. This is delightful, but occasionally strenuous, walking country along the great cliffs from Durdle Door to Lulworth, then on to St Alban's Head, the most southerly point of the Isle of Purbeck. Just round the corner lie Swanage, Poole Harbour and busy Bournemouth, where

BOAT TRIPS

Going to sea from the Dorset coast is irresistible and there are various cruises from all the resorts, including a specially equipped glass-bottomed boat that operates on the **Fleet Lagoon** behind **Chesil Beach**, giving a remarkable insight to the undersea world. For a great day-trip you can even head for France or the Channel Islands aboard a Condor Ferries fast catamaran. It can take as little as two hours to get from **Weymouth** to **Jersey**, **Guernsey** or **St Malo** (you will need your passport for a French visit), with plenty of time to enjoy your destination.

The harbour at Lyme Regis, famous for its breakwater known as The Cobb

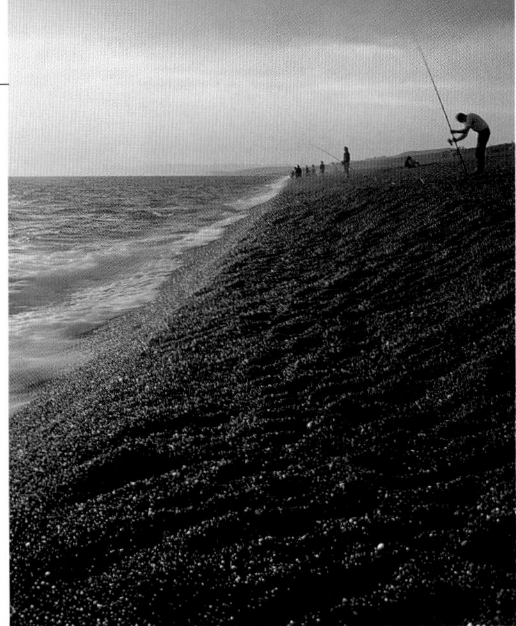

Fishing enthusiasts line the ridge of shingle at Chesil Beach

Cerne Abbas Walk

WALK

The Mystery of the Cerne Abbas Giant

START/FINISH: Cerne Abbas, Dorset
DISTANCE: 5 miles (8km)
ASCENT/GRADIENT: 575ft (175m); gradients are gradual
TERRAIN: fields and country lanes; very sticky and slippery mud after rain
PARKING: limited parking available in the village, and also at the viewpoint of the figure beside the A352 Dorchester to Sherborne road

From one of Dorset's most picturesque towns it is just a short walk to one of Britain's most mysterious figures, a giant carved in the chalk downland high above the Cerne Valley.

1 In Cerne Abbas, make your way to the church, which stands in Abbey Street and walk along the street with the church to your right. To your left is an elegant row of timbered houses complete with overhangs.

2 Go past the village pond, to the right. Ahead now is beautiful Abbey Farm.

3 Just beyond the pond, go right, under an arch and diagonally across the cemetery – the site of Cerne Abbey. Leave the cemetery through another arched gateway and cross the field diagonally beyond – the abbey ruins are to your left. Go over a stile to reach the base of Giant Hill.

4 Now follow a clear path beneath the Giant – which lies beyond the fence on your right. The figure, which is believed to have been cut just before or after the Roman invasion (AD 43), is 180ft (55m) tall and holds a club 120ft (37m) long. It is outlined by trenches cut into the chalk, each trench being 2ft (60cm) wide and deep. When the fence ends, continue along the obvious path, eventually crossing a stile and then maintaining direction to reach a waymarker near a barn. Go to the right past the barn, and follow the hedge on the left for about 380yds (346m) to reach a gate, also on the left.

5 Go through the gate and across the field beyond to reach another gate. Go through and maintain direction, passing several waymarkers to reach a gate. Cross the field beyond to reach a track, following it to a

you will find all the bright and breezy diversions you could ask for.

Bournemouth was planned for pleasure. It was described rather sniffily by Thomas Hardy as 'the Mediterranean lounging place on the English Channel', but Queen Victoria approved of it. Until the first houses were built here in 1810, there was nothing but heathland between the great inlet of Poole Harbour and Hengistbury Head. Even then, Bournemouth did not flourish until the coming of the railways in the late 19th century, after which it became the most fashionable of the south coast resorts. The modern resort has lost none of its sunny charm and friendliness. Low heathy cliffs make the perfect frame for Bournemouth's 7 miles (11km) of golden sands. 'Britain's Baywatch' is the modern epithet, proudly promoted by Bournemouth, and though the surf might not be entirely Californian, these are award-winning 'Blue Flag' beaches maintained to the highest standards and with excellent facilities.

The central axis of the town is the green ribbon of the Leisure Gardens that runs for 2 miles (3km) inland from the pier. Bournemouth's garden theme is continued along its east and west shores. As well as beach 'lounging', you will find all types of activities and attractions here, from traditional tennis, golf and bowling, to beach volleyball and even *pétanque* (a type of French bowls), with a lively nightlife to keep you going after dark. If it all gets too much, and you fancy an alternative, then there's all that wonderful coast and countryside within easy reach.

SKY VIEWS

You can get a great view of Bournemouth from 500ft (150m) up in the gondola of a tethered balloon. The **Vistarama** balloon drifts gently above the town's Lower Gardens and there are 'flights' every 15 minutes. It's well anchored so you won't go anywhere you don't want to! There's even disabled access to the gondola, and in clear weather the views are superb.

For an entirely different aerial view you can take a helicopter ride from Bournemouth airport or have a helicopter flying lesson.

POOLE POTTERY

They've been making pottery at Poole for over 125 years and the Poole Pottery of today has everything for enthusiasts, young and old. Located on **The Quay**, the pottery has a museum that outlines its history and is packed with superb work by master craftspeople. There's a factory tour as well, during which you can see the whole process, including potting, glass-blowing and hand-painting of pots. And if you're itching to try your hand, there's a special 'Have a Go' area, where children in particular can enjoy themselves. A restaurant, bar, and gift and factory shopping add to the attractions.

BROWNSEA ISLAND

Within sight of the lively bustle of Poole and Bournemouth is tranquil Brownsea Island (below), acquired by the National Trust in 1962. There are regular boat trips out to Brownsea from Poole Quay, Swanage, Bournemouth and Sandbanks. Brownsea is a marvellous antidote to too much seaside fun on the mainland. Throughout its 500 acres (202ha) there are many walks across the heathland and through the woods. There are also guided walks through the nature reserve, home to numerous species of birds and to red squirrels. Facilities for wheelchair users are good and all boats cater for them.

WATERSPORTS

The Dorset coast is ideal for watersports, provided you are properly equipped and are accompanied by experts if you are a novice. There are diving opportunities in the **Portland** area and you can book diving trips and courses. **Weymouth's** sheltered bay is ideal for sailing, windsurfing and canoeing. **Poole** and **Swanage** are both major centres for watersports and you can take lessons in sailing and windsurfing, or book a trip on a motor boat. At **Sandbanks Beach**, all types of water-based fun are available, including surf canoes, pedaloes, banana boats, ringo rides and even parascending.

crossing of tracks. Turn left (signed main road) and follow the track (which becomes metalled) through Minterne Parva to the A352.

6 Turn left and follow the road, with great care, for 220yds (200m), then turn right along the road for Up Cerne. Follow this narrow, but quiet, road through beautiful Up Cerne, reaching the village 'square'. Continue uphill: there is a fine view of the Manor House from here.

7 Just beyond a white gate marked 'Private', go left along a field path, heading towards the modern barns, regaining the road and following it to its junction with the main road.

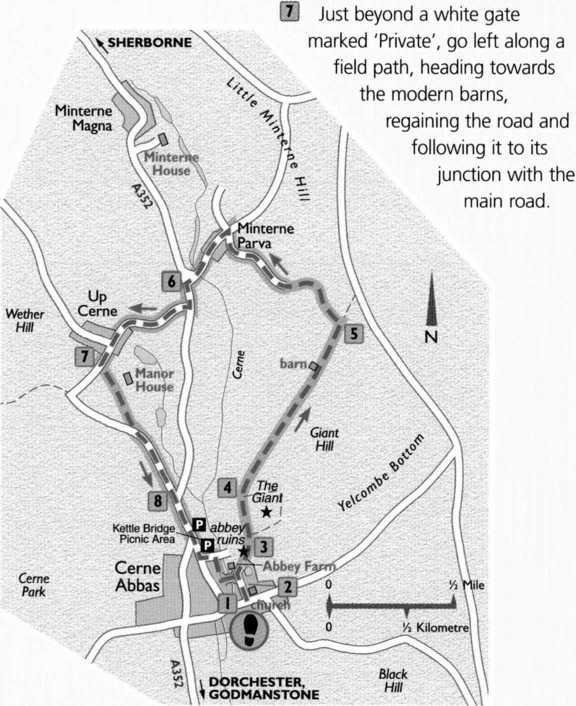

8 Cross the main road, bearing right and then left along the minor road towards the village, soon reaching the Kettle Bridge Picnic Area. Turn left (signed village centre), then follow the sign for the pottery. Before crossing the bridge, turn right along a path (river on your left). After 200yds (182m) turn left over a footbridge and continue to the village.

DORSET VILLAGES & SALISBURY

On the smooth, chalk downs of Dorset, prehistoric settlers first staked a claim to Island Britain. Just inland from Chesil Beach and the ancient town of Abbotsbury, a line of grass-covered barrows, or tumuli, crowns the ridge that links Bronkham Hill, Black Down and Portesham Hill. These were the graveyards of Bronze-Age farmers. They were also territorial markers, symbolic 'Keep Out' signs to outsiders and would-be invaders, warning them that here was an occupied land.

A sense of history pervades deepest Dorset, especially at sites such as Maiden Castle above Dorchester, a vast fortified hilltop camp used from the early Stone Age to the Iron Age. Dorchester itself,

Dorchester author and poet Thomas Hardy (1840–1928)

Over 4000 years old, Maiden Castle is one of the largest prehistoric sites in Europe

TOP FIVE HOUSES AND GARDENS

Aurelia Gardens

These unusual gardens present blocks of brilliantly coloured flowers set out in maze-like patterns. The gardens are near Ferndown and also keep rare breeds of poultry.

Athelhampton House

Located near Dorchester, this 15th-century manor house has many magnificent rooms with fine period furnishings. The architectural gardens contain pavilions, fountains and topiary.

Edmondsham House

There are Georgian additions to this original Tudor manor house and an octagonal Victorian dairy to add to the variety. In the walled gardens you will find organic gardening in practice.

Kingston Lacy (NT)

Near Wimborne Minster, this beautiful 17th-century house (above) is set amid 250 acres (100ha) of wooded parkland. The exquisite interiors contain a fine collection of paintings.

Cranborne Manor Gardens

These historic gardens were first laid out in the 17th century and enlarged during the 20th century. There is a series of walled gardens with special themes and the garden centre has some old-fashioned roses and other plants for sale.

Wilton Cycle Ride

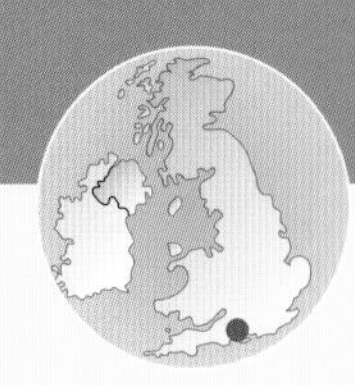

CYCLE RIDE

Through the Nadder and Ebble Valleys

START/FINISH: Wilton. Small town on the A30, 3 miles (5km) west of Salisbury
DISTANCE: 21 miles (33.5km)
ASCENT/GRADIENT: 800ft (244m); undulating; two steep climbs
ROADS: country lanes; short stretch of B-road
PARKING: free car-park in South Street

The picturesque valleys of the Nadder and Ebble rivers to the west of Salisbury provide the setting for a delightful ride along undulating lanes. Dramatic open chalk downland flanks the narrow Ebble Valley, complete with timeless villages, contrasting with the gentle wooded landscape in the Nadder Valley.

1 Turn right out of the car-park and leave town to ascend (gently at first) Bishopstone Down. Descend into the Ebble Valley, turning right at the T-junction, signed to Broad Chalke. Skirt Bishopstone village, pass The White Hart and take the second lane left, signed Stoke Farthing. Cross the River Ebble then, at a T-junction, turn left and then right into Broad Chalke. Turn left again opposite the church and follow the lane through the village. Broad Chalke comprises some fine examples of stone, cob and timber-framed thatched cottages as well as some large and imposing manor houses, notably 18th-century Reddish Manor and stone-built King's Old Rectory, former home of the 17th-century diarist John Aubrey.

2 On leaving the houses, turn right down a narrow lane (post box), passing watercress beds and crossing the river to reach the main valley road. Turn left and pass Fifield Bavant church (13th century), one of the smallest churches in England, 35ft (10.5m) long and 15ft (4.5m) wide, perched on top of a grassy hill. Keep left at a fork to enter Ebbesborne Wake, a quaint, unspoiled village of neat, thatched cottages congregating around the 15th-century church and The Horseshoe pub.

3 Ascend out of the village to West End, turning left at a T-junction and shortly enter Alvediston. Turn right opposite the Crown Inn and pass St Mary's Church. Sir Anthony Eden, Prime Minister between 1955 and 1957, spent his last days in the adjacent manor and is buried in the

Thomas Hardy's 'Casterbridge' and a bustling market town today, supplanted Maiden Castle after the Romans put a brutal end to native British resistance there. East of Maiden Castle and just north of Bournemouth, at Wimborne Minster, is the mighty Iron-Age camp of Badbury Rings. From here the Roman Road, known by a much later misnomer as Ackling Dyke, runs north to Old Sarum and Salisbury across the rolling downs of Cranborne Chase. The entire length of this old road offers glorious walking where it cuts its confident line across the flinty landscape, past the ancient earthwork of Bokerley Dyke and alongside the striking cluster of Bronze-Age barrows at Oakley.

Scattered throughout this ancient landscape are countless villages and hamlets, many of which began as medieval settlements. Villages such as Evershot, Nettlecombe and Cerne Abbas all have Norman churches, rose-hung, sandstone cottages and traditional inns, while deep within the countryside stand historic houses such as Athelhampton. North Dorset is classic Thomas Hardy country. At Sturminster Newton in Blackmore Vale, Hardy wrote *The Return of the Native*. The village names of Okeford Fitzpaine, Fontmell Magna and Gussage All Saints speak of an older, mellower England. At the northern end of Blackmore Vale stands the town of Shaftesbury, famous for its steep cobbled street of Gold Hill, the ultimate image of Olde England in old Dorsetshire, though nowhere as old as Ackling Dyke and Maiden Castle.

Older than most is 'Sarum', the historical Salisbury, a double-act composed of the Iron-Age hilltop site of Old Sarum and the cathedral city that supplanted it in the 13th century as New Sarum. Modern Salisbury has numerous brick and stone buildings, many of them timber-framed, that represent periods from medieval times through to our own. It is a prosperous, friendly city, where a sensible control of high-rise development has left the mighty spire of the cathedral dominant over the skyline. The name 'Salisbury' derives from that of Salzburg, and was borrowed by New Sarum's Norman founders in a bid for prestige. Modern Salisbury has prestige enough, and more than a hint of cosmopolitan life in its delightful market square, with its European alfresco café culture and street entertainment.

TOP FIVE FUN PLACES FOR CHILDREN

New Barn Field Centre, Bradford Peverell Re-created Iron-Age homestead; also wild-flower reserve and nature trail.

Brit Valley Llamas, Beaminster One of Dorset's more unusual species provides a different way of seeing the countryside, with a llama-trekking excursion.

Brownsea Island, Poole Harbour A short ferry ride leads to lovely walks and the chance to see the only red squirrels in southern England.

Charmouth Heritage Coast Centre A must for those who like fossils and rock pools.

Dorchester Dinosaur Museum Unique museum with hands-on exhibits.

The Salisbury Giant parades through the city's streets on St George's Day

churchyard. Ascend steeply to the top of Middle Down then drop sharply to a crossroads with the A30.

4 Cross straight over into Ansty, look out for its maypole which at 96ft (30m) is thought to be highest in England, and turn left at the T-junction towards Tisbury. Take the first lane right and continue to a T-junction on the edge of Tisbury. Turn left if wishing to visit the village and its fine 13th-century church. The churchyard contains a massive 1,000-year-old yew tree and the grave of Rudyard Kipling.

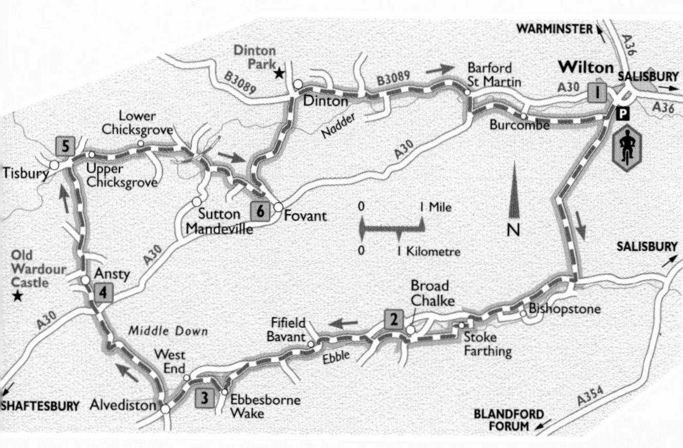

5 Otherwise, turn right, signed to Chicksgrove. On your left is a splendid thatched 15th-century tithe barn. Proceed along a gently undulating lane through the Nadder Valley, passing a right turn for Sutton Mandeville, then turn right just before a sharp left bend, signed to Fovant. Pass under the railway bridge, then pass by Sutton Mandeville village sign and cross the River Nadder. Keep left at a junction (village signed right) and shortly descend into Fovant.

6 At a T-junction by the village hall, turn left into Dinton Road for Dinton. Keep to this lane for about a mile (1.5km), crossing the River Nadder into Dinton. Turn right at the crossroads on to the B3089 towards Salisbury. Proceed for 2 miles (3km) to Barford St Martin and the A30. Turn right, cross the Nadder and turn first left (no sign). Pass through Burcombe then, in 1 mile (1.5km), turn left at a T-junction back into Wilton, which is best known for carpet-making.

THE GREAT DORSET STEAM FAIR

Steam fairs put all other forms of power in their place. There is something eternally fascinating about the hissing and clanking of great mammoth-like machines lovingly tended by their dedicated engineers and enthusiasts. The Great Dorset Steam Fair is a major international event and is held in the heart of Hardy Country, at **Tarrant Hinton**, near Blandford Forum at the end of August each year. It runs for several days and includes an old-style steam funfair, all types of steam engines at work, vintage tractors and motorcycles, shire horses, country crafts, trade stands and masses of entertainment from brass bands to pop groups.

SALISBURY PLAIN TO THE VALE OF THE WHITE HORSE

The chalk hills that run in a great swath across Salisbury Plain and the Marlborough Downs were Dark-Age Britain's last line of resistance to waves of influence and incursion from Europe. After the end of Roman rule in the 5th century AD, Romano-British tribes erected the mysterious Wansdyke, the great earth rampart that runs from the border of modern Hampshire across the downs to Bath and then on to the Bristol Channel. The Wansdyke was more for show than serious defence. It was a clear signal to Anglo-Saxon and Danish intruders that the West Country was 'Old Britain' and therefore out of bounds. Unfortunately, it was a forlorn hope.

On the downs there are even older memorials than the Wansdyke. Stonehenge, at the heart of Salisbury Plain, is the most conspicuous and the most famous of England's ancient monuments, but the smaller, rougher stone circles of Avebury, between the Plain and the Marlborough Downs, are perhaps the more haunting. The surviving line of the ancient track of the Ridgeway on the crest of the Berkshire Downs above the Vale of the White Horse, is a more enduring memorial still. Later Roman roads sliced their way

The ancient Ridgeway, an 85-mile (137-km) track which follows the Berkshire Downs

unerringly across the landscape, whereas the Ridgeway followed the lie of the land.

Today's downs have been thoroughly tamed by intensive farming and are crisscrossed with a network of main roads. Yet these ancient downlands at England's heart are exhilarating in their spaciousness and in the powerful sense of history that survives amid their ancient monuments. You travel across the downs between islands of remarkable archaeological treasures. At Uffington on the Ridgeway, the great White Horse, finest of all the carved figures that pepper the chalk landscape, overlooks the Vale of the White Horse

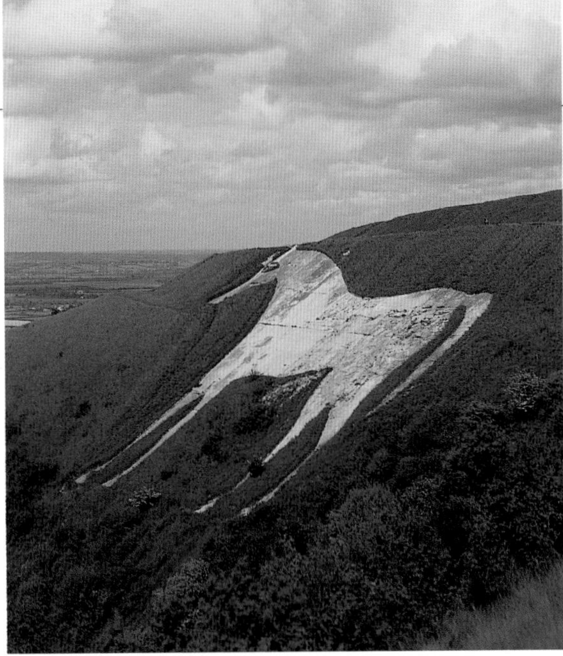

The Westbury White Horse, one of eight etched into Wiltshire's chalk hills

Devizes Drive

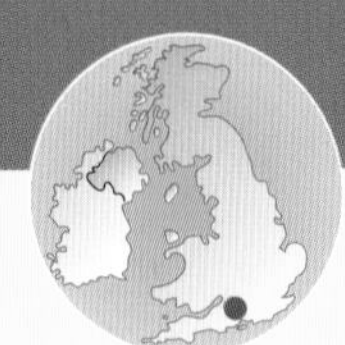

DRIVE

Land of our Forefathers

START/FINISH: Devizes. On the A361 between Marlborough and Trowbridge

DISTANCE: approx. 90 miles (144km)

This drive takes in many of the legacies of Britain's ancient inhabitants, including the mysteries of Avebury and Silbury Hill, and incorporates castles, market towns and villages.

1 From the market town of Devizes, with its flight of 29 locks on the Kennet and Avon Canal, follow the A361, signed Swindon, northeast to the A4. Turn right, signed Marlborough, and pass Silbury Hill, a conical, man-made prehistoric earthen mound on the left. Continue on the A4 to a lay-by after 1 mile (1.5km) and a waymarked footpath on the right for West Kennet Long Barrow, a prehistoric chambered tomb.

2 Head west for half a mile (800m) then take the B4003 (not signed) right to Avebury, one of the largest prehistoric stone circles in the world, enclosing two smaller stone circles. Return to the A4 via the A4361 and turn right. In 6 miles (10km) enter Calne. Continue west on the A4 and soon bear off left on to a minor road to Derry Hill to Bowood House.

3 Return to the A4. Turn left and shortly head south on the A342 towards Devizes. After 2 miles (3km) take the minor road right for Lacock, a beautiful village (NT) with a 13th-century abbey. Continue to the A350 (Melksham to Chippenham road). Turn right, then left in half a mile (800m) to follow a minor road into Corsham. Turn right, signed Chippenham A4, past Corsham Court, an Elizabethan mansion. Continue to the A4 and go straight over towards Biddestone.

4 Pass through Biddestone and continue to the A420 and turn left (west) to Marshfield. After 6 miles (10km) turn right on to a minor road, signed Castle Farm, and follow it towards Dyrham, crossing the A46 at a staggered junction to reach the village and Dyrham Park (NT), an impressive 17th-century mansion. Return to the A46. Head south towards Bath and turn left at a roundabout along the A4 and drive towards Batheaston. At a roundabout take the A363 south to Bradford-on-Avon (7 miles/11.5km), a delightful town noted for its fine

WILTSHIRE'S WHITE HORSES

The famous White Horses of Wiltshire are mainly the products of a fashion for monumental gestures in both the 18th and 19th centuries.

Uffington White Horse – the most famous White Horse of all, thought to date back 900 years.

Westbury White Horse – in its present form it dates from 1778, but there was a chalk figure on the site for centuries before this.

Cherhill White Horse – dating from 1780, it stands on the flanks of Oldbury Castle, near Avebury, and once had a glittering eye made from upturned bottles.

Pewsey White Horse – redesigned 1930s version of a much older horse.

Marlborough White Horse – dates from 1804.

Alton Barnes White Horse – dates from 1812.

Hackpen Hill White Horse – commemorates Queen Victoria's coronation in 1837.

Millennium White Horse – cut near Devizes to commemorate the year 2000.

There is a long-distance walk of 80 miles (128km) called the White Horse Trail that takes you past a string of these chalk figures. Details at local TICs.

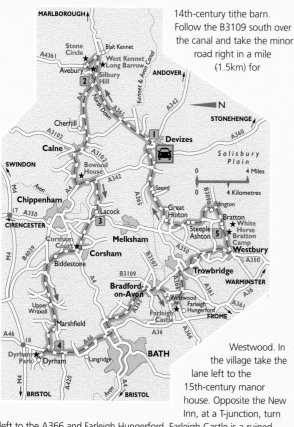

14th-century tithe barn. Follow the B3109 south over the canal and take the minor road right in a mile (1.5km) for Westwood. In the village take the lane left to the 15th-century manor house. Opposite the New Inn, at a T-junction, turn left to the A366 and Farleigh Hungerford. Farleigh Castle is a ruined 14th-century castle with surviving chapel. Turn left at the T-junction.

5 Head east along the A366 to Trowbridge, then take the A363 and A350 south, towards Warminster, to Westbury. Turn left on to the B3098 for 2.5 miles (4km) to Bratton, passing Bratton Camp, an Iron-Age earthen fort, and the 18th-century Westbury White Horse carved on the hillside on the right. Continue through Bratton to Edington. Just before leaving Edington, take a minor road left to the charming village of Steeple Ashton. Continue north, taking a minor road right through Great Hinton to the A361 and east for 5 miles (8km) back to Devizes.

where it runs its broad course along the edge of the Berkshire Downs from Swindon to Abingdon. Near Avebury, the still unexplained artificial pyramid of Silbury Hill links the Avebury circles to the longbarrow burial chamber of West Kennet, one of the finest examples of an early Bronze-Age monument in Europe. The people who created these stunning monuments travelled under their own power, or on horseback, and today walking, cycling and riding are the most satisfying ways of exploring this exhilarating countryside and its rich history.

Long after the ancient centres of Avebury and Stonehenge were abandoned, the centralised and static farming culture of the Saxon and then the Norman periods saw the development of towns such as Warminster, Chippenham, Devizes and Marlborough, now the main urban centres of these chalk downlands. Marlborough's High Street is a lesson in medieval and post-medieval English history. Here Elizabethan façades stand side by side with later Georgian and Victorian additions. Chippenham is a Saxon town, with medieval and Georgian additions, and Devizes has old coaching inns and a fine market place. From Devizes the Kennet and Avon Canal winds eastwards between Salisbury Plain and the Marlborough Downs, a much later, yet still man-made 'way' across the downs, than the old Wansdyke.

CROP CIRCLES

The appearance in Wiltshire each year of intricate circles made in trampled crop fields, has never been explained. Magic or manipulation? Such circles often display the most complex designs and have been recorded worldwide. Some of the finest have appeared in fields of wheat, barley or oats on the Marlborough Downs and in Pewsey Vale. Their proximity to so many deeply symbolic ancient sites has prompted speculation about their possible 'magical' Earth Mystery origins. Scientists, as well as the spiritually inclined, still agonise over the causes of crop circles, while sceptics explain them as the products of a genuinely ancient, but very human, skill in mischievous trickery!

A FLIGHT OF LOCKS

The Caen Hill flight on the Kennet and Avon canal, just west of Devizes, is one of the jewels of the inland waterway system. Built between 1801 and 1810 by the celebrated Scots engineer John Rennie, this flight of 29 locks rises 237ft (71m) in just 2 miles (3km). The **Caen Hill Discovery Trail**, starting at Devizes Wharf, is 6 miles (9.5km) long and takes about 3 hours.

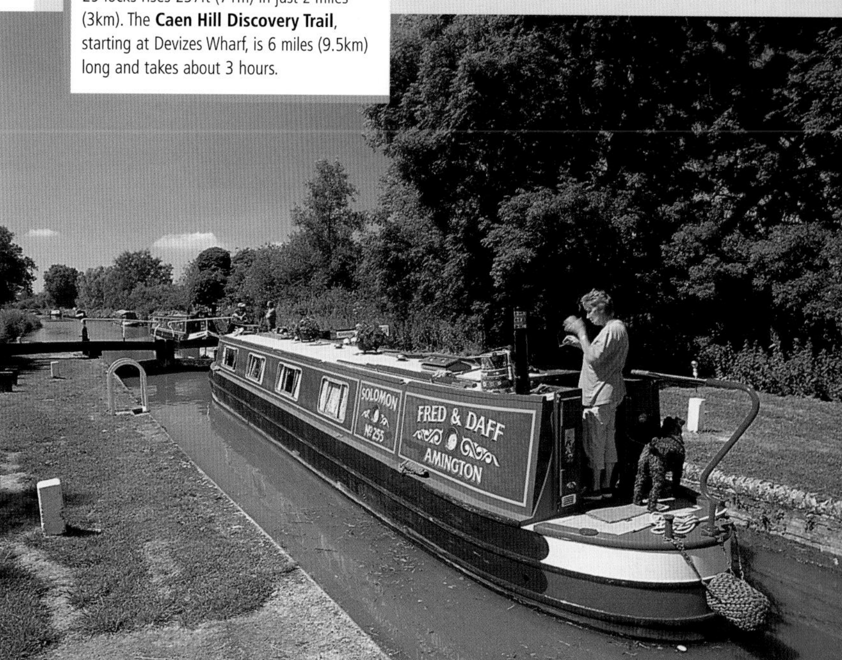

A barge drifts past the village of Great Bedwyn on the Kennet and Avon Canal

THE FOREST OF DEAN & THE SEVERN VALLEY

The Severn Valley lies between the Cotswolds in the east and the Forest of Dean in the west. The Forest, in its turn, lies like a green wedge between the Severn and the smaller River Wye, and seems to push the two river valleys ever further apart. The Severn begins in Wales but runs for most of its course through England, while the Wye is essentially Welsh, both in its beginnings and in the way it defines the border between Wales and England all the way to the sea. Ancient forest, rolling hills, meandering rivers and wooded escarpments all combine to produce a unified landscape, while the cities and towns of the area – Gloucester, Hereford, Tewkesbury, Monmouth and Ross-on-Wye – together with a host of picturesque villages, enhance the richness and beauty of this historic region.

Gloucester Cathedral
The magnificent tower of Gloucester Cathedral dominates the city's skyline. The cathedral dates from the 12th century and has a powerful and imposing presence at the centre of the Cathedral Green. Its nave is lined with Norman arcading and the 14th-century East Window is the largest of its kind in Britain.

Tewkesbury

Tewkesbury has a well-preserved medieval townscape emphasised by its handsome abbey. Church Street and High Street have numerous timber-framed buildings interspersed with later Georgian façades.

SYMONDS YAT

Symonds Yat, East and West, face each other across the River Wye beneath Huntsham's Hill and can be reached from each other by chain ferries. The nearby cliffs of Yat Rock and Coldwell Rocks rise to a height of 400ft (121m) above a spectacular meander of the Wye.

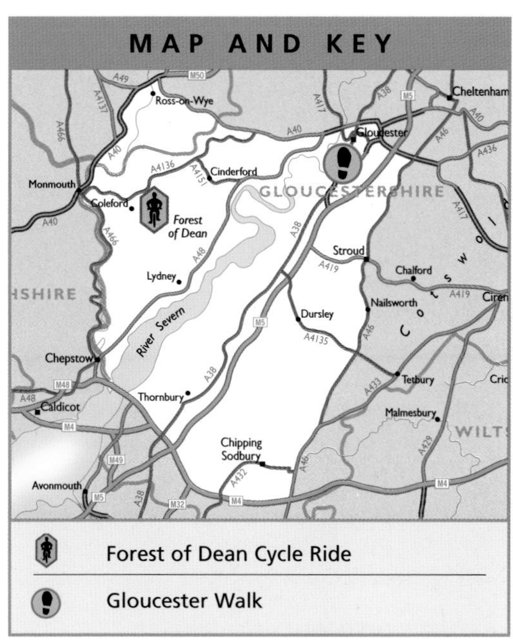

TINTERN ABBEY

Cistercian monks founded Tintern Abbey at the heart of the Wye Valley in the 12th century. Abandoned at the Dissolution of the Monasteries in 1536, the abbey became ruinous, yet what remains today is impressive. The Saxon earthwork of Offa's Dyke runs along the top of the wooded escarpment to the east.

Chepstow

Chepstow is the gateway to Wales. It stands close to the mouth of the River Wye and its splendid Norman castle occupies a commanding position above the river cliffs. This was the first Norman stronghold to be built in stone. The town itself retains its medieval walls and gate.

THE WYE VALLEY & THE FOREST OF DEAN

The River Wye is one of the great rivers of Britain, yet for most of its length it is not particularly wide. In its lower reaches especially, the river is contained narrowly between wooded escarpments until north of Monmouth where the valley widens and the river begins a series of great, swirling meanders through low-lying water meadows. The Wye played a part in the 18th-century Romantic movement. Its picturesque forms, the wooded cliffs and promontories that contained it and the ivy-hung ruins of Tintern Abbey all appealed to landscape painters and to poets such as J M Turner and William Wordsworth. The Wye Valley was even more popular with the fashionable tourists of the time, yet 19th-century industry was also important in the river's history. The rich iron ore of the Forest of Dean was processed at Redbrook, just south of Monmouth and during the 18th and 19th centuries the banks of the river clattered and hummed with the sound of iron mills and foundries.

FIVE GOOD PLACES FOR BIRD-WATCHING

Aylburton Warth, west bank of the Severn Waders and wildfowl, best seen when the high tide concentrates birds nearer the shore.

RSPB reserve, Nagshead, Forest of Dean Many woodland species including over 50 pied flycatchers.

Symonds Yat, Wye Valley Great spot for peregrines, with RSPB staff in attendance.

Walmore Common, Severn Valley Open damp grassland with huge flocks of wildfowl in winter.

Slimbridge Headquarters of the Wildfowl Trust; vast numbers of geese, swans and ducks, especially in winter.

The Jacobean Old House in Hereford, which includes 17th-century furnishings

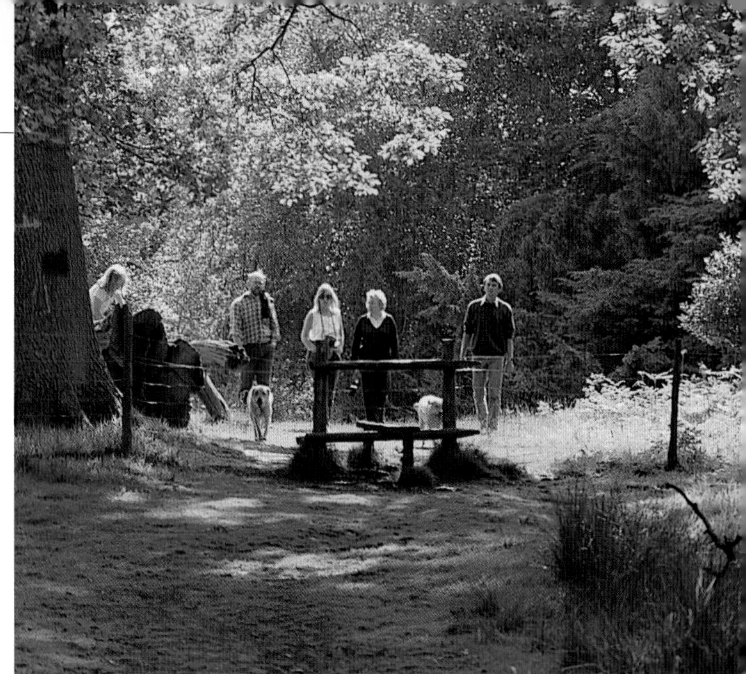

The Forest of Dean, former royal hunting ground, provides beautiful scenery for walks

Forest of Dean Cycle Ride

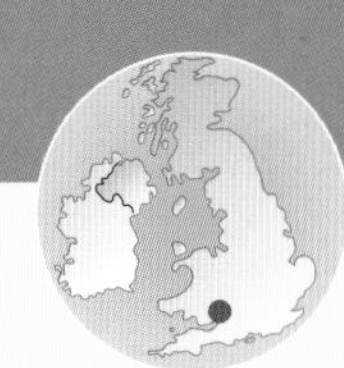

CYCLE RIDE

Ancient Forests and Woods

START/FINISH: Coleford. A small town on the B4028 and B4228 Chepstow road, 1 mile (1.5km) off the A4136 east of Monmouth

DISTANCE: 17.5 miles (27km); shorter ride options

TERRAIN: hilly with long, steady climbs and descents on narrow lanes

ROADS: B-roads and country lanes

PARKING: there are three car-parks in the centre of town

This route covers some of the most beautiful and unspoiled countryside in Britain. There is a wealth of interest in the area, ranging from old industrial sites, a fascinating heritage centre and a steam railway, to nature and woodland trails and spectacular views from the hilltops.

1 From the car-park drop downhill to the traffic lights and turn right on to the B4028 towards Cinderford. After a mile (1.5km), turn right on to the B4226, signed Cinderford. Gently climb into Broadwell and out into the Forest of Dean. Enjoy a long descent past Hopewell Colliery and soon undertake a long, gradual ascent, passing Beechenhurst Lodge (picnic site), to reach the Speech House Hotel. Descend into lower Cinderford.

(Shorter ride option: at the crossroads beyond Hopewell Colliery, turn right heading south on the B4234 past Barn Hill Plantation. Gently climb up to Parkend, then turn right to rejoin the main route.)

2 Climb up the rise, turning right at the White Hart Inn into Ruspidge. Follow the road downhill, pass the Rising Sun Inn and shortly re-enter the forest.

3 Follow the road around to the left and over the bridge into Upper Soudley. The large lake on the left is Upper Soudley Pond, with many nature trails and information boards on this fascinating site. On the right is the Dean Heritage Centre, a converted mill housing craft workshops, a café, forester's cottage, beam engine and Museum of the Forest. The

FOREST AND RIVER WALKS

The Wye Valley and the Forest of Dean both offer wonderful scenic walking opportunities in the area.

Offa's Dyke – the Dyke is an 8th-century earthwork, 150 miles (240km) in length, erected by the Mercian King Offa. It runs from the North Wales coast to the Severn, and was intended to mark out the political boundary of Offa's kingdom, defining the English–Welsh border, beyond which the wild Welsh were permitted only under strict control. Today there is a well-established National Trail along the length of the Dyke and you can easily reach the Wye Valley section south of Monmouth.

Wye Valley Walk – a riverside route running for 110 miles (176km) from Chepstow to Monmouth and on to Ross-on-Wye, Hereford, Hay-on-Wye and Rhayader.

Sculpture Trail – one of numerous walks in the Forest of Dean. Starting at Beechenhurst, the 4-mile (6.5-km) walk passes various sculptures illustrating the life and work of the forest. The walk is suitable for pushchairs.

The Wye has survived centuries of human use with its natural beauty intact. From Chepstow, where the river is overlooked by magnificent Chepstow Castle, all the way to Ross-on-Wye, the valley is a designated Area of Outstanding Natural Beauty. Notable towns along its length include medieval Monmouth, with its handsome entrance gateway and bridge over the River Monnow, and Ross-on-Wye, where narrow streets converge on the lively market square. Hereford is also an attractive market town and a cathedral city. But it is the river landscapes that are most compelling: the spectacular viewpoints of Wintour's Leap, Wyndcliffe and Yat Rock and charming riverside villages, such as Brockweir and Llandogo.

The ancient Forest of Dean covers an area of 35sq miles (90sq km), a marvellous natural enclave of broad-leafed trees and conifers, crisscrossed with roads, tracks and pathways. Once the royal hunting ground of Norman kings, it still harbours fallow deer in its leafy glades. The best way to enjoy the natural beauty of the forest is on foot or by bicycle, and there are easily accessible attractions throughout the area, ranging from the craft workshops at the Dean Heritage Centre between Cinderford and Blakeney, to the fascinating Clearwell Caves near Coleford.

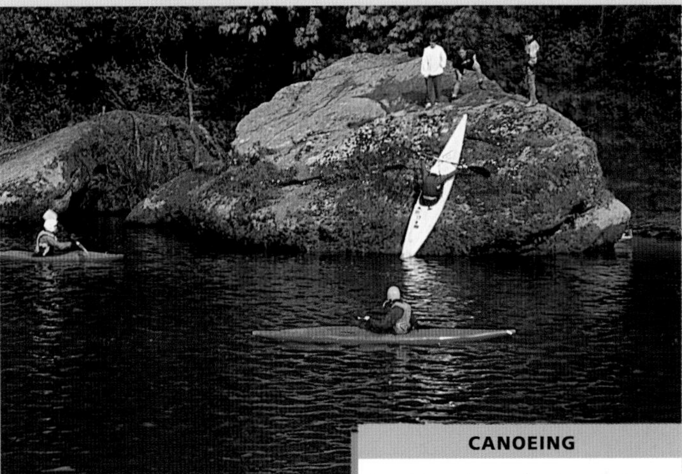

CANOEING

One of the best ways of exploring the Wye Valley and its river is by canoe. The River Wye has ideal sections for most levels of canoeing and there are several companies that organise trips. You have a choice of kayaking or Canadian canoeing and family groups are well catered for at most centres. If you are not very experienced, you should always canoe with organised centres. Many offer multi-activity holidays so that you can tie in canoeing with sports as diverse as archery, raft-building and rock-climbing.

ANGLING

The well-watered border area is noted for its fishing, not least on the River Wye where there is excellent salmon and trout fishing. There are also several smaller rivers and well-stocked reservoirs where you can enjoy a day's fishing, or sit peacefully, with rod in hand, on the banks of the **Monmouthshire and Brecon Canal**. Some private fisheries allow fishing and permits are required for most venues.

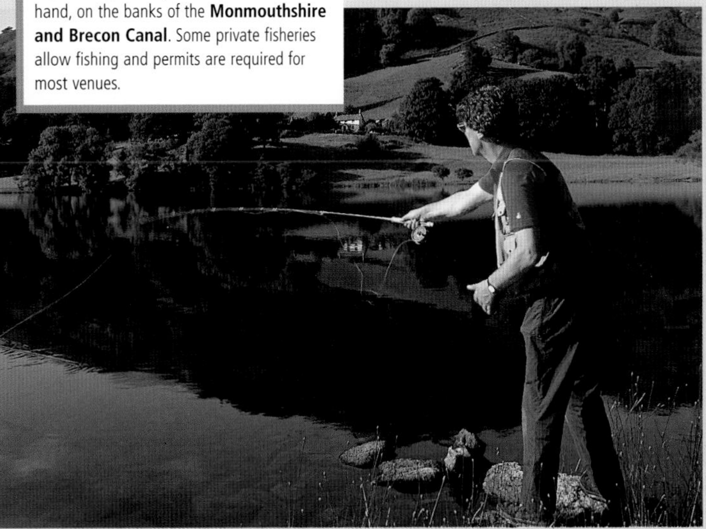

road swings over the river and bears left heading along the opposite bank. Climb the road, descend to Brain's Green and continue to the A48.

(Shorter ride option: ignoring the initial left turn, instead turn right and follow the road gently uphill. After about 1 mile (1.5km) follow the main run of the road gently right, and descend to the main road. Turn right and rejoin the main route.)

4 Turn right on to the A48 for about 200yds (180m) then right again,

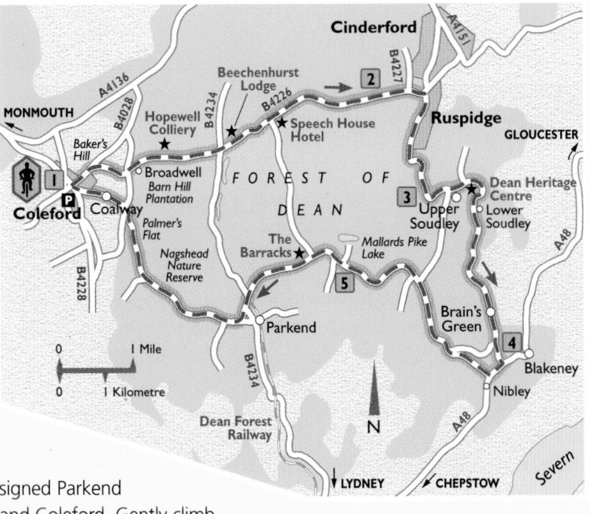

signed Parkend and Coleford. Gently climb through this now heavily wooded area (picnic tables alongside the stream), remaining on the road towards Coleford.

5 Pass the turning for Mallards Pike Lake and terraces of houses called The Barracks, to reach Parkend. Continue towards Coleford, freewheeling down through the houses to the bottom and a left turn to the Dean Forest Railway. Steam locomotives, coaches, wagons and railway equipment are on show at this popular attraction. Carry straight on to pass Nagshead Nature Reserve, noted for bluebells, pied flycatchers, butterflies, dragonflies, and its autumn colour. Continue to Palmer's Flat and pass the Crown Inn at Coalway before dropping down into Coleford, turning right on to the B4228 and back to the town centre.

GLOUCESTER & THE SEVERN VALLEY

Gloucester was founded as a Roman town and later became a Saxon capital. Later, the Normans established an abbey church that was to become the city's magnificent Cathedral of St Peter. In Tudor times Gloucester became a major inland port on the River Severn and remained so until the docks went into decline in the 19th century. Today, the hub of Gloucester is The Cross, from which radiate the principal streets – Northgate, Eastgate, Westgate and Southgate. Gloucester Cathedral is situated just to the north of The Cross. Cathedral Green is surrounded by a fine array of houses from the 16th, 17th and 18th centuries, as well as the 15th-century half-timbered Parliament Room, where Richard II held parliament in 1378.

Each of the radiating 'gates' has buildings of historical note, such as Northgate's medieval New Inn with its beautiful galleried courtyard. In Westgate is the Folk Museum, housed in fine half-timbered houses, while in Southgate you will find the splendid Church of St Mary de Crypt. Southgate leads to the docks where many of the old warehouses have been reincarnated as offices, restaurants and museums, including the National Waterways Museum. At the north end of the docks is the Old Customs House, now home to the Regiments of Gloucestershire Museum.

The modern city may have lost much of its old character to commercial development, but there is a lively bustle to busy Westgate Street, the main shopping area. Gloucester is a specialist centre for antiques as exemplified by the Gloucester Antiques Centre, containing some 60 shops in a converted warehouse.

The Severn Valley has always been a great commercial artery that facilitated the movement of goods, and social and cultural influences, deep into the heart of England and Wales. From Upton-upon-Severn to Gloucester, the valley flood plain is a

Kiting on Haresfield Beacon near Stroud, with panoramic views across the Severn Vale

The village green at Frampton on Severn, the largest in England

Gloucester Walk

WALK

The Heart of Gloucester

START/FINISH: Gloucester. Cathedral city located off M5 (J11a) between Bristol and Worcester

DISTANCE: 4 miles (6.5km)

GRADIENT: flat

PATHS: pavements, pedestrian areas, shopping malls and alleys

PARKING: Gloucester railway station car-park

A pleasant stroll through the centre of old Gloucester, exploring the shopping areas, ancient architecture and the historic docks.

1 From the station car-park cross the dual carriageway and head along Bruton Way, turning right at the roundabout into Station Road. Head towards The Chambers pub and turn left into Kings Walk, then right at the entrance to the shopping mall and walk along The Oxebode to the T-Junction.

2 Turn right, then left into St John's Lane and, at the end of the church building on the left, turn right again through the pillars and arches of the nearby building and turn left towards the cathedral. Bear right, following signs for the Kings School, and at the Infirmary Arches bear right towards the red post box and turn left into Pitt Street. At the junction cross the road into Archdeacon Street, turn right through a gap in the hedge and walk past the ruins of St Oswald's Priory. Join the path on the left and exit the park, turning right on to Archdeacon Street. Turn left into Westgate Street, right at Berkeley Street and at the junction cross the road to the Transport Museum.

3 Turn left into Barbican Road, following the signs for the Maritime Walk, cross the road at the lights and enter the docks. Keep straight ahead on the footpath with the dock on the right. Turn left, then right over a bridge and pass the Robert Opie Collection, Advertising & Packaging Museum. Cross the car-park, skirting the dock and go to the National Waterways Museum.

SLIMBRIDGE

Established as the Severn Wildfowl Trust in 1946, the saltmarshes around the Gloucester and Sharpness Canal and the River Severn have now become the home of the greatest collection of waterfowl in the world. The Trust was the inspiration of the late Sir Peter Scott, artist and naturalist.

Today, Slimbridge boasts 180 different kinds of waterfowl, swans and flocks of migrating wild geese. The Trust also harbours the more exotic flamingoes and a tropical house containing delicate humming-birds. There are excellent viewing facilities and you can hire binoculars for a spot of serious bird-watching.

landscape of orchards and meadows scattered with charming villages of half-timbered houses. Upton is a lovely Worcestershire village, from where the river winds through quiet countryside to medieval Tewkesbury and then on to Gloucester. South of Gloucester, the Severn becomes more estuary than river. Here the valley is defined on the east by the rough bounds of the Cotswold fringe and by the peaceful Vale of Berkeley, fertile farming country where rural tranquillity has survived.

Just south of Gloucester the Severn widens and then makes a spectacular westerly loop at Arlingham, where there is fine walking along the river shore. Near by is the village of Frampton, the loveliest in the Vale, and just south is Slimbridge, where the Wildfowl and Wetlands Trust reflects the importance of the Severn Estuary to bird life. At Sharpness, the Gloucester and Sharpness Canal leads off from the river while further south, at the heart of the Vale, is the magnificent 850-year-old Berkeley Castle. Beyond Berkeley the suburban fringe of Bristol and main road and motorway soon dominate.

Exhibit at the Robert Opie Collection

4 From the museum, exit the docks on to Llanthony Road, cross the canal bridge and follow the road to Llanthony Secunda Priory. Return by the same route, pass the museum on the left and head across the docks to the Regiments of Gloucestershire Museum, turn left, pass the Health Authority building and turn right to exit the docks. Retrace your steps to the Transport Museum and turn right into Longsmith Street.

5 Turn right into Ladybellgate Street, left into Blackfriars, then cross Southgate Street and continue along Greyfriars to the junction. Turn right into Brunswick Road, fork right on to Parliament Street, turn right into Southgate Street, and left into Westgate Street.

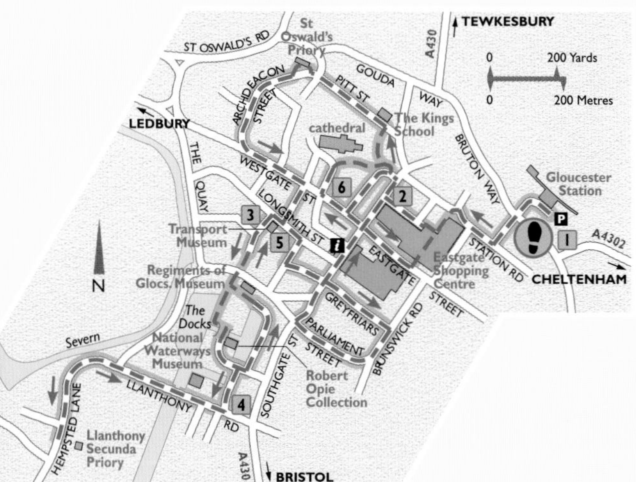

6 Turn right at College Court, enter the Cathedral Grounds and turn right. Pass the cathedral on your left, turn right into Cathedral Way, go through the arch and turn right into St John's Lane. Turn left at Westgate Street, continue along Eastgate Street then turn left into Eastgate Shopping Centre. Exit this on to Kings Walk and from here retrace your steps to the station.

FIVE PLACES TO SEE THE SEVERN BORE

The Severn Bore is a tidal wave that moves upriver through the Severn Estuary as far as Bristol. It can measure up to 9ft (3m) high and is made even more spectacular in certain wind conditions. It is caused by the tidal movements of the Bristol Channel and the Severn Estuary, which experience the second greatest tidal range in the world.

Newnham, near Westbury-on Severn Good view from the churchyard as the bore rounds Horseshoe Bend.

Minsterworth Popular spot just off the A48, but with limited parking. Severn Bore Inn allows observation in comfort.

Lower Parting Here the bore splits into the two channels of the river.

Overbridge Where the A48 crosses the Severn.

Maisemore Bridge The highest point of the bore; a weir prevents it running any further. A reflex wave flows back down the river ten minutes after the bore.

SEE CONTACTS SECTION FOR ADDITIONAL INFORMATION

WALKING THE LONG-DISTANCE TRAILS

A letter to Tom Stephenson, open-air correspondent of the *Daily Herald* newspaper, from two American girls visiting Britain in 1935, was the starting point for Britain's fast-growing system of long-distance walking and riding trails. He worked out for them a 'Long Green Trail' – starting at Edale in the Peak District and crossing the Pennines, over Hadrian's Wall and the Cheviots, and finishing at Kirk Yetholm. It was another 30 years before the first long-distance footpath, the 250-mile (412-km) Pennine Way, was opened in 1965.

Today there are 18 official long-distance paths – now termed National Trails – some of which, such as the Ridgeway and Peddars Way, double as bridleways and are also available to cyclists. The only National Trail specifically dedicated for horse-riders is the incomplete 208-mile (335-km) Pennine Bridleway, which will run from Carsingston Reservoir in Derbyshire to Kirkby Stephen, along the western edge of the Pennines.

Walkers enjoy the clifftop views along the Pembrokeshire Coast Path

The longest National Trail is the 515-mile (982-km) South West Coast Path, which hugs the roller-coaster coastline of the southwest peninsula between Minehead in Somerset to Poole in Dorset. This clifftop walk includes stunning coastal features such as Land's End, the Lizard Peninsula and the soaring cliffs of Dorset. Another coastal trail is the 168-mile (299-km) Pembrokeshire Coast Path which follows the flower-decked sea-bird sanctuaries of the Pembrokeshire Coast National Park between St Dogmaels and Amroth.

Easier walking is provided by the 100-mile (161-km) South Downs Way, which runs the length of the proposed South Downs National Park between Eastbourne and Winchester. The 93-mile (150-km) Peddars Way and Norfolk Coast Path is a bridleway which starts on the sandy tracks of Breckland, near Thetford in Norfolk, and heads north to the glorious north Norfolk coast near Hunstanton, before turning east to Cromer.

If you like your walking seasoned with history, then the 85-mile (137-km) Ridgeway National Trail between Overton Hill, near Avebury, and Ivinghoe Beacon, on the Bedfordshire Chilterns, is hard to beat. Another National Trail steeped in history is the 177-mile (285-km) Offa's Dyke path which threads the English–Welsh border between Chepstow on the Severn estuary and Prestatyn on the Irish Sea coast. The latest National Trail is the 100-mile (161-km) Cotswold Way, which follows the crest of the limestone escarpment from the honey-stoned town of Chipping Campden to the Georgian city of Bath.

Joining the club north of the border is the 93-mile (150-km) West Highland Way, situated between Milngavie near Glasgow and Fort William in the shadow of Ben Nevis, taking in Loch Lomond and Glen Coe. Also in Scotland is the 60-mile (96-km) Speyside Way and the 212-mile (341-km) Southern Upland Way, between Portpatrick and Cockburnspath.

Celebrated walker Alfred Wainwright popularised his unofficial 190-mile (305-km) Coast-to-Coast Walk, between St Bees Head in Cumbria and Robin Hood's Bay, which is reckoned by many connoisseurs to be the finest of all the hill-walkers' trails. It is one of many other unofficial 'ways' which have sprung up as the popularity of walking has grown. This has also spread to horse-riding routes, where the 250-mile (402-km) Heritage Ride through Lincolnshire and Yorkshire is among a number of unofficial riding trails.

A Ridgeway signpost at Uffington

WALKERS' CROSSROADS

The pretty little former lead-mining village of Keld in Swaledale, in the Yorkshire Dales, has a special place in the world of the long-distance walker. At the bridge over the Swale, the routes of the Pennine Way and the Coast-to-Coast Walk intersect. At this point the Pennine Wayfarer has covered 120 miles (192km) of his marathon, and the Coast-to-Coaster has completed 95 miles (152km) – so both walkers are exactly halfway on their trek across England.

The northern section of the Pennine Way, passing through Northumberland's Cheviot Hills

LIQUID HISTORY

There's a good reason why England's longest river, the Thames, has been dubbed 'liquid history'. The 179-mile (288-km) Thames Path, which follows the river from its source in the Gloucestershire Cotswolds to the Thames Barrier at Woolwich, provides a walk through history, passing a number of important sites, including Kelmscott Manor, the city of Oxford, Windsor Castle, Hampton Court, the Tower of London and the Houses of Parliament.

Offa's Dyke footpath above Knighton, on the Welsh–English border

The unofficial Coast-to-Coast walk takes hikers through the Lake District

This map shows the National Trails and long-distance bridleways.

SOUTHEAST ENGLAND

Bluebells at Great Maytham Hall, Kent

FROM ISLAND TO FOREST & DOWNLAND

Between the bright lights of London and the green West Country hills, this wedge of southern England has something for everyone. Nature-lovers can escape to the woods and heaths of the New Forest, where humans take second place to animals. For walkers there are towpaths and riverside trails, ancient tracks and high chalk ridges. Boaters can mess about on canal barges, and sun-and-sport-seekers will make for the Isle of Wight, a holiday island with a family atmosphere, ringed with wide beaches. It may be only a stone's throw from the metropolis, but this is still a world of village greens and country churches, solitary farms and traditional market squares. You won't find much dramatic landscape or dynamic city life here, but if you're searching for a slice of rural England at its gentle, intimate best – look no further.

Winchester Cathedral
It took 300 years to build the cathedral, which resulted in a mish-mash of architectural styles. The foundations were laid in 1079, in marshland, and early in the 20th century the heroic efforts of diver William Walker saved the building by laying concrete to replace the rotting timbers. Among the royal tombs are those of Canute and William Rufus, son of William the Conqueror, and near the font is a stone commemorating a clergyman's daughter – Jane Austen.

HMS *VICTORY*

Nelson breathed his last on this ship, at the Battle of Trafalgar in 1805. Nowadays it's hard to believe that this elegant vessel, with her high masts, carved woodwork and shiny brass fittings, had any connection with war. At Portsmouth you can wander through the quarters where 820 crew lived and fought, and see where they ate their 'square meals' – rations served on square wooden platters.

Lymington

Cobbled streets, Georgian houses and waterside walks make this little harbour town a real treat. Sitting right at the edge of the New Forest, it is linked by ferry to the Isle of Wight, and always has a cheerful, holiday atmosphere, especially at the Saturday market. Trails wind through the coastal reedbeds, busy with waterfowl, and skirt the quayside, where you can watch the yachts skim by.

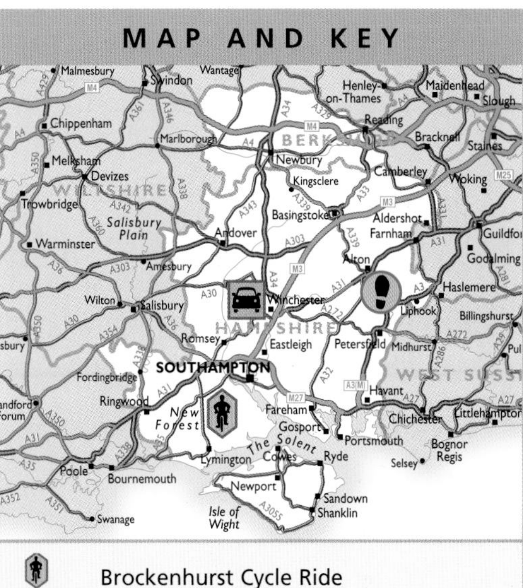

Brockenhurst Cycle Ride

Winchester Drive

Selborne Walk

The Needles and Alum Bay

At its western tip the Isle of Wight is a kaleidoscope of colours, petering out to sea in the three dazzlingly white chalk stacks called The Needles. You can visit these by boat from Alum Bay, where the cliffs are layered in different shades of red and orange, and the ochre sand was used by Victorian painters to spice up their colours.

THE NEW FOREST & THE ISLE OF WIGHT

A more accurate name for the New Forest would be the Old Heathland. This swath of scrubland, fields and woods was earmarked as perfect hunting country by William the Conqueror in 1079. A new law threatened all kinds of gruesome punishment against any locals caught poaching the King's deer; in return, the Commoners were allowed to collect firewood and peat, and graze their animals. About 3,000 diminutive ponies still graze freely across the forest's 130sq miles (336sq km) – and the Crown's deer are still there, too. You can watch them from viewing platforms at the Bolderwood Walks, west of Lyndhurst, the forest's 'capital'.

It may not look like the average forest, but the king's old playground does have some very grand old trees. Take the 19th-century Bolderwood Ornamental Drive to see the 380-year-old Knightwood Oak, and the Rhinefield Ornamental Drive, to the south, for neck-straining views of giant firs and redwoods.

Motor enthusiasts will love the National Motor Museum at Beaulieu, but if you've had enough of the road, head down the Beaulieu River to Exbury Gardens, with its blaze of azaleas and rhododendrons, or to Furzey Gardens, at the pretty thatched village

WALKS ON THE ISLE OF WIGHT

Bring your sturdiest boots to the Isle of Wight: in all there are 500 miles (805km) of footpaths here. In May there's an annual walking festival, marking the island's status as the first British county to hit the Countryside Commission's target for public rights of way. Popular routes include the 12-mile (19-km) **Tennyson Trail**, which runs along the high ridge between Freshwater Bay and The Needles, and the island's highest point, 764-ft (235-m) St Boniface Down, overlooking the spa resort of Ventnor on the sunny south coast.

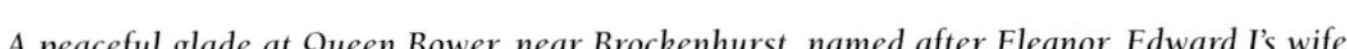

A peaceful glade at Queen Bower, near Brockenhurst, named after Eleanor, Edward I's wife

A clifftop walk affords spectacular views across Alum Bay on the Isle of Wight

Brockenhurst Cycle Ride

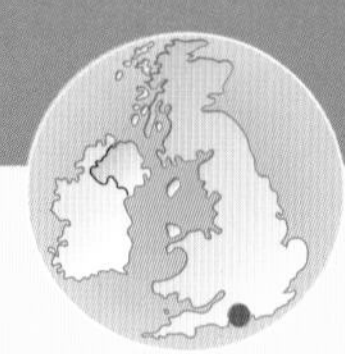

CYCLE RIDE

New Forest Heathland

START/FINISH: Brockenhurst. On the A337, midway between Lyndhurst and Lymington

DISTANCE: 23.5 miles (37.5km), with 6.5 miles (10.5km) off-road

GRADIENT: gently undulating

ROADS: country lanes, gravel tracks, short sections on B-roads

PARKING: Balmerlawn Forestry Commission car-park (free) at the junction of the A337 and B3055, just north of the village

A delightful ride through peaceful New Forest heathland and enclosures via excellent gravel tracks and along gently rolling Forest fringe lanes, with views across the Solent to the Isle of Wight. Take time out to visit the National Motor Museum at Beaulieu and the historic village of Bucklers Hard.

1 Leave the car-park and turn right along the B3055, then after 400yds (366m) bear off left on to a gravel track (arrowed 'Car Park') across heathland. Pass Tilery Lane car-park and soon curve left to the car-park at Standing Hat. Keep right, pass beside a barrier and shortly go through a gate close to a cottage. Proceed along a forest track to a crossing of tracks. Turn right towards a gate and soon cross a railway bridge.

2 After the railway bridge, take the first track left, then after a mile (1.5km) turn right at a crossing of five ways and follow a gently ascending track to a gate. Proceed straight on to a further gate, then descend to a crossing of tracks and turn left. Keep left uphill where a track merges from the right and remain on this forest track for three-quarters of a mile (1km) to a gate beyond a brook. Climb a heathland track, then bear right to merge with a metalled lane at Furzey Lodge and soon reach a crossroads at Hatchet Pond.

3 Turn left along the B3054 for 1 mile (1.5km). Continue downhill for 200yds (192m) and turn right, to visit Beaulieu village. Keep to the B-road for a further half a mile (1km) if you wish to visit the National Motor Museum and Beaulieu Abbey. Return out of Beaulieu on the B3054 and turn left, signed Bucklers Hard. Follow the lane uphill and keep left with Bucklers Hard signs to reach the historic, riverside village.

GETTING AROUND THE NEW FOREST

There's a network of cycle trails linking Brockenhurst railway station with the main villages and attractions. You can hire cycles near the station, at the **New Forest Cycle Experience**, which gives details of routes such as the **Ornamental Loop**, 8–15 miles (12–24km), passing through the deer sanctuary at Bolderwood, and the **Northern Link**, which at 35 miles (56km) might leave you a little saddle-sore. You can even combine bike and boat, taking a ferry-ride to the Isle of Wight on the **Bite of Wight** route.

Visitors are discouraged from approaching the ponies, but there are plenty of other four-legged foresters to meet. You can ride out Wild-West-style from **Burley Villa**, along trails that wind through the western part of the Forest; and horse-drawn wagons set out from **Brockenhurst** and **Burley**, through villages and forest enclosures.

of Minstead. Further downriver is the place for sea-dogs: Buckler's Hard, where ships were built for Lord Nelson.

Good, old-fashioned family fun is the theme on the Isle of Wight, a ferry-ride across the Solent from Lymington. Only 23 miles (37km) long and 13 miles (20km) wide, this diamond-shaped haven has three valuable assets: sand, sea and sun. Even Queen Victoria was amused here – she and Prince Albert opted for peace and quiet, building villa-style Osborne House as a summer getaway (complete with private beach and bathing machine). Alfred, Lord Tennyson took a liking to the place, too, and entertained the literati at his house near Freshwater.

There's always a flutter of sails around the island, with yachting enthusiasts congregating at Yarmouth, with its harbour and castle built by Henry VIII, and at the sailing mecca, Cowes.

Once a thriving shipbuilding yard, it features a fascinating little maritime museum that recalls this tradition and cottage displays re-create 18th-century life.

4 Continue along the lane to a T-junction. Turn left, signed St Leonards, and shortly pass the ruins of a tithe barn and a chapel. Bear right and proceed along this level lane. Keep straight on at the next two junctions to reach East End. Keep left at a junction, then in 100yds (91m) turn right, signed Norleywood. Pass through the hamlet to reach the B3054.

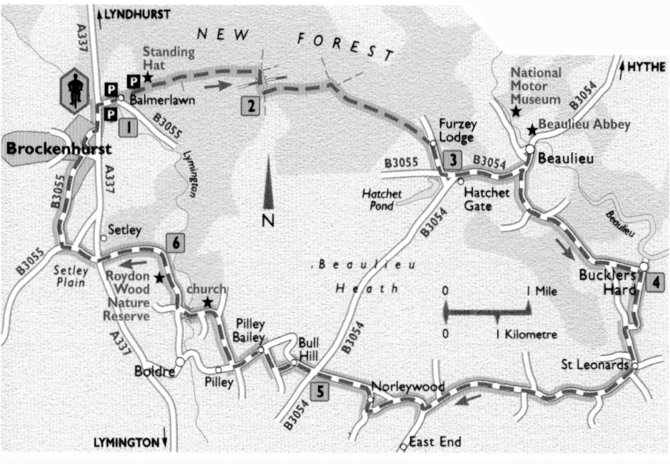

5 Cross over in to Bull Hill, signed to Pilley. Proceed through Pilley Bailey, then just before reaching The Fleur de Lys pub, turn right into Church Lane. Shortly, reach the isolated and interesting Boldre Church, noted for its memorials to HMS *Hood*. Descend, ignore the turning left, cross the Lymington River then, at a crossroads, turn right along a 'No Through Road', which soon becomes a gravel bridleway through Roydon Wood Nature Reserve.

6 Keep to the main bridleway as it bears left through the woodland. Cross a cattle grid, pass a house and keep left to the A337. Cross over and cross Setley Plain. Turn right on to the B3055, following it into Brockenhurst. Go straight on at a crossroads, then turn left on reaching the A337 for the short ride back to the car-park.

NEW FOREST WILDLIFE

The New Forest isn't just a treat for people: it's also an important area for wildlife. The ancient Court of Verderers still sits at Lyndhurst, and appoints Agisters to look after the forest ponies and cattle. Badgers, pigs, foxes, snakes and even wild boar roam the area – see them on the guided trails organised by **Nature Quest**, at **Ashurst**. You can also book places at the glass-walled hides run by **Badger Watch**, and enjoy close encounters with the animals during the evenings between March and November.

SEE CONTACTS SECTION FOR ADDITIONAL INFORMATION

Yachts compete every August during world-famous Cowes Week on the Isle of Wight

WINCHESTER & THE CHALK RIVERS

King Arthur's alleged Round Table, which hangs in the Great Hall at Winchester

Winchester might not look like a great capital, but for centuries this was a royal city – and it was from here that Alfred ruled his Saxon kingdom, Wessex. Hiding round corners and tucked away in little nooks are reminders of that proud past. A detour from the High Street, with its quirky mix of shops, takes you through a passageway to an impressive 'secret garden' – the tranquil Cathedral Close, surrounding the longest cathedral in Europe (556ft/169m). Narrow streets ramble south to Winchester College, England's oldest school, founded in 1382. Carry on to the top of the High Street and the only surviving part of Winchester Castle – the Great Hall, with its huge Round Table, said to be where King Arthur sat in conference with his noble knights. Near by you can climb the medieval gateway, Westgate, to look back down the High Street towards Broadway and the bronze statue of Alfred, wielding his sword at passers-by. It's only a stroll away from the royal presence to the trout-filled River Itchen: a riverside walk takes you to the lush water meadows, where a trail leads to the medieval almshouse of St Cross.

The Test River is a favourite with trout-fishers, flowing west of the city past the Augustinian priory of Mottisfont with its glorious

WALKS AND TRAILS

Winchester is a good base for several long-distance walks.

Clarendon Way – 24 miles (38km) from Winchester to Salisbury.

Itchen Way – following the river from its source near Hinton Ampner to Southampton Water, 27 miles (43km) away.

South Downs Way – 99 miles (159km) from Eastbourne to Winchester.

Test Way – 66 miles (106km), between Inkpen Beacon and Totton.

Other good places for shorter walks are **St Catherine's Hill**, 1 mile (1.5km) from the city centre and, further afield, the 13-acre (5-ha) Iron-Age fortress at **Danebury**, southwest of Andover, made up of three high circular ditches and ramparts.

Spice Island in Old Portsmouth, formerly an area of inns and brothels popular with sailors

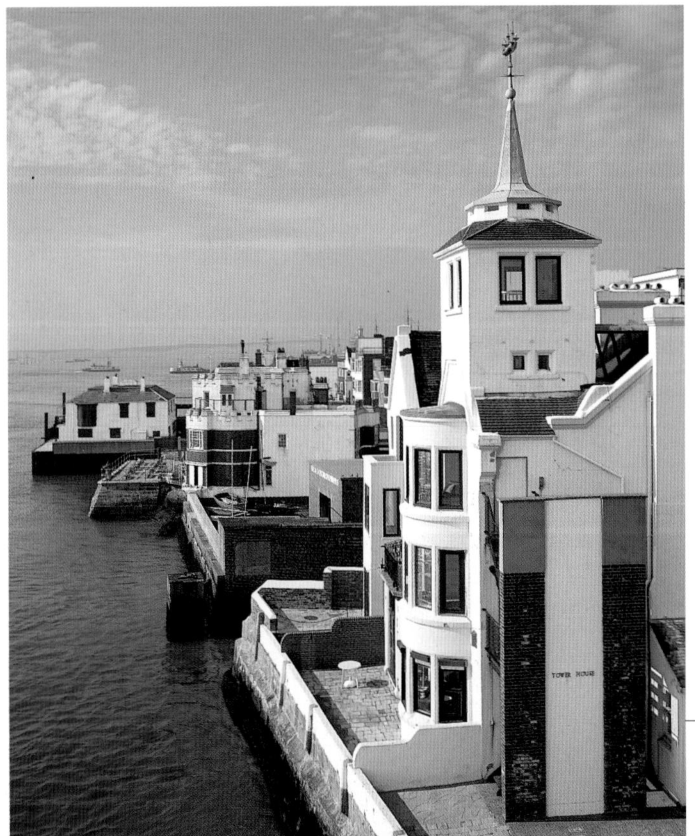

Winchester Drive

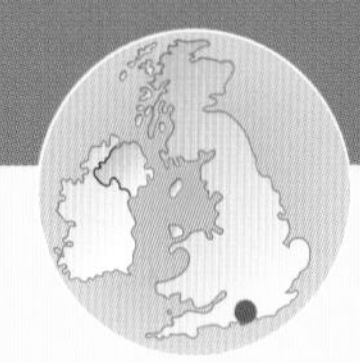

DRIVE

Test Valley and the Chalk Uplands

START/FINISH: Winchester. Cathedral city off the M3 between Basingstoke and Southampton

DISTANCE: 55 miles (88.5km)

This tour starts at Winchester, the county town and England's ancient capital. It passes through the lush valley of the River Test, homely villages of brick, thatch and timber, and encompasses the high chalklands of central and western Hampshire.

1 Leave Winchester on the B3040 heading west towards Romsey. At the roundabout turn right on to the B3041 then left into Sarum Road. Continue to Farley Mount Country Park, go over the crossroads and pass the Country Park car-parks. Turn right at the junction, pass through Ashley and continue to King's Somborne.

2 In King's Somborne turn right at the T-junction, then left on to the A3057. Turn right on to the unclassified road, signed Horsebridge. Turn right at the mill and cross the many streams of the Test into Houghton. Follow the road to the left and keep straight on heading south down the Test Valley to Mottisfont. Turn right at the post office to reach the B3084. Turn left, cross the level crossing and turn right at the Mill Arms on to the minor road, signed Lockerley.

3 Turn right in Lockerley, go under the railway bridge and keep straight ahead. Continue to East Tytherley and then bear right, signed Broughton. Continue for 2 miles (3km), bear left on to the B3084 and then turn right into Broughton. Turn left in Broughton, bear right over the Wallop Brook, then immediately left to pass Manor Farm, signed Middle Wallop. Cross the A30 to Nether Wallop. Go over the crossroads to Middle Wallop, then cross the A343 on to the B3084 into Over Wallop. Turn right by the village war memorial into King Lane and continue past Sunnyside Farm, over a crossroads and under the railway to Grateley.

4 Turn left through Grateley and then right, signed The Church. Turn right again and bear left with the road to pass through Quarley. Go under the A303. Turn right at the junction and turn right then right again into Thruxton. Follow the road to the left and go under the A303.

rose gardens, and the busy town of Romsey. Between Winchester and Romsey is a gardener's paradise – the Hillier Gardens and Arboretum, where no fewer than 42,000 plants and trees thrive on the land cultivated by green-fingered nurseryman Sir Harold Hillier.

The Itchen and the Test finally reach the sea at Southampton, whose historic centre was all but flattened during World War II. Remnants of the medieval town are tucked into a small area south of the shopping centre, but this is definitely a busy, modern town with a real tang of the sea. For a look at seafaring history, head along the coast to Portsmouth, where masts and rigging tower over the docks at the Royal Naval Base. You can step aboard Nelson's flagship, HMS *Victory*, or the first iron battleship, HMS *Warrior*; or go further back in time and see the dripping carcass of Henry VIII's ship *Mary Rose*, as well as the everyday Tudor knick-knacks that went down with her 700 crewmen when she sank in the Solent in 1545.

QUEEN ELIZABETH COUNTRY PARK

Straddling the A3, Queen Elizabeth Country Park has two distinct halves. In one, wildlife trails and waymarked walks lead through beech forests; in the other, a slice of open chalk downland gives wide views, and has a demonstration Iron-Age farm (right). Hang-gliders and paragliders take off into the wide, blue yonder from breezy **Butser Hill**. The earthbound can explore the park on mountain bikes, on hire from the Gravel Hill car-park on weekends and school holidays.

Timeless towns and pretty villages are dotted all about the chalk downs. One village with a proud claim to fame is Hambledon, in the lovely Meon valley – the birthplace of cricket. A monument marks this turning-point in history, near the aptly named Bat and Ball Inn. Steam trains still connect Alresford, with its neat Georgian streets and curiosity shops, to Alton, an old brewing town, whose main street forms part of the Bronze-Age Trackway, or Pilgrims Way.

Jane Austen lived just south of Alton, at Chawton, and wrote her best-known books in the red-brick house in the middle of the village.

THE WATERCRESS LINE

The 10-mile (16-km) steam-driven **Mid Hants Railway** links **Alresford** with **Alton Station** and the steamless railway system, stopping *en route* at Ropley, with its 100-year-old topiary, Medstead and Four Marks, the highest station in southern England at 630ft (192m) above sea-level. Known as the Watercress Line, it opened in 1865, carrying the watercress-growers' harvest in wooden panniers to be sold at London's markets. Nowadays you can eat a gourmet meal while travelling across country, or even drive and fire one of the engines yourself.

Turn left at Amport to the crossroads in the village of Monxton. Go straight over and across the railway to Abbotts Ann.

5 In Abbotts Ann turn right and then left beside the Eagle pub. Continue past the church and follow the road to the left and right to Little Ann. Turn left along the A343 and then right into Anna Valley, signed The Clatfords. Continue to Upper Clatford, following the valley of the River Anton, and carry straight on to Goodworth Clatford. In 1.25 miles (2km) go over a crossroads and continue to Longstock.

6 Continue to the A30 crossroads. Turn left on to the A30 over the Test into Stockbridge. Go over the roundabout along the B3049 for three-quarters of a mile (1km). Turn right on to an unclassified road (no sign), through Little Somborne, over the crossroads and pass the turning to Up Somborne on the right. Cross the B3049 to Crawley. Continue and turn right on to the A272 and return to Winchester.

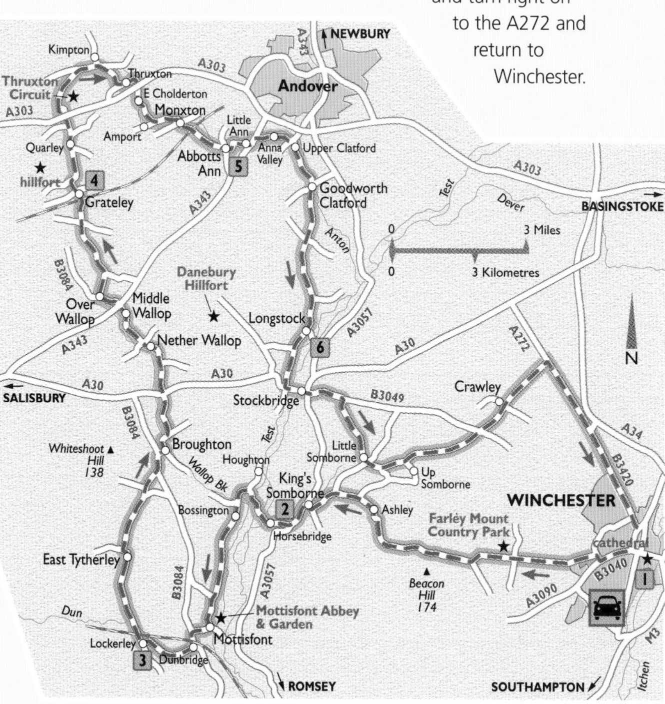

HAMPSHIRE & BERKSHIRE DOWNLAND

Stepping off the train at Basingstoke, you might be tempted to think that this is just commuter country, where, despite the bustling shopping mall and angular concert hall, The Anvil, all roads really lead to London. But you don't have to go much further to discover the rural charms of northern Hampshire and Berkshire's chalk downs: gentle, wooded hills and open fields; historic market towns and huddling hamlets; cosy country pubs, where you can linger over your pint by a roaring log fire. And then there are the country mansions, reminders of a less frantic age: just 2 miles (3km) north of Basingstoke is The Vyne, built for one of Henry VIII's courtiers, with meandering woodlands and a serene lake.

Across the county boundary in Berkshire, handsome Newbury still looks good on the proceeds of its 17th- and 18th-century golden age, at the peak of the cloth trade. Next to the town museum (in the 1626 Cloth Hall) are the rickety cottages where the hard-working cloth-weavers lived. The cloth was transported to market along the Kennet and Avon Canal, now a peaceful waterway used by boaters and ducks. On the northwestern edge of town is Donnington Castle, with its massive twin-towered gatehouse and earth ramparts that were built during the Civil War, when Sir John Boys was fending off the Roundheads.

Another 'castle', southwest of Newbury, is actually a Victorian

Finkley Down Farm Park introduces children to rural life and farmyard animals

MILESTONES

Street scenes of the past are re-created in Milestones, **Basingstoke's** new museum. Lampposts, drain covers, enamel advertising signs, postboxes and even freeze-dried mice and stuffed pigeons have been gathered together to add authentic touches to the re-created streets of the 19th and 20th centuries. You can view vintage steam engines and lorries, go shopping 1930s-style, see how home life has changed with the evolution of vacuum cleaners, sewing machines and electric irons, and even drink Hampshire's local Gales Ales beer in a traditional spit-and-sawdust pub.

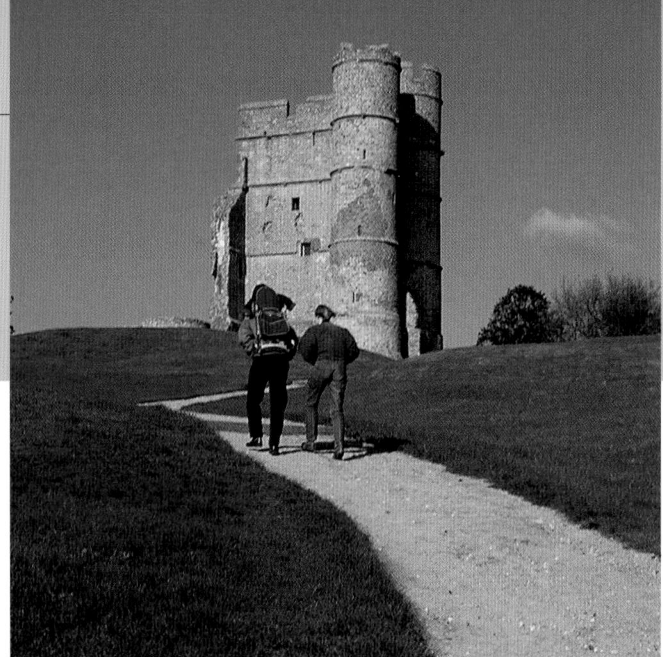

Walkers approach the remains of the gatehouse at Donnington Castle

Selborne Walk

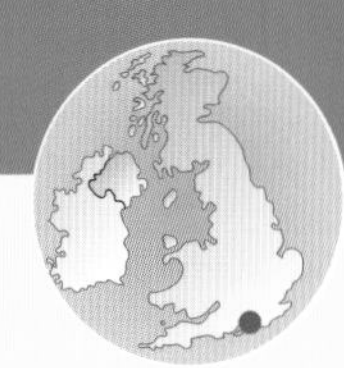

WALK

Selborne and the Hangers Way

START/FINISH: Selborne
DISTANCE: 7.5 miles (12km)
ASCENT/GRADIENT: 770ft (235m); mostly gradual, some steep descents
TERRAIN/PATHS: fields and woodland; paths generally good, can be very muddy
PARKING: car-park at the back of the Selborne Arms, Selborne

A circular walk through the wooded hill country of East Hampshire, in the footsteps of Gilbert White.

1 Selborne's fame is largely due to the writings of Gilbert White (1720–93). The Natural History of Selborne is one of the first accounts of local ecology in the 18th century. From the car-park, take the no through road by the pub, signed near the main road as the Hangers Way. Ignore the footpath to the Zigzags and the Hanger. Pass a tennis court on the right after 150yds (146m) and, at the junction by a garage on the left, take the left fork continuing to follow the Hangers Way. At Kingsfield Cottage take the footpath to the left side of a fence and continue on a narrow path past stables and a field. As another path comes up from the left, cross a stile into a field and continue on its left-hand edge into another field. Go through a stile at the edge of the next field and pass a red-brick house. Pass over a stile and follow yellow arrows around the field fencing, turning left at the corner to reach a road.

2 Cross the road and follow the minor metalled road, signed Noar Hill. Continue down the lane and, just before a red-brick cottage on the right, turn left up the track signed Hangers Way. Continue uphill to Noar Hill. There were chalk quarries here in medieval times and it is now a nature reserve. Stay on the chalky lane ignoring gates into the reserve on the right and a bridleway off to the left. At the fork take the left track signed Hangers Way.

3 Continue along the bridleway uphill. Ignore a right turn at the top of hill, instead contour around on a bridleway, eventually bearing right at the junction. At a meeting of paths, take the first left, the Hangers Way, down the hill. Emerge at the bottom of the hill into open fields by a stile. Cross the stile and continue to the opposite corner of the field. Cross the stile and continue with a hedge on the left to a stile and a road by a ford.

mansion: Highclere Castle was built in grand style for the designer of the Houses of Parliament, Sir Charles Barrie. The 5th Earl of Carnarvon was a later resident, and kept some of his Egyptian souvenirs there after unearthing the tomb of Tutankhamun.

Between Basingstoke and Newbury there used to be another lively town – but it has long since vanished. The Roman town of *Calleva Atrebatum* (Silchester) was a buzzing regional capital in the 3rd century; now it's a bumpy field, surrounded by the best-preserved Roman walls in Britain, running around the site. The little amphitheatre and its gory, rowdy shows were situated beyond the town confines.

INLAND WATERWAYS

Kennet and Avon Canal – built in 1810 to link the Thames with the Bristol Channel. In its heyday, it carried hundreds of thousands of tons of freight – mainly coal – and provided the power for mills, breweries and factories along its 87-mile (140-km) length. In the 1950s the railway and the road had all but killed it off, but volunteers rescued it, and it is now a popular beauty spot. The canal's history is traced at Newbury Wharf's 18th-century granary and at the visitor centre in Aldermaston Wharf's 19th-century wharfinger cottage. Boat trips set out from **Hungerford, Newbury** (motor barges from both) and **Kintbury** (horse-drawn barges).

Basingstoke Canal – a towpath trail runs 33.5 miles (54km) from Penny Bridge, east of Basingstoke, to its junction with the River Wey at Woodham. Boat trips can be arranged at the visitor centre at **Mytchett**, roughly halfway along the towpath; these include half-hour cruises with commentary on the traditional narrow boat *Daydream*.

Down on the River Test, south of Basingstoke, is a reminder of the more recent past – handsome Whitchurch silk mill, built in 1800 and still fully operational. You can watch the old looms and water-powered machines as they turn out top-quality silk fabrics which are destined to be shown off on the stage or in stately homes.

One of Britain's oldest roads – the Ridgeway – passes through Goring, north of Berkshire's most impressive Georgian mansion: Basildon Park, a magnificent creation in golden Bath stone, set in gardens and woods above the Thames Valley. It narrowly escaped being sold to the United States in the early 20th century; some of the house's fitments did change hands, though – they found a new home in the Waldorf Astoria Hotel, New York.

EXPLORING ON FOOT

Watership Down and its rabbits were immortalised in Richard Adams's book, and this open country between Whitchurch and Newbury is a great place for windswept walks. A steep climb leads to the summit of nearby **Beacon Hill**, named after the beacons that used to send messages across country as far afield as the Midlands.

Berkshire's recreational routes include a 2-mile (3-km) trail around **Wash Common**, west of Newbury, scene of a bloody battle during the Civil War; and from **Inkpen** to **Walbury Hill**. The **Ridgeway** is now a long-distance path, covering 85 miles (137km) between **Avebury** and **Ivinghoe Beacon** in Buckinghamshire. On its way it passes the locks and weirs of **Goring**, an attractive spot with a 12th-century church, 17th-century vicarage and 18th-century almshouses.

4 Cross the ford by a bridge and immediately turn left over two stiles and across the middle of the next field. Pass into another field to the left of a red-brick house. Keep to the fence on the right and cross the field to the opposite corner. Cross a stile on to a road. Turn left for a few paces then go right uphill on a byway. Pass Priors Dean Vineyard on the left and continue to join Keyham Farm access road. Continue to a road junction.

5 Go straight across to a track between hedges, following it left as it is joined by a track from the right from Goleigh Farm. Descend to a road. Turn right for 200yds (196m), passing a crossroads, then turn left uphill to the woods on Selborne Common.

6 Follow blue posts to a junction and take the middle footpath right, following a wide cleared way through the woods on to the common. Continue to bear slightly right ahead across a flat area, eventually dipping downwards towards a white house on the right. Ignore paths to the Hanger to the left. A metal bench and a stone mark the top of the Zigzags. Descend the Zigzags and go through a kissing-gate. Continue down the lane to the village, emerging back at the car-park.

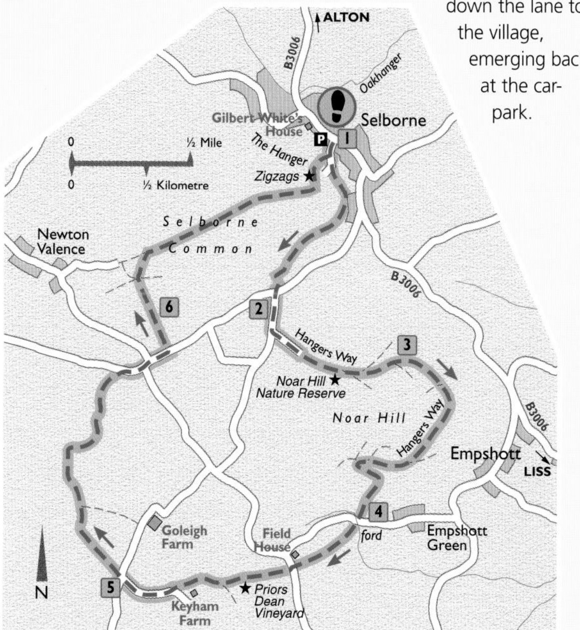

SOARING ON THE DOWNS

The chalk hills of Hampshire and Berkshire, rising to 974ft (297m) at Walbury Hill, offer excellent gliding. **Lasham Gliding Society** is one of the biggest in the country and the **Shalbourne Soaring Society** at Rivar Hill has superb soaring from thermals and a north-facing ridge. In a northerly wind **Inkpen Gibbet** is a good spot for hang-gliding.

THE WEALD & SOUTH COAST

Good, clean, salty sea air blows through the towns and villages of the South Downs coast, from the eccentric fun of Brighton, where café society thrives, to old holiday favourites such as Worthing and Eastbourne, and the historic charms of Chichester, Rye and Winchelsea. Rivers cut their lazy course through soft chalk hills to the sea: the Ouse, the Cuckmere and the Arun, flowing through fertile farmlands and wide water meadows on their way. As the coast runs eastwards, it leaves behind its majestic white cliffs and reaches the flat, ghostly Romney marshlands, whose networks of water channels were once a secret known only to the smugglers born and bred in that strange landscape. But only a few miles inland there's a different world: one of mellow villages, hop fields, pastures and pear, plum, cherry and apple orchards, bursting into bloom every year across the beautiful Weald of Kent.

THE ROYAL PAVILION, BRIGHTON

It's been lauded and reviled, and described (by the 19th-century writer William Cobbett) as 'a square box, a large Norfolk turnip and four onions'. Whatever you think of Brighton's pavilion, you can't ignore it. Originally it was a relatively modest affair, built by Henry Holland to a Classical design in 1783, but in 1812 the Prince Regent asked John Nash to add a few finishing touches, and the final version was a riot of pinnacles, domes, minarets and mind-bogglingly exotic 'Chinese' interiors.

Sissinghurst
Writer Vita Sackville-West created the gardens of this Tudor mansion east of Tunbridge Wells with her husband, Sir Harold Nicolson, in the 1930s. They followed the traces of vanished parts of the house to design several 'rooms' with different themes. Best known is the White Garden, where flowers and foliage are in shades of white and silver.

FISHBOURNE ROMAN PALACE

This 100-room palace was built for Cogidubnus, a Celtic leader who embraced the Roman way of life and was rewarded with the status of viceroy. Along with all mod cons – including underfloor heating and baths – the palace boasted elaborate mosaics: the most famous shows a winged boy riding a dolphin. The gardens have been redesigned to a Roman style, and an audio-visual display describes life in Roman Britain.

Dungeness

Denge Marsh reaches the sea in a remote, flat shingle headland, made all the more surreal by the vast nuclear power station built here in the 1960s, which offers guided tours around the plant. Two lighthouses stand within view of each other – one having taken over active duty from the 1904 'old lighthouse' (which is open for visits), itself the fourth version to be built on that site. Colonies of sea birds can be seen gathering at the RSPB reserve here: the visitor centre is off the Lydd road.

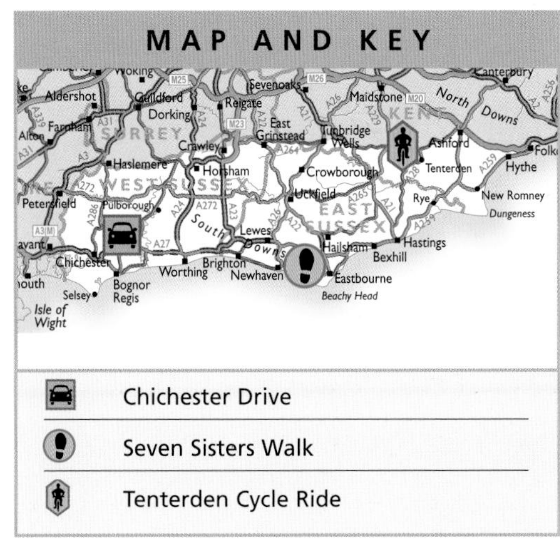

Chichester Harbour

A cluster of little villages lies along the inlets of Chichester Harbour – including Bosham, whose red-roofed cottages and Saxon church (featured on the Bayeux Tapestry) perch on a peninsula between two creeks; and yachters' favourite, Birdham, where Turner painted views of the harbour. You can take walks along the waterside at Apuldram, to spot the widgeon, waders and shelduck that flock here.

Seven Sisters and Beachy Head

The best sea view along this coast is from Beachy Head (575ft/175m), whose name comes from the French beau chef, or 'lovely head'. Between here and Cuckmere Haven, the elements have carved out a series of bright, white 'sister cliffs' – West Hill Brow, Baily's Hill, Flagstaff Point, Bran Point, Rough Brow, Short Brow and Haven Brow. Walking tracks lead along the clifftops and across the Seven Sisters Country Park.

THE SOUTH DOWNS

Bathing huts, bracing walks along the prom, end-of-pier shows and fish-and-chip suppers … the British seaside holiday is at its most traditional along this stretch of the southern coast. Generations have passed through the guesthouses and sat around the bandstands of Bognor Regis, Worthing, Hayling Island and Littlehampton, and a visit to any of these resorts will still take you back to an age of simple pleasures. Beyond the amusement arcades and crazy-golf courses there's a calm, unspoiled coast, where rivers meander between the soft chalk hills, and long, marshy fingers of land stretch out to form the inlets of Chichester Harbour.

Chichester is a small city with a long history: its streets and walls are reminders of the original Roman layout; there are stylish houses built on the profits of the port in the 18th and 19th centuries; and the 12th-century cathedral has pride of place. The Romans sailed up the Fishbourne Channel in the 1st century, and made a point of building lavish homes to show off their wealth and power. The biggest and best was Fishbourne Roman Palace, found near the village of Fishbourne, 2 miles (3km) west of Chichester.

Clinging to a hillside on the edge of the downs, with its castle perched on the top, Arundel isn't all it seems. Once upon a time it was a thriving

The village of Arundel with its imposing castle, the ancestral home of the Dukes of Norfolk

A demonstration of traditional turning at the Weald and Downland Museum

A view from Devil's Dyke on the South Downs, an ideal location for hang-gliding

Chichester Drive

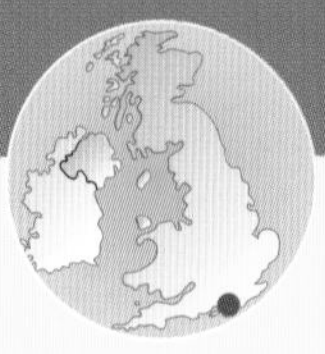

DRIVE

Chichester and West Sussex

START/FINISH: Chichester. Located on the A27 between Portsmouth and Brighton

DISTANCE: 58 miles (93km)

This tour climbs up over the South Downs and then crosses the valley of the River Rother to historic Petworth. It circles through the western tip of the Weald to the spectacular Devil's Punchbowl and returns to the downs via Midhurst.

1 Leave Chichester from the Ring Road (east side) by following signs for Bognor Regis A259. Veer left of the Four Chestnuts pub into Oving Road (minor road). In half a mile (800m), at the traffic signals, go forward, signed Oving, over the Chichester By-Pass, then in half a mile (800m) go forward, signed Tangmere. In 1.5 miles (2km) bear left to pass the airfield at Tangmere and the entrance to the Military Aviation Museum.

2 In Tangmere village, turn right following the sign to Boxgrove (A27). At the next roundabout (junction with A27), take the second exit towards Boxgrove and Halnaker. Continue through Boxgrove to Halnaker and turn right on to the A285 Petworth road. Ascend to reach the top of Duncton Hill. Descend through Duncton village. Cross the River Rother to enter Petworth and leave by following the A283 Guildford road to enter Surrey. Petworth House (NT) houses fine paintings and is surrounded by a magnificent deer park.

3 Continue through Northchapel to Chiddingfold and in a further 2 miles (3km) cross a railway bridge then turn immediately left, on to a minor road, signed Sandhills and Brook. In half a mile (800m) bear left and on reaching the edge of Brook, cross the main road (no sign). After 2.5 miles (4km) turn sharp left on to the A3 towards Petersfield. Ascend and pass the Devil's Punchbowl, a huge natural amphitheatre, on the right before entering Hindhead.

4 At the traffic signals in Hindhead turn sharp left on to the A287, signed Midhurst, and descend. At Shottermill, turn right for Midhurst, then at the traffic signals turn right again on to the B2131 Liphook road. At the roundabout turn right, then 2 miles (3km) further on bear

port – hard to believe, now that it sits 5 miles (8km) up the wandering Arun River. The castle is a Victorian version built on to the ruins of the Norman original; and the Roman Catholic cathedral is another 19th-century addition. Alongside the river, thousands of waterfowl find their own sanctuary in the Wildfowl and Wetlands Trust reserve.

One way to hang on to the past is to move it to a safe place. The Weald and Downland Museum, north of Chichester, has rescued historic buildings from demolition and rebuilt them here, stone by stone and brick by brick. There are medieval farmhouses and workshops, a village school and a blacksmith's forge – all full of people plying their trades for the benefit of modern-day visitors.

If you fancy a flutter, it's not far to Goodwood racecourse, 3 miles (5km) northeast of Chichester, laid out around 18th-century Goodwood House, which competes for attention with its grand stables. This was the home of the glamorous daughters of the 2nd Duke of Richmond. Nearby Trundle Hill is the site of an Iron-Age fort and an even older neolithic camp.

Tangmere was a name on everyone's lips during some of the darkest days of World War II. It was from the RAF base at this little village east of Chichester that pilots took off in 1940 to engage in 'dogfights' over southern England, known as the Battle of Britain. Today you can 'fly' a Spitfire at the Military Aviation Museum, which also houses the Meteor and Hunter jets that smashed the world air-speed records in 1946 and 1953.

CHICHESTER FESTIVAL

Chichester has established itself as one of the cultural hotspots of southern England, thanks to its summer theatre festival in June. Plays are staged at the six-sided **Festival Theatre**, built in 1962. Its first Artistic Director was Sir Laurence Olivier, who later founded the National Theatre in London, using actors from the Chichester company. The theatre now mounts about 750 performances a year, many of them going on to play at London's West End and in other cities all over the world.

GLORIOUS GOODWOOD

Set on its high, green hill, 500ft (152m) up at the heart of the South Downs, Goodwood is a special place, not just for race-goers. There are 18 flat-racing days a year, but everybody who's anybody comes for one particular meeting: Glorious Goodwood, held over five days in late July or early August. This is where the social élite and fashion leaders come to be seen, having recovered from the exertions of Ascot in June.

BY THE SEASIDE

Until the late 18th century, **Bognor** was just a quiet fishing hamlet, minding its own business as it had done since Saxon times. Then it was discovered by Georgian trend-setters; it acquired Regency houses and beach chalets, and grew even more during the Victorian seaside craze, when trains began to bring the masses to the coast. In 1928 Bognor became Bognor Regis when King George V convalesced at nearby **Aldwick** and gave it his stamp of approval. Nowadays, Butlin's **Southcoast World** still draws the crowds.

Worthing had its own royal boost in 1798, when Princess Amelia, the Prince Regent's sister, took a break at what was then a small fishing village. Fishing boats are still drawn up on the shore here, and sell their catch fresh off the decks, but Worthing is now a fully fledged seaside town, with 5 miles (8km) of sea-front, a flower-decked prom and regular variety shows at the Pavilion Theatre.

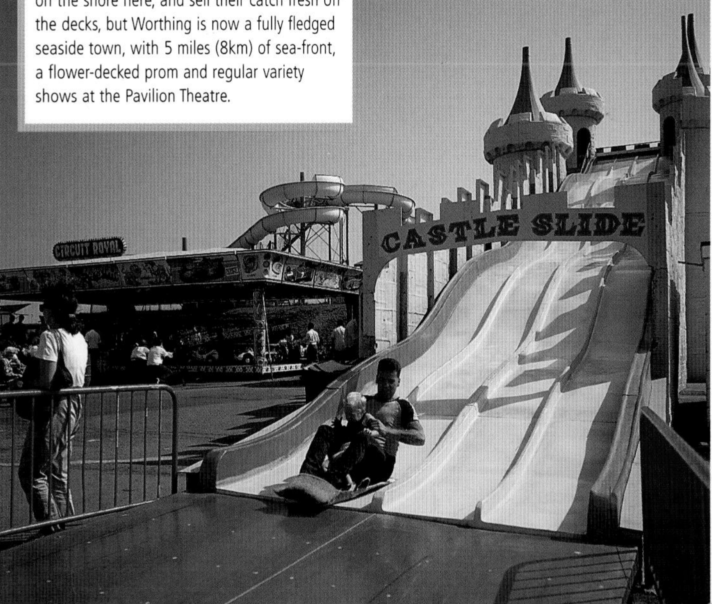

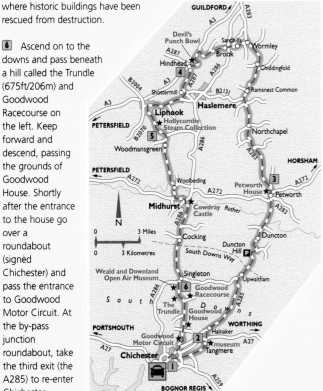

Traditional seaside amusements at Littlehampton's all-weather funfair

right to enter Hampshire and Liphook. At the town centre turn left at a mini-roundabout and keep ahead across several roundabouts, following signs to 'Station'. Shortly pass the entrance to Hollycombe Steam Collection.

5 Continue with the Midhurst signs and in 1.5 miles (2.5km) turn left, signed Woolbeding. Descend to Woolbeding and bear right to pass the church. Shortly re-cross the River Rother and turn left on to the A272 for Midhurst. At the mini-roundabout turn right on to the A286 towards Chichester. (Turn left for Midhurst town centre and Cowdray Castle.) Pass through Cocking and, on the far side of Singleton, turn left, unclassified, on to the Goodwood road. Pass the entrance to the Weald and Downland Open-Air Museum, where historic buildings have been rescued from destruction.

6 Ascend on to the downs and pass beneath a hill called the Trundle (675ft/206m) and Goodwood Racecourse on the left. Keep forward and descend, passing the grounds of Goodwood House. Shortly after the entrance to the house go over a roundabout (signed Chichester) and pass the entrance to Goodwood Motor Circuit. At the by-pass junction roundabout, take the third exit (the A285) to re-enter Chichester.

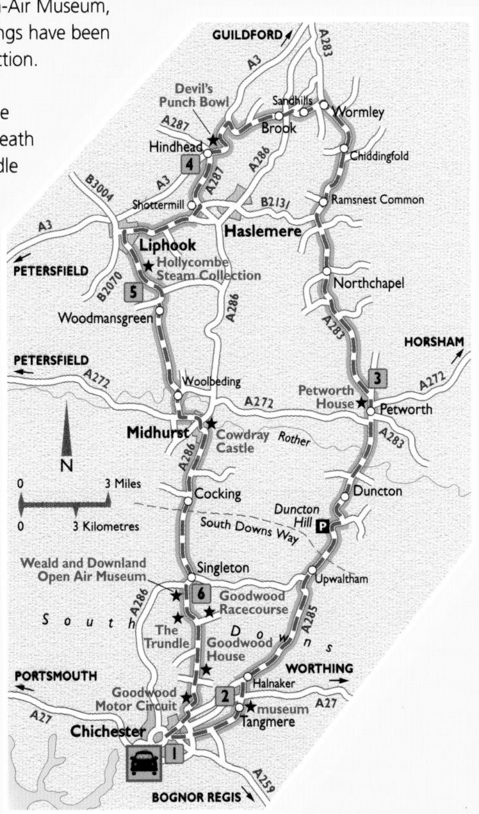

BRIGHTON & THE COAST

If it hadn't been for a certain Dr Richard Russell and his faith in sea air, there'd be no stuccoed terraces, no saucy postcards, no Royal Pavilion and its Christmas-tree baubles. But Dr Russell's spin did the trick, and in the mid-18th century the stressed and the ailing flocked to the coastal village of Brighthelmstone. Within a few years it was transformed into Brighton, England's top seaside resort, and today it still lives up to its history, with two piers, a long prom, trendy cafés and shops and, still the real star, the Prince Regent's Pavilion.

If you can tear yourself away from Brighton's eccentric charms, you'll find an irresistible mix of grassy hills, river valleys and spectacular cliffs, along with picture-postcard villages and stately seaside towns. The most breathtaking views are from the Seven Sisters, a switchback of majestic chalk cliffs reaching their climax at Beachy Head, south of Eastbourne. The South Downs Way loops down to these clifftops on the last leg of its 99-mile (159-km) journey from Winchester. Eastbourne itself is a neatly planned Victorian town looking out across the Channel towards France in one direction, and back over the rolling downs in the other.

A participant in the town criers' festival held at Hastings

One of the high points of the downs is Ditchling Beacon, 813ft (248m) up and a steep walk from the lovely village of Ditchling, where sculptor Eric Gill once lived. Other attractive downland

The Victorian seaside resort of Eastbourne, complete with promenade and bandstand

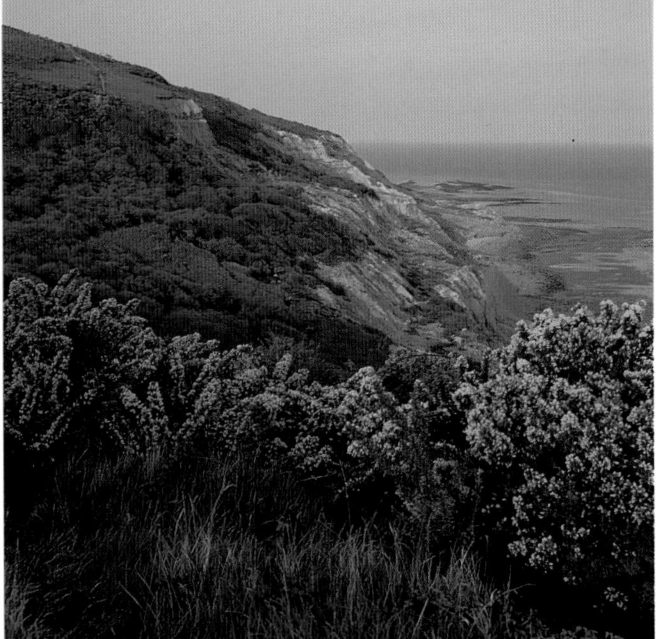

Walkers can enjoy beautiful coastal scenery at Hastings Country Park

Seven Sisters Walk

WALK

Up and Down on the Seven Sisters

START/FINISH: Exceat. On the A259 between Eastbourne and Seaford

DISTANCE: 7 miles (11km)

ASCENT/GRADIENT: 250ft (76m); some steep sections on Seven Sisters

TERRAIN/PATHS: forest, fields, downland; wide forest rides; good field paths

PARKING: car-park opposite Seven Sisters Country Park Visitor Centre

From wide forest rides linking timeless, secluded hamlets, this varied and testing walk traverses the open downland and cliffs of the famous Seven Sisters – up and down, up and down – on steep grassy paths with magnificent views, to the Seven Sisters Country Park at Cuckmere Haven.

1 From the car-park cross the road, and with the visitor centre on your left, walk up the grassy hill, on the South Downs Way, to a flint wall at the top. Climb over the wall, turn slightly to the right and take the Friston Forest Forestry Commission signpost. The path soon leads steeply to steps down to Westdean, a hidden flint-built hamlet, where the manorial rights are said to have been held by King Alfred. Today there is a pretty pond, a fine manor house, a tiny church and a rectory claimed to be the oldest inhabited one in the country.

2 Take the road on the right of the pond, signposted Friston and Jevington, and continue on into Friston Forest. Follow the ride between the trees until it curves left. Do not follow this, but take the wide fork straight ahead and continue until this meets a narrow track.

3 Cross this narrow track and go straight on to an open field, the Gallops, with a tower in the far distance. Continue up and down until you come to a road with a converted barn opposite.

4 Turn left, signposted Friston, and follow this as it curves downhill to the right and uphill to a gate on the right. Go through this into a field, with an electric fence on your right, and walk to the gate at the far end.

villages include quaint Pevensey, one-time haunt of smugglers, which is dwarfed by its sprawling castle ruins. The Romans were able to sail up the river right to Pevensey's gates, but the sea has receded now, and the village has been left high and dry. Tiny Westdean is reached down steep steps from Seven Sisters Country Park, and makes a good base for walks – through Friston Forest, or to Alfriston, an ancient clutch of buildings on the Cuckmere River. A little further to the east is the Long Man of Wilmington, a giant 231-ft (70-m) figure leaning on two sticks – or perhaps brandishing two spears – cut into the chalk of Windover Hill.

Lewes, the county town of East Sussex, is charming, with its elegant, curving high street, countless lanes and alleys, splendid half-timbered and stone houses, and castle remains to crown it all.

Hastings is a name to quicken the blood of history lovers, but handsome as the town is, with its pier and terraces, and fishing boats putting out from the beach, it isn't the place where William the Conqueror won his battle in 1066. That was 7 miles (11km) away, at the town known aptly as Battle. There was no town at the time, of course, and even today most of the battlefield is open and untouched – except by sheep!

The romantic, moated castle of Herstmonceaux, southwest of Battle, was built three centuries after William had conquered. It sits a mile (1.5km) from the village of the same name, which has made a good living for nearly two centuries from making gardening trugs.

GET ACTIVE!

There's no problem getting out and about in this part of the country and there are many popular pastimes.

Hang-gliding – over Devil's Dyke, a cleft in the South Downs giving great views across the hills. Local legend claims the Devil made the dike to flood the land and end the growth of Christianity.

Golf – at Waterhall golf course which is hilly and challenging, but shorter than Hollingbury Park, which has wonderful sea views.

Swimming – at Hove's sea-front King Alfred's leisure centre, with wild-water slides, and facilities for jet skiing.

London to Brighton veteran car run – during the first week of November. This is one of several events, including the **London to Brighton bike ride**, which attract spectators.

SHOPPING IN BRIGHTON

You can still map out the old village of Brighthelmstone in the network of cobbled courtyards and walled paths or 'twittens' that twist from North Street to the sea-front. Known as **The Lanes**, they're crammed with wonderful old buildings, and the North Laine (*sic*) is an Aladdin's cave of more than 350 shops, selling antiques and bric-à-brac, vintage clothes and ethnic jewellery, local crafts and catwalk fashion. There are also plenty of cafés strategically placed for foot-slogging consumers.

5 Walk diagonally across the next field. Climb over the stile at the end, up some steps on to a minor road which leads to the A259 at Friston church and pond. Cross the road. The porch door of the early Norman church is dedicated to the composer Frank Bridge, who was Benjamin Britten's first teacher.

6 Follow the no-through road next to the church, past the National Trust car-park, and down the tarmac path to the secluded hamlet of Crowlink, where Edith Nesbit, author of *The Railway Children* lived. Walk through a gate to a grassy path and follow this until the downs open up. In the summer over 45 different species of tiny wild-flowers grow on the downland, and there are skylarks, wheatears and stonechats, and the lovely chalkhill blue butterfly. Bear right up the hillside to tackle Brass Point (160ft/50m), Rough Brow (216ft/67m), Short Brow (214ft/66m), and the last Sister before Cuckmere Haven, Haven Brow (also the highest at 253ft/78m).

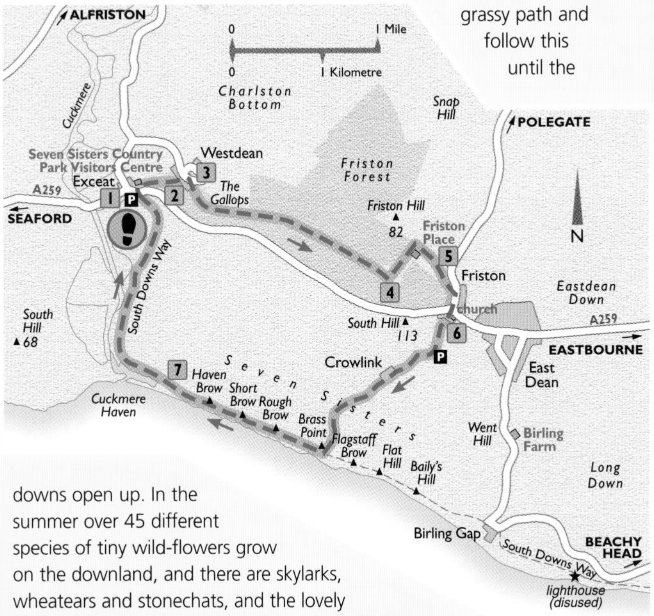

7 At a signpost follow the South Downs Way down to Cuckmere Haven, with a wire fence on your left. Turn right along a concrete path which leads back alongside the meandering River Cuckmere to Exceat car-park.

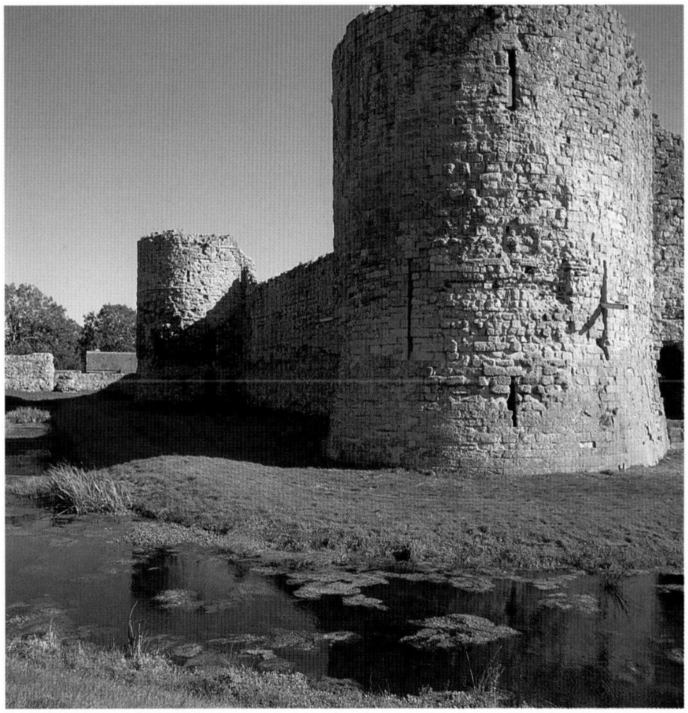

Originally built by the Romans as a fortress, Pevensey Castle still survives today

THE WEALD & ROMNEY MARSH

The Weald of Kent – whose name is from an ancient Saxon word meaning 'wild, wooded hills' – was once a place of deep oak forests, full of legend and magic. Now it's the garden of England, rich with orchards and farms and hop gardens guarded by their distinctive witches'-hat oast-houses. Weatherboarded houses give the villages their particular Kentish charm, while splendid mansions sit in vast green acres. Towards the coast and the Strait of Dover are the eerie landscapes of Romney Marsh, where medieval churches loom over misty flatlands and deeply cut dikes. This old smugglers' haunt juts out to sea at Dungeness, a shingle headland which is the site for thousands of birds on the RSPB's reserve, and an enormous nuclear power station. You can toil up the 169 steps of the Old Lighthouse to the giant lens, and then venture on to the balcony for views (on a good day) of France.

The Pantiles arcade in Tunbridge Wells, where the town's spring was discovered

There's more conventional charm in the walled town of Rye, with its cobbled streets, ancient half-timbered Mermaid Inn and golden 'quarter boys', figures that march out of St Mary's Church clock to strike every quarter hour. On the opposite hill is Winchelsea, a peaceful, pretty town built by Edward I to replace the original version, which was swallowed up by stormy seas. It was planned as a port, but the sea played another trick and receded, leaving the harbour to silt up and the town to settle into tranquillity. Rye and Winchelsea were added as 'limbs' to the confederation of Cinque Ports, the King's string of coastal defence ports (see page 85). Among the original five ports was New Romney, the biggest town on Romney Marsh, which is the headquarters of the famous Romney, Hythe and Dymchurch steam railway.

A traditional Kent oast-house in the village of Biddenden, used for drying hops

UP, UP AND AWAY

You can get a bird's-eye view of the Wealden fields and orchards from a hot-air balloon: flights are organised by **Sky Trek**, who have 'launch pads' in **Frant**, near Tunbridge Wells. They take to the skies every year between 1 March and 31 October, and flights usually last about an hour – at sunrise, from about 6am, or at dusk, between 5 and 7pm. Within that time the balloons cover around 10–15 miles (16–22km), and reach heights of between 500 and 1,500ft (150 and 460m). Landing sites vary according to the wind direction, but the ground crew will meet you as you come down to earth, with a glass of champagne and a Land Rover to take you back to your car.

Tenterden Cycle Ride

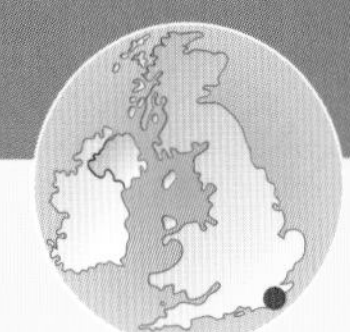

CYCLE RIDE

Tenterden and the Weald of Kent

START/FINISH: Tenterden. Situated between Ashford and Hastings on the A28

DISTANCE: 30 miles (48km), with 1 mile (1.5km) off-road

GRADIENT: mainly level; a few gentle climbs

ROADS: country lanes; short sections of busy A-road

PARKING: pay-and-display car-park in Bridewell Lane (south side of the High Street)

From the appealing country town of Tenterden, with its historic houses and steam railway, this delightful ride gently climbs to Sissinghurst and its famous castle and gardens, and then continues along the level roads of the Weald of Kent, passing through attractive villages in a landscape dominated by gentle farmland.

1 From the car-park turn left into the High Street (A28) and leave the town. Descend the hill, and after a short distance turn right on to a minor road, signposted Cranbrook. Keep on this road for 6 miles (9.5km), passing straight over the crossroads by the Castleton's Oak pub and through Hemsted Forest, to reach the crossroads at Golford. Turn right here and descend, before climbing to a T-junction in Sissinghurst. Turn right on to the A262 and in half a mile (800m) turn left along the drive to Sissinghurst Castle and Gardens (NT). Although the castle is really the remains of a splendid Elizabethan mansion, the renowned gardens are the main attraction, having been established by Vita Sackville-West during the 1930s.

2 Go straight on at the Castle Farmhouse sign, to pass in front of the castle and garden entrance. Bear right after the main buildings, just before the NT shop, to pass a white hexagonal summer house on the right. Ignore the marker and track to the right but keep straight ahead on a track, rising across a field (may be muddy), and meet the road by an iron gate. Bear right, and in quarter of a mile (500m) fork left on to a lane (no sign). At the next T-junction, turn left and continue for 3 miles (5km), passing through Lashenden and crossing the A274 to reach The Bell pub. Turn right shortly after the pub and follow the road into Smarden, one of Kent's prettiest villages. In the summer, the

Further inland, the Weald country begins with Tenterden, an old wool-trading town with lovely white weatherboarded houses and warm brick-and-tile homes built in the 18th century. Oddly enough, this was another 'limb' of the Cinque Ports – its link with the sea was at Smallhythe quays, on the river, 2 miles (3km) south. The great actress Ellen Terry lived near by at Smallhythe Place, a half-timbered 16th-century National Trust house. Head west, further again into the Weald, to see Vita Sackville-West's outstanding garden at Sissinghurst Castle (actually a Tudor mansion).

At the heart of the Weald is Royal Tunbridge Wells – an elegant old spa town which entertained the royals of Regency days, and looked to Beau Nash for guidance in fashion and society. You can still imagine the dandies of the day parading along the Pantiles, a street paved with tiles and lined with arcaded shops and houses.

THINGS TO DO

Biddenden, north of Tenterden, offers cider and apple juice to taste, made from local fruit, as well as wine produced in the county's oldest commercial vineyards.

Tenterden Vineyard Park, at **Smallhythe**, has more wine to sample and buy. Stroll around the herb gardens and spend some time in the countryside museum.

Bewl Water, near **Lamberhurst**, has the biggest lake in the southeast, where you will find walks, woodlands, watersports, fly-fishing and cycle hire.

South of England Rare Breeds Centre, at **Woodchurch**, east of Tenterden, allows you to make friends with the farm animals here. There are woodland trails, play areas and trailer rides, and the children can pet the animals in the barn.

The tranquil, watery landscape of Romney Marsh provides an ideal habitat for birds

THE BIDDENDEN MAIDS

Biddenden village is worth a visit – not just for the vineyards, but for its high street, paved with limestones embedded with fossils and its half-timbered houses, some of them old weavers' workshops. While you're there, look out for the village sign, which pictures Mary and Eliza Chulkhurst, the Biddenden Maids. The sisters were born in 1100 joined at the hip and shoulder, and lived for 34 years. When one died, the other refused to be separated, announcing: 'As we came together, so we will also go together'; she died six hours later. The sisters gave land to fund a village charity, which still exists, providing for the needy.

FULL STEAM AHEAD

Romney, Hythe and Dymchurch Railway – in the late 1920s, Captain J E P Howes achieved his dream by building a 13.5-mile (22-km) steam railway. Saved from closure by volunteers, the line still carries its gleaming, one-third size locomotives along the coast from Hythe, via New Romney and Dymchurch to Dungeness.

Kent and East Sussex Railway – opened in 1900, this line ran for 61 years and was reopened in 1974, again thanks to the dedication of steam-locomotive enthusiasts. It runs 7 miles (11km) from Tenterden, via Rolvenden and Wittersham Road to Northiam, and serves first-class meals on the luxurious Wealden Pullman.

Bluebell Railway (below) – situated over to the east, beyond the Weald. This line runs 10 miles (16km) from Sheffield Park, a garden with five lakes linked by cascades, and ends up at East Grinstead, after travelling through magical bluebell woods.

white-boarded cottages make a perfect backdrop for the colourful cottage gardens.

3 Negotiate a narrow Z-bend into the village and turn right. Go past the church gate on the right and over a narrow bridge. Shortly, bear left at a fork towards Bethersden. Proceed for 3 miles (5km), following signs to Bethersden, to meet the A28 by the Bull Inn. Turn left and immediately left again into Bethersden village. The churchyard has some unusual burial vaults.

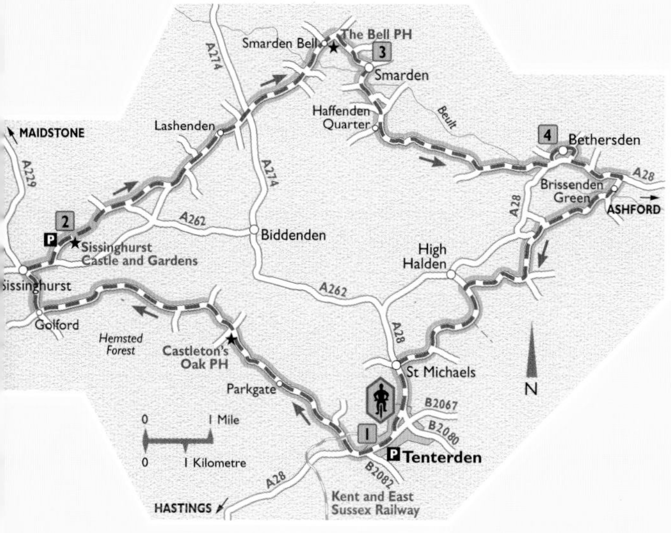

4 Follow the road which loops around the village to rejoin the A28. Turn left and continue for 1 mile (1.5km) before turning right into a minor road, signposted Woodchurch. Take the first turning right in Brissenden Green, signed High Halden. Keep left by a converted oast-house to meet a crossroads at Cuckold's Corner and turn right, signposted High Halden. After a mile (1.5km) turn left, at a sharp bend, into Harbourne Lane, signed St Michaels. Continue for 2 miles (3km) to reach the A28 in St Michaels. Turn left here to return to Tenterden.

THE NORTH DOWNS & THE KENT COAST

Always on the move – that's the first impression of the counties that skirt the capital to the south. There's the daily traffic in and out of London as commuters head in to their offices and city-dwellers rush out to enjoy the Kent coast and countryside. There's the constant toing and froing between France and the ferry and train terminals of Folkestone and Dover. And there's the slow shifting of the land itself, as the sea and its rivers deposit their silt and leave former ports such as Sandwich stranded inland, and former islands such as the Isle of Thanet welded to the mainland. But despite all this change, there's something timeless about this area, too. The rolling chalk downs stretching from Farnham in the west to the white sea cliffs of the east have a serene beauty. And nothing compares with summer in Kent, when the orchards are in bloom, the hops are ready to pick and cricket games are following their slow course on every village green.

LEEDS CASTLE

This fairy-tale castle, complete with turrets and wide moat, was built in 1120 and served as a royal palace for 300 years. Catherine of Aragon, Henry VIII's first wife, lived here – as did Elizabeth I, against her will, when she was still a princess and a prisoner. The castle stands on its two islands among 500 acres (200ha) of romantic grounds, where there's a vineyard, a maze and grotto, woodland, water gardens and the Culpeper Garden, growing old-fashioned flowers and herbs.

WHITE CLIFFS OF DOVER

You can gaze at these majestic white cliffs as you sail through the busiest shipping lanes in Europe on boat trips setting off from De Bradelei Wharf in Dover. Or you can enjoy the views across the Straits of Dover from the cliffs themselves, at the Gateway building on Langdon Cliffs, or South Foreland Lighthouse, from where Marconi sent his first ship-to-shore radio transmission. Guarding the cliffs is mighty Dover Castle.

Hop-picking

The heavy scent of hop flowers has been filling the fields of Kent every summer since the 16th century, when the crop was first introduced as an ingredient of beer. At one time there were about 30,000 acres (12,140ha) given over to hops, which were handpicked, often by migrant workers from London. The process is mechanised today, but you can still see how it all works at the Whitbread Hop Farm in Paddock Wood, which has the world's biggest group of Victorian oast-houses.

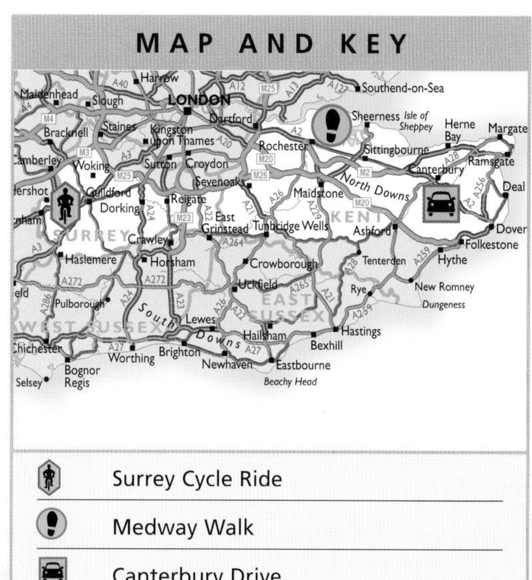

Pilgrims' Canterbury

A single candle marks the spot where Thomas à Becket was murdered in Canterbury Cathedral by two knights determined to rid Henry I of his 'turbulent priest'. His shrine has drawn thousands of pilgrims to the church, built in 1071 on the site of the country's first cathedral from the 6th century. Geoffrey Chaucer described a colourful party of 14th-century pilgrims in his bawdy Canterbury Tales, *and an exhibition in the city centre re-creates their journey and the sights, sounds and smells of medieval England.*

The entrance to Canterbury's Cathedral Close, showing the magnificent West Front

THE NORTH DOWNS & THE MOLE VALLEY

According to Charles Dickens, Guildford's High Street was 'the most beautiful in the kingdom' – and even today, it's easy to see why. Built on a hill, looking down towards the River Wey and the green hills beyond, this cobbled road is lined with shops and historic buildings, including The Angel, last of the old coaching inns, and the famous guildhall clock, a landmark since 1683, when John Aylward gave it to the city in return for permission to set up shop there. Beyond Guildford are the open downlands and woods of the North Downs, rising towards Box Hill, one of the best viewing points in Surrey, where trails zigzag up to the 563-ft (171-m) summit. Antiques hunters can spend hours browsing through shops in Dorking, to the south, at the mouth of the River Mole, before setting out to explore the Mole Valley and its unspoilt villages – Mickleham, Betchworth and Brockham. Polesden Lacey, near Dorking, is a 19th-century National Trust house with a gorgeous display of roses in the summer.

Make for Leith Hill, 965ft (294m) up, to see the 1766 tower built by Richard Hull, who is buried there. You can climb the hill the hard way – straight up from the road – or the gentle way, from the Abinger road. Abinger Hammer, north of Abinger itself, was once an industrial hothouse, hammering out iron from its 17th-century forge. There's still a working smithy, and the figure of a blacksmith strikes the hour on the village clock.

West of Guildford, the North Downs narrows into a

WISLEY

Only 3 miles (5km) east of the busy commuter town of Woking is the Royal Horticultural Society's flagship garden, Wisley. Covering over 240 acres (97ha), the garden manages to look stunning all year round. It has alpine meadows carpeted with wild daffodils in the spring, roses, mixed borders and the rhododendron-covered Battleston Hill in the summer, and rich foliage providing colour in the autumn, as well as the exotic greenhouse collections (including orchids and fuchsias) to warm you on chilly days. Wisley is a research site as well as a feast for the eyes, and there are trial grounds, model gardens and horticultural experts among the staff ready to apply their minds to your gardening problems. Sundays are reserved for members of the Royal Horticultural Society.

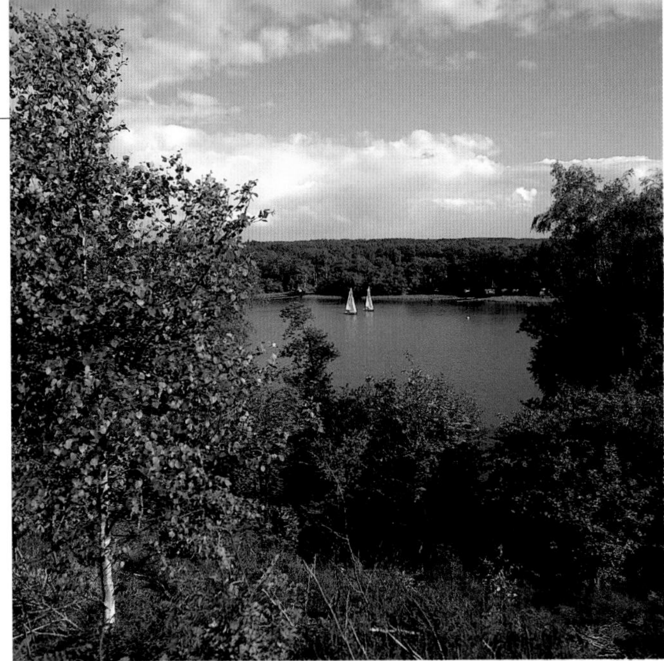

Frensham Great Pond, which was created to supply fish for the Bishop of Winchester

Surrey Cycle Ride

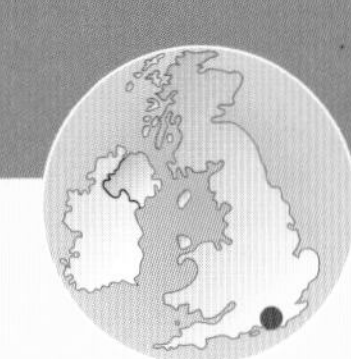

CYCLE RIDE

Heath and Woodlands

START/FINISH: Frensham Great Pond. Just off the A287 Farnham–Hindhead road

DISTANCE: 16.5 miles (26.5km), with 8 miles (13km) off-road

GRADIENT: gently undulating; one short, steep climb on a bridleway

ROADS: quiet country lanes and bridleways; latter may be muddy

PARKING: car-park and toilet facilities by the Great Pond (9am–9pm all year)

This is a delightful ride along quiet Surrey lanes and tracks, taking in several areas of classic heathland around both Frensham Great and Little Ponds. Various parts of the route follow rivers and streams which, apart from the ponds themselves, add another dimension to a ride already rich in flora and fauna.

1 From the car-park facing the water, turn right, follow the edge of the water to the road, and turn left on to the main road around Great Frensham Pond. This area abounds with wildlife, where mammals include roe deer, foxes and badgers, along with approximately 200 species of birds, notably the rare Dartford warbler. Bear left at Frensham Pond Hotel, then soon turn right on to a bridleway. Once past Coppice Cottage ignore the left fork and continue to join the drive. Turn left and go up a steep hill turning left at the road. At the T-junction turn left on to the A287 then turn right towards Tilford.

2 Continue past the Pride of the Valley pub and go straight over the crossroads towards Thursley and Elstead. After 2 miles (3km) turn left on to a bridleway, signed Hounsdown Lane. Go over the bridge, bear right and carry on along the road past Chailey Wood and past a cemetery to a T-junction. Turn left and after 1 mile (1.5km) turn left again into Westbrook Lane by St James's Church.

3 Pass a farmyard to a triangle and bear right along a bridleway past Hankley Farm on the right, following the blue marker arrows. At Stockbridge Pond bear right following the red arrows to Tilford.

windy ridge, with panoramic views – the Hog's Back – where medieval pilgrims would tramp along their route from Winchester to Canterbury. This runs towards Farnham, a dignified town full of stylish Georgian buildings, which made its money as a corn market. Nearby Aldershot is an army town with some excellent military museums, including the Army Medical Services Museum at Keogh Barracks, where you can follow the sometimes gruesome history of army nursing and dentistry from 1660.

WEY NAVIGATION

Hire a narrow boat or a rowing boat from **Guildford Boat House** to cruise along the Wey Navigation, 20 miles (32km) of the River Wey that once provided an important trading route, and is now owned by the National Trust. An electric river-boat launch takes passengers from the Town Wharf to Dapdune Wharf, which has been restored to give an idea of what life was like at the peak of the river-trading days. There are interactive displays in the old Carbide Store, stable and smithy, and you can potter round the revamped Wey barge *Reliance*. Walks follow the towpath along the Navigation out into the Surrey countryside.

4 The route does not go into Tilford. Instead, go straight across the road (there is a car-park on the left) on to the byway, then fork left following the red marker arrows and turn right at the public conveniences. To visit Frensham Little Pond carry straight along the byway for about 150yds (140m), turn right and the car-park is on the left. Following the bridleway marked 513, bear right past Keeper's Cottage across the bridge, through the farmyard and bear right, passing through a gate, along a bridleway. Bear left through the woods to the end and turn left.

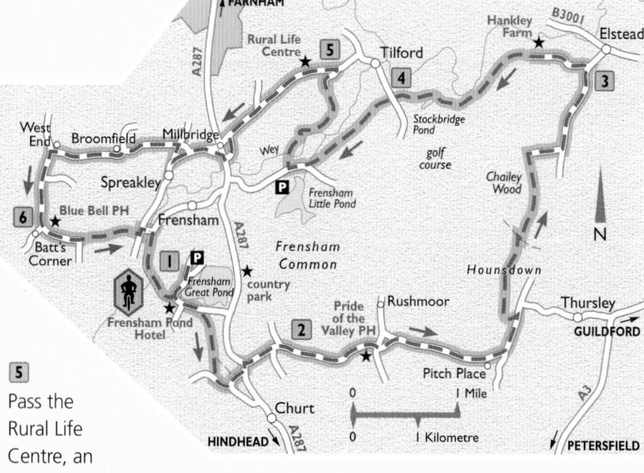

5 Pass the Rural Life Centre, an extensive museum complex containing one of the biggest private collections of village and rural life in the country, on your right and continue to the main road, opposite the Mariners Hotel. Turn right and then first left. Turn left past The Holly Bush pub then turn right, signed Broomfields and West End, and bear left into West End Lane past converted oast-houses. Turn left at a T-junction and then take the second left past The Blue Bell pub.

6 Carry straight on to a bridleway to reach the road. Turn left, then first right over the river and right again through the gates of The Old Mill House. A bridleway is straight ahead up the hill. Follow this along the river bank, keeping left, to the end, where you turn left and then first right to take you back to Frensham Great Pond and the car-park.

If you need a breath of fresh air, head south of Farnham to Frensham Ponds: the Great Pond and the Little Pond are both super places for boating, fishing and bird-watching, and there are wide views from the three nearby hills known as the Devil's Jumps. There's more good walking country on Hindhead Commons, where springs have formed a natural crater called the Devil's Punchbowl. Legend has it that the area was used for satanic rites and witchcraft. This was a no-go area during the 18th century: highwaymen and cattle-rustlers haunted the high heathland around Hindhead village, and three men were hanged at nearby Gibbet Hill for murdering a sailor.

BIRDWORLD

Birds of every size, shape and colour imaginable live at Birdworld, 3 miles (5km) south of Farnham on the A325. Attractions include a seashore walk, Penguin Island, animal-handling sessions, a tropical walk and the rare birds breeding centre. Children can make friends with the young animals on Jenny Wren Farm, and there are woodland trails, shops and picnic sites in the grounds. The complex also includes Underwater World, a tropical aquarium.

DID YOU KNOW?

Box Hill was named after the evergreen box trees that grew there alongside the yews. People came up to sit in their shade and enjoy a picnic as far back as the 1660s, but during the 18th century many of the trees were cut down for their dense wood, which was used to make blocks for engravings. A celebrated engraver, Thomas Bewick, boasted that he'd used one of these blocks 900,000 times – and it was still going strong.

THE NORTH DOWNS & THE MEDWAY ESTUARY

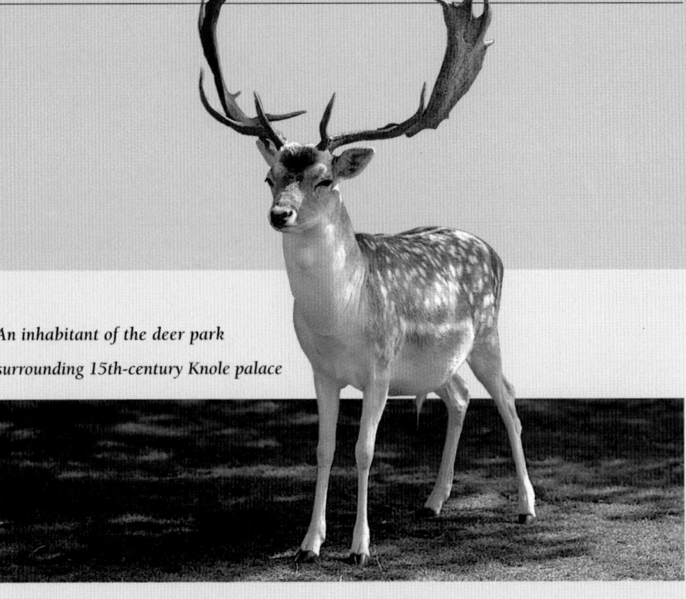

An inhabitant of the deer park surrounding 15th-century Knole palace

This area is full of unexpected treats. Packed commuter trains travel up and down to London every day, but the capital's 'green belt' has kept its character and beauty, with glorious manors and sweeping parkland among the still unspoilt North Downs, and the River Medway flowing through Kent to its estuary and cluster of historic ports.

Busy Maidstone is Kent's county town, built on the Medway, which flows past the 14th-century Archbishop's Palace, where Canterbury's archbishops used to come to get away from it all. Further upriver, Tonbridge is a pleasant market town where Jane Austen's father taught at the boys' school, and where boats can be hired for a little relaxed river-cruising.

Sevenoaks, north of Tonbridge, is on the main route from London, but gives access to the wide green park of Knole, a medieval house that's more of a palace, with, it's said, a courtyard for every month of the year, a staircase for every week and a room for every day. Thomas Sackville moved here during Elizabeth I's reign; his descendant, Vita Sackville-West, designed the magnificent gardens at Sissinghurst (see page 70).

Castles and grand houses seem to be round every corner in this part

COUNTRYSIDE ROUTES

The North Downs Way – long-distance footpath winding its way through northern Kent *en route* from Farnham to Canterbury, looping up towards Rochester and giving sweeping views of the coast to one side and hop farms, fields and orchards on the other.

Greensand Ridge – 440 acres (178ha) of perfect walking country around Toys Hill and Ide Hill, where the National Trust protects the classically English village green, pubs and hilltop church.

High Weald Country Tour – a 70-mile (112-km) route circling through some of the most seductive Kentish countryside between Penshurst and Tenterden; ideal for cyclists.

CRICKET IN COBHAM

Kent is cricketers' county: every summer weekend, village teams compete on the greens, their whites sparkling in the sunshine, while the air resounds with the 'thunk' of leather against willow. Many of the game's greats have wielded their bats in the village of Cobham, including the most famous Victorian player of all, W G Grace. Ivo Bligh was another hero, who started off as captain of the Cobham team and went on to lead the English team to Australia in the 1880s. Cobham's half-timbered pub, the Leather Bottle Inn, has its own, non-cricketing claim to fame – it features in Dickens's novel *The Pickwick Papers*.

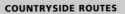

Medway Walk

WALK

Historic Medway Towns

START/FINISH: Rochester. Located on the A2 between Gravesend and Sittingbourne

DISTANCE: 5.5 miles (9km)

TERRAIN: city streets

PARKING: Rochester Station

A rich and varied past is all around you on the streets of Rochester and Chatham. Follow the river to the birthplace of the Royal Navy and the town which inspired Charles Dickens, taking in Chatham's dockyard, Rochester's cathedral, castle, and High Street, the latter full of Dickensian associations.

1 From Rochester Station turn left, go under the rail bridge and walk right, down to the main road. Turn left along Medway Street, follow the road round, then turn left again up Dock Road, signed Historic Dockyard. Pass Fort Amherst, a Napoleonic complex of underground tunnels built to protect the Royal Naval Dockyard from attack, then a gateway above which sits a coat of arms erected on the 50th anniversary of D-Day to commemorate Chatham Dockyard's role in support of Operation Overlord – the Allied invasion of occupied Europe.

2 Keep walking up this busy road. Go straight on at the roundabout, then left into the Historic Dockyard. Henry VIII used to winter his ships on the Medway and many of the ships that defeated the Spanish Armada sailed from these docks. It was here too that Drake, and later Nelson, learned their seamanship. Leave the dockyard and turn left. Go over the roundabout, then past the Medway Tunnel. Cross the road at the next roundabout and walk up to the submarine *Ocelot*, the last warship to be built for the Royal Navy at Chatham.

3 Follow the road back into town. At the clock, cross over to the Pentagon Shopping Centre. Turn right up a pedestrianised street (Military Road), then go right along a quiet part of Chatham High Street. Keep going straight ahead, back to Rochester Station.

4 Pass the station, walk up to the main road, cross over and walk down the pedestrianised High Street. Just after Eastgate House turn left, up Crow Lane. Cross over at Restoration House and follow the sign

CHATHAM DOCKYARD

For 300 years, Chatham Dockyard was the most important base for the Royal Navy, and its tradition of shipbuilding carried on until the closure of the yards in 1984.

They opened again, but as a living museum, showing how the docks developed from their beginnings in Henry VIII's reign, through the 17th century, and the flourishing Georgian era. You can see where ropes were made for the ships, in the country's longest room, a quarter of a mile (600m) from end to end, and try your hand as an 18th-century ship's apprentice in the Wooden Walls gallery.

Moored near the docks are three battleships – the last Victorian sloop, *Gannet*; a World War II destroyer, HMS *Cavalier*, and the spy submarine *Ocelot*, where you can experience the crew's limited living space. A paddle steamer, *Kingswear Castle*, takes visitors round the dockyard during the summer.

of the country. The most impressive is Leeds Castle, just east of Maidstone, while Hever Castle, west of Tonbridge, is a romantic, moated manor house, once the home of Henry VIII's wife, Anne Boleyn, and kitted out with the best of Edwardian décor by American millionaire William Waldorf Astor in the early 20th century. Chartwell, to the north, is on a more modest scale, but has the distinction of being Sir Winston Churchill's home from 1922 to 1964. Between Tonbridge and Hever there's Penshurst Place, a stunning example of a medieval manor house, all courtyards and galleries, with an exceptional Barons' Hall. Ightham Mote, a magical moated mansion near the half-timbered village of Ightham, was saved for posterity by American C H Robinson, who fell in love with it while on a cycling holiday. He duly went home and made his fortune, bought the house lock, stock and barrel and bequeathed it to the National Trust.

The Medway winds past the flatlands of the Isle of Sheppey and the Isle of Grain, where cherry orchards and oil refineries have replaced the wheatfields that gave the area its name. At the mouth of the river are Chatham and Rochester, both associated with Charles Dickens, who lived in Chatham as a child and wrote more about the cathedral city of Rochester than any other place bar London. Rochester still has pockets of old-world charm and a huge castle keep – 125ft (38m) high – built by Henry I to defend the Medway crossing against invaders. Nowadays it has an easier time, watching over the yachts and dinghies that skim around the estuary waters.

for Centenary Walk, which leads over a small park. Charles Dickens loved the town and it featured a lot in his work. Restoration House, for instance, a forbidding brick building, became Satis House in *Great Expectations*. Today its iron gate still keeps the outside world at bay, just as it did for mad Miss Havisham.

5 Turn right at the end, go down the hill, then left at the bottom. Pass the cathedral, which was founded in AD 604, cross the road and turn left round the castle, following the Centenary Walk signs. Built by the Normans on the remains of an

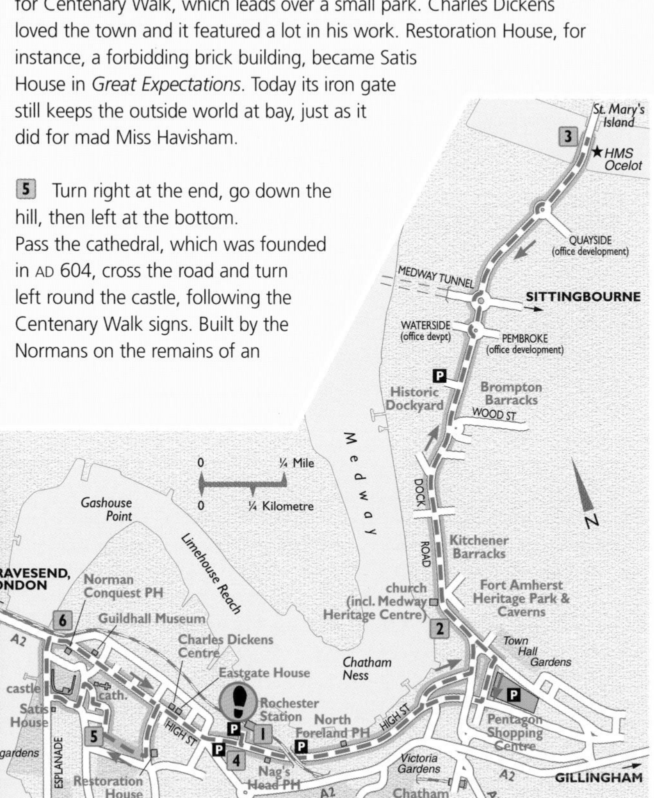

earlier Roman fort, this magnificent milky castle, with a four square stone keep, has walls 12ft (3.5m) thick in places. Continue ahead and pass Satis House, turn right at the river, then turn right again by the bridge.

6 Walk right along the High Street, taking time to explore the small alleys and passageways leading off the main route. Cross the road at the end and walk back to the station.

SAILING ON THE MEDWAY ESTUARY

The Medway Estuary is a favourite challenge for sailors. A combination of tricky currents and changing winds between the creeks branching off this winding stretch of water brings the competitive and the adventurous here in their droves. The **Medway Regatta** has been held here since 1888, when an Australian skiff was beaten in a race with a local helmswoman. The week-long event in July includes dinghy races and cruiser/keelboat races.

On the southern shore of the estuary you can still see the Thames barges in all their glory. These red-sailed, high-masted ships used to be the east coast's traditional cargo vessels: there were over 2,000 still fully operating at the turn of the 20th century. Only a handful are sailed now, but groups can book them for pleasure trips along the river or shore, as well as parties, and jazz or murder mystery cruises, run by **Topsail**.

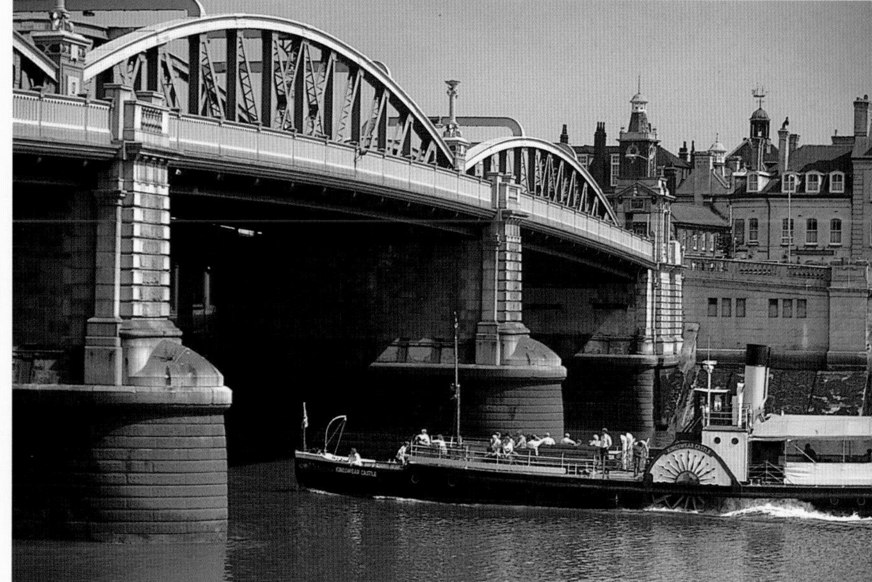

PILGRIMS WAY – FROM CANTERBURY TO DOVER

For centuries pilgrims trudged over the downs along the Pilgrims Way (now part of the North Downs Way), *en route* to visit Thomas à Becket's shrine in Canterbury Cathedral. And thousands of years before them, prehistoric travellers followed the same upland track across country. Along the shore, ancient ports have seen countless kings and queens, armies and merchants come and go across the Channel to France or the Netherlands – and today there's more traffic than ever, as holiday-makers and business travellers hurry through the gateway of England to catch the ferry or take the train through the Channel Tunnel. Yet amid all this bustle, the serenity of historic towns, atmospheric old streets, tranquil villages and calm wooded landscapes dotted with farms, manor houses, churches and pubs, remains.

There's Canterbury itself, with its glorious old cathedral soaring above the huddle of pedestrianised streets and old buildings – a wonderful place to explore on foot, around the medieval walls or along the River Stour, where in summer you can take a guided punt tour. Further along the Stour, southwest of the city, is the perfect Kentish village of Chilham, with its mellow brick-and-stone cottages, its immaculate gardens and square, and the Jacobean castle, whose gardens slope down to the water's edge. Up towards the coast, Faversham is a quirky market town where the old sailing barges still glide past Iron Wharf, and strung along the shore to the east is a series of jolly seaside resorts.

At Whitstable you can forget the diet and make the most of the famous local seafood, before browsing through the colourful craft shops on the harbourside, or ambling along the clifftop Tankerton Slopes, with fine views of the narrow shingle ridge known as The Street,

THE WORLD IS YOUR OYSTER

If you like seafood, a stroll along **Whitstable harbour** will soon have you smacking your lips. There's a thriving oyster industry here, celebrated every July in the week-long Oyster Festival, and described in the Oyster and Fishery Exhibition on East Quay. One of the best places to indulge is the roomy **Whitstable Oyster Company**, located in a former warehouse at Horsebridge. Here you can tuck into the house speciality, as well as mussels and other types of seafood from the morning's catch, while watching the boats in the harbour.

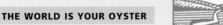

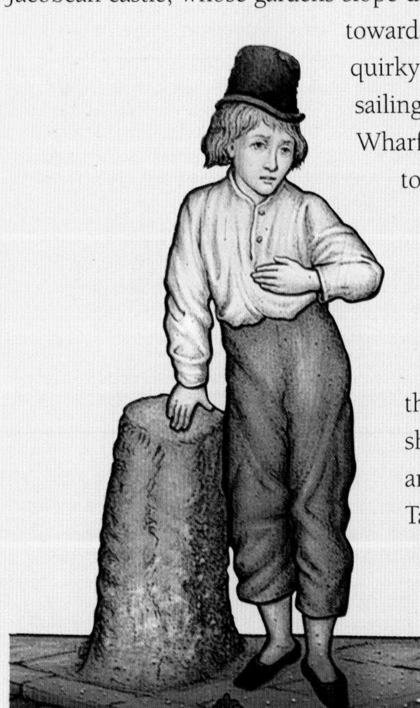

An image of David Copperfield at the Dickens House, Broadstairs

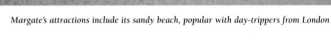

Margate's attractions include its sandy beach, popular with day-trippers from London

Canterbury Drive

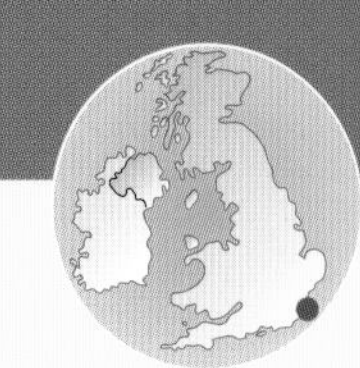

DRIVE

From Cathedral to Cliffs

START/FINISH: Canterbury. Cathedral city on the A28 between Ashford and Margate

DISTANCE: 107 miles (172km)

Cathedral and castles, steep cliffs and flat marshes are part of this drive, which also takes in green countryside, oast-houses, thatched cottages, and the Cinque Ports on the Kent coast.

1 From the city centre take the A28 Ashford road to Chartham and Chilham. Chilham has a charming village square lined with unspoilt Tudor and Jacobean houses, and a fine castle (not open), built for Henry II in 1174. From Chilham return to the A28, head south for 2 miles (3km) then turn off on to unclassified roads to Wye.

2 Return to the A28 for 5 miles (8km) to Ashford. This old market centre for Romney Marsh and the Weald of Kent is now a thriving shopping and business centre, and an important international terminus for Eurostar.

3 Follow an unclassified road, then the A259 across Romney Marsh to Rye. Rye is an enchanting little town, with cobbled streets and a wealth of historic buildings, including a Norman church, a 13th-century tower and 16th-century inns. It is the first of the Cinque Ports to be visited on this drive – a group of maritime towns which were originally responsible for providing ships and men to guard against invasion. Return on the A259 to East Guldeford, then take an unclassified road through Camber to Lydd to join the B2075 to New Romney. The Romney, Hythe and Dymchurch narrow-gauge railway opened in 1927, with locomotives and carriages which are one-third full size.

4 Take the A259 again, then unclassified roads for 9 miles (14km) to Lympne, then via the B2067 to the A261 which leads eastwards to Hythe. The 11th-century castle at Lympne (pronounced Lim) stands on top of a cliff which was once a coastline. Port Lympne Wild Animal Park is set in 300 acres (121ha) of gardens surrounding a mansion. Hythe is a popular seaside resort. Follow the A259 from Hythe to Folkestone, another resort town and cross-Channel ferry port. The Museum and Art Gallery in Grace Hill has displays on the town's maritime history, and Spade House was the former home of the author H G Wells. Head

stretching out to sea. Then comes Herne Bay, a Victorian town with safe beaches and good sailing; and a little further along is a ring of resorts grouped around the Isle of Thanet, once cut off from the mainland by the rivers Stour and Wantsum. Margate is the biggest and brashest, with funfairs, amusement arcades and donkey rides, while Ramsgate is more of an old-world town with a long sea-going tradition. At Broadstairs, between the two, old houses cluster round the jetty and sun-lovers gather on Viking Bay, in the shelter of the high chalk cliffs. Dickens was a fan of Broadstairs, and wrote *David Copperfield* here.

TUNNEL VISION

It took 160 years for the tunnel linking Britain and France to progress from idea to reality. Building had started on both sides of the Channel as far back as the 1880s, but fears of invasion put Queen Victoria off the whole idea and the plans were subsequently abandoned. Funding problems led to another false start, in the 1970s, but eventually the project got underway, and by 1994 trains were thundering through the tunnel between **Folkestone** and **Sangatte**.

All that digging threw up a lot of muck, and it's been ingeniously put to use as a wildlife site at **Samphire Hoe**, off the A20 between Dover and Folkestone. It's become a haven for wild-flowers and birds, and you can go there to fish, walk or cycle. Guided walks and other events are regularly organised.

There's good fishing at Deal, on the southern Kent shore, where Georgian houses line the streets and lanes that twist here and there to divert the driving Channel winds. Three of the original Cinque Ports guard this curve of coast – Sandwich, Dover and Hythe – once all-important strategic towns. Sandwich and Hythe have gone into peaceful retirement, but Dover is still businesslike, ushering traffic in and out of its ferry terminal, sending travellers off or greeting arrivals with the famous view of its towering white cliffs.

Conquest House, one of the surviving half-timbered buildings in Canterbury

SEE CONTACTS SECTION FOR ADDITIONAL INFORMATION

inland on the A260 to Hawkinge. The Kent Battle of Britain Museum lies to the west of the village.

5 Take unclassified roads eastwards from Hawkinge, eventually heading south on to the A256 for Dover. Dover, famous for its white cliffs and magnificent castle, was the chief Cinque Port. The Painted House, discovered in 1970, dates from about AD 200. More recent is the Old Town Gaol, which shows the dismal conditions of Victorian prison life, and the White Cliffe Experience, a lively museum about Dover's history. Take the A258, then an unclassified road to St Margaret's at Cliffe. Massive chalk cliffs dominate the scene, and sheltered beneath them is the Pines Garden, created in the 1970s with trees, shrubs and a lake. Rejoin the A258, then take the B2057 from Ringwould to Walmer. The fine coastal fortress here, built by Henry VIII and shaped like a Tudor rose, is now an elegant stately home with beautiful gardens.

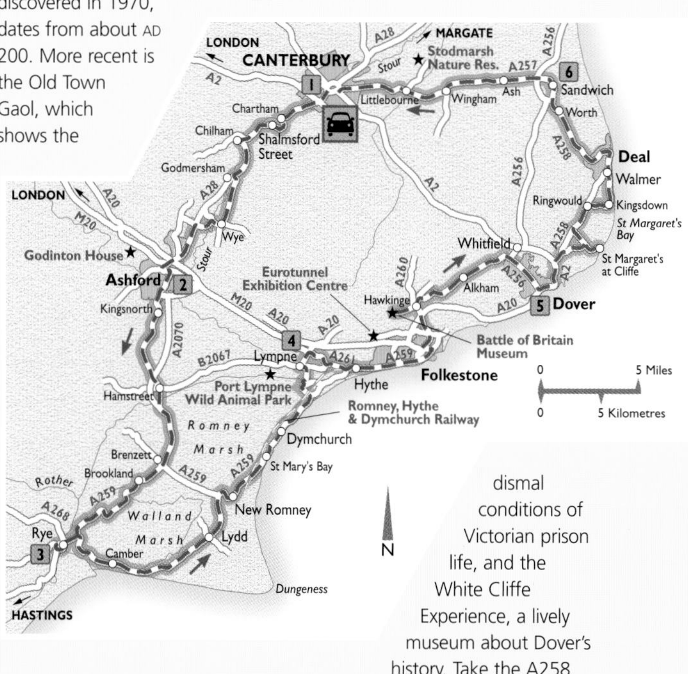

6 Take the A258 to Sandwich. The oldest of the medieval Cinque Ports, Sandwich is separated from the sea by 2 miles (3km) of sand dunes. Follow the A257 for 6 miles (10km) to Wingham. Continue along the A257 for the return to Canterbury (6 miles/10km).

THE CINQUE PORTS

In the Middle Ages five ports took on the main burden of defending the coast and providing able seamen and fighting men. They were **Dover**, **Sandwich**, **Hythe**, **New Romney** and **Hastings**, and in 1278 Edward I drew up a charter naming them the Cinque ('five' in French – but pronounced 'sink') Ports. The king granted them special rights to hold their own courts and collect their own taxes, in return for helping him out in times of need. **Rye** and **Winchelsea** were later added to the confederation. Over time some of the ports lost their importance as their harbours silted up, and as a professional, national navy took over the job of defence, they became obsolete. The confederation was officially ended – and the towns' privileges lost – in 1685.

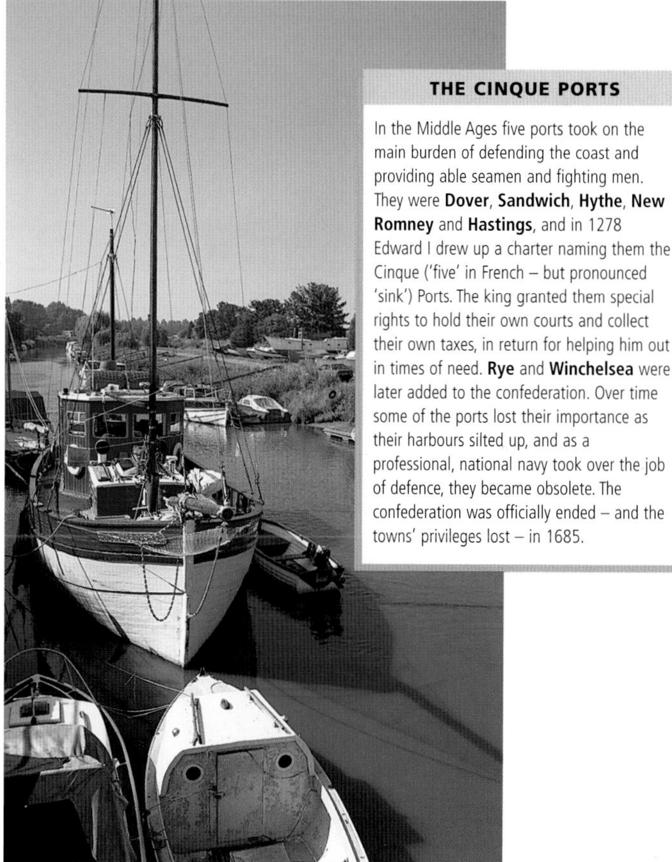

Sandwich, situated on the River Stour, is the oldest Cinque Port

LONDON

London pulsates with life: hectic, buzzing and vibrant, there won't be a dull moment. Visit the great historic sights, take in the museums and 'shop 'til you drop' in the department stores and exciting street markets. Even here you can find green spaces and great outdoor activities, and escape the crowds to see the city from the air, the river or the top of a bus – or you can simply explore on foot. From the elegant shops and Royal Parks of the west, to the modern development of the Millennium Dome at Greenwich and Docklands in the east, you will discover new delights at every turn.

BUCKINGHAM PALACE

This vast, sprawling, 600-room house, world famous as the London home of the royal family, was built mostly between 1820 and 1837, although the familiar East Front public face of the palace was not added until 1913. Visit the Queen's Gallery and the Royal Mews, and check for the limited summer opening to view the grand State Rooms. Don't miss the Changing of the Guard, still the most popular reason for visiting the palace.

The River Thames
The story of London is the story of the Thames – all the city's early buildings centred on the river. From Hampton Court, Henry VIII's palace to the southwest, to the hi-tech Thames Barrier at Woolwich in the east, London's most under-utilised highway twists and turns for 30 miles (48km) past parks and houses, offices and pubs, and beneath a dozen or more bridges. It's a great way to see the city.

COVENT GARDEN PIAZZA

London's first fashionable square was built by Inigo Jones in 1630, but lost its grandeur to become London's principal flower, fruit and vegetable market from 1670 until 1974. The site was then developed as a pedestrian area and has become one of the most lively areas of London with plenty of street entertainment thrown in! It is thronged with shoppers and sightseers by day, and theatre-goers and revellers by night.

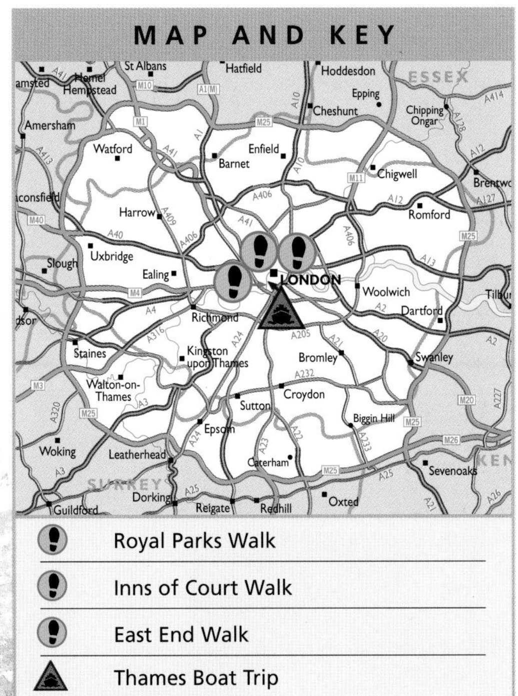

Trafalgar Square
This is the geographical and symbolic centre of London; all road distances in Britain are measured from here and at its centre is Nelson's Column, one of the city's most enduring symbols. Here you will find the grandiose National Gallery, home to one of the finest and most comprehensive collections of Western art in the world.

St Paul's Cathedral
Sir Christopher Wren's masterpiece, completed in 1720 after 35 years, is where most great ceremonies of state take place. Its most notable feature is the Whispering Gallery, a perfect circle around the base of the dome, where a whisper can be heard as it travels round the circumference.

Tower of London
London's foremost historic site, the Tower has served as castle, palace, prison, jewel house and site of execution during its 900 years. Started in 1078 by William the Conqueror, it was completed by the early 14th century during the reign of Edward I. There is much to see, but arrive early to see the Crown Jewels before the queues grow.

HYDE PARK & THE WEST

Hyde Park, once a royal hunting ground of Henry VIII, was first opened to the public in the early 17th century during the reign of James I and subsequently became a fashionable place for walking and horse-riding. The park and adjoining Kensington Gardens cover around 615 acres (248ha) of trees, flowers and greenery creating the largest of central London's open spaces. Kensington Gardens provide a relatively quiet area, surprisingly rich in wildlife. Herons and grebes can be seen on the willow-fringed Long Water to the north of the lovely Serpentine bridge, built in 1826. Close by is the Serpentine Gallery, which hosts exhibitions of 20th-century art in the summer months, and to the southwest is the Albert Memorial.

West from here is the Round Pond, where children and adults come to sail model boats. In the gardens you can visit Kensington Palace, the birthplace of Queen Victoria and well known as the home of the late Diana, Princess of Wales. Hyde Park is more a place of recreation and entertainment, with boats to rent on the Serpentine in summer; bandstand music at lunchtime in June, July and August; and occasionally fairs, concerts and firework parties. Battersea Park and Holland Park in west London are worth a visit and are good places to escape the crowds.

The western region of London has some of the

Speakers' Corner in Hyde Park

NOTTING HILL CARNIVAL

London meets Rio at the Notting Hill Carnival, which was founded in 1966 as a local neighbourhood festival, but has since grown to be the biggest Caribbean-style carnival in Britain. It is held over the August Bank Holiday weekend rather than the traditional carnival date of Mardi Gras (Shrove Tuesday), in deference to the English weather. Drawing half a million people, it consists of processions of colourful floats, street stalls, steel-band music and non-stop dancing, and there are prizes for the best costumes and music.

Chelsea Pensioners, retired soldiers who live at the Royal Hospital

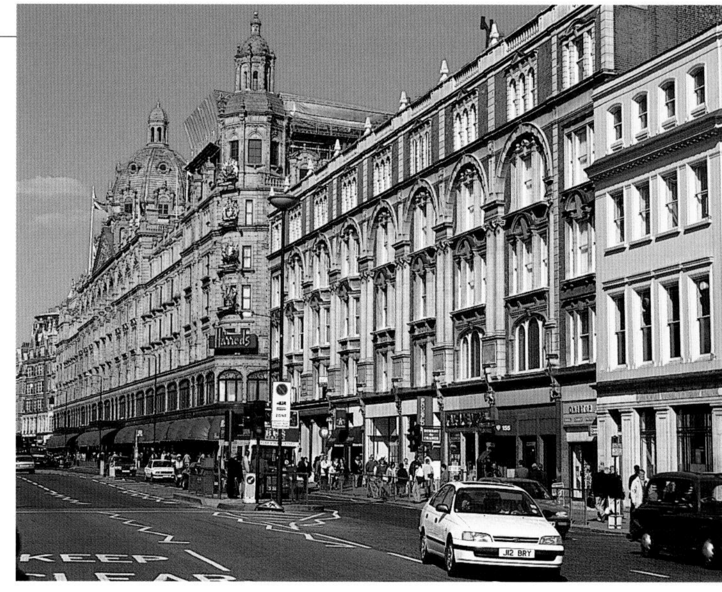

A view down to Harrods' elegant and distinctive store in Knightsbridge

Royal Parks Walk

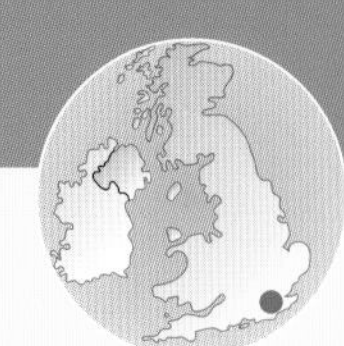

WALK

The Royal Parks

START: Houses of Parliament
FINISH: Regent's Park
DISTANCE: 4.5 miles (7km)

The Royal Parks are wonderful oases of green escape in the very heart of London; this walk links four of them.

1 Begin from Westminster, opposite the Houses of Parliament. Cross Parliament Square and go into Great George Street. Take the first right, and turn into St James's Park. St James's is the oldest and most attractive of the central London parks, established by Henry VIII in the 1530s.

2 Keep to the left of the lake until you can cross it by a bridge. The views from the bridge are equally stunning in both directions; face the impressive buildings of Whitehall, and behind you lies Buckingham Palace.

3 Over the bridge, turn left, and soon go up to join The Mall. Cross this and walk towards Buckingham Palace. Keep right, along the edge of Green Park, and up Constitution Hill. Tackle the Green Park and Hyde Park Corner subways, as if going to Hyde Park Station, but continuing

City-dwellers enjoy a stroll along the Serpentine in Hyde Park

RIVER AND ROAD

Riding on the top deck of a London bus is a great way to see the capital. The Big Bus Company's hop-on, hop-off **Blue Route** covers the **Hyde Park** area and stops include Harrods, the South Kensington museums (the Victoria and Albert, the Science Museum and the Natural History Museum) and Kensington Gardens.

Various services operate on the river and you can take a boat from **Westminster Pier** down past Chelsea, Battersea, Putney, Chiswick and on to Kew.

The **Thames Path** follows the well-marked foot path on either side of the river. Make use of the bridges and riverside inns to invent circular routes of various length. The path is well maintained and there is no need for walking boots, just comfortable shoes.

smartest shopping and the most expensive residential areas in the capital. Wander around the exclusive streets of Chelsea and Knightsbridge, whose elegant houses and gardens convey an image of class and gentility. Chelsea has two faces; on the one hand are the graceful tree-lined streets, the Royal Hospital, the home of the annual flower show and Chelsea Physic Garden, while on the other is the King's Road, which has long stood for youthful rebellion. Its boutiques were the first to sell mini-skirts in the 1960s and punk was born here a decade or so later.

KNIGHTSBRIDGE – ABSOLUTELY FABULOUS

Harrods – Britain's largest department store is much more than just a shop, it is an internationally famous institution. Don't miss the stylish Food Halls (right).

Harvey Nichols – famous for its designer clothes and accessories and the food hall on the top floor.

The Scotch House – founded in 1830 and still stocking traditional tweeds and tartans.

Jasper Conran, **Issey Miyake**, **Emporio Armani** – designer shops in the Brompton Road, to name but a few.

The Brompton Road in Knightsbridge has a clutch of chic shops and restaurants and is where some of the world's best-known designers have their boutiques. Further west along the Cromwell Road is another tourist magnet: the Victoria and Albert Museum, the Science Museum and the Natural History Museum. Continuing west is another popular shopping area, Kensington High Street, with its fashionable indoor clothing markets and Barkers, the former department store, with its striking art-deco façade.

When London becomes too hectic, seek out fresh air and space by visiting riverside places such as Barnes and Chiswick. Travelling by boat can give some of the best views. As you sail past the Hammersmith and Chiswick riverside malls, with their pubs and boathouses, and on further west between tree-lined banks through a series of riverside villages, you will soon feel far from the noise and fast pace of the city.

PARK PURSUIT

Hyde Park – try rowing on the Serpentine or play tennis near Lancaster Gate tube station. If a view from horseback appeals, head for Hyde Park Stables. All rides are supervised in either the indoor arena or around the 5-mile (8-km) circumference of the park itself. The park is also a mecca for rollerblading fans. You can also use the cycle track or just enjoy a leisurely stroll along the tree-lined avenues.

Battersea Park – the 200-acre (81-ha) park includes tennis courts, a running track and an old English garden.

Holland Park – this park has peacocks, an adventure playground, a summer theatre and the Kyoto Garden (below) created for the Japan Festival in 1991.

SEE CONTACTS SECTION FOR ADDITIONAL INFORMATION

instead up to the park. Hyde Park originally belonged to the Church, until Henry VIII seized it to use as hunting grounds.

4 By keeping to the eastern side of the park you eventually find your way to Marble Arch. Go through the subway complex here, to exit 14. Go forward into Oxford Street until you can turn left into Portman Street. Turn right into Portman Square and, when you reach Wigmore Street, go left along another side of Portman Square, and forward into Baker Street. At the far end of Baker Street, continue the short distance to reach Regent's Park, the last of the Royal Parks.

5 You can return from Baker Street Station.

CENTRAL LONDON & THE CITY

London is considered one of the ten greatest cities in the world, and landmarks such as Big Ben, Tower Bridge and Buckingham Palace are familiar to millions. It is a city rich in history that everyone should see at least once in a lifetime. The 'City of London', a commercial centre since Roman times, and today recognised as a centre of theatre, classical music, pop music and television, is also one of the world's three major financial powerhouses.

Certainly the famous sites should be visited and the fashionable shopping districts viewed. Covent Garden with its street theatre and Neale Street with its trendy shops should be explored, but also try to experience a flavour of local London and visit the more off-the-beaten-track areas. Discover a greener, more active London and see where you can escape the crowds and the queues. View the city by foot, on the top of a red London bus or an open-top bus, explore the river by boat or walk along the towpath.

Leave behind the West End and shop in Hampstead instead, and have a meal or drink overlooking Hampstead Heath, which has one of the best views over London. Visit and enjoy the leafy areas of London at Regent's Park, Parliament Hill Fields and

REGENT'S PARK

Though it is world-famous for **London Zoo**, there are several cheaper activities to be found in the park.

Regent's Park Golf and Tennis School – floodlit driving range and three tennis courts, which can be booked in advance. Professional tuition available. Open daily from 8am to 9pm. Non-members are welcome.

Boating Lake – forget the pressures of the city and take out a rowing boat to enjoy the splendid scenery and birdlife. Pedaloes for smaller children are also available.

Regent's Canal (above) – take a narrow boat trip from Camden Lock to London Zoo and Little Venice, or walk along the towpath.

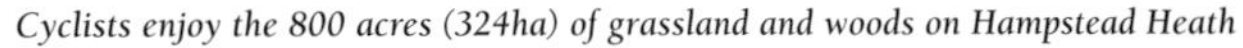

Cyclists enjoy the 800 acres (324ha) of grassland and woods on Hampstead Heath

VIEWS OVER LONDON

British Airways London Eye (left) – the world's largest observation wheel towers 444ft (135m) above the banks of the Thames allowing a bird's-eye view over London. On a clear day you can see all of London's towers and spires and beyond the city 25 miles (40km) in each direction, from Windsor in the west to Dartford in the east.

Tethered balloons – one in Vauxhall and one near Tower Bridge. Rising to a maximum of 500ft (152m) above the ground, the 15-minute trips offer some terrific views. Subject to weather conditions.

Inns of Court Walk

WALK

Around the Inns of Court

START: Temple Underground Station (closed Sun)
FINISH: Chancery Lane Underground Station (closed Sun)
DISTANCE: 2.5 miles (4km)

Gray's Inn, with gardens stretching from High Holborn to Theobald's Road

This walk should be done on a weekday as the nearest underground stations are closed on Sundays and several areas within the Inns are closed at the weekend.

1 Turn left out of Temple Underground Station, go up the steps and turn right into Temple Place, which leads (via a car-park entrance) to Inner Temple. Turn left up the steps to Fountain Court. The splendid Elizabethan hall and the adjacent gardens are occasionally open.

2 Continue straight on beneath the archway following the sign to Lamb's Buildings into Middle Temple. Go up the steps to the left of the building ahead to find Temple Church, famous for its effigies of 13th-century Crusader knights. Leave Temple by the alleyway adjacent to Dr Johnson's Buildings. At the end is the doorway to Prince Henry's Room, a rare Elizabethan survivor with a fine 17th-century interior.

3 Cross Fleet Street, turn left and then right alongside the monumental Royal Courts of Justice into Bell Yard. At the end of Bell Yard turn left and, by Legastat printers, turn right into New Square, the

A view of London's skyline from St Paul's Cathedral, looking east towards Canary Wharf

Highgate. London's famous attractions are popular, so visit early in the day or in the late afternoon. In between, discover a greener city. There are secret gardens to be found in the City, such as the one behind St Stephen Walbrook, the Lord Mayor of London's parish church in Walbrook, which is open weekday lunchtimes. If you stay over a weekend walk through the often-deserted City and drop into the Conservatory at the Barbican, with its 197-ft (60-m) high tropical paradise. There are places in central London and the City where you can swim, join a gym class and ice skate, some only a stone's throw from Covent Garden and Oxford Street.

Visit the regenerated parts of Camden, Islington and King's Cross. New walks and special trails have been, and are still being, devised to introduce visitors to fascinating streets and architecture, canals, markets, and quirky and unusual shops in a district hitherto seen as uninteresting and a virtual no-go area.

There is so much to see and do in central London, it is often hard to know where to start and you certainly won't do it all in one trip. Once you have experienced all the big attractions, you have the opportunity to explore and discover the delights of the 'other' London.

KEEP FIT

The Oasis – located in Endell Street, it offers a wide range of health and fitness facilities. There are heated indoor and outdoor pools, a fully equipped gym and a choice of 70 exercise classes including yoga and ju-jitsu. Open to all.

The Jubilee Hall Club – in Covent Garden. The club has a wide range of classes run by experienced instructors, including kick-boxing, karate and yoga.

The Broadgate Centre – a great venue for skating in the outdoors from October to March.

Parliament Hill Fields – offers a full-sized athletics track and an open-air lido in summer. You can take inspiration from the Highgate Harriers who train here. Great for flying kites, too.

SHOP 'TIL YOU DROP

Jermyn Street – one of London's finest collection of small specialist shops.

Burlington Arcade – specialist up-market shops in a historic setting.

Neale Street – close to Covent Garden, it's the place for the latest in style.

South Molton Street and St Christopher's Place – for smart fashion and accessories.

Chancery Lane – the London Silver Vaults house over 30 shops in an underground arcade selling old and modern silver.

Charing Cross Road – for antiquarian and second-hand books.

Camden Market (below) – trading along Camden High Street and Chalk Farm Road, where shops lining the street spill on to the pavement offering street cred to trendsetters, leading where fashion follows.

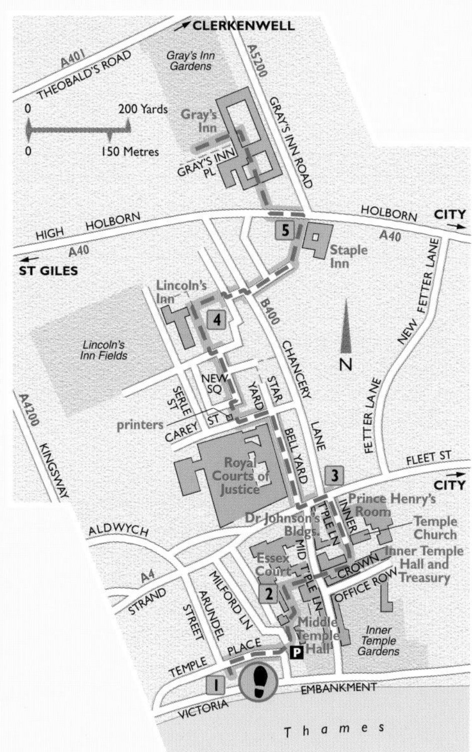

heart of Lincoln's Inn. Lincoln's Inn's splendid hall (to the left) isn't open but you can visit the chapel (to the right), built in 1620.

4 Continue through the Inn and exit right at the corner of Stone Buildings. Cross Chancery Lane, turn right, then go left into Southampton Buildings, which leads to Staple Inn. This is a former Inn of Chancery (a prep school for the Inns of Court); note its Elizabethan façade on High Holborn.

5 Cross High Holborn, turn left, then, by the Cittie of York pub, go right into Gray's Inn. Duck beneath the arch to the left of the hall (closed) to Gray's Inn Gardens. Return to High Holborn for Chancery Lane Underground Station.

GREENWICH & THE EAST

The fastest-changing area of London is east of the City along the Thames from Tower Bridge down into the Isle of Dogs, where the river forms a huge loop, and continuing downstream past Greenwich and the site of the Millennium Dome and on to Woolwich. New offices, shops and restaurants, houses and flats have been built, and old wharves and warehouses have been renovated and converted. The Docklands Light Railway (DLR) connects with the underground network making the area very accessible for commuters and visitors alike. There are even city farms, a dry-ski slope and a host of sporting activities in which to participate.

Along the river are many well-known sights and a river trip provides the best view. Sailing up from Westminster to Greenwich you pass the Tower of London, then continue east by Canary Wharf, London's newest business district, worth visiting for its 90 or so shops, cafés, riverside bars and restaurants. From the 17th century these docks were the base of London's world-wide trading network. By 1964, changes in technology – in particular containerisation – signalled the demise of this area and the quays remained derelict until the 1980s, when the government began the world's largest urban redevelopment project to date. Use the DLR to buzz around this region and you will get some fine views too.

Travel on the DLR for scenic views of Canary Wharf and the Millennium Dome

To reach Greenwich you can take the train from London Bridge, but it is much better to use the DLR or go by boat. You can even walk along the towpath or on the Lee Valley Pathway which extends from Hackney through the East End and down to

MARKETS

Greenwich – among London's best set markets, and all within walking distance of each other, are Greenwich Arts & Crafts Market in a central square, the Flea Market on Thames Street, the Antiques Market on High Road and the Central Market on Stockwell Street.

Brick Lane (left) – a bargain hunter's paradise in the East End. From new and second-hand merchandise, bicycles and furniture to leather goods and fruit and veg. Surrounding streets are lined with aromatic Asian shops and restaurants.

Petticoat Lane – London's most famous and largest market. Listen out for Cockney rhyming slang.

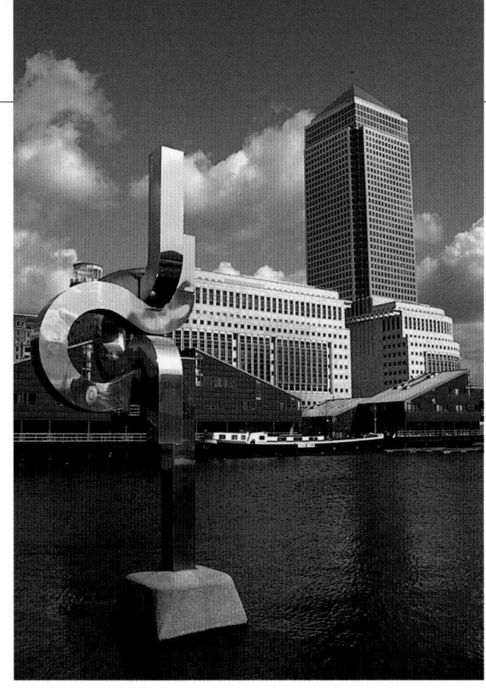

Canary Wharf at West India Docks, not just a business centre but a place to eat and shop

East End Walk

WALK

In London's East End

START/FINISH: Tower Thistle Hotel, Tower Bridge

DISTANCE: 6.5 miles (10.5km)

PARKING: NCP St Katharine's Way car-park, next to Tower Thistle Hotel, by Tower Bridge

Discover the intriguing landmarks of a thousand years of popular history in the streets between Docklands and the City. From the Tower of London and Tower Bridge, to historic riverside pubs, scenes of notorious murders, and modern, glass office towers, this lesser-known part of London has plenty to offer the explorer on foot.

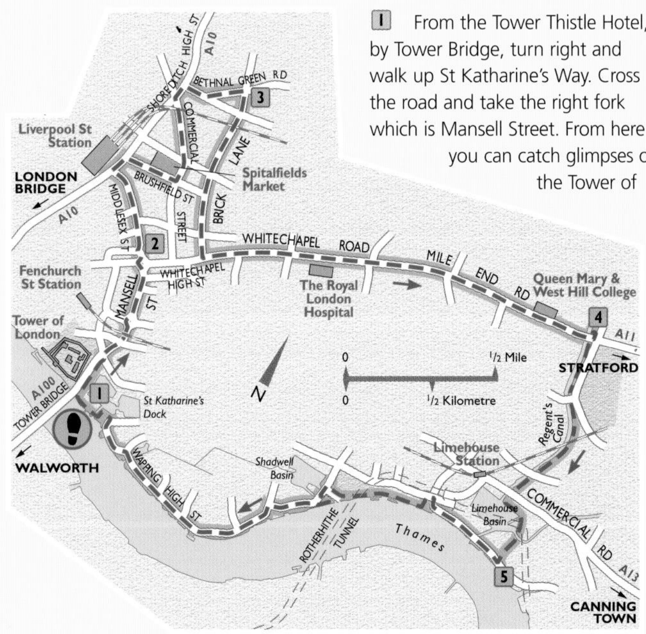

1 From the Tower Thistle Hotel, by Tower Bridge, turn right and walk up St Katharine's Way. Cross the road and take the right fork which is Mansell Street. From here you can catch glimpses of the Tower of

Greenwich. Greenwich still merits its Saxon name 'green village', thanks to the vast areas of lawns and huge Greenwich Park. Since Tudor days, Greenwich has been synonymous with ships. Visit the *Cutty Sark*, in its time the fastest of all the clipper ships bringing tea from China. Other highlights include the National Maritime Museum, the Royal Naval College, Queen's House (1616) and the Old Royal Observatory, now a museum. Although often crowded in summer, Greenwich has lots of small shops, excellent markets and plenty of open space to escape to.

DOCKLANDS WATERSPORTS

Docklands Watersports Club – located on board the *Tereza Joanne*, a vessel complete with bar and food. Jet-ski hire available together with tuition.

Docklands Sailing & Watersports Centre – offers dinghy sailing, canoeing, dragon-boat racing and rowing. Open to the general public, but ring first.

Peter Chilvers Windsurfing Centre – specialises in teaching complete beginners, but is also suitable for experts.

Surrey Docks Watersports Centre – offers a range of sailing, windsurfing, canoeing and powerboat courses.

Royal Victoria Dock Watersports Centre – sailing, canoeing and bell boating (two huge canoes strapped together and paddled by a team).

Shadwell Basin Outdoor Activity Centre – provides sailing, canoeing, diving, angling, dragon-boat racing and, for those who want to keep out of the water, wall climbing.

When considering trips out to Greenwich and the east, don't forget to have a closer look at London's East End, best seen by foot. Wrapped around the City to the north and east are scores of small communities such as Spitalfields, Whitechapel and Bethnal Green.

London, London's most enduring symbol of this great city, nestling by the River Thames and dwarfed by Tower Bridge, as you make your way to Aldgate. Go under the subway and take exit 14 which is marked Middlesex Street (Petticoat Lane). Today, all that remains of Aldgate is the name, but it is the site of one of six original gates into the Roman city of *Londinium*.

2 Walk up Petticoat Lane, famous for its Sunday street market selling clothes and all sorts of domestic goods, to Bishopsgate. Turn right, then take the second turning on the right, Brushfield Street. Walking down Brushfield Street you have a superb view of the serene white stonework of Christ Church (1723), acknowledged as the masterpiece of Nicholas Hawksmoor, a pupil of Sir Christopher Wren. Pass old Spitalfields Market and at the end turn left and along Commercial Street. At the crossroads turn right along Shoreditch High Street, then right down Bethnal Green Road.

3 Turn right down Brick Lane. The brick- and tile-making industry flourished here in the 16th century and grimmer history is recalled in Hanbury Street, the scene of one of the notorious Whitechapel Murders committed by 'Jack the Ripper' in 1888. He was never caught and his identity is still unknown. At the end turn left and go along Whitechapel High Street, which eventually becomes Mile End Road. Keep walking ahead until you reach the bridge over the Regent's Canal. Go over the bridge and immediately turn left. Take the steps down to the canal and at the bottom walk down to the left. The Regent's Canal was completed in 1820 to link the Grand Union Canal at Paddington with the Thames. It was laid out by Nash who was one of the investors in it.

4 Walk down to Limehouse Basin, designed by Thomas Telford, under the Docklands Light Railway (opened in 1987 and operates between the City and Docklands) then turn left. Go over a bridge and through a play area.

5 Turn right at the converted wharves and follow the signs for the Thames Path and Riverside Pubs, taking the riverside links off left wherever possible. Not all are continuous and you'll need to return to the road on occasions. You'll pass some of London's finest historic pubs. Most notable is the Prospect of Whitby, frequented at various times by Pepys, Dickens, Judge Jeffreys and J M W Turner. When you reach St Katharine's Dock, follow the signs through the dock and come out on the other side at Tower Bridge.

OUT AND ABOUT

Mudchute Park and Farm – the largest city farm in the country with a riding school and farm animals.

Docklands Equestrian Centre – provides riding and tuition.

Mile End Climbing Wall – in Mile End Park, with several climbing rooms, each offering a different terrain and catering for all levels of climber. Beginners' classes on Tuesdays, Saturdays and Sundays.

Lee Valley Cycle Circuit – the only comprehensive bicycle track in the country, offering everything from a mountain bike course to a BMX track. The 1-mile (1.6-km) cycle circuit and 2-mile (3-km) road are set in 45 acres (18ha) of land.

Beckton Alps Ski Slope – offers skiing on the 656-ft (200-m) artificial slope.

City Cruises – leisurely hop-on hop-off ferry trips around the old Pool of London wharves.

Each began as a small village with a parish church, a manor house and cottages surrounding a green. Rapid population growth in the 19th century turned them into one vast metropolitan sprawl. Even so, they each have a strong identity and are worth exploring for a different view of London. Some have become run down over the years but there is a huge effort to clean up and attract visitors, with interesting guided walks and museums, such as the Geffrye Museum, the Ragged School Museum and Bethnal Green Museum of Childhood.

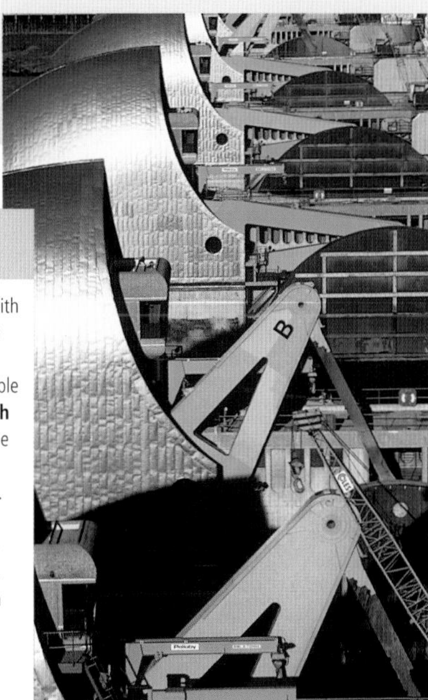

THAMES BARRIER VISITOR CENTRE

Flooding has always threatened London, with the danger coming from rising water levels and surge tides funnelling water up the Thames. In 1984, the world's largest movable flood barrier was inaugurated at **Woolwich Reach**. Seven stainless-steel shells span the 1,705-ft (520-m) width of river; between these are four main gates five storeys high. Each weigh 3,700 tonnes and take 30 minutes to raise; the visitor centre explains all. The best time to visit is when the gates are being raised – ring in advance. You can picnic on the riverside embankment and stroll along the bank, and there is also a children's play area.

GREATER LONDON

Visitors to London may not automatically think of visiting the outer boroughs or suburbs, the area lying between central London and the M25 orbital motorway. Visions of continuous streets of residential houses and unsightly industrial areas, with little open space and limited activities spring to mind. There are, however, not only many pleasant green areas but plenty of attractions to see and sports to participate in, with fewer crowds and queues than in the centre of the capital.

The exotic pagoda in the grounds of Kew's Royal Botanic Gardens

For those keen on the river, cruise a little further upstream and make a trip out to Kew, with its famous gardens, to Richmond and on to the magnificent Hampton Court. The main palace dates from the early 16th century and is well worth a visit – don't forget to navigate the maze, first planted in 1690, with 2,460ft (750m) of paths enclosed by a 6-ft (1.8-m) high yew and privet hedge. The area from Kew in the east to Hampton Court in the west has undoubtedly some of the finest open spaces with parks and fascinating historical houses to view – Gunnersbury Park, Osterley Park, the Old Deer Park and Richmond Park, and Bushy and Hampton Court Park. You will find plenty of history and recreation, with excellent walking – guided walks of Richmond, Twickenham and Kew are available – cycling, swimming, tennis, golf and much

Escape to Epping Forest for a peaceful stroll, starting your walk from the Forest Centre

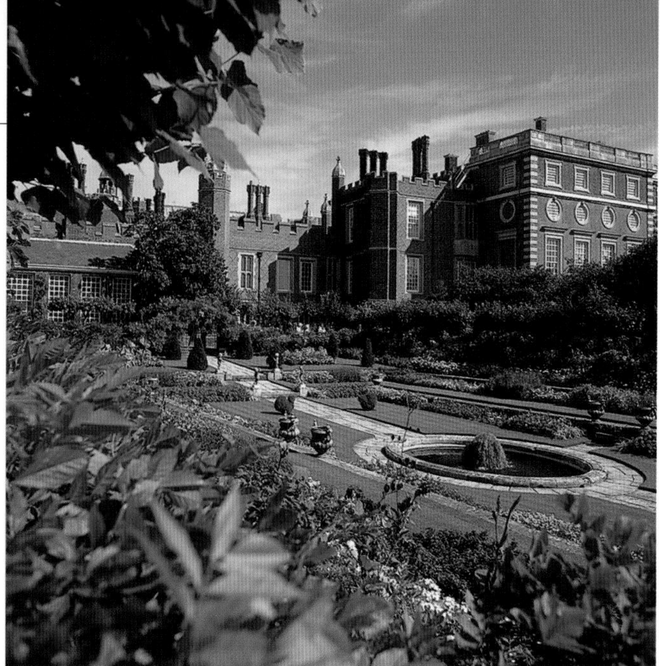

The delightful Tudor garden at Hampton Court, the country palace built for Henry VIII

Thames Boat Trip

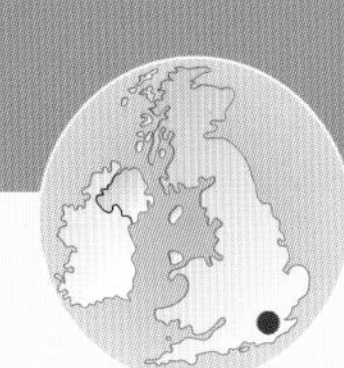

BOAT TRIP

Westminster to Hampton Court

START: Westminster Pier, Westminster Bridge (Tel: 020 7930 2062 for times and booking)

FINISH: either complete the round trip or there are stations at Hampton Court, Richmond and Kew Bridge with regular trains back to London Waterloo

DISTANCE: approx. 22 miles (35km) each way

PARKING: NCP Abingdon Street car-park. Alternatively, park at Hampton Court, take the train to Waterloo and cross the river to Westminster

From the heart of London follow the twists and curves of the River Thames, once a major highway to and from London, past ancient villages and grand houses to one of Britain's loveliest palaces. The Thames Link towpath allows you to follow the same route on foot or bicycle, with easy access on and off to a number of tube and trains stations, and some celebrated pubs for refreshment *en route*.

1 At the start is a view of the London Eye, the world's largest ferris wheel, before the boat passes under Westminster Bridge with Big Ben and the Houses of Parliament on the right and Lambeth Palace on the opposite bank. After Lambeth Bridge, the right bank is dominated by the classical Tate Gallery. Through Chelsea Bridge, the right bank is occupied with the elegant Chelsea Royal Hospital and Garden.

2 A number of famous people have lived in the elegant houses of Cheyne Walk, on the right. At the end of the Walk is the new development of Chelsea Harbour, with its yacht marina. The river banks now feature a delightful mix of old houses and churches, derelict warehouses and wharves, and a growing number of luxury apartments.

3 After Wandsworth Bridge, the buildings start to retreat and open space begins to appear, including the grounds of Hurlingham Park, home of croquet. Putney Bridge marks the start of the annual Oxford & Cambridge Boat Race, which finishes at Mortlake by Chiswick Bridge.

4 Moored on the river's embankment are huge Thames barges, which once carried goods on this main highway, and are now homes,

THRILLING DAYS OUT

Thorpe Park – located close to the M25 in Surrey. Provides fun for all the family. Big-thrill attractions include the world's first and only pitch-black, backwards ride, called 'No Way Out!' Remember to take your swimwear for a range of water thrills. Railway, craft centre, farm and lots, lots more.

Chessington World of Adventures (left) – offers more thrills for the brave. The scariest is probably 'Samurai', a mind-blowing 360-degree triple rotation ride from an intimidating height of 60ft (18m). Don't forget there is the more peaceful zoo to visit and animal shows to see.

nightclubs and restaurants. At Kew, the south bank is occupied by the grounds of tiny Kew Palace, the country retreat of King George III. On the opposite bank is a junction with the Grand Union Canal and the magnificent Syon House, set in its extensive park. There are no buildings visible along this stretch of the river until the village of old Isleworth. On the south side of the river is the Old Deer Park, part of Richmond Park.

5 Richmond's elegant 18th-century houses climb dramatically up the steep banks. Around the next bend are two of greater London's most stunning stately homes – Marble Hill House and Ham House. Eel Pie Island, one of the largest islands on the river, was a popular destination for both Victorian trippers and 1960s rock fans.

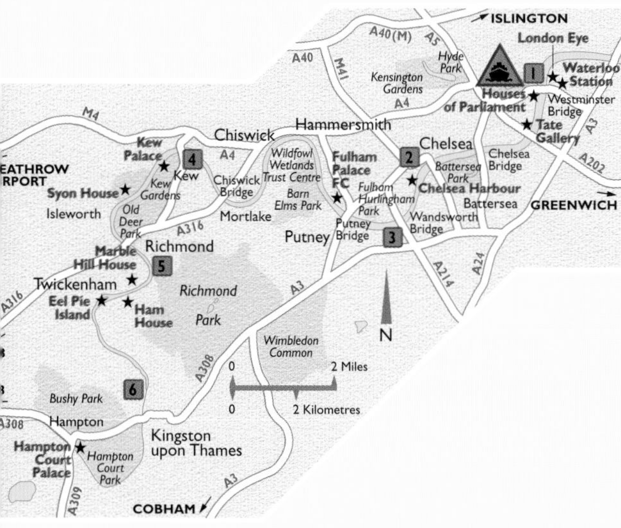

6 At Teddington you pass through the lock and the river life changes, with working boatyards and marinas among the smart houses of Kingston. The boat turns north towards the final stop, Hampton Court Palace – the country home to kings and queens for over 200 years.

more. There are good shopping opportunities at Richmond and Kingston, and the area has great pubs and restaurants, too.

Moving away from the affluent and attractive environs of Richmond, you will find other boroughs may have fewer stately homes and less history, but there are still places worth exploring. To the north, on the Essex/Hertfordshire border, is the great expanse of Epping Forest, a former royal hunting ground. Here, too, is the valley of the River Lee, stretching from the City, through Essex and on to Hertfordshire, offering a wealth of recreational possibilities.

Travelling east and south takes you towards the Kent border. Around the Bexley area you can find good walks and an interesting heritage. There is some excellent walking in these parts, including sections of the London Loop, a 150-mile (240-km) walk around the capital. In total, there are 24 sections covering some superb countryside. Not far away at Chislehurst, join a tour of over 20 miles (32km) of underground caverns and passages, including a Druid altar and prehistoric fossils.

Boroughs such as Ealing, Enfield and Hounslow may not appear appealing at first glance, but they all have their hidden historical secrets and places where the city meets the countryside. Discover the woodlands, meadows and parklands offering escape from the city. Whether north, south, east or west, plan a few trips out of town and explore the less-talked about London.

OUTDOOR PURSUITS

Chingford Golf Course – just two minutes' walk from the station and surrounded by a beautiful forest. A challenging 18-hole course. Players must wear a red outer garment whilst on the course.

High Elms Golf Course – delightfully situated in the parklands of Orpington, offering a relaxed but challenging 18 holes at a reasonable price.

Original Bike Hire Company – hire a bike and cycle here in Richmond for an hour or a whole weekend.

Ealing Riding Centre – gives horse-riding lessons from beginner to intermediate level, for groups or individuals.

Mount Mascal Stables – has one-to-one or group lessons in 600 acres (242ha) of woodland at Bexley.

SKI, SKATE AND SAIL

Hillingdon Ski Centre – the place to have a go at skiing or polish up your parallel turns and smarten up your slalom technique.

Bromley Ski Centre – you can ski or snowboard. Lessons offered. Open all year.

Silver Blades – in Streatham. Individual or group lessons or just skate for fun. Special course for children aged five and under.

Thames Young Mariners – an outdoor centre based at Ham, with a man-made lake fed twice daily with fresh water from the Thames. One-, two- or five-day introductory courses available in kayaking, canoeing, sailing and windsurfing.

A boat trip up the Thames from Westminster will bring you to the town of Hampton Court

THE CHILTERNS & THE NORTHERN HOME COUNTIES

An Area of Outstanding Natural Beauty, the Chilterns run in an arc from Goring in the Thames Valley to a point near Hitchin in Hertfordshire. The most extensive beechwoods in Britain can be found in the Chilterns. Surrounding these ancient woodlands are the northern Home Counties – Buckinghamshire, Hertfordshire and Bedfordshire and bordering on the Thames Valley areas of Berkshire and Oxfordshire. Much of this region is an easy ride from London and provides excellent walking and cycling country, together with historic towns, new towns such as Milton Keynes, historic houses and outstanding river scenery.

Windsor Castle
Only 25 miles (40km) west of London, this towered and turreted complex is the oldest and largest inhabited castle in the world. From its hilltop position it overlooks the cobbled streets of Windsor, the famous public school of Eton College, the River Thames and the Home Park. Magnificently restored after a disastrous fire in 1993, the castle and the surrounding area make a great day out.

HATFIELD HOUSE

Lying to the east of St Albans is Hatfield House, one of stateliest showplaces in Britain. It was built early in the 17th century for Robert Cecil, principal minister of Elizabeth I and James I. Its fine contents include the National Collection of Model Soldiers, and portraits of Elizabeth who spent much of her childhood under house arrest in the nearby Old Palace, of which only one wing remains.

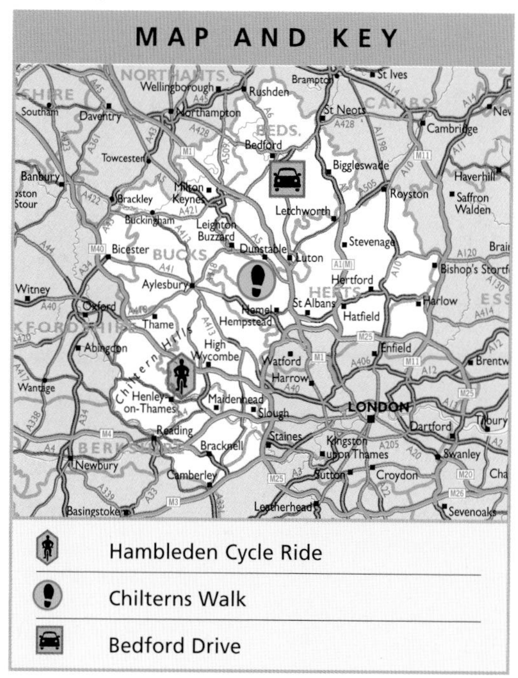

Woburn Abbey

Eighteenth-century Woburn Abbey, the seat of the Dukes of Bedford, is one Britain's most famous stately homes. The palatial house contains superb state apartments and a magnificent art collection, which includes works by Gainsborough, Rembrandt, Reynolds and Van Dyck to name a few. The 3,000-acre (1,214-ha) park was landscaped by Humphrey Repton and is home to nine species of deer, as well as many other rare animals and birds.

Chiltern Open-Air Museum

Five centuries of life in the Chilterns are reflected in this collection of farmhouses and other local buildings. As far as possible, the original building methods and materials are employed in all the reconstructions. There is also an Iron-Age house reconstructed from archaeological evidence, from which a nature trail explores some of the 45 acres (18ha) of local woods and chalk grasslands. Lots of activities and special events make for an entertaining visit.

THE RIVER THAMES & THE SOUTHERN CHILTERNS

This attractive region stretches from Wallingford in Oxfordshire in the west, along the Thames Valley to Windsor, and north to the southern Chiltern Hills in Buckinghamshire. Much of the ridge of the southern Chilterns is covered with beechwoods – dense, green-gladed places, full of paths, mossy banks and running streams. In the springtime it is covered with bluebells and cherry blossom. Worth a visit in this area are the town of Beaconsfield, the caves at West Wycombe and the villages of Great Hampden and Hambleden. The ancient tracks of the Icknield Way and the Ridgeway pass through this landscape and provide excellent walking and cycling.

The River Thames flows past the Berkshire Downs offering distant views of these beech-clad Chilterns. Below Wallingford the countryside is varied with hills and woods extending to the water's edge. The river continues through the gentle gorge of Goring Gap, between the downs and the Chilterns towards

ACTIVITIES

Skiing and snowboarding Wycombe Summit Ski Centre at High Wycombe makes spectacular use of its steep hillside with the longest dry-ski run in Britain at over 985ft (300m). Open throughout the year, it attracts many enthusiastic skiers and snowboarders.

Skating and tobogganing At the John Nike Leisuresport Complex at Bracknell you can chose between an Olympic-size ice rink, artificial ski-slope or toboggan run. Or try tobogganing at Hemel Hempstead Ski Centre.

Ballooning and helicopter rides Try ballooning over the Thames Valley and the Home Counties or take a helicopter ride over London, taking off from Marlow, flying down the Thames and over the city.

HENLEY ROYAL REGATTA

Henley-on-Thames is world-famous for its annual rowing regatta. The first, in 1839, was raced in a single afternoon, but today's regatta is a five-day event. Ending on the first Sunday in July each year, the regatta has become part of the social as well as the sporting calendar. For those few summer days, rows of marquees line the banks, the river is alive with craft of all kinds and spectators throng town and riverside alike. At the centre of it all are the duels between pairs of rowing crafts – single oarsmen, pairs, fours and eights race up from the start at Temple Island towards the finishing line near the town bridge.

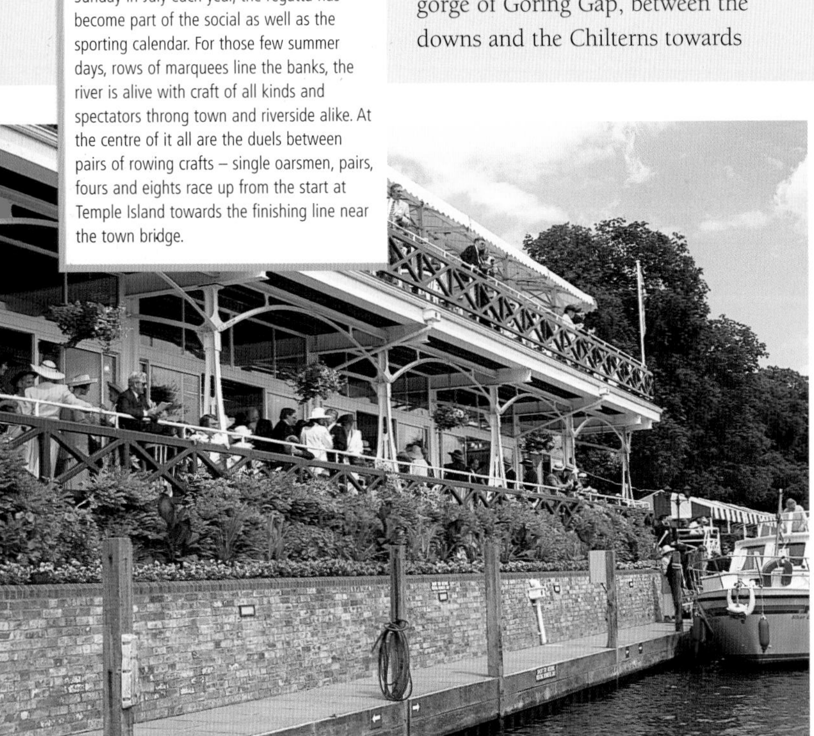

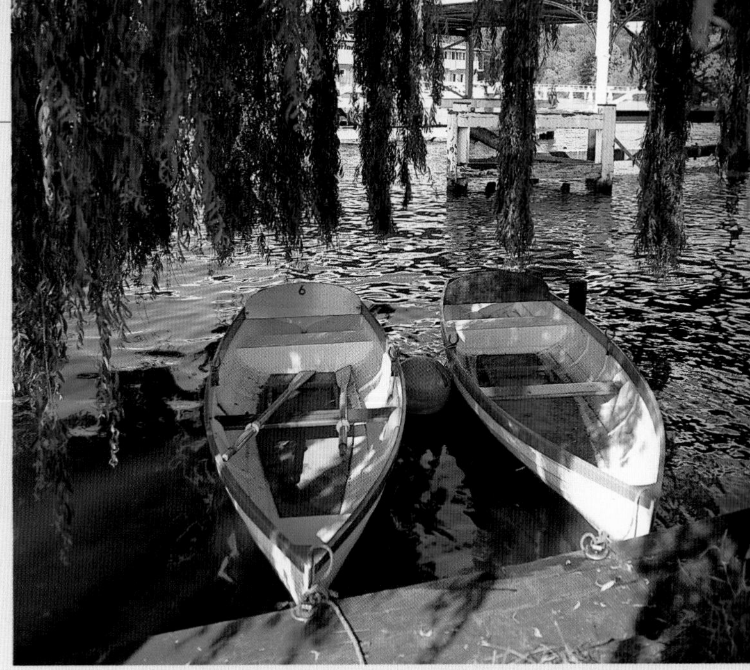

Row boats moored on the Thames at Cookham, an area popular for riverside activities

Hambleden Cycle Ride

CYCLE RIDE

Hambleden & the Southwest Chilterns

START/FINISH: Hambleden. Situated 1 mile (1.5km) north of Mill End which is itself situated midway between Henley and Marlow on the A4155

DISTANCE: 20 miles (32km), with diversion of 3.5 miles (5.5km)

GRADIENT: undulating; one severe climb

ROADS: single-track country lanes; short stretches of B-road

PARKING: village car-park (free) alongside the Stag and Huntsman pub

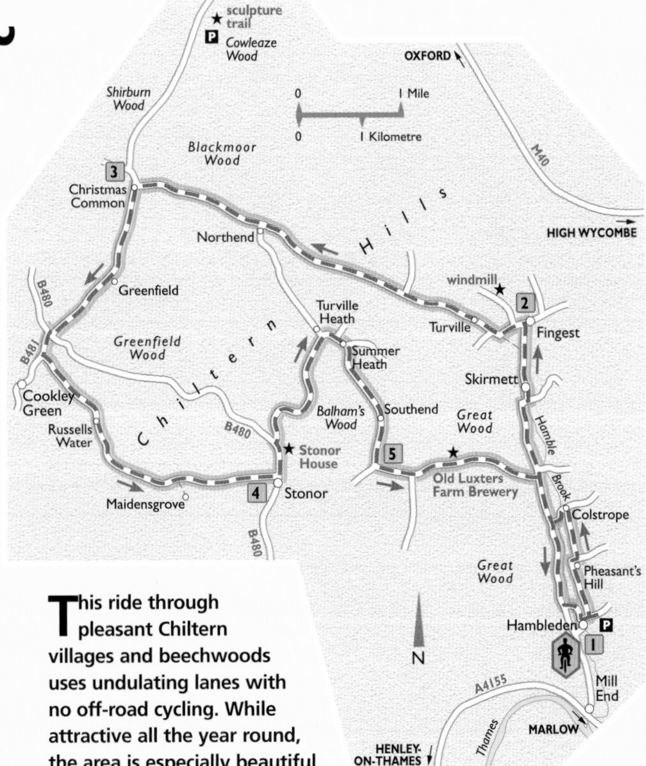

This ride through pleasant Chiltern villages and beechwoods uses undulating lanes with no off-road cycling. While attractive all the year round, the area is especially beautiful

Pangbourne, an attractive town with some fine 17th- and 18th-century buildings where Kenneth Grahame, the author of *The Wind in the Willows* (1908), lived.

From Sonning downstream past Henley, Marlow, Maidenhead and eventually to Windsor and Eton, the ever-widening Thames looks at its finest. Great beechwoods roll down softly contoured hills to the water's edge, and along the river's course are pretty meadows, islands, weirs, locks, historic houses and ancient abbeys. In summer the river is alive with all manner of craft – boats, punts and canoes. Stop at Henley, internationally famous for its Royal Regatta, and enjoy its villagey atmosphere – a pleasant place to shop and have a bite to eat. Following the river you will come to Marlow, where the riverside is dominated by the spire of All Saints Church. The High Street and George Street still have attractive Georgian houses and interesting individual shops, and there are good walks along the river below Marlow Lock and in Quarry Wood.

Flowing on past Bourne End the river reaches Cookham, captured by local artist Stanley Spencer (1891–1959). His works are exhibited in King's Hall, Cookham. Meanwhile the river steers a straight and narrow course to Boulter's Lock and on through Maidenhead. Near Windsor the river is congested with motor cruisers, steamers and punts, but still it retains its stateliness. The ramparts of Windsor Castle dominate the busy town, a popular destination for shoppers and tourists alike. On the north bank of the river stands the historic town of Eton, with its famous school – and still the majestic river continues on its journey, to the City of London and out to the sea.

MESSING ABOUT ON THE RIVER

If you want to get on the river for the day, or just a few hours, you can hire one of the small craft available from a number of operators along the river. Anything from rowing boats to large family cruisers will give you the chance to experience at first hand the delights of boating on the Thames. Alternatively, board a pleasure boat for a trip. Vessels operate regularly from **Henley**, **Marlow**, **Maidenhead** and **Windsor** during the summer months. The wider waters of the middle Thames provide space for sailing as well as rowing and canoeing, and there are lots of opportunities to fish along the Thames, but you will need a licence.

THE THAMES PATH

Following the course of the Thames for 184 miles (296km) from its source in Gloucestershire to the Thames Barrier near Greenwich, the Chiltern Thames section of the Thames Path follows the river through **Hambleden** (right), **Medmendham**, **Marlow**, **Bourne End** and **Taplow**.

Alternatively, try the 7 miles (11km) between **Windsor** and **Maidenhead** or the shorter walks at **Eton**, **Boveney** and **Bray**. Walking is along level, easy-to-follow routes and there is a variety of pubs and restaurants for a break along the way.

in early autumn, when the beech trees are probably at their most colourful.

1 Turn left downhill from the car-park and turn right with the church on your left to follow the lane to the sharp right-hand bend at Pheasant's Hill. Immediately after the bend, turn left along Bottom Hill to the T-junction at Colstrope. Turn left down the hill and follow the lane over the Hamble Brook to the junction with the Hambleden Valley road. Turn right and continue through Skirmett until you reach the outskirts of Fingest, after 2 miles (3km).

2 Turn left, signed to Turville and Ibstone, at the top of the short hill just before Fingest church. The tower of this Norman church is crowned by an unusual saddle-back roof and its walls are almost 4ft (1m) thick. Ignore the right turning to Ibstone, and continue to the fork in the road. Take the right fork to Turville, a quintessential English village with tiled and gabled cottages, a small green, timbered pub, and a restored windmill on a nearby hill. Continue through the village and up the valley, ignoring the right-hand turning. Climb steeply through woodland to reach the T-junction near Northend after 2 miles (3km). Turn right on to a level road and continue for a further mile (1.5km) to Christmas Common. (Optional 3.5 mile/5.5km diversion right to Cowleaze Wood picnic area and the Sculpture Trail, which features 17 exhibits made from both natural and man-made products.)

3 Bear sharply left at the junction, pass The Fox and Hounds, and proceed for 2 miles (3km) to the next crossroads (B480/B481 junction). Turn right and then shortly left to join the B481, signed Nettlebed. In 400yds (365m) turn off left down a single-track road. Continue for 3 miles (5km), passing through Russells Water and by Maidensgrove, descending through beechwoods to the B480 at Stonor.

4 Turn left with care and pass the entrance to Stonor House, a fine old mansion surrounded by a magnificent deer park. Shortly, turn right, signed to Turville Heath, and climb steadily on the narrow road, forking right just before the Turville Heath sign, then right again after 50yds (45m). Turn right at a signpost for Southend and continue through Southend to a T-junction.

5 Turn left, and after 500yds (450m), where the road bears sharply right, go straight ahead on another single-track road. Proceed for 2 miles (3km) passing the Old Luxters Brewery and Chiltern Valley Winery before dropping steeply down (take care) to the T-junction. Turn right and continue for 1.5 miles (2.5km) to the outskirts of Hambleden; then bear left to return to the car-park.

DAYS OUT

Legoland, Windsor (below) – dedicated to children, with plenty of hands-on enjoyment. Its 40 or more rides and attractions are based around five main activity areas and surrounded by gardens and parkland. There's even a Lego Millennium Dome!

Shire Horse Centre, Maidenhead – meet the gentle giants, take a dray ride and watch the working farriers and harness makers.

Odds Farm Park, High Wycombe – created with children in mind, the park provides opportunities to observe animals – including many rare breeds – closely. Play areas and special theme weekends complete the package.

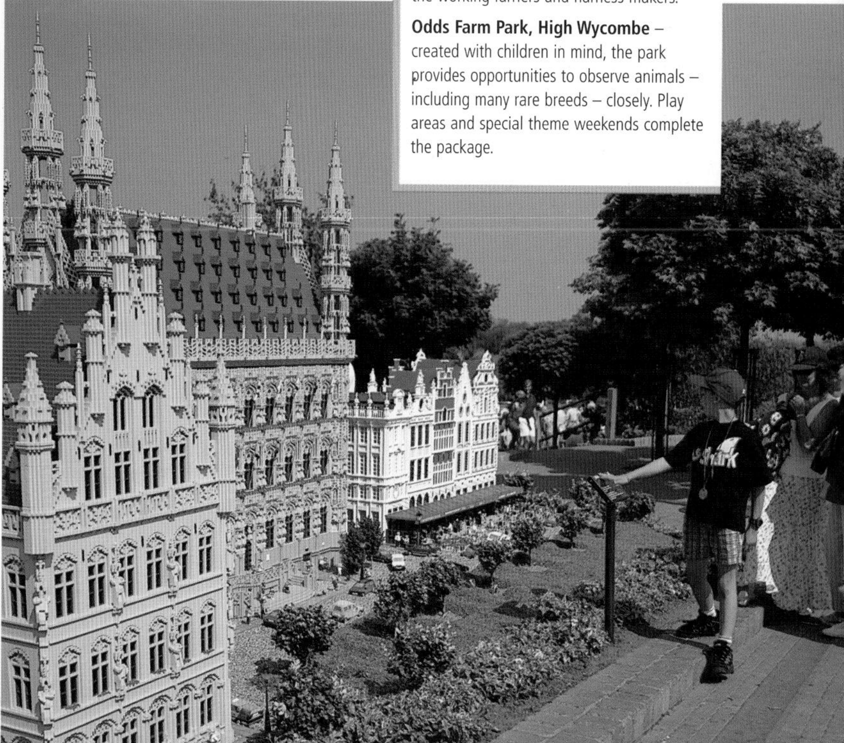

HERTFORDSHIRE & THE NORTHERN CHILTERNS

Main roads – from the Romans' Watling Street to the modern M1 motorway – have always sliced through Hertfordshire. But between Hitchin, close to the northernmost part of the Chiltern Hills, is a belt of unspoilt countryside that is typical rural Hertfordshire. Leafy lanes zigzag through the countryside only a few miles from two traffic-laden motorways; large trees – reminders that Hertfordshire used to be densely wooded – soften the contours of grassy hills and steep little valleys. Thatch, half-timbering, tiles and weather-boarding are the dominant styles in west Hertfordshire, because the county lacks durable stone for building as it consists mainly of undulating chalklands, such as the gentle eastern slopes of the Chilterns.

To the south lies St Albans, an important centre since the Romans chose it as the site of *Verulamium*, one of their finest towns in Britain. You can visit the museum of everyday life in Roman Britain and also the Roman hypocaust, or heating system, in Verulamium Park. Near by at Bluehouse Hill you will find the remains of the only Roman theatre open to visitors in Britain. Visit the town market, held on Wednesdays and Saturdays, as popular now as it was when it was first established in AD 948. There is also an art market held on summer Sundays. From St Albans it is an easy drive to the west of the Chiltern region towards Tring, with its wonderful zoological museum and its reservoirs connecting with the Grand Union Canal – perfect for boating, fishing and walking. Further west, towards Aylesbury, pretty villages are set among woods on the northern edge of the Chiltern escarpment affording spectacular

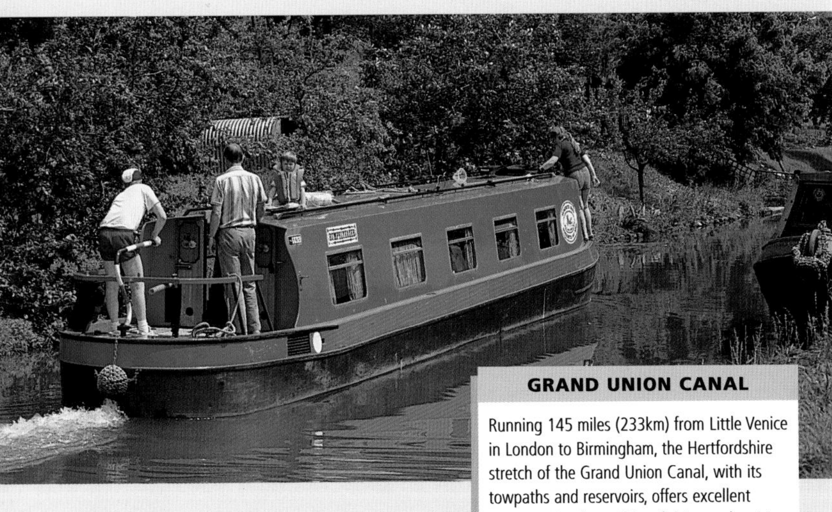

GRAND UNION CANAL

Running 145 miles (233km) from Little Venice in London to Birmingham, the Hertfordshire stretch of the Grand Union Canal, with its towpaths and reservoirs, offers excellent opportunities for walking, fishing and cruising in beautiful scenery with some excellent riverside pubs along the way. There are several canal walks in the county, including the wildlife haven of **Tring Reservoirs**. Cycling is permitted where the towpath offers suitable conditions. Permits are needed for cycling and fishing.

The imposing St Alban's Cathedral, built on the site where St Alban was beheaded

Chilterns Walk

WALK

Historic Routes across the Chilterns

START/FINISH: Aldbury. Located northeast of Tring off the A41
DISTANCE: 7.5 miles (12km)
ASCENT/GRADIENT: 1,100ft (335m); moderate gradient, two steeper sections
TERRAIN/PATHS: farmland, downland and woodland; paths are good; can be muddy
PARKING: by the village pond

Along the Ridgeway to Ivinghoe Beacon, then back through beechwoods, this is a trail steeped in history – for over 2,000 years people have crossed the Chilterns through the Tring Gap.

1 At the village centre, facing the Greyhound Inn, go right, up the road for 300yds (273m), past a sports ground on the left, to the bridleway on the left, by Greenings Farm. Follow this for 500yds (455m), ignoring a path off left, to a footpath on the right. Cross a stile and continue through a golf course to woodland at the top of the course.

2 Go through a fence gap, cross a track and enter woodland. Shortly, turn right to join the Ridgeway National Trail, continuing down to the edge of the wood to the nature reserve interpretative panel. This section of the Ridgeway National Trail follows the Upper Icknield Way. Retrace your steps for 30yds (27m) and follow the Ridgeway National Trail up to the left. Continue through woods to a gate and open grassland above the remains of Pitstone Quarry on the left. From Pitstone Hill the Chiltern escarpment curves to the south and west, carrying the Icknield Way towards its Thames crossing at Goring. Below, the Grand Union Canal and the London-to-Glasgow railway wend their way northwards.

3 Follow the Ridgeway path on to the ridge then go straight ahead across a road, aiming for the right side of Steps Hill ahead. As the bowl of Incombe Hole cuts in from the left, traverse its edge to Steps Hill and follow the track to a gap in the fence in the far corner, ignoring a gate and stile on the right. Follow national trail signs through the woods, then descend to the road.

4 Cross the road and take the left-hand track along the ridge to the National Trust panel on Ivinghoe Beacon. Retrace your steps to the road

IN THE SWIM

The region offers an excellent range of outdoor pools, where you can swim or sunbathe during the summer months.

Hitchin Swimming Centre – in a lovely park setting where facilities include a 25-m indoor pool with separate learner pool, plus a 50-m outdoor pool (summer only) with sunbathing terrace.

Letchworth Open-Air Pool – is possibly the best outdoor pool in the area. It is open throughout the summer and offers a 50-m pool, as well as a paddling pool and sunbathing area.

Hoddesdon Open-Air Pool – the heated pool has grassy banks where you can picnic and sunbathe. A bubble cover means the pool can open early March and remain open until late October.

views, in particular at Coombe Hill near Wendover, the highest point of the Chilterns.

From the earliest times, good roads from the south coast through London have taken travellers hurrying across Hertfordshire on their way to the North. Ermine Street, built by the Romans, ran from Pevensey in East Sussex to York. The Great North Road became the backbone of the country and divided it in half as effectively as a natural barrier. Modern motorways have taken the dismemberment of the county a stage further. Between the main roads to the North, however, are pleasant unspoilt routes running west to east. An exceptional number of Elizabethan and Jacobean houses, such as Hatfield House, were built in this area, which had the advantages of being near London and offering good hunting in the forests, some of which still survive in scattered patches. This region is great for walking, cycling and horse-riding.

The continuing growth of London has encroached on Hertfordshire a great deal. Britain's first garden city, Letchworth, was planned in 1903, with the second, Welwyn Garden City, in 1920. Then came the new towns in the 1940s and 1950s: Stevenage and Hatfield. These, set amid pleasant countryside, offer good shopping and leisure facilities. Despite its proximity to London, however, and a great deal of modern building, the area has managed to retain some of the prettiest landscapes in southern Britain.

Sailing enthusiasts are catered for on the quiet waters at Fairlands Valley Park, Stevenage

and turn left, down hill, following the Icknield Way signs, over a stile then along the edge of a field and hill. Cross a stile and enter woods after 500yds (455m). This route predates the Roman Ermine Street, visible to your left from Aldbury Nowers, which used the Tring Gap to travel through the Chilterns. In the late 18th century, the same road became a turnpike, so the northern cattle drovers who used this route to London went back to the ancient Icknield Way to avoid paying the tolls.

5 After a steep ascent, turn right into a farmyard. Turn right in front of the house and follow the farm road to a minor road and turn right. After 50yds (46m) turn left to follow a path into the woods. The path swings right, then left, crossing an estate boundary path.

6 Cross two stiles out of the woods to emerge in fields. Keep to the right edge until over the brow. Go ahead down to a metalled lane by the entrance to Duncombe Farm. Cross and bear left through two fields to join a track. Follow this into woods.

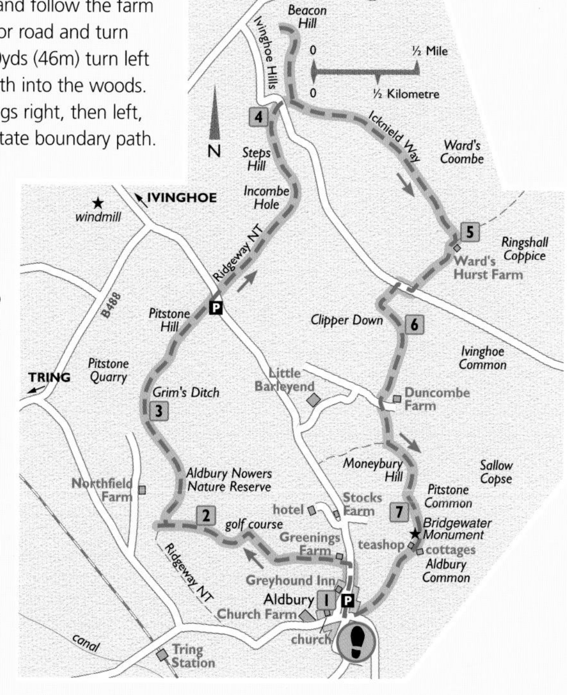

7 As the path levels out, take the right fork above a cottage, then bear left into a clearing by the Bridgewater Monument. Facing the monument turn left and descend a track to the right of cottages. Descend quite steeply down a sunken lane, staying right at any junctions, to emerge in Aldbury. Turn right back to the village centre.

CLIMBING UP THE WALL

Why not try the climbing wall at **Phasels Wood Climbing Complex** at **Kings Langley**? The complex is an exciting, free-standing, outdoor climbing structure, 38-ft (11.5-m) high, and includes almost every climbing feature you could expect to find in a natural mountain environment. It incorporates a steeply overhanging competition-style wall, as well as a chimney, and welcomes both novices and experts.

CYCLEWAYS AND FOOTPATHS

Take to your bike or enjoy the countryside on foot on the following trails, both part of the National Cycle Network.

The Alban Way – this 6.5-mile (10.5-km) former railway line is now used by cyclists and walkers. Linking St Albans and Hatfield, its hedge-lined banks, laden with wild-flowers during late spring and early summer, are perfect for a ride or stroll.

The Nicky Line – an 8.75-mile (5.5-km) route, also a former railway line, which links Harpenden, Redbourn and Hemel Hempstead. It is ideal for walkers and cyclists, with excellent opportunities for spotting wildlife.

BEDFORDSHIRE & MILTON KEYNES

The southernmost tip of Bedfordshire has the county's most varied scenery. The chalk Chilterns stretch northeast from Buckinghamshire, their steep slopes facing northwest and providing an ideal launching ground for gliders at Dunstable Downs. From the downs there are views over nine counties and you can see Five Knolls, the county's best-known ancient burial site where a Bronze-Age skeleton was found. To the north is a low ridge of sandstone rising to its highest point at Woburn, and the landscape is one of low hills covered with pine trees or open heathland.

Most of this area is in the valley of the River Great Ouse, a broad, wandering river that enters the county from Buckinghamshire near Harrold, runs northeast past Odell, loops southwards to Bedford, then meanders past Willington, Roxton and Eaton Socon towards the Cambridgeshire border. Tributaries flow through water meadows to join it, their routes marked by willows and alders and lined by paths popular with anglers. The villages to the north of Bedford are lonely and unspoilt, linked to the outside world by broad lanes. Many of their houses

TRANSPORT THROUGH THE AGES

The Shuttleworth Collection (below right) is part of the Old Warden Park estate. It is a museum of vintage aircraft from Blériot's plane to a Spitfire, together with cars, motorcycles and horsedrawn carriages from around 1880 to 1942. Most are in working order and are flown or driven at air displays from May to October.

Stondon Transport Museum at Henlow is the largest private collection in the country with over 400 exhibits including cars, motorbikes, army vehicles, fire engines, buses, light aircraft and a full-size replica of Captain Cook's ship *Endeavour*.

Leighton Buzzard Railway (below) lets you experience the vanished world of English light railway travel. The 65-minute journey features sharp curves, steep gradients, level crossings and unique roadside running.

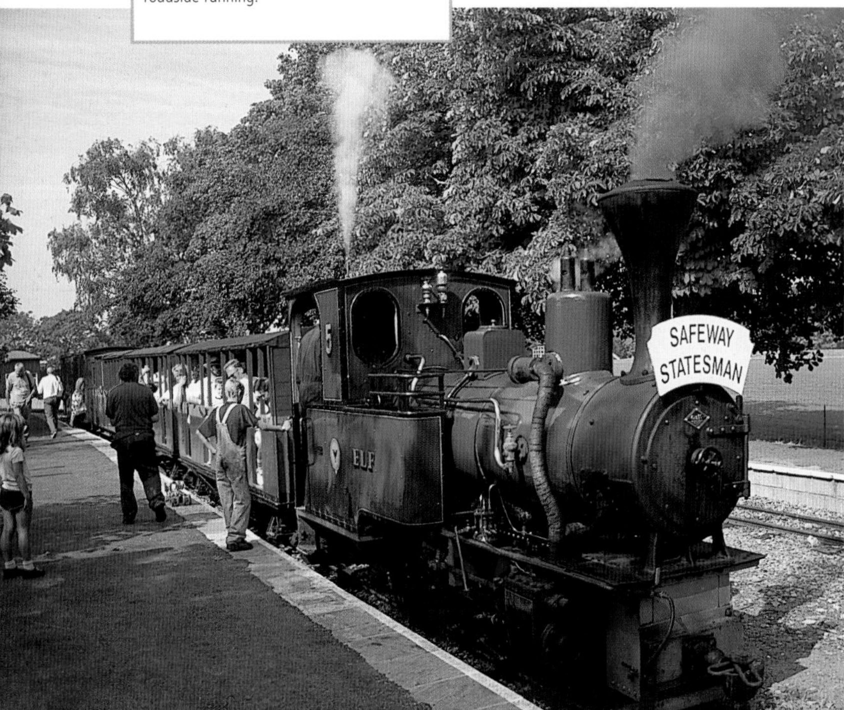

A thatched, timbered cottage in Flitton. The village's De Grey Mausoleum houses aristocratic monume

Bedford Drive

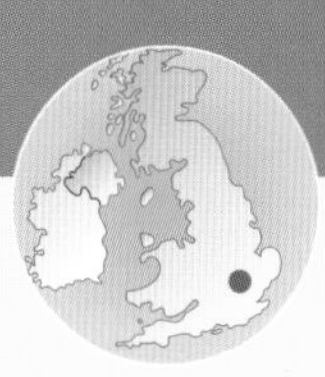

DRIVE

Progress through Bunyan's Country

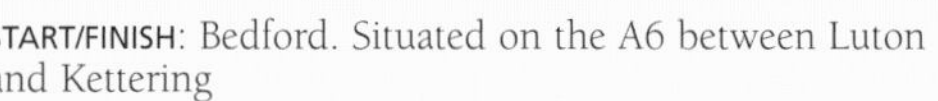

START/FINISH: Bedford. Situated on the A6 between Luton and Kettering

DISTANCE: 58 miles (93km)

Across the fertile Bedfordshire plain strode Christian in Bunyan's *Pilgrim's Progress*; from these fields, too, in October 1930, the airship *R101* began its ill-fated maiden voyage. Roads wind through green pastures and broad arable fields, linking medieval villages, bustling market towns and a modern garden city.

1 From Bedford, a busy market town on the River Great Ouse, take the A6 south and turn left through Elstow. John Bunyan was born here in 1628 and the late 15th-century Moot Hall is now a museum illustrating 17th-century life and traditions associated with Bunyan. Rejoin the A6 and continue south.

2 After 2.5 miles (4km) turn right and pass through Houghton Conquest, then turn left on to the B530. Houghton House, now a ruin, may have been the original 'House Beautiful' in *Pilgrim's Progress*.

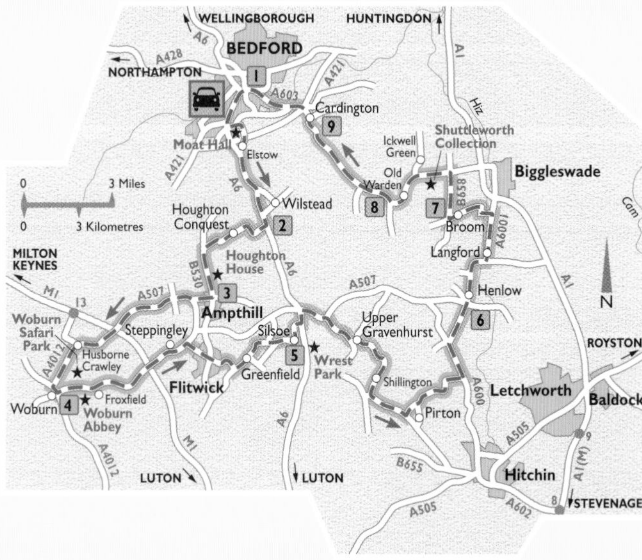

HORSE-RIDING

The open countryside provides excellent opportunities for those keen on riding. Of particular interest is the **Skylark Ride**. The full route is 20 miles (32km) long and travels through the countryside in east Bedfordshire with a section in Cambridgeshire. It follows bridleways and some sections of road. There are also circular sections of the ride which range from 6 to 20 miles (10 to 32km). There are stables in the region at **Steppingley**, near Woburn, at **Shillington** and **Northill** near Biggleswade.

have thatched roofs, and the churches around which they cluster are built in the Northamptonshire tradition, with stone spires and fine square-hewn masonry in brown ironstone. John Bunyan was a frequent preacher outside these churches and on village greens.

The county town, Bedford, has existed since Saxon times and is now a thriving commercial and industrial centre on both banks of the River Great Ouse. The town is proud of its Bunyan connection and his statue can be seen on St Peter's Green. You can also visit his birthplace in the nearby village of Elstow. The attractive market town of Olney, set on the edge of three counties – Buckinghamshire, Bedfordshire and Northamptonshire – is home to the famous pancake race held every Shrove Tuesday.

Milton Keynes is Britain's newest town, founded in 1967. Loosely based on American architect Frank Lloyd Wright's scheme for Broadacre City in the United States, Milton Keynes was designed with much thought given to landscaping and separating pedestrians and traffic. Despite its modern image within the borough, there is a wealth of history dating back to the Romans, including historic towns such as Newport Pagnell, Bletchley, Stony Stratford, Woburn Sands, Wolverton and Olney. Two-thirds of the borough is rural and within Milton Keynes there are 4,000 acres (1,619ha) of public open space and parkland, with more than 470 acres (190ha) of lakes and waterways. Leisure and shopping facilities are excellent and include a new Sports Village, a theatre and multi-screen cinema complex, and Midsummer Place, a new shopping centre.

ON THE WILD SIDE

Woburn Safari Park, created by the Duke of Bedford in 1970, is a 300-acre (120-ha) park offering the experience of driving through open reserves close to some of the most beautiful and dangerous animals in the world, including a number of endangered species. In addition there are plenty of exciting attractions in Wild World Leisure Area.

At **Whipsnade**, you can enjoy 2,500 animals in 600 acres (243ha) of parkland near Dunstable. The park is one of Europe's largest wildlife conservation centres and part of the Zoological Society of London, a major worldwide conservation charity. Visitors can observe the animals by taking a railway safari through the grounds.

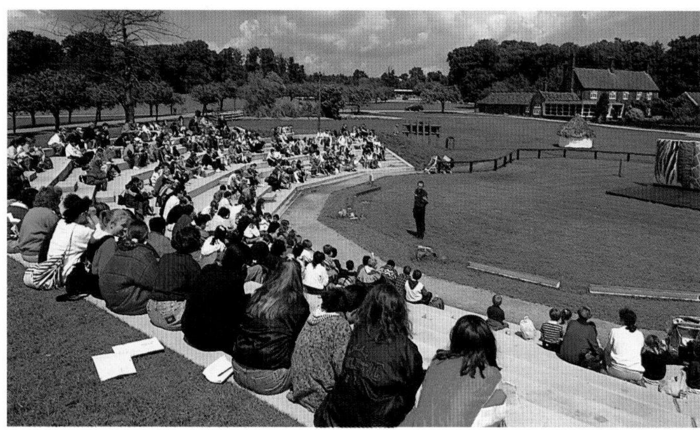

Visitors to Whipsnade Zoo take time out to relax and enjoy a bird demonstration

3 In 2 miles (3km) enter Ampthill and turn right at a double mini-roundabout to leave the town. Turn right on to the A507 for 4.5 miles (5.5km), then follow the A4012 to Woburn. Standing in 3,000 acres (1,214ha) of parkland, Woburn Abbey, a palatial 18th-century mansion, was originally a Cistercian Abbey, and the Dukes of Bedford have lived here since 1547. The state apartments contain a valuable art collection, 18th-century furniture, silver and porcelain. Woburn Safari Park occupies 300 acres (121ha) and visitors can drive through enclosures of animals.

4 Turn left on to Park Street by the Bedford Arms Hotel and go down the rhododendron-lined drive of Woburn Abbey, to eventually pass by Froxfield. Follow signs firstly to Steppingley and then to Flitwick. In Flitwick, turn left over the railway, then right into King's Road and immediately left, signed to Greenfield. Pass through Greenfield, turning right at Flitton and following signs to Silsoe.

5 Turn left at Silsoe High Street to join the A6 (or right to visit Wrest Park, an elegant 19th-century mansion with beautiful formal gardens), then turn right at the roundabout. After a mile (1.5km), turn right to Upper Gravenhurst and then follow signs to Shillington. Pick up signs to Pirton, forking left on a hairpin bend by cottages. Pass Pirton Hall Nursing Home and follow the road round into pretty Pirton village. Follow signs to Holwell, pass through the village and soon reach the A600 north of Hitchin. Turn left, then take the third exit at the roundabout on to the A6001.

6 Continue through Henlow towards Biggleswade. Pass through Langford before taking the next road left, signed to Broom.

7 Go through Broom, then turn right on the B658. Turn left at the roundabout, to follow the Old Warden road. Old Warden Aerodrome is home to the Shuttleworth Collection. Housed in seven hangars, 40 working historic aeroplanes span the progress of aviation with exhibits ranging from a 1909 Blériot to a 1941 Spitfire. Historic motor and horsedrawn vehicles are also on display.

8 After passing through Old Warden, with its Swiss Garden attraction, turn right to Cardington. Looming over the flat countryside surrounding the village are the giant airship hangars, built in the days when airships seemed to be the aerial transport of the future. The ill-fated *R101* began its journey here.

9 After 4 miles (6.5km) enter the village, then turn left by the King's Arms pub to join the A603 for Bedford.

SKIES OVER BEDFORDSHIRE

The **Dunstable Downs** are the perfect setting for learning to glide. At the **London Gliding Club** you can have a trial lesson, take part in a gliding day or book a one- or five-day course. The club has been on its present site since the 1930s and is part of aviation history. Nearly 100 gliders, from colourful vintage aircraft to sleek modern machines, operate from this beauty spot. Alternatively, you can watch the hang-gliders or fly a kite on the downs.

The 'brave new world' of Milton Keynes is captured in the town's unusual sculpture

EAST ANGLIA & CAMBRIDGE

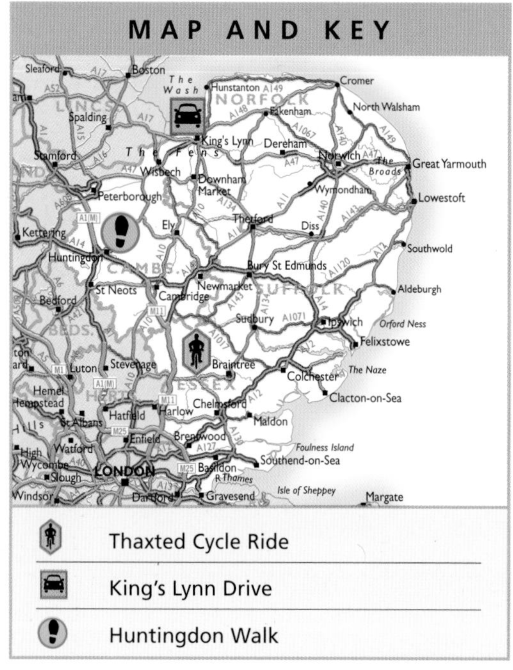

A delightful corner of the country, East Anglia has an attractive gentle landscape dotted with picturesque villages, unique fens and broads with superb habitats for wildlife, together with the spectacular coastlines of Norfolk, Suffolk and Essex. Here you can find a heritage dating from pre-neolithic times, through Roman Colchester, Britain's oldest recorded town, to the Georgian splendour of towns like Bury St Edmunds. The area remains largely quiet and unspoilt, a wonderful place to get on your bike, sail or walk to explore its hidden byways and backwaters.

KING'S COLLEGE CAMBRIDGE

The unforgettable sight of Cambridge is the view across the River Cam and the Backs to the stately Gothic chapel of King's College. The Christmas service of lessons and carols televised from King's College Chapel draws attention every year to one of the most breathtakingly beautiful buildings in Britain. With its superb fan-vaulted ceiling and magnificent stained glass, it is one of the glories of Western civilisation.

Suffolk Heritage Coast

Stretching from Lowestoft in the north to Felixstowe (above) in the south, this coastline is ideal for sailing and bird-watching. It is peppered with estuaries and creeks, providing interest to sailors as well as a home for bird life. Much of the coastline is being encroached by the sea – visit Dunwich to learn about the lost town beneath the waves.

CONSTABLE COUNTRY

The country in the valley of the River Stour on the border of Essex and Suffolk was already known as 'Constable Country' in the painter's own lifetime. It was here, in the village of East Bergholt, that John Constable was born in 1776, and he used local subjects for his well-loved paintings – among them Flatford Mill, Willy Lott's Cottage and Dedham Vale, all of which you can visit today.

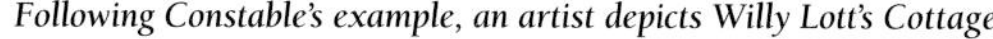

Following Constable's example, an artist depicts Willy Lott's Cottage

Norwich and the Broads

All of Norfolk is said to be in Norwich on a Saturday and it certainly proves to be an attractive and popular city. Drawing from a largely rural population, the shopping is good and the buildings sublime. Norwich has almost 1,000 buildings listed as of historic and architectural interest. Within easy reach of the city are the Norfolk Broads, Britain's most recent National Park, a haven for wildlife and a must for any boat enthusiast.

ESSEX & SUFFOLK

They may not have the rugged beauty and mountains of Wales or the spectacular cliffs of Cornwall, but the counties of Essex and Suffolk have plenty to offer, both visually and actively. This driest part of the British Isles is the ideal region to get out and about on foot or on a bike. With few major hills to climb you can cover a good deal of ground quickly and you will be able to feast your eyes on some of the most picturesque villages in Britain. And if you love water the sailing and watersports are excellent in the coastal region with its estuaries and lonely creeks.

The many different faces of Essex show a changing landscape offering a variety of pursuits. The south borders on the suburban London boroughs but open spaces are to be found, most notably at Epping Forest, approximately 6,000 acres (2,428ha) of beautiful woodland. The area of the Thames Estuary is sombre with its docks and factories but near by is one of the earliest seaside resorts at Southend-on-Sea, London's own Blackpool. Don't miss the attractive coastal towns of Burnham-on-Crouch, Bradwell-on-Sea and the small town of Maldon which offers river trips on restored Thames barges once used to transport straw to London.

The two other main areas of Essex popular with visitors cover the northwest and northeast. The Rodings, centred on the attractive town of Saffron Walden which dates from the Middle Ages, is a region of handsome timber-framed and plaster-fronted cottages, pretty villages and small towns such as Great Dunmow, Thaxted and Finchingfield. To the northeast you will find Roman Colchester and

TOP FIVE BIRD-WATCHING SITES

Minsmere Nature Reserve, Westleton, Suffolk

A large area of heath, woodland, reedbeds and lagoon with a great variety of birds.

Abberton Reservoir Nature Reserve

Run by Essex Wildlife Trust in a specially protected area for wild duck, swans and other water birds. Look for goldeneye, widgeon, gadwall, shovellers and cormorants.

Fingringhoe Wick Nature Reserve

Covers 126 acres (51ha) of stunning mixed habitat on the Colne Estuary.

Crouch Estuary, Essex

Bird-watching and seal-sighting river trips to the mouth of the river.

Titchwell Marsh Nature Reserve

One of East Anglia's most popular reserves has freshwater reedbeds, lagoons, wild saltmarshes, sand dunes and shingle. A superb habitat for a wide variety of birds.

TO HORSE

Horse-riding can be enjoyed throughout the region. Essex County Council has devised six country rides taking in some of the best bridleways and byways in Essex.

Take a carriage drive near **Framlingham** (left) in Suffolk which can be combined with a pub meal. Horse-and-carriage drives are also available in the summer around **Bury St Edmunds**.

The National Stud at **Newmarket** has 75-minute conducted tours to see the stallions and up to 100 mares and foals, sometimes less than a day old.

Thaxted Cycle Ride

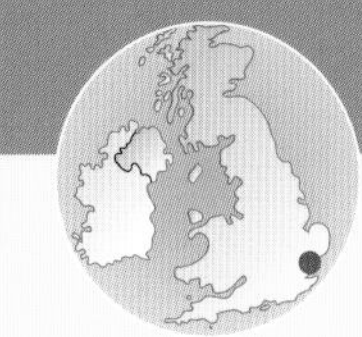

CYCLE RIDE

Windmills around Thaxted

START/FINISH: Thaxted. Located on the B184 between Great Dunmow and Saffron Walden, 5 miles (8km) north of Great Dunmow

DISTANCE: 18 miles (29km)

GRADIENT: gently undulating

ROADS: country lanes

PARKING: long-stay car-park (free), east of the High Street in Margaret's Road

This is an easy all-road ride linking the picturesque villages of Thaxted, Finchingfield and Great Bardfield via gently rolling country lanes. Each village boasts a charming fully-restored windmill, historic buildings and interesting local museums. Along the way, note the grand country hall houses that were built by wealthy merchants in medieval times.

1 Turn left out of the car-park, then turn right along Weaverhead Lane to a T-junction and bear right again to reach the High Street. Established in the 14th century, Thaxted became a flourishing market town and features well-preserved old houses, a 15th-century church that soars cathedral-like above the main street, and a magnificent timbered and jettied guildhall dating from 1390. Built in 1804, the windmill houses a fascinating rural museum. Turn left along the B184, then after 200yds (185m) take the left turning, signposted The Bardfields. Gradually climb out of the village, bearing left at a fork of roads after half a mile (800m) towards Little Sampford.

2 Continue on this quiet narrow lane for 2.5 miles (4km), past a no-through road on the left, to a T-junction, and bear right for Little Sampford, signed to Gt Bardfield and Finchingfield. In half a mile (800m), turn left in front of Little Sampford church and descend to a T-junction with the B1053. Turn left, then immediately right on to a lane beside a thatched cottage. Proceed gently uphill and keep to this peaceful lane for over a mile (1.5km), passing a fine moated farmhouse on the left, to an unsigned T-junction.

3 Turn right, then on reaching a further T-junction turn right towards Finchingfield. Pass the lane for Cornish Hall End and continue

weaving villages such as Coggeshall, with its beautiful timbered wool-merchant's house Paycocke's (*c* 1500), while still further east is the yachting centre of Mersea and the seaside resorts of fun-loving Clacton and prim and sedate Frinton.

The Stour Valley, straddling Essex and Suffolk, was home to the artist John Constable (1776–1837) and is one of the prettiest parts of the region with its picturesque medieval villages and towns, of which Lavenham is one of the best preserved. It boasts timbered halls, fine churches and houses covered in ornamental plasterwork. Other villages worth a look, and a mecca for antiques lovers, are Long Melford, Clare and Cavendish. Moving north you will discover the open farmlands of central Suffolk, great cycling and walking country peppered with villages and interesting towns. Visit Georgian Bury St Edmunds to the west, central Stowmarket and Framlingham in the east, and don't miss the home of British horse-racing, the National Stud at Newmarket.

TOP WALKS AND CYCLE TRAILS

The Essex Way An 81-mile (130-km) footpath across the county, passing through ancient woodlands, open farmland, tree-lined river valleys, historic towns and picturesque villages.

The Suffolk Way A 109-mile (175-km) walk through rural and coastal Suffolk and parts of North Essex, including Constable Country.

The Stour Valley Path A 60-mile (96-km) route through attractive scenery stretching from Newmarket to Cattawade alongside the River Stour.

Suffolk Coastal Cycle Route A 75-mile (120-km) circular signed route linking Felixstowe, Framlingham and Orford. Cycle hire is available.

Punch and Judy entertain at Clacton

for 2 miles (3km) on this rolling lane, passing the magnificent Spains Hall on your left, before descending into the charming village of Finchingfield. At a T-junction turn right and pass the windmill to reach the village centre. Possibly the most photographed village in Essex, Finchingfield is a picture-book settlement complete with a church on a hill, a picturesque postmill, a hump-backed bridge and a village green with a duckpond surrounded by quaint cottages.

4 Bear left uphill at the village green before the bridge and duckpond. Pass the church, then turn right by The Three Tuns pub into Vicarage Road. Leave the village and in half a mile (800m), keep right at a T-junction to pass Daw Street Farm. Descend to a bridge over the River Pant and climb steadily into tiny Walthams Cross. At the top of the hill, by a small postbox, turn right, signed Gt Bardfield and remain on this lane to a T-junction in the village centre. A feature of this old market town is a restored windmill that stands on a green overlooking the pleasant mixture of colour-washed old cottages and pargetted houses.

5 Turn right uphill through the village, keeping left at the top of the rise, by the memorial cross, along the B1057. In a short distance, turn right beside a timbered cottage, signposted to Thaxted. Continue through Little Bardfield and after 4 miles (6.5km) reach the B184 in Thaxted and retrace the outward route back to the car-park.

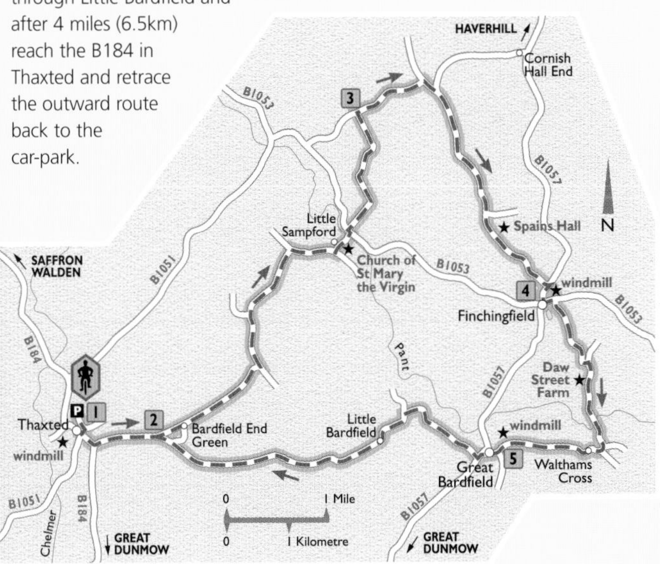

ON THE WATER

Sea-fishing is available all along the Essex and Suffolk coast, including **Southend** and **Burnham** in the south and **Aldeburgh** and **Southwold** in the north. Skipper-operated charter boats can be taken from **Bradwell** and **West Mersea** in Essex.

Sailing and watersports enthusiasts will find plenty to keep them active from the Thames Estuary right up to the north Suffolk coast. For different watersports try the inland **Gosfield Water Ski Club** near **Halstead** in north Essex where beginners are welcome, or scuba-diving in **Chelmsford**. Also popular are canoeing and rowing to be found at **Brandon** in Suffolk and **Flatford** on the Essex/Suffolk border.

Be sure not to leave out Suffolk's coastline, a wonderland of birds and estuaries, old-fashioned seaside towns and eroding cliffs. Visit Woodbridge, set on slopes above the River Deben, the castle at Orford, Aldeburgh for its musical festival and regatta, and Snape for its concert hall. Further up the coast is Dunwich, steadily being devoured by the sea and Southwold, an elegant small town and a favourite for artists.

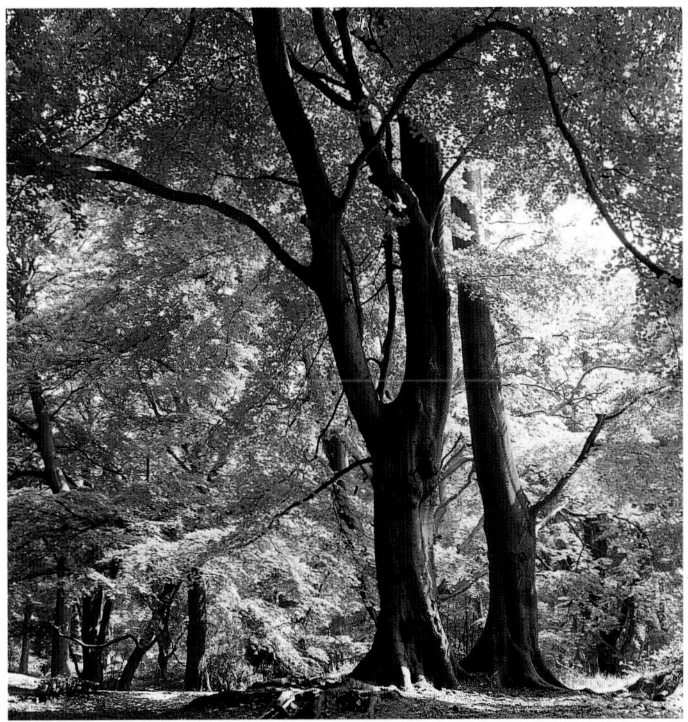

Paths through the ancient oaks and beeches of Epping Forest are perfect for walks

NORFOLK & THE NORTHEAST COAST

One of the great attractions of a visit to Norfolk is to experience tranquil places where uncongested lanes lead to fields, woodlands and meandering river valleys. With the vibrant city of Norwich at its heart, Norfolk provides a wonderful mix of history and outdoor pursuits. The coastal strip of north Norfolk, curving from Happisburgh in the southeast to Blakeney in the northwest, is heavily fortified against the never-ending assault of the sea. The joy of this little-explored corner of English coast is its isolation. The area has a wonderful sense of place and history and much to interest the naturalist. Dutch gables, flints, huge medieval 'wool' churches and weather-beaten coastal villages supply the man-made elements – saltmarshes (Europe's largest expanse), vast sand beaches, prolific bird life and dramatic skyscapes are among the natural attractions. Whether you are a bird-watcher or a windsurfer, a walker or a swimmer, the Norfolk coast is waiting to be explored.

One of the most popular holiday areas in the county is the Broads, situated in the triangle of Norwich, Lowestoft and Sea Palling. Here you will find 30 'broads' or open expanses of water with navigable approach channels. Together with linked rivers, lakes, streams and man-made waterways they provide 124 miles (200km)

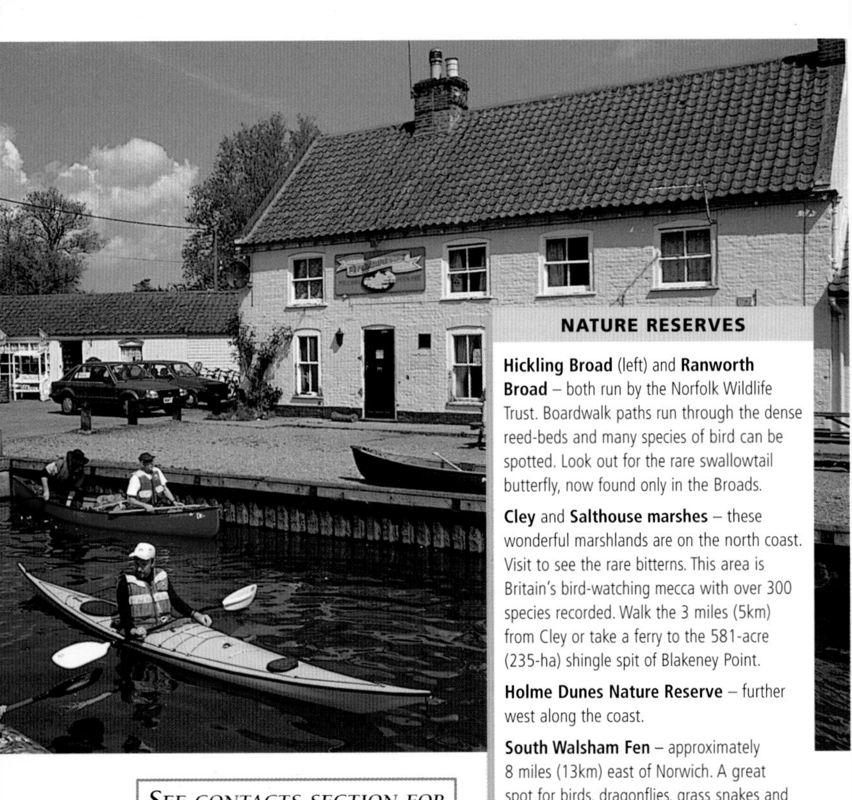

NATURE RESERVES

Hickling Broad (left) and **Ranworth Broad** – both run by the Norfolk Wildlife Trust. Boardwalk paths run through the dense reed-beds and many species of bird can be spotted. Look out for the rare swallowtail butterfly, now found only in the Broads.

Cley and **Salthouse marshes** – these wonderful marshlands are on the north coast. Visit to see the rare bitterns. This area is Britain's bird-watching mecca with over 300 species recorded. Walk the 3 miles (5km) from Cley or take a ferry to the 581-acre (235-ha) shingle spit of Blakeney Point.

Holme Dunes Nature Reserve – further west along the coast.

South Walsham Fen – approximately 8 miles (13km) east of Norwich. A great spot for birds, dragonflies, grass snakes and rare plants.

SEE CONTACTS SECTION FOR ADDITIONAL INFORMATION

ARTS AND CRAFTS

Candles The village workshop at Stokesby gives demonstrations of candlemaking and there are candles to buy. The Candle Shop at Little Walsingham sells a huge range.

Craft Centres Great Walsingham Barns. Albany Crafts at Erpingham. Tavernham Nursery Craft and Country Shopping Centre. The Village Experience, north of Great Yarmouth, has a variety of craft shops.

Pottery Holkham Pottery has a series of craft workshops. Sutton Pottery for wheel-made stoneware pottery. Made in Cley for hand-thrown domestic and sculptural pottery in stoneware and raku.

Gifts Norfolk Lavender offers tours of the distillery and a wide choice of gifts. Langham Glass has a collection of workshops including glass-blowing, as well as shops, a restaurant and a museum.

King's Lynn Drive

DRIVE

Fen, Farm & Coast

START/FINISH: King's Lynn. Located off the A47 between Wisbech and Swaffham

DISTANCE: 84 miles (91.5km)

Through flat fields and across the fenland, you are drawn to the magnificence of Ely's cathedral, then on to the undulating ground of rural Norfolk. The farming landscape continues to the coast, before ending with lavender and a royal residence.

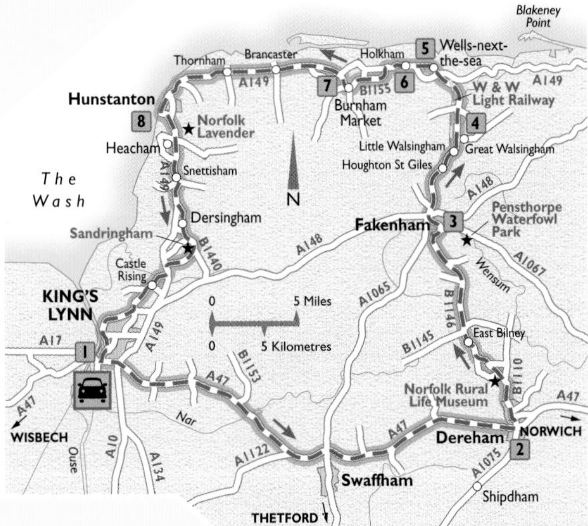

1 Leave King's Lynn on the A47 heading east, crossing the River Nar and the A1065, to Dereham. The town has some fine Georgian buildings, and Bishop Bonner's Cottage has attractive pargeting. At Gressenhall is the Norfolk Rural Life Museum and Union Farm, which has rare breeds and a museum on farming.

2 Continue north on the B1110, then the B1146 to Fakenham, a delightful small market town which dates from Saxon times. Pensthorpe Waterfowl Park covers 200 acres (81ha), with five lakes which are home to the largest collection of waterfowl and waders in Europe.

for sailing or motor-boat cruising. Once you have left the boatyard you can meander quietly through the fields, woodlands and marshes, taking breaks at the waterside villages, pubs and restaurants along the way. Many footpaths run along the Broads' 40 shallow lakes and five rivers, so picnicking, fishing, bird-watching, cycling and exploring couldn't be easier.

Another area of Norfolk, which provides excellent opportunities for outdoor enthusiasts, is to the southwest in the region known as Breckland. Here you can discover good cycling routes, bridleways and long-distance walks, where you can enjoy the flat landscapes with twisty leafy lanes and enormous skies with a church tower on nearly every horizon. This is a unique area of countryside, with neolithic flint mines, the largest area of lowland pine forest in Britain, England's tallest medieval earthwork and one of the best climates in the UK.

No trip to Norfolk would be complete without a visit to Norwich, tucked away inside a flat loop of the River Wensum. The city has grown up around its three Norman landmarks: the cathedral, the castle and the market-place. Steeped in history, and with a wealth of museums and medieval churches, it also offers good shopping including the attractive cobbled Elm Hill with its antiques and specialist shops, the excellent 900-year-old market of 200 stalls open six days a week and the network of charming old streets, alleys and art-nouveau arcade. Don't miss the famous Coleman's Mustard Shop and Museum; Jeremiah Coleman started milling mustard in Norwich in 1814.

Norfolk has long been popular with artists and craftspeople lured by its peace and beauty. Throughout the county, towns and villages are full of workshops and galleries. Landscape and seascape painting, silver plating, pottery, woodcarving and glass-blowing can be found across the region, adding another dimension to getting out and about in Norfolk.

COASTAL DELICACIES

Norfolk is well-known for a variety of regional seafoods including:

Yarmouth for bloaters – whole unsplit herrings, slightly salted and smoked, and kippers – herrings split, slightly salted and smoked. Visit the smoke house in Yarmouth and the renovated vessel *Lydia Eva*, the last herring drifter.

King's Lynn for shrimps.

Cromer, world-famous for its crabs.

Wells-next-the-Sea for whelks and cockles.

Stiffkey for cockles – the best ones are the dark grey-blues known as Stewkey Blues.

Samphire is a plant found on the edge of tidal waters and marshes. It is eaten during late July and August, pickled or cooked and served with butter, and is known as 'poor man's asparagus'.

TOP CYCLING ROUTES

Whether you are an experienced tourer or a complete novice, Norfolk lends itself to the view from the saddle. The vast, flat fenlands in the south give way to gentle slopes with villages nestling in the hollows as the land nears the sea – all superb cycling country with a network of quiet country lanes and bridleways to explore. Bring your own bike or hire on site.

The Bittern Track – a network of nine cycle routes, ranging from 6 to 30 miles (10 to 48km), centred around the Norwich–Sheringham railway.

Reepham Station – 25 miles (40km) of former railway route for traffic-free cycling.

Wensum Valley – there is excellent cycling in the Upper, Mid, and Lower sections of the valley.

Norfolk Coast Cycleway – you can cycle along the coast or enjoy seven circular routes to explore the inland landscapes and villages.

Broads Bike Hire – a network of hire points to enable exploration of the Broads by all-terrain bike.

A view across the windswept sand dunes of Norfolk's coastline

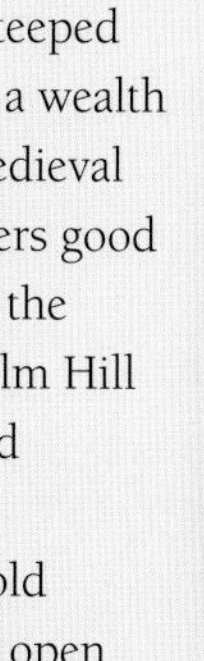

3 Cross the A148 and follow an unclassified road to Houghton St Giles. This attractive village has old links with nearby Little Walsingham, which has been a Christian shrine since 1061. Great Walsingham is noted for its textile centre.

4 Return to the unclassified road from Great Walsingham and follow to the 18th-century town of Wells-next-the-Sea. The Wells and Walsingham Light Railway runs through 4 miles (6km) of countryside to the famous pilgrimage villages of Walsingham.

5 Follow the A149 west for 2 miles (3km) to Holkham. In a beautiful deer park with a lake landscaped by 'Capability' Brown, is the 18th-century mansion of Holkham Hall, just south of the village of Holkham.

6 Continue along the A149, then left on to the B1155 to Burnham Market. This upmarket village has a handsome, wide village green surrounded by elegant 18th-century houses.

7 Return to the A149 for 12 miles (19km) to Hunstanton. Hunstanton developed as a seaside resort in the 19th century, and is famous for its red-and-white striped chalk cliffs and excellent beaches.

8 Head south on the A149, then the B1440 from Dersingham to Sandringham, and further south to Castle Rising. The royal estate of Sandringham covers 20,000 acres (8,094ha) and was bought by Queen Victoria for the Prince of Wales in 1862. At Castle Rising are the ruins of a splendid Norman castle. Take the B1439 back to rejoin the A149, then an unclassified road back to King's Lynn.

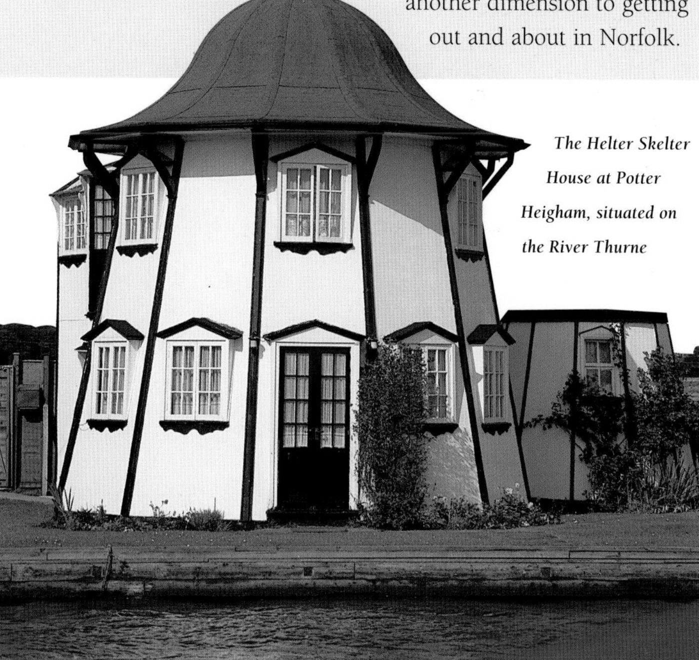

The Helter Skelter House at Potter Heigham, situated on the River Thurne

CAMBRIDGE & THE OUSE VALLEY

Wide fenland horizons, interrupted only by an occasional church spire or the distinctive outline of a solitary windmill, lend a sense of exhilaration to the flat landscapes of the Cambridgeshire fens. Old towns and villages hug the banks of the meandering River Great Ouse and in Cambridge punts drift by under the willow trees along the River Cam. This region provides fine walking and cycling country where the flat terrain will enable you to cover a great deal of ground and discover the area's unique natural beauty.

The Romans were the first to raise causeways above the treacherous surface of the Fens. They also opened drainage channels to divert water and carry food to garrisons further north. After their departure most of their work fell into disrepair and it was not until the 13th century onwards that sporadic attempts were made to set up comprehensive drainage schemes. By the 19th century steam engines began to replace the windmills, which had been used for centuries for fen drainage. The rich dark peat soils have sustained cereal and root crops, apples, soft fruit, flowers and bulbs for hundreds of years and the habitat is a wonderful haven for wildlife.

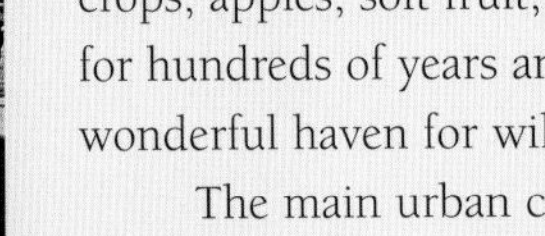

The main urban centres of the area are Cambridge, Huntingdon and Ely, with their fine buildings and strong sense of history. Cambridge, renowned for its university, boasts

PUNTING ON THE RIVER CAM

The River Cam offers a different perspective of Cambridge, so why not try your hand at punting on the famous university Backs – it's not as easy as it looks! If you are not brave enough to try, you can always take a chauffeured punt tour which will take in the important sights, including the Bridge of Sighs, King's College Chapel and the Wren Library. Rowboats and river cruises are also available on the Cam.

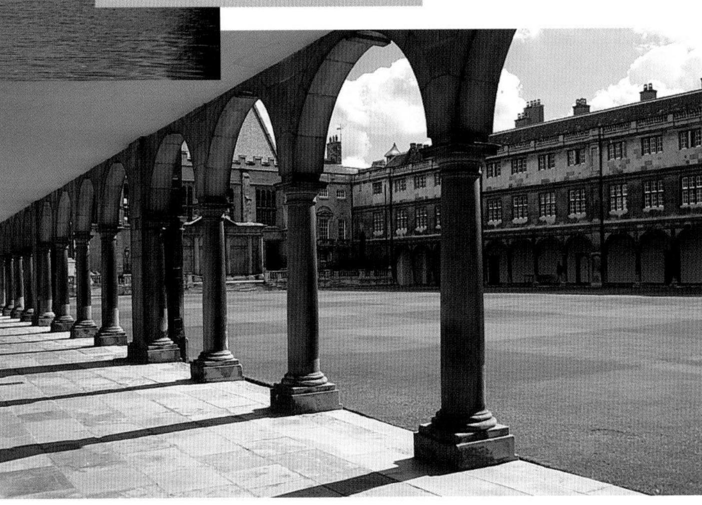

Founded in 1546, Trinity College boasts a library designed by Sir Christopher Wren

RETAIL THERAPY IN CAMBRIDGE

Cambridge has a variety of shopping facilities to suit all tastes, from large department stores to small, specialist outlets, with some of the country's best new, second-hand and antiquarian bookshops.

The city has two shopping centres; one based on the old, traditional market-place and the other at the Grafton Centre, with the usual high-street names.

The best areas for specialist shops can be found in Green Street, Bridge Street, King's Parade and All Saints' Passage. There is an excellent daily market, with a farmers' market on Sundays.

Huntingdon Walk

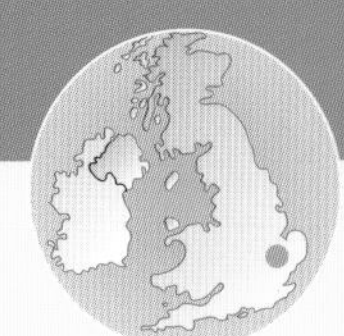

WALK

Oliver Cromwell's Huntingdon Home

START/FINISH: Huntingdon. Off the A14/A1 16 miles (26km) northeast of Cambridge

DISTANCE: 8 miles (13km)

ASCENT/GRADIENT: negligible

TERRAIN/PATHS: meadows, riverside, some streets; good paths, but muddy after rain; flooding possible in winter

PARKING: car-park in Malthouse Close off Princess Street, opposite bus station

The spirit of the commoner who rose to extraordinary power during the Civil War, haunts his former homeland around the Ouse Valley. This walk guides you past the principal Cromwellian sites before heading out into the countryside of the Ouse Valley.

1 From Princess Street, follow Literary Walk to the High Street and turn left to All Saints' Church, the Falcon Tavern and the Cromwell Museum. Continue past the church and turn left into George Street. Cromwell was born in the town in 1599, and was a landowner and farmer before becoming an MP. Several sites can claim a connection: All Saints' Church holds his baptismal record, the Falcon Tavern was used frequently by Cromwell between 1642 and 1644, and the Cromwell Museum was formerly the grammar school where he was educated.

2 Go straight on at the traffic lights. When the road bends to the right, turn left along a footpath to Mill Common. Go diagonally left to a road and turn right, past Castle Hill, under the A14 and over a brook to join the Ouse Valley Way in Port Holme Meadow.

3 Walk straight across to a footbridge at Godmanchester Lock. Having crossed, turn left to reach Chinese Bridge. Cross into Godmanchester, leaving the Ouse Valley Way. Cross the B1043 to Cambridge Street, then left into Chadley Lane to St Mary's Church. Crossing Port Holme Meadow, and walking along the Cambridge road through Godmanchester and by the River Great Ouse near Houghton, you are treading footpaths and bridleways used by Cromwell himself.

4 Turn right through a churchyard, then right again to follow East Chadley Lane to Cambridge Road by the White Hart pub. Turn left, go

superb architecture and peaceful river backwaters. The university grew from small beginnings at the start of the 13th century with the first college, Peterhouse, founded in 1281. Other colleges followed, including King's, Trinity, St John's and Magdalen, all in easy reach by foot of the city centre.

Huntingdon, at the centre of a rich agricultural area, is an attractive town of fine Georgian buildings and is famed as the birthplace of Oliver Cromwell in 1599. The meandering River Great Ouse, one of the country's largest navigable rivers, attracts many visitors to the town, with opportunities for boating, fishing and walks along the towpath.

One of the most breathtaking sights in Cambridgeshire is Ely Cathedral, one of Britain's most outstanding cathedrals, and its huge size appears to dwarf the little fenland market town that surrounds it. Here the River Great Ouse continues its journey to the Wash, again providing boating and fishing possibilities, together with riverside pubs, restaurants and an antiques centre on its banks in the town.

As the river maintains its course between Huntingdon and Ely, it features a succession of lovely towns and villages. St Ives recalls in its museum the time when locals used to skate on the frozen river. A little further afield you can visit the cathedral town of Peterborough, with its modern shopping facilities. Just beyond, you can explore lovely mellow stone villages including Wansford, Barnack, Helpston and Ufford.

ON THE GO

Hot-air ballooning over Cambridgeshire is available from **Lakeside Lodge**, at **Pidley** near **Huntingdon**, which also offers a par-72 golf course and pitch-and-putt course, rally karting and a ten-pin bowling centre.

Have a day out at the **Mepal Outdoor Centre** in the middle of the Cambridgeshire fens. Try a host of interesting activities including rock-climbing, archery and trampolining. Watersports include canoeing, sailing and windsurfing on the sheltered lake.

Cool off in **Jesus Green swimming pool**, an open-air pool in an idyllic position by the river in **Cambridge**. One of the longest pools in the country, it is open from mid-May until mid-September.

GRAFHAM WATER

Three miles (5km) long and 1.5 miles (2.5km) across at its widest point, these 1,600 acres (675ha) of open water provide a wide range of attractions for visitors of all ages. You can have a go at trout fishing, sailing or windsurfing. Out of the water there is a 10-mile (16-km) circuit for walking, jogging or cycling around the lake and through the quieter wooded areas of the nature reserve. As a Site of Special Scientific Interest it is excellent for bird-watching. Restaurant and picnic areas are available.

DID YOU KNOW?

The Mathematical Bridge in Cambridge was supposed to have been constructed without nails, purely on geometric principles. Look at the sundial at Queen's College at night-time and you will find you can even tell the time by the shadow cast by the moon.

Go to Whittlesey in January and you'll find the inhabitants dancing in the streets, parading behind the 'Strawbear' which is said to bring fertility to crops in spring.

In May, in the village of Stilton, you can witness the spectacle of cheese being rolled down the High Street in a contest. And believe it or not, the World Pea Shooting Championships really do take place at Witcham, near Ely, every July.

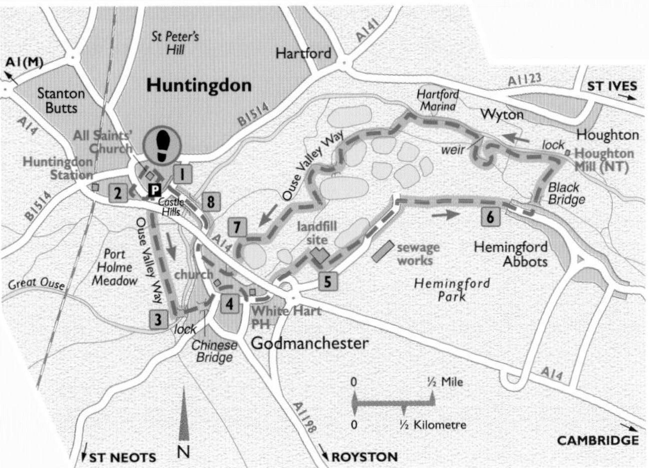

under the A14, shortly join a footpath on the left and pass a pool then turn right past a young plantation. Cross a landfill site access track and continue by a fence.

5 Ignore access to Cow Lane and carry straight on, climbing on to an embankment to walk along the top. At the far end descend to Cow Lane. Turn left, then join the second path on the right, a bridleway running beside a dismantled railway across a common.

6 After passing a pond, the bridleway veers slightly right to join Common Lane at Hemingford Abbots. Go straight on to reach Meadow Lane and turn left. Cross Black Bridge and Hemingford Meadow to Houghton Lock. Houghton Mill (NT) is a large timber-built water-mill on an island in the Ouse, with much of its 19th-century machinery still intact. Turn left beside the river, rejoining the Ouse Valley Way, and follow the waymarkers.

7 Take an underpass beneath the A14 and head for Godmanchester. Pass a housing estate to intercept a footpath/cycleway and turn right to the B1043. Turn right towards Huntingdon, crossing at the lights. A wealth of period buildings and a 14th-century bridge link the two towns.

8 Cross a footbridge spanning the Great Ouse. Follow the road left, then walk through Castle Hills and along a passageway to Castle Hill. Proceed to Mill Common and turn right to Princess Street.

Peterborough's town centre, a mix of modern shops amid medieval and Tudor buildings

WATCHING WILDLIFE

If wildlife watching is your main reason for going out into the countryside, then the best places to spot the rarities are at the many bird and nature reserves around the country. There are a total of about 2,500 reserves throughout Britain, the cream of which are the 170 National Nature Reserves (NNRs), which have been specially designated by the government because of their national or international importance. The largest in England is The Wash NNR, which covers nearly 24,460 acres (9,900ha), and the smallest, like Swanscombe in Kent, are only about 5 acres (2ha) in extent. The first NNR to be set up in Britain was the magnificent 11,860-acre (4,800-ha) Beinn Eighe reserve on Scotland's rugged west coast. In addition to its rare, semi-Arctic flora, the Beinn Eighe reserve is home to the shy wildcat and pine marten, which are rarely found elsewhere in Britain.

Most of the other reserves are local nature reserves which are usually managed by the individual county wildlife trusts, such as the strange, end-of-the-world shingle spit of Spurn Point on the Humber Estuary, which is run by the Yorkshire Wildlife Trust. Others are owned and run by the National Trust, like Wicken Fen in Cambridgeshire, the only remaining piece of native fenland left in East Anglia and home to the spectacular swallowtail butterfly, and Selborne Hill in Hampshire, the outdoor laboratory of the pioneer naturalist Gilbert White.

In addition to the many nature reserves, there are 130 specialist bird reserves managed by the Royal Society for the Protection of Birds (RSPB) which are open to the public. These range from the reed-fringed meres of Leighton Moss on the Morecambe Bay coast of Lancashire, a haunt of the rare, booming bittern and the equally elusive otter, to the wild Highland landscapes of Loch Garten, part of the Abernethy Forest Reserve in Strathspey, where the fish-eating osprey successfully returned in 1959.

Feeding the flamingoes at Martin Mere Wildfowl and Wetlands Trust Reserve near Ormskirk, Lancashire

Islands provide some of the finest bird reserves, where huge populations of screaming sea birds roost and nest. Examples of these include the National Trust island of Lundy off the north coast of Devon, where there are populations of puffins, guillemots, razorbills and kittiwakes; Skomer Island off the rugged coast of Pembrokeshire, which is known for its guillemots, kittiwakes, puffins and burrow-nesting Manx shearwaters; and the Farne Islands off the Northumberland coast which, in addition to a fascinating bird life, have a large colony of grey seals.

Other coastal sites include perhaps the most famous bird reserve of all, Minsmere in Suffolk, where you can find avocets, the elegant black-and-white wader which became the emblem of the RSPB after its successful return here, and the dizzy cliffs of Flamborough Head and Bempton on Yorkshire's North Sea coast, where thousands of sea birds cling to the 400-ft (120-m) cliffs and give out an unforgettable cacophony of sound.

Many of the larger reserves have information centres and hides where you can watch the wildlife in comfort, and at some you can hire binoculars for the day. Examples of these are at Loch Garten, where you can watch the ospreys from a visitor centre, and Leighton Moss, where one of the hides even has easy chairs and carpets!

BIRD-WATCHING FOR BEGINNERS

- Wear warm, waterproof clothing
- Don't wear clothing which is bright or noisy
- Keep as still and quiet as possible
- Leave the dog at home
- Don't forget the binoculars and identification guide
- Be patient, something will turn up eventually

Wicken Fen, Britain's oldest reserve, is home to the warbler and breeding snipe

Inverpolly National Nature Reserve in the western Highlands

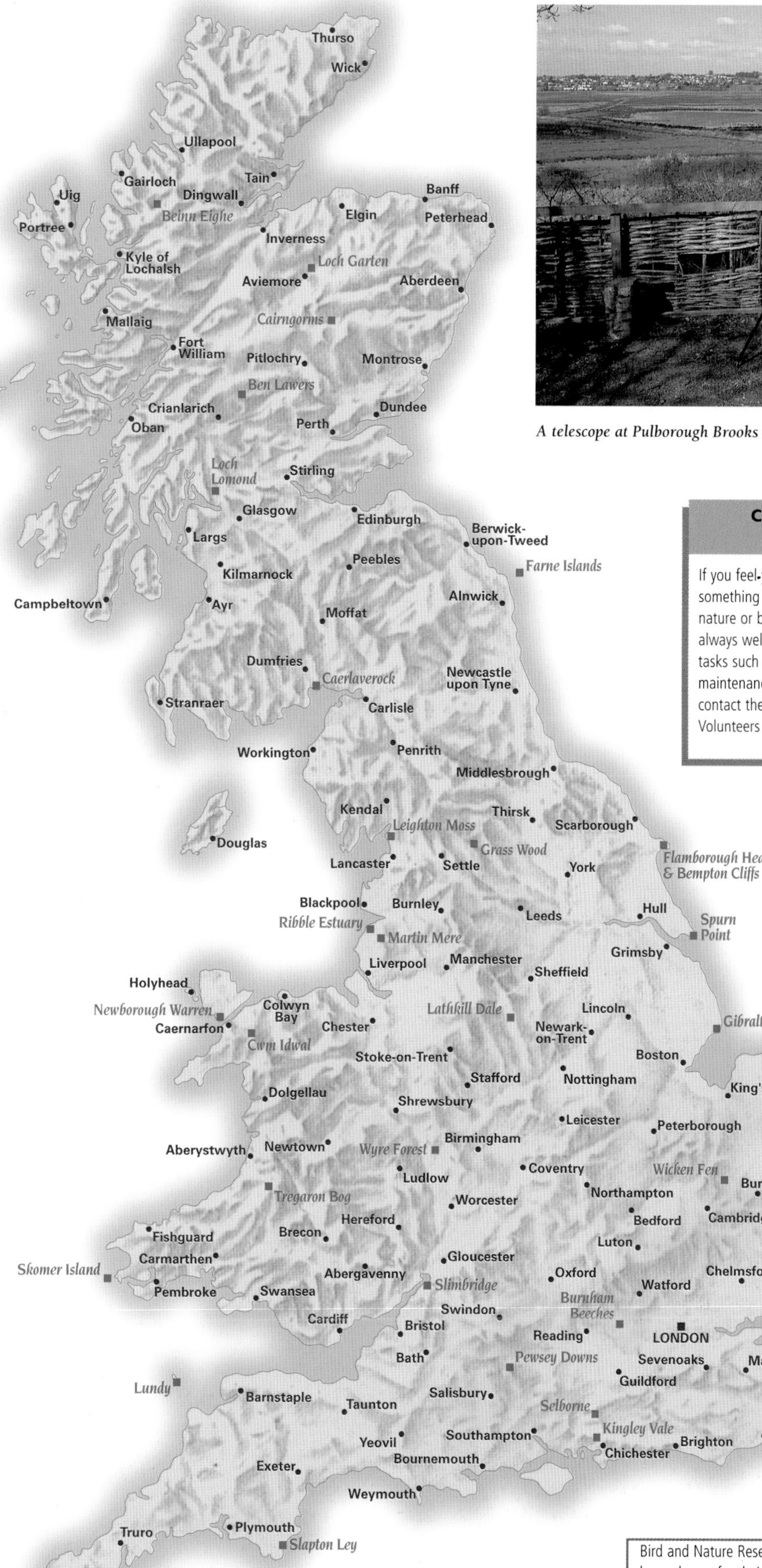

A telescope at Pulborough Brooks allows a closer view

CONSERVATION VOLUNTEERS

If you feel you would like to 'put something back' and help out at a nature or bird reserve, volunteers are always welcome to do conservation tasks such as scrub clearance or path maintenance. Ask at the reserve, or contact the British Trust for Conservation Volunteers (Tel: 01491 839766).

Bird and Nature Reserves shown on the map have been chosen for their particular interest or attraction and to give a good geographical spread. It is not possible to show every one on the map.

CENTRAL ENGLAND

Painswick Beacon, Gloucestershire

THE COTSWOLDS & OXFORD

One of the most quintessentially 'English' areas of Britain, this high, limestone plateau is chiefly noted for its beautiful villages. Created from honey-coloured stone and often tucked into delightful wooded valleys, they are enhanced by sparkling streams and contrasted with high, open meadows. From the steep escarpment of the western Cotswolds, carved by the River Severn, and the elegant spa town of Cheltenham, the plateau slopes eastward as far as the golden city of Oxford. Between Shakespeare's Stratford in the north and the River Thames in the south is a stunning area waiting to be explored.

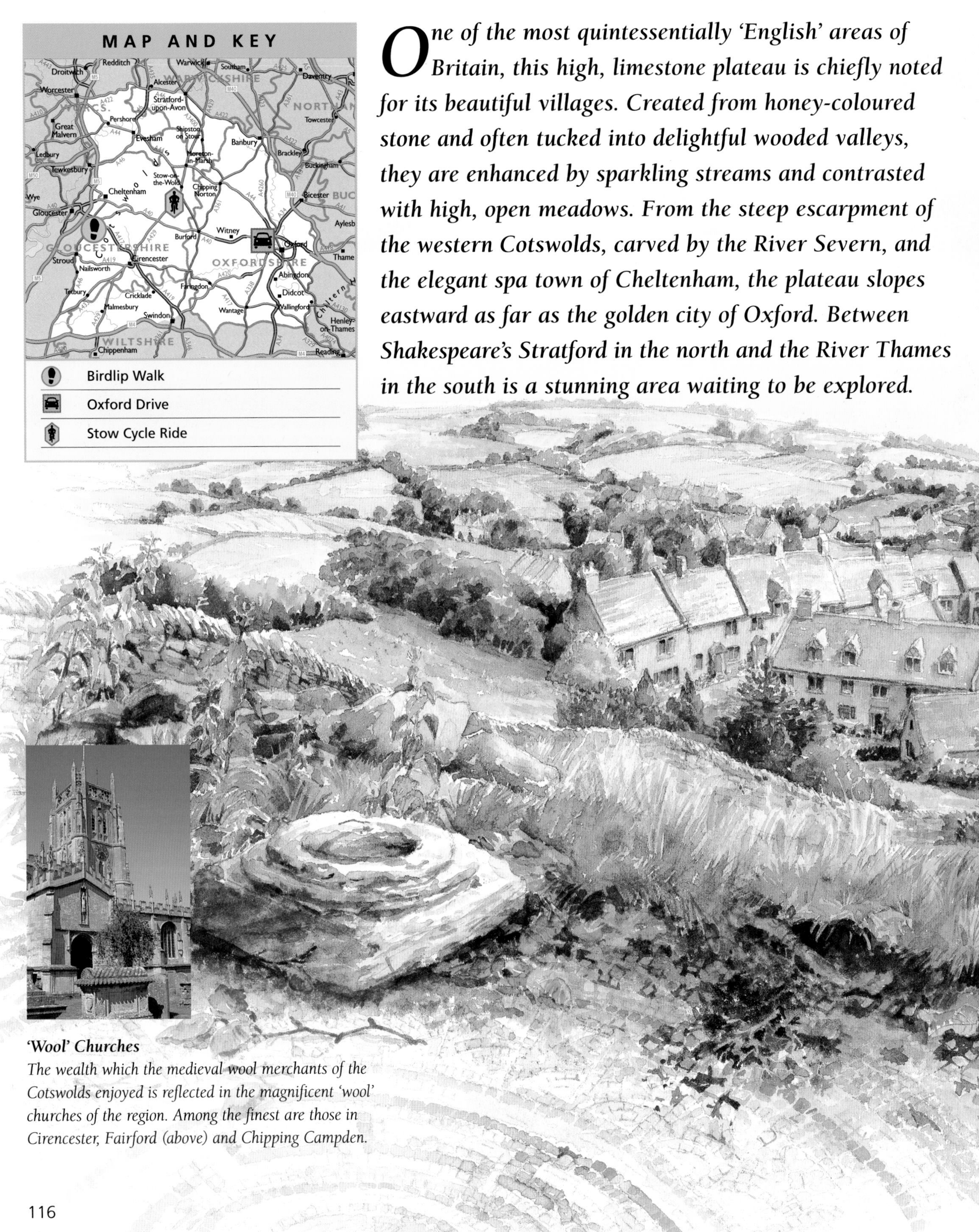

'Wool' Churches

The wealth which the medieval wool merchants of the Cotswolds enjoyed is reflected in the magnificent 'wool' churches of the region. Among the finest are those in Cirencester, Fairford (above) and Chipping Campden.

WALKING IN THE COTSWOLDS

The Cotswolds offer a wide range of walking opportunities, from the strenuous roller-coaster of the 100-mile (160-km) Cotswold Way, which traverses the western edge between Bath and Chipping Campden, to many far gentler, waymarked circular walks from the beautiful villages which shelter in the combes beyond the escarpment.

Roman Mosaics

Cirencester was an important centre for the production of mosaics in Roman Britain. Good examples can be seen in the Corinium Museum in the town, and at the Chedworth Roman Villa 8 miles (13km) to the north, where the famous 'Four Seasons' mosaic shows life as it was in the Cotswolds through the Roman year.

City of Oxford

Oxford's raison d'être *is its university, one of the oldest in the world, which was established in 1214. Within a square mile (1.5sq km) the heart of the city contains 653 listed buildings, most of them built in golden Cotswold stone. The towers and turrets of colleges such as Christ Church, Oriel and Merton, seen from the banks of the Isis or the Cherwell, are one of the great symbols of the world's cultural heritage.*

THE SHAKESPEARE TRAIL

Stratford-upon-Avon is forever linked with England's greatest playwright, William Shakespeare, born here on St George's Day in 1564. As well as his birthplace in Henley Street (above), you can visit the site of his last house, New Place, where he died in 1616; Holy Trinity Church where he was buried; and the Grammar School, where he received his education, all in a short walk around the town.

THE SOUTHERN COTSWOLDS

Although the escarpment of the Cotswolds is lower in the south, the valleys are steeper and the dappled stone is heavier and more silvery. The medieval wool industry moved from the high wolds to these steeper valleys to make use of the fast-flowing streams, especially in the Stroud Valley. Pretty villages abound, particularly along the Coln Valley, while memories of an even earlier time when the Cotswolds flourished – during the Roman occupation – are to be found in Cirencester and the village of Chedworth.

In Roman times Cirencester, now a busy market town, was the most important city in England after London, and during the Middle Ages it regained something of its former glory when it became the most influential of the wool towns. In common with many of the area's towns, Cirencester has a wealth of exquisitely crafted buildings created for the wealthy wool merchants. These span from the Middle Ages until the 18th century, when the wool and cloth trades disappeared from the area. Many towns and villages have particularly magnificent churches built to display this immense wealth derived from the 'Golden Fleeces'. Cirencester church is notable for being one of the largest in England, but Chipping Campden, Fairford and Lechlade all have very fine examples.

A detail of the stained glass at St Mary's Church, Fairford

Near Cirencester is a charming village called Chedworth, usually associated with the remains of one of the finest Roman villas in England. The villa, discovered in 1864, is just outside the village. Many of the finds from the villa, and the numerous other Roman remains scattered over

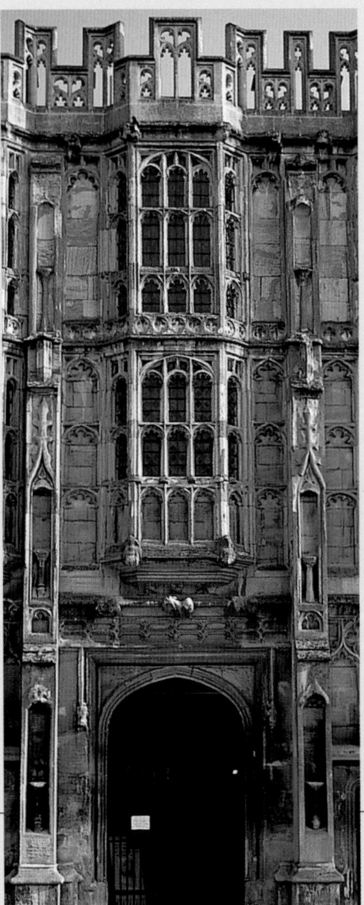

The elegant gatehouse of Cirencester's Norman abbey

Arlington Row, a terrace of 17th-century weavers' cottages by the riverside in Bibury

Birdlip Walk

WALK

Birdlip and the Cotswolds

START/FINISH: Barrow Wake viewpoint on the A417 east of Gloucester, near the Air Balloon pub
DISTANCE: 7.5 miles (12km)
ASCENT/GRADIENT: 400ft (120m); gradual climbs
TERRAIN/PATHS: fields and open grassland; waymarked Cotswold Way, good paths
PARKING: Barrow Wake viewpoint car-park

Passing through venerable beech woods and returning across the high wold, the walk follows part of the Cotswold escarpment, affording far-reaching views across the Vale of Gloucester to the Brecon Beacons.

1 From the panorama board and memorial in the car-park, bear left along the Cotswold Way to a stile into beech woodland. There is a fine view to the right, but it is even better if the short detour is taken to The Peak. From here return to the Cotswold Way and follow it through beech woods. In spring some areas of the wood are carpeted in bluebells, others with the white-flowered, pungent ransoms, which belong to the garlic family. After passing a high bank on the left, a distinct path goes off left.

2 Turn left, bearing left at a fork to a gate. Follow the wall on the right across the field beyond to reach a road (B4070). Cross the road, footbridge and a waymarked stile and cross the field beyond to another stile (don't cross). Turn left along field edge to a stile on to the A417. Look out for the quick slate-blue flash of a sparrowhawk, hovering kestrels or buzzards.

3 Cross with care and go over the stile opposite. Follow the hedge on the right to a waymarker post. Continue along the hedge on the right (beyond the gap), pass another waymarker and turn left in the corner to continue beside a hedge. Follow the hedge sharp right along a wide track. After 30yds (27m) turn left, walking with a hedge on your right and turning left with it, then following a wall on the right to its end. Here step right, around the wall end, and turn left beside a hedge. Here, on the high wolds, Cotswold sheep once outnumbered people, growing fleeces that made the area the richest in England in medieval times.

the Cotswolds, are gathered into the award-winning Corinium Museum in Cirencester.

The Cotswolds are ideal for both walking and cycling, and there are over 500 miles (800km) of routes recommended by tourist information centres for both activities. If you prefer to explore by car, the 'Romantic Routes' have been planned to take you through some of the prettiest villages in the area.

Just to the north of Cirencester is a string of villages along the small River Dunt. Known as the Duntisbournes, they have a special character given by their unusual saddleback church towers, which have something almost French about them.

On the escarpment not far from Cheltenham, the River Coln, a tributary of the Thames, rises. This is arguably the prettiest of the many rivers that ripple through the Cotswolds. It gently descends the slopes of the plateau, passing through a number of picturesque villages *en route*, most notably Bibury, before going on to Fairford and Lechlade. Bibury is celebrated for its row of 17th-century weavers' cottages, with the trout-filled Coln sliding along outside their doors. Near by is Bibury Trout Farm, where you can catch your own or buy from the shop.

The Cotswold towns and villages are particularly good for shopping, whether it be for local produce from the farms, crafts or antiques. Shopping is unhurried and there is plenty of variety. Malmesbury and Tetbury are typical of the region with a mix of attractive buildings, quaint streets, a selection of individual shops, restaurants and B&Bs.

The area is also known for its riding and hunting – and the most famous name of all is Badminton. In the Great Park of Badminton House, home of the Duke of Beaufort, the international three-day equestrian event has been held every year since 1949. It is also possible to arrange for horse-riding holidays at a number of venues in the Cotswolds, following a network of bridleways.

GETTING AIRBORNE

Cotswold Gliding Club, at **Aston Down Airfield** near Stroud, has superb soaring on thermals rising from the high limestone ridges. Launches are made by both motor pulley and aerotow, and there is a fleet of aircraft for all abilities, including Ka13 dual-seat trainers, Ka8s for early solo pilots, plus a Ka6 and an Astir for more experienced pilots. The club has residential accommodation, toilets and showers, and caravan and camping facilities.

WATERY WONDERLAND

Over 100 lakes created by gravel extraction near South Cerney now make up the popular **Cotswold Water Park**. The park provides facilities for nature-lovers and watersports enthusiasts alike. Activities include coarse and game fishing, sailing, water-skiing, plus walks, cycle routes and cycle hire. There are three nature reserves and the wetlands attract millions of wildfowl, particularly in the winter.

DOWN IN THE FOREST

Garden-lovers flock to the magnificent **Westonbirt Arboretum**, near **Tetbury**, where over 13,000 trees thrive in 600 acres (242ha) of glade, with 17 miles (27km) of footpaths. It was started in 1829 by Sir Robert Holford of Westonbirt House. Now managed by the Forestry Commission, the arboretum contains one of the most important collections of trees and shrubs in the world, and is beautiful at any time of year – marvellous displays of flowers in spring, shady glades in summer, the mellow russets and yellows of autumn, and the Siberian grandeur of winter.

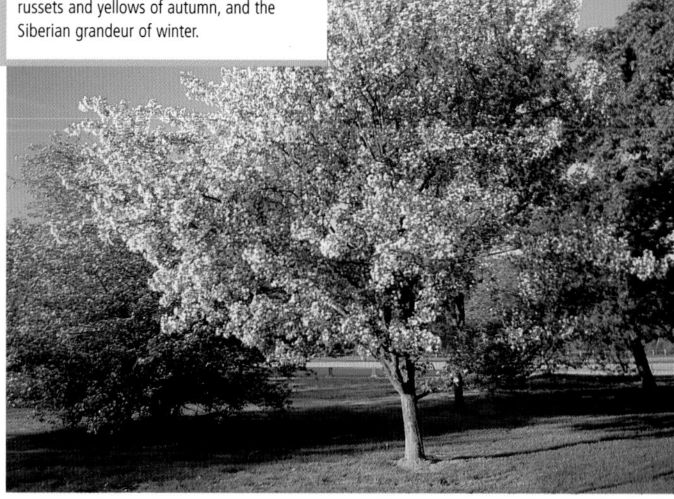

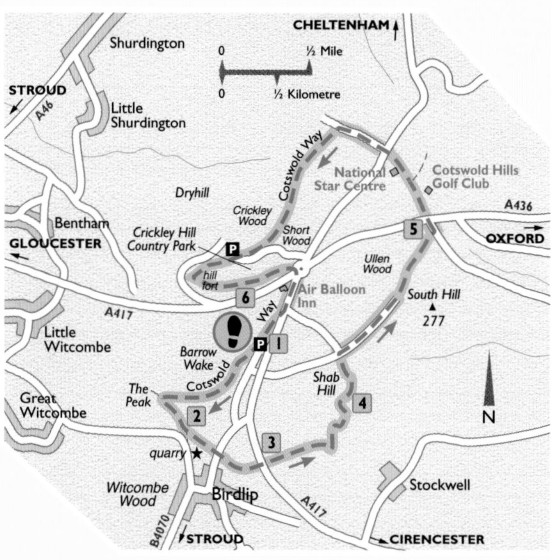

4 Follow the hedge to where it turns left and turn left along a broad, grassy swathe to a gate. Follow the lane beyond between houses to reach a road by the masts. Turn right and follow the road, but where it goes right, continue ahead, soon forking left along a metalled lane. Where the lane bears right at a mast and transformer, bear left along a track, following it downhill between deer fences to reach a road. Bear left for a few steps to the main road.

5 Cross and take the road opposite, following it past the golf club and the National Star Centre. Between the two the Cotswold Way joins from the right. Go across the next crossroads, following the Cotswold Way. When the road descends, go left up steps and follow the Way, crossing two stiles before descending into Short Wood. Stay close to the right edge, and soon go through the car-park at Crickley Hill Country Park, passing the visitor centre. Follow the Way across the hillfort to reach a wall, turning left to walk with it.

6 Go through a gate, through the ramparts of the extensively excavated fort and a wood to reach the A417 by the Air Balloon Inn. Cross the road and follow the roadside path uphill. Bear right, away from the road, but where the Cotswold Way turns right, continue along the path to return to the start.

OXFORD & THE EASTERN COTSWOLDS

The distinctive character of the Cotswolds does not respect county boundaries. Where Gloucestershire ends, the villages of honeyed limestone, watered by pretty streams and set amid rolling sheep pastures, continue east into Oxfordshire. With the well-known exceptions of Burford and Woodstock, many of these unspoilt villages, with their medieval 'wool' churches and charming cottages, are frequently and undeservedly overlooked.

Porcelain figures, part of the collection at the Ashmolean Museum in Oxford

Chipping Norton is the highest town in Oxfordshire at 650ft (197m), and as a thriving market town has a varied collection of shops, hotels and houses, mainly 18th century. It is distinguished by a large Victorian tweed mill, now converted into flats, that sits to the west of the town. This area of the Cotswolds hides villages well in its folds and on its shelves, such as Charlbury, a small, busy town that looks across the Evenlode valley in happy isolation towards Wychwood Forest. Even more concealed are the villages of Great and Little Tew, until quite recently kept in a time warp by their eccentric owner. Near by is Hook Norton, with its celebrated brewery and a waterfowl sanctuary.

Just off the A40, Burford is a sedate collection of handsome inns and charming cottages. The wide main street, lined with shops and pubs, crosses the Windrush on a medieval bridge. Quarries near

FIVE PRETTIEST COTSWOLD VILLAGES

Bibury Described by William Morris as 'the most beautiful village in England'.

Bourton-on-the-Water The Windrush flows along the main street beneath a succession of bridges, earning the village the title 'Venice of the Cotswolds'.

Broadway The handsome grass-verged main street has a host of lovely houses in Cotswold stone.

Chipping Campden Delightful village with a wealth of beautiful architecture.

Snowshill Tucked into a beautiful combe at the edge of the Cotswolds, known for its Tudor manor house.

The evening sun adds to the golden hue of Burford's 15th-century High Street

Elizabethan Kelmscott Manor, home to the artist William Morris from 1871 to 1896

Oxford Drive

DRIVE

Oxford and the East Cotswolds

START/FINISH: Oxford. Historic city off the A40/A34

DISTANCE: 69 miles (110.5km)

The sheer homeliness of Oxfordshire is its greatest asset. Gentle and unspectacular, the countryside is made up of farming land, low hills and sluggish rivers. North of Oxford's dreaming spires the tour follows a belt of limestone stretching across from the Cotswold Hills, dotted with timeless villages and small towns.

1 An ancient and picturesque university city dating back to the 8th century, Oxford sits comfortably on the rivers Cherwell and Thames. Leave the city centre by the High Street, then cross Magdalen Bridge and, at the roundabout, branch left and soon go straight on at two sets of traffic lights to climb Headington Hill. Continue through Headington then at the roundabout take the second exit (Bayswater Road), for Stanton St John. In half a mile (800m) turn right, then on reaching the T-junction, turn right then immediately left into Stanton St John.

2 Continue through the village and follow the signs to Oakley. Turn right at the B4011 then take the next left for Brill, standing 700ft (213m) above the Vale of Aylesbury. At the war memorial keep left and turn left into Windmill Street. Pass the fine 17th-century post mill and shortly join the B4011 to Blackthorn. After 3.5 miles (5.5km) turn left on to the A41.

3 Take the B4100 into Bicester and follow the one-way system around the town centre, eventually turning left at the lights on to the A34, signed Oxford. Soon turn right on to the B4030 towards Witney. After 2.5 miles (4km) enter Middleton Stoney. Cross the main road and continue for 3 miles (5km) to the edge of Lower Heyford. Turn left, cross the River Cherwell and, after a mile (1.5km), turn right on to the A4260, signed Deddington. Continue to Deddington.

4 Turn left on to the B4031 Chipping Norton road, pass through Hempton and in 3 miles (5km) turn left on to the A361. Turn left on to the B4022 and in 1 mile (1.5km) turn left on to a minor road for Great Tew. Bear right in the village then in half a mile (800m) turn right, and turn left at the next crossroads to re-join the B4022, signed Enstone. After 2.5 miles (4km) go over a staggered crossroads, skirt Enstone, and

Looking down on the spires of All Souls College, Oxford, from St Mary's Tower

by produced stone used to build some of England's finest buildings – Blenheim Palace, St Paul's Cathedral and various Oxford colleges. About 10 miles (16km) from Oxford, Blenheim Palace, designed by John Vanbrugh for the 1st Duke of Marlborough, is perhaps the greatest stately home in England, set in a stunning 2,000-acre (800-ha) park. Adjoining the gates of the palace is Woodstock, a small town of some charm and numerous antiques shops.

South of Burford is Filkins, a quiet village which has a distinctly bypassed feel about it. The village is best known for its working woollen weaving factory, one of the last in the Cotswolds. Adjoining buildings contain more workshops devoted to other traditional crafts as well as a shop.

Lechlade has an individual quality deriving from its rivers. Once it was a busy river town, being at the confluence of three waterways – the Coln, the Leach and the Thames – and at the highest navigable point on the Thames. From 1789 the Thames was linked to the Severn here by the Thames and Severn Canal. The bustle of commercial river life has long gone from Lechlade, although pleasure craft can still be hired from the boatyard near the Ha'penny Bridge. Passing Lechlade along the river bank is the Thames Path, a cycling and walking route running from the source of the Thames near Cirencester as far as the Thames Barrier in London.

Boating, especially punting – using a flat-bottomed boat pushed along by a pole – has a great tradition in Oxford. Punting mainly takes place on the River Cherwell, whereas the Thames is popular for rowing and motor-boats. Oxford, one of England's premier university cities, is famous for the 'dreaming spires' of its colleges. Built mainly in the Middle Ages from golden Cotswold stone, these ancient establishments are usually bustling with students or tourists.

LEGEND OF THE ROLLRIGHTS

There is a long-standing legend of how the Bronze-Age circle of the Rollright Stones, near Long Compton, came about. Long ago a band of soldiers met a witch who told them that if their leader were to take seven long strides and 'If Long Compton thou canst see, King of England thou shall be.' The aspiring monarch risked all, saw nothing and, along with his followers, was turned to stone, creating the stones of the circle known as the King's Men, with the now railed monolith of the King Stone standing isolated just across the road. The Whispering Knights, a nearby burial chamber, are the traitors who planned to overthrow the king once he became ruler of England.

HOT-AIR BALLOONING

Floating over the Oxford spires and the Thames Valley on a hot summer's afternoon is a tranquil way to spend a few hours. Several companies offer flights in the area: Adventure Balloons, Hot Air Balloons, Southern Flights, Virgin Balloon Flights and The Great Balloon Experience.

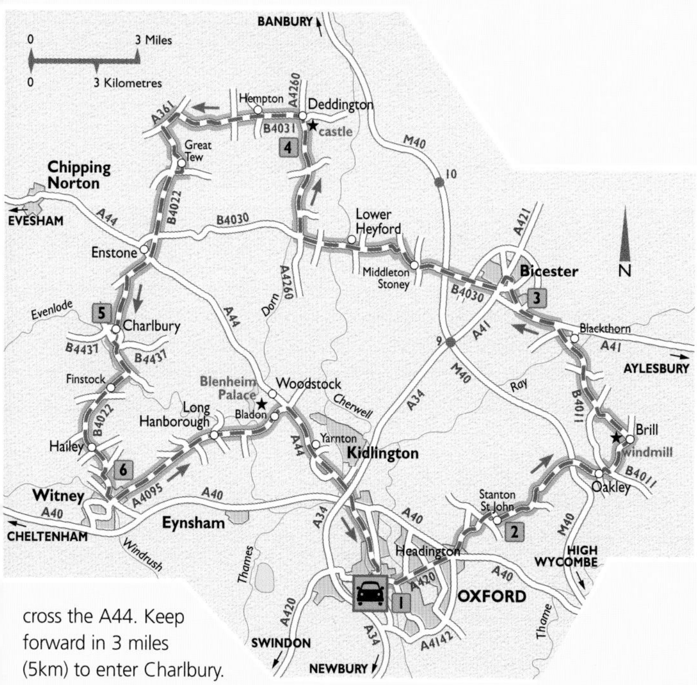

cross the A44. Keep forward in 3 miles (5km) to enter Charlbury.

5 Set in the Evenlode Valley, Charlbury is a compact little town with many narrow streets containing 18th-century buildings. Go over the staggered crossroads, signed Witney, and at the end of the town turn right, then immediately right again. Continue on the B4022 to Witney, a pleasant market town famous for making blankets.

6 Turn left at the first roundabout and then, to avoid the town centre, turn left at a double roundabout and leave by the A4095 Bicester road. Continue through Long Hanborough to Bladon. Prime minister and war leader Sir Winston Churchill, his wife and both his parents are buried in the churchyard here. Churchill was born at nearby Blenheim Palace in 1874 and, if time allows, this magnificent building and its gardens and grounds should be visited in the town of Woodstock. A mile (1.5km) beyond the village, at the junction with the A44, turn right for Oxford. In 4 miles (6.5km), keep straight on over the mini-roundabout, until you bear right to pass under the A34 at a large roundabout, and follow signs to City Centre for the return to Oxford.

THE NORTHERN COTSWOLDS & STRATFORD

Cleeve Hill, the highest point in the Cotswolds, viewed from the village of Winchcombe

The northern part of the Cotswold escarpment is higher and notable for hills offering wonderful views across the Severn Vale to Wales. Best known is Cleeve Hill, at 1,083ft (333m) the highest point in the Cotswolds, a windswept plateau straddling the way between Cheltenham and Winchcombe. This ancient common where birds, orchids and butterflies are still profuse, is a popular riding area. There is a pleasant walk across the hill to Winchcombe, an attractive little town, which in Saxon times was the capital of Mercia. Near by is the superb Sudeley Castle, which has eight delightful gardens and a wildfowl sanctuary. Close to Winchcombe is Toddington, where you can take a ride on a steam train along a restored part of the Honeybourne Line, which will eventually be reopened all the way to Cheltenham.

The landscape north of Tewkesbury is dominated by the bulk of Bredon Hill, a 960-ft (295-m) outlier (outcrop of rocks), an excellent place for rambling. At nearby Beckford, silk continues to be printed by traditional hand methods and sold in the factory shop.

On the very edge of the Cotswolds, overlooked from Cleeve Hill, is the elegant spa town of Cheltenham, celebrated for its beautiful 18th-century buildings, most notably The Promenade. Its sophisticated shops and restaurants make an irresistible outing for the shopaholic. This former Regency resort is also well known for its international festivals of music and literature, and for its racecourse.

First-class racing at the annual Cheltenham Gold Cup

CHEESE ROLLING

This strange annual ritual takes place every Spring Bank Holiday Monday on Cooper's Hill, just outside the village of **Brockworth**. Its precise origins are obscure, but it is thought to date back to the 16th century in its current form. The competitors line up across the top of the steep (1-in-3) hill, and the cheeses are launched down the slope, to be pursued hell-for-leather by the racers, whose task it is to retrieve one of them before it reaches the bottom. Anyone who does so keeps the cheese!

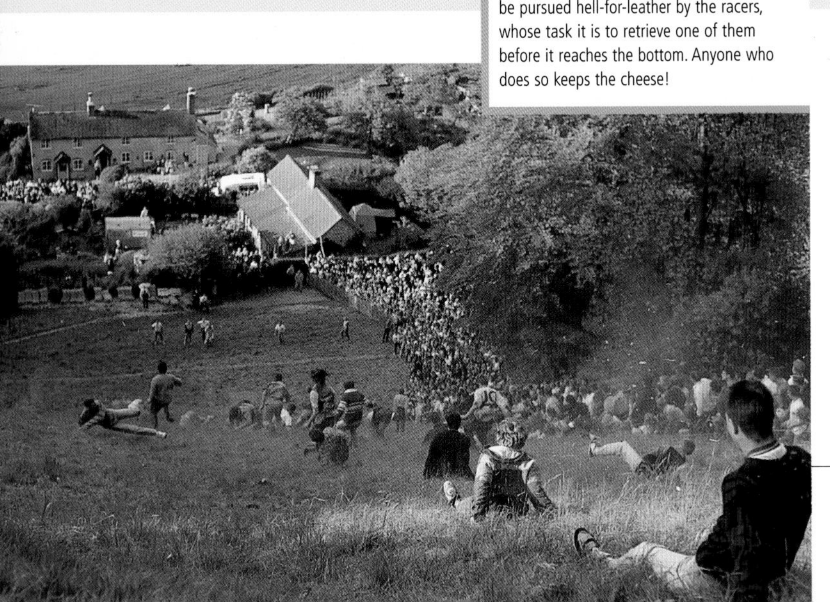

Stow Cycle Ride

CYCLE RIDE

A Cotswold Tour from Stow-on-the-Wold

START: Stow-on-the-Wold. Hilltop town located where the A424 crosses the A429 between Cheltenham and Banbury
DISTANCE: 25 miles (40km)
GRADIENT: undulating; one long climb at Little Rissington
PARKING: car-park on the south side of town, near the Bell Inn

Starting from the popular wool town of Stow-on-the-Wold, this route explores one of the loveliest corners of the Cotswolds. Look out for mud on the lanes, and don't expect to stay on your bike to the top of every hill!

1 Stow-on-the Wold is a quiet town with a large market square and a pleasing muddle of old houses and inns. Climb the main street through the town square and turn right on to the A429. Turn left at the traffic lights, then left again on to the B4077, signed Upper Swell. Descend, cross a hump-backed bridge, then climb into Upper Swell. Turn left (minor road) signed to Lower Swell, and make a steady ascent before dropping down past the church into Lower Swell. At the bottom go straight over, keeping the war memorial on your left. Turn right along the main road, then first left, signed The Slaughters. Beyond the village, fork right towards Upper Slaughter on a narrow lane (not signed).

2 After 1.5 miles (2.5km) descend into Upper Slaughter, and take the sharp right-hand bend with caution. Follow the road round to the left. Turn right down here to explore the village; otherwise, keep straight on, heading away from the river, to turn left at the T-junction. Following signs for Lower Slaughter, bear left after half a mile (800m). Enter Lower Slaughter, parallel with the river, and turn right immediately past the phone box. The road rises gently; at the top turn left, signed Bourton-on-the-Water. Turn left at the next junction, and soon reach the Fosse Way (A429). Turn right, then left into Lansdowne, following the river into the popular beauty spot of Bourton-on-the-Water.

3 Bear right at the end of the main street into Rissington Road. Pass Birdland, and climb towards Little Rissington. Climb through the village, up the long hill to reach a crossroads. Go straight over, signed to Burford, and continue for half a mile (800m) to the A424. Turn left and take the first turning right, to Church Westcote. Proceed through

On the edge of the escarpment, where the Cotswolds join the Vale of Evesham, is the charming town of Broadway, noted for its antiques shops and the 16th-century Lygon Arms. The town is overlooked by Broadway Tower, a glowering piece of Gothic folly set on a hill where you can enjoy country park walks. A few miles north is Stratford-upon-Avon. Birthplace of William Shakespeare, it attracts huge numbers of tourists, many of whom visit the Royal Shakespeare Company's theatres on the banks of the River Avon. Due south of Stratford is Chipping Campden. 'Chipping' means 'market' and the main street boasts a fine Jacobean Market Hall, together with individually embellished houses.

THE COTSWOLD WAY

The Cotswold Way is a challenging long-distance footpath of 100 miles (160km), along the western escarpment of the Cotswolds between Bath and Chipping Campden. It takes about nine days to complete if attempted in one go, otherwise it is possible to walk short sections of the route. The trail passes a number of important historical sites, and provides extensive views westwards across the Severn Valley towards Wales.

A Cotswold-style model village captivates children at Bourton-on-the-Water

On the plateau above lies windswept Stow-on-the Wold, the highest town in the Cotswolds. At the meeting point of eight roads, and lying on the Roman Fosse Way, Stow's main claim to fame was as a prosperous and busy market town. At its heart is the old market square, still surrounded by attractive pubs and coaching inns, shops and restaurants. Near by is the Cotswold Farm Park, the home of rare-breeds conservation, where there are nearly 50 breeding flocks and herds of ancient breeds of livestock.

The busiest honeypot in the area is Bourton-on-the-Water, where the River Windrush flows along the main street beneath a succession of graceful footbridges. Bourton is best avoided if rural calm is what you yearn for, but the village does have a lot to offer in the way of attractions, including a bird zoo and a motor museum.

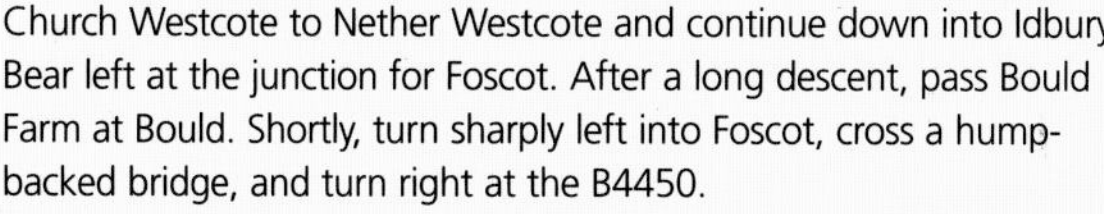

Church Westcote to Nether Westcote and continue down into Idbury. Bear left at the junction for Foscot. After a long descent, pass Bould Farm at Bould. Shortly, turn sharply left into Foscot, cross a hump-backed bridge, and turn right at the B4450.

4 Cross the railway by Kingham Station, then where the main road bends right, bear left towards Kingham. Follow the road into the village, passing St Andrew's Church and the post office, and follow signs for Daylesford and Cornwell. Ignore the left turn to Stow and proceed straight ahead. Pass Kingham Hill School, then at the crossroads, turn left to reach the A436 in almost a mile (1km).

5 Bear left towards Stow, then take the right turn to Adlestrop. Take the first left and tour round the village. Carry on left on to the main lane, heading for Broadwell. Turn left before Evenlode, crossing the railway and the river, to reach Broadwell. Turn right into the village, signed to Stow. Soon turn left signed Stow, go round the village green, turning left again. After a mile (1.5km), turn left at the A429 into Stow-on-the-Wold. Pass through the traffic lights and turn left for the town square.

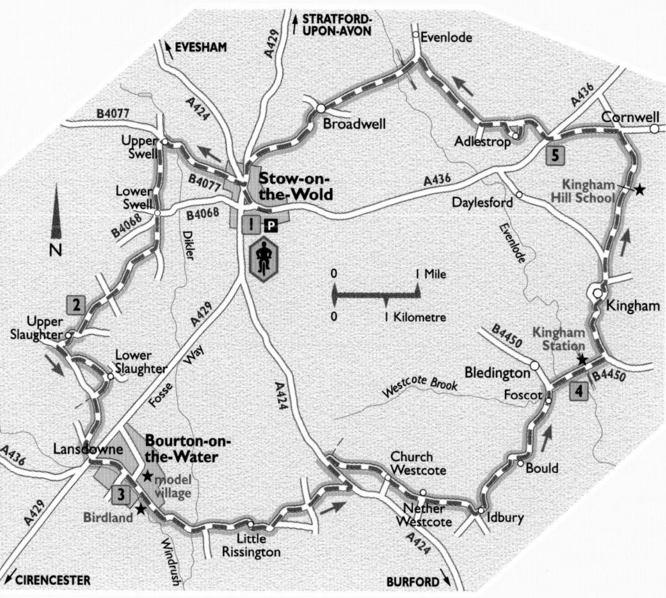

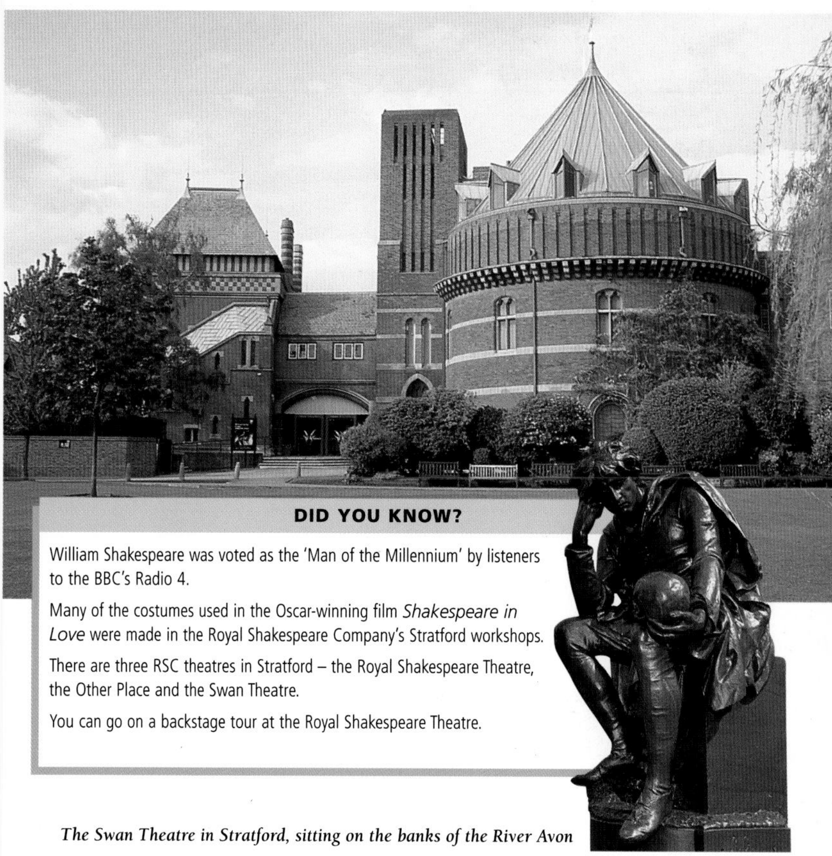

DID YOU KNOW?

William Shakespeare was voted as the 'Man of the Millennium' by listeners to the BBC's Radio 4.

Many of the costumes used in the Oscar-winning film *Shakespeare in Love* were made in the Royal Shakespeare Company's Stratford workshops.

There are three RSC theatres in Stratford – the Royal Shakespeare Theatre, the Other Place and the Swan Theatre.

You can go on a backstage tour at the Royal Shakespeare Theatre.

The Swan Theatre in Stratford, sitting on the banks of the River Avon

HEREFORDSHIRE & SHROPSHIRE

The border country of Herefordshire and Shropshire contains some of the finest of England's countryside, which together with the great cathedral cities of Worcester and Hereford still has the air of medieval timelessness. Bracketed by the breezy summits of the Malvern Hills in the south and the rugged, heather-covered heights of the Shropshire Hills in the north, the mighty River Severn runs like a silvery thread from north to south along the eastern edge of this rich, pastoral countryside, past half-timbered gems such as Tewkesbury teetering on the edge of the Cotswolds. In sharp contrast, the very foundations of British industrial society were forged at Ironbridge, now a World Heritage Site, and near by, the new town of Telford and the busy towns of Bridgnorth, Kidderminster and Stourbridge are all testimony to industrial development.

The Iron Bridge
The graceful, airy cast-iron structure of the world's first iron bridge was designed by Thomas Pritchard and assembled at Ironbridge over the River Severn by Abraham Darby III in 1777, using 370 tons of iron cast in his furnaces at nearby Coalbrookdale. The bridge was constructed using carpentry joints, since bolts and rivets had not been invented.

BRIDGNORTH CLIFF RAILWAY

The Bridgnorth Cliff Railway has been taking people between Bridgnorth's Low Town, which sits on the banks of the Severn, and High Town, perched on a sandstone cliff rising sheer from the opposite river bank, since 1892. It operates twin carriages on parallel tracks, connected by a pair of steel cables. The carriages counterbalance each other, so that when one is at the top, the other is at the bottom. At least 150 trips are made daily by this simple, yet efficient system.

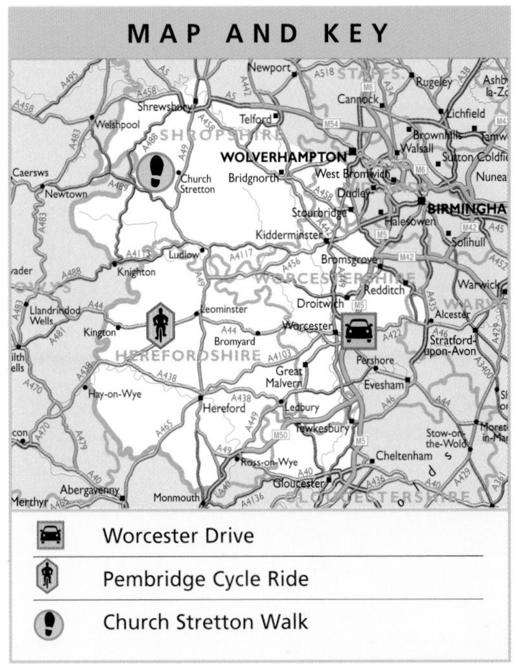

The Mappa Mundi
The greatest treasures of Hereford Cathedral are its chained library and the 14th-century Mappa Mundi, one of the earliest known maps of the world. As with most maps of that period, it shows Jerusalem at the centre of the known world, and many strange creatures around the edges. It is now housed in a special darkened exhibition.

Severn Valley Railway
The 16-mile (26-km) Severn Valley Railway follows an idyllic stretch of the western bank of the River Severn between Bridgnorth and Kidderminster. With stops at Hampton Loade, Highley, Arley and Bewdley, the line and its period stations are regularly featured as the backdrop for films and TV programmes.

WORCESTER & THE MALVERN HILLS

The mighty River Severn is the ribbon that binds together these lush fields, bordered by the whaleback spine of the Malvern Hills to the west and Bredon Hill and the Cotswolds to the east. Rising dramatically from the surrounding countryside, the impressive miniature mountain range of the Malvern Hills was an inspiration for the composer, Edward Elgar, who was born in their shadow at Lower Broadheath. Now you can follow a signposted Elgar Route by car, or take the 'Elgar Variations' cycle routes around the Malverns.

The Malverns stand on the border between upland and lowland Britain, and the views from their 5-mile (8-km) ridge are stunning. They played an important role in Britain's early history as the Herefordshire Beacon, rising dramatically to 1,114ft (340m), made a splendid lookout point. It was the site of an impressive Iron-Age hillfort, known as the British Camp. Formed from ancient pre-Cambrian rocks, the name 'The Malverns' – from the Welsh 'Moel Bryn' or 'bald' (i.e. treeless) hill – echoes their frontier role.

A view of the 11th-century church in the former spa town of Great Malvern

THE SEVERN WAY

The Severn Way is claimed to be the longest riverside walk in Britain. It is a 210-mile (337-km) long-distance footpath which follows the River Severn from its source in the peaty wastes of Plynlimon in mid Wales to finally reach the sea at Bristol. Passing through **Worcester**, **Tewkesbury** and **Gloucester**, it features some of the most beautiful scenery in the Midlands, and is waymarked throughout with the symbol of an old Severnside sailing trow.

There are excellent walks all over the Malverns, but be prepared for a stiff climb!

Sprawling on the lower slopes of these dramatic hills is the spa town of Great Malvern. With its rambling houses and steeply climbing streets, the town retains an air of faded gentility. Its neighbours of

MALVERN HILLS

The 10-mile (16-km) stretch of the Malvern Hills ridge is one of the finest walks you can take in the Midlands, with wonderful views to the broad plain of the Severn Valley to the east and the hills of Wales to the west. The ridge starts from the highest point of the **Worcestershire Beacon** (1,385ft/422m) in the north and crosses Wyche Cutting to Wynds Point then on to the British Camp on **Herefordshire Beacon**, before continuing to **Midsummer Hill**, where there is another Iron-Age hillfort.

Worcester Drive

DRIVE

East Worcestershire

START/FINISH: Worcester. Cathedral city located off the M5 (J7) between Cheltenham and Birmingham

DISTANCE: 59 miles (95km)

Gently undulating countryside, watered by small rivers and streams between the Severn and Avon, reaches a hillier climax in the north at the Clent and Waseley Hills. Woodlands, historic houses and attractive villages with half-timbered or mellow brick cottages add their charms to this leisurely drive.

1 The ancient city of Worcester, compact enough to wander round comfortably, is rich in old buildings, in particular timber-framed Greyfriars (NT) built in 1480 and now housing a folk museum. Leave Worcester on the A44 towards Evesham. At a roundabout keep left along the A422, signed Stratford-upon-Avon. Pass Spetchley Park Gardens and continue through Broughton Hackett to Inkberrow. In a mile (1.5km) take the second turning left (B4092), signed to Redditch, then turn left along a minor road towards Feckenham and Bradley Green. Shortly, turn left on to the B4090 (no sign) to Feckenham.

2 Continue on the Droitwich road to Hanbury, and turn sharp right (B4091) towards Bromsgrove to pass the road to Hanbury Hall, a William and Mary style red-brick house (1701). Go forward through Stoke Prior and pass the Avoncroft Museum of Historic Buildings. At Stoke Heath, turn right on to the A38 towards Birmingham. At the roundabout, continue ahead, signed Birmingham, to the junction with the M42. Take the first exit on the roundabout to the junction with the M5. At the roundabout take the second exit (A491) for Stourbridge, and in half a mile (800m) turn right along the B4551, signed Romsley.

3 Pass the road towards Waseley Hills Country Park and in 1 mile (1.5km), at the start of the descent, turn left on an unclassified road towards Clent. At the trunk road, turn left and in a mile (1.5km) turn left again into Chapel Lane, signed Clent. At the crossroads turn right, signed Lower Clent, and at the Fountain Inn, turn left towards Broome. At the roundabout, take the first exit for Bromsgrove and at the crossroads turn right into Belbroughton Road, for Belbroughton. Go forward on to the B4188, and at the end branch left on an unclassified road for Chaddesley Corbett. At the far end turn right along the A448 Kidderminster road.

Malvern Wells and Edward Elgar's resting place Little Malvern, which climbs up the hills to the pass of Wynds Point, contain many villas built at the height of its health-spa heyday.

Worcester, dominated by its beautiful cathedral, is a city rich in ancient buildings, such as the Guildhall, the Tudor House Museum and the Commandery. This fine 15th-century timber-framed building was the headquarters of Charles II's army during the Battle of Worcester in 1651 and is now England's only Civil War Centre. This area played a critical role in the Civil War and it is possible to take 'Battle walks' around Worcester and nearby Tewkesbury. Worcester is also famous for its porcelain and the world's largest collection is displayed at the Dyson Perrins Museum, next door to the Royal Worcester factory which has an excellent shop for bargains in china and glass.

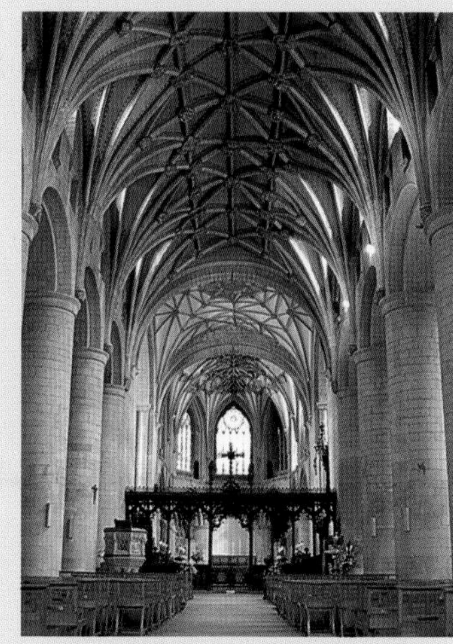

The elegant vaulted nave of Tewkesbury's Norman abbey

Here, as at Tewkesbury and Gloucester, the River Severn provides endless activity and a variety of river craft can be hired: row or paddle boats for the more energetic, or take a river steamer for the longer but more leisurely view. Along the banks is the clearly marked route of the Severn Way, for cyclists and walkers.

Composer Edward Elgar's grave at St Wulstan's Church in Little Malvern

Ledbury, with its leaning, half-timbered cottages and narrow winding alleyways, is for many people the quintessential small English market town. Ledbury has long been a favourite place for poets and painters, from Wordsworth to the Brownings. Hops are widely grown in this fertile region as proclaimed by Worcester's Hop Market and Ledbury's popular Hop Fair which celebrates the harvest. There are also many craft centres selling decorative items created from hops and other local produce. Near Ledbury, in the grounds of Eastnor, a fairy-tale castle, there are some excellent nature trails through an arboretum, a deer park and by a lake.

4 At the Mustow Green roundabout take the first exit (A450), signed Worcester, and in 2 miles (3km) at the roundabout, go forward. Go under the railway bridge, turn left on to the A449, and then turn right on to the B4193, signed Stourport, to Hartlebury. Bear right and pass the turning to Hartlebury Castle on the right, the historic home of the bishops of Worcester. At the roundabout go forward along the A4025. Shortly, turn left (one way) and follow the Town Centre signs into Stourport-on-Severn, England's only town created directly as the consequence of a canal: the Staffordshire and Worcestershire Canal.

5 Leave on the A451, signed Great Witley, cross the River Severn and turn left on to the B4196 for Worcester. Pass through Shrawley and Holt Heath, proceeding over the crossroads on to the A443 to Hallow. Shortly, join the A44 and enter Worcester.

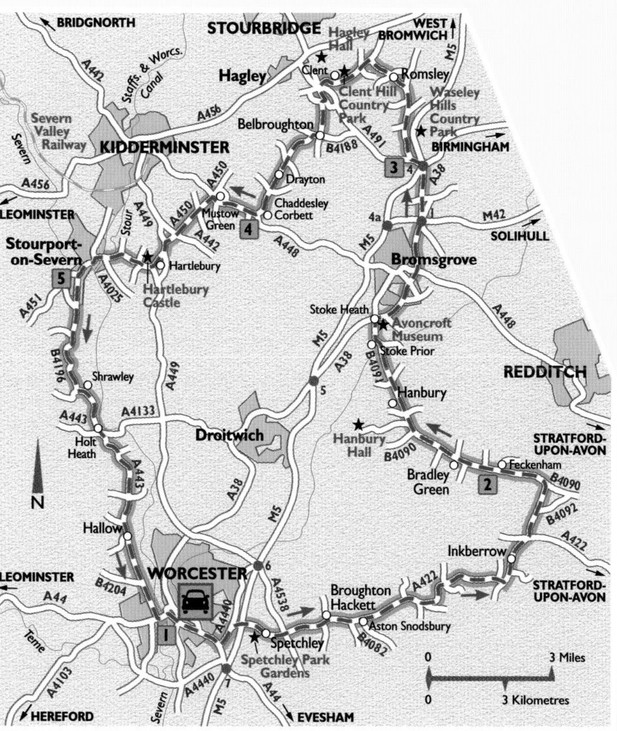

THREE CHOIRS FESTIVAL

The Three Choirs Festival has featured the choirs of **Worcester** (below), **Gloucester** and **Hereford** cathedrals for over 300 years. Held annually in August at each of the cathedrals in turn, it provides a musical and cultural link between the three cities. Walkers can now make their own link by following the 100-mile (160-km) **Three Choirs Way** through the beautiful Severnside countryside between the three cities.

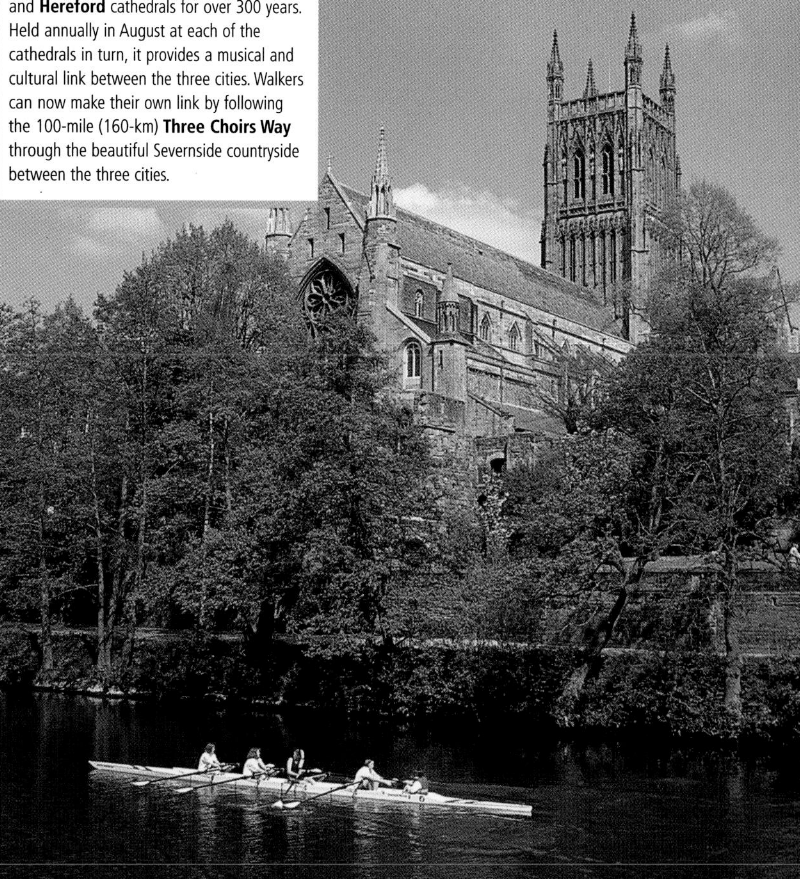

THE UPPER WYE VALLEY & HEREFORD

The meandering River Wye coils down through green pastureland as it makes its way south from the Black Mountains of Wales, winding through Herefordshire to the Forest of Dean. This is prime agricultural land, where the dusty red soil matches the sandstone of the rocks and the coats of the Hereford cattle.

The River Wye, as it twists and turns through the county, is a constant artery. Its ever-changing nature provides the opportunity for many activities, from kayaking, canoeing and white-water rafting to trips on pleasure craft around the towns of Hereford and Ross-on-Wye. Along the banks there are places to enjoy abseiling or follow the Wye Valley Walk on foot or by bike. In the shelter of the Black Mountains lies the Golden Valley, an area celebrated for its unspoilt nature. The hilly terrain of western Herefordshire gives opportunities for caving, mountain biking, gorge walking and horse-trekking.

A local craftsman at the medieval village of Pembridge fashions a terracotta pot

The first town on the river is Hay-on-Wye, famous throughout the world as the premier venue for second-hand books. The narrow streets are crowded with bookshops, stalls and shoppers, giving it a lively air, especially when the International Festival of Literature is being held.

Hereford is the bustling county town with a thriving arts and crafts centre. Its small Norman cathedral, with its great forest of pink sandstone columns lining the nave, is one of the

A timber-framed house in Hay-on-Wye doubles as a bookshop and B&B

A riverside view of Ross-on-Wye, with the spire of St Mary's Church in the distance

Pembridge Cycle Ride

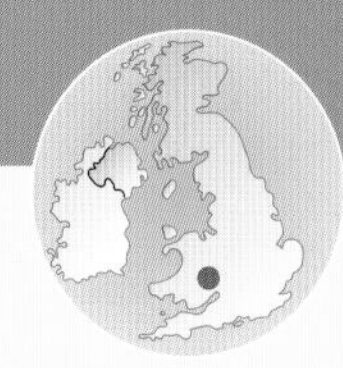

CYCLE RIDE

The Black-and-White Villages

START: Pembridge. Village on the A44 7 miles (11km) west of Leominster
DISTANCE: 27 miles (43km)
GRADIENT: level
ROADS: country lanes; short stretches of main road
PARKING: public car-park behind Visitor Centre

This route is an easy, level tour around several of the best-known and most attractive black-and-white villages of Herefordshire. The route threads through a network of quiet, well-surfaced country lanes around Pembridge and Weobley.

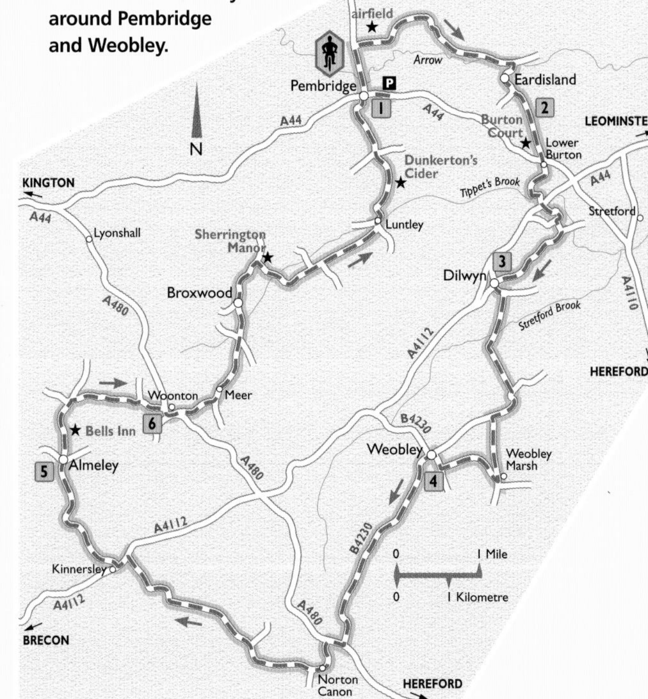

Real Herefordshire Cider
Direct from the Orchard
WILLIAM PULLING & Co., HEREFORD.
ESTABLISHED 1780.

finest in England. Hereford Cathedral has a magnificent chained library, claimed to be the largest in the world, containing some 1,500 volumes, each attached to its bookcase with an individual chain.

The area is traditionally celebrated for its fruit growing and orchards form a distinctive feature throughout rural Herefordshire, Shropshire and Worcestershire. Apples are the most well-known crop and this is famous cider country. There is plenty of opportunity to visit cider-makers to sample the produce and buy. More recent additions to the fruit crop are grapes for winemaking. Along the Three Choirs Way a few vineyards offer a similar opportunity for tasting.

THE CIDER ROUTE

The orchards of Herefordshire are the home of real cider. The combination of specially grown cider apples, soft Herefordshire water and the traditional skills of the cider-makers have won the county its reputation. Visitors can follow the Cider Route and visit places such as **Bulmer's Cider Mill and Visitor Centre**, the **Cider Museum** and **King Offa Distillery** (which produces cider brandy).

The top five traditional cider and perry producers include:

Lyne Down Farm, Much Marcle – tiny producer making only 35 barrels annually using a 100-year-old mill.

Westons Cider, Much Marcle – family business founded in 1880 and making award-winning ciders and perries.

Dunkerton's of Pembridge – superb ciders, including the single varietal Kingston Black.

Franklins Cider Farm Shop, Little Hereford – ciders and perries from apples and pears grown in the Teme Valley.

Broome Farm, Peterstown – naturally produced cider from orchards on the slopes of the Wye Valley.

Another fine Herefordshire market town is Ross-on-Wye, standing on a bluff overlooking a sweeping meander of the River Wye, with marvellous views across to the Welsh hills to the west. There are splendid views, too, of the Wye Valley from The Prospect, near the churchyard.

To the north of Hereford are many small villages celebrated for their black-and-white style, among them Eardisland, reputed to be the prettiest village in the Midlands. These villages were protected from the border disputes between the Welsh and the English by Offa's Dyke, which runs all along the Welsh border.

Leominster (pronounced 'Lemster') is an old wool town lying amid hopfields and orchards of cider apples on the River Lugg. The fine-textured wool, known as Lemster Ore, was the source of the town's medieval wealth, and sheep farming is still important in the area. The town is an antiques hunter's dream, with numerous shops, many still offering the possibility of a bargain.

HEREFORDSHIRE TRAILS

Lower Wye Valley Walk – 112 miles (180km) between Chepstow and the source.

Mortimer Trail – 30 miles (48km) between Ludlow and Kington.

Three Choirs Way – 100 miles (160km) linking Hereford, Gloucester and Worcester.

Marches Way – 60 miles (96km) between Orleton and Pandy.

Offa's Dyke – 177 miles (285km) between Prestatyn and Chepstow.

SEE CONTACTS SECTION FOR ADDITIONAL INFORMATION

1 Before setting off take a closer look at the village, especially the old wool market behind the timbered New Inn, and the church with its unusual detached timber bell-tower. Take the road north towards Shobdon, cross the River Arrow and in half a mile (800m) turn right just before the old railway station (narrow lane). Pass Shobdon airfield on the left. In 2.5 miles (4km) at Eardisland, turn right at the T-junction to ride through the village and turn left, signed Burton Court.

2 Pass the 18th-century mansion of Burton Court, on the right and cross the A44 towards Lower Burton. Pass a narrow track on the left and bear right, then turn off left opposite a yellow hydrant and driveway on to a narrow lane. On reaching the A4112, cross straight over (with care) and follow the lane opposite. In 875yds (800m), opposite a pair of garages, turn left (just before Beaford B&B), then right at the next T-junction and continue for 1 mile (1.5km) into Dilwyn.

3 In Dilwyn bear left on to the main road at the church. Turn left towards Stretford at the village green, then in a short distance turn off right towards Weobley Marsh. After 1.5 miles (2.5km) turn right at the T-junction, then in half a mile (800m) turn left to pass through Weobley Marsh, a traditional village common complete with grazing animals. Just after the common turn right towards Weobley, then turn right at the T-junction into Weobley, and soon bear left for the village square, passing the Unicorn Inn.

4 Ride down the main square, bear left by the Red Lion Hotel and, at the T-junction, turn left along the B4230 towards Hereford. In 3 miles (5km) turn right (A480) towards Lyonshall, then in half a mile (800m) turn left for Norton Canon. Proceed for 3.5 miles (5.5km) to the A4112 near Kinnersley, turning left towards Brecon, then shortly right into the narrow lane to Almeley. This quiet village offers a seat next to the village pump, and views across to the Black Mountains.

5 Pass the Bells Inn and three-quarters of a mile (1km) beyond the village turn right, beside a stone wall immediately before a green, and follow this narrow lane to the A480 at Woonton.

6 Turn right and soon fork left into a lane to Meer and Broxwood. Go left at the next T-junction and continue through Broxwood. In half a mile (800m) turn right towards Sherrington Manor, and continue for 2 miles (3km) to Luntley. Turn left here to pass a much-restored dovecote (1673), then cross the bridge and turn right towards Dunkerton's Cider. Continue for 2 miles (3km), past the cider company, back to Pembridge.

One of the area's renowned black-and-white thatched cottages at Leominster

SHREWSBURY, TELFORD & THE UPPER SEVERN VALLEY

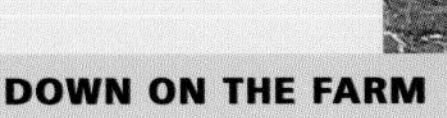

DOWN ON THE FARM

Acton Scott Working Farm and Museum near **Little Stretton** is a marvellous place for children and adults to experience farming as it was in the Shropshire hills before the days of tractors and combine harvesters. Shire horses are used for most of the heavy work, such as ploughing and pulling carts, and there is a range of farming and craft demonstrations in a lovely setting.

Shropshire life is governed by the influence of the apparently endless River Severn in the east and its 'blue remembered hills' of Long Mynd, Caer Caradoc, The Stiperstones and Wenlock Edge, with the Clee Hills to the west. It is a surprisingly wild part of the Midlands, where heather-covered hills rise dramatically from steep-sided valleys, and where fortified houses tell of a troubled past.

The towns that grew up along the Severn's arterial highway flourished through hundreds of years of trade: Kidderminster, Bridgnorth and Shrewsbury. But in the 18th century Ironbridge burst on to the scene, becoming the heart of the Industrial Revolution, while in the 1970s Telford new town was created to accommodate Birmingham's expanding population. The river still provides activity, but now it is for leisure pursuits such as canoeing, sailing or fishing – all of which are easily available.

A sculpted head from the ruins of Wenlock Priory

The pretty, Severnside town of Bridgnorth is divided into two parts – High Town and Low Town – and they are linked by the famous Cliff Railway, which has been transporting people up and down the 111-ft (34-m) sandstone cliff since 1892. Alternatively, the energetic – or very fit – can climb the seven 'stairways to heaven', which were cut in the rock in earlier times so goods could be carried up from the busy river port below. This enchanting town is also the base and northern terminus of the 16-mile (25.5-km) Severn Valley Railway. This steam railway follows the river from Kidderminster, halting at Severn

A DREAM CASTLE

Stokesay Castle is a perfect, romantic example of a 13th-century fortified manor house which stands frozen in time at the end of a lane. Its North Tower is uniquely topped with a half-timbered construction, the earliest part of the house, begun around 1240. It has a massive polygonal South Tower (1291) and an Elizabethan gatehouse, and was the home of the Say and Ludlow families, before passing to the Cravens (of Craven Arms) and the Baldwyns from nearby Diddlebury.

Church Stretton Walk

WALK

Over the Long Mynd

START/FINISH: Church Stretton. On the A49 between Shrewsbury and Ludlow

DISTANCE: 9 miles (14.5km)

ASCENT/GRADIENT: 1,150ft (350m); fairly steep early on, gentler ascent to the top

TERRAIN/PATHS: heather moorlands buttressed by steep hill slopes; mostly clear, firm paths; some boggy areas

PARKING: car-parks on Easthope Road

The long, heathery crest of this rugged mountain remains markedly wilder than the surrounding cultivated lowlands. To climb the Long Mynd and trek its moorlands is to appreciate the true scale and wilderness qualities of the place.

1 Church Stretton assumed its current form in Victorian and Edwardian times, while the railway brought tourists into the area, who were quick to discover the Carding Mill Valley and the heather-covered moorland of the Long Mynd. From the car-park, leave town by walking along the Shrewsbury Road. Turn left into a road signed Carding Mill Valley and golf course. Fork right up a winding road at Trevor Hill, eventually turning left to reach the golf course. Go through the gate to the right of the clubhouse marked Public Footpath to the Hills. Turn right and walk alongside beeches, then turn left and follow marker posts up a valley and across the golf course. The path runs around the head of a valley and passes a shelter, then climbs a rise before heading off to the left. Keep following the marker posts, passing a black hut, until you overlook the Carding Mill Valley scored into the moorland hills.

2 Go through a gate at the top of the golf course, bear right and follow a path gently uphill, around Haddon Hill. Use the most well-trodden path. Cross two boggy patches and step over a tiny stream a little further on. The path descends slightly and crosses a wider, fast-flowing stream before continuing to contour round the hillside. Negotiate another stream, turn left uphill on a faint path to intercept a wide track.

3 Turn left and rise along the broad track over extensive heather moorlands. Ignore other paths, keeping to the broad track. At one junction there is a view down Carding Mill Valley to Church Stretton. Keep straight on, rising gently to reach a complex junction. Simply step to the right to follow a narrow track uphill. The track leads finally to the top

Valley country park so passengers can have access for walks.

Ironbridge, with its elegant, eponymous bridge, the first of its kind to span any river, is now a World Heritage Site. While further upstream, Shrewsbury stands on an enormous loop of the River Severn, which is crossed by two bridges – the English and the Welsh – reflecting its role as a border town. It is full of romantic, half-timbered houses, with an equal wealth of fine Georgian buildings.

Scattered among the hilly countryside are many attractive villages and towns, linked by quiet twisting lanes that keep the outside world at bay. A well-known 'magpie' village is Much Wenlock, a pretty settlement at the northern end of Wenlock Edge. Wenlock Edge is a deeply wooded 10-mile (16-km) escarpment of limestone to the south of Much Wenlock. It is a splendid viewpoint for the Shropshire Hills and an excellent location for horse-riding. Riding is a particularly good way to see this area and there are numerous stables for hiring horses. Much Wenlock is crossed by the Jack Mytton Way, a 72-mile (115-km) trail also covering Long Mynd and the Welsh Borders. This trail is just part of the 3,000 miles (4,800km) of walks across hills, along lakes and canals, and through the lovely towns of Shropshire.

One of Britain's best-preserved medieval towns, Ludlow, has a wealth of black-and-white houses and a massive red-sandstone castle. Sited on the confluence of three rivers, the town is well known as an activity centre and has a reputation for some particularly fine restaurants. Church Stretton is the capital of Shropshire's hill country, situated at the eastern end of the Carding Mill Valley, one of the most beautiful of the approaches to the Long Mynd, a 10-mile (16-km) whaleback hill, which looms over the town. Cheerful tearooms and a range of shops are a feature of this pleasant little village. The Mynd is the most southerly grouse moor in England, with plentiful heather on the broad plateau.

STEPPING BACK IN TIME

You will need a full day to explore the **Ironbridge Gorge Museum** (above), which includes the original hearths used by the Darby family for smelting, the houses where their workers lived, and the inclined plane which took materials down from the Shropshire Canal to a wharf on the Severn. The **Blists Hill Open-Air Museum**, a re-created town of the 1890s covering 42 acres (17ha), enables visitors to really step back in time and experience how people lived and worked. Two miles (3km) downstream at **Coalport** there is a museum on the site of the original Coalport China Works.

of the Long Mynd (1,696ft/517m). There is a trig point and a toposcope. Walk straight on down to a narrow road and turn right. After passing Pole Cottage (a black hut surrounded by trees) take a grassy path on the left.

4 The path curves right and, after about 440yds (400m), joins a broad, grassy track. In bad visibility you can follow the road for another 220yds (200m) and join this track where it leaves the road. Follow the track as it rises over Round Hill then descends to a saddle. The path rises to the right, then goes round a steep slope to reach another saddle. The gentle gradient eventually gives way to a steep descent to a gate by a stream. Ford the stream and cross a footbridge to reach a lane.

5 Turn right along the lane, then left and left again in Little Stretton. Note All Saint's Church at the crossroads, with the Ragleth Inn opposite. Follow the road as it passes through fields to return to Church Stretton.

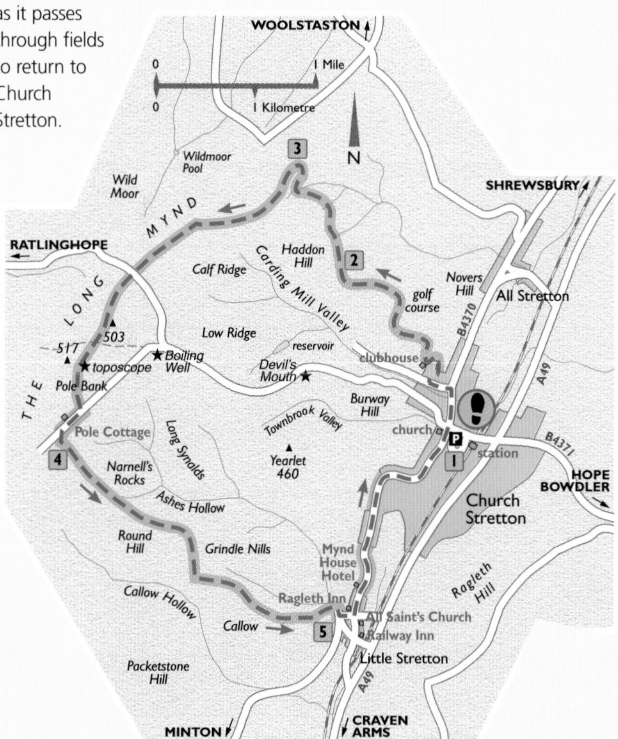

Looking across the banks of the River Severn to the railway town of Bridgnorth

THE MIDLANDS

The Midland shires are truly at the very heart of England. In many minds they are dominated by the urban sprawl of Birmingham, the Black Country and the West Midlands conurbation. However, this region still retains much beautiful countryside extending into leafy Warwickshire and Northamptonshire in the south and to the heath-covered heights of Cannock Chase in the north. Warwickshire is known for its stately homes and magnificent castles, such as Warwick and Kenilworth, and for its magnificent trees, whose ancestors were once part of the Forest of Arden. The huge web of peaceful canals which cross the area, once the arteries of Britain's industrial past, have been restored as leisure routes and the former coalfields of Leicestershire, Staffordshire and Derbyshire are slowly being transformed into the new, amenity-led National Forest. The ancient cities of Birmingham and Coventry have come through the Industrial Revolution to reinvent themselves as thriving cultural and entertainment centres.

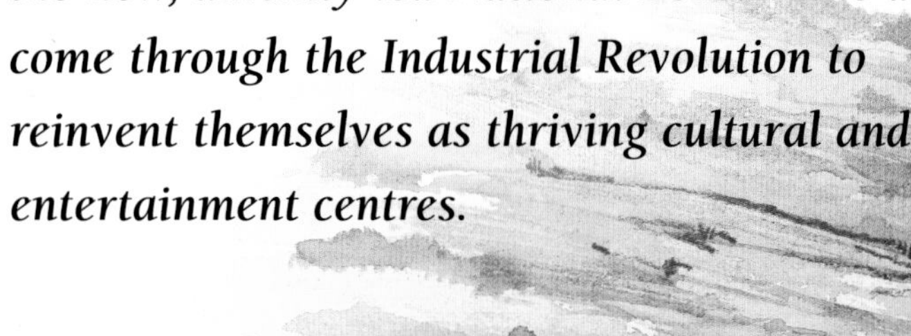

COVENTRY CATHEDRAL

Rising phoenix-like from the ashes of the 1940 Blitz, Sir Basil Spence's magnificent new Coventry Cathedral has been voted Britain's most popular modern building. Completed in 1962, this wonderful, airy cathedral is filled with the work of some of Britain's finest craftsmen, from Graham Sutherland's superb altar tapestry to John Piper's engraved west window.

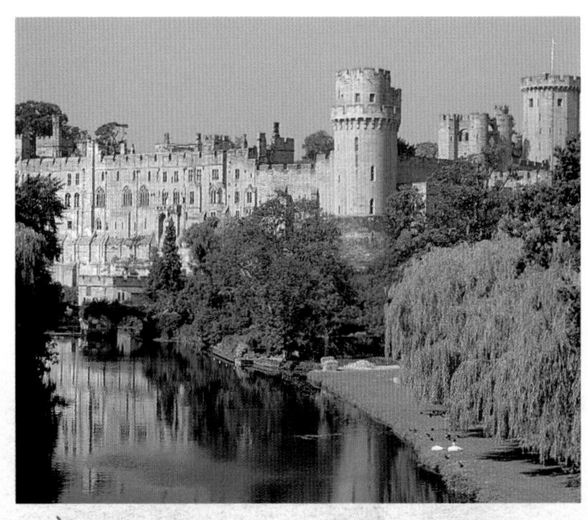

Warwick Castle

The magnificent sight of Warwick Castle's turrets and battlements rising above the River Avon is a 'must see' on any Midland explorer's list. Originally a Saxon fortification, the castle was adapted by successive earls of Warwick into the wonderfully complete medieval fortress we see today, and which has become one of the most visited places in the Midlands.

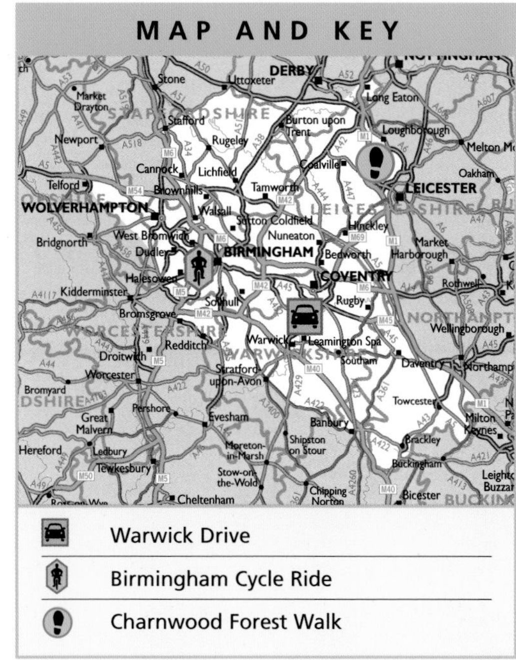

The Thrill of the Chase

Cannock Chase was once a Norman hunting ground, and still has fallow and red deer which thrive in the unspoilt environment. Several vantage points – Coppice Hill, the Hednesford Hills, and the Castle Ring Iron-Age hillfort – offer excellent views across the Chase and the Trent Valley for walkers, cyclists and riders. The Forestry Commission has waymarked several routes to aid exploration of the Chase and there is a visitor centre at Marquis Drive.

ART IN THE CITY

The Birmingham City Museum and Art Gallery, located in Chamberlain Square in the heart of the city, has one of the world's finest collections of Pre-Raphaelite art. Works by artists such as Rossetti, Burne-Jones and Millais are held here, in a collection which successive city councils have amassed over many years, and which today is often in demand internationally.

THE HEART OF ENGLAND

Amid the Midlands countryside are many pleasant surprises including, at Kenilworth and Warwick, two of the finest castles in the country – one a romantic ruin, the other hardly changed in hundreds of years. Perhaps the most unexpected joy is the wealth of unspoiled, pretty villages throughout Warwickshire, Northamptonshire and Leicestershire. As soon as you leave the main roads, you will quickly discover some delightful villages such as Hampton Lucy, Stoneleigh or Foxton.

An unusual way to explore the area is via the West Midlands Way, 152-mile (245-km) circular long-distance walk that encompasses the conurbation of the West Midlands. It runs between Birmingham and Coventry, passing through Warwickshire and visiting Berkswell and Kenilworth, and starting and finishing from the cross on the village green at Meriden.

Coventry, so often dismissed as industrial sprawl, has also retained some medieval streets and has a wonderful modern cathedral. Coventry's most celebrated citizen is probably Lady Godiva, who rode naked through the city in protest at the heavy taxes imposed by her Saxon husband, Earl Leofric. Reflecting Coventry's reputation as the birthplace of Britain's motor industry is the Museum of British Road Transport, close to the city centre, which contains over 400 vehicles.

Vintage vehicles at Coventry's Museum of British Road Transport

Warwick is a small town of great historical importance, noted above all for its magnificent castle, which is in a miraculous state of preservation. Set on an outcrop towering above the River Avon, with huge towers, ramparts and crenellated walls, it is every child's vision of a medieval castle. A short walk brings you to the town centre, an attractive mix of Georgian and medieval architecture. Both Warwick and nearby Royal Leamington Spa have an excellent selection of small, individual shops offering a choice of unusual goods. Leamington was once a fashionable spa town with seven springs

Lady Godiva's statue takes pride of place in Coventry city centre

The superb 15th-century Beauchamp Chapel in St Mary's Church, Warwick

Warwick Drive

DRIVE

Canals and Castles at England's Centre

START/FINISH: Warwick. Historic town off the A46 15 miles (24km) south of Coventry

DISTANCE: 53 miles (85km)

In England's heartland a great castle stands above the River Avon, Regency terraces grace a royal spa and farming research is conducted in the grounds of a Georgian mansion.

1 The majestic walls and towers of 14th-century Warwick Castle rear above the town, where Georgian houses built after a fire in 1694 blend happily with buildings which survived the blaze. Attractions at the castle include the grand State Rooms, the Great Hall, and the gloomy dungeon and torture chamber. In the town, look out for the Lord Leycester Hospital, a series of fine half-timbered buildings that were built in the late 14th century and adapted to almshouses by the Earl of Leycester in 1571. From Warwick town centre, take the A429. Turn left at the Crown and Castle pub, then turn right on to the B4115 to Stoneleigh.

2 Turn right into Birmingham Road in the pretty village of Stoneleigh, with its timber-framed houses and cottages standing on high grassy banks in the main street. The original abbey at Stoneleigh was founded in around 1154 by Cistercian monks. In the grounds of the present 13th-century abbey is the National Agricultural Centre, where research is carried out into farming techniques. Turn right on to the B4113, then after half a mile (800m) turn left to reach Baginton, signed Coventry. Just outside Baginton, on Coventry Road, is The Lunt, a reconstructed turf and timber Roman fort from around the end of the 1st century. An Interpretation Centre is housed in the granary. At the T-junction turn right on to the A45, signed to Birmingham. In 445yds (400m) turn around at the roundabout to travel back on the A44, signed Coventry.

3 Take the A45 to Ryton-on-Dunsmore. Turn right and then left (B4455) to reach Stretton-on-Dunsmore after 7 miles (11.5km). It is a peaceful village with a tiny triangular green flanked by timber-framed houses and red-brick farm buildings, and a stream spanned by low brick bridges. Turn right in the village to Princethorpe. At the T-junction, turn right on to the B4453, then left on to the A423 to Marton. Enter the village and follow signs to the Museum of Country Bygones (Louise

THE CENTRE OF ENGLAND

The weathered medieval cross shaft on the village green at **Meriden** (left), midway between Coventry and Birmingham, traditionally marks the centre of England. A Cyclists' Touring Club Memorial near by makes the same claim, but other claimants include High Cross near **Copston Magna**, where the Roman roads of the Fosse Way and Watling Street cross.

whose zenith was reached during the late 18th and early 19th centuries. The town still exudes something of the elegance of that period, with Regency terraces and crescents. More hints of its genteel past can be found in the Pump Room and Assembly Rooms, as well as in the pretty Jephson Gardens.

Above all, the area is associated with water. The rivers Avon, Stour and Soar are significant waterways among a tracery of small rivers and streams that help keep the countryside fertile. There is plenty of opportunity for travelling on the rivers, while a number of lakes, such as at Draycote Water, Kingsbury or Daventry, provide the opportunity for sailing, canoeing, fishing or bird-watching.

However, as throughout the Midlands, the most influential watercourses are the canals. The Stratford-upon-Avon Canal, the Coventry, the Oxford and the longest of all, the Grand Union, all weave their way across the countryside. Once they carried coal, steel and other merchandise to London or Liverpool via Birmingham, but now they provide a leisurely way to enjoy the countryside. The towpaths alongside the canals make delightful trails for walkers and cyclists. One of the many excellent cycle routes runs parallel with the Ashby Canal and passes the 200 acres (80ha) of woodland at Burbage Common, plus numerous attractive villages along the way to Foxton on the Grand Union Canal. Foxton, near Market Harborough, is celebrated for its complex flight of ten locks, completed in 1814.

A RIGHT ROYAL EVENT

The **Royal Agricultural Show**, held in the first week of July every year, is the largest single agricultural event in Britain, with over 1,500 stands, including 200 from the Royal Crafts Association, attracting over 200,000 people. It is held at the National Agricultural Centre at **Stoneleigh**, near Kenilworth, which is the permanent headquarters of many farming and rural-based bodies, and which also plays host to the Town and Country Festival in August.

Close, off the High Street), which includes craftsmen's tools, dairying implements and agricultural machinery. Turn left through Birdingbury.

4 To visit the country park at Draycote Water at the foot of Hensborough Hill, continue through Leamington Hastings and turn left along the A426. From the hilltop there are fine views across the reservoir and surrounding countryside. Return along the A426 and then left to Napton on the Hill, crossing the A425 into the village. Napton Hill stands 500ft (152m) above the Oxford Canal, and the village clings precariously to its southern and eastern slopes in terraces of houses and cottages.

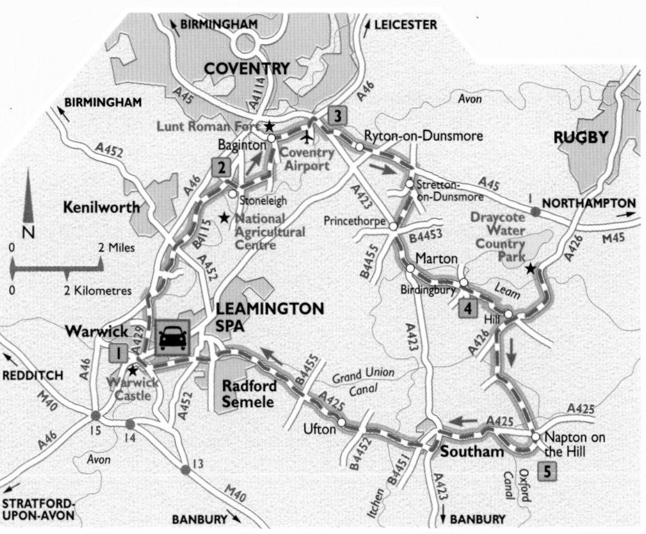

5 Turn right through the village to join the A425 to Southam. The town developed on the old cattle droving road from Wales to London; less peaceful visitors were the Royalist and Parliamentarian troops during the Civil War, and Charles I stayed here overnight on his way to the first major battle of the war at Edgehill in 1642. Rejoin the A425 for 7 miles (11.5km) to Royal Leamington Spa. Leamington became 'Royal' in 1838 when Queen Victoria visited the spa, and during the 19th century the town reached the peak of its fame as those with ailments flocked to take advantage of the town's mineral springs. Remain on the A425 to return to Warwick.

TOP WARWICKSHIRE HOMES

Charlecote Park

Elizabethan mansion, rebuilt in the 1830s. The interior is fascinating and you can picnic in the deer park.

Packwood House

Timber-framed house (above) dating from between 1556 and 1560, with 17th-century additions. Contains an important collection of tapestries and textiles, including fine Bargello work.

Baddesley Clinton House

Romantically sited medieval moated house, dating from the 14th century.

Warwick Castle

Formidable 14th-century fortress with towers, ramparts and crenellated walls, built on the site of a Norman castle.

Coughton Court

An impressive central gatehouse dating from 1530. The south wing contains some notable furniture, porcelain, portraits and relics of the Throckmorton family who have lived here since 1409.

SEE CONTACTS SECTION FOR ADDITIONAL INFORMATION

BIRMINGHAM & THE WEB OF CANALS

As Britain's second largest city, Birmingham has become one of the most vibrant centres of British culture, with an exceptionally good nightlife. The city of Birmingham centres on Victoria and Centenary Squares, fringed by impressive civic buildings built during the 19th century to advertise the region's great industrial wealth – the Council House, the Town Hall and the City Museum and Art Gallery. Largely pedestrianised, the heart of the city has been completely revitalised and is now a major shopping and leisure destination. With a mixture of restored arcades, such as the Great Western, modern malls and old-fashioned markets of New Street, there is something for everyone. The main shopping area runs along New Street to the City Plaza. The Jewellery Quarter, where there is a discovery centre in Vyse Street, and the wholesale clothing markets are also magnets for shoppers. The celebrated Bull Ring is in the throes of major redevelopment and at Brindleyplace there is an award-winning complex of bustling bars and cafés beside Birmingham's revived canal network. Here you will find the National Sea Life Centre where there are over 50 displays of marine life.

Interactive displays at Cadbury World, where you can also sample the chocolate

Birmingham is at the heart of Britain's unrivalled web of canals and their restoration has contributed enormously to Birmingham's

Displays of Birmingham's industrial heritage at the Museum of Science and Industry

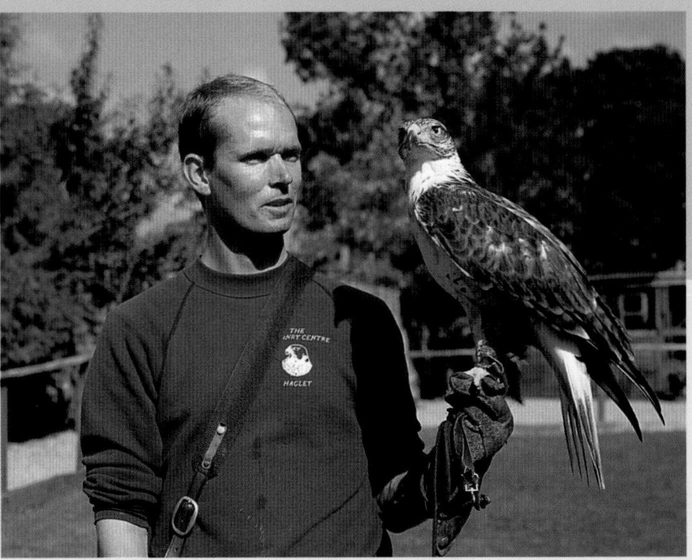

Birds of prey displays can be enjoyed at the Falconry Centre near Stourbridge

Birmingham Cycle Ride

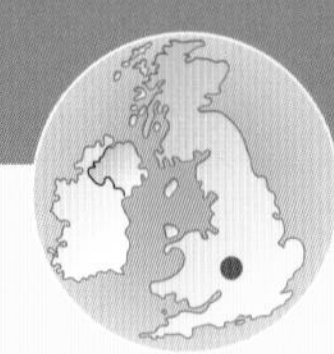

CYCLE RIDE

Birmingham and Black Country Canal Cycleway

START/FINISH: Birmingham
DISTANCE: 16 miles (25km), 15 miles (24km) off-road
GRADIENT: level
ROADS/PATHS: city streets/canal towpath
PARKING: car-park at Brindleyplace, just off Broad Street by the canal

Ride the Birmingham and Black Country Canal Cycleway on a tour through the industrial heartland of the Midlands.

1 From the car-park at Brindleyplace turn left, first right then left again. Go down the steps to the canal towpath and turn right. Turn left across the bridge at Gas Street Basin and head left along the towpath on the opposite side. Birmingham's first canal opened in 1769 and within three years had been extended to Wolverhampton. The original canal, constructed by James Brindley, followed the contours of the land, twisting and turning through the countryside, serving countless wharves and basins along its length.

2 The cycle path is well marked with signboards at all the major entry/exit points. At Smethwick Junction, 3 miles (5km) from Gas Street Basin, follow the directions, crossing the bridge and taking the left branch of the canal.

3 After 5 miles (8km), at Sponlane Locks, cross to the opposite towpath by the footbridge. In a further 4 miles (6.5km), at Factory Bridge Locks, cross the canal again, this time by the small footbridge at the first lock. With so much industry to serve along its length, canal traffic increased to such an extent that special steam pumps had to be installed to re-circulate the water. At Factory Bridge Locks the congestion got so bad that even working them around the clock, seven days a week, could not cope with the demand. Thomas Telford eventually built Birmingham's Main Canal, which incorporated some of Brindley's original canal and solved the traffic problem.

4 At Coseley Tunnel dismount and walk the 360yds (330m) along the fenced towpath. Then cycle to the end of the canal where a bridge takes

AT THE HUB

Birmingham and the Black Country lie at the hub of the British canal system, with Birmingham alone having eight canals within its boundaries, covering 32 miles (53km). After the canals were gradually abandoned in favour of the cheaper and more efficient railways, they assumed a new role as leisure amenities. The old towpaths also make excellent walk and cycleways, such as the **Birmingham and Black Country Canal Cycleway**, which runs along the **Birmingham Canal Navigation** from Birmingham city centre to Wolverhampton.

renaissance. From Wolverhampton and Cannock to the north and Stourbridge to the south, this area had 212 working locks, with 550 factory-side basins, forming the greatest concentration of industrial canals in the country. There are still 130 miles (210km) of navigable canals in the area. The canals have been given a new lease of life as leisure routes, for boating, walking and cycling, and Birmingham's Gas Street Basin is once again alive with brightly coloured narrow boats.

Surrounding Birmingham there are numerous places to visit. A steam train will take you from Birmingham to Stratford-upon-Avon, the birthplace of Shakespeare. Major visitor attractions, such as Cadbury World or Drayton Manor Theme Park, will appeal to children.

Dudley has a well-known zoo, located in its castle's 40 acres (16ha) of grounds, which houses one of the largest collections of animals in the country. A mile (1.6km) from the town centre is the award-winning Black Country Living Museum, a re-creation of an industrial village, with shops and a pub, cottages and a chapel. There is a canal dock with narrow boats and trips into the Dudley Tunnel. Visitors can also go underground into an 1850s mine.

INDOOR SKIING

Tamworth Snowdome is the largest indoor skiing and snowboarding facility in Britain. It has a 460-ft (150-m) real snow slope and caters for beginners and experts of all ages. There are two bars and restaurants with views of the slope, and swimming pools as part of the complex.

Just 10 miles (16km) north of the centre of Birmingham is the 2,400-acre (5,930-ha) Sutton Park, an amazing survivor of a medieval landscape of ancient oak woods, heath, wetlands and pools. Sutton Park is now a National Nature Reserve and a wonderful wilderness area, much loved by cyclists, walkers and naturalists. It is also a venue for the RAC motor rally and other events.

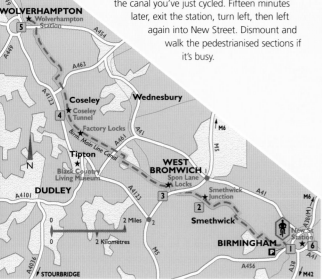

A cook's confectioner's shop at the Black Country Living Museum, Dudley

you up to the road. Cross this and rejoin the towpath, following the cycle signs for Wolverhampton town centre. To get some idea of what life was like when this was the industrial heart of England, leave the canal at Tipton and cycle a short distance to the Black Country Living Museum (opposite Dudley Guest Hospital). Here, in a re-creation of a Black Country village, complete with cottages, a chapel, bakery and a pub serving real ale, costumed guides and demonstrations bring the buildings to life.

5 At Broad Street Basin turn right and exit via the footpath to the cycleway. Turn right over Broad Street Bridge, turn left at the traffic lights, then right on to the pavement following the cycle route signs for the railway station. Take a train back to Birmingham New Street, along the length of the canal you've just cycled. Fifteen minutes later, exit the station, turn left, then left again into New Street. Dismount and walk the pedestrianised sections if it's busy.

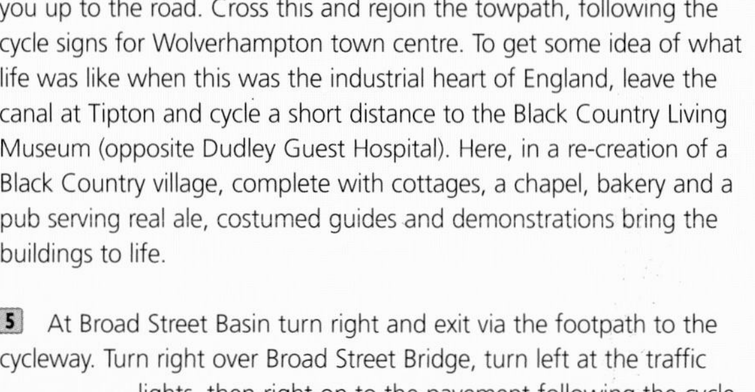

6 Circle left on Victoria Square, go up to Fletchers Walk and dismount. Walk through the shopping area, exit on to Centenary Walk, keeping left, then join Broad Street at the pedestrian crossing and go right. At the pedestrian crossing, where Broad Street crosses the canal, turn right, following the line of the canal back to your starting point and from there to the car-park.

NEW & ANCIENT FORESTS

This area of the East Midlands is one of old and new forests. While Staffordshire has Cannock Chase, Nottinghamshire will forever be associated with the ancient royal hunting forest of Sherwood, which extended over much of the East Midlands, and is traditionally linked to Robin Hood. The Merry Men would not find much that is familiar today, however, as many acres of the former forest are now fertile farmland.

Although Sherwood Forest has dramatically shrunk, a recent introduction has been the new National Forest covering 200sq miles (518sq km) and aimed at creating a multi-purpose forest for the future. Surrounding Burton upon Trent, Swadlincote, Ashby-de-la-Zouch and Coalville, the forest offers opportunities for walking through woods, by lakes or canals, riding, cycling, coarse and fly fishing, dinghy and board sailing, and bird-watching. Particular care has been taken to ensure disabled access to many of these forest activities. There are a number of interesting houses to visit in the forest and the Snibston Discovery Park offers wild-water experiments and a trip down a colliery. Several large craft centres display and sell local work.

ROBIN HOOD

The popular English folk hero was first mentioned in 1377 in William Langland's *The Vision of Piers the Plowman*. According to legend he was a 12th-century gentleman robber who used his skill with the longbow to poach the land of Sherwood Forest and rob the rich to help the poor. But in fact, no one can be sure that Robin Hood ever really existed, although some people think he may have been a Yorkshire yeoman, or merely the personification of the Green Man, or spirit of the woods. As for Maid Marian, Friar Tuck, and the others, they appear to derive from a variety of sources, notably Hollywood.

A former miner introduces visitors to life in a colliery at Snibston Discovery Park

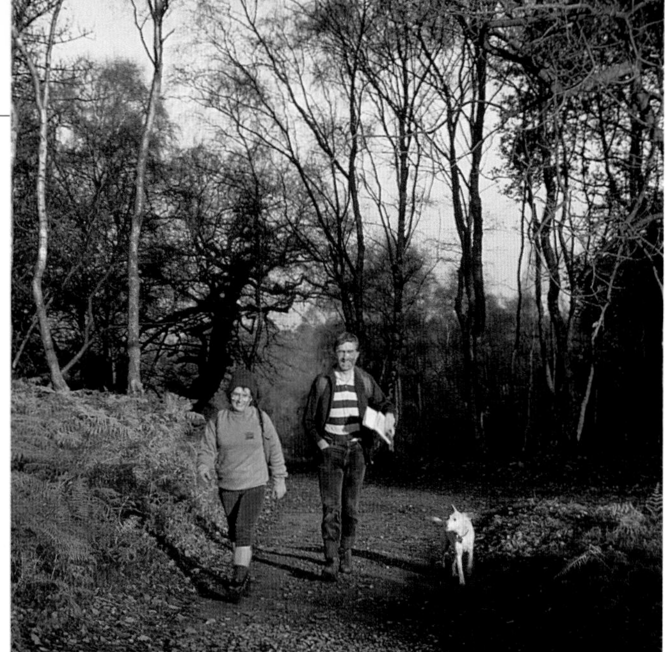

Walkers enjoy one of the many waymarked paths through Cannock Chase

Charnwood Forest Walk

WALK

A Woodland Walk in Charnwood Forest

START/FINISH: Woodhouse Eaves. Off the A6 between Loughborough and Leicester

DISTANCE: 5 miles (8km)

ASCENT/GRADIENT: 655ft (200m); gradual climbs

TERRAIN/PATHS: woodland, heathland, fields and farmland; firm paths on Beacon Hill, but can be muddy around Broombriggs

PARKING: Broombriggs car-park on B591 Beacon Road above Woodhouse Eaves

A country park and a farm trail illustrate the varied countryside and traditional farming practices of this fascinating corner of Leicestershire.

1 From the car-park, cross Beacon Road, walk uphill a few paces and turn right into Beacon Hill Country Park. A woodland path climbs to join a broad path. Turn left on this path, pass tall oak, beech and birch trees. Open heath is reached, which is being cleared of bracken and scrub.

2 Keep straight on, climbing gradually, while off to the right is the bare summit of Beacon Hill. Climb over grass and rocks to reach a trig point and an old AA toposcope. Bronze-Age settlers cleared Beacon Hill 4,000 years ago and built ramparts of earth and stone around the summit. As the woods were cut back, a flowery heath developed. This is managed so that heather, sheep sorrel and other wild flowers can flourish.

3 Continue along the path, curving right as it descends. Banks of bilberry precede denser woods. When a gateway and car-park are reached at the bottom, detour left to look at the Native Tree Collection, returning to the car-park later. There are 28 trees native to Britain and they are all on this walk. Notice boards provide interesting insights into their growth and the habitats they support. To continue the walk, exit from the car-park near the toilets and follow a path uphill signed Broombriggs. Cross the road to return to the Broombriggs car-park.

4 At Broombriggs, a traditional farm is equipped with a waymarked farm trail. The trail offers an insight into the methods used to farm what

The village of Castle Donington is famous for its motor-racing track and the Donington Collection, the largest assembly of single-seater racing cars in the world. Many of the cars were raced by the world's greatest drivers – Juan Fangio, Stirling Moss and Ayrton Senna. Donington is situated just near where the turbulent River Trent flows into Nottingham. The Trent is very popular for canoeing and, along with the River Dove, white-water slalom. Alongside the Trent is the Trent and Mersey Canal, part of the network of waterways including the Birmingham and Fazeley and the Ashby Canals which serve the North Midlands. A steam railway, the Battlefield Line, runs beside part of the Ashby Canal. Starting at Sutton Cheney, the site of the Battle of Bosworth, the track goes north to the village of Shackerstone.

Although dominated by huge breweries, at the heart of Burton upon Trent is the River Trent. Once an 'inland port' bustling with river trade, the valley of the River Trent is today serene and tranquil and there are numerous footpaths crossing the Trent 'washlands'. Several cycle paths, including a millennium route, and walking trails take the visitor along both the river and the Trent and Mersey Canal. Boating is, of course, popular and river trips up and down both the Trent and the Trent and Mersey Canal can be booked in Burton.

THE STAFFORDSHIRE WAY

This delightful trail starts in the Cannock Chase country park and crosses the centre of Staffordshire near Blithfield Reservoir, passing the pretty village of Abbots Bromley, which appears to have changed little for hundreds of years. The route continues through Bagot Forest and just north of Uttoxeter National Hunt Racecourse, it crosses the River Dove, following the course of the river towards the Weaver Hills. The trail returns into Staffordshire along the Churnet Valley.

INLAND SAILING

Even though Burton upon Trent is about as far from the sea as you can get, it is still possible to go sailing. **Burton Sailing Club** was founded in 1902 and originally sailed on the Trent. The club has now moved to the 230-acre (93-ha) Foremark Reservoir, equidistant from Burton, Derby and Ashby-de-la-Zouch. The fleet includes many classes from International 505s to Lasers.

is really a rather difficult area to cultivate. The farm can produce crops of wheat, barley, oats and oilseed rape. Cross a stile and walk up through fields, parallel to Beacon Road, to enter Bluebell Wood. When the farm access road is reached, turn left, then turn right to pick up the next section of the trail. A broad, grassy strip has been fenced off and this climbs above the Hall Field to reach the Trust Field. There are good views westwards.

5 Follow field boundaries, passing through gates and crossing several stiles. As the trail descends it turns left and runs to the right of Long Stye Wood. Notice boards explain about farming at Broombriggs, with further reference to the surrounding countryside. Quite apart from the rich woodlands, fields and flowers in this part of Charnwood Forest, a variety of birds can be seen. There is an option to turn right at the bottom of the wood and detour into Woodhouse Eaves.

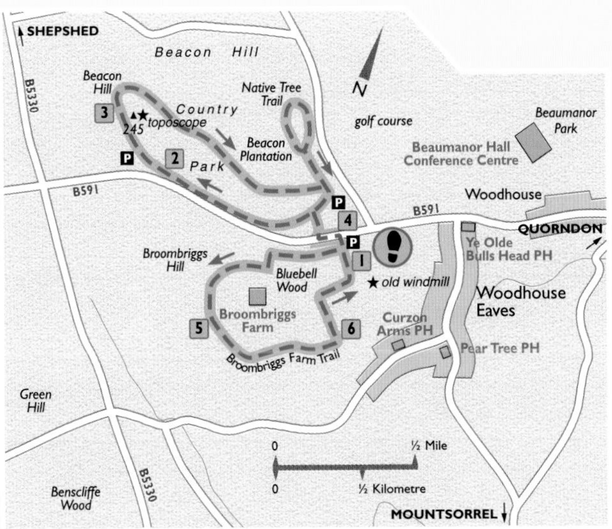

6 The farm trail turns left, away from Woodhouse Eaves, passing through a couple of fields. Take the path on the right, rising towards Windmill Hill. When a path junction is reached at the top of the field, turn left. This will lead you down through fields to return to the car-park at the start of the walk.

BASS MUSEUM OF BREWING

Burton upon Trent, on the borders of Staffordshire and Derbyshire, is synonymous the world over with brewing, and the Bass Museum of Brewing in Horninglow Street illustrates the traditions and history of beer, which has been brewed in Burton for centuries. You can follow the Brewing Trail through the town, or take a stroll along the Trent and Mersey Canal which winds through this mainly Victorian town.

The East Staffordshire market town of Uttoxeter is perhaps best known for its National Hunt steeplechase racecourse, while near by are Jacobean-style Sudbury Hall and the Earl of Lichfield's home of Shugborough, as well as the large reservoir at Blithfield. Blithfield, popular for sailing and bird-watching, is just north of Cannock Chase. Officially designated as an Area of Outstanding Natural Beauty (AONB), Cannock Chase is 20,000 acres (8,100ha) of heath and woodland, an ideal spot to walk, cycle or enjoy a picnic.

Fast-paced action at Castle Donington, with the British Touring Car Championship

NORTHAMPTONSHIRE & THE LINCOLNSHIRE WOLDS

The broad acres of England east of the M1 motorway could be loosely described as the Shires and Wolds. This part of the East Midlands and Lincolnshire typifies the idea of English countryside, from the hedged hunting shires of Northamptonshire, Nottinghamshire and Leicestershire to the gently rolling landscapes of the Lincolnshire Wolds. There is a strong historical legacy, with the great cathedral city of Lincoln as the hub of its huge county, and the castles at Belvoir, Newark-on-Trent and Rockingham providing enduring reminders of a troubled past. More recent are the many airfields of Lincolnshire, from where the Bomber Command crews of World War II took the fight into the heart of Germany. The industrial heritage of the East Midlands is also evident in the great cities of Leicester, Northampton and Nottingham, while through it all runs the Grand Union Canal and the River Trent.

THE LINCOLN IMP

Most visitors try to find the Lincoln Imp, a little cross-legged devil, who can be seen high among the Gothic arches of the Angel Choir in Lincoln's magnificent cathedral. Begun in the 11th century, the triple-towered cathedral was not completed until the 14th century and is one of the finest examples of Gothic architecture throughout the world.

The Wash and Fens

The fertile, low-lying Fens, around the great rectangular bay of The Wash, are the result of a centuries-long battle against water – fresh and salt – since the Romans built the first sea-wall on the north shore. Generations of drainage engineers have produced an environment in which the triangulation points seldom reach double figures, its horizons broken only by church towers and grain silos – the only landmarks in a landscape that is two-thirds sky.

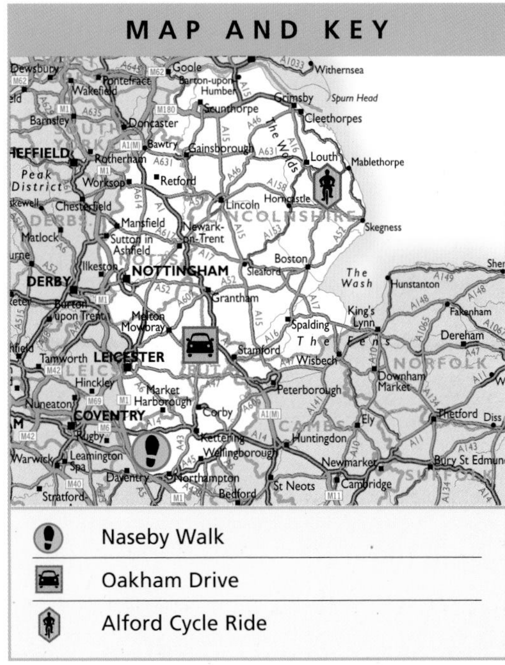

Rutland Water

Rutland Water, at 3,100 acres (1,254ha) one of the largest expanses of man-made water in Europe, is popular for all kinds of water-based sports and recreational activities. There is a thriving watersports centre at Whitwell, where you can hire anything from a canoe to a rowing boat. Or you can cruise on the smooth waters in the passenger-carrying Rutland Belle.

BELVOIR CASTLE

Belvoir Castle, home of the Dukes of Rutland, dominates the broad vale which takes its name. Its fairy-tale appearance, a popular backdrop for medieval battle re-enactments, dates only from the 19th century, when the house was extensively rebuilt, but there has been a castle on the site since the 11th century. Among the many treasures inside are paintings by Van Dyck, Murillo, Holbein and other famous artists.

THE NENE VALLEY TO THE WASH

Historical footwear at Northampton's museum

There is plenty to do and see in this area, including several good castles and fine estates, farm parks, the world-famous Silverstone motor-racing circuit – where you can have a go yourself – rivers and canals, and many small towns selling antiques and specialist gifts. As Northamptonshire gives way to hilly Leicestershire and then Lincolnshire, the valley leads east across reclaimed levels and out to The Wash and the North Sea.

The county town of Northampton, home to the shoe-making industry

You can take boats on the River Nene, which also has excellent fishing, or on the Welland Canal, or try windsurfing or sailing on Thrapston Lakes, or Eyebrook and Pitsford reservoirs. Because the terrain is so varied it provides superb thermals and at Welland there is the opportunity for gliding and flying light aircraft. Near the delightful town of Oundle you will find the only dragonfly reserve in Europe.

DID YOU KNOW?

More than half the bulbs grown in Britain come from the flat fields around Spalding, which is sometimes known as 'Tulip Land'. The tulip industry was introduced by the Dutch 90 years ago, and now thousands of visitors drive around the tulip fields or enjoy the Flower Parade every April, which fills the town with numerous flower-decked tableaux.

The central market square of the county town of Northampton is one of the largest in Britain and its museum specialises in the history of footwear, a traditional local industry. West of the town is Althorp House, family home and burial place of

The Elizabethan towers of Burghley House, whose grounds are used for annual horse trials

Naseby Walk

WALK

The New Model Army at Naseby

START/FINISH: Naseby. Off the A508 7 miles (12km) south of Market Harborough
DISTANCE: 8 miles (13km)
ASCENT/GRADIENT: 165ft (50m); very gradual climbs
TERRAIN/PATHS: gently rolling cultivated fields crossed by roads and paths; mostly firm underfoot but can be muddy in wet weather
PARKING: recreation ground on the Haselbech road in Naseby

This walk takes you through the thick of the battle, from Naseby to Sibbertoft, where Cromwell led his soldiers to change the course of British history.

1 To appreciate the battle, and this walk, visit the Naseby Battle and Farm Museum (on the Cottesbrooke road) before setting off. From the car-park, walk into Naseby village. Follow the road signed Sibbertoft, leaving the village and turn right along a minor road, rising over the A14, crossing over Mill Hill and several gentle humps.

2 On the left is a stone monument marking the spot where the battle took place; an information board sketches out the salient points of the battle. At 9am on Saturday 14 June 1645, some 9,000 men on the Royalist side were ranged against 13,500 in the New Model Army on Parliament's side. You are standing in Parliament's front line, facing the King's men on Dust Hill opposite. Continue along the minor road, rising over Dust Hill, so that you can turn around and see things from the Royalists' point of view. When a road junction is reached, Sibbertoft is signed to the left. Prince Rupert, the King's nephew and a seasoned warmonger, led the first charge, uphill and against heavy fire, yet he devastated the western wing of the New Model Army. Cromwell, on the eastern side, led a similarly devastating charge against the Royalists. It could have gone either way, but the eventual Cromwellian victory sealed the fate of King Charles and heralded a new era of British government.

3 A bridleway is signed at a gateway to the left of the junction. If the fields have just been ploughed, note that the signpost points exactly to the crucial gap in a hedge giving access to the next field. At that point, a gateway can be seen leading on to the next road. Turn left to Sibbertoft.

Diana, Princess of Wales, which also exhibits a collection of some of her dresses.

The former steel town of Corby lies in a pleasant location at the edge of Rockingham Forest, where there are lovely walks at Stoke Wood and Stoke Albany. Rockingham Castle is near by, towering above Rockingham village. The town is also well located for Brigstock Country Park, Kirby Hall, Deene Park House and King's Wood, a nature reserve of ancient woodland.

Wicksteed Leisure Park, near Kettering, is a giant playground founded in 1920 by the industrialist and philanthropist Charles Wicksteed. It has over 50 rides to tempt the children – and the bravest adults! However, antiques collectors may prefer the Market Harborough Antique and Collectors' Fair held every Sunday in the Market Hall. There are 55 stalls selling antiques and bric-à-brac.

TOP FIVE PRETTIEST NORTHAMPTONSHIRE VILLAGES AND TOWNS

Rockingham

Charming village with a steep main street lined with stone houses and overlooked by Rockingham Castle (left).

Badby

An attractive village on a hillside, with thatched cottages and Badby Wood, which is covered in a vibrant carpet of bluebells in spring.

Fotheringhay

Mellow old cottages and the willow-hung banks of the Nene create a tranquillity in this tiny hamlet where historic Fotheringhay Castle, with its grim associations, once stood.

Oundle

This delightful little town, surrounded on three sides by the River Nene, has picturesque inns and old houses.

Raunds

A village best known for its 13th-century church, with medieval murals depicting the parable of the deadly sins.

4 To continue the walk, turn left without actually entering Sibbertoft, then left again signed Naseby. At a sharp left bend, keep straight ahead along a signed bridleway, and turn right to follow a track past a brick building. When a junction of tracks is reached, turn right. At this point, put yourself in the position of a villager trying to get across country without getting involved in the battle and imagine your fear as the battle suddenly shifts westwards towards Sulby.

5 The track loses its firm surface and can be muddy. Go through a gate on your left, then bear right to a small gate leading into a woodland. Follow a muddy track through the wood and up to a quiet minor road.

6 Turn left towards Naseby. Shortly, cross the A14 and enter the village. Naseby Obelisk is in sight from the car-park, and is easily visited by anyone wanting a short extension to the walk.

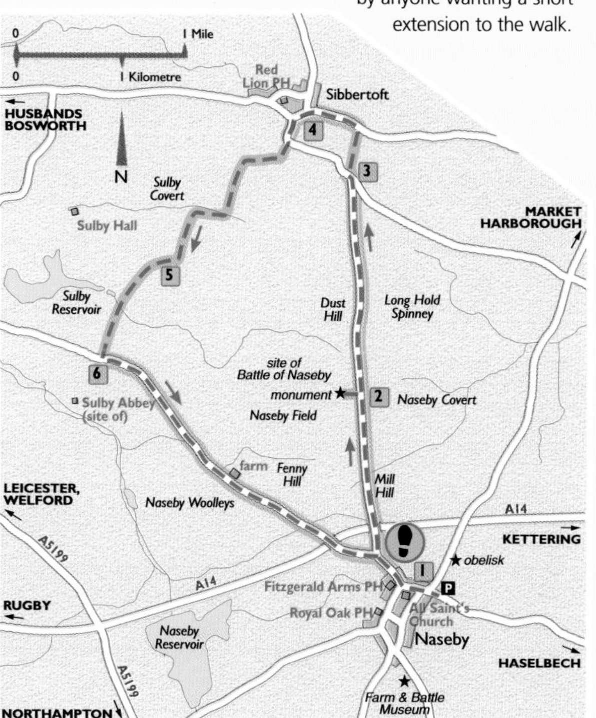

Stamford is, without doubt, one of England's finest small towns. It retains a timeless air with winding streets of golden houses and cobbled alleyways. Just outside Stamford stands Burghley House, a masterpiece of late Tudor architecture, venue for the international Burghley Horse Trials.

As the River Nene nears the sea, the land takes on a distinctly 'Dutch' appearance – flat fen country, crisscrossed by drainage ditches. At the heart of this is Spalding, where acres of tulips are grown each spring. It is a peaceful market town, characterised by grand Georgian terraces flanking the River Welland, which flows out to the salt marsh expanses of The Wash at Fosdyke.

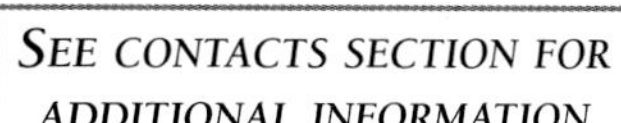

SADDLING UP

Northamptonshire, with its rolling hills, has long been riding country. **Rockingham, Salcey** (below) and **Whittlewood Forests** were originally part of the Royal Hunting Grounds and famous hunts such as the Quorn are still active. There are plenty of stables offering rides: Boughton Mill Riding School, Chapel Brampton; Evergreen Riding Stables, Gayton; Butterfield Liveries and Riding School; Harringworth Manor Stables, near Corby; Manor Farm Riding School, Wellingborough.

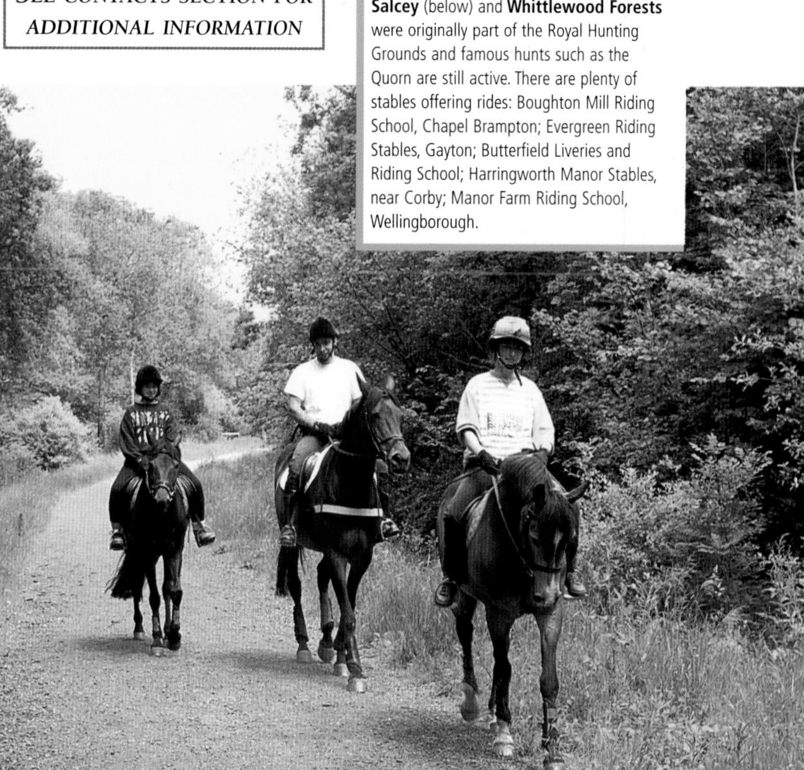

RUTLAND WATER & THE VALE OF BELVOIR

Rutland, England's smallest county – about 150sq miles (389sq km) – lies at the heart of the English Shires. Oakham, Rutland's county town, is a small market town of stone terraces and Georgian villas. Oakham is on the edge of Rutland Water, a 3,100-acre (1,254-ha) artificial lake – one of the largest in Europe. Created in the 1970s, it has now become a valued part of the landscape and a popular venue for sailing, fishing and bird-watching. A cycle track skirts all around the reservoir and cycles can be hired at the visitor centres. There is more sailing on Ashforby's lake and a jet-ski centre at Six Hills near Melton Mowbray.

STILTON CHEESE

A real taste of the shires is provided by the blue-veined Stilton cheese – renowned as 'the king of English cheeses'. It can only be made in Leicestershire, Nottinghamshire or Derbyshire, and although its origins are uncertain, it is claimed that it was first marketed from the 17th-century coaching inn called the Bell at Stilton. Of six modern producers, four are in the Vale of Belvoir.

Melton Mowbray is the place for speciality food shopping. Famous for its pork pies, the shops in the town sell other famous local produce – sausages, Stilton and Leicestershire cheese, and Melton Hunt Cake. There are a number of markets as well as a cattle market and horse auction. Near by is the fertile Vale of Belvoir (pronounced 'Beever'), watched over by its stately castle.

Amid the timeless countryside of Leicestershire and Nottinghamshire there are cities with a strong historical and industrial heritage. The county town of Leicester is known for its lively multi-cultural population, and one of the joys of a visit is the chance to sample one of the city's renowned Indian restaurants. The past is not forgotten, though, with many museums and historic places. Riverside Park stretches all the way through Leicester – a 12-mile (19-km) long green corridor along the River Soar and the Grand Union Canal. This

GREAT CENTRAL RAILWAY

The Great Central Railway runs for 6 miles (10km) along the old Manchester, Sheffield and Lincolnshire Railway. It has over 20 steam locomotives and an extensive selection of rolling stock, and was the first preserved railway to offer a regular dining service. Each station reflects a different age: Loughborough Central Station is typical of the 1960s; Quorn and Woodhouse Station re-creates the 1940s; and Rothley Station captures the Edwardian period.

A view across the heathland of Bradgate Park, a good spot for walks and picnics

Oakham Drive

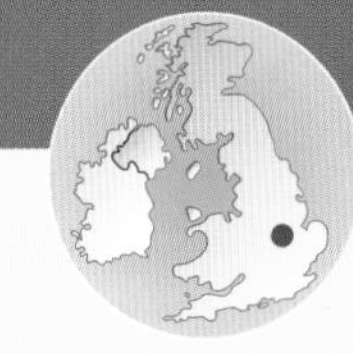

DRIVE

Oakham & Melton Mowbray

START/FINISH: Sykes Lane Car-Park and Information Centre on the north shore of Rutland Water. On the A606 just east of Oakham or 6 miles (10km) west of the A1 and Stamford

DISTANCE: 60 miles (100km)

A leisurely drive through the rolling countryside of tiny Rutland and the unspoilt Wolds on the Leicestershire/Lincolnshire border, taking in some attractive Wolds villages and the historic market towns of Oakham, Melton Mowbray and Grantham.

1 Sykes Lane Car-Park contains the Anglian Water Butterfly Farm and Aquatic Centre. From the car-park drive towards Oakham on the A606, the same road that will take you on to the next town, Melton Mowbray. Rutland Water was created by damming the River Gwash in 1976. It is the second-largest artificial lake in England and a host of leisure facilities have grown up along its shoreline. Oakham is the county town of Rutland and has a long history as a commercial centre. Take time to find the L-shaped market place and the old town stocks, and perhaps the Rutland County Museum.

2 Leaving Oakham, head north on the A606 to Melton Mowbray. Most of Melton Mowbray is Victorian, but St Mary's Parish Church is medieval and worth taking time out to find – you can't really miss its 100-ft (30-m) tower. The town is renowned for its pork pies, a tasty snack if you stick to the smaller ones – don't attempt to eat a full-grown Melton Mowbray pie!

3 Having negotiated the one-way system in Melton Mowbray, head along the A607 to Grantham, passing through Waltham on the Wolds, an attractive Wolds village of ironstone houses, some thatched, others with pantiled roofs. There is also a television transmitter station (note the mast). As you head along the A607 note the views of Belvoir Castle, home of the Dukes of Rutland, away to your left. Continue through Harlaxton, passing Harlaxton Manor, a grand building that is the home of the University of Evansville, USA. Continue on the route to Grantham.

beautiful flood plain, along with gravel pits, has been turned into a country park for bird-watching, watersports, fishing, cycling and walking. The park can also be reached via a stop along the Great Central steam railway. Northwest of Leicester is Bradgate Park, providing 30sq miles (76sq km) of heathland, woodland and rock outcrops for a variety of leisure activities.

ON YOUR BIKE

The quiet Shire country around Rutland and the Vale of Belvoir is just made for cycling, and there are a number of Shire Cycle Trails which follow selected routes along minor country lanes. These include the **Melton and Rutland Trek**, taking in Market Harborough, the Welland Valley and Stamford; and the **Vale of Belvoir and Rutland Trek**, which also takes in Rutland Water, where there are day-ride cycle-hire facilities at Whitwell.

Built on a strategic point on the River Trent, Nottingham has been an important town for many centuries. The huge Old Market Square and surrounding streets have stately buildings from its industrial heyday. The castle now houses a collection of British paintings, silver and ceramics. There are many other museums, including one for lace, for which Nottingham has become famous. Beneath the city is a network of 700-year-old man-made caves. Nottingham was recently nominated one of the top shopping venues in the UK. It has over 1,300 shops, including designer outlets. The county has a well-established reputation among antiques hunters and also offers top-quality craft centres.

On the outskirts of the town, on the River Trent, is the National Watersports Centre at Holme Pierrepont Country Park. There are superb facilities and tuition for all kinds of watersports including white-water slalom and water-skiing.

A few miles northeast of Nottingham is Newark-on-Trent.

Melton Mowbray's original pork pie shop, which has been baking pies since 1850

ROCKBLOK

Rutland is not normally the place you might associate with rock-climbing, but Rockblok, the new outdoor climbing centre at **Whitwell** on Rutland Water, is just the place to burn off some energy. Tuition and equipment are provided for novices and children.

4 From Grantham, simply head south on the A1. Grantham is renowned for its connections with scientist Sir Isaac Newton. At the Colsterworth sign, it is worth taking a detour and heading for Woolsthorpe by Colsterworth. Sir Isaac Newton was born at Woolsthorpe Manor, which is now a National Trust property.

5 Turn off the A1 on to the A606 to head back towards Rutland Water. However, if time allows, historic Stamford is well worth a visit. It is also worth exploring the road to the south of Rutland Water.

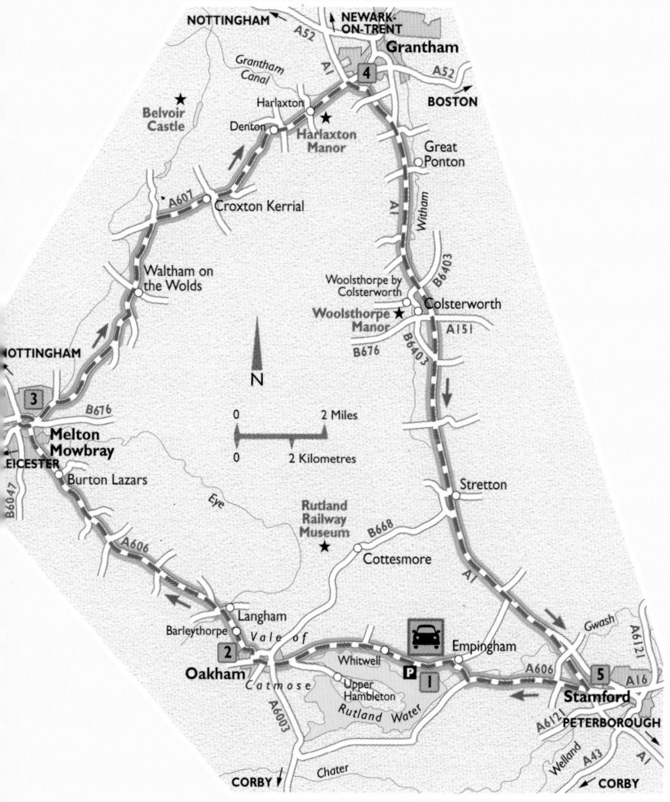

A yacht takes to the calm misty waters from Rutland's sailing club

This busy riverside town is perhaps best known for its ruinous castle and Civil War defences. Markets are held most days and boat trips can be taken along the river.

North of Nottingham are the remains of the great forest of Sherwood. A shadow of its former self, it is still extensive enough to provide excellent waymarked trails. The limestone gorge at Welbeck has a network of caves to explore.

TWITCHING AT RUTLAND

There are no less than 17 hides for bird-spotters within the 450 acres (182ha) of designated nature reserve at the **Anglian Water Birdwatching Centre** at **Egleton**, found at the western end of Rutland Water. The centre has a viewing gallery overlooking three lagoons where up to 20,000 wildfowl overwinter, and there is a re-introduction programme for ospreys. Egleton is also home to the British Birdwatching Fair held annually each August.

THE LINCOLNSHIRE WOLDS

Lincolnshire has an undeserved reputation for being flat. True, there is extensive fenland, but anyone visiting the beautiful Lincolnshire Wolds will find open, rolling hills and steep, deep-sided valleys officially recognised as an Area of Outstanding Natural Beauty. The rolling Lincolnshire countryside extends out to the coast with its long sweeping beaches and popular seaside resorts. This is a very rural county with many unusual buildings including churches, great houses, castles and windmills. There are few towns of any size, but there are still 30 which have traditional markets and Brigg has one of the last great horse fairs. From Brigg, there is an interesting circular route to cycle or drive through the pretty Ancholme and Trent valleys.

Lincolnshire was the home of the man who invented longitude and the meridian line for 0 degrees runs through the county in a line from Cleethorpes to Boston. An interesting cycle ride between these destinations passes through Snipe Dales Country Park and some of Lincolnshire's most delightful villages.

THE VIKING WAY

Lincolnshire's outstanding long-distance footpath is the 147-mile (237-km) Viking Way which runs through the county from the Humber Bridge to Oakham in Rutland. It passes to the east of the Wolds escarpment, through many pretty villages before following a disused railway track to Woodhall Spa, then east to Lincoln and south to Rutland Water and Oakham. Waymarked by a horned Viking helmet, the footpath recognises the influence of the Danelaw on the county's history.

Boston had been a flourishing seaport since the 13th century, when the opening up of the New World diverted trade to west-coast ports. The lively market town is dominated by the splendid tower of St Botolph's church, universally known as the Boston Stump, which can be climbed for far-reaching views over the Wolds and the Wash.

Donkeys provide traditional seaside fun along the flat sands of Skegness

A traditional street market in Boston's town centre, still a popular sight in Lincolnshire

Alford Cycle Ride

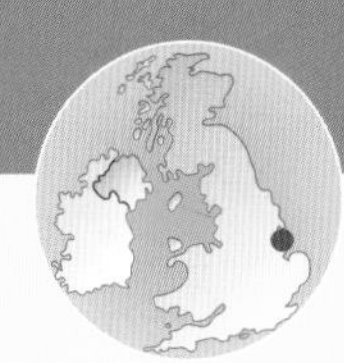

CYCLE RIDE

Alford and the South Lincolnshire Wolds

START: Alford. 15 miles (24km) southeast of Louth by the A16 and the A1104

DISTANCE: 21.5 miles (34.5km)

GRADIENT: generally flat; two or three taxing Wolds hills

ROADS: quiet country lanes

PARKING: South Market Place car-park, behind the library

This ride combines winding lanes on flat land with the gently rolling countryside of the south Lincolnshire Wolds. Tiny villages offer plenty of interest, for those with time to explore, and magnificent views across the Wolds and to the North Sea can be savoured towards the end of the ride.

1 Alford is a busy market town with narrow streets of Georgian and Victorian houses set around a 14th-century church and a market place. Leave the town centre heading southwest along the A1104 towards the A6, and turn right into Tothby Lane, signed Ailby. In 2 miles (3km) turn left towards Aby, continue to a T-junction and turn left away from Aby. Pass a right turn to Belleau and continue up a short rise, passing a limestone quarry on the left. Carry straight on past the next junction on the left and soon turn right, at The Vine Inn, into South Thoresby.

2 Proceed through the village to meet the A16 at a staggered junction. Go straight across and continue to Calceby Manor. Turn right, with the ruins of Calceby church behind and above you as you turn. Climb a long, shallow hill for 1.5 miles (2km) and turn left on reaching the crossroads. The Massingberd Arms is on the right on the road to South Ormsby. The glass in the south aisle window of the parish church came from Notre Dame in Paris during the French Revolution.

3 Fork left by the church and old school, signed Brinkhill, passing the fine thatched Bishop's Cottage on the left, and continue to Brinkhill. Pass through the village, following the main road, and after half a mile (800m) and a short steep climb, bear right at the junction and head downhill towards Harrington. Pass the Hall as the road bends right and turn left after about 200yds (180m). Look for Harrington church (to the left of the Hall, partially hidden by the trees), with its tower and 'ting-tang' bell, and a carpet at the altar which was used in Westminster

BOMBER COUNTRY

The **North Kesteven Airfield Trail** links the airfields of Lincolnshire which were the base for some of the key missions of World War II. The trail includes **RAF Coningsby** (left) which has the Battle of Britain Memorial Flight Visitor Centre exhibiting a Lancaster, Spitfires and Hurricanes, and the **Lincolnshire Aviation Heritage Centre** in East Kirkby which offers an insight into the workings of a 1940s bomber base.

At the centre of the county, Lincoln has one of the great cathedrals of the world. Rising high above the gentle Lincolnshire countryside and the north banks of the River Witham, the third-largest medieval cathedral in the country is a wonderful sight, towering over the city and the surrounding countryside. Many of Lincoln's other attractions are concentrated around the cathedral – the impressive castle, narrow cobbled streets of ancient buildings, particularly along the well-named Steep Hill, and the Norman vaulted High Bridge, still carrying timber-framed buildings.

Lincolnshire is crisscrossed with waterways, including the rivers Lymm and Witham, several canals and numerous drainage dikes or 'delphs'. The River Trent continues across the county on its lengthy journey to join the River Humber, which forms the county's northern boundary. Boating activities are immensely popular and almost any sort of craft can be hired.

ANYONE FOR GOLF?

Lincolnshire's 'Poacher Country' is well known to golfers as the home of the English Golf Union (EGU), which is based at Woodhall Spa. The **Hotchkin** course at **Woodhall** is in the top 30 of the world golf rankings, and the EGU has recently completed a second course, the **Bracken**. There are other excellent courses at **Horncastle**, **Louth**, **Woodthorpe**, **West Ashby** and along the coast.

Another significant feature of Lincolnshire is its lengthy coastline. Miles of sandy dunes running from Grimsby at the mouth of the River Humber, down to the mudflats of The Wash. Even at the height of the season most of the coast remains the solitary preserve of wading birds. There are nature reserves, trails and access points all along the coast – a delight for walkers and bird-watchers.

There are several popular seaside resorts along the coast, such as Mablethorpe, Sutton-on-Sea, Cleethorpes and Skegness. These were favourites with the Victorians and Cleethorpes still has an elegant pier. There are numerous modern attractions at these resorts as well as illuminations and clean sandy beaches. At Grimsby, once a major port, is the National Fishing Heritage Centre offering a taste of the hard life of a North Sea fisherman.

BIRDS OF GIBRALTAR

A number of rare migrating birds might be seen among the sand dunes of the **Gibraltar Point Nature Reserve**, on the northern entrance to The Wash, south of Skegness. These include: red-breasted flycatchers; pied flycatchers; spotted flycatchers; Pallas's warblers; little terns; ringed plovers and short-eared owls.

Apart from Grimsby, the largest town is Scunthorpe, once one of the world's leading steel producers. An interesting heritage trail through the town includes a restored industrial village, viaducts and native woodland. Just north of Scunthorpe, at Normanby Hall, there is also the opportunity to saddle up and go pony-trekking.

Abbey for the Queen's coronation in 1953. At the next junction go straight on towards Hagworthingham, and soon reach Stockwith Mill. A truly tranquil spot, this fine mill houses a tearoom and craft shop, and homemade food is served by the mill pool, the water wheel and the mill race (March to October).

4 Retrace your route back to the last junction and turn right towards Aswardby. At the crossroads in Aswardby keep straight on and, in half a mile (800m), turn left into Langton with its packhorse bridge beside the red-brick church. Both Dr Johnson, the great English scholar, and poet Sir John Betjeman, loved and admired this church, with its noble three-decker pulpit and the unusual inward-facing box pews. Go through the village, noting the unusual circular thatched house on the left, climb through mixed woodland for almost a mile (1.5km) and cross the A16 at the staggered junction towards Skendleby. Continue through Fordington and climb a short, steep hill to the A1028.

5 Bear left at The Open Gate Inn, and shortly right into Ulceby village, passing the red-brick church of All Saints. Go through Ulceby, then on reaching the A1104, turn right for a welcome 2.5-mile (4-km) downhill ride back to Alford and the car-park.

THE PEAK DISTRICT

The Peak District, covering 555sq miles (1,438sq km), was England's first National Park, reflecting its importance as a landscape of rare drama and beauty. Surrounded by some of the largest industrial cities and towns of northern England, it remains an area of uncompromising uplands, where former industry has ebbed from the dales leaving a legacy of discarded millstones and the abundant remains of lead mining. Farming has shaped the open moors and dry-stone walled pastures, influenced by the harsh climate and thin soils. The harsh grey gritstone of the Dark Peak counterpoints the pale limestone of the White Peak; the Dark Peak's high edges and tors overlook the flower-studded pastures and deep, wooded dales of the White. No other part of England has such diversity in such a small area, touched but unspoilt by old industries, busy with visitors yet full of wide open spaces where walkers, although close to 'civilisation', can feel as though they are in a real wilderness.

CHATSWORTH

Often known as the 'Palace of the Peak', Chatsworth House is the Derbyshire home of the Duke of Devonshire. The present, mainly 17th-century, Palladian-style building dates from the 1st duke's rebuilding, and the house itself, standing in superb parkland and gardens, is a treasure-house of works of art.

BAKEWELL

Bakewell is the unofficial capital of the Peak. A market town for probably a thousand years, it is still the meeting place for farmers from all over the district who attend the livestock market every Monday. The old town stands on an important crossing of the River Wye, still spanned by a splendid 13th-century bridge.

Well-dressing

The ancient art of well-dressing, originally peculiar to the villages of the White Peak, probably has its origin as a pagan thanksgiving for the gift of water on the fast-draining limestone plateau. Nowadays, over 30 villages 'dress' their wells or springs and the floral mosaic tableaux usually have a Christian theme.

MAP AND KEY

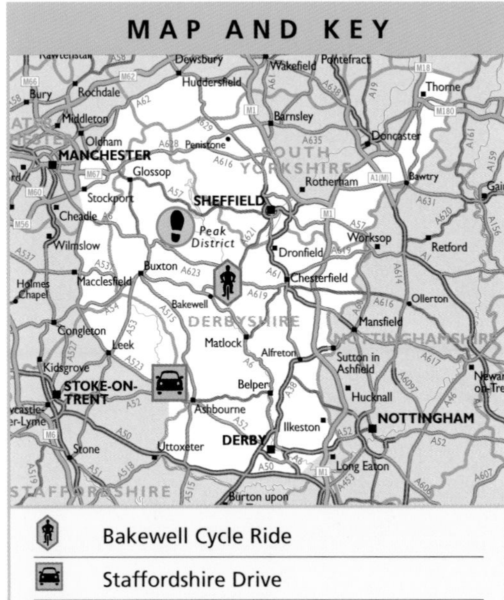

Bakewell Cycle Ride

Staffordshire Drive

Castleton Walk

Arbor Low

The enigmatic stone circle and henge monument of Arbor Low stands in glorious isolation near Middleton-by-Youlgreave, high on the White Peak plateau. It is thought to have been built around 4000 BC. The whole monument measures 250ft (76m) across and must have been an important ritual centre for the first settlers in the Peak District.

STANAGE EDGE

The crags of the Peak District, such as Stanage Edge above Hathersage, have provided the nursery of some of the finest rock-climbers in the world, who later went on to conquer Himalayan giants such as Everest and K2. Joe Brown, Don Whillans and Doug Scott all started their climbing careers on Peak District gritstone.

THE WHITE PEAK & THE DERWENT VALLEY

The pale limestone plateau of the White Peak is crisscrossed by miles of dry-stone walls and dissected by steep-sided dales, some carrying streams, while others are dry. The rivers Wye and Derwent flow through the White Peak carving out broad shale valleys. The Peak District is a rambler's paradise with 1,600 miles (2,560km) of public footpaths crossing wild moor, along river banks or past sleepy villages.

The White Peak is crossed by the Tissington, High Peak and Monsal Trails: former railway lines now converted to leisure routes for walkers and cyclists.

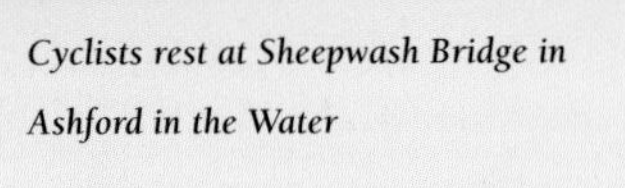

Cyclists rest at Sheepwash Bridge in Ashford in the Water

Bakewell, on the River Wye, is the only town within the National Park, and is celebrated for its Bakewell pudding. Just downstream is the romantic medieval pile of Haddon Hall, frequently used as a backdrop for films, such as Franco Zeffirelli's recent *Jane Eyre*. Ashford in the Water, 2 miles (3km) upstream on a bend in the river, is one of the most attractive of all the Peak villages, while Ashover is the setting for Carlton TV's *Peak Practice*.

The Derwent flows down from the northern Peak District, watched over by the 'edges' of Froggatt, Curbar, Baslow and Stanage, winding through a mellow valley, skirted by woods, meadows and

Baskets of local treats at the Old Original Bakewell Pudding Shop

The five-arched stone aqueduct at Monsal Dale, which spans the River Wye

Bakewell Cycle Ride

CYCLE RIDE

Bakewell Village and Chatsworth House

START/FINISH: Bakewell. On the A6 7 miles (12km) north of Matlock

DISTANCE: 19 miles (30km), with 7 miles (11km) off-road

ASCENT/GRADIENT: reasonably level, some hilly sections

ROADS/PATHS: dirt tracks, stone and paved surfaces with some muddy sections

PARKING: car-park at the Bakewell Agricultural Centre, in the centre of town, signed off the main road

Forgotten railway lines, sleepy, secluded villages and stately homes in the Peak District National Park.

1 Bakewell is a market town and tourist centre for much of the Peak District. Leave the car-park on a path heading north towards Wyeburn house and the Long Meadow House B&B on the right. Turn right on to Coombs Road and continue for half a mile (800m) to reach a viaduct.

2 Climb the embankment steps and at the top turn left and ride along the old railway track to the bridge with the sign No Exit for Cyclists Beyond this Point. Climb up to the road, go left and continue to a T-junction in Great Longstone and turn left. The railway line that ran through here from 1863 to 1968 is now the Monsal Trail, a cycleway and footpath, created by the Peak District National Park.

3 Take the first road left and exit the village past the church. At the T-junction at All Saints Church, go left then take first right, signed Baslow, just beyond the Eyre Arms. Turn left at the junction in Baslow then right over the bridge.

4 Turn right on to the main road, keep ahead at the small roundabout, then follow the A619 for Chatsworth House at the large roundabout at the end of the village. After about 1 mile (1.5km) when the A619 turns right, keep left on the B6012.

5 Inside Chatsworth Park it is worth taking a detour round Edensor, a classic, unspoilt estate village, and then visiting Chatsworth House before continuing on the B6012. The entrance to Chatsworth House is a few

pretty villages. On the banks of the river, whose course was altered to enhance the park, is magnificent Chatsworth House.

Joined by the Wye, the Derwent flows through a narrow gorge where the little town of Matlock has been built. Overlooked by the cliffs of the Heights of Abraham, Matlock is a tourist honeypot. Old Matlock is on the east bank of the Derwent, where the turbulent waters through the gorge are ideal for white-water rafting and kayaking. In the immediate

TOP FIVE STATELY HOMES

Haddon Hall

Beautiful 14th-century manor house with magnificent gardens.

Eyam Hall

Fine 17th-century house built and still occupied by the Wright family.

Kedleston Hall

Elegant neo-classical mansion designed by Robert Adam in beautiful parkland.

Renishaw Hall

A 17th-century manor built by the Sitwell family, with Italian-style gardens.

Chatsworth House

Built in 1707 and with a park landscaped by 'Capability' Brown. One of the great stately homes of England.

HEIGHTS OF ABRAHAM

Rising dramatically above the village of Matlock Bath in the valley of the River Derwent, the Heights of Abraham have an unusual means of access – a five-minute cable-car trip. Once at the top there are woodland and hilltop trails, caverns and a restaurant – and the views down into the Derwent Gorge are stunning. For those with strong legs, there is a steep path which reaches the top in about half an hour.

locality are a number of caves: Great Masson and Great Rutland caverns can be reached by a cable-car ride across the Derwent Gorge to the Heights of Abraham. High Tor, above Matlock Bath, is also a magnet for climbers, as is Chee Tor in the valley of the Wye and the millstone grit edges above the Derwent.

The restored Peak Railway runs from Matlock and at nearby Clay Cross, where George Stephenson pioneered the new railway route to Leeds, is the 'mile long' Clay Cross Tunnel and the Barrow Hill Engine Shed, the last working roundhouse in Britain.

Just to the east of the White Peak is Chesterfield, a town celebrated for its amazing twisted church spire. The town has a lively market on summer Saturdays and a variety of shops and outlets for the famous local Denby Pottery and another local industry, glassware. Chesterfield is the ideal base from which to arrange horse-riding or trekking jaunts in the Peaks. Near the town there are several reservoirs at Linacre and Ogston, which are excellent for rambling or bird-watching, and south of Matlock is Carsington Water, a popular venue for fishing and various watersports.

FAVOURITE GRITSTONE EDGES FOR CLIMBING

Stanage Edge – near Hathersage, 3 miles (5km) long, up to 70ft (21m) high and with hundreds of routes.

Birchen Edge – near Baslow, a lovely little crag with good routes in the lower grades.

Froggatt Edge – over 100 routes, including some of the classics of the Peak.

Curbar Edge (below) – fierce and steep, with some fine crack climbing.

Millstone Edge – the highest of the edges (up to 120ft/36m) with fine corners, cracks and arêtes.

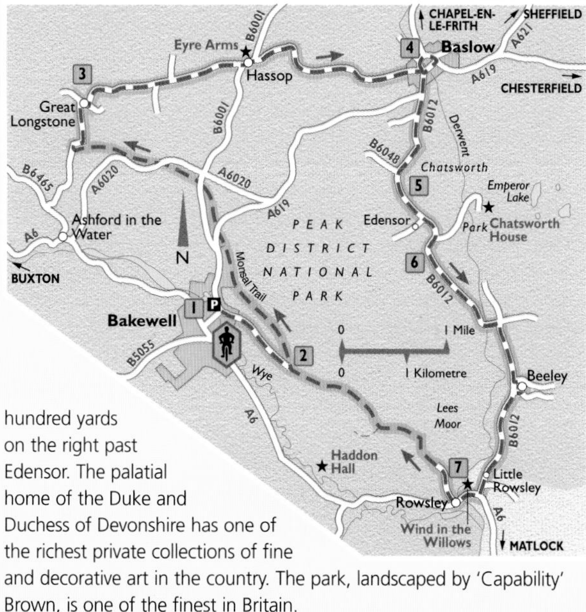

hundred yards on the right past Edensor. The palatial home of the Duke and Duchess of Devonshire has one of the richest private collections of fine and decorative art in the country. The park, landscaped by 'Capability' Brown, is one of the finest in Britain.

6 Follow the B6012 towards Rowsley and turn left at Beeley. Much of Beeley, a fine estate village, was laid out by Paxton for the 6th Duke of Devonshire. Older buildings include the early 17th-century Old Hall and the attractive Devonshire Arms which forms the nucleus of the village. Go through the village and then rejoin the main road which is narrow here and can be busy. On reaching the A6 in Rowsley turn right, then right again, into Church Lane, at the Peacock Hotel. Nearby Haddon Hall is a romantic, battlemented mansion that has hardly changed for 400 years. It is, perhaps, the most perfect example of a medieval manor house in England, the oldest part being the painted chapel.

7 Follow this lane as it climbs the steep hill and continue when it turns into a rough track (this section is not easy terrain). When you reach the junction barred by two gates go left. Keep left at the next fork and continue downhill. At the next junction turn right, ignoring the bridleway to Chatsworth, and continue downhill on the path marked Bakewell. Go under the railway bridge and follow the road back to the car-park.

THE WESTERN MOORS & SOUTHERN DALES

The Peak District is usually associated with Derbyshire, but half of the western moors lie in Staffordshire. The hills of the Peaks begin to rise as far south as Uttoxeter, where the River Dove and its tributaries have cut many narrow wooded valleys, reached by twisting country lanes. It is in this rural area that Britain's most celebrated theme park, Alton Towers, is found. Popular with thrill-seekers it has five heart-stopping rides – Oblivion, Nemesis, Ripsaw, Corkscrew and Blackhole! Further up the little River Churnet is the Churnet Valley Railway, which runs from Consall to Leek.

Walkers stop to admire the scenery along one of the trails through Dovedale

A typical stone bridge at Wetton Mill crosses the river along the Manifold Valley

Leek, which was built on the silk industry, is where the first hills of the Peak rise up suddenly from the Staffordshire Plain. These heights are known as the Staffordshire Moorlands and marked by outcrops such as The Roaches and neighbouring Ramshaw Rocks and Hen Cloud. They are very popular with hang-gliders, and there

Buxton's magnificent Georgian buildings, created by the 5th Duke of Devonshire to rival Bath

Staffordshire Drive

DRIVE

Staffordshire Peak and Plains

START/FINISH: Ashbourne. Off the A52 midway between Derby and Stoke-on-Trent

DISTANCE: 55 miles (88km)

North and west of Ashbourne lies the Staffordshire part of the Peak District, less well known than its Derbyshire counterpart but equally beautiful. One bank of the far-famed Dovedale lies within this underrated county, and the towns and villages on the edge of the hills are full of interest.

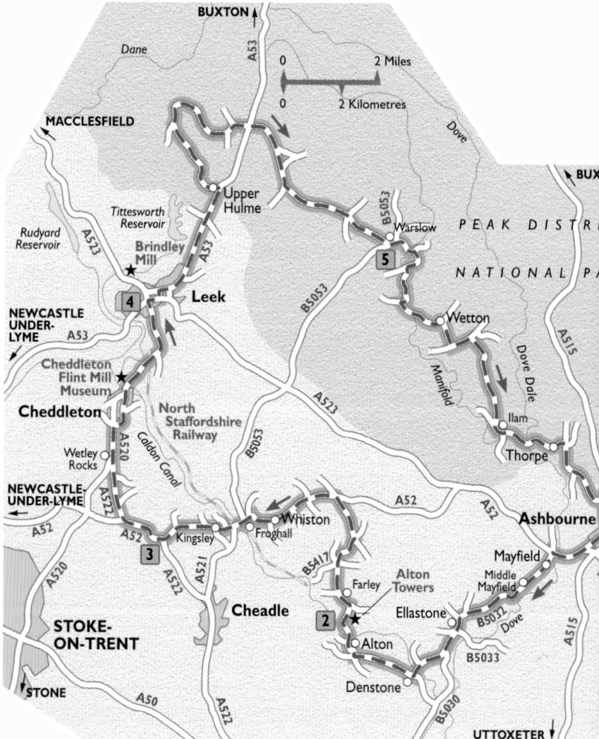

is a school for beginners at Upper Hulme in the shadow of The Roaches. Beneath The Roaches, near Leek, two large reservoirs, Rudyard and Tittesworth, are popular for boating, windsurfing, fishing and bird-watching. You can also take a boat along the edge of the western Peaks on either the Caldon or the Macclesfield canals.

The wild western moors are quieter and less frequented than those in the east and north. This air of remoteness has helped to spawn many myths and legends about solitary heights such as Ramshaw and Windgather Rocks, and The Roaches, which are a favourite haunt of rock-climbers.

Ashbourne, a market town celebrated for its gingerbread, is at the gateway to Dovedale. Dovedale is the most famous and popular, of all the Peak District dales. The 7-mile (11-km) stretch of Dovedale, from the Stepping Stones to Hartington, is best avoided on a summer Sunday or Bank Holiday. The upper reaches of Dovedale can be explored from the little hilltop village of Longnor, which sits on a ridge between the Dove and the Manifold. There are many wonderful walks to be enjoyed from the cobbled market-place of this charming village, including exciting excursions to the sharply pointed reef limestone hills of Chrome and High Wheeldon.

MILLSTONE MARKERS

Most of the main roads into the Peak District National Park carry boundary stones, on which rest millstones of various types. They recognise the fact that the beauty of Britain's first National Park rests on centuries of industrial exploitation, from lead mining to the manufacture of thousands of these millstones, carved from the millstone grit of many of the Peakland 'edges'.

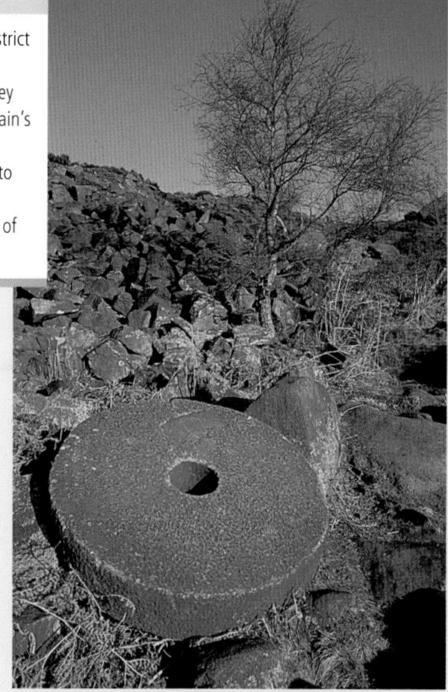

Just to the east is the equally stunning, twisting gorge of Manifold Valley. The valley has one of several cycle trails which follow the tracks of disused railways. Many people's favourite dale is the Lathkill, part of the Derbyshire Dales National Nature Reserve and lovely at any time of the year.

The elegant spa town of Buxton lies practically in the centre of the Peak District. Its many buildings of note include the Royal Crescent and the beautiful Opera House. Opposite the Crescent is St Ann's Well, the source of Buxton's heated spa water and near by is the awesome gulf of Poole's Cavern, the Peak's most accessible cave.

ON THE ROCKS

The Roaches near **Leek** were the scene of some of the greatest advances in rock-climbing during the 1950s. It was here that the 'working class revolution' in climbing took place, and Manchester plumbers Joe Brown and Don Whillans pushed gritstone rock-climbing to previously unheard of limits, using their new hand-jamming techniques and the minimum of equipment. Routes such as **The Sloth** and **Valkyrie** on The Roaches still engender deep respect among modern climbers.

1 Often described as the most perfect Georgian town in Derbyshire, Ashbourne has some fine architecture. Look out for the Elizabethan grammar school and the elegant parish church, one of the best examples of Early English style in the North Midlands. Leave Ashbourne on the A52 towards Stoke and cross Hanging Bridge. Turn left in Mayfield on to the B5032, signed to Uttoxeter. At Ellastone, bear left then in 1 mile (1.5km) branch right, signed to Denstone. At Denstone, bear right and in 2 miles (3km) turn right on to a minor road, signed Alton. At Alton bear left and descend (1-in-10) to cross the Churnet Valley.

2 Pass the entrance to Alton Towers – one of Europe's biggest pleasure parks, featuring exhilarating rides, shows and attractions. Continue to Farley and, in a mile (1.5km), turn right on to the B5417, signed to Ashbourne. At the next crossroads, turn left on to a minor road, signed Winkhill. Turn left on reaching the A52 (towards Stoke) and continue through Whiston and Froghall to reach Kingsley.

3 At the T-junction beyond Kingsley, bear right, keeping on the A52. Shortly, branch right on to the A522. At Wetley Rocks turn right on to the A520 towards Leek. Continue through Cheddleton and pass the Flint Mill Museum. In 2.5 miles (4km) turn right on to the A53 and enter Leek.

4 Leek's modern importance was founded on silk products and dyes, and the old mill buildings are now used by modern industry. At the roundabout take the second exit into Ball Haye Street then turn right on to the A53 towards Buxton. After 3 miles (5km) turn left (minor road), signed to Upper Hulme. Very shortly, branch left at Harold's Leap and keep left (gated road). After 2.5 miles (4km) pass through two gates. In a further 2 miles (3km) keep left. Turn right at the T-junction, cross the main road and bear right in 1 mile (1.5km), signed to Leek and Bottomhouses. In another mile (1.5km) branch left (no signs) and, at the T-junction, turn left and follow signs to reach Warslow.

5 Turn left on to the B5053, towards Buxton, take the next right, signed to the Manifold Valley, and soon turn right again. Descend to the T-junction and turn right. Cross the river bridge and turn right for Wetton, then turn immediately left through the tunnel. In 1.5 miles (2km) keep ahead, then shortly bear left and ascend (1-in-7). Keep forward into Wetton. Just after Yew Tree Farm (towards the end of the village) turn right (not signed). Turn left at the crossroads and descend, soon to turn right for Dovedale and Ilam. At Ilam, a neat estate village, turn left at the war memorial, passing Dovedale Car-Park. Continue on this road back to Ashbourne.

THE DARK PEAK & THE NORTHEAST

The Dark Peak is uncompromising high country, lying on a bed of millstone grit beneath the peat. The surface is a skin of bog moss or cotton grass, the home of grouse, curlew and golden plover. Only two or three roads cross this wilderness that, surprisingly, still exists less than a dozen miles from the cities of Manchester and Sheffield. It is here that the Pennine Way, Britain's first and toughest long-distance footpath, has its southern terminus at Edale, in the shadow of the Peak's highest hill, Kinder Scout, which rises to 2,088ft (636m). This National Trail runs for 256 miles (412km) up the backbone of England to Kirk Yetholm, just across the Scottish Border.

The small Yorkshire town of Holmfirth, which has become a TV-inspired tourist destination

In the Hope Valley near by, there is so much of interest that Castleton sometimes suffers from a surfeit of tourists, as this delightful little village is a good base for exploring the area. Castleton is presided over by the impressively sited ruins of Peveril Castle. Deep beneath the castle is Speedwell Cavern, an old lead mine which descends 2,000ft (600m), part of which can only be accessed by water. Three other showcaves are open to the public in Castleton: Treak Cliff Cavern, Blue John and Peak Cavern. For the more adventurous, the Peak District has some of Britain's deepest and most challenging cave systems within its limestone core, waiting to be explored. There are several activity centres around Castleton that provide safe caving and pot-holing.

The curtain of high hills at the head of the valley rises up a dramatic cliff face to 1,695ft (517m) at Mam Tor, less than 2 miles (3km) to the northwest of the village. Bands of shale and gritstone give the hill the nickname of the 'Shivering Mountain', because the whole hillside is gradually slumping down into the valley.

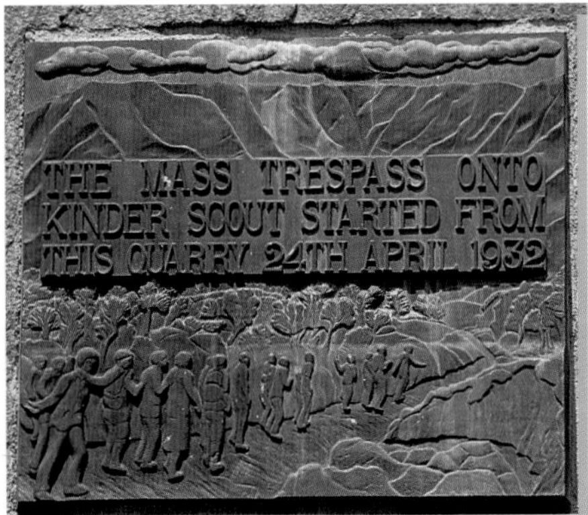

THE BATTLE OF KINDER SCOUT

The 'Mass Trespass' on Kinder Scout which took place on 24 April 1932, started as a peaceful protest to gain access to the hills. About 400 walkers climbed the public footpath out of Hayfield to William Clough. A brief scuffle took place when the protesters left the path and were met by a group of gamekeepers, but nobody actually trespassed on to the boggy summit of Kinder. Even so, six protesters were arrested and five were sent to jail, which resulted in huge publicity for the ramblers and ensured a place in history for the 'right to roam'.

Looking east on the ascent out of Tintwistle, on the northwestern edge of the Peak District

Castleton Walk

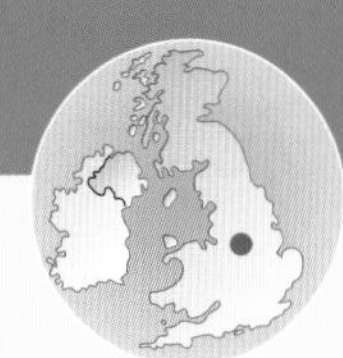

WALK

The Wonders of the Peak at Castleton

START/FINISH: Castleton. On the A625 between Sheffield and Chapel-en-le-Frith

DISTANCE: 5 miles (8km)

TOTAL ASCENT/GRADIENT: 1,035ft (315m); one steep 1,000-ft (305-m) ascent to the Mam Tor ridge

TERRAIN/PATHS: rocky start, easy going on ridge and through fields; can be muddy if wet; ridge mostly paved

PARKING: main village car-park

Where the White Peak meets the Dark, this walk takes in Castleton's 'wonders', the celebrated Peak, Blue John and Treak Cliff Caverns, and Mam Tor, the 'Shivering Mountain', with its fine views over the Hope Valley.

1 The attraction of Castleton is founded on its position, standing on the great geological divide of the Peak District, where the rolling limestone plateau of the White Peak meets the sombre moors of the Dark Peak. From the car-park turn left up the main street, turning left again by the primary school and going straight ahead down the walled packhorse route known as Hollow Ford Road. Cross Tricket Bridge and keep left at Hollow Ford Training and Conference Centre.

2 Go through a gate and ascend for just over a mile (1.5km), with fine views to the left of the 'shivering' east face of Mam Tor. The top of the ridge at Hollins Cross (1,260ft/384m) is marked by a viewfinder, and has wonderful views north across the Vale of Edale to the plateau of Kinder Scout, the highest point of the Peak District.

3 Turn left and follow the heavily eroded ridge path along Cold Side until you reach a newly paved section, which leads up through the embankments of an Iron-Age hillfort which crowns Mam Tor. It encircles the 1,695-ft (517-m) summit, which is characterised by its sheer, crumbling east face, which gives it its alternative name, the 'Shivering Mountain'. If the weather is fine, catch your breath on the summit, and take in the fabulous views over Castleton, Edale and the Hope Valley.

4 An easy staircase of slabs leads down through the fortifications to Mam Nick (a pass). A stile gives access (left) to a path which descends through a pasture, crossing the A625 by a pair of ladder stiles. The

Many of the dales of the Dark Peaks have been drowned under reservoirs to feed the thirsty industrial cities of Manchester to the west, Sheffield to the east, and the Huddersfield-Halifax-Bradford conurbation to the north. The water-filled valleys have, however, become a major leisure attraction offering watersports, fishing and bird-watching as well as riding, cycling and walking trails in the countryside around.

At the head of the Derwent are three reservoirs, the largest being Ladybower, which flooded 2 miles (3km) of the Derwent Valley. The rising waters drowned the villages of Derwent and Ashopton whose foundations are sometimes revealed in drought conditions.

Over a century ago, the waters of the Etherow were dammed to create five reservoirs near Glossop. Now sailing dinghies and kayaks pirouette on the Torside and Woodhead reservoirs. Railway lines that were once laid to link the great industrial cities of Manchester and Sheffield, following the River Etherow up to Woodhead and through a 3-mile (5-km) tunnel below the moors, have been transformed as part of the Trans Pennine Trail and the Longendale Cycle Trail.

The remote moorland to the north of the Peaks is marked by a sharp fall into the Calder Valley. One of the few roads drops dramatically into the small town of Holmfirth, familiar as the backdrop to the TV series *Last of the Summer Wine*.

CASTLETON GARLANDING

Oak Apple Day, 29 May, is celebrated in Castleton by a glorious pub crawl, involving a procession led by the 'King' and 'Queen', both in Restoration costume and on horseback. The King is completely covered in a great cone of flowers, the Castleton Garland, which is hoisted to the top of the tower of the parish church at the end of his tour around the village. A silver band plays the traditional tune 'Pudding in a Lantern', girls dance and everyone welcomes the coming of summer.

SNAKE BY NAME ...

Weather warnings on television and radio have made the Snake Pass famous. When the sun is shining across the rest of the Peak, the A57 between Sheffield and Manchester may well be closed because of severe blizzards. Drivers using the Snake Pass, could be forgiven for thinking that it derived its name from the serpent-like twists and turns of the road. Not so. The snake comes from a device on the crest of the Cavendish family, the Dukes of Devonshire. The Snake Inn was built in 1821 as Lady Clough House, when the original medieval track was turned into a turnpike road.

SEE CONTACTS SECTION FOR ADDITIONAL INFORMATION

second stile (opposite) leads down to the Windy Knoll cave, where Victorian excavators found the bones of many prehistoric animals.

5 Cross the B6061 and take the slanting path to a fence stile. Turn left downhill to pass the entrance to the Blue John Mine showcave. This is the source of the banded fluorspar known as Blue John.

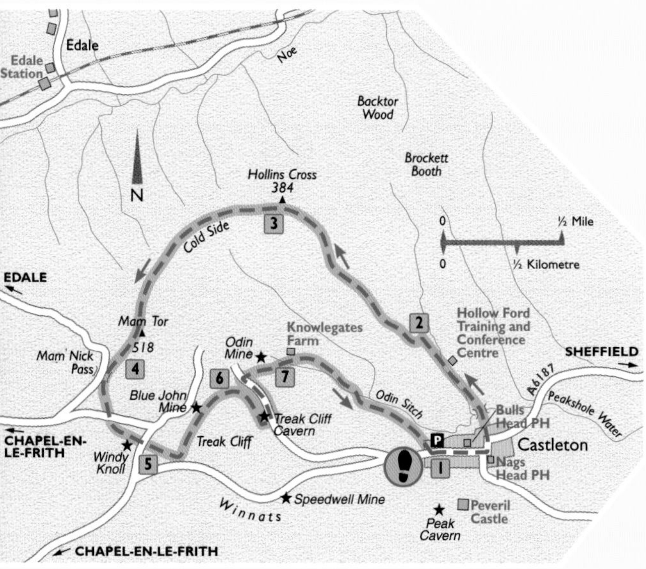

6 Take the path which contours around Treak Cliff, crossing two stiles to reach the hillside entrance to Treak Cliff Cavern, another of Castleton's showcaves. Take the steps down from the cave entrance to the road, which was abandoned in the 1970s after it collapsed beneath the shifting face of Mam Tor. It is a short distance left up the old road to the mysterious crevice of Odin Mine, on the left, one of the oldest recorded Peak District lead mines.

7 Opposite the mine, cross a fence stile and pass the lead-crushing circle to descend across the stream, and go through a landscape of lead spoil tips to another stile. Continue through bracken, pass a farm, and return to Castleton alongside Odin Sitch via stiles.

Hikers enjoy glorious walking country through the Ashopton Valley

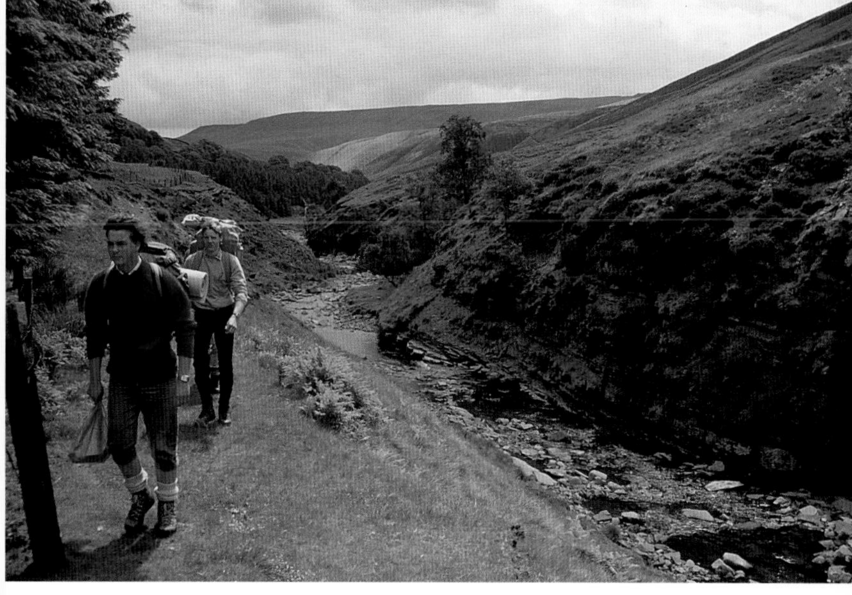

CHESTER & THE POTTERIES

For most people, Cheshire and Staffordshire are just two of the green counties of Central England, viewed merely in passing as they dash up or down the M6. But for those who turn off the motorway, the area has much to offer, from the glorious medieval cities of Chester and Stafford to the industrial heritage of the six towns of Stoke-on-Trent and the Potteries. The varied, ever-changing countryside ranges from the moorland foothills of the Staffordshire Pennines to the first hills of Wales around Oswestry. A network of canals provides a peaceful way to explore this wonderful landscape. The forest of Delamere provides yet more opportunities for the outdoor enthusiast, with mile after mile of inviting trails and paths to tempt you from your car.

Going to Pot

The six north Staffordshire towns of Tunstall, Burslem, Hanley, Fenton, Longton and Stoke – now incorporated into the city of Stoke-on-Trent – have produced some of the finest pottery in the world during the last 300 years. The names of Wedgwood, Minton, Spode, Coalport and Copeland are synonymous with the craft and have been exported all over the world.

Chester's Walls

Parts of Chester's ancient red sandstone city walls date back to Roman times, when the city was known as Deva, but most of the towers and gates which you see today were constructed in the Middle Ages. The 2-mile (3-km) stroll around the walls is one of the finest ways to admire this bustling Deeside city.

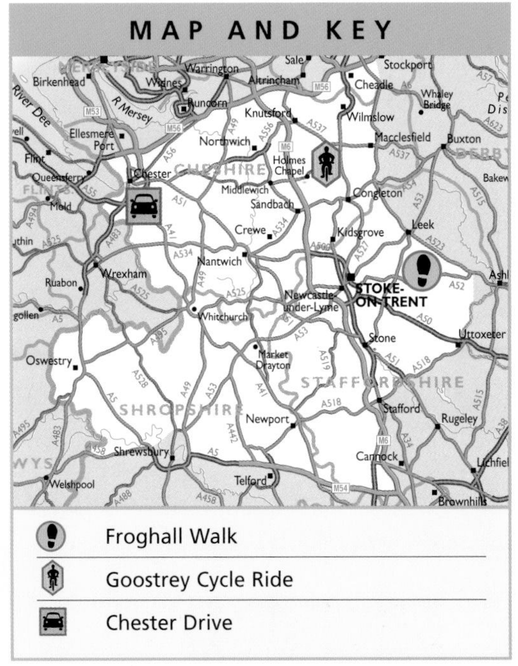

Canal Cruising

The Cheshire Plain and Upper Trent are crossed by miles of canals, from the major highway of the Trent and Mersey to the much smaller Shropshire Union or Montgomery canals. And there are few more relaxing ways of enjoying the gentle pastoral landscapes of the area than from the deck of a narrow boat.

'Magpie' Houses

Cheshire is famous for its black-and-white, half-timbered 'magpie' houses. Usually box-framed in construction, most date from the 16th century and have a free-standing, brick-built chimney. They have had their timbers blackened and their plaster panels whitewashed over the years, although the wood was originally naturally stained. Good examples can be seen at Little Moreton Hall (right) and Bramall Hall, although most villages have them.

THE POTTERIES & TRENT VALLEY

The heavy industrial image of the Potteries and Upper Trent Valley means they have often been overlooked by visitors, but Staffordshire has some beautiful countryside, threaded by canals, wonderful historic houses, and an industrial heritage that is well worth exploring, particularly in Stoke-on-Trent.

Stoke-on-Trent actually consists of the six towns of Stoke, Burslem, Hanley, Longton, Tunstall and Fenton. Each of these was part of the flourishing pottery industry that made this area so famous. Today, while still producing some of the world's finest china, modern Stoke-on-Trent gives its visitors a real experience of Britain's industrial heritage, through working museums and new leisure amenities based around the revitalised canals and abandoned railway lines.

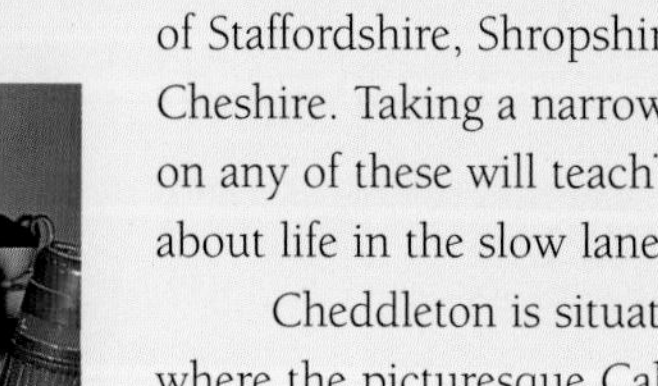

Saxon reindeer horns are used in a medieval hunting rite at Abbots Bromley

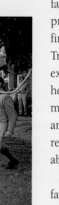

There are more than 40 factory outlets and pottery museums scattered over the six towns. Many of the famous china producers offer factory tours, including Royal Doulton, Coalport, Wedgwood and Spode – the oldest manufacturing ceramic factory on its original site. At Hanley is one of the most magnificent collections of china and pottery and Longton has a working 19th-century pottery. Mining was also an important local industry and at Tunstall former miners guide you down the shafts.

The River Trent played a vital part in the industrialisation of the region and is pivotal to the network of canals that covers so much of Staffordshire, Shropshire and Cheshire. Taking a narrow boat on any of these will teach you about life in the slow lane!

Artists demonstrate their decorative skills at the Wedgwood Visitor Centre

Cheddleton is situated where the picturesque Caldon Canal runs parallel with the River Churnet. It was once important for the grinding of flint, used in the production of slip for the pottery industry. Its twin mills, with their water wheels, were last worked commercially in 1963, although they continue to turn through the dedication of volunteers. Also in Cheddleton is the headquarters of the North Staffordshire Railway Company, which runs a museum

An old pottery factory, strategically placed on the banks of the canal in Stoke-on-Trent

Froghall Walk

WALK

Along the Caldon Canal

START/FINISH: Froghall. On the A52 between Stoke-on-Trent and Ashbourne, 3 miles (5km) north of Cheadle

DISTANCE: 6.5 miles (11km)

ASCENT/GRADIENT: very steep sections to climb, otherwise flat or downhill

TERRAIN/PATHS: canal towpath, fields, forest roads and tracks; good paths; muddy in parts

PARKING: descend hill in Froghall (A52), turn right, signed Foxt, to car-park at Froghall Wharf picnic site

A linear walk along a canal towpath and through woodland in the heart of the Potteries.

1 Josiah Wedgwood was one of the main forces behind the construction of the Trent and Mersey Canal and its branch, the Caldon, initially built for the transportation of lime and limestone, was also used as a supply of water for the Trent

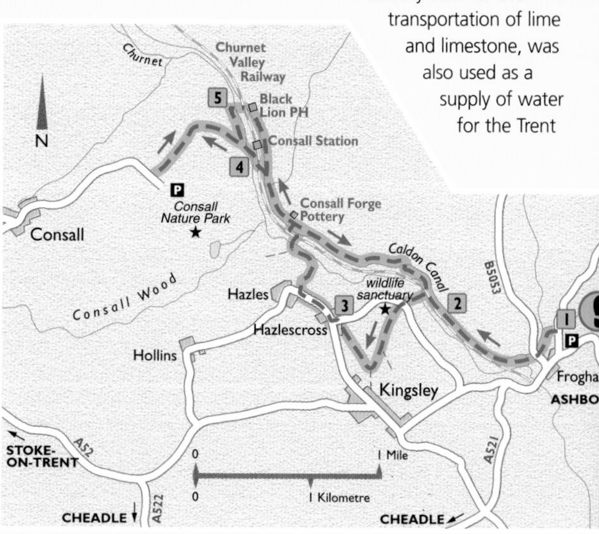

and occasional steam trains. At Blythe Bridge, the Foxfield Light Railway offers steam-powered trips through delightful countryside.

In spite of the giant conurbations, there are numerous small towns and villages scattered throughout the area, with footpaths and cycleways to explore them. Stafford, the ancient county town of Staffordshire, is still a pleasant town and boasts the Ancient High House, a classic black-and-white building and the largest timber-framed town house in England. Stafford has a lively indoor market, while at Newcastle-under-Lyme there are regular flea markets. The fertile countryside has encouraged an interest in gardening and Bridgemere Garden World, at 25 acres (10ha), is Europe's largest garden centre. Antiques and craft shops are found in many of the small towns, such as Market Drayton. The town's famed gingerbread biscuits are said to have aphrodisiac qualities if dunked in port!

CALDON CANAL

The Caldon Canal runs for 17.5 miles (28km) from the main line of the Trent and Mersey Canal at Etruria, near Stoke, to Froghall and passes through 17 locks. Completed in 1778, its main purpose was the transport of limestone, and horse-drawn tramways were built to link Froghall with the quarries. The Caldon Canal was never officially closed down and constant pressure from the volunteers of the Caldon Canal Society finally led to its re-opening in 1974.

TOP STAFFORDSHIRE STATELY HOMES

Shugborough Hall

Magnificent 900-acre (365-ha) seat of the Earls of Lichfield (above). The 18th-century mansion has fine collections of silver, paintings and French furniture.

Weston Park

Fine mansion, built in 1671, standing in elegant gardens and a vast park designed by 'Capability' Brown.

Moseley Old Hall

Elizabethan timber-framed building which was encased in brick in the 19th century. Charles II sheltered here after the Battle of Worcester in 1651.

Boscobel House

Built around 1600, the house contains a number of hiding places, one of which was used by Charles II after his defeat at the Battle of Worcester.

Chillington Hall

Home of the Giffard family since the 12th century, the present porticoed red-brick building dates from the 18th century.

AN URBAN WALK

Stoke-on-Trent's unique linear geography lends itself nicely to a walk that takes in the six towns, with the added advantage of never being far from a bus stop. The full walk, of 11.5 miles (18.5km), starts at Chatterley Whitfield Mine Site and finishes at the Wedgwood Visitor Centre. The walk can be shortened to 8 miles (13km) by starting at Westport Lake, to 6 miles (9.5km) by starting at Canal Marina, to 4 miles (6.5km) by starting in Stoke itself, or to a mere 1.5 miles (2.5km) by starting at the Trentham Hotel.

and Mersey which had suffered shortages. From the car-park at Froghall Wharf picnic site turn left and head along the canal towpath to Froghall Tunnel. Cross the road and rejoin the towpath on the other side.

2 Look for a stile on the left with waymarks for the Staffordshire Way, Moorlands Walk and Red Walk. Cross here and follow the Red Walk markers, go over a footbridge and turn left under the railway bridge. The railway line was closed in the 1960s but has since been re-opened by the Churnet Valley Railway, a preservation society running weekend and special steam trains on the line from their base at the Victorian station in Cheddleton. The line is open to Consall with plans to extend this to Froghall Wharf. The climb is quite steep from here. The path crosses a road and continues uphill, past the animal sanctuary and through a gate on to meadowland. Cross the field, go over a stile and continue through a gate. Before another gate at the end of the field, marking the Moorland Walk, turn right and head for the gate marked the Red Walk. Go through the gate and continue to a narrow road.

3 Turn left at the houses and at the T-junction with Hollins Lane, turn right and follow the Red Walk markers. Look for a signpost pointing right towards Consall Forge and descend this path following purple markers. When the Purple and Moorland Walks paths are intersected by another track, turn right and continue descending. Follow this track, eventually crossing a footbridge over the River Churnet and walk across the railway. Continue on to a forest road beside the canal (the towpath is on the opposite bank) and turn left.

4 The forest road eventually crosses the canal, railway and river, and leads uphill to Consall Nature Park (RSPB) on the left. Call in at the visitor centre. Retrace your steps and rejoin the road heading west downhill. At the white post marker, join the path through the wood until you reach a kissing-gate on your left. Go through the gate and follow the track ahead and the signpost for the Black Lion pub.

5 Cross the river and canal by the bridge opposite the Black Lion and turn right on to the towpath. Where the canal flows through Staffordshire's 'Little Switzerland' the Churnet Valley, on its way to Froghall Wharf, it runs beside the River Churnet and the railway line. The valley is so narrow here that at Consall Station there is a unique platform, engineered to hang out over the canal. Pass Consall Railway Station and Consall Forge Pottery and return to Froghall, crossing bridges where the towpath changes sides.

The sham Gothic castle of Mow Cop, near Biddulph, built by a local squire in 1754

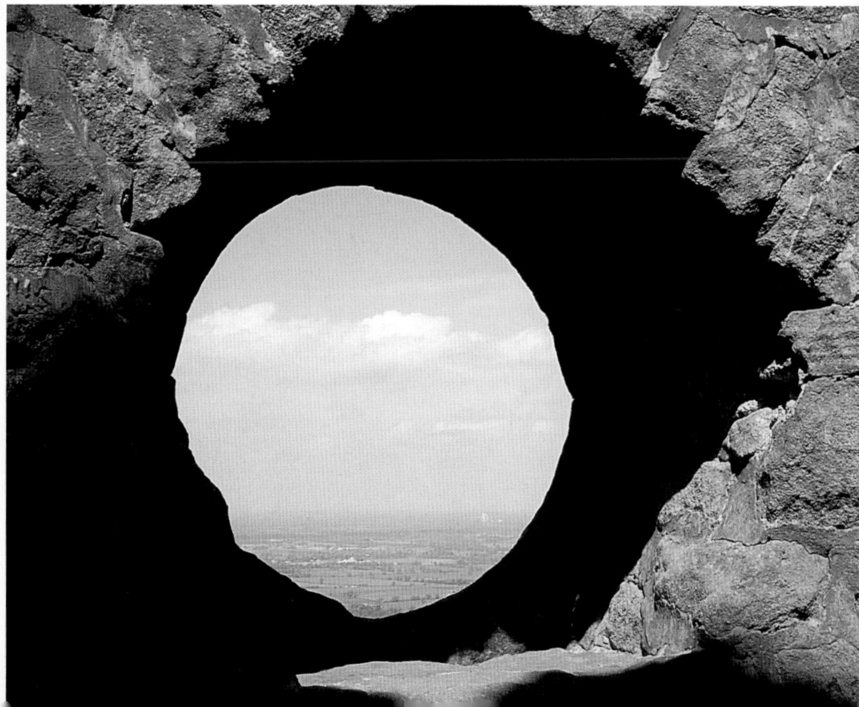

CHESHIRE WATERWAYS

The broad and fertile Cheshire Plain has sometimes been described as a vast parkland. Threaded by the M6 motorway that slices its noisy way through this pleasant, pastoral landscape, this part of Cheshire was once renowned for its salt workings. The legacy left by this industry are the numerous 'meres' or 'flashes' – small lakes or ponds left where the ground has subsided over old salt workings. These meres are popular for fishing and bird-watching. The flat plain was also perfect for creating canals: the main arteries of the Trent and Mersey Canal connect Staffordshire with Liverpool in the northwest and Hull in the northeast, joining the Staffs and Worcs Canal, it also connects the region with the River Severn and thence to Bristol. The Shropshire Union Canal links the Staffs and Worcs Canal to Ellesmere Port via the River Severn. Numerous shorter canals branch off these, creating endless opportunities to explore the hidden byways of England and Wales.

The flatlands of the Cheshire Plains are dotted with a host of unspoilt towns and villages among winding lanes negotiating numerous streams and bogs, known as 'mosses'. Between the villages there are several country parks offering cycling and walking opportunities. Near Little Budworth is the motor-racing track of Oulton Park.

Cheshire is not unrelentingly flat, for the land begins to climb towards the Peak District. Those who climb the cliffs of Alderley

The sun sets over the radio telescope dishes at Jodrell Bank Science Centre

A multi-levered signal box is preserved at the Crewe Railway Age Museum

TOP FIVE CHESHIRE GARDENS

Cholmondley Castle Gardens

A magnificent 800 acres (320ha) of parkland and water gardens.

Ness Botanic Gardens

Rhododendrons and azaleas, plus an outstanding collection of Himalayan and Chinese plants.

Arley Hall

Twelve acres (5ha) with two walled gardens, plus tea, fish and herb gardens, and a double herbaceous border reputed to be the oldest in England.

Hare Hill

A 10-acre (4-ha) ornamental woodland garden in a tranquil setting.

Tatton Park

One of the finest National Trust gardens (below), reflecting almost every aspect of English garden design.

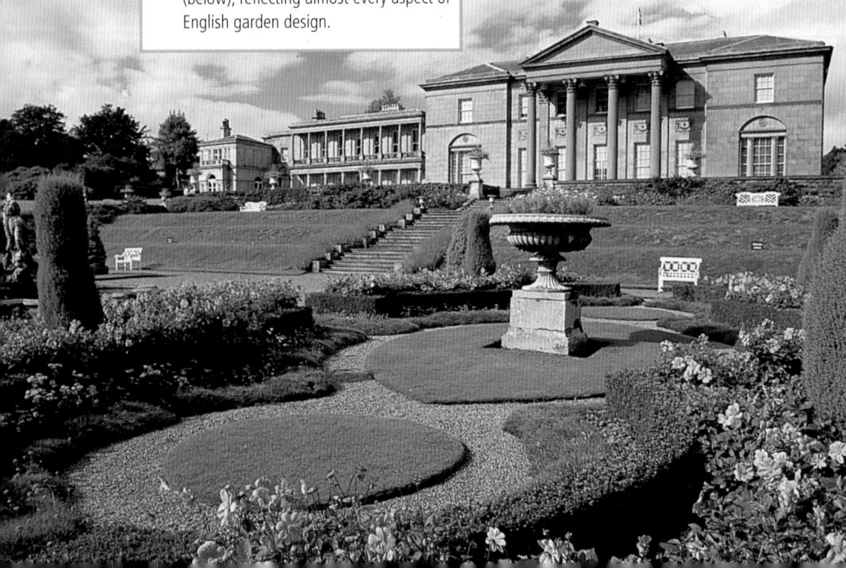

Goostrey Cycle Ride

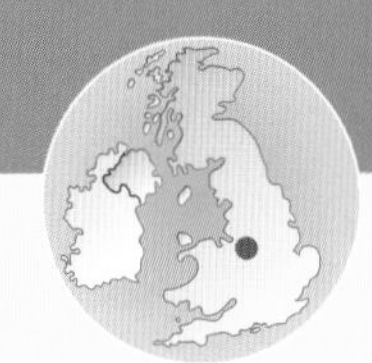

CYCLE RIDE

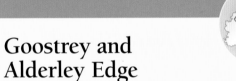

Goostrey and Alderley Edge

START/FINISH: Goostrey. East of Chester, 2 miles (3km) north of Holmes Chapel

DISTANCE: 27.5 miles (44km), with 547yds (500m) off-road

GRADIENT: level then undulating; one steep climb (optional) up Alderley Edge

PARKING: Goostrey Station car-park, between Goostrey and Twemlow Green; Alderley Edge National Trust car-park provides an alternative starting point

A gentle ride through pasturelands, with delightful contrasts in landscape and architecture between park and farm, halls and cottages, old water-mills and the Jodrell Bank radio telescope.

1 Turn left out of Goostrey Station to Twemlow Green. Go left at the T-junction and then immediately left and right over the A535 on to Forty Acre Lane. After 1.5 miles (3km) turn right, signed to Swettenham, on to Congleton Road, and in just under a mile (1km) turn left signed Swettenham Heath. Soon turn left again at a T-junction. Go over the crossroads towards Marton, turning left at the T-junction to join Marton Hall Lane and take the immediate left fork, unsigned, to Marton. Cross the A34 and continue past Pikelow Farm to the A536 (3 miles/5km). Cross on to Maggoty Lane. At the crossroads turn right, and proceed to Gawsworth Hall, a magnificent black-and-white Tudor manor house.

2 Return back to the crossroads and continue straight across, up a slight incline, and continue to the A536. Cross straight over, following Dark Lane to the T-junction with the B5392. Go right and left over the B5392 on to Bearhurst Lane. At the T-junction turn left and then right opposite cottages, signed Chelford, skirting Henbury Hall. Cross the A537 on to Birtles Lane and pass Birtles Hall. Immediately after St Catherine's Church, Birtles, take the tarmac bridleway left. At the three ways in front of farm buildings, take the stony track on the left through a gate, soon to reach tarmac at Shawcross crossroads, where there is a choice of routes. (To take a short cut and avoid a moderate climb, go left here on the byway, which can be muddy in places, then after a mile (1.5km) bear left on to Bradford Lane and continue to Nether Alderley. Here turn left on the A34 and then soon right on to Sand Lane to regain the route at Welsh Row.) Otherwise, take the road opposite, Slade Lane, and continue to the B5087 and turn left. After half a mile (800m) there is a car-park

Edge will be rewarded with a fine view over the Cheshire Plains. The Cheshire Ring Canal Walk beside Macclesfield, once a major silk-producing town, forms a pleasant circuit, partially alongside the Macclesfield Canal which skirts the edge of the Staffordshire Moorlands. Around here there are also some challenging mountain-bike trails, as the land climbs so steeply.

Also on the edge of the Staffordshire Moorlands is Lyme Park, one of many historic houses in Cheshire, used in the filming of the BBC's popular adaptation of *Pride and Prejudice*. Just by Lyme Park, the Gritstone Trail starts its 19-mile (30-km) route to Rushton Spencer, through some of the most rugged and spectacular scenery in Cheshire. At Rushton Spencer, you can join the Mow Cop Trail along the Congleton Edge.

DID YOU KNOW?

The Reverend Charles Lutwidge Dodgson, better known as Lewis Carroll, author of *Alice's Adventures in Wonderland*, was born at **Daresbury** in north Cheshire, in 1832. The village church, set amongst meadows, has a colourful stained-glass window depicting Alice, the Mad Hatter, the Mock Turtle and the other characters which appear in Alice's adventures.

(NT) on the right, just before The Wizard, where it is possible to take a short walk around The Edge for great views across the Cheshire Plain.

3 Turn left, opposite The Wizard, on Artists Lane, and descend to cross the A34 on to Welsh Row at Nether Alderley. After crossing over the railway bridge, continue along Soss Moss Lane. Go right along the A535 for 547yds (500m) at Great Warford, then turn left on to Merryman's Lane, past Warford Hall, and then almost immediately left again on to Mill Lane, past the Stags Head pub and on through Little Warford.

4 Continue along Sandlebridge Lane to Marthall. Cross the A537 on to Sandhole/Snelson Lane, go over the crossroads on to Mill Lane which soon becomes Boundary Lane. In 1.5 miles (2km) turn left signed Bate Mill.

5 Climb to the T-junction, and turn right, Jodrell Bank Science Centre is soon on your left. Adjacent to the huge Lovell radio telescope, this science centre features a planetarium and exhibits. The Environmental Discovery Centre is also worth visiting. Go left at the T-junction in Goostrey and continue on Station Road to return to Goostrey Station car-park.

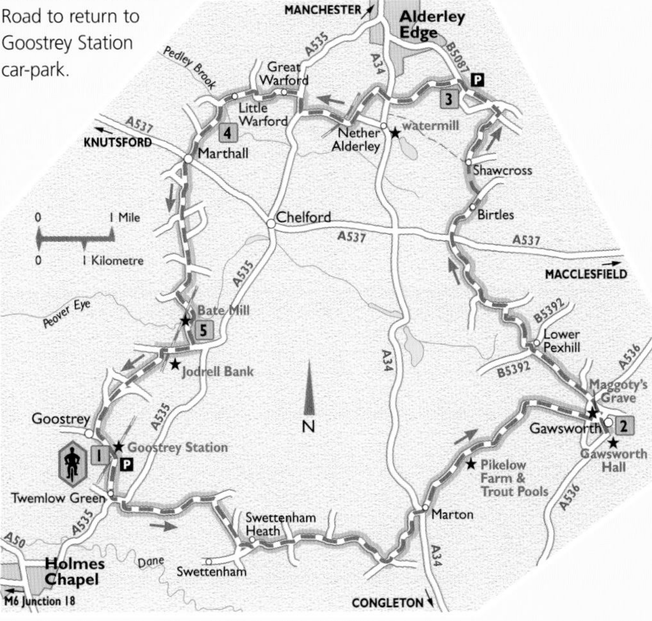

Near Nantwich, one of Cheshire's former salt-mining towns, is the massive Stapeley Water Gardens which, making the most of the resulting 'meres', offers Europe's largest selection of water plants and angling equipment. Fishing is a popular activity in the region: at Biddulph Moor there is fishing in the extensive grounds of Biddulph Park, as well as at the Knypersley Reservoir in the nearby Greenway Bank Country Park and at Tatton Park.

DOWN IN THE FOREST

Delamere Forest is a great place to explore, either on foot or by bike on one of the many waymarked trails. Originally part of a medieval hunting forest used by the Earls of Chester, these pine-clad heights are now in the care of the Forestry Commission, and usually open to the public to enjoy. Favourite spots include the lovely, reed-fringed pools of Hatchmere and Oakmere, and there is a Dark-Age hillfort on Eddisbury Hill.

Around Nantwich and Crewe there is long a circular walk, or around Congleton along the Biddulph Valley Way or from Sandbach through some pretty valleys and canalside scenery. The Vale Royal Round crosses the heart of Cheshire, linking a number of other trails, and is best enjoyed over a couple of days.

CHESHIRE WALKS

The Dane Valley – a 4.5-mile (7-km) walk through rich dairy country following a wooded river valley.

Raw Head – a more strenous walk of 5.5 miles (9km) with some steep climbs among rugged sandstone outcrops, reaching 747ft (227m) at Raw Head.

Parkgate – a gentle estuary walk of 3 miles (5km) with thousands of wading birds on the marsh in winter.

Utkinton – a 5-mile (8-km) route across a patchwork of fields and country lanes, with great views of the Peckforton Hills.

Shutlingshoe – a walk of 6.5 miles (10.5km) across Cheshire's gritstone hill country, reaching 1,664ft (506m) at Shutlingshoe.

CHESTER & THE BORDER COUNTRY

Inland from its muddy estuary, a haven for bird-watchers, the River Dee, with its intricate twists and turns, marks the border between England and Wales. This area was a turbulent battlefield for hundreds of years, which is made clear by the castles scattered near the border and the defensive walls of the beautiful city of Chester. The bustling county town of Cheshire, Chester is famous for its red sandstone city walls and two-storey galleried medieval shops known as The Rows. Originally it was a Roman fortress called *Deva* and if you take a city tour around Chester your guide may be dressed as a Roman soldier! Chester is now an excellent city for shopping, with a varied selection of individual and high street shops, many aimed at an upmarket clientele. Just outside Chester is Cheshire Oaks, Europe's largest designer outlet. Other delights to purchase are creamy Cheshire cheese or salmon fresh from the River Dee.

South from here, the broad, fertile meadows of the Cheshire Plain enter Shropshire around Whitchurch. The countryside near by is scattered with numerous lakes or 'meres', and is known as Shropshire's 'Lake District'. At the centre of the 'Lake District' is Ellesmere, which stands close to seven attractive meres, which are rich in wildlife, particularly wildfowl. They include the 116-acre (47-ha)

The mere at Ellesmere, a watery home to numerous wildfowl

WHERE BATS FLY FREE

Chester Zoo is claimed to be the largest in the country, and makes an exciting day out for the children at any time of the year. Not for the faint-hearted, however, is the Twilight Zone Bat Cave, where rare bats fly free as visitors walk through a simulated nightscape. Among the other latest attractions is the Penguin Pool, where you can watch through viewing ports the superb and graceful underwater antics of these comical little flightless birds. And there's always a batch of new baby animals to see, as the zoo has a vigorous breeding programme.

A busker entertains by the cross in Chester's medieval streets

Chester Drive

DRIVE

Cheshire's Deeside

START/FINISH: Chester. Cathedral city located off the A55/M53 south of Birkenhead

DISTANCE: 54 miles (86.5km)

From historic Chester, this relaxing drive follows the River Dee south, passing through quiet Cheshire countryside where charming villages invite exploration. The return journey north tours the well-wooded Peckforton Hills, dotted with historic sites, and passes through the ancient Forest of Delamere.

1 Leave Chester by following the Whitchurch road from the Ring Road. At the gyratory system follow the signs to Farndon to leave on the B5130. First settled by the Romans, Chester has a fascinating history. The Grosvenor Museum tells the story. Visit the unique galleried streets, known as The Rows, and the walk around the city's defensive ramparts.

2 Just beyond Churton turn left to follow the B5130, signed Stretton Watermill. Passing Farndon on the right, turn left along the A534, signed Broxton. On the edge of Barton, turn right towards Tilston. In just under a mile (1.5km) turn left on to a single-track road, signed Stretton Watermill. Pass the mill, a fully restored, 17th-century water-powered corn mill, keep forward and shortly turn right for Tilston. At Tilston turn left and continue to Malpas. Passing the market cross on your right, turn left down the side street, signed No Man's Heath.

3 Cross the A41, signed Bickley, and turn left on reaching the A49. Shortly, turn left again along a minor road, signed to Egerton and Bickerton. Pass the grounds of Cholmondeley Castle and continue, unclassified, for 2 miles (3km). Cholmondeley Castle (not open), a Gothic-style 18th-century building, is surrounded by romantically landscaped gardens. At the T-junction turn right, then at Bickerton church keep straight on, signed Broxton. Turn left along the A534 and take the next right (by the Coppermine pub) on to the Harthill road.

4 Pass Harthill church and in half a mile (800m) turn right for Burwardsley. A mile (1.5km) beyond Burwardsley turn right for Beeston. In 2.5 miles (4km), at the foot of the castle hill, bear right for the village of Beeston, passing Beeston Castle, a ruined 13th-century stronghold with views to the Pennines and the Welsh hills. At the end of the village

mere at the eastern end of the town, which is popular for boating, fishing and picnics.

To the west, the first hills of Wales mark the Border Country around Oswestry. This picturesque market town is in every sense a border town, and was constantly fought over by the English and the Welsh. Now its reputation is as the hot-air ballooning capital of the world. Here Per Lindstrand tests his round-the-world balloons and several companies offer the chance to take fabulous flights over the Welsh hills or Long Myndd and the Shropshire Hills. Parachuting or flying lessons are also options.

Not far from Oswestry is part of Offa's Dyke long-distance footpath, wending its way up past the ruins of Chirk Castle to North Wales. Mountain biking is popular around Oswestry and gentler cycling paths cross the county to the east. Another option for exploring the area is by horse and, of course, we must not forget the canals and rivers. The Shropshire Union and the Llangollen canals meander across the county. As they enter the hilly west, some staggering feats of engineering have created the 70-ft (21-m) high Chirk Aqueduct across the Ceiriog Valley and the Pontcysyllte Aqueduct which carries boats over the River Dee at 126ft (38m).

To the east of the county, near the small market town of Wem, is an amazing man-made landscape. Lost for many years through neglect and decay, the extraordinary park at Hawkstone is an excellent place to let off steam. A few hundred years ago the natural cliffs and gorges were constructed into a fantasy landscape that has recently been partially restored. From the top of the monument, which crowns the park, a number of counties can be seen on a clear day.

STAND AND DELIVER

The area southwest of Oswestry is known as **Kynaston Country** after Humphrey Kynaston, an 18th-century highwayman who is supposed to have leapt the River Severn on his horse. You can still see his hideaway, a cave carved out of the sandstone at the **Nesscliffe Hill Country Park**, which he was supposed to have used when he was hiding from the long arm of the law.

CITY IN THE SKY

Old Oswestry, traditionally the home of Queen Guinevere, wife of King Arthur, is one of the finest Iron-Age hillforts in the country. It stands on a 500-ft (152-m) hill just north of Oswestry and provides an easy walk with fine views from the extensive ramparts which contour around the hilltop. At its height during the 1st century, between 200 and 250 people lived here, probably using it as an administrative or trading centre, as much as a defence against their enemies.

SEEING THE DEE

The Dee, Cheshire's most famous river, descends from the Welsh mountains to meander its way through the broad, fertile Cheshire Plain before reaching Chester. A good way to see it is by river boat; cruises from Chester (below) go upstream as far as Thomas Telford's great wrought-iron bridge at Aldford. Downstream from Chester, the Dee estuary offers plenty of opportunities for bird-watching.

keep left towards Tiverton and soon turn left on to the A49. Skirt Tiverton and, at the A49/A51 junction, go straight ahead on to the B5152, signed Eaton. Continue through Eaton and turn right, signed Little Budworth, on to a minor road to Oulton Park. Pass the entrance to Oulton Park Motor-racing Circuit, then turn sharp left, signed to Sandybrow and Chester.

5 Continue to the A49 and turn right, then left on to the A54 towards Chester. At the Fishpool Inn, turn right on to the Delamere Forest road, B5152. Cross the A556, signed Frodsham, pass Delamere Station on the left to enter Delamere Forest, a popular recreation area with picnic areas and miles of waymarked walks. In 1 mile (1.5km), at the crossroads, turn left, signed to Marley and Moldsworth, along a minor road for 2 miles (3.5km) to a crossroads. Proceed straight on, signed Tarvin, turn left on to the B5393 (no sign) and pass through Ashton. Turn right on reaching the A54, skirt Tarvin and join the A51 for the return to Chester.

TRAVELLING THE CANALS & WATERWAYS

Every year, one in six of Britain's population uses part of Britain's 2,000 miles (3,200km) of canals and waterways for recreation. British Waterways, who manage the network, estimate that the waterways welcome 10 million visitors a year. The 200-year-old network of canals – built to transport goods and raw materials and providing the vital underpinning for the success of the world's first Industrial Revolution – has never been more popular. But today, the canals are mainly used for leisure purposes, and they are valued not only for their boating opportunities, but also for activities such as angling, walking or cycling, provided by the towpaths.

In addition to the canals, the navigable waters of the major rivers enable the water-borne visitor to safely enjoy some of England's great historic rivers, including the Severn, the Weaver, the Ouse and the Trent. And there are over 130 miles (209km) of navigable waters in the Norfolk and Suffolk Broads National Park.

The boats which use the waterways can range from canoes and sailing boats to cabin cruisers and converted narrow boats and barges. As well as privately-owned powered craft, there are nearly 1,500 powered boats for hire. Added to this, about 150 day-trip, restaurant and hotel boats provide inland cruises for those who prefer to let someone else take the helm.

A traditionally painted narrow boat on the Kennet and Avon Canal at Newbury

There are few finer or more relaxing ways of enjoying Britain's ever-changing countryside than on a narrow boat holiday. As you gently chug through some of the quietest countryside, often miles from any road, you are likely to encounter a side of Britain which few other visitors will see. Wildlife is everywhere, so nature-lovers will have unrivalled opportunities to study their subjects close at hand. Along the waterways, there are over 600 miles (965km) of hedgerows and 1,000 wildlife conservation sites, including nature reserves, which encompass over a hundred Sites of Special Scientific Interest (SSSIs), and a few Ramsar sites, which are internationally-recognised wetland areas.

There are 100,000 anglers who fish the waterways regularly. The opportunities for coarse fishing in these waters are excellent, but you must have a National Rod Licence, issued by the Environment Agency, and the permission of the landowner. Most of the British Waterways network is leased to local fishing clubs who control the day-to-day fishing on these stretches. Most clubs, however, allow non-members to fish their waters for a daily fee.

Walking the 1,500 miles (2,413km) of available towpaths is becoming increasingly popular and several routes have been made into long-distance walking trails. These include: the Grand Union Canal, 147 miles (236km) from London to Birmingham; the Thames Path, 180 miles (290km) from its source in Gloucestershire to the Thames Barrier; the Kennet and Avon Canal, 87 miles (140km) from Reading to Bath; and the Caledonian Canal across the Highland Fault 'neck' of Scotland.

Generally speaking, the towpaths are freely available for walkers, joggers or cyclists. However, there is no legal right of way for cyclists on towpaths, and you will need to display a special cycle permit available from local British Waterway offices. British Waterways is committed to a programme of improving towpaths to expand the mileage currently available to cyclists.

CITY OF CANALS

It's Birmingham's proud boast that it has more miles of canals than Venice, and the 35 miles (53km) of waterways which thread Britain's second city are a wonderful way to see it. The tastefully restored Gas Street Basin, close to the city centre where the Worcester and Birmingham Canal joins the Birmingham Main Line, is at the hub.

Neptune's Staircase on the Caledonian Canal near Fort William

Colourful houseboats moored at Aylesbury on the Grand Union Canal

Thurso
Wick
Ullapool
Gairloch
Tain
Uig
Dingwall
Banff
Elgin
Peterhead
Portree
Inverness
Kyle of Lochalsh
Aviemore
Aberdeen
Caledonian Canal
Mallaig
Fort William
Montrose
Pitlochry
Crianlarich
Dundee
Oban
Perth
Stirling
Glasgow
Edinburgh
Berwick-upon-Tweed
Largs
Peebles
Kilmarnock
Campbeltown
Alnwick
Ayr
Moffat
Dumfries
Newcastle upon Tyne
Stranraer
Carlisle
Workington
Penrith
Middlesbrough
Kendal
Thirsk
Scarborough
Douglas
Settle
R Ouse
Lancaster
York
Blackpool
Burnley
Leeds
Hull
Huddersfield Narrow Canal
Bridgewater Canal
Grimsby
Liverpool
Manchester
Sheffield
R Weaver
Peak Forest Canal
R Trent
Holyhead
Colwyn Bay
Lincoln
Caernarfon
Pontcysyllte Aqueduct
Chester
Newark-on-Trent
Stoke-on-Trent
Boston
Stafford
Nottingham
King's Lynn
Dolgellau
R Severn
Norwich
Great Yarmouth
Shrewsbury
Leicester
Peterborough
Norfolk and Suffolk Broads
Birmingham
Aberystwyth
Newtown
Gas Street Basin
Coventry
Grand Union Canal
Ludlow
Northampton
Bury St Edmunds
Worcester
Stratford-upon-Avon Canal
Bedford
Hereford
Cambridge
Ipswich
Stoke Bruerne Waterways Museum
Fishguard
Brecon
Monmouthshire & Brecon Canal
Luton
Carmarthen
Gloucester
Abergavenny
Chelmsford
Pembroke
Swansea
R Thames
Oxford
Watford
Swindon
Cardiff
Reading
R Thames
Bristol
LONDON
Bath
Kennet & Avon Canal
Sevenoaks
Maidstone
Guildford
Dover
Barnstaple
Salisbury
Taunton
Yeovil
Southampton
Chichester
Brighton
Hastings
Bournemouth
Exeter
Weymouth
Truro
Plymouth

Cruising along the Shropshire Union Canal at Llangollen

CANAL CULT CENTRE

The Barge Inn in the tiny hamlet of Honeystreet, near Alton Barnes in Wiltshire, is well named as it stands on the Kennet and Avon Canal, where the waterway winds across the Vale of Pewsey beneath the rolling Pewsey Downs. Typical of many canalside pubs, The Barge has, however, gained another claim to fame as the unofficial headquarters of the crop circle cult, and the interior is decorated with their weird and wonderful designs.

Canals and waterways shown on the map have been chosen for their particular interest or attraction and to give a good geographical spread. It is not possible to show every one on the map.

NORTH ENGLAND

Ambleside, Cumbria

LANCASHIRE & LIVERPOOL

Manchester, for so long tarred with the dark brush of industrial grime and deprivation, has undergone an urban make-over unequalled in Britain, while Liverpool, the city that produced the Beatles, is renowned for its acerbic wit and a remarkable community spirit. These northern industrial conurbations have always been close to beautiful landscape and rural retreats to rival any in England. Explore the pretty villages and hamlets of Lancashire, historic Lancaster on the edge of the Forest of Bowland, and the sweeping flat sands of Morecambe Bay flanked by the hills of the Lakes and the Pennines. The cities, the countryside, the seaside and tacky, technicolour Blackpool are all part of that lively mixture of friendliness and sheer exuberance which brings people back to the North.

The Lowry, Manchester
This magnificent modern building, close to Harbour City Metrolink tram station, is the main millennium building for the Northwest of England. Resplendent in gleaming silver, it has something of the air of the Guggenheim Museum in Bilbao, Spain. Those who think they know the work of the artist L S Lowry will be surprised at his range of styles.

FERRY ACROSS THE MERSEY

The ferry from Liverpool to Birkenhead, celebrated in song, film and folklore, is legendary. The first ferry across the Mersey was operated by the monks of Birkenhead Priory when Liverpool was a mere village. Ferries now run from Liverpool's Pier Head, where splendid Victorian buildings create a skyline that is dominated by the Royal Liver Building. There is no better way to view the city's waterfront and architectural heritage.

Croxteth Hall and Country Park
This fine historic mansion and its 500-acre (203-ha) park, on the outskirts of Liverpool, was once the home of the Earls of Sefton. The rooms of the hall are a wonderful re-creation of its Edwardian heyday, with period pieces and people dressed in character. The park there has a Victorian walled garden and a unique collection of rare breeds of farm animals.

MAP AND KEY

- Liverpool Walk
- Martin Mere Cycle Ride
- Morecambe Drive

BLACKPOOL

There can be few better-known landmarks in the country than Blackpool Tower. The town's soaring ambitions as a holiday resort were confirmed by the building, in 1894, of this 519-ft (158-m) replica of Paris's Eiffel Tower. There are lifts to the top, from where there are magnificent views over the resort and miles of coastline. The long-established Blackpool Pleasure Beach is one of the most visited amusement parks in England. Four of the original wooden roller-coasters remain, along with many other rides.

LIVERPOOL, MANCHESTER & THE SHIP CANAL

Liverpool, a city with two cathedrals, gazes out across the River Mersey to the sea, as it has done for centuries. In its long history as a port it has unloaded cargoes of tobacco, cotton and cane sugar from across the Atlantic. Many of those ships continued on to West Africa, taking wretched human cargoes back to the Americas to be sold into slavery.

Albert Dock, built in 1864 to accommodate sailing ships, proved too shallow for steamships and by the turn of the century had become largely obsolete. Comprising the largest collection of Grade I listed buildings in the country, the dock has been sensitively restored to become the city's recreational centre-piece. Around the dock is a fascinating array of attractions, including the award-winning Merseyside Maritime Museum, the HM Customs and Excise National Museum, the northern outpost of the Tate Gallery, the Museum of Liverpool Life, and the greatest draw of all, The Beatles Story.

THE BEATLES STORY

More than a quarter of a century after they broke up, The Beatles are a bigger tourist attraction than ever, and The Beatles Story tells the remarkable tale of the four local lads who conquered the world with their music. You can take a trip to Hamburg, 'feel' the Cavern beat, 'tune in' to flower power, board the Yellow Submarine and battle with a Beatle brain computer.

THE BIRKENHEAD PACKET

At East Float Dock are two vessels – the frigate HMS *Plymouth* and submarine HMS *Onyx* – that played important roles in the Falklands conflict. These are just two of the waterfront attractions that, along with the tram and transport museum and Woodside Visitor Centre, comprise the 'Birkenhead Packet'. Vintage trams now carry visitors between the museum and the ferry.

An elegant masted ship moored in Liverpool's historic Albert Dock

Liverpool Walk

WALK

Liverpool and The Beatles

START/FINISH: The Beatles Story, Albert Dock, Liverpool
DISTANCE: 5 miles (8km)
GRADIENT: slight
TERRAIN/PATHS: city centre; pavements

This gentle walk begins from Liverpool's historic Albert Dock and explores the city's streets, passing places associated with The Beatles, including The Cavern Club and numerous pubs.

1 Before you start the walk, visit the tourist office at Albert Dock and buy a copy of *Discover Beatles' Liverpool*. This tour guide and pocket map will take you to even more places with Beatles' associations. From The Beatles Story turn left, then right along the front of the dock by the river. Turn right at the end, signed Maritime Museum. Pass the museum and exit the docks, turning left on to the main road, then left again at the major junction into Mann Island.

2 Turn right along Pierhead, right again to reach the front of the Royal Liver Building at George's Dock Gates, and cross the busy road with care to turn left into Water Street. Continue up past the India Buildings on the

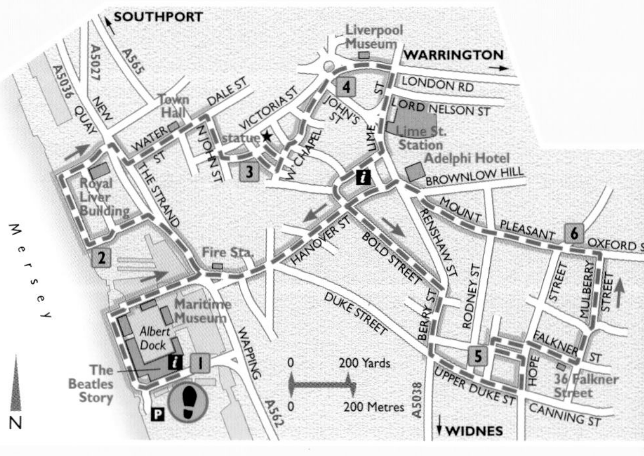

Only the width of the River Mersey separates Liverpool from Birkenhead, just a hamlet until the shipbuilding boom of the 19th century. The town contains the oldest building on Merseyside – Birkenhead Priory – where interpretative displays describe the daily routine of the monks.

Prescot, to the east of Liverpool, is well worth a visit if you are interested in horology. The Museum of Clock and Watch Making illustrates the main industry of the area. It includes a reconstruction of part of a traditional watchmaker's workshop and displays of the equipment used to make the intricate parts of clock and watch movements. Just to the north of Prescot is Knowsley Safari Park, with a 5-mile (8-km) drive through reserves containing lions, tigers, elephants, rhinos, monkeys and many other animals. Children can get closer to (tame) animals in the pets' corner, and there is also a reptile house and an amusement park.

The 36-mile (58-km) long Manchester Ship Canal was opened in 1894 to give ocean-going vessels access from the Mersey estuary to Manchester. Mersey Ferries' MS *Mountwood* takes you from Salford Quays to the Pier Head at Liverpool through an industrial heartland of factories and wharves, locks and bridges, motorway viaducts and surprising rural stretches.

Cotton manufacture brought prosperity to Manchester and the network of canals and railways set the seal on the city's lasting importance. A legacy of handsome Victorian buildings, both civic and industrial, is testimony to the city's prosperity. Manchester now attracts more than one-and-a-half million visitors each year. Among its wealth of museums and galleries are the City Art Gallery, the Whitworth Art Gallery and the Manchester United Museum & Tour Centre, at Trafford.

GRANADA STUDIOS

At Granada Studios you can enter the magical world of TV and film and experience its drama, comedy and sheer excitement. You can go behind the scenes and in front of the cameras, walk on famous sets and experience the cinema of the future. The main attractions include the back-stage tour, the Baker Street experience, the Coronation Street experience, Motion Master (the cinema of the 21st century), the 3D Galactic Hunter, House of Commons Debate, The All New Sooty Show and a live magic show.

PORT SUNLIGHT

A short ferry ride across the River Mersey from Liverpool lies the Wirral peninsula. Late in the 19th century Lord Leverhulme built a 'model' village for the workers at his soap factory. Port Sunlight offered tree-lined roads, open spaces and good housing – a fine example of social engineering at a time when very few employers gave much thought to their employees' well-being. A heritage centre tells how the garden village, now a conservation area, was planned and built, and you can explore it by following the village trail.

URBAN RENEWAL

Britain's first Urban Heritage Park, the **Castlefield** area of Manchester is being transformed into a major recreational amenity. The original castle made way, during the late 18th century, for the building of the country's first canal, the **Bridgewater Canal**. Castlefield gradually slipped into dereliction, a decline halted in recent years by a massive restoration scheme. Now there are festivals, carnivals and exhibitions throughout the year to supplement permanent attractions that include the Museum of Science and Industry and tours of the Granada Television Studios.

right and Town Hall on the left, turn right into North John Street at the top and then take the third left, Mathew Street. The Cavern Club is on your right, at 10 Mathew Street, but it's not the original. That disappeared in a spate of redevelopment but has been reconstructed, partially on the original site, using some of the original bricks. Paul McCartney played here in 1999.

3 Turn second right into Rainsford Gardens (*not* Rainsford Square), left at Button Street and left again into Whitechapel. Almost immediately after, turn left up Stanley Street to see the Eleanor Rigby statue on the right. Return to Whitechapel, turn left, cross the street and continue to the end, well beyond the shops, crossing Crosshall Street along the way. Bear left round the top of the major junction which leads into the Birkenhead tunnel. Throughout the Cavern Quarter are tributes to The Beatles, a Yellow Submarine, statues of John Lennon and Eleanor Rigby, even a Cavern pub. You can still have a quiet drink in the Beatles' two favourite pubs, The Grapes and the White Star.

4 Turn right into William Brown Street, walking uphill past the Liverpool Museum, Central Library and the Walker Art Gallery. The imposing building on the right is St George's Hall. Cross the road with care at the top (pedestrian lights) and turn right down Lime Street and past the Empire Theatre. Once past the taxi ranks on the far side of the station, cross the road with care and go down Elliot Street, down the modern steps by St John's shopping precinct and continue to the bottom of the pedestrian area. At the corner with Church Street, turn left and look up the long straight road which is Bold Street. Cross Hanover/Ranelagh Street to reach it and go all the way to the top. Turn right into Berry Street, left into Upper Duke Street, and up past the impressive Anglican Cathedral before turning left into Hope Street. Turn down into Mount Street.

5 Turn right at Pilgrim Street, right again into Rice Street and left back into Hope Street. Go first right into Falkner Street, left on to Catharine Street, continue as it changes to Mulberry Street and turn left down Oxford Street. You can walk past 36 Falkner Street where John and Cynthia first set up home, the Art School where they studied and drink in Ye Crack Pub in Rice Street where John met Stu Sutcliffe 'the fifth Beatle'.

6 Keep on this road as far as the Adelphi Hotel, cross the road and turn left into Ranelagh Street. Continue in this direction as it joins Hanover Street. As you cross Paradise Street look straight ahead and you will see Albert Dock in the distance. Cross the main road by the Fire Station at Canning Place and return to Albert Dock.

Manchester's network of canals and railways, which aided the city's commercial prosperity

FROM FORMBY SANDS TO THE MOORS

Even in this industrial heartland of England, once engulfed in the black smoke of 'dark satanic mills', you are never far from open countryside and coast. The dunes of Formby Sands, the genteel resort of Southport, the solid Victorian respectability of Preston, industrial Blackburn and the lovely Ribble Valley are a microcosm of 19th-century England where the Industrial Revolution wrought changes in an ancient rural landscape.

Preston is the administrative, commercial and retail capital of Lancashire, with a colourful and vibrant market and Victorian shopping arcades. Crisscrossed by over 160 miles (257km) of public footpaths and bridleways, including the famous 'Round Preston Walk' and part of the Ribble Way, the town is surrounded by beautiful countryside. Mentioned in the Domesday Book, it is one of the oldest boroughs in the country. It was a wealthy market town in the 17th century and became an important centre of the cotton and textile industries in the 19th century. Preston has a superb choice of open spaces, from moorland and woodland to the Victorian splendour of formal ornamental gardens. Moor Park is the town's largest open space, dating back to 1726.

FRESHFIELD RED SQUIRREL RESERVE

The reserve consists of predominantly coniferous woodlands which were planted in the 1920s to stabilise the dunes and shelter the town of Formby. The squirrels are active during the day, spending three-quarters of their time above ground in trees and shrubs. You are most likely to see red squirrels. Though they are native to Britain, the squirrel reserve is one of the few remaining places where the red squirrels have survived in competition with the larger grey squirrel.

Steam locomotives on the East Lancashire Railway stop at the unspoilt town of Ramsbottom

Late 19th-century worthies of Preston would have holidayed at Southport and the town retains that feel of solid Victorian gentility. Classical municipal buildings, gardens, mature trees and fountains line up opposite brass-plated shop-fronts with wrought-iron canopies. But you can also try out stomach-churning rides at the amusement park, investigate the education and conservation programme at the zoo or take a trip on the *Southport Belle*, a Mississippi-style paddle steamer on the Marine Lake. On the

Martin Mere Cycle Ride

CYCLE RIDE

Lanes and Villages Around Martin Mere

START/FINISH: Burscough Bridge railway station. On the A59 between Liverpool and Preston, 2 miles (3km) north of Ormskirk

DISTANCE: 14 miles (22.5km)

ROADS: quiet back lanes and short stretches of busy A-road

PARKING: free parking south side of the station (near The Cambridge pub). Visitors to the Martin Mere Centre could also start from there

An easy, level ride that follows quiet back lanes through fertile fields between the settlements of Burscough Bridge and Rufford. Allow time to visit a 16th-century half-timbered hall and one of Britain's most important wetland sites, Martin Mere, where you can view a wide variety of birds and wildfowl.

1 From Burscough Bridge station join the main A59 road which crosses the railway tracks. It is busy, so wheel your bike across the road and walk left down the pavement for 70yds (64m) to Warpers Moss Lane on the right. Ride along the lane and soon reach the countryside; the narrowing lane winds its way beneath two railway bridges to a junction. Burscough Bridge, known for corn-milling and basket-making, developed in the late 18th and early 19th centuries with the coming of the Leeds and Liverpool Canal and the railways.

2 Go left and cross the Leeds and Liverpool Canal at Lathom. Ignore Sutch Lane but take the second left, Daisy Lane (concealed entrance), to a junction at a level crossing. Take the right fork, Bleak Lane, to a crossroads of tracks. Go right here to reach the end of Wood Lane. At this junction turn left into Wanes Blades Road.

3 The road bridges the River Douglas into Mains Lane and meets the B5246 below Bispham Green. Turn left into Hall Lane and continue for 2.5 miles (4km) to Rufford. The road bends sharp left into the village, over the Leeds and Liverpool Canal and the railway line. Pass St Mary's Church in Rufford and meet the A59. Turn right for Rufford Old Hall (437yds/400m). This splendid 16th-century half-timbered hall (NT), home to the Hesketh family for centuries, contains a range of fine furniture, arms, armour and tapestries.

Youngsters are catered for with rides at Southport's funfair

4 Otherwise, cut left to ride along the old Liverpool Road (A59), then follow the right-hand feeder lane to join the B5246, opposite the Central Garage. (It is better to dismount and walk across.) After 437yds (400m) turn left into Cousins Lane. Turn right into Tootle Lane. At the fork, take the right branch into Mere Lane which runs through fields for half a mile (800m) to a sharp right turn before reaching a few dwellings. Go left here to reach a T-junction at a busier road.

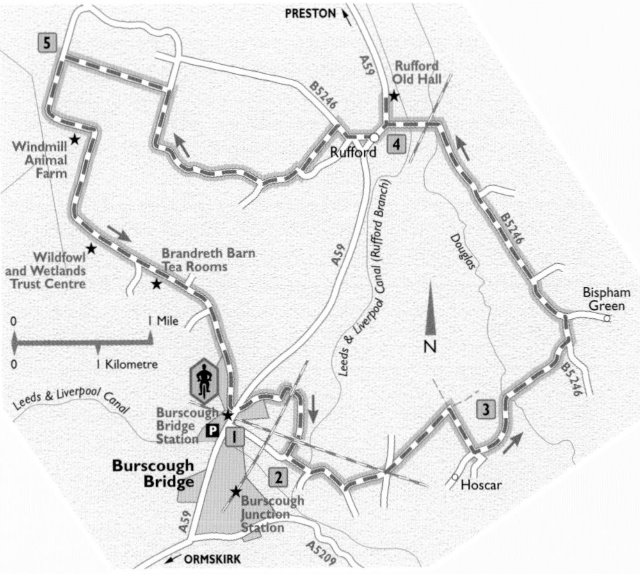

5 Turn left and follow this road, passing a windmill and Windmill Animal Farm. The road bends sharp right round the farm and then, after another straight section, left to Martin Mere Wildfowl and Wetlands Trust Centre. Martin Mere was once an extensive lake covering some 3,000 acres (1,200ha), much of which has been reclaimed, and the Trust Centre is home to a wide variety of birds. Continue along Fish Lane, which becomes Tarlscough Lane, to Burscough Bridge for just under 2 miles (3km), passing Brandreth Barn Tea Rooms in just under half a mile (800m). Enter the outskirts of Burscough Bridge and soon turn left back to the railway station.

MARTIN MERE

This Wildfowl and Wetlands Trust Centre near **Ormskirk** has birds from all over the world, including ducks, geese, swans and flamingoes which can be observed from hides overlooking the floodwaters. In winter the bird population is swelled by the arrival of huge numbers of pink-footed geese and migrating Whooper and Bewick's swans, which can be viewed from the many hides or from the comfort of the heated Raines Observatory. The centre also has the Wetland Adventure for children, an exciting expedition through simulated wetland, via a swaying bridge, to a pond maze.

northern outskirts of Southport lies the village of Churchtown, with thatched fishermen's cottages dating back to the 18th century.

Inland to the south are Wigan, Bolton and Bury whose workers would have travelled to the coast at Southport for day-trips. Wigan Pier is one of the best industrial heritage museums in the country, with a host of attractions from Music Hall to factories to children's games. Bolton, situated on the lower slopes of the West Pennine moors, played a significant role in the industrial development of Lancashire. Samuel Crompton's invention of the 'spinning mule' changed the cotton industry from cottage- to factory-based production. Gone now are the mills which dominated the skyline, the smoking chimneys, blackened terraced houses and cobbled streets. On the outskirts of Bolton both Samuel Crompton's home of Hall-i'th'-wood and nearby Smithills Hall recall an even older way of life. Here you can gain an impression of life in Lancashire from the Middle Ages to the Victorian era.

From Bury, the East Lancashire Railway runs steam and diesel services to Rawtenstall, where the local countryside offers relaxing walks through fells and moorland, unchanged since medieval times. Bury boasts a thriving indoor market selling traditional East Lancashire goods, as well as many specialist shops on its cobbled main street.

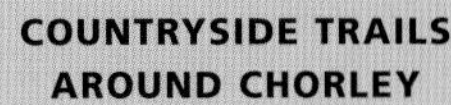

COUNTRYSIDE TRAILS AROUND CHORLEY

Chorley Circular – 9 miles (14.5km) taking in Duxbury Woods and the Yarrow Valley Park.

Rufford and Mawdsley – 6 miles (9.5km) over varied countryside including the Douglas Valley.

Whittle-le-Woods – 6 miles (9.5km) tracing the route of the Walton Summit Branch of the Leeds and Liverpool Canal.

Botany Bay Circular – 11 miles (17.5km) taking in the Withnell local nature reserve and the hamlet of White Coppice in the shadow of the West Pennines.

Brindle to Withnell Fold – 4 miles (6.5km) over undulating farmland.

The heritage museum at Wigan Pier, which evokes scenes from Victorian life

BOWLAND FOREST & BLACKPOOL

A carpet of buttercups covers a meadow near Whitewell in the Forest of Bowland

The resorts of Lancashire are where the North of England has traditionally gone on holiday. Whole mill towns would decamp here during 'Wakes Week' (the annual holiday). Blackpool and Lytham St Anne's still attract millions, and from Morecambe Bay to Lytham St Anne's much of the coastline remains unspoilt, with miles of empty beaches. In sharp contrast are the bleaker beauties of the surrounding hills, the Lake District, visible to the north, and the Pennines to the east, with their tumult of moors and stormy skies.

The delightful Toy & Teddy Bear Museum at Lytham St Anne's

Morecambe is famous for its 4-mile (6.5-km) seaside promenade, which provides holiday entertainment from theatres, funfairs and amusement arcades to a modern Superdome and Bubbles Leisure Park. The Marineland Oceanarium and Aquarium was the first of its kind in Europe and its performing dolphins are still the star turn. Morecambe grew from the little fishing village of Poulton-le-Sands, and boats still fish locally for whitebait, cockles and shrimps.

Brash, brazen and bustling, Blackpool wears its heart on its sleeve; there is nothing subtle about the attractions of the Pleasure Beach and the celebrated Golden Mile – part of a promenade that runs along the sands. When the sky turns leaden there are plenty of undercover amusements, including the attractions at the base of the famous tower and the Sea Life Centre, which has a walk through the largest

LEIGHTON HALL

Three miles (5km) north of **Carnforth**, set against a dramatic backdrop of Lakeland fells, is Leighton Hall, an Adam-style house with a splendid neo-Gothic façade. A fortified manor was first built on this site in 1246, but during the 1715 rebellion it was sacked and burnt by government troops. Rebuilt in 1763 by George Townley, it then passed into the hands of the Gillow family, whose cabinet-making business, based in Lancaster, is well represented throughout the house. A replica of a Maryland mansion, built in the 1870s and containing 1,200 antique fittings, is just one of its many treasures.

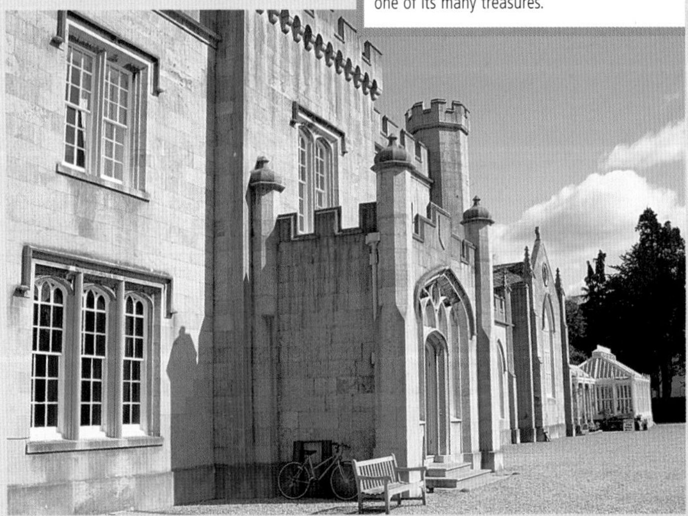

Morecambe Drive

DRIVE

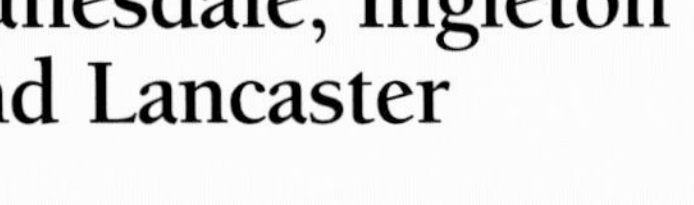

Morecambe, Lunesdale, Ingleton and Lancaster

START/FINISH: Morecambe. On the coast northwest of Lancaster and the M6 (J34)

DISTANCE: 75 miles (120km)

One of the loveliest northern rivers, the Lune carves a gracious valley in its southwesterly course from the Pennines to the sea in Morecambe Bay. Green pastures and limestone uplands contrast with the wild moors of Bowland Forest, while historic Lancaster links beautiful countryside with a holiday coast.

1 Leave Morecambe from the Clock Tower and follow the A5105 Marine Road East to Hest Bank. In 1 mile (1.5km) turn left on to the A6, signed to Kendal and Carnforth, to Bolton le Sands and Carnforth. Once in Carnforth, branch left at traffic lights on to minor road (one-way) towards Warton and Silverdale and, at a T-junction next to the railway station, turn left. Pass the Steamtown Railway Centre and continue to Warton.

2 Follow signs to Yealand Conyers and shortly bear right then left into the village. Pass the road to Leighton Hall. This castellated neo-Gothic mansion, home to the Gillow family, famous Lancashire furniture-makers, contains examples of early Gillow furniture. Continue forward to Yealand Redmayne. Before reaching Leighton Moss RSPB Reserve, a man-made fen with open water, marshes, woodland and an abundant bird life, turn right, signed to Milnthorpe. Cross the main road, the railway, canal and the M6, then at the T-junction, turn left, signed to Crooklands and Kendal, then immediate right towards Kirkby Lonsdale.

3 In 4.5 miles (7km) turn left and soon bear left. Cross the main road, signed to the town centre, and, at the T-junction, turn right then branch left (one-way), signed to Old Town. Shortly, at the foot of a descent, turn right on to the B6254 (not signed) to the town centre. This delightful market town has an ancient three-arched bridge (Devil's Bridge) and scenic walks that follow the footsteps of John Ruskin, the 19th-century writer and painter. Go forward to the A65 and turn left towards Skipton. Reach Cowan Bridge and in 4 miles (6.5km) cross the River Greta and, at the Bridge Inn, turn left on to Main Street and continue towards Ingleton.

shark display in Europe. In autumn the famous illuminations, along 7 miles (11km) of sea-front, still attract thousands of visitors, and a tram ride is one of the best ways to view them.

Until 1923, Lytham and neighbouring St Anne's were two distinct communities. Lytham, mentioned as a port in the Domesday Book, is separated from the shore by the expanse of the Green and the town's most distinctive landmark – a beautifully restored windmill dating back to 1805. St Anne's was created by Victorian entrepreneurs as a health resort. Rainy day attractions here are more genteel.

Inland, the Forest of Bowland is one of the most dramatic natural features of the Lancashire landscape. A vast plateau of rolling hills and moors rises to over 1,800ft (550m) above sea-level, dissected by deep valleys, such as the Pass of Bowland, once notorious as the haunt of smugglers and highwaymen. Drive from Quernmore, near Lancaster, to Dursop Bridge, 12 miles (19km) to the southeast, to get a taste of this lonely, rugged hill country. Better still, discover its waterfalls, sweeping views and wildlife on foot.

On the edge of the Forest of Bowland, and in contrast to the largely Victorian seaside resorts, is Lancaster, originally a Roman fort (*castrum*). A medieval castle, which houses the county courts and prison, takes pride of place in the city. Exploring the network of streets below the castle offers pleasant reminders of Lancaster's wealth in Georgian times. A maritime museum, occupying the former Custom House on St George's Quay, tells the fascinating story of Lancaster's trading past.

FISH TO FRY

Blackpool and its hinterland offer varied opportunities for fishing. **Blackpool's North Pier** is a popular spot, while further north **Fleetwood** has a flotilla of boats for offshore angling. The rivers give fine sport: the **Lune** has salmon, sea trout and brown trout; the **Ribble** and **Wyre** hold salmon and sea trout and have good coarse fishing in their lower reaches. Inland you'll find numerous reservoirs and ponds, as well as the **Lancaster** and the **Leeds and Liverpool Canals**.

CARNFORTH STATION

Situated at the junction of the scenic Settle to Carlisle and the main London to Glasgow railway lines, Carnforth Station has unlikely romantic associations. It was the setting for the classic 1940s film, *Brief Encounter*, starring Celia Johnson and Trevor Howard. Film and railway buffs should not miss the working collection of steam engines at **Steamtown Railway Centre**, where children will love to ride on the miniature railway, complete with scaled-down stations and signals.

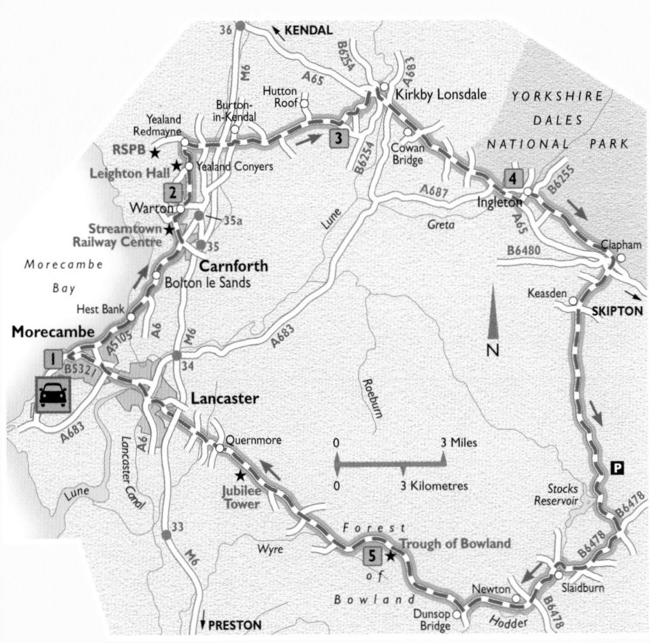

4 Bypass Ingleton village centre, turn right for Hawes then shortly, at the crossroads, turn left on to the B6255. Take the second turning right in half a mile (800m), to Clapham. In Clapham turn left at the T-junction then right into Station Road, just before the bridge (ignoring the first lane called Station Road). Cross the main road, signed to Keasden, and shortly bear left under the railway bridge and keep right towards Slaidburn. Make a long ascent, then a descent (1-in-7) and pass Gisburn Forest car-park. In 2 miles (3km), at the crossroads, turn right on to the B6478 and continue to Slaidburn. Bear left, signed to Lancaster, Clitheroe and the B6478, to Newton and continue on a minor towards Dunsop Bridge. Go forward then turn right and ascend to Trough of Bowland Summit.

5 Make a gradual descent to Jubilee Tower (fine views) and soon descend and ascend two 1-in-6 hills to reach a crossroads beyond Quernmore. Go straight across then, at the T-junction, turn right. At the crossroads, turn left to Lancaster, predominantly a comfortable, Georgian county town. Turn left on to the A6 and follow the signs A6, North. Follow the signs for Morecambe and join the A683. In 2 miles, at the third roundabout, take the second exit (B5321) to return to Morecambe.

LEIGHTON MOSS RESERVE

The Royal Society for the Protection of Birds has turned this man-made fen, which was drained around 1920, into a bird-watcher's paradise. Open water, reed beds, marshes and woodland offer a variety of habitats to attract abundant bird life, which can be observed from a network of footpaths and hides. Escorted wildlife events, such as otter and deer watches, allow visitors to see some of the other rare inhabitants of the reserve.

The lifeboat museum and distinctive 19th-century windmill in Lytham St Anne's

WEST YORKSHIRE & THE BRONTË COUNTRY

From time immemorial, sheep have grazed the windswept moors of Yorkshire, and the history of these times is written across the landscape. Many of the old farmsteads have been abandoned in these unforgiving moors, but paths and signposts to the isolated dwellings remain. You can walk over the moors to lonely Wuthering Heights and imagine the isolation of such a spot 200 years ago. The Industrial Revolution changed the area's way of life completely, attracting the rural population to factories and mills in the towns of Leeds and Bradford. This industrial heritage remains, although factory chimneys no longer fill the sky with their black reek. Harrogate is content to offer echoes of a more leisurely age. The Brontës would scarcely recognise the world around Haworth today and yet the town itself remains in a time warp, little changed since those days when the family lived in the parsonage and walked out across the moors.

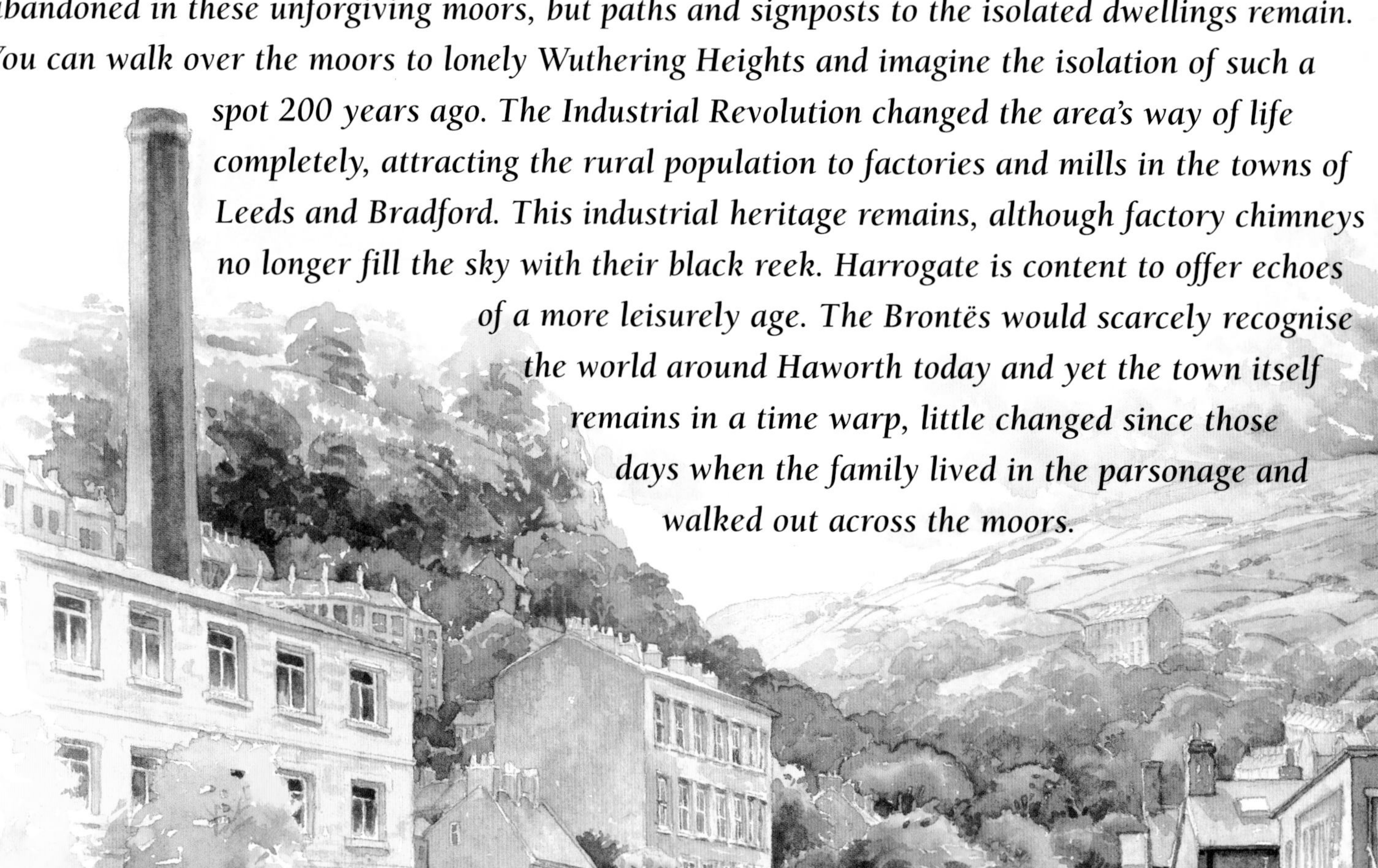

COW AND CALF ROCKS

On Ilkley Moor, near the White Wells, are the dramatic Cow and Calf Rocks. A local giant supposedly chased his wife across Ilkley Moor and tripped over the large Cow Rock, chipping off a chunk which landed near by to form Calf Rock. Local climbers practise on these sheer surfaces and successive generations have carved messages here.

Corn Exchange Leeds
Built in 1863, the Corn Exchange was modelled on the one in Paris, and the magnificent domed glass roof once threw light on market dealings below. Now restored to its former glory, it bustles with designer shops, craft fairs and exhibitions, with plenty of café tables where you can watch the world go by.

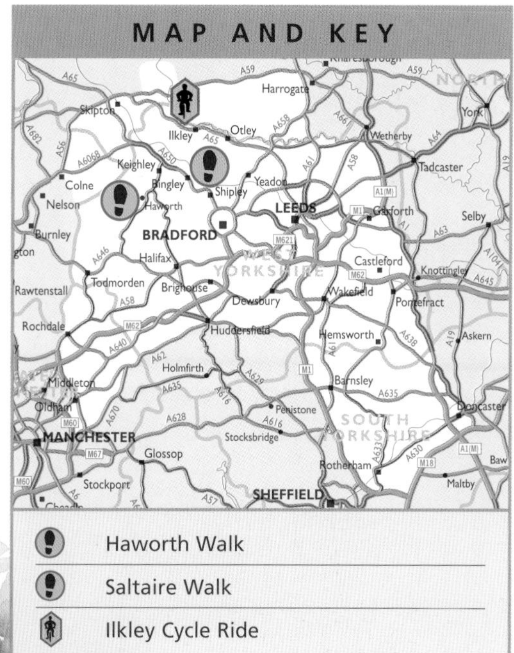

Oakworth Station
Oakworth Station on the Keighley Worth Valley Line remains unchanged since Edwardian days. The station is easily recognisable from the 1970 film The Railway Children. *It has never been connected to electricity and the original gas lamps are still in working order.*

HAREWOOD HOUSE

The delightful Robert Adams rooms of Harewood House are unrivalled essays in elegance, and the great house is filled with fine Chippendale furniture, porcelain and paintings. The Terrace contains an Italian-style garden with ornate fountains, a stunning parterre with symmetrical flower beds and glorious views over 'Capability' Brown's 18th-century landscaped grounds. The lake is surrounded by enchanting woodlands dappled with shade and covered in spring bulbs and rhododendrons.

BRONTË COUNTRY

Set in the moors where the River Aire runs by on its journey eastwards to the North Sea, Haworth owes its position as one of Britain's most popular tourist destinations to chance. If the Reverend Patrick Brontë had not produced the literary offspring that he did, Haworth today would be an appealing but quiet town, noted for a steep cobbled street that leads up to its church, but no more. Instead, visitors flock from all over the world to the Brontë Parsonage Museum, while beyond on the moors, footpath signs in several languages direct thousands to the sites that inspired *Wuthering Heights*. Outside the parsonage is the parish church where all the Brontës except Anne are buried in the crypt.

A view of terraced houses in the steep cobbled town of Haworth, home to the Brontë family

KEIGHLEY AND WORTH VALLEY RAILWAY

The Keighley and Worth Valley Railway, a 5-mile (8-km) stretch of branch line, run by enthusiasts, links with the Leeds–Settle–Carlisle main line at Keighley Station. At the station, the concourse and booking hall have been beautifully restored to their late 19th-century splendour, complete with a glass canopy, and there is also a locomotive turntable on display, but the main attractions require a trip on the train. The line begins at Keighley and passes through **Ingrow**, **Oakworth** and **Haworth** to the terminus at Oxenhope. The railway organises a popular programme of events for families and enthusiasts alike, including Thomas the Tank Engine weekends and seasonal Santa Specials.

Other Brontë links include the Black Bull Inn where Branwell drank, and the Old Apothecary where he bought his opium.

Haworth itself is bulging with tearooms and souvenir shops, as well as a reconstruction of one of Yorkshire's last handloom weaving workshops, which were once the hub of industry in many northern towns. There are regular spinning and weaving demonstrations, and visitors have the opportunity to buy some of the goods in the shop.

HACKING ON THE MOORS

The moors around Airedale are splendid riding country, offering the chance to brood, Heathcliff-like, in the saddle, or just enjoy some magnificent countryside.

True Well Hall Riding Centre provides children's residential riding holidays, **Wharfedale Riding School** offers treks over Ilkley Moor on moorland and mountain ponies, and **Moorside Equestrian Centre** at Shipley treks the heights of Baildon Moor. Wilsden, between Haworth and Shipley, has **Shaygate Riding School** and the **Salter Royd Equestrian Centre**.

Haworth Walk

WALK

Haworth and the Brontë Moors

START/FINISH: Haworth. Off the A6033 south of Keighley
DISTANCE: 7.5 miles (12km)
ASCENT/GRADIENT: 575ft (175m); gradual climbs
TERRAIN/PATHS: mostly open moorland; well-defined paths; stout footwear advisable
PARKING: car-park near Brontë Parsonage, Haworth

The moors above the Brontë's West Yorkshire home were a source of both inspiration and solace in their briefly flourishing lives. This ramble escapes bustling Haworth, crossing the wild Yorkshire moors to a romantic ruin, following, literally, in the footsteps of the three precociously talented sisters.

1 The little gritstone town of Haworth has become a literary mecca to rival Grasmere and Stratford-upon-Avon, attracting visitors from all over the world seeking an insight into the books of Charlotte, Emily and Anne Brontë. The sisters were brought up by their father, Reverend Patrick Brontë, who lived at the Georgian parsonage. Now a museum, it has been painstakingly restored to reflect the lives of the Brontës, with rooms filled with their personal treasures. From the car-park, go through gate posts opposite the museum and turn right. The lane soon becomes a paved field path that leads to the Haworth–Stanbury road. Walk left along the road and, after about 80yds (75m), take a left fork, signed to Penistone Hill. Continue along this quiet road to a T-junction.

2 Take the track straight ahead, soon signed Brontë Way and Top Withins, gradually descending to South Dean Beck where, within a few paces of the stone bridge, you'll find the Brontë Waterfall and Brontë Seat (a stone that resembles a chair). Cross the bridge and climb steeply uphill to a three-way sign.

3 Keep left, uphill, on a paved path signed to Top Withins. The path soon levels out to accompany a dry-stone wall. Cross a stile and then keep left. Cross a tiny beck on stepping stones; a steep uphill climb brings you to a waymarker by a ruined building. A short detour of 200yds (182m), left, uphill, is needed if you want to investigate the lonely ruins of Top Withins, which is believed to have inspired the setting of Emily's great novel *Wuthering Heights*. Turn right at the waymarker,

Although only about 3 miles (4.5km) north of Haworth off the A629, industrial Keighley is a world away. The first stop in Keighley should be the Cliffe Castle Museum, a 19th-century mansion northwest of the town. The museum specialises in the geology and natural history of the region and has hands-on opportunities as well as touring exhibitions. There are Victorian toys, general local historical items and a working beehive, where the bees come in and out through a tube which leads to a hole in the wall.

A northern town which expanded due to the Industrial Revolution, Keighley still harbours a great deal of the wildlife that lived here before the looms and mills came along. The local Naturalists' Society has devised a 2-mile (3-km) walk which incorporates a stretch of the Leeds and Liverpool Canal and the industrial heartland of the town, where visitors are reminded that they are still in Airedale by the presence of wildlife such as rabbits, foxes and the occasional badger.

A mile (1.5km) northeast of the town is the National Trust's East Riddlesden Hall. This 17th-century Yorkshire manor house is set in 12 acres (5ha) of land with attractive gardens, a duck pond and a particularly fine medieval tithe barn which houses a collection of old agricultural implements. The gardens include a monastic fishpond and a restored walled garden. Inside the hall itself are mullioned windows, panelled rooms and collections of furniture, pewter, embroidery and kitchen utensils, as well as the impressive original kitchen – and plenty of ghost stories!

BRONTË PARSONAGE MUSEUM

The one-time home of Patrick Brontë and his children (Emily, Charlotte, Anne and Branwell) is now a museum of their lives and literary endeavours. Manuscripts and paintings attract as much attention as their living rooms, or the room in which Emily died at the early age of 30. It is an interesting place to visit for anyone who has ever read *Wuthering Heights* or *Jane Eyre*, but it is advisable to avoid Bank Holidays and summer weekends when coach parties crowd the rooms. There is rather more space to browse in the modern extension which houses most of the literary artefacts.

OXENHOPE STRAW RACE

On one Sunday in July of each year, the village of Oxenhope near Haworth is transformed by this event, which dates back to 1975. Rival teams compete to carry a bale of straw around the village, visiting – and drinking in – as many pubs as possible on the way! The race, which has a serious purpose in raising money for local hospitals, took off in a big way and now several hundred people take part (many in fancy dress) and thousands gather to watch. There are also other activities during the weekend.

on a paved path, downhill, signed to Stanbury and Haworth; you are now joining the Pennine Way. You have a broad, easily-followed track across the wide expanse of moorland. By now you'll have certainly left the crowds well behind, you'll probably only have grouse for company, and perhaps some hardy Pennine Wayfarers. Pass a white farmhouse – Upper Heights Cottage – then bear immediately left at a fork of tracks (still signed as Pennine Way). Walk past another building, Lower Heights Farm. After 550yds (500m), where the Pennine Way veers left, continue on the track straight ahead, signed to Stanbury and Haworth. Follow the track to meet a road near the village of Stanbury.

4 Bear right along the road through Stanbury, then take the first road on the right, signed to Oxenhope, and cross the dam of Lower Laithe Reservoir. Immediately beyond the dam, bear left on a road that soon reduces to a track, uphill, to meet a road by Haworth Cemetery. From here you retrace your outward route: walk left along the road, soon taking a stile on the right, to follow the paved field path back into Haworth. No matter how crowded this little town becomes, it is always possible to escape to the moors that surround Haworth.

Walking country at Penistone Hill Country Park, south of Haworth

LEEDS, BRADFORD & OUR INDUSTRIAL HERITAGE

The Industrial Revolution changed the face of the north of England more than any other part of the country, with great conurbations developing around the coalfields and the ports. Though these areas may not immediately suggest themselves as tourist attractions, many have been revitalised in recent years and have much to offer, from their proud museums to their industrial heritage, imaginative new uses for redundant sites, lively arts and entertainments and superb sporting venues.

Brick-built Leeds and stone-built Bradford are the closest of neighbours and were once vital cogs in the engine room of the Industrial Revolution. Cosmopolitan Bradford is a bustling city with a wealth of fine Victorian architecture. The Wool Exchange, textile mills and the warehouse district of Little Germany are evocative reminders of a time when Bradford was the woollen capital of the world. The story is vividly told at the Industrial and Horses at Work Museum in a former spinning mill in Eccleshill, which includes working machinery, horse-drawn rides, textile workers' cottages and the mill-owner's house.

Leeds, the largest urban development in Yorkshire, owes its growth, during the 19th century, to wool and to its position on the Leeds and Liverpool and Aire and Calder canals. As such, it formed a link between Liverpool and Hull from where goods were transported world-wide. The city's other early industries include clocks and furniture-making – Thomas Chippendale began his furniture business here. Leeds is rapidly changing to meet new

A display of typical pub hand-pumps at Tetley's Brewery Wharf, Leeds

Bradford, capital of the 19th-century woollen trade, and now a thriving multicultural city

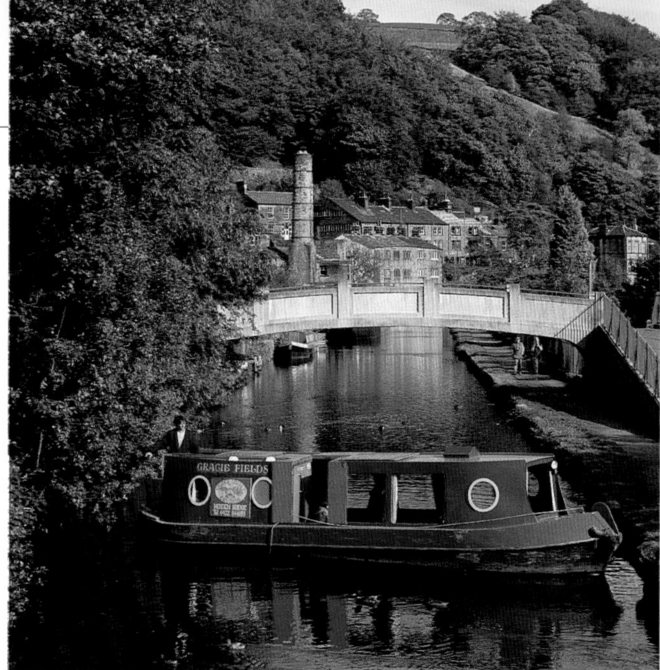

South of the Pennine moors, a barge drifts along Rochdale Canal at Hebden Bridge

Saltaire Walk

WALK

Saltaire's Model Streets and the Five Rise

START/FINISH: Saltaire. Off the A650 west of Shipley
DISTANCE: 8.5 miles (13.5km)
ASCENT/GRADIENT: 430ft (131m); some steep sections
TERRAIN/PATHS: canal bank, woodland and open moorland; generally clear and well-signed paths; boggy in places
PARKING: at Hirst Wood, 1 mile (1.5km) along Hirst Lane from A650 Saltaire roundabout

Titus Salt built his vision of an industrial village beside the engineering triumph of the Leeds and Liverpool Canal. This walk follows the canal through the Aire Valley to the spectacular Five Rise Locks at Bingley, then skirts the lower slopes of Ilkley Moor to return along the valley heights above Shipley Glen.

1 Saltaire, an early example of a planned industrial village, was founded by Sir Titus Salt. He made his money by cornering the market in alpaca wool, which he wove into high-quality cloth in the huge mill which dominates the start of this walk. Cross the canal by the swing bridge, turn left on to the canal towpath and follow the canal for 2 miles (3km) to Five Rise Locks. One of the major engineering structures on the 127-mile (204-km) Leeds and Liverpool Canal, the Five Rise Locks were opened in 1770. Each of the five staircase locks – with the top gate of each lock acting as the bottom gate of the next – is 66ft (20m) long and 14ft 4in (4.5m) wide, and holds 90,000 gallons (409,140 litres) of water. It alters the level of the canal by 60ft (18.5m), and it takes at least 30 minutes for each boat to pass through. At the locks' summit turn right over the metal bridge and walk up the road. Just before a road joins from the right, turn left up a narrow metalled lane between two walls.

2 Follow this path uphill, cross two roads and pass through a small housing estate, to reach the hilltop on Lady Lane, and turn right.

3 Turn left down College Road and walk towards the stone houses, with Lady Park Nursing Home to your right. Bear left through a small estate called Nicholson Close to a signed footpath. You are now leaving the valley of the River Aire to cross the lower slopes of the famous Ilkley

challenges: smoke-blackened mills are giving way to new developments overlooking the River Aire and the Leeds and Liverpool Canal, creating riverside walks and, at Granary Wharf, a labyrinth of speciality shops. Leeds was dubbed the 'Knightsbridge of the North' when the first Harvey Nichols store outside London opened here. Colourful Kirkgate Market, where Marks and Spencer began in 1884 as the Penny Bazaar, has bustling market stalls selling fresh produce. The restored Corn Exchange has antiques and bric-à-brac piled high in elaborate Victorian arcades. Further afield, within the workaday brick walls of historic factory mills, designer labels and local crafts share space with towels and fine linen. Bobbins and shuttles still fly at Armley Mills Industrial Museum, showing all the stages of production, from sheep to clothing; and the history of the English pub is illustrated at Tetley's Brewery Wharf, where actors take visitors through the ages, via a medieval ale-house, and Elizabethan, Jacobean, Georgian and Victorian hostelries.

Halfway between Leeds and Harrogate lies one of Yorkshire's finest and stateliest homes, Harewood House. On the outskirts of Leeds, on the banks of the River Aire, is Kirkstall Abbey, founded in 1152 and one of the finest monastic sites in the country. Near by is the Abbey House Museum, with Victorian shops, workshops and cottages.

A TASTE OF INDIA

Bradford is undoubtedly the place in England to sample authentic Indian dishes. There are countless curry houses and the food is excellent. Places to look for are the basic establishments with formica tables, tiled walls and no cutlery where you will find the curry of the day served with chapattis for the price of a snack, but wherever you go, it is almost impossible to find a bad curry in Bradford.

NATIONAL MUSEUM OF PHOTOGRAPHY, FILM AND TELEVISION

Re-opened after a major renovation, the National Museum of Photography, Film and Television is the top tourist attraction in Bradford – and it's free. It portrays the past, present and future of media using special effects, computer imaging, dramatic reconstructions and interactive devices. Ride a magic carpet, become a newsreader for a day or try your hand at vision mixing. The main attraction, for which you need to buy a ticket, is IMAX, the UK's largest cinema screen at over five storeys high.

SALTAIRE

Built between 1852 and 1872 by Sir Titus Salt, the village of Saltaire, on the River Aire, is a perfectly preserved vision of his industrial utopia, modelled on buildings of the Italian Renaissance. It was originally constructed in open countryside to provide his mill workers with the benefits of fresh air, though it is now surrounded by urban sprawl. The mill, which is larger than St Paul's Cathedral in London, was once the biggest factory in the world, and was the centre of a small conglomeration of schools, hospitals, houses, parks, baths and washhouses.

SEE CONTACTS SECTION FOR ADDITIONAL INFORMATION

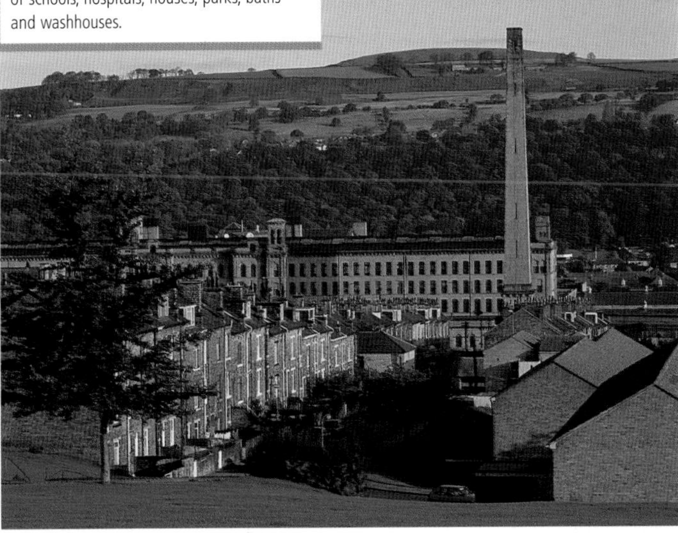

Moor. Go over a stile, turn right and follow the waymarkers through two fields to a stone stile. Cross and go left, passing farm buildings to a road. Turn left and then first right down a track. This paved, switchback track is part of a former packhorse route that crossed the moors to link up the Aire and Wharfe valleys.

4 After a right-angled bend beyond the cottages turn left, downhill on the packhorse track between walls. Pass the reservoir to reach a road, then turn right to reach 17th-century Eldwick Hall on your right. Turn left opposite the hall and follow the path through fields to reach a signpost. Turn right, along the Dales Way Link. On reaching a farm, go left over a stile and follow the farm drive to the road.

5 Cross the road to a farm and follow a path next to a beck until you reach a road, which you follow past the Bracken Hall Countryside Centre, where you can learn more about the wildlife and geology of the area, to the Glen Tramway entrance. Take the tramway down the hill, or the path beside it. At the foot of the hill go straight ahead through Roberts Park. Cross the river by a footbridge, then go straight on to the canal towpath, turning right to reach Hirst Wood after 1 mile (1.5km).

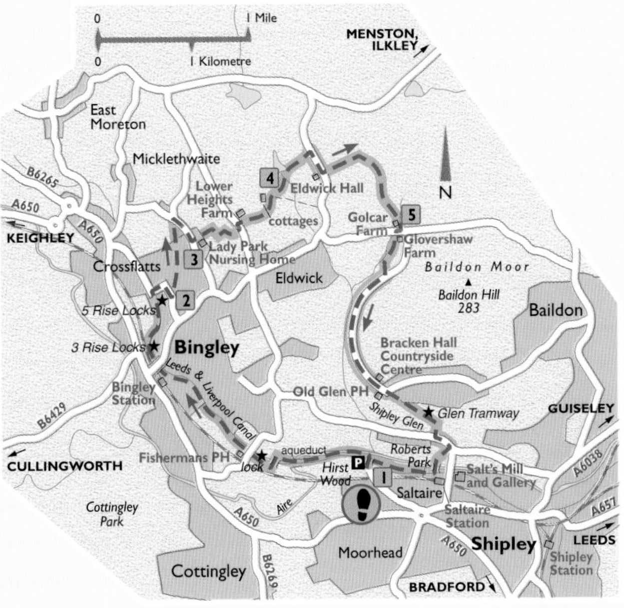

HARROGATE & ILKLEY

This region may not be the 'real' Yorkshire Dales as we know them, but it does mark their start. Here the industrial regions of Yorkshire give way first to the moors around Ilkley and then to the more open Dales landscape and the National Park to the north. It is an area which spawned the unofficial Yorkshire anthem *On Ilkley Moor B'aht 'At* and provided the location for the popular TV soap *Emmerdale*. Ilkley and Otley are both in Wharfedale, while refined Harrogate, with its colourful parks and gardens, lies at the outer edge of the dales and moors.

The discovery of spring water – and their restorative powers – by William Slingsby in 1571, transformed the sleepy little village of Haregate into the bustling spa town of Harrogate. It is now an attractive and lively place with theatres, cinemas and good restaurants, and a large number of hotels and modern conference centres. An important feature of Harrogate is its greenery, especially the wide swathes of grass and flower beds known as the Stray that sweeps right through the town. These 200 acres (80ha) are protected under an ancient law. There are more flowers as well as a boating pond, children's playground, crazy golf and other activities in the Valley Gardens, Harrogate's main park.

Curious dangling objects, solidified by lime, at eerie Dropping Well in Knaresborough

Nearby Knaresborough, perched on ridges of rock above the River Nidd, is one of the most picturesque market towns in the Dales. A viaduct crosses high above the river, while old houses peek through the trees on one side, to the parkland and woods which conceal Mother Shipton's Cave on the opposite bank. The market-place has a busy Wednesday market and the oldest

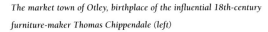

The market town of Otley, birthplace of the influential 18th-century furniture-maker Thomas Chippendale (left)

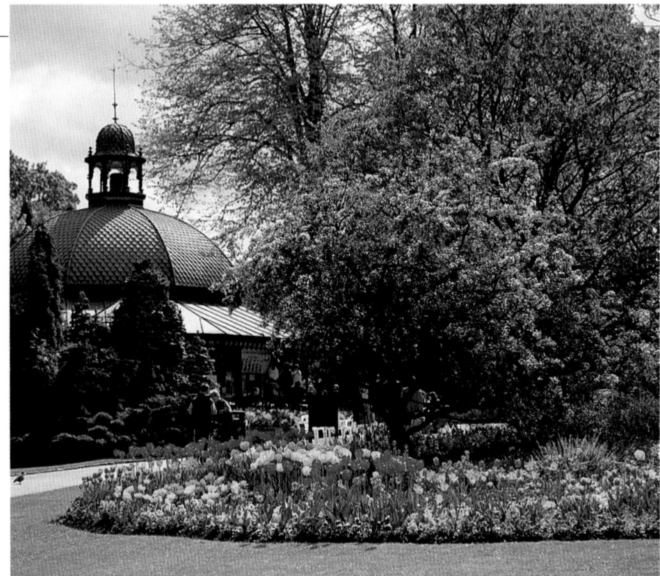

Spring tulips in bloom in Harrogate's beautiful Valley Gardens

Ilkley Cycle Ride

CYCLE RIDE

Through the Wharfe Valley

START/FINISH: Ilkley. Located on the A65 10 miles (16km) north of Bradford

DISTANCE: 21 miles (33.5km)

ROADS: mainly B-roads and country lanes; very short off-road section

PARKING: on-street parking near railway station

Country estates with woodland and historic buildings, typical Yorkshire stone in Dales' villages and farms, combine to form a rich mosaic on this leisurely cycle ride along the River Wharfe.

1 Regarded as the gateway to Upper Wharfedale, Ilkley stands on the site of a Roman fort beside the River Wharfe, which flows beneath a gracious bridge dating from 1673 (closed to traffic). The town is surrounded by the fine scenery of Ilkley Moor. From the railway station turn right, first right again, go through the traffic lights and downhill over the bridge. Turn left into Denton Road and keep ahead at the small roundabout. Turn first left into Nesfield Road. Continue on a narrow road through the golf course to Nesfield.

2 Go through Nesfield and continue for 2.5 miles (4km) on the narrow lane to Beamsley. Follow the lane to its T-junction with the A59 and turn left. Shortly turn left to follow the Bolton Bridge cycleway signs on to the track and under the road bridge, emerging on a small lane. From the station, near Bolton Abbey village, it is possible to travel, and return, along 4 miles (6.5km) of preserved steam railway, through Dales scenery. This operates every Sunday and daily in the summer months.

3 Turn left, go over a narrow bridge (views of the abbey to your right) then turn right on to the B6160 at the Abbey Tea Rooms. Continue on this road for 1.5 miles (2.5km) to Bolton Abbey village. Visit the information centre by the car-park here (an alternative start point) before turning right down the drive to Bolton Priory, a ruined 12th-century Cistercian monastery on the banks of the Wharfe. The repaired nave is now the Priory Church of St Cuthbert and St Mary. There are several woodland walks across the estate, including one from the car-park by the Cavendish Pavilion, to a powerful stretch of water called The Strid, where the river boils through a 12-ft (3.5-m) constriction of its gorge.

chemist's shop in the country, believed to have been first established on the site as long ago as the 13th century.

Ilkley is well situated, with the heart of the Dales to the north, easy access to Harrogate to the northeast and Leeds to the southeast. The River Wharfe runs through the town, and above it stands Ilkley Moor itself where the original spa was located. Antiques shops rub shoulders with expensive dress shops, which attract customers from all over the country, and The Box Tree Inn has one of the best restaurants in the north of England. In the gardens in Queens Road is the Panorama Stone, the most accessible of several prehistoric carved rocks in and around Ilkley. On Ilkley Moor are the dramatic Cow and Calf Rocks, and even if you lack the time or the inclination to venture on to the moor itself, you should try to see these striking features.

Otley, in Lower Wharfedale, is a busy working town with attractive 17th- and 18th-century buildings and streets with ancient names, such as Kirkgate, Bondgate and Boroughgate. When the television series *Emmerdale* looked for a town with a bustling livestock market for filming, Otley was chosen. There are cattle markets on Monday and Friday, with general street markets on Friday and Saturday. Otley also boasts one of the oldest agricultural shows in the country, dating back to 1796. It is a highlight of the Otley calendar and includes rare breeds and splendid Shire horses.

SHIPLEY GLEN AND TRAMWAY

Shipley Glen is a large plateau scattered with gigantic boulders, whose sheer faces and impossible overhangs provide a challenge, even for experienced climbers. There are plenty of paths for those who'd rather keep their feet firmly on the ground.

The Shipley Glen Tramway, dating from 1895 and open from Easter to October and at Christmas, will haul you up to the plateau in an open carriage. You can walk from Ilkley across Ilkley Moor and Rombalds Moor to Shipley Glen and then take the train from Shipley back to Ilkley.

Row boats lined up along the River Nidd at Knaresborough

HARROGATE TURKISH BATHS

Harrogate is one of the few places where you can enjoy a Turkish bath in original 19th-century splendour at the Harrogate Turkish and Sauna Suite in the Royal Baths Assembly Rooms. Its Victorian exterior masks a beautifully renovated tiled interior, with a cold plunge bath, several hot rooms, a steam room, massage room and a relaxing rest room for afterwards. There are both male and female sessions, so check first if you are thinking of going along.

Continue on the drive to emerge back on the B6160, turning right past the memorial. After 3 miles (5km) pass Barden Tower on the right and turn immediately right, towards Appletreewick.

4 Go downhill, cross Barden Bridge and follow the road round to climb the hill at the other side. Ruined Barden Tower is a 12th-century hunting lodge; adjacent Priest's House is now a tearoom and restaurant. Near the top of the hill take the Hazlewood and Storiths single-track road to the right. Follow this for 4 miles (6.5km) to the junction with the A59.

5 Turn right and after 1 mile (1.5km) at the roundabout turn left on to the B6160. After 2 miles (3km), at the T-junction in Addingham, turn left at the Crown Inn.

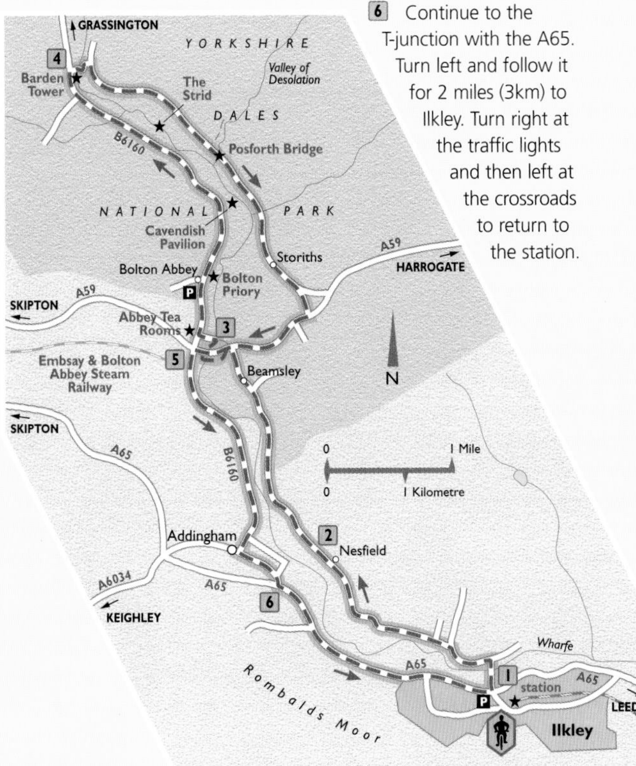

6 Continue to the T-junction with the A65. Turn left and follow it for 2 miles (3km) to Ilkley. Turn right at the traffic lights and then left at the crossroads to return to the station.

Looking across to Ilkley from rocky crags on the moor above the town

THE YORKSHIRE DALES

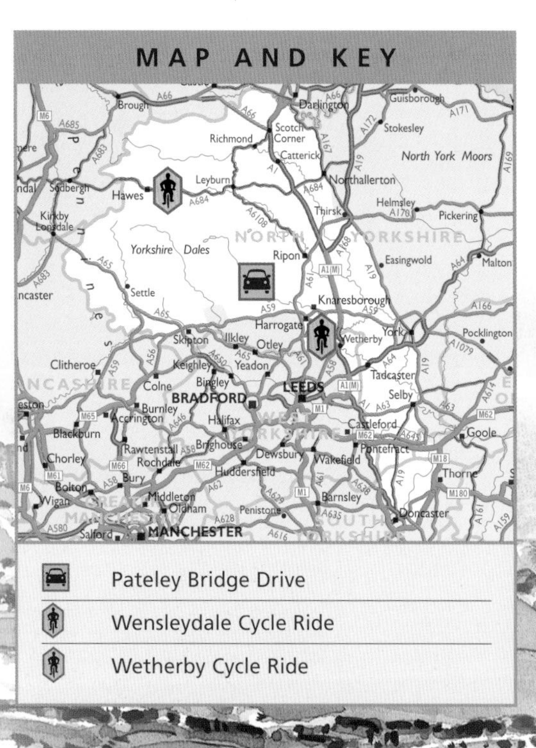

The Yorkshire Dales are a land of hills and valleys, of waterfalls and rivers, of caves, country shows and sheep. It is a landscape for walkers and artists, for those who love their food and drink and appreciate the hospitality of the friendly people who live there. Over 300 million years ago this area was beneath a tropical sea. Bones and shells from sea creatures were compressed into a block of limestone as the sea drained, forced into huge mounds, and cut by glaciers to form gorges and valleys. Settlers moved in to farm the land and it is still farmed today. Now ten million visitors arrive each year to marvel at the area's beauty.

NEWBY HALL

The charming 18th-century mansion of Newby Hall, southeast of Ripon, was designed by Robert Adam and incorporates an elaborate tapestry room and two galleries of Roman sculpture. The billiard room is particularly splendid, there is a fine statue gallery, a great deal of Chippendale furniture to admire, an overwhelming tapestry room whose walls are covered in 18th-century French tapestries, and, by way of contrast, an amusing collection in the chamber-pot room.

Jervaulx Abbey

This Cistercian monastery, founded in 1156 and mostly in ruins, is an evocative place, filled in summer with the scent of the many wild flowers which grow around the crumbling grey stones. Though the buildings are in ruins, there is still plenty to see, such as the remains of the staircase known as the Night Stairs, which led the monks down from their dormitory to night services in the church.

YE OLDE NAKED MAN CAFÉ

This café in Settle kept the name of an inn, previously on the site, called the Naked Man, as a satire on the over-elaborate dressing habits of the time. Take a look behind the café and you will see Bishopdale Court, typical of the many old yards and alleyways hidden away in Settle's streets. Ye Olde Naked Woman is in Langcliffe, which is near by.

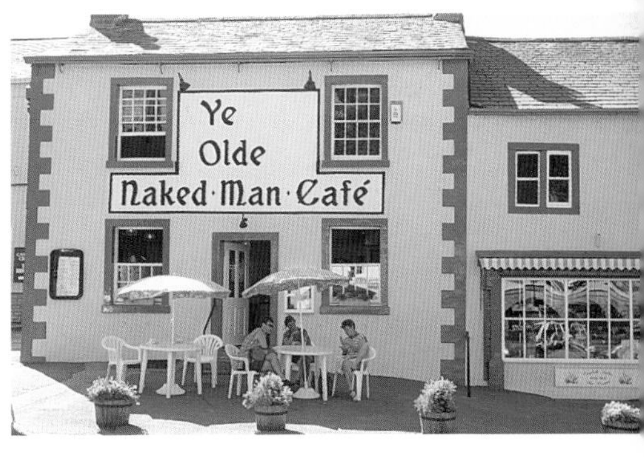

How Stean Gorge

To the north of Pateley Bridge, near Lofthouse, How Stean Gorge is popularly known as Yorkshire's 'Little Switzerland'. The ravine of up to 80ft (24m) deep was hacked out in the Ice Age, and pathways lead along by the fast-flowing river through ferns and by lush, dank undergrowth. There are bridges on different levels and fenced galleries on rocky ledges.

WHARFEDALE & NIDDERDALE

This is the heart of the Dales. It has the highest peaks – Ingleborough, Whernside, Pen-y-ghent and Buckden Pike – and the biggest caverns, including the exciting White Scar Caves, potholes galore and attractive villages and towns. It is a landscape both rolling and rugged, a place for walkers, climbers, cavers and fell runners.

Skipton, the 'Gateway to the Dales', buzzes with life, its busy market filling the main street four days a week. It has modern shops, ancient inns, churches, a museum, restaurants and hotels, as well as a 900-year-old Norman castle in a wonderful state of preservation. There are pleasant walks along the canal-side towpaths where the Leeds and Liverpool Canal joins the Ellerbeck and Springs Canal.

At the centre of Wharfedale, Bolton Abbey Estate, owned by the Duke and Duchess of Devonshire, is a popular amalgamation of the recreational, the historical and the geographical. The small and sleepy town of Grassington, with its cobbled market square, was a thriving lead-mining town from the 17th to the 19th centuries. Modern Grassington has a National Park Centre and the Upper Wharfedale Folk Museum, a tiny but enjoyable collection housed in two 18th-century lead-miners' cottages.

GAPING GILL POTHOLE

The interior of Gaping Gill is about 120ft (37m) high and 500ft (152m) long, and the stream of Fell Beck plunges down into it from the surface, making it one of the highest waterfalls in Britain at 364ft (111m). This breathtaking sight is normally reserved for experienced potholers, but twice a year, on spring and summer Bank Holidays, local caving clubs set up a winch and bosun's chair and allow members of the public to share the experience.

The Ribble Way footpath passes the spectacular 24 arches of the Ribblehead Viaduct

The cobbled streets and stone lead-miners' cottages of Grassington

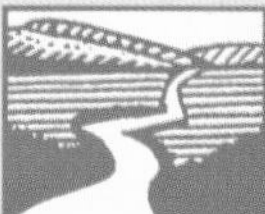

Pateley Bridge Drive

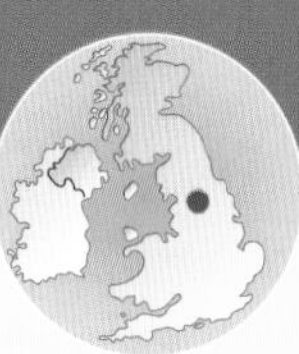

DRIVE

To Small Towns and Large Villages

START/FINISH: Pateley Bridge. Small town on the B6265 between Ripon and Grassington

DISTANCE: 75 miles (120.5km)

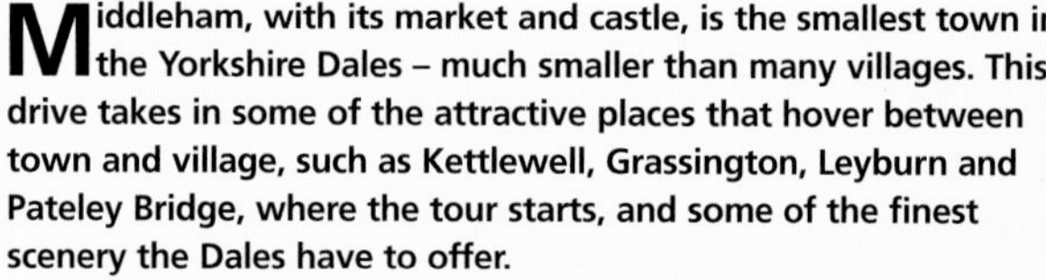

Middleham, with its market and castle, is the smallest town in the Yorkshire Dales – much smaller than many villages. This drive takes in some of the attractive places that hover between town and village, such as Kettlewell, Grassington, Leyburn and Pateley Bridge, where the tour starts, and some of the finest scenery the Dales have to offer.

1 From the centre of Pateley Bridge, a lively market town in the heart of Nidderdale, take the minor road that leads north from near the bridge itself, towards Ramsgill and Lofthouse. Pass Gouthwaite Reservoir on your right. In Lofthouse turn right and take the steep road out of the village, over the moors towards Masham. Continue for about 6 miles (9.5km), passing two more reservoirs on the right. Take the third left turn, as you approach Healey, towards Ellingstring, turning left again to the junction with the A6108.

2 Turn left at the crossroads and continue to the junction with the A6108. Turn left towards Leyburn passing the impressive remains of Jervaulx Abbey on the right. The abbey, founded in 1156, is in complete contrast to the grand and busy Fountains Abbey, yet in its day it was one of the most important Cistercian abbeys in Yorkshire. Continue on the A6108 and pass through Middleham, considered to be 'the Newmarket of the North', with its 16 or so racing stables. The ruined castle was much favoured by Richard III, whose son Edward was born here in 1473.

3 Continue to Leyburn, a busy Wensleydale town, and turn left then left again, to join the A684 through Wensleydale towards Hawes. Continue for 6 miles (10km) through West Witton and turn left on to the B6160, signed to Grassington. Alternatively, remain on the A684 for a mile (1.5km) to visit Aysgarth Falls. Although they consist of three different sections, only the Upper Falls are visible from the road. The other sections can be reached by footpath from the National Park Visitor Centre. Near by are a mill, a carriage museum and tearooms. Return to the B6160.

To the west, Malham is a magnet for visitors. The half-mile (800-m) walk to Malham Cove, one of Britain's most impressive natural features, is signed from the centre. Look out for the two old bridges in the village. The New Bridge was built in the 17th century, then widened in the 18th. Malham's older bridge, the Wash-Dub or Moon Bridge, dates from the 16th century.

The day to visit Settle is Tuesday, when stalls are crammed into Market Square and visitors jostle with locals from the surrounding farms and villages. Old yards and alleyways and old-fashioned family-run stores add to the appeal of its 18th- and 19th-century buildings.

MALHAM COVE

The limestone rock face of Malham Cove seems to tumble down the 250-ft (76-m) cliffs, and extends for about 1,000ft (305m). This natural amphitheatre was formed by movements of the earth's crust and is simply the most visible part of the Craven Fault. It is a steep climb to the top, but the reward is an exhilarating view over the moors around Malham, north to Malham Tarn and over the limestone pavements which stretch away from beneath your feet. These slabs are known as clints, while the gaps between them are grikes; it is in these grikes that some of the area's unusual plants can be found.

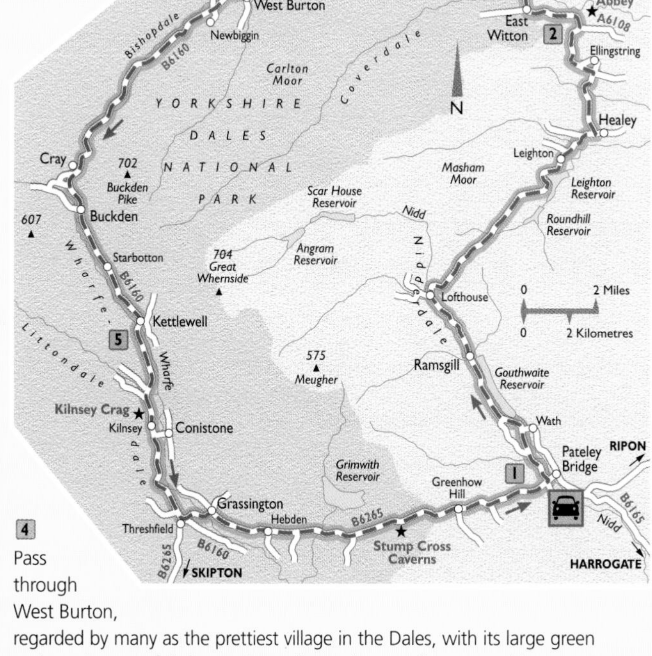

4 Pass through West Burton, regarded by many as the prettiest village in the Dales, with its large green and nearby waterfall, Burton Force, just a short stroll away, and keep to the B6160. The road takes you along the lovely and lesser-known Bishopdale, over Kidstones Pass to Buckden in Wharfedale. Pass Kettlewell on the left, a small busy town and a centre for walkers on nearby Great Whernside. It is also on the Dales Way long-distance footpath, and was once a centre of the lead-mining industry.

5 Continue ahead and look out for Kilnsey Crag on your right, which juts out dramatically towards the main road. Kilnsey Crag is popular with climbers, film-makers and peregrine falcons. Continue on the B6160 then turn left into the centre of Grassington – a large village with narrow cobbled streets, 17th- and 18th-century houses, pubs and a museum of Upper Wharfedale life. Drive around the centre of Grassington, leave on the B6265 and return to Nidderdale and Pateley Bridge.

The Three Peaks Challenge Race, taking in Pen-y-ghent, Whernside and Ingleborough, starts and ends in Horton-in-Ribblesdale every year. The Pennine Way weaves through the village, which also has a station on the Settle–Carlisle line.

Whernside is the highest point in the Dales, reaching to 2,415ft (736m). The two most popular approaches are from the Ribblehead Viaduct or Chapel-le-Dale. Ingleborough can be approached from Clapham, Ingleton, Horton and Chapel-le-Dale, and each is an invigorating climb to the peak (2,373ft/723m). From Clapham the walk is about 4 miles (6.5km), passing Ingleborough Cave on the way. White Scar Caves, near Ingleton, have underground rivers and waterfalls, making for an exciting hour-long guided tour.

The climb up to the summit of Pen-y-ghent is steep in places, with a bit of scrambling, but not beyond the capabilities of anyone who is reasonably fit. Once up there, walkers can revel in the views across to the other peaks, north across the fells of Langstrothdale Chase, and south over Ribblesdale and Lancashire's Forest of Bowland.

BOLTON ABBEY

There are several marked nature trails near the river and through Strid Wood, which is a Site of Special Scientific Interest, with over 60 different varieties of plants and about 40 species of birds nesting there every year. Spring brings snowdrops and later whole rivers of bluebells, and in summer the air is thick with dragonflies, butterflies and bees. The 13th-century Augustinian priory lies in evocative ruins in a meadow by the banks of the River Wharfe. The adjoining 1220 priory church of St Mary and St Cuthbert is one of the finest churches in the Dales. Now magnificently restored, it has breathtaking stained glass and wall paintings.

WENSLEYDALE & SWALEDALE

Wensleydale is the longest of the Yorkshire Dales, running for over 40 miles (64km), and has some of the prettiest landscapes in the region. Where other dales have rugged features, Wensleydale's are more soft and rounded, the slopes of its hills lush and green, grazed by large flocks of sheep.

Hawes is the first of the old-fashioned towns and villages that lie strung out along the dale. Family businesses on the main street stock good local produce, and on Tuesday's busy market day, stalls line the street and farmers conduct their business at the livestock market.

Farmers show off their prize sheep at a show held on the summit of Tan Hill

Askrigg was the unspoilt Dales town chosen to represent the fictional Darrowby in the TV series *All Creatures Great and Small*, based on James Herriot's books. To the south of the village is Yorkshire's largest natural lake, Semer Water, ringed by three pretty little villages – Countersett, Marsett and Stalling Busk – with a fourth settlement said to be lying on the bed of the lake! It is popular with anglers, watersports enthusiasts, walkers and those who simply want to admire the splendid views.

From Aysgarth on the road to Carperby lie the Aysgarth Falls, reached by a stroll through one of the last remnants of the ancient

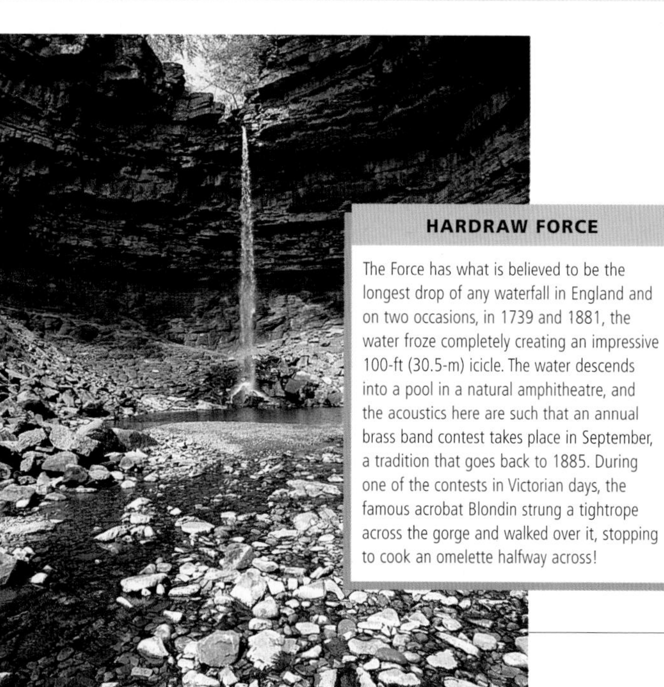

HARDRAW FORCE

The Force has what is believed to be the longest drop of any waterfall in England and on two occasions, in 1739 and 1881, the water froze completely creating an impressive 100-ft (30.5-m) icicle. The water descends into a pool in a natural amphitheatre, and the acoustics here are such that an annual brass band contest takes place in September, a tradition that goes back to 1885. During one of the contests in Victorian days, the famous acrobat Blondin strung a tightrope across the gorge and walked over it, stopping to cook an omelette halfway across!

Askrigg, which became known as James Herriot's fictional town of Darrowby

Wensleydale Cycle Ride

CYCLE RIDE

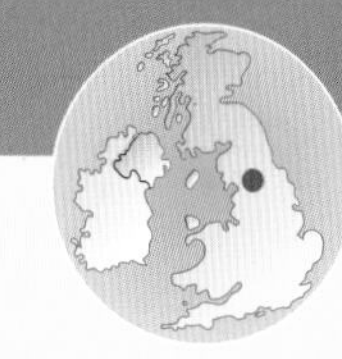

Wensleydale and the Yorkshire Dales

START/FINISH: Hawes. Market town on the A684 northwest of Ripon

DISTANCE: 25.5 miles (41km)

GRADIENT: undulating; some very steep ascents and descents

ROADS: quiet lanes; stretches of main A684

PARKING: free car-park in town next to Market House; pay-and-display at Dales Countryside Museum and in Gayle Lane

The main A684 is the principal east–west route through the Yorkshire Dales National Park, making Wensleydale probably the most accessible of the Dales. But this ride explores both sides of this attractive valley by using quiet side-roads. On the route you can see the highest market town in the country, two of Yorkshire's most famous waterfalls and some of the finest countryside in the Yorkshire Dales.

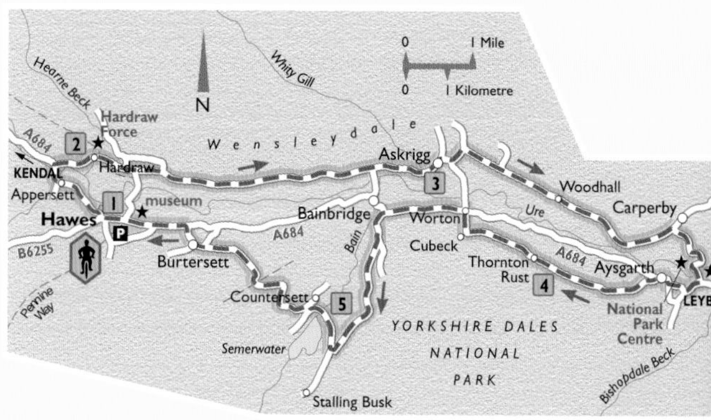

1 The 'capital' of Upper Wensleydale, Hawes is a busy little town – especially on Tuesday, market day. The Dales Countryside Museum is home to a splendid collection of tools, bygones and curios that help to show what dales life was like in earlier times. Leave Hawes travelling

forest of Wensleydale. Further on is Castle Bolton, a one-street village leading to Bolton Castle, where Mary, Queen of Scots was imprisoned for six months. To the south of Carperby is the beautiful village of West Burton with its delightful waterfall, Burton Force. Below the fall is a packhorse bridge, which adds to the charm of the scene. The main road bypasses the almost timeless village green, where children play and horses graze and visitors feel they have stepped back 50 years in time.

Wensley was the first place to receive a market charter, as long ago as 1202, retaining the only market in the whole of the dale for the following 100 years. When plague struck the village in 1563, the focus of Wensleydale life shifted to Leyburn. Leyburn now has the largest auction centre outside London, and holds general and specialist sales two or three times a month, ranging from the mundane bric-à-brac of house clearances to expensive collections of fine antiques, old cars and ceramics.

The rugged beauty of Swaledale is more appealing to some than the prettier and busier Wensleydale. It is a dale of fast-flowing streams and waterfalls, of small villages with harsh-sounding Norse names such as Keld and Muker. At its eastern end stands Richmond, as busy and civilised a market town as you could wish for, with its castle and no less than three museums. At its western end, visitors will feel they have left civilisation far behind as the road climbs and curves through some dramatic scenery towards Mallerstang.

Approaching Richmond from Swaledale, the road winds through wooded valleys, eventually revealing Richmond Castle standing on its hill high above the river. Behind the castle is Richmond's huge cobbled market-place, with its market cross and the unusual sight of Holy Trinity Church with shops and a museum built into the base of the building.

HIGH ON THE PENNINES

Between Wensleydale and Swaledale, 2349ft (716m) above sea-level, stands **Great Shunner Fell**, an excellent viewpoint for those with the requisite stout walking shoes and equally stout legs. The round-trip from Hardraw, along the Pennine Way, is 12 miles (19km), but from the summit the panorama is superb: to the south lie Pen-y-ghent, Whernside and Ingleborough, and far to the west are the fells of the Lake District.

Looking across the River Swale to the imposing Norman ruins of Richmond Castle

westwards along the A684, towards Sedbergh. Enter the hamlet of Appersett and cross two bridges before bearing sharp right, signed to Hardraw and Askrigg.

2 After half a mile (800m) enter Hardraw. Make sure to visit Hardraw Force, a spectacular waterfall that crashes over the lip of a limestone crag into a pool 96ft (29m) below; entry to Hardraw Force is through the Green Dragon pub. Continue along this level road to Askrigg, through the enticing landscape of this gently sloping U-shaped valley. Wensleydale's river – the Ure – is visible at most points during the ride; look out for typical waterside birds, such as the dipper, yellow wagtail and the huge grey heron.

3 The road winds up through Askrigg, best-known today as the TV location for James Herriot's *All Creatures Great and Small*, although well worth exploring in its own right. Leaving the village, your route is signed towards Carperby and Leyburn. A steep climb is followed by level riding, through a typical Dales landscape of dry-stone walls, field barns and scattered farmsteads. Just after the Carperby village sign, turn right, signed to Aysgarth Falls and National Park Centre. To investigate the trio of waterfalls (on foot) turn right after almost a mile (1km) into the Aysgarth Falls National Park Centre. To continue on the route, carry on steeply down the road, cross the River Ure, and climb (or walk) a very steep hill to the A684. Turn right, pass through the village of Aysgarth and turn left, signed to Thornton Rust. Climb steadily, enjoying panoramic views across Wensleydale. Most of the Dales (Swaledale, Wharfedale, Airedale, etc.) are named after the rivers that run through them. Wensleydale is an exception, taking its name from Wensley, a village further down the dale.

4 After 2 miles (3km) pass through Thornton Rust and, in a further mile (1.5km), the hamlet of Cubeck (no sign), then freewheel downhill to the A684 at Worton. Go left, signed to Bainbridge. Just before the road descends into Bainbridge, bear left on a road signed to Semerwater and Hawes. Climb uphill, keeping right when the road forks, to arrive at an almost Lakeland scene: Semerwater in the valley bottom hemmed in by hills. Keep right at the next fork, overlooking the lake (ignore a sign to Stalling Busk), and ride down to the lake.

5 Cross the River Bain, and negotiate a 1-in-4 hill up to a T-junction. Go right, and immediately left, signed to Burtersett and Hawes. A steep climb is followed by a long descent into Burtersett. Continue downhill to the A684 and turn left to cycle the last mile (1.5km) back into Hawes.

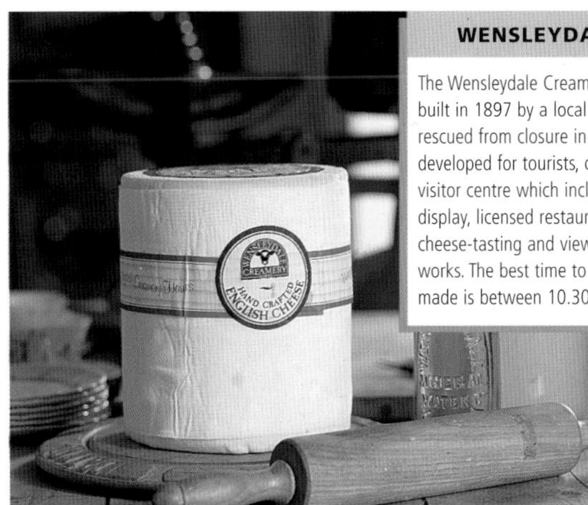

WENSLEYDALE CHEESE

The Wensleydale Creamery at Hawes, first built in 1897 by a local corn merchant, was rescued from closure in 1935. It has been developed for tourists, creating a flourishing visitor centre which includes a museum, video display, licensed restaurant, shop, free cheese-tasting and viewing platforms into the works. The best time to see cheese being made is between 10.30am and 3pm.

RIPON & THE VALE OF YORK

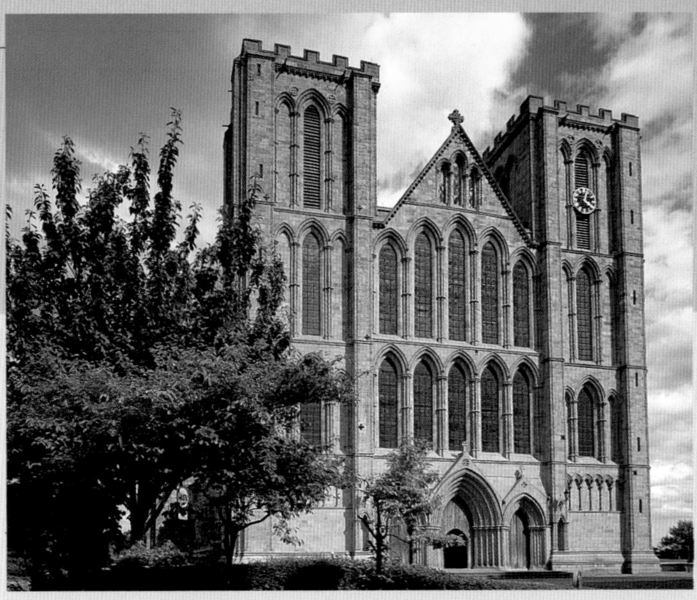
Magnificent Ripon Cathedral, which houses an ancient Saxon crypt dating from AD *672*

This is the 'civilised' corner of the dales, where the landscape is pleasantly rolling, appealing to drivers and those who like strolling round sights, rather than to serious walkers who prefer to trek across the wilder dales.

Masham's huge cobbled market-place is an indication that it was once much more important than it appears today. Between the sheep-filled hills of Wensleydale and the flatter crop-growing fields of the Vale of York, it was also within easy reach of Fountains Abbey to the south, and Jervaulx Abbey to the north. Near the market-place stands the parish church of St Mary, which was mentioned in the Domesday Book.

Towards Wensleydale, Bedale is an attractive old market town which gained its market charter in 1251, with a market cross that dates from the 14th century. On the wide main street stands Bedale Hall, a grand Georgian mansion with huge ballroom, which today serves as impressive council offices. Inside is the Tourist Information Centre and a tiny museum, whose main exhibit is a fire engine from 1748.

THEAKSTON'S

Theakston's brewery at **Masham** is open for inspection, with a visitor centre and the chance to see some of the country's few remaining coopers at work, building barrels. Full guided tours must be booked in advance. The same applies to the **Black Sheep Brewery**, so called because it belongs to a renegade member of the Theakston family.

TOP FIVE GARDENS

Thorpe Perrow Arboretum

Over 2,000 species of plants and trees thrive in these 85 acres (137ha) of garden and woodland. Visit when the bluebells, cherry blossom and daffodils are in bloom.

Studley Royal

Paths wind around these gardens which adjoin Fountains Abbey, taking in the temples and cascades and the River Skell which flows through the grounds.

Harlow Carr Botanical Gardens

Set in 68 acres (27ha), these gardens are a lovely mix of formal and informal, with a gardening museum, plant and gift shops.

Newby Hall Gardens

These award-winning gardens (below) were created to offer something different for every season of the year. The Woodland Discovery Walk is particularly attractive.

Ripley Castle Gardens

Ripley contains the National Hyacinth Collection, as well as walled gardens, old hothouse buildings and a walk through wooded grounds to a gazebo.

CYCLE RIDE

Wetherby Cycle Ride

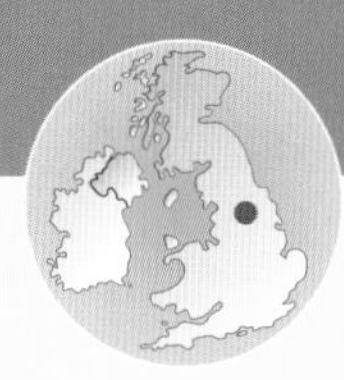

Between Wharfe and Nidd

START/FINISH: Wetherby. On the A1 12 miles (19km) north of Leeds

DISTANCE: 28 miles (45km), with 7 miles (11.5km) off-road

GRADIENT: level along the old railway, otherwise undulating

ROADS: quiet lanes; short sections on A-road; bridleway (can be wet in winter)

PARKING: Wilderness car-park, just off the A661 in Wetherby by the bridge over the Wharfe

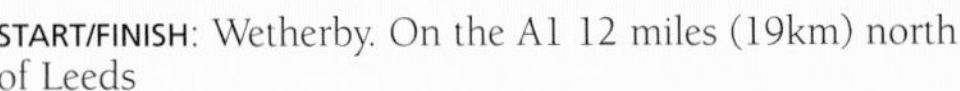

This scenic circuit offers much of interest, and options for off-road cycling along the former Wetherby–Spofforth railway.

1 From the car-park cycle north up the B6164 past the Brunswick pub. Look for the blue cycle route sign and join the Harland Way under the steel bridge; fork left where path divides. Continue on this route for about 3 miles (5km) to Spofforth; turn right on to the A661 along the High Street. Go straight over the mini-roundabout, signed To Castle. Pass the remains of 13th- to 15th-century Spofforth Castle on your left.

2 Continue north on Castle Street and keep right at the fork beyond the village, climbing gradually to Follifoot. Turn right at the T-junction opposite Rudding Gates, descending to cross Crimple Beck, then rising to the A661. Turn sharply right here, descend, and turn left to Plumpton Rocks. Amazing rock formations are to be found here in a woodland setting around a small, deep lake. Beyond East Lodge the path is a bridleway – continue up the driveway to the northwest corner of Plumpton Hall Farm. Now ride on the bridleway west through a gap in the wall going north, then east and north again (turn left) along the edge of Birkham Wood to the busy A658. Cross carefully, pass through the gate opposite, and follow the bridleway through the wood, and continue on a track to the Lido Caravan Park. Go through the park and at the exit turn left and left again, on to the B6164 into Knaresborough.

3 At Grinbald Bridge cross the River Nidd and turn immediately left on to Abbey Road (private). Go over the crossroads with the B6163 into Waterside; to visit the castle and town centre, walk up the path or by Water Bag Bank, beyond the railway viaduct. Retrace the route on Waterside to the low bridge and turn right on to the B6163, up Bland's

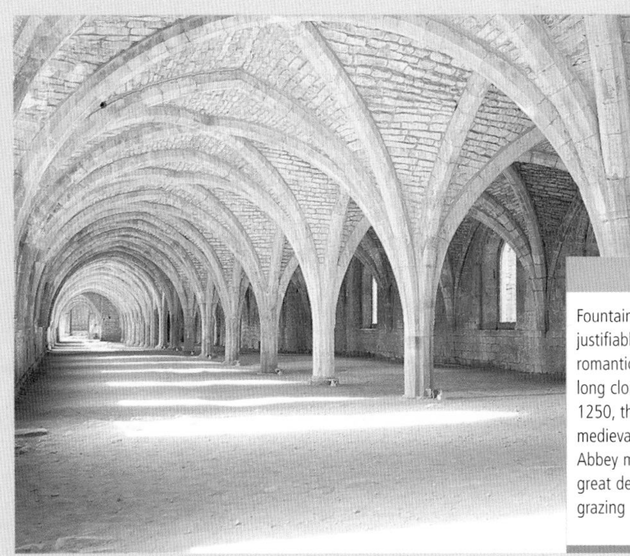

FOUNTAINS ABBEY

Fountains Abbey, the largest monastic ruin in Europe, was justifiably designated a World Heritage Site in 1987. The romantic ruins you see today, including the 312-ft (93.5-m) long cloisters, were mostly constructed between 1150 and 1250, though the North Tower is a 16th-century addition. In medieval times the Cistercian order of monks at Fountains Abbey made it the richest monastery in Britain; it owned a great deal of the land in the Yorkshire Dales, and used it for grazing large herds of cattle and sheep.

Heading south, attractions such as Fountains Abbey and Newby Hall vie for attention around Ripon. A complete Saxon crypt, built by St Wilfrid in AD 672, lies below Ripon Cathedral. The West Front of this splendid cathedral dates from 1220, the East Front from 1290, and inside there are 500-year-old woodcarvings, a 16th-century nave and some exceptional stained-glass work. Close by, in St Mary's Gate, visitors move from God to the godless, in the Ripon Prison and Police Museum. Housed in the cell block of what was first the Ripon Liberty Prison and later its police station, the museum tells the vivid story of Yorkshire law and disorder through the ages. It has some chilling displays. The Lightwater Valley Amusement Park, with its enormous roller-coasters and other rides, is high on the list for families, and there is the Lightwater Village, a shopping centre with factory, fashion and food shops.

Further south lies Ripley, an estate village built around Ripley Castle, which has been home to the Ingilby family since the 1320s. There are fine collections of weaponry and furniture, as well as secret hiding holes and passageways. The village was largely built in the 1820s by Sir William Amcotts Ingilby, an affable eccentric who modelled it on a village he had seen in Alsace-Lorraine. The delightful result is the only place in Yorkshire which has a 'Hotel de Ville' rather than a Town Hall, and the cobbled market square with its stocks, the listed cottages, and the 15th-century church all make this an unusual and pleasurable place to visit.

Hill. Take the second turning right by The Union pub on to Forest Moor Road. In 1 mile (1.5km) turn left at the crossroads, then pass the cemetery to cross the A661 into Rudding Lane.

4 Descend, then climb gradually, passing Rudding Park on the left. At the next junction turn right, signed Pannal, and continue west across Follifoot Ridge to Pannal. At the golf club turn sharp left into Drury Lane and continue to the A658. Turn right and immediately left, eventually descending into Kirkby Overblow. Turn left at the T-junction, and continue along a ridge, to pass a chapel in a mile (1.5km).

5 Bear left, and shortly keep left, continuing northeast to Sicklinghall. Descend through the village, heading towards Wetherby. Beyond Linton Spring Country Hotel, fork right to Linton. In the village turn sharply left opposite a public byway. Pass the golf course, and then turn right at a junction with Linton Road, returning to the car-park in Wetherby.

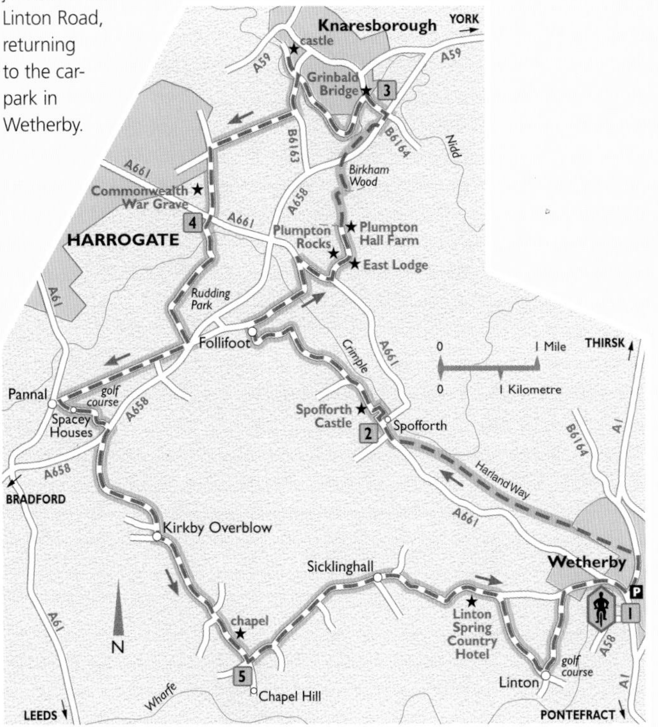

OUTDOOR ADVENTURES IN THE DALES

Ballooning A balloon flight over this lovely area gives a unique perspective on the scenery, whether skimming the treetops or high in the clouds. Airborne Adventures at Skipton launch from three sites – Skipton, Settle and Gisburn – depending on the weather and wind direction.

Caving Visitors flock to Britain's biggest show cave – White Scar Cave – but there are more caves used by those interested in adventure activities. With a qualified leader you can explore the caves around Ingleton at very little expense. Introductory caving trips can be booked at the National Park Centre in Grassington.

Climbing and abseiling The Cow and Calf Rocks on Ilkley are popular for climbing. In the vicinity of Ingleton, local instructors can take you out climbing and abseiling. Inglesport, the largest outdoor equipment specialist in the Dales, operates an indoor climbing wall here.

Driving Drive a single-seater, race saloon or rally car under the expert guidance of professional instructors at the Croft Racing Circuit. For thrills, nothing can compare with this unforgettable experience.

SEE CONTACTS SECTION FOR ADDITIONAL INFORMATION

YORK, NORTH YORK MOORS & THE EAST RIDING

From the North York Moors to the Humber, from fishing ports and holiday resorts on the coast to historic York, this is a fascinating and diverse area. The Moors and the Wolds are havens of peace and solitude, rich in wildlife and scant in population. The chalky escarpment of the Wolds is cut by deep and winding dry valleys, contrasting with the heather moorland and green valleys of the Moors. The Moors are crisscrossed by long marches of dry-stone diking, while the irregular hedges of the Wolds enclose smaller fields. The North Sea coast has miles of sandy beaches around the holiday resorts of Filey, Bridlington and Hornsea, contrasting with the dramatic chalk cliffs at Flamborough Head. Finally, the incomparable city of York, in the Vale of York, at the heart of Yorkshire and of England's history, is perhaps the most beautiful city in all this green and pleasant land.

White Horse of Kilburn
This hill figure is a very distinctive and much-loved landmark for miles around. It was cut into the slope by Thomas Hodgson in 1857 after visiting the famous White Horse of Uffington in Oxfordshire. The White Horse is almost 325ft (99m) from head to tail, and 227ft (69m) in height. It is now the only major landscape figure in the north of England.

DUNCOMBE PARK

The splendid 200-room mansion of Duncombe Park, southwest of Helmsley, sits in 600 acres (243ha) of tranquil parkland. It

was designed by William Wakefield in 1713 as a family home for the Duncombe family and their descendants, the Fevershams. There is public access to both the house and the landscaped parkland, which boasts a delightful terrace walk, with Ionic and Tuscan temples to lend an air of romance.

Robin Hood's Bay

The houses of Robin Hood's Bay, reached by narrow alleyways and steps, seem to tumble down the side of the cliff in a charming jumble of whitewashed walls and red-tiled roofs, almost tipping into the sea at the bottom. Notorious as a haunt of smugglers, it is easy to imagine the scene as they heaved the contraband kegs and chests through this maze to the top of the village.

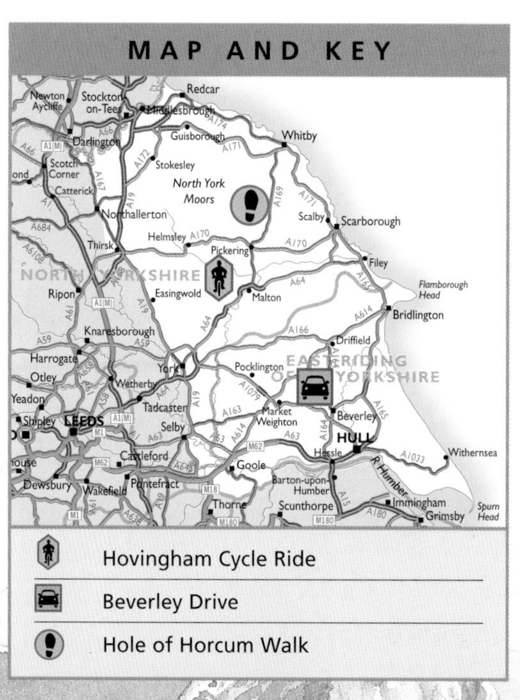

Flamborough Head

The landscape of Flamborough Head is dominated by the undulating Yorkshire Wolds countryside which drops spectacularly into the North Sea creating chalk cliffs, stacks, caves and coves. The cliffs and rocky shores here support a great diversity of marine communities. The RSPB reserve at Bempton provides unrivalled facilities for watching the thousands of sea birds which nest on the cliffs.

York Minster

The magnificent Minster, at the heart of York, took 250 years to build and was completed and consecrated in 1472. Its stained-glass windows, spanning 800 years and including some of the oldest examples in the world, are acknowledged as a collection of international importance. There are over a hundred windows including the magnificent Rose Window and the immense East Window, the largest area of medieval stained glass in the world.

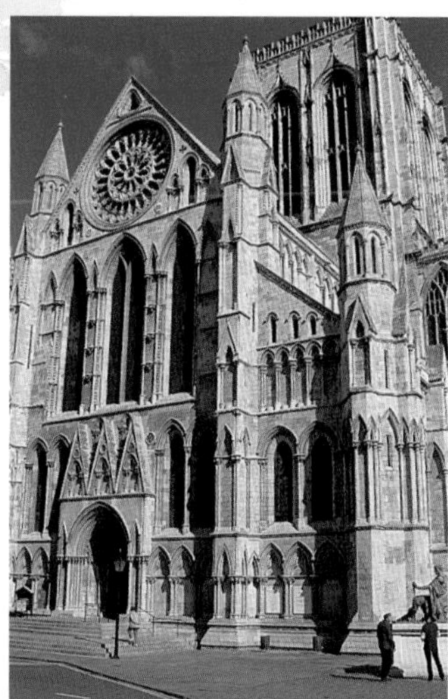

YORK & THE DERWENT VALE

York is a truly medieval city, from the moment you enter through the gates in the ancient city walls or explore the narrow winding Shambles and come upon the soaring Minster, suddenly and unexpectedly, immense and beautiful before you. You can walk around almost the entire city on the walls, interrupted by the impressive battlements of the four gates on which the heads of traitors were once gruesomely displayed.

Begun in AD 71, *Eboracum*, as it was called, was an important Roman administrative centre for several hundred years. The name 'York' comes from the Viking settlement, Jorvik, re-created at the Viking Centre in Coppergate, complete with the sights, sounds – and even smells – of village life. The Castle Museum is outstanding, with reconstructed Victorian and Edwardian streets and shops, plus the cell in which the highwayman Dick Turpin spent his last night as a condemned man.

THE WORLD OF JAMES HERRIOT

Alf Wight, the creator of James Herriot, began his career as a veterinary surgeon in **Thirsk** in 1939. Step back 50 years as you cross the threshold of his surgery into original interiors lovingly re-created with help and advice from Wight's family. Even the carbolic smells of the 1950s permeate the house. The kitchen and laundry have ancient stoves and mangles and shelves of preserves. The dispensary is filled with jars, tins, strange potions and liniments. There's an excellent audio-visual, a re-creation of a Yorkshire farmyard, and Alf Wight's pride and joy – his garden.

CASTLE HOWARD

Castle Howard, designed by Sir John Vanbrugh in 1699, took 100 years and numerous architects to complete. Familiar as the setting of the TV series *Brideshead Revisited*, its majestic sweeping lines, richly carved façades and the famous dome are set in 1,000 acres (405ha) of glorious parks and woodlands. The interior, which still has the feel of a family home, is richly furnished with a notable collection of pictures including works by Gainsborough, Reynolds, Rubens and Holbein. The grounds are a delight with rare roses in the walled garden, a unique collection of magnolias, hydrangeas and wild roses in the woodland garden and various fountains, bridges and follies, as well as the mausoleum.

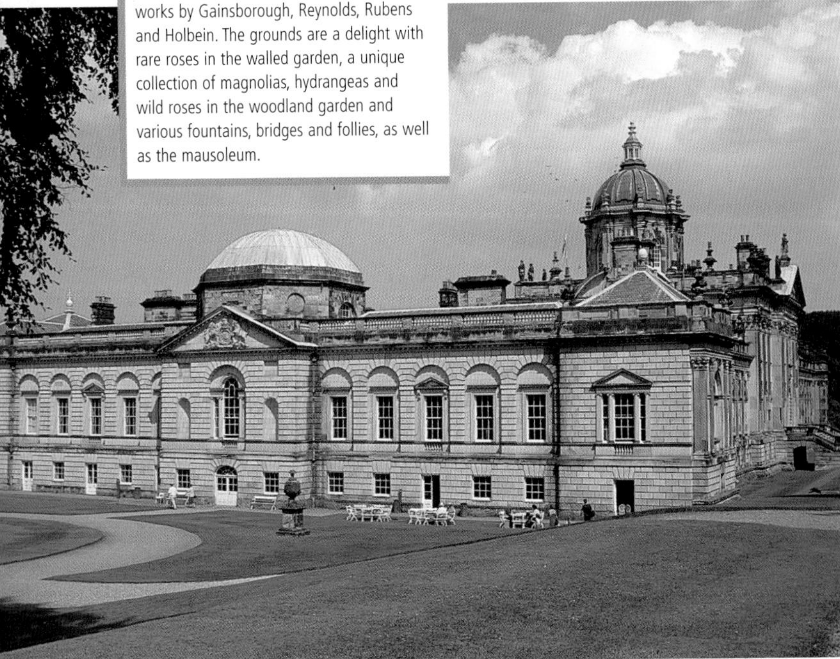

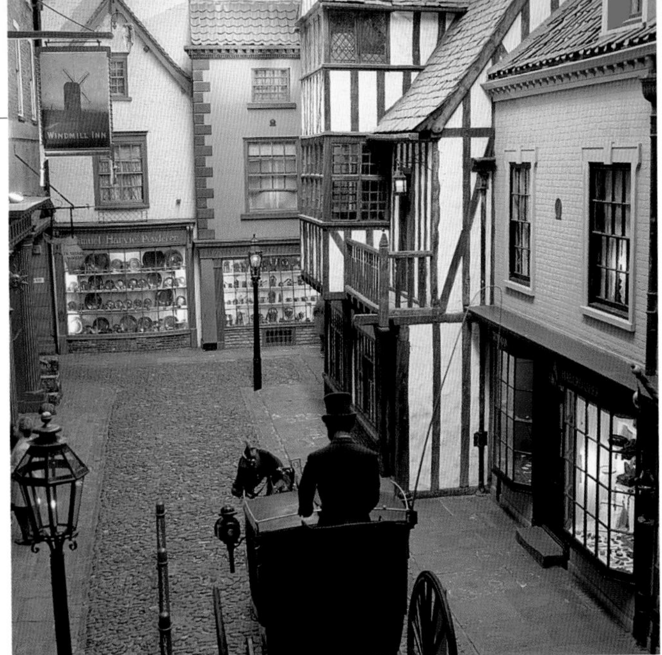

A horsedrawn carriage passes through historical streets at York's Castle Museum

CYCLE RIDE

Hovingham Cycle Ride

Touring the Howardian Hills

START/FINISH: Hovingham. On the B1257 8 miles (13km) west of Malton

DISTANCE: 22 miles (35km)

GRADIENT: undulating

ROADS: country lanes, B-class roads and tracks

PARKING: car-park opposite Hovingham Hall

This gentle ride, with a choice of on- or off-road routes, takes you through the rich countryside around Castle Howard. The undulating roads pass castles and stately homes, visit pretty villages and woodland, and offer panoramic views.

1 Hovingham has been an estate village since Roman times. Hovingham Hall (not open) is owned by Sir Thomas Worsley, whose family links date from 1661. Turn left from the car-park and head for Malton on the B1257.

2 Off-roaders: turn right after 1.5 miles (2.5km), signed Baxton Howe, and climb to Fryton Wood. The lane becomes a farm track. Continue ahead across a bridleway, keep left, descend to a stream, then ascend to a T-junction on the woodland edge (2 miles/3km). Turn left when the track reaches a road. Descend through woodland to the gatehouse at Coneysthorpe, looking across the Great Lake to Castle Howard. The road option continues on the B1257 to the village of Slingsby, with its ruined 18th-century castle. Turn right here, signed Castle Howard, and follow the quiet road as it climbs the Howardian Hills. Stop at the top to enjoy the views. Descend to the Coneysthorpe junction and the Great Lake.

3 Cycle up to the obelisk (turn left for Castle Howard) and on through the stone gatehouse; look left for the Black Pyramid. Proceed through a second mock fortified archway to a crossroads and turn right towards Terrington. Over 1,200 acres (490ha) of parkland flank Castle Howard, a magnificent stately home built between 1699 and 1726.

4 In half a mile (800m) turn right towards Slingsby and climb gently to Brandrith Farm. Off-roaders: turn left through a gate, signed Bridleway, past the farmhouse and follow a track for half a mile (800m) across fields and down past fish ponds. Ascend, bear right into a farmyard, then left and continue to climb to reach the road. Descend into Terrington. Road riders continue past Brandrith Farm to Ganthorpe and then to Terrington.

North of York, the small Yorkshire market town of Thirsk lies between the Yorkshire Dales National Park and the North York Moors National Park. Alf Wight, better known as the vet James Herriot, had his surgery here at 23 Kirkgate. At the centre of Thirsk the cobbled market square with its clock tower is surrounded by shops and places to eat.

Heading east from Thirsk, the road climbs the 1-in-4 incline of Sutton Bank. The view from the top is one of the finest in Yorkshire. Spread out below you is the flat plain of the Vale of York. On a clear day, armed with a pair of binoculars, you can see York Minster and the Three Peaks of the Yorkshire Dales.

THE SHAMBLES, YORK

This short, narrow street of almost perfectly preserved medieval buildings was where the city's butchers once plied their trade. The buildings huddle so close together that attic-dwellers could shake hands across the street. The narrow street kept direct sunlight away from the meat – a wise precaution in the days before refrigeration. The butchers' shops are all gone, though many of the shop-fronts still incorporate the wooden ledges on which meat used to be displayed.

YORKSHIRE GLIDING CLUB

The Yorkshire Gliding Club operates from the top of **Sutton Bank**, exploiting the thermals rising up the scar. Powered planes tow the gliders over the edge. With the addition of hang-gliders, microlight aircraft and soaring birds, the skies beyond Sutton Bank can get very busy indeed.

A delightful walk hugs the edge of Sutton Bank, taking in graceful gliders from the flying club, the White Horse of Kilburn and Lake Gormire, once imagined to be bottomless.

Visitors to Kilburn should not miss the workshops and showrooms of the renowned woodcarver and cabinet-maker, Robert Thompson, where craftsmen can still be found demonstrating their skills. His handiwork, carrying his unique trademark – a little carved mouse – can be found in York Minster and Westminster Abbey. A chapel in Kilburn's parish church was dedicated to the 'Mouseman' shortly before his death in 1958. East of Kilburn, picturesque villages are strung out along the Ampleforth Valley, flanked by the Howardian Hills and the moors. Ampleforth is best known for its public school and monastery. At Nunnington look over the delightful 17th-century, three-arched bridge over the River Rye to spot basking trout, superbly camouflaged against the sandy river bed.

NATIONAL RAILWAY MUSEUM

The National Railway Museum in York, the largest railway museum in the world, tells the story of the railway from Stephenson's *Rocket* to Eurostar. The museum has every type of railway carriage from open wagons with wooden benches and royal palaces on rails, to spartan third-class carriages and opulent elegance in first class. There are various hands-on displays from the intricacies of the signalling system to sorting the mail. The 7¼in-gauge miniature railway takes visitors on a fun ride through the museum's play and picnic area, specially designed for younger visitors.

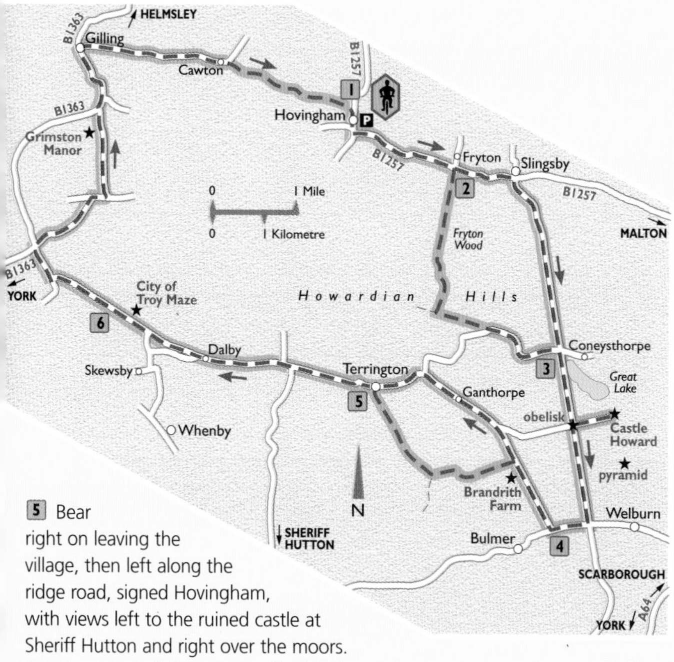

Malton on the River Derwent, a market town just to the northeast of the Howardian Hills, has been the historic centre of Ryedale since Roman times. North of the Roman fort site is the quaint town of Old Malton, with ancient stone houses and the most beautiful Gilbertine prior, where you can also find a working farm giving demonstrations. Nearby is magnificent Castle Howard, designed for the 3rd Earl of Carlisle. To the south of Malton is Wharram Percy, a 'lost' medieval village, depopulated by economic forces in the 15th century.

Woodcarving skills on display at Robert Thompson's workshop in Kilburn

5 Bear right on leaving the village, then left along the ridge road, signed Hovingham, with views left to the ruined castle at Sheriff Hutton and right over the moors. Continue past a left turn to York, then bear left, signed Dalby, as the main road bends right. Pass through Dalby, and proceed to the Whenby/Skewsby junction. Stay on the ridge; just ahead on your right is the ancient City of Troy Maze. This little turf maze is the only surviving example in North Yorkshire of the ancient game of 'treading the maze'.

6 Continue to a junction and follow the road right towards Helmsley. At a major road junction turn right, signed Hovingham, and proceed to another T-junction. Turn right, then left in 330 yards (300m) along a lane to Gilling. Soon descend past Grimston Manor to a T-junction; turn right on to the B1363 and enter Gilling. This quiet village nestles in pleasant wooded countryside beneath its castle (now part of a school). Turn right at the Fairfax Arms to Cawton. As the road turns sharp left at the village end, a chalk track continues straight on, with Spring Farm Cottages on the right. This is an easy 2-mile (3-km) off-road section to Hovingham, which can be ridden on slick tyres. Go through a gate by the children's playground, and follow the lane to emerge by the ford and bakery.

THE EAST RIDING OF YORKSHIRE

The Yorkshire Wolds extend from the Humber estuary to the North Sea coast near Scarborough. Formed from chalk, they rise gently from the east to a dramatic escarpment at the eastern edge of the Vale of York. Although not particularly high, the escarpment offers splendid views over the flat Vale of York. The coastal stretch of east Yorkshire from Flamborough Head to Spurn Head at the mouth of the Humber forms a huge marshy peninsula about 30 miles (48km) long. The finest cliff scenery is between Bridlington and Filey, where the chalk cliffs rise 300ft (90m) out of the sea. Traditional seaside towns include Hornsea, with its 2-mile (3-km) long freshwater Mere, and Bridlington.

The seaside resort of Bridlington has miles of sandy beaches to the south and north, backed by the chalk cliffs of Sewerby and the Headland. Visitors can watch the hive of activity in the harbour from a safe viewing area as keel boats and coble boats (an ancient design dating back to the 5th century) land cod, haddock, whiting, plaice, salmon, sea trout, lobsters and crabs. Bridlington is also the home of the Royal Yorkshire Yacht Club and during the summer almost 100 yachts compete in racing in the bay.

A row of terraced, thatched cottages in the village of Warter, near Pocklington

The Humber Bridge, looking towards Hull, is the world's longest single-span bridge

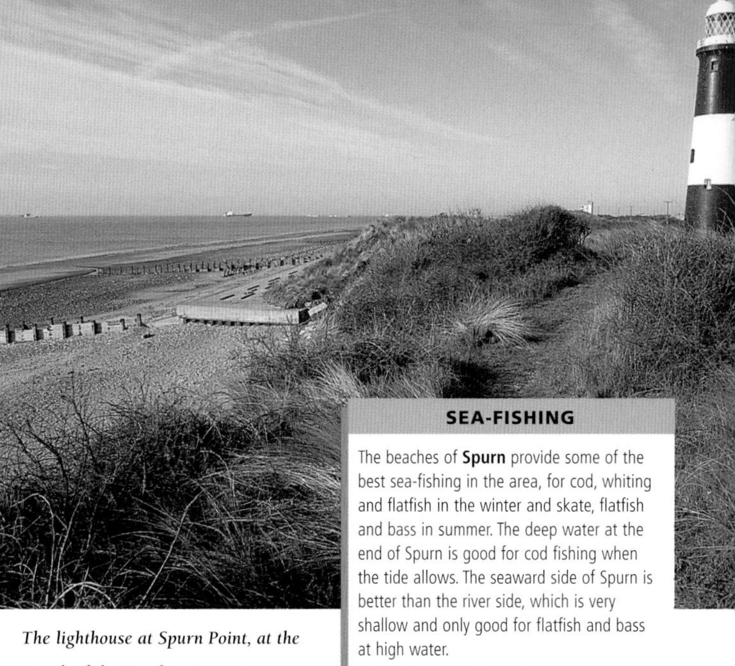

The lighthouse at Spurn Point, at the mouth of the Humber Estuary

SEA-FISHING

The beaches of **Spurn** provide some of the best sea-fishing in the area, for cod, whiting and flatfish in the winter and skate, flatfish and bass in summer. The deep water at the end of Spurn is good for cod fishing when the tide allows. The seaward side of Spurn is better than the river side, which is very shallow and only good for flatfish and bass at high water.

Beverley Drive

DRIVE

Heartland of the Wolds

START/FINISH: Beverley. On the A1035 8 miles (13km) north of Hull

DISTANCE: 49 miles (78.5km)

Historic Beverley is the southeastern gateway to Britain's most northerly area of chalk country, where broad, sweeping wolds are broken only by secretive, green, dry valleys. Hedged roads and lanes link the few, scattered villages in ordered landscapes of the 18th century.

1 The North Bar, built in 1409, is the only surviving gateway to historic Beverley, an attractive town with medieval streets dignified by handsome Georgian buildings. The twin bell towers of Beverley Minster, one of England's finest Gothic churches, dominate the town and the surrounding flat pastures. Leave Beverley by following the signs to York (A1079) and, at the roundabout, take the third exit (A1079) for Market Weighton. Embowered in trees, graced with a large green and two ponds with well-fed ducks, stately beeches, chestnuts and sycamores, and groups of attractive brick or half-timbered cottages, Bishop Burton is a gem of a village.

2 Continue on the route to Market Weighton, following signs to the town centre and, at the near end of the main street, turn right signed Londesborough. At the roundabout, keep forward towards Londesborough, then at the T-junction turn right for Londesborough. Go over the crossroads, signed Nunburnholme, then keep straight on at the next crossroads and descend to the outskirts of Nunburnholme. This straggling village along a chalk stream has white-painted brick cottages with pantiled roofs, and a tiny church with a fine Saxon cross. Turn right, signed to Warter, and after 1 mile (1.5km) turn right again, signed Huggate, into Warter.

3 Turn right on to the B1246 towards Driffield and shortly turn left on to a minor road, signed to Huggate. At the edge of Huggate turn left for Millington, then turn right, signed to Fridaythorpe. In 2 miles (3km) take the right fork by two large ornamental stones, then right again at the A166 for Fridaythorpe. At the end of the village, turn left on to the

POCKLINGTON CANAL

Pocklington Canal has a good towpath and is popular with walkers and wildlife enthusiasts. Angling can also be enjoyed on sections of the canal that are free from weed. The most tranquil part is the section between **Melbourne** and **East Cottingwith** where the canal flows alongside the Wheldrake Ings nature reserve. The whole canal lies within three Sites of Special Scientific Interest (SSSI) because of the rich variety of wildlife. The unrestored section of the canal above Melbourne, with its surrounding network of ditches, becks, hedgerows, grasslands and scrub, is one of the most important canal sites in England for wildlife. Many birds breed here, including kingfishers, reed and sedge warblers, reed buntings and tufted ducks, and otters are known to use its quiet waters.

THE WOLDS WAY

One of nine National Trails in England, the Wolds Way stretches 79 miles (127km) from the Humber Bridge to the North Sea along the escarpment of the Yorkshire Wolds. It is dominated nearly all the way by the crest of the chalk escarpment, which runs first north from the Humber and then east, to terminate abruptly in the 400-ft (120-m) cliffs of Bempton. This complex and varied trail leads you up to lonely windblown wold tops and down through remote sheep-grazed valleys. The peace and quiet of country life still dominate and the gentle charm of the Yorkshire Wolds leaves the walker refreshed in body and spirit.

Sewerby Hall and gardens enjoy spectacular views across Bridlington Bay

Spurn Head, at the mouth of the River Humber, is a hook-shaped peninsula, some 3.5miles (5.5km) long and as little as 50yds (45m) wide in places. Spurn is made up of sand and shingle banks held together with marram grass and seabuckthorn and has occasionally been breached by the sea, as the Victorian sea defences are now crumbling. There are fossils and all manner of things to find among the soft sand, pebbles and shingle of the beaches.

The River Humber separates Yorkshire from Lincolnshire and marks the transition from the North of England to the Midlands. The magnificent Humber Bridge, one of the world's longest single-span suspension bridges, crosses the River Humber at Hessle. Hull is the third-biggest port in England after Liverpool and London and has been described as 'the biggest fishing port in the world'. It also has important ferry links to Zeebrugge and Rotterdam in Europe. In medieval Hull, known as the Old Town, the 14th-century church of Holy Trinity incorporates some of the earliest uses of brick – a brickyard was recorded in Hull as early as 1303. Wilberforce House, the birthplace of the anti-slavery campaigner William Wilberforce, is now a museum dedicated to the history of the slave trade.

Market Weighton and Pocklington are market towns situated near the edge of the Wolds between Hull and York. Pocklington has a 13th-century church and a grammar school dating from 1514 which was attended by William Wilberforce.

B1251, signed 'Bridlington, scenic route', to Fimber. Continue through Fimber and at the roundabout, take the second exit to Sledmere. The vast Sykes estates spread across the Wolds around Sledmere. The present elegant house dates largely from the late 18th and early 19th centuries.

4 Go forward on to the B1252 towards Driffield. After 2 miles (3km) pass Sir Tatton Sykes Monument on the right, a 120-ft (33-m) high tower which dominates the Wolds skyline. In 1.5 miles (2.5km) turn left on to the A166 into Garton-on-the-Wolds. Turn right on to a minor road, signed Kirkburn, then on reaching the A163 turn right towards Bainton/Beverley. At the roundabout, turn left to Bainton. Branch left on to the B1248 and 9 miles (14.5km) further, at the roundabout, take the second exit (A164) and return to Beverley.

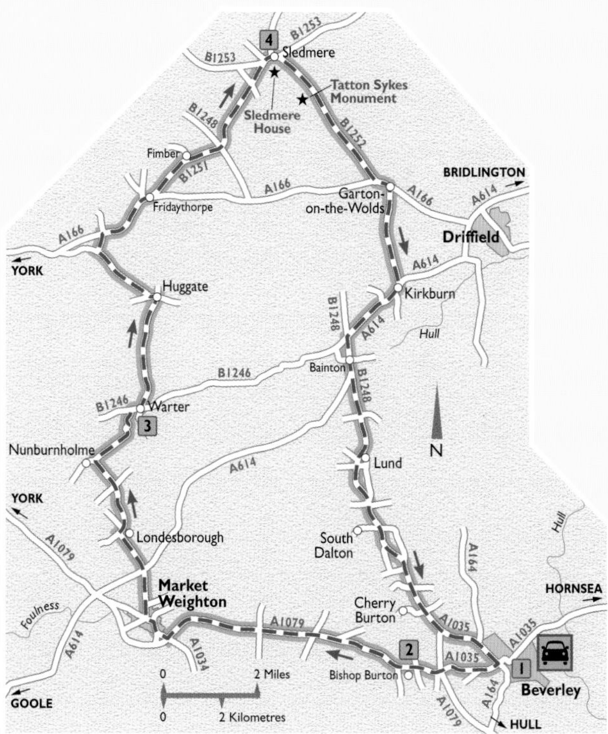

BEMPTON CLIFF

With over 3 miles (5km) of sheer chalk cliffs, rising to 400ft (120m), Bempton is the best place in England to experience the sights, sounds and smells of over 200,000 breeding sea birds and England's only gannetry. Five safe viewing points give spectacular close-up views of puffins, gannets, guillemots, razorbills, kittiwakes and fulmars between April and mid-August. At other times there are migrating birds to be seen and possibly seals and porpoises.

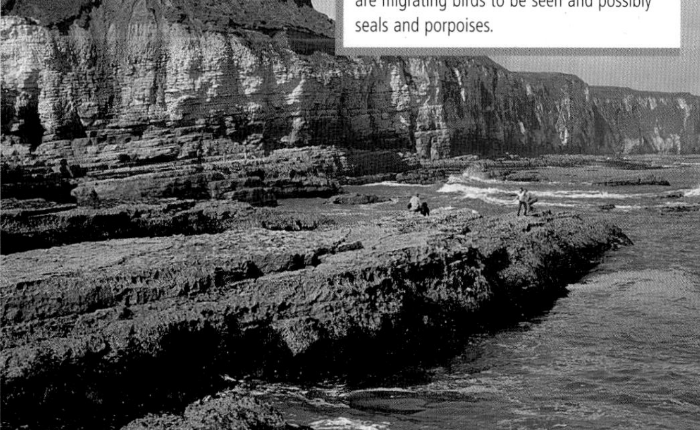

THE NORTH YORK MOORS

The North York Moors is the most extensive area of moorland in England or Wales. Rolling hills blaze with purple heather in late summer and rock-strewn streams chatter through pretty green valleys and rough gorges. Most settlements are villages, usually centred on a bridge over a river; the cottages are built of stone with distinctive red pantiled roofs. Spectacular views over this scenery can be enjoyed from the steam trains of the North York Moors Railway, running from Pickering to Grosmont, and along the Cleveland Way footpath, which skirts the northern and western edges of the moors and then follows the coast towards Scarborough.

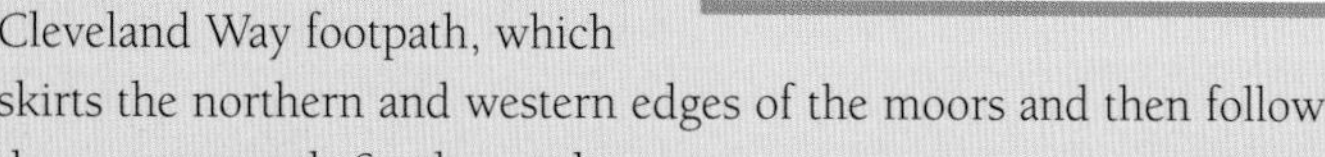

To the west, Helmsley, a handsome little market town, is the administrative centre of the National Park. On the long scenic valley of Bilsdale, from Helmsley, towards Stokesley in the north, look out for The Sun Inn, about 8 miles (13km) north of Helmsley. Each licensee has been called William Ainsley for 200 years. Just yards from the pub is a much earlier thatched inn, of cruck-frame construction, that dates back to the 16th century.

The delightful drive through Bransdale from Helmsley to Kirkbymoorside passes through open heather moorland patched by dry-stone

THE CROSSES WALK

This challenging walk of about 53 miles (85km) was created to be undertaken in a single day. Starting and finishing in the village of **Goathland**, it uses 13 prominent crosses as waymarkers. An interesting custom was for well-heeled travellers to leave coins on top of the crosses (many had a recess for this purpose) for the benefit of the needy.

NORTH YORKSHIRE MOORS RAILWAY

The Whitby–Pickering line has a new lease of life as the North Yorkshire Moors Railway, where steam-hauled trains take you deep into the moors. The steepest section of the line was known as the Beck Hole Incline, so steep that the earliest carriages had to be hauled up and down using a system of counter-balanced weights. Though tiny and unspoilt today, **Beck Hole** was briefly, during the middle of the last century, a busy centre of ironstone mining. The Newtondale Halt has no road access, making it the most isolated station on this most scenic of restored lines.

The former whaling port of Whitby, home to the explorer Captain James Cook

Hole of Horcum Walk

WALK

In the Hole of Horcum

START/FINISH: car-park on the A169, 12 miles (19km) north of Pickering and 3 miles (5km) north of Lockton

DISTANCE: 8.5 miles (13.5km)

ASCENT/GRADIENT: 1,015ft (309m): moderate ascents; some steep sections

TERRAIN/PATHS: moorland ridges and wooded valleys; good tracks and woodland paths; often muddy

An invigorating trek across fell and woodland that explores this spectacular dip in the moorland plateau, traces signs of civilisation from the Iron Age, and features a preserved steam railway and a remote farming village.

1 The vast, bowl-shaped depression of the Hole of Horcum has been created by springs which have cut their way through the flat-topped hills of the North York Moors to carve out one of the most spectacular sights of the area. From the car-park cross the road and walk north, following the road's sharp left bend and then going ahead over a stile on to an uphill track as the road hairpins right. Follow this track for 2.5 miles (4km), alongside an Iron-Age ditch, built to protect the early settlers whose farmstead stood on a nearby ridge, passing left of a pond, to reach a signpost by a second pond.

2 Turn right (signed Station) with the pond on your right. Go ahead at a crossing track, walk beside a wall for 200yds (182m), then descend the ridge to the valley road and turn left. As you leave the moor and descend into Newtondale you may hear the sound of a whistle or see the smoke of a steam-drawn train. This is the route of the North Yorkshire Moors Railway, a spectacular preserved steam railway.

3 After 200yds (182m) take a signed track to the right. Follow bridleway signs to reach a gate by a wood. The track curves through the wood to a stile, then across fields.

4 At the second gateway take the track uphill, through a gate into woodland. Continue uphill where a track joins from the right, turning left at a crossing track, which eventually becomes metalled.

5 After 500yds (457m), turn right along a bridleway, going downhill

CYCLING IN ROSEDALE

The old Rosedale railway line is ideal for cycling along much of its length, as it is relatively level and surfaced with ash ballast. The best section is from **Rosedale Bank Top** to **Blakey Junction**, near the Lion Inn (4 miles/6.5km) and then across the moors to **Ingleby Bank Top** another 7 miles (12km). You could even cycle down the incline, but remember what goes down must come up!

walls and scattered farmsteads of well-dressed, honey-coloured stone, harmonising perfectly with a timeless landscape. The moors, with barely a tree to be seen, echo to the calls of the curlew, red grouse and lapwing.

Further east, the daffodils of Farndale are justifiably famous, but this is a lovely valley to visit at any time of year. Hutton-le-Hole is one of Yorkshire's 'picture postcard' villages, with houses set back from Hutton Beck, a watercourse spanned by a succession of pretty little bridges. The village green is the size of a meadow, with the grass cropped short by grazing sheep.

To the north the River Esk rises near Westerdale, meandering through a string of pretty villages to the North Sea at Whitby. The National Park's Visitor Centre, close to the Esk, near Danby, is a perfect spot to enjoy a picnic or a riverside stroll. A few yards downstream is an arched packhorse bridge, intriguingly named Duck Bridge. The Esk Valley Walk, a waymarked route, begins at Castleton and follows the river to the coast at Whitby. Ramblers can alight at Egton Bridge, on the Middlesbrough to Whitby line, and walk along the Esk Valley to Lealholm to catch the next train home.

RYEDALE FOLK MUSEUM

The Ryedale Folk Museum in pretty **Hutton-le-Hole**, illustrates over 2,000 years of local history with an array of fascinating bygones. This is one of Britain's most remarkable open-air museums, with a reconstructed cruck house, Elizabethan manor and cottages from three different centuries. The museum also contains the oldest daylight photographic studio in England and a small glass-making furnace of 1590 from Rosedale Abbey. The cruck-framed house contains a witch post, elaborately carved from mountain ash, to ward off evil spirits.

Cyclists enjoy scenic trails through Dalby Forest near Scarborough

From Grosmont you can take the North Yorkshire Moors Railway to Goathland, famed as the location for the popular television series, *Heartbeat*. Of the delightful waterfalls around the village, the best known is the 70-ft (21-m) Mallyan Spout.

The coastline between Whitby and Scarborough offers spectacular cliffs, hidden coves, sandy beaches and fascinating rock formations. Numerous sea birds can be found nesting on the cliff ledges and soaring out to sea. Robin Hood's Bay, with its cobbled streets and tiny cottages is one of the loveliest fishing villages in the country, while Scarborough is Yorkshire's premier seaside resort.

and left at a crossing track. The path winds through woodland and eventually reaches a road, where you turn left up into Levisham, a remote farming village typical of the area.

6 At the top of the green take the lane to the right of The Horseshoe Inn. At a stile beside a gate across the lane, go right and descend to follow a path along the narrowing valley, beside the stream. To the left of the lane by which you leave the village there are the remains of pits from which iron has been dug since the Iron Age.

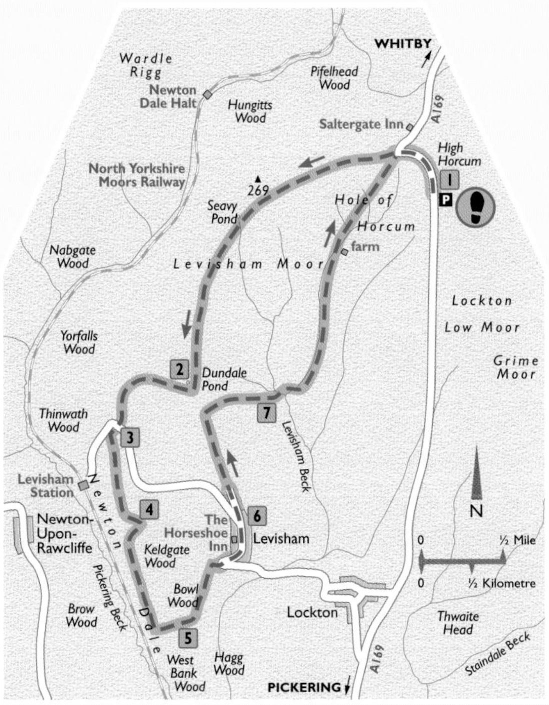

7 At a signpost for Saltergate turn left, go over two footbridges and turn left at the waymark beyond. The path follows the valley into the Hole of Horcum, passing a former farmhouse, then ascends to a ladder stile beside the A169. Turn right to the car-park. If in need of refreshment, turn left for the Saltergate Inn, whose peat fire is reputed to have been kept alight for more than 200 years.

THE LAKE DISTRICT & EDEN VALLEY

MAP AND KEY

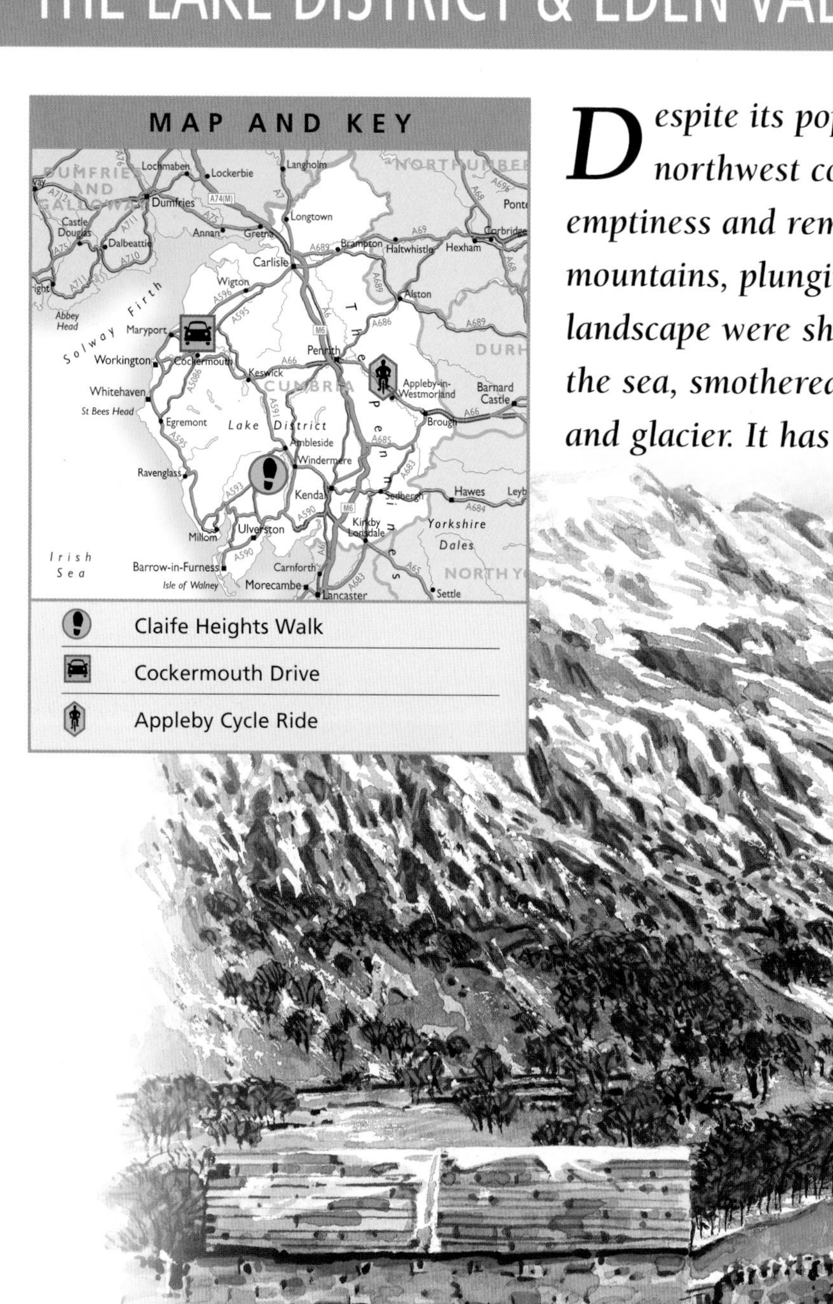

- Claife Heights Walk
- Cockermouth Drive
- Appleby Cycle Ride

Despite its popularity, much of this beautiful northwest corner of England retains its air of emptiness and remoteness. The narrow passes, soaring mountains, plunging waterfalls and lakes of this dramatic landscape were shaped millions of years ago, slaked by the sea, smothered in dust-storms and sculpted by deluge and glacier. It has inspired poets, writers and artists for

Langdale Pikes

The distinctive silhouette of the Langdale Pikes is one of the views that seems to typify the Lake District. The twin humps of Harrison Stickle (2,415ft/736m) and Pike of Stickle (2,323ft/708m) are glimpsed from many different vantage points. Those who know the Lake District well will recognise them from their outline alone.

STEAM YACHT *GONDOLA*

Originally launched in 1859 to convey tourists in some luxury, the steam yacht *Gondola* remained in service for 80 years before falling into dereliction. Her boiler was sold to a sawmill and her hull was converted into a houseboat. Since 1980 visitors to Coniston Water have once again been able to enjoy Victorian elegance while cruising the lake. The delightful round trip takes about an hour.

200 years and Wordsworth, Coleridge, Ruskin, Beatrix Potter, Arthur Ransome and Melvyn Bragg have all made their home here. Visit Wordsworth's Dove Cottage, gaze across the incomparable Tarn Hows towards the beautiful backdrop of rolling hills and the Langdale Pikes, steam along the scenic Haverthwaite–Lakeside Railway followed by a leisurely cruise on Windermere, negotiate the twists and turns of the spectacular Hardknott Pass, and mingle with the mountain climbers and country walkers.

Castlerigg Stone Circle

Two miles (3km) east of Keswick is one of the most dramatic and atmospheric stone circles in Britain. Dating from around 2000 BC, the 38 stones in the circle itself, including a further ten at the centre, are surrounded by high fells, with Helvellyn (3,116ft/950m) to the southeast. They are made of volcanic Borrowdale rock, brought here by the glaciers of the Ice Age.

Jaws of Borrowdale

The Jaws of Borrowdale are where the high crags on either side of the valley almost meet, squeezing the road and the river together as they both try to get through. Both do, and the road then swings round to the west, through the village of Seatoller, to climb through the equally dramatic Honister Pass, linking Borrowdale with Buttermere.

HADRIAN'S WALL

Above the dramatic Irthing Gorge, with its picnic area now looking out over it, the remote remains of the Roman fort and settlement at Birdoswald have the longest visible remaining stretch of Hadrian's Wall. At its busiest it would have housed up to 500 foot soldiers, there to protect this length of wall, and in particular the bridge across the River Irthing, from the Scots.

THE SOUTHERN LAKES

William Wordsworth foresaw that his beloved Lakeland would be spoiled irretrievably by the influx of visitors when the railway came to Windermere. Certainly the railway opened up the landscape to ordinary working people and was changed inevitably in the process. On the other hand, millions of people are now able to enjoy the unrivalled scenery.

The town of Windermere grew up around its railway station, and gradually spread along the lakeside into Bowness. At Bowness Bay, sleek clinker-built dinghies can be hired by the hour. The less energetic can enjoy a cruise on England's largest lake, via Waterhead and Lakeside. Trips are also available on a Victorian steam launch from the Windermere Steamboat Museum. Picturesquely situated at the head of Windermere, with mountains on three sides, the attractive Victorian town of Ambleside was popularised by the Lakeland Poets, a number of whom lived in or near the town.

To the east, Kirkstone Pass, rising to 1,489ft (454m), is the highest road in the Lake District. Charabancs used to labour up the long haul, from either Ambleside or Troutbeck, a typical hillside village, now designated a Conservation Area. The Kirkstone Pass continues through magnificent scenery, before dropping down into Patterdale.

The village of Grasmere is set in a valley surrounded by hills, a short stroll from Grasmere lake. Literary pilgrims have flocked to Grasmere since William Wordsworth produced some of his finest romantic poetry there.

To the west, the Langdales, undoubtedly two of the most beautiful valleys in the Lake District, are recognisable from the distinctive silhouette of the Langdale Pikes. There are challenging climbs and scrambles here, as well as lowland rambles for those who

GRIZEDALE FOREST

On the hills above Brantwood is Grizedale Forest, the first Forestry Commission enterprise which actively encouraged visitors by providing special facilities. Grizedale has some of the best nature trails in the country (red squirrels and roe and red deer can all be seen), with forest walks, picnic areas, a tree nursery and a wildlife museum. The **Theatre in the Forest** was founded over 40 years ago to present a wide range of events including dance and drama, classical and jazz music, and variety and folk concerts. Sculptors were regularly sponsored to create artworks in woodland settings; there are now more than 80 pieces forming a unique Sculpture Trail through the forest.

Classic boats from the Victorian era at Bowness Steamboat Museum

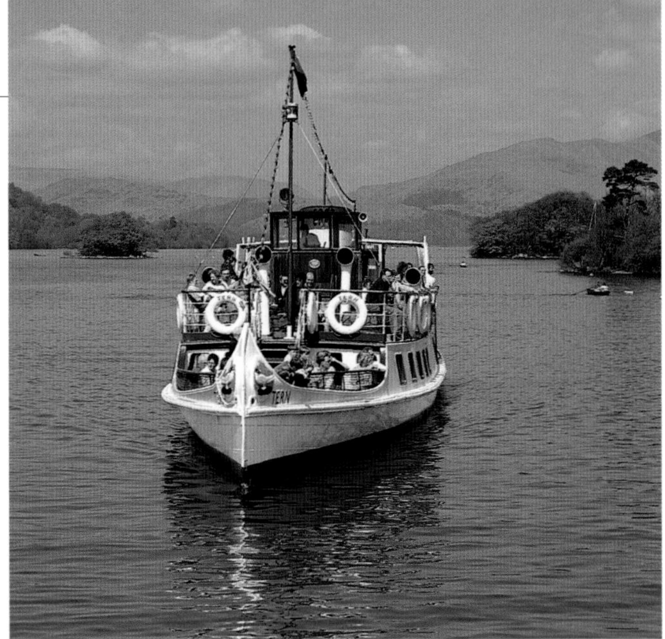

A steamer takes visitors on a leisurely cruise around Windermere

Claife Heights Walk

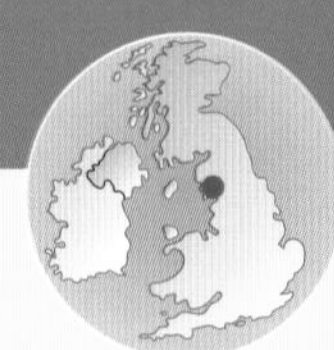

WALK

Claife Heights and the Victorian View

START/FINISH: Harrow Slack National Trust car-park, off the B5285 on the west shore of Windermere, 200yds (182m) along the lakeside lane northwest of Bowness Ferry

DISTANCE: 8 miles (13km)

ASCENT/GRADIENT: 495ft (151m); some steep sections

TERRAIN/PATHS: woodland, open moorland, farmland; mainly good paths, but some rough and boggy sections

A subtle balance between artifice and nature in the Lake District is revealed in this pleasant lake and moorland walk through the National Trust estate at Claife.

1 Turn left (north) out of the car-park and follow the lakeside for 2 miles (3km). The metalled lane soon becomes a track through woodland. The shoreline of the lake has the character of parkland in which nature's rougher edges have been trimmed and tamed. The grounds were laid out early in the 19th century by the Curwen family of Belle Isle, the curious circular mansion that can just be glimpsed through trees out on its private island.

2 As the track approaches Belle Grange turn left just before the house up a steep bridleway, signed to Letterbarrow and Near Sawrey. Ignoring a path to the left, continue on uphill (signed to Hawkshead) until the path levels out and reaches a broad bridleway at a complex intersection.

3 Cross the bridleway and follow the path (signed to Sawrey via Tarns) that bears slightly to the left. Cross another intersection, still following signs to Sawrey, up a steep and stony path. Join a broader track and pass through a gate and stile to reach the open moorland on Claife Heights. The views are unexpected and superb, of open moorland backed by distant prospects of the Furness Fells and Langdale Pikes.

4 Follow the faint path down towards the nearest tarn, where the route becomes much clearer. Follow the trackway as it swings to the left below an old stone dam, passes through a gate and dips down to Moss Eccles Tarn. Continue on the track as it drops down from the moor and runs between stone walls.

TOP FIVE HISTORICAL HOMES

Townend

A fine example of a yeoman farmer's house in the Troutbeck valley. Home to the same family for over 300 years, it remained virtually untouched and offers a fascinating glimpse into the domestic life of Lakeland's wealthier farmers.

Hill Top

An unpretentious 17th-century farmhouse at Near Sawrey, with a delightful cottage garden, where Beatrix Potter wrote and illustrated many of her books between 1905 and 1913.

Dove Cottage

The home (left) of William Wordsworth and his sister, wife and young family from 1799 to 1808. Here he wrote some of his finest poetry in 'the loveliest spot that man hath ever found'. An exhibition centre next door displays his manuscripts and memorabilia.

Rydal Mount

William Wordsworth's home from 1813 until his death in 1850 is still occupied by members of the Wordsworth family. In the gardens, designed by Wordsworth himself, are the terrace and shelter where many of his later poems were composed.

Levens Hall

A 14th-century pele tower incorporated into a more elaborate Elizabethan building. In 1688, Colonel James Graham engaged a Monsieur Beaumont to create a marvellous topiary garden, in which yew trees were clipped into a variety of shapes. It remains much as it was when first designed three centuries ago.

just want to enjoy the view. Beyond the village of Chapel Stile, Great Langdale opens up in spectacular fashion, patched with stone walls and farmsteads, set against the mountain peaks.

Near the northern tip of Coniston Water, overlooked by the bulk of the Old Man of Coniston (2,627ft/801m), the little grey town of Coniston enjoys a superb setting. A short drive takes you to the delightful Tarn Hows, studded with islands, surrounded by woodland and rolling hills. You can also explore the architectural anarchy of nearby Hawkshead, with its intriguing maze of tiny alleyways, arches and 17th-century whitewashed houses.

Kendal, the gateway to the Lakes, is famous for its mint cake, the essential standby of hill-walkers. The steep streets of this busy market town are dominated by the hilltop ruins of the castle. Narrow enclosed yards, where the weavers lived and worked, survive behind the shop-fronts of Stricklandgate and Highgate.

To escape the crowds in Langdale and Borrowdale, you can still find solitude in the little village of Kentmere. From here you can explore the head of the valley on foot, or walk 'over the top' into the Troutbeck valley.

GRASMERE SPORTS

The famous Grasmere Sports (the first recorded meeting was in 1852), held on the third Sunday after the first Monday in August, have become the Lake District's most celebrated event. One of the most popular sports for spectators is fell racing, which involves competitors tackling an arduous route to the top of the nearest fell followed by a wild dash back down to the arena. Other events include hound trailing and Cumberland and Westmorland wrestling. Traditional Lakeland sports are also held at **Ambleside** on the Thursday before the first Monday in August.

LAKESIDE AND HAVERTHWAITE RAILWAY

Originally a branch of the Furness Railway, the line used to carry goods and passengers from Ulverston to connect with the Windermere steamers at Lakeside. After it closed in 1967, a group of rail enthusiasts bought the branch line and re-opened it as a recreational line in 1973, using steam-hauled trains. As in the railway's heyday, the scenic journey can be combined with a leisurely cruise on Windermere.

5 Where the track forks to Near and Far Sawrey, bear left through a gate and follow a bridleway down to join a lane into Far Sawrey. Turn left to the Sawrey Hotel.

6 Just beyond the hotel car-park bear left up a track signed to the ferry. The footpath skirts the gardens of a private house, then drops towards the lake beside a high stone wall. Continue on across a driveway, down a path through overhanging rhododendrons, to the road.

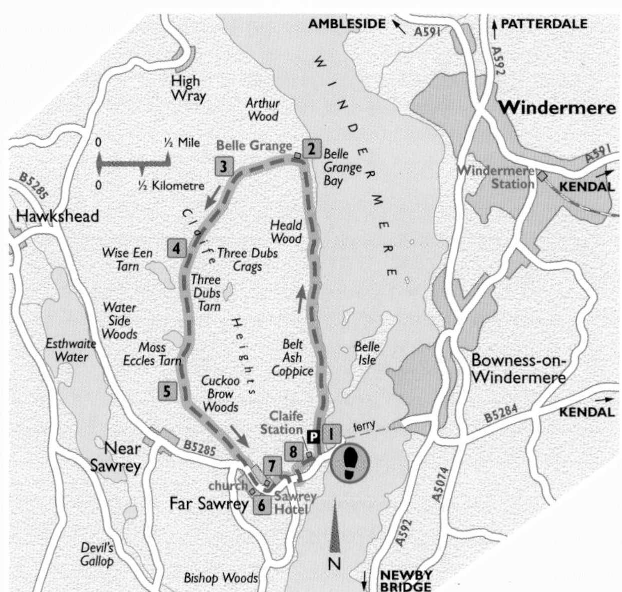

7 Turn left downhill and cross the road on to a footpath separated from the traffic by a wall. Follow the path downhill and across the road, through woodland to a car-park.

8 At the far end of this car-park, take the footpath into the woods and up the steps to Claife Station. Built in 1799, visitors would pay to see framed landscapes. At the top of the steps, turn right along the terrace walk, which drops down to the road. Turn left, then bear immediately left along a narrow lane to return to the car-park.

THE NORTHWEST & THE BORDERLANDS

On the border between England and Scotland, where warfare was endemic until the mid-18th century, this beautiful landscape and its sparse settlements bear the marks of continual violence. The most striking feature of all is Hadrian's Wall, 73 miles (117km) long and almost 2,000 years old, marking the northern boundary of the Roman Empire.

Carlisle is the only historic English town not mentioned in the Domesday Book, because it was in Scotland at the time. Its castle and city walls were begun by William Rufus, who recaptured it from the Scots in 1092. The award-winning Tullie House Museum and Art Gallery in Castle Street traces the town's history and also has good natural history exhibits, including an illuminated microscope.

When the Lakes first began to attract tourists in numbers in the 19th century, many of them came to Keswick. From Keswick, Skiddaw was the peak they all climbed, and it's easy to see why. To the north are the mountains of Scotland, and in the far west the Isle of Man. The peaks of the Pennines rise towards the east, while all around are Lakeland's other hills and dales. Derwent Water, attractively dotted with islands, can be explored by one of the ferries that ply between the seven landing stages around

THE BOWDER STONE

The stone is signed along a path east of the B5289 Borrowdale road, south of the village of Grange. It weighs about 2,000 tonnes and appears to be balanced, ready to topple over. A set of steps leads up to its top (36ft/11m), and despite the attempts of almost everyone who visits to give it a push, it hasn't fallen yet. It was set in place by a glacier, which later melted around it.

HADRIAN'S WALL

Taking advantage of a prominent natural ridge in AD 122, the Emperor Hadrian built a massive fortification some 73 miles (117km) long from coast to coast. It succeeded in holding back the Picts for over 200 years. Now a World Heritage Site, this tremendous achievement can still be appreciated, including substantial portions of both the stone section, running from Newcastle to Gilsland, and the turf rampart from Gilsland to Bowness. Excavations, most notably at **Housesteads**, have revealed the forts and living quarters of the garrisons. Other Roman sites worth visiting are **Chesters Fort and Museum** at Walwick, **Corbridge**, **Carrawburgh** and **Vindolanda (Chesterholm)** at Bardon Mill.

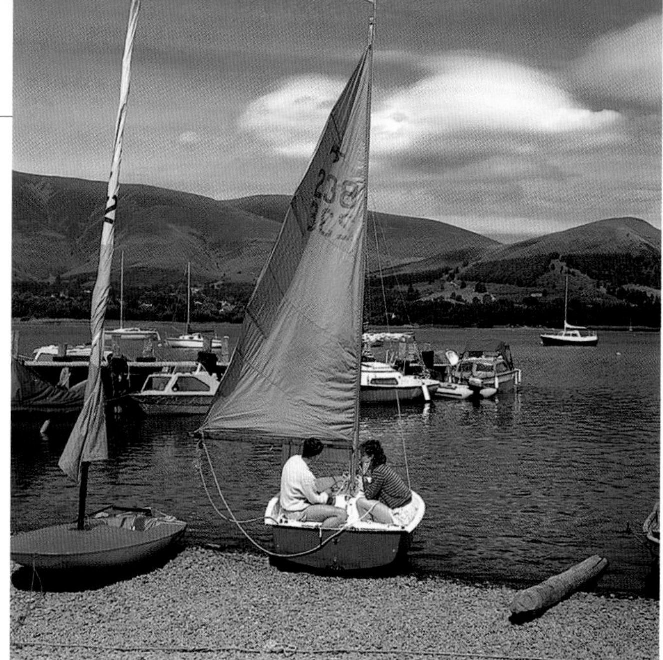

Derwent Water, a popular place to take to the water by sail or motorboat

Cockermouth Drive

DRIVE

From the Mouth of the Crooked River

START/FINISH: Cockermouth. On the A66 8 miles (13km) east of Workington

DISTANCE: 58 miles (93km)

From Cockermouth, famous for being the birthplace of Wordsworth, this drive hugs the north Cumbrian coastline, passing through small fishing villages and a designated Area of Outstanding Natural Beauty. Heading inland, it takes in small villages and pretty market towns and crosses the boundary of the National Park before returning to Cockermouth.

1 After a walk around this ancient market town, visiting Wordsworth House (the poet's birthplace) in Main Street, take the A594 out of Cockermouth and drive for 7 miles (11km) to the Roman town of Maryport. Visit the harbour and Maritime Museum, then go up the hill to the Roman Museum.

2 Leave Maryport on the A596 Carlisle road, then turn left on the B5300 and continue for 2 miles (3km) to a car-park on the right for Saltpans, the site of a 17th-century saltworks and a Roman milecastle. Continue to Allonby, which retains much of its appeal from when it developed as a Georgian and Victorian bathing resort. Across the Solway you can see Scotland and the Galloway hills.

3 Continue north for 6 miles (10km) on the B5300 to Silloth. Until 1857 Silloth was a small fishing village, then it expanded as a port when linked by rail with Carlisle; the town still preserves its Victorian spa atmosphere. Continue straight on past the green and drive for about 1.5 miles (2.5km) to Skinburness.

4 Continue on a narrow road from Skinburness for a further 2 miles (3km). Turn left on to the B5302 and drive through Calvo to Abbey Town. Leave Abbey Town on the B5302, then just beyond Waverbridge turn left on to an unclassified road, signed Aikhead and Station Hill. On reaching the A596, turn left and then right into Wigton and soon right again into the town centre. Note the gilded granite fountain, dedicated to George Moore, who made his fortune in London.

EGREMONT CRAB FAIR

The crabs at the Egremont Crab Fair are crab apples – not crustaceans! The fair dates from 1267, and on the third Saturday in September the Apple Cart parade passes through the town, and apples are thrown to people lining the route. There are athletics competitions, animal shows, hound trails and a greasy pole competition. In the evening the World Gurning Championship takes place. Whoever can make the ugliest grin (gurn) while peering through a horse collar (a braffin), is declared world champion.

the lake, allowing visitors to get off and walk the many footpaths through the surrounding woods. Borrowdale, a glorious wooded valley running south from Derwent Water, contains two of the Lake District's most dramatic natural features – the Bowder Stone and the Jaws of Borrowdale.

The western lakes and shores of Cumbria have features which rival the most beautiful in the area, as well as an industrial history of mining coal, slate and iron ore. Today there are museums and heritage centres looking back on the past, forming a contrast to the better-known face of the Lakes.

CUMBERLAND PENCILS

Graphite is the reason for the existence of the **Cumberland Pencil Museum** in **Keswick**. It is one of those delightfully quirky specialist collections which shows that even something as humble as a pencil has a fascinating history. You can see modern production methods and the world's largest pencil. An entertaining video includes a clip from the animated film *The Snowman*, drawn by artist Raymond Briggs using Cumberland pencils.

Lorton Vale sweeps south from the small market town of Cockermouth through Loweswater, Crummock Water and finally Buttermere before ending in the lofty Honister Pass. Cockermouth has a number of museums including the birthplace of William Wordsworth and the intoxicating Jennings' Brewery, which dates from 1828.

Whitehaven was the third-largest port in Britain, thanks to the local industries. Today it has a small fishing fleet, and its harbour has been declared a conservation area. St Bees is the start of Wainwright's famous 190-mile (304-km) Coast-to-Coast walk to Robin Hood's Bay in North Yorkshire. This part of the coast is Cumbria's only Heritage Coast, and part of the cliffs form St Bees Head Nature Reserve.

SEE CONTACTS SECTION FOR ADDITIONAL INFORMATION

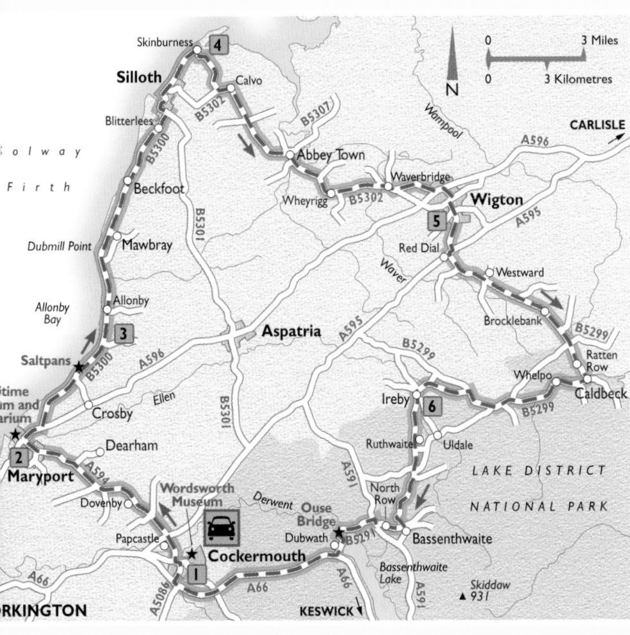

5 Leave Wigton on the B5305 and then soon the B5304. Cross the A595 and continue for about 7 miles (11km) on an unclassified road, to arrive in Caldbeck on the B5299. This is an attractive village with a green, duck pond and the ancient Church of St Kentigern. The gravestone of the huntsman, John Peel, is near the church on the left. Leave Caldbeck in the direction by which you came, but this time bear left at the Oddfellow's Arms on to the B5299. After 3 miles (4.5km), at a fork, keep to the B5299 and continue for another mile (1.5km) to a sign for Ireby.

6 Turn left and descend into the village, turn left again and follow signs for Bassenthwaite. Reach a junction where a road from Uldale comes in on the left. About a mile (1.5km) past here take a narrow road left, signed Robin Hood. Descend steeply to Bassenthwaite village and turn right through North Row to reach the A591. Turn right, then at Castle Inn, turn left on to the B5291. Keep on the B5291, turning left over Ouse Bridge where there is parking. This is good place to take a walk in beautiful scenery. Continue on the B5291 to meet the A66, turn right and return to Cockermouth.

WORDSWORTH'S BIRTHPLACE

The grandeur of Wordsworth's birthplace in **Cockermouth**, a Georgian town house dating from 1745, comes as a surprise when compared to modest Dove Cottage in Grasmere, where the poet later lived. Wordsworth House has been faithfully restored by the National Trust and has seven rooms – including a spotless kitchen and an elegant drawing room with an original fireplace – furnished in mid-18th-century style, with some of Wordsworth's own personal effects.

THE EASTERN FELLS & THE EDEN VALLEY

To the south and west of this corner of the Lake District, expanses of water – Haweswater and Ullswater – are surrounded by soaring mountains such as Helvellyn (3,116ft/950m). Further east lies the rolling green landscape of the Eden Valley and, beyond, the Pennine mountains.

Penrith, at the centre of the area, was the capital of the ancient Kingdom of Cumbria. Penrith Beacon on Beacon Hill was lit to warn the inhabitants of impending raids by border reivers (robbers), and today makes a good viewpoint.

To the west, on Ullswater, a series of splendid waterfalls tumbles down through the wooded gorge of Aira Beck. William and Dorothy Wordsworth were walking near here when Dorothy observed the now famous 'daffodils so beautiful ... they tossed and reeled and danced'. The southern tip of the lake below the shoulders of Helvellyn is reached through the dramatic Kirkstone Pass. At Pooley Bridge on the lake's northern tip, a fish market used to be held in the main square, and this area is still known for its trout and salmon. From the pier near the bridge, two 19th-century steamers take visitors down the lake. A popular option is to combine a cruise with a walk between Howtown and Glenridding.

EDEN BENCHMARKS

Eden Benchmarks is a series of ten imaginative sculptures on paths beside the River Eden between its source in Mallerstang and its mouth at Rockcliffe. It is promoted by the East Cumbria Countryside Project, which also sponsors an award-winning programme of guided and self-guided walks and tours throughout the Eden Valley and the north Pennine area.

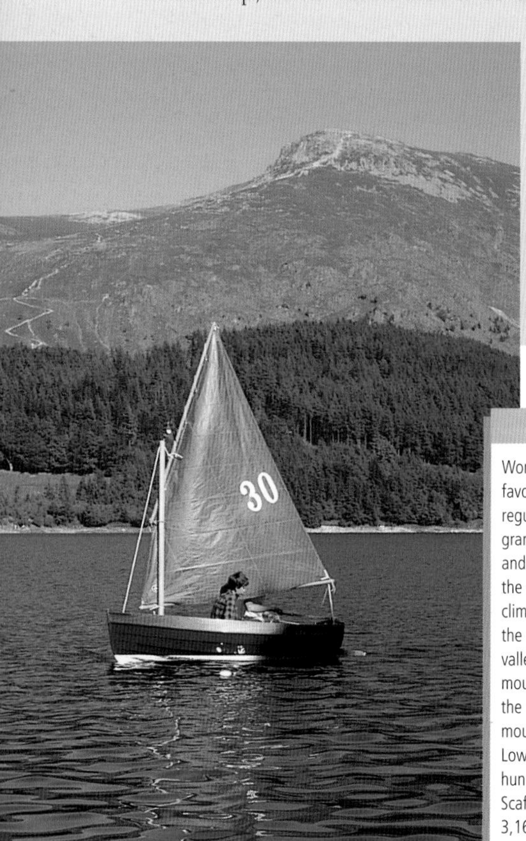

HELVELLYN

Wordsworth's favourite mountain is also the favourite of countless thousands, who regularly trek to its summit. It is indeed a grand climb, but it has its arduous stretches and on no account should it be undertaken if the weather forecast is bad. The arduous climb may take your breath away, and so will the views from the top – north along the valley towards Keswick, and east beyond the mountain lake, Red Tarn, to the high peaks of the Pennines. There are 6 miles (10km) of mountains here, with other peaks such as Lower Man and Great Dodd just a few hundred feet less than Helvellyn itself. Only Scafell Pike, at 3,205ft (977m), and Scafell, at 3,162ft (964m), are higher than Helvellyn.

A ferry drifts across the still surface of Ullswater at Pooley Bridge

CYCLE RIDE

Appleby Cycle Ride

The Vale of Eden

START/FINISH: Appleby-in-Westmorland. Just off the A66 13 miles (21km) southeast of Penrith and the M6

DISTANCE: 34 miles (54.5km)

GRADIENT: hilly

ROADS: country lanes; short stretch along the busy A66

PARKING: pay-and-display car-park in Chapel Street

The Eden Valley is a hilly area running from north to south between the Lake District mountains to the west and the long, high line of the Pennines to the east. It is a quiet, unspoiled area offering panoramic views, and contrasting lush farmland with wild upland scenery.

1 Appleby is a quiet historic town with a fine wide main street, Boroughgate, an ancient two-storied Moot Hall, a Norman castle and peaceful riverside walks. It is famous for its horse fair in June. Leave the car-park by Low Wiend, which is opposite the park, signed town centre, join Boroughgate in front of the cloisters, and bear left into Bridge Street to cross the Eden Bridge. At the T-junction turn right, signed Brough. After 300yds (270m) turn left into Drawbriggs Lane, signed Hilton. Pass under the railway bridge and turn left at the T-junction, just beyond the cheese factory. Follow this undulating road, signed Hilton, for 3.5 miles (5.5km), going under the A66, and following Hilton Beck into Hilton.

2 Passing by Hilton, follow the road to the left and continue along the fellside. This is the highest point of the route, with High Cup Nick, an extraordinary cleft in the hill, visible to the right. In 3.5 miles (5.5km) turn right and proceed into Dufton. Along this side of the Pennine range there are many quiet villages such as Hilton, Dufton and Milburn, with spacious greens bordered by squat 18th-century sandstone houses.

3 Leave Dufton, continue down the hill and after 1.5 miles (2.5km) pass through Knock. Ignoring lanes left and right, proceed for 2 miles (3km), passing through Silverband to reach a T-junction. Turn right, signed Milburn. Pass the Stag Inn and shortly bear right into Milburn. Leave the village from the bottom of the green, signed to Newbiggin, and in 100yds (91m) bear left. Shortly bear right, signed Newbiggin.

TOP FIVE GARDENS

Hutton-in-the-Forest

The stately home of the Vane family since 1600. Monthly 'Meet the Gardener' walks round the grounds offer a chance to hear about the problems and pleasures of a garden this size. It includes a wild-flower meadow, a walled garden which dates from the 1730s and a lake where nature is largely allowed to take its course.

Acorn Bank Garden

Particularly noted for its walled herb garden, which contains the largest collection of medicinal, culinary and narcotic herbs in the north of England – some 250 species. There are traditional orchards and fine collections of roses, shrubs and herbaceous borders, as well as a host of golden daffodils.

Grange-over-Sands

Renowned for its ornamental gardens. Sheltered by the Lakeland Fells, its mild climate has made it a gardeners' paradise, with plants growing here that would be unlikely to survive elsewhere on the west coast.

Holker Hall

The home (right) of the Cavendish family, retaining the atmosphere of a family home. The 25 acres (10ha) of formal gardens and woodland are justifiably famous.

Mirehouse

A 17th-century home to the same family since 1688. It has a wild-flower meadow and a walled garden, while inside is a fine collection of furniture, literary portraits and manuscripts.

Haweswater is a reservoir, created in the 1930s. Beneath its surface lies the village of Mardale and the one-time dairy farms of the Haweswater valley. Wildlife is abundant – peregrine falcons, buzzards, sparrowhawks and even golden eagles now breed in the valley. An observation post allows visitors to watch the activities of the eagles. Otters have also colonised the area, and other mammals include both roe and red deer and a population of red squirrels. Ancient Naddle Forest lies to the east, refuge of wood warblers, tree pipits, redstarts and several species of woodpecker.

To the east, Appleby, once the county town of Westmorland, with a royal charter dating from 1174, sits in a loop of the tree-lined River Eden. The village of Morland, 7 miles (11km) northwest of Appleby, has the Highgate Farm Animal Trail, a delightful hands-on farmyard experience, where you can have a go at milking a goat.

East of the gentle Eden Valley, Alston marks the start of the narrow-gauge South Tynedale Railway which uses steam and diesel engines to take visitors along the valley. Alston was built around the lead-mining industry and you can go prospecting for lead at Nenthead Mines Heritage Centre, which vividly evokes past life and work in this remote upland landscape.

CUMBRIAN SHEEP

Ten per cent of England's sheep are in Cumbria, and the distinctive Cumbrian breed is the white-faced Herdwick. Their fleece is notable for being black when young and growing greyer with age. This hardy breed produces an equally hardwearing wool, used more for carpets and rugs than clothing. Herdwicks are known to have been here when the Romans were building Hadrian's Wall, and like the Wall their dwindling numbers are in need of preservation.

4 In 1 mile (1.5km) bear right, signed Newbiggin. Follow this road for 2 miles (3km), passing the crossroads in Newbiggin and the left turn to Temple Sowerby, to reach Acorn Bank Gardens. Once owned by the Knights Templar, it is now looked after by the National Trust.

5 Retrace the route and turn right towards Temple Sowerby. Pass through the village, turn left at the A66 (take great care) for 350yds (320m) and turn right into a lane, signed Morland.

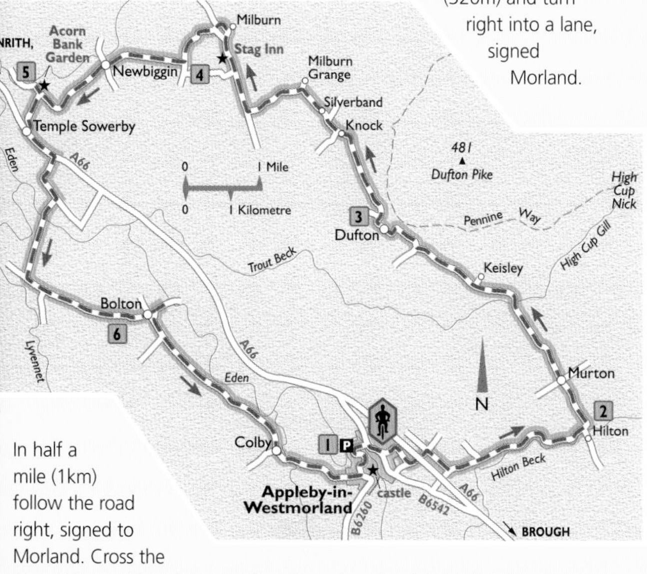

In half a mile (1km) follow the road right, signed to Morland. Cross the River Eden and turn left at a T-junction, signed to Morland, Bolton and Appleby.

6 In 2 miles (3km) enter the village of Bolton, and keep left to visit the church. Return to the junction and turn left at the post office, then shortly left again, and follow this undulating road through Colby back to Appleby. At the T-junction turn left, then bear immediately right (if not visiting the castle, turn left down Doomgate and turn right into High Wiend which bears right [Chapel Street] back to the car-park), and climb the steep hill to High Cross. Go down the hill, turn left before the post office, then first right back to the car-park. If time allows, visit the castle (April to October), with its fine keep, Great Hall, Clifford family paintings and some items of the Nanking Cargo.

A steam locomotive on the South Tynedale Railway starts off on a journey from Alston

NORTHUMBRIA & NEWCASTLE

Northumbria is a vast swathe of northeast England, from the fiercely contested Scottish border to the boundary of Yorkshire, from the High Pennines – England's last wilderness – to the golden sands along Northumberland's coast. It encompasses the smooth Cheviot Hills, deep river valleys, expansive Kielder Water and huge tracts of forest, as well as vibrant Newcastle upon Tyne, historic Durham, the secret valleys of the Tees and Wear, and the fascinating industrial history of the Tyne. The borderlands were fought over for centuries. Stone-Age and Iron-Age people dug hilltop forts, Hadrian constructed his Wall, and the great castles of the Middle Ages were built as protection against Scottish raiders. St Aidan, St Cuthbert and St Godric made this a centre of early Christianity while the Venerable Bede wrote his Ecclesiastical History. *The industrial age produced inventors, including George Stephenson and Lord Armstrong, and grinding poverty among working people, poignantly evoked by the novels of Catherine Cookson.*

DURHAM

Built within a loop of the River Wear, on a high sandstone outcrop above a deep ravine, the city of Durham has one of the most dramatic skylines. The 11th-century cathedral and castle, towering high on a bluff above the river, are an unforgettable composition of Norman splendour, now part of the famous university, England's third oldest, after Oxford and Cambridge.

Holy Island

This island has been so-called since the 11th century, although its Celtic name, Lindisfarne, is just as familiar. It was one of the main centres of Christianity in the 7th century, when the teachings of St Aidan and St Cuthbert attracted pilgrims. In St Mary's Church a copy of the famous Lindisfarne Gospels, illuminated in AD 698, can be found. Next to the church are the remains of 12th-century Lindisfarne Priory, the stones from which were used to build Lindisfarne Castle, imaginatively restored by Edwin Lutyens in the early 20th century.

BLANCHLAND

Blanchland is one of the most perfect villages in England – a cluster of stone houses, which glow golden in the sunlight, set in a deep, wooded valley among high moorland. Most of the cottages were built in the mid 18th century for Lord Crewe, Bishop of Durham, who owned the estate. When the mines closed and the miners departed, Blanchland remained in the hands of the Crewe Trustees, undisturbed in its beauty.

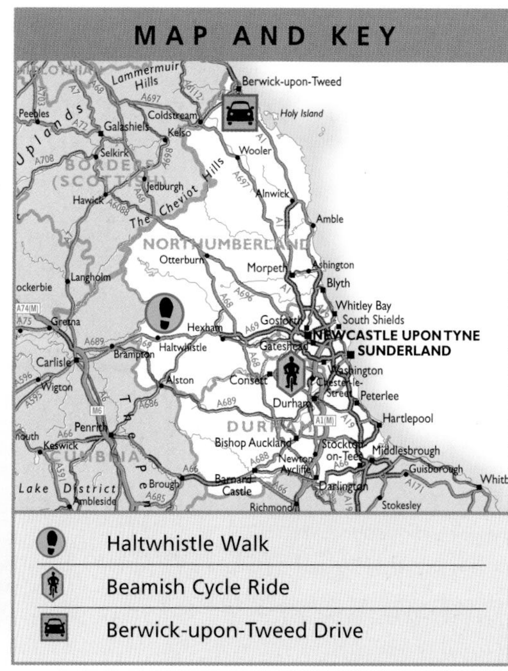

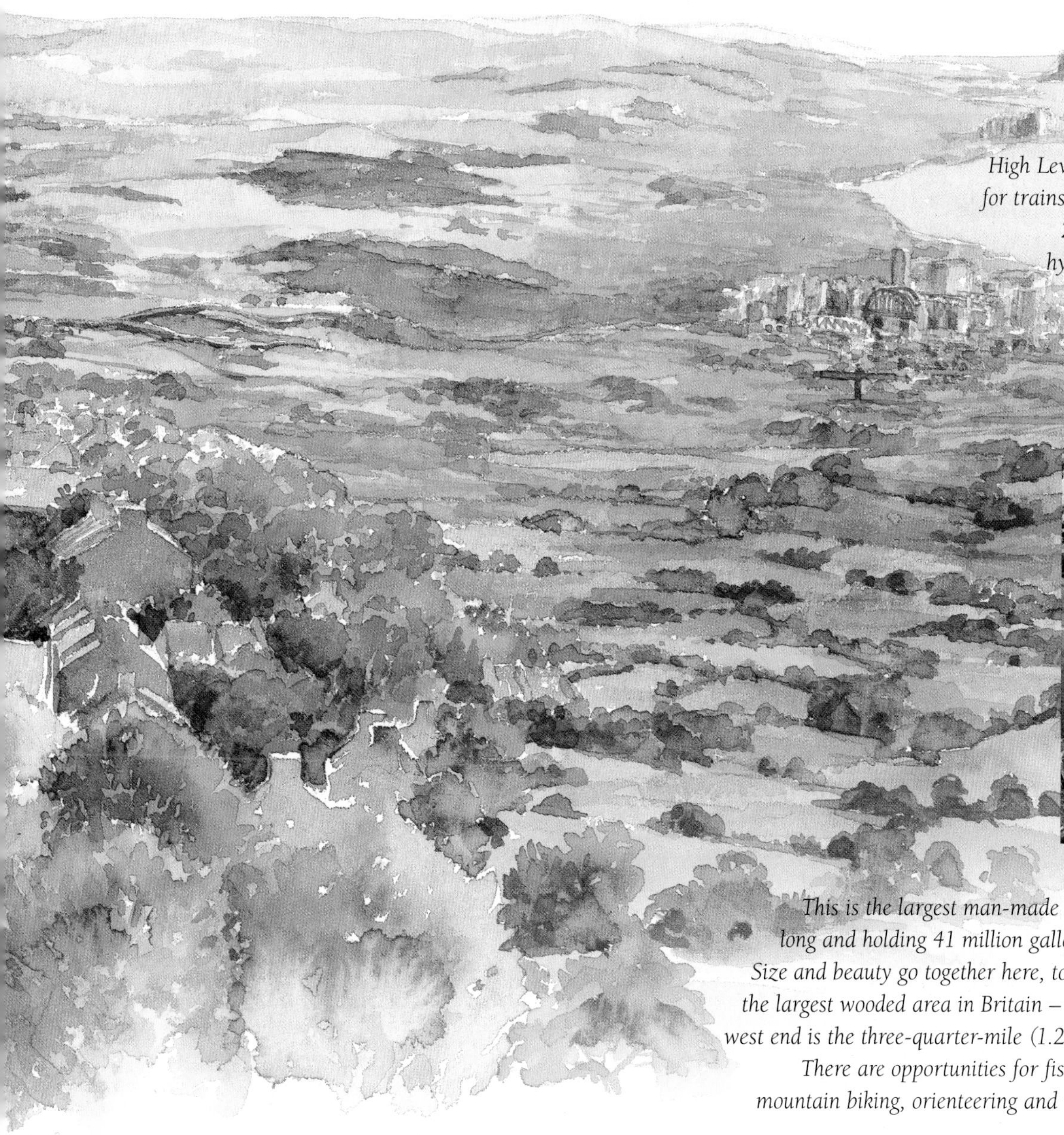

The Tyne Bridges

The River Tyne is crossed by three of Newcastle's most famous bridges. Robert Stephenson's High Level Bridge of 1849, has twin decks for trains and cars. The Swing Bridge built 25 years later was once driven by hydraulic engines. The semicircular Tyne Bridge immediately says 'Newcastle' to homesick Geordies all over the world.

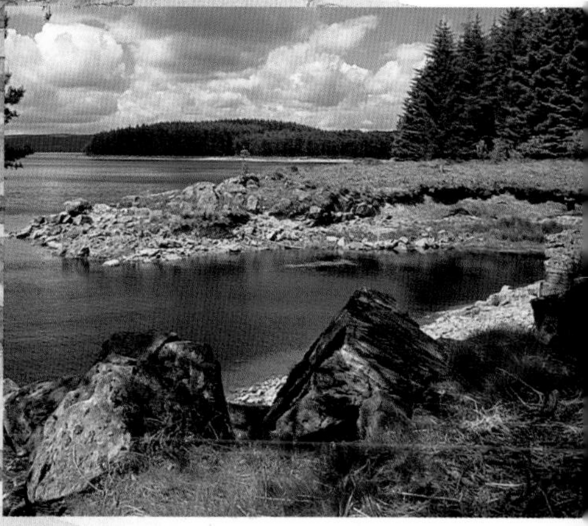

Kielder Water

This is the largest man-made lake in Europe, 9 miles (14.5km) long and holding 41 million gallons (186,385,000 litres) of water. Size and beauty go together here, too, with the huge Kielder Forest – the largest wooded area in Britain – coming down to the shore. At the west end is the three-quarter-mile (1.2-km) long dam, finished in 1982. There are opportunities for fishing, sailing, windsurfing, riding, mountain biking, orienteering and walking along well-signed tracks.

THE NORTHERN PENNINES

The High Pennines combine the majestic sweep of high moorland with deep valleys, where waterfalls thunder over sheer crags. The villages are peaceful now, but they were once thriving industrial centres, the focus of Britain's lead-mining industry.

Northumbria's former capital, Corbridge, suffered badly from invasion by Danes and Scots. Not surprisingly, there are two defensive pele towers. One dating from the 13th century has been converted into a comfortable house; the other, built of Roman stones, was probably constructed in the 14th century. The large Roman site here, built to protect the River Tyne, includes remains of a storehouse, plus temples, granaries, and houses.

Hexham is a good town to stroll around, with some stunning Victorian shop-fronts and fine houses. The street names, too, have a particular charm – St Mary's Chare and Priestpopple, for example.

KILLHOPE LEAD-MINING CENTRE

Just southwest of Allenheads, this restored 1870s lead-crushing mill brings Victorian mining to life. You can try your hand at separating the lead ore from waste material using primitive machinery, and follow a discovery trail around the site to see displays of mining through the ages. The highlight of Killhope is its huge overshot waterwheel which has been restored to working order.

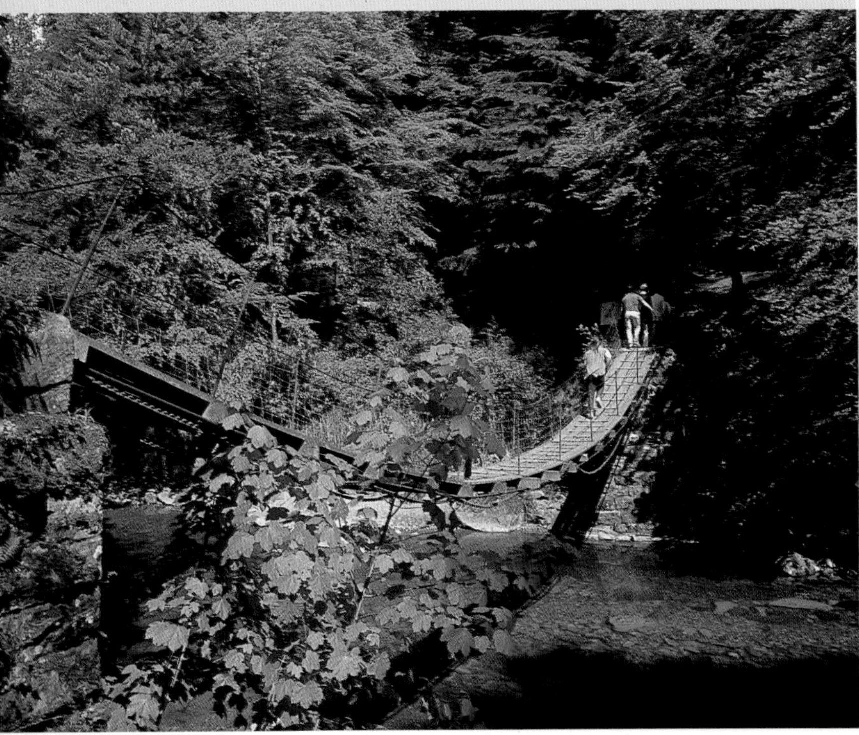

Riverside walks lead across a suspension bridge at Allen Banks

The Bowes Museum is housed in this French-style chateau in the town of Barnard Castle

Haltwhistle Walk

WALK

The Edge of an Empire on Hadrian's Wall

START/FINISH: Haltwhistle. Just off the A69 between Hexham and Brampton

DISTANCE: 6 miles (9.5km)

ASCENT/GRADIENT: 560ft (171m); gradual ascents

TERRAIN/PATHS: fields, open country; mostly good paths but can get boggy

PARKING: by Haltwhistle Station

No monument to the Roman invasion of Britain in 55 BC is more important, or more impressive, than the wall built by the Emperor Hadrian. This exhilarating walk takes you back to paths once tramped by Roman soldiers.

1 From the station, walk straight ahead to the main street, then right along Westgate. Follow the main road, then turn left up steps, immediately before the Grey Bull Hotel. Cross the next road, to join a private road to a kissing-gate and path down to Haltwhistle Burn.

2 Near the burn, bear left alongside a playing field to a lane. Shortly, turn right beyond some old works, over the bridge and left through a gate. The sound from the brick-glazing works, old collieries and abandoned quarries must once have echoed the length of the gorge. After 200yds (182m), bear left, re-cross the burn and turn right on a lane to Lees Hall Farm. Keep to the right of the farm to a gate. Follow the track and cross the main road, turning right, then left by a house. Keep on the tarmac road, through a gate and across the burn until you reach a farm – the site of *Aesica*, Great Chesters Fort.

3 Within the fort, turn left towards a round fenced area. Go through the gap in the wall and follow the Pennine Way markers, over ladder stiles and past Cockmount Hill Farm, keeping along Hadrian's Wall. This took six years to build and ran for 80 Roman miles (73 modern miles or 117km) across Britain. You are rewarded with glorious views to the north where the North Tyne valley stretches out to meet the Scottish border.

4 Turn left off the Pennine Way after a ladder stile beyond Turret 44B.

OFF-ROAD DRIVING

Slaley Hall, near **Hexham**, offers the chance to test your driving skills in a variety of vehicles. There is the 4x4 'extreme course' tackled by Land Rover, quad-biking for all ages, Honda pilot racing, grass hovercrafts and the 'Italian job' auto test using specially prepared Minis.

Haltwhistle Burn flows into the South Tyne east of the attractive town of Haltwhistle, and there are pleasant walks alongside the burn up to Hadrian's Wall. This once-thriving industrial town is a good centre for exploring the north Pennines. Some of its Victorian station buildings, including the stationmaster's house, waiting room and ticket office, date from as early as 1838.

Set 800ft (244m) up among spectacular Pennine scenery, Allendale Town is the geographical centre of Britain. The dale has two rivers – the East and West Allen – fed by many peaty burns which cascade from the surrounding high hills. At Allen Banks, 5 miles (8km) north of Allendale Town, a suspension bridge links the two sides of the heavily wooded gorge.

Turn left again at a muddy lane, then after 200yds (182m), turn right on a path signed Fell End. Go through the gate to the left of a building, then follow the wall around to the left. Just beyond a waymarker, go down the course of an old wall and straight on where it ends to the far side of the field. Pass through a gate then bear left to ascend to the lowest gap in the ridge ahead. Near the top, pass through a gate and cross the next field to a stile at the main road.

5 Cross the road signed Haltwhistle and after 400yds (366m), where the road bends left, turn right on a path signed Birchfield Gate. Head across the field to a ladder stile. Go down the centre of the next field towards a house. At the next gate, bear right, cross a burn and head for the left corner of a barn. Turn left here, re-cross the burn and ascend to the right-hand corner of the field. Cross four stiles to a field on the left. Continue, to the left of Woodhead Farm, through two more gates and keep ahead, crossing a stile in the right-hand corner of the field.

6 Continue to a road and, after a school, turn right down an alley to a service road. Bear right on Greenholme Road, turning right at the end, then left into Greencroft Avenue. At the bottom keep forward for the railway station.

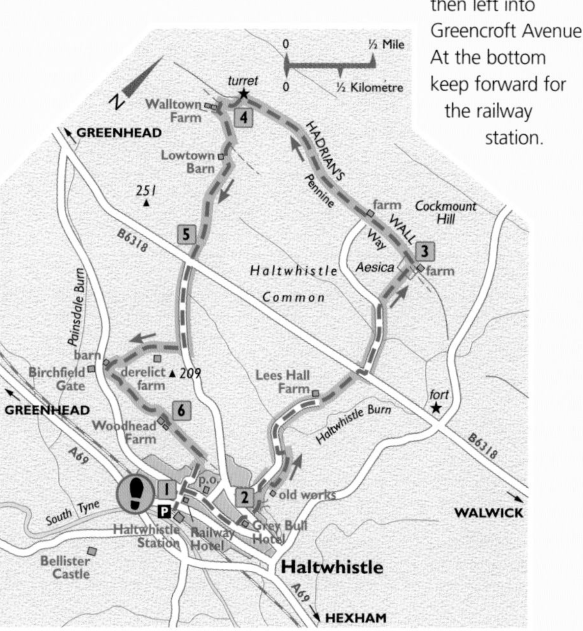

FIVE BEST CASTLES

Alnwick

Alnwick has Norman walls and towers, with a Renaissance interior. The parkland was landscaped by 'Capability' Brown and the Brizlee Tower was designed by Robert Adam.

Bamburgh

This castle (above) looks so completely medieval that film crews use it as a backdrop to historical romances and adventures. However, the interior is the result of late-Victorian renovations.

Chillingham

Much of Chillingham dates from 1344, when it had a moat, now a huge tunnel under the south lawn. The gardens include topiary and woodland walks.

Durham

Begun in 1072, the castle now houses University College. The highlight of a tour is the Norman gallery and chapel.

Raby

Raby Castle is one of the most beautifully positioned castles in the country, with nine towers and battlements overlooking the lake, and superb gardens.

Middleton is the best centre for exploring the wild landscapes of Upper Teesdale. Upstream from Middleton the River Tees is increasingly spectacular. You can walk to Gibson's Cave, where 20-ft (6-m) Summerhill Force has formed a hollow in the soft rock. Over the Tees is Wynch Bridge, Europe's earliest suspension bridge, originally built in the 1740s. Just above the bridge is Low Force, a series of picturesque waterfalls. Best of all is High Force, one of the highest single-drop waterfalls in England. The Tees plunges over the Great Whin Sill here, and roars into the huge gorge, at 70ft (21.5m).

Romaldkirk, with its irregular greens, complete with traditional stocks and pump, and a large church, is full of interest. The 17th-century Eggleston Bridge crosses the Tees to Eggleston. The gardens of Eggleston Hall, with their fine shrubs, mature trees and greenhouses, are open to the public, and you can buy herbs and other plants, fruit and organically grown vegetables.

Cotherstone is set above the River Tees, its pretty houses following the winding road. A minor road alongside the Balder will take you to a chain of reservoirs, where you can enjoy waymarked walks, water-skiing and fishing.

The market cross at Barnard Castle is a handsome octagon of 1747. The colonnade provided shelter to the butter-sellers, and the upper floor was the town hall. The Bowes Museum, housed in a remarkable French-style chateau, has an astonishing collection, with Roman altars, porcelain, furniture, paintings by Goya and El Greco, costumes and toys.

CITIES & SAINTS

Even in the north's great cities, you are never far from peaceful landscapes, pretty villages and stunning scenery. The cities of Newcastle, Durham and Sunderland, at the heart of southeastern Northumbria, each have a distinctive character and history. Ruined abbeys and ancient churches testify to the area's role in spreading Christianity, while Roman remains and medieval castles tell the story of its often violent past.

Newcastle upon Tyne is a vibrant and friendly place with plenty of character, its active nightlife sitting comfortably alongside the many fine museums and galleries. This area is also the industrial centre of the North. The town centre is a monument to the Victorian Gothic revival. Its railway station, with huge curved train shed, supported by slender iron columns, was much imitated. To the south is elegant Grey Street, lined with columned buildings, curving down towards the Tyne and the famous bridges.

The popular author Catherine Cookson has put South Shields on the map, thanks to her historical novels.

George Stephenson's Locomotion No. 1, *at North Road Station, Darlington*

NORTH OF ENGLAND OPEN-AIR MUSEUM

At **Beamish**, 4 miles (6.5km) northwest of Chester-le-Street, set in 200 acres (80ha) of beautiful countryside, the North of England Open-Air Museum has reconstructed a northern town *circa* 1900. Costumed staff welcome visitors to shops stocked with period goods, and to the pub and newspaper office. You can take part in a lesson in the village school, worship in the Methodist chapel, ride on a tram, catch a train or experience the hard life of the pit. For some, the ultimate horror might be a visit to the dentist, especially after sampling the sweet factory! Home Farm, with its traditional farm animals, used to supply Beamish Hall, once owned by the Shafto family.

Anthony Gormley's arresting steel figure, Angel of the North, *south of Gateshead*

Beamish Cycle Ride

CYCLE RIDE

Iron and Steel

START/FINISH: North of England Open-Air Museum, Beamish. Off the A693/A6076 2 miles (3km) north of Stanley

DISTANCE: 27 miles (43km)

GRADIENT: downhill then a hilly section

ROADS/PATHS: old railway lines, bridle paths, mud trails and fields

PARKING: car-parks at Eden Picnic Area, near entrance to North of England Open-Air Museum

A nostalgic trip, from an industrial museum along the tracks of the world's oldest railway.

1 Set in 200 acres (81ha) of beautiful countryside, the open-air museum at Beamish vividly re-creates life in the north of England in the early 20th century. You can stroll down the cobbled streets of the town to see fully stocked Co-operative shops, a dentist's surgery, working pub, sweet shop and sweet factory. Guided tours are given underground at a real drift mine in the colliery village and a row of miners' cottages show how pitmen and their families lived. From the left-hand car-park join the cycle path. Cross the road, turn right, then left downhill and turn right on to the National Cycle Path heading to Stanley.

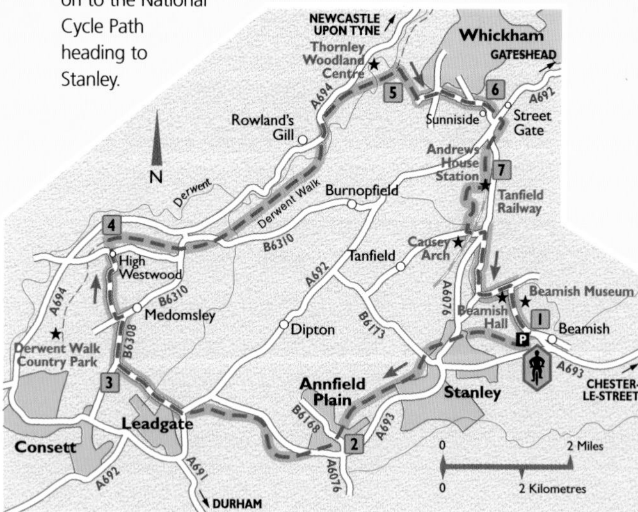

Visitors can follow the Cookson Trail and visit a re-creation of her childhood home in the museum.

Jarrow is famous for the crusade of 1936, when malnourished and desperate workers marched to London, stirring the nation's sympathy. The Venerable Bede, early historian and author of *Ecclesiastical History of the English People*, lived at Jarrow monastery. Incredibly, the church he knew – dedicated in April 685 – still survives and its nave has become the chancel of the present building.

Sunderland was a small port until coal transportation and shipbuilding caused its spectacular growth in the 18th and 19th centuries. In warm weather crowds flock to the sands of Roker and Seaburn, north of the river.

NEWCASTLE HOPPINGS

For a real taste of Geordie enjoyment, go to **Town Moor** in the last full week in June for the largest travelling fair in the country during 'The Hoppings'. There are stalls and rides – complete with flashing lights and raucous music – stretching for more than a mile, from midday (2pm on Sunday) to late into the evening. The jollifications began last century as a temperance festival.

The MetroCentre at Gateshead, Europe's largest out-of-town shopping complex

Once at the heart of the ancient kingdom of Northumbria, Durham's importance is reflected in the fact that its cathedral and castle have been declared a World Heritage Site. Climbing from the market-place up Saddler Street you immediately get the feel of the place, with small Georgian houses interspersed with shops and university buildings. Colleges cluster in the streets around the castle and cathedral, while elsewhere the city becomes more work-a-day, though the churches are worth exploring.

Bishops have lived at Auckland since the 12th century, but Auckland Castle has been their main residence since Durham Castle was given to the university in 1832. An 18th-century gatehouse leads from the market square of Bishop Auckland into the extensive grounds of Bishop's Park, complete with Bishop Trevor's pretty Gothic deerhouse and mature, majestic trees.

The first passenger railway, the Stockton and Darlington, was built by George Stephenson and opened in 1825. The former North Road Station at Darlington, opened in 1842, now houses Darlington Railway Centre. Its prize exhibit is Stephenson's *Locomotion No. 1*, the first engine to be used on a public railway.

2 At Annfield Plain cross the road opposite the Co-op supermarket, leave the path and turn left along St Aidans Crescent and from there head back to the cycle route. After the football park turn right and follow signs for Consett. At the junction, cross the road, turn right. After 50yds (46m) turn left through a gap in the hedge. Follow the C2C and Consett & Sunderland Cycle Path signs, crossing another road, until you reach the roundabout. At the roundabout take the road to the right of the Jolly Drover, signed Medomsley.

3 At the top of the hill turn right on to the B6308, then left at the next T-junction. Turn right on to the road to The Deane. The road bends sharp right at Westwood Primary School. After 100yds (91m) turn left on to a public byway.

4 Turn right on to the old railway, cross several viaducts and roads then exit on to Stirling Lane, Rowland's Gill, cross the road and turn left on Burnopfield Road passing a garage before turning right on to a bridleway at Derwent Walk Country Park. Miles of old railway line have been converted to cycling and walking paths. The prettiest section is along the line of the Derwent Walk, which follows the old Derwent Valley Railway, gently downhill, to the Derwent Walk Country Park.

5 Beyond the sign for Thornley Woodland Centre, follow the sign on the right to Clockburn Lonnen. Go uphill and turn left on to an unsurfaced road. Cross a main road and continue to a T-junction.

6 Turn right then right again on to Kingsway. At the second public footpath sign (opposite Farm Close) turn right then left on to the path. Cross the road and follow the track which splits; both tracks lead to Tanfield Railway. Turn right and follow the Tanfield Railway Path. The Tanfield Railway, the oldest existing railway in the world, has been in operation since 1725.

7 At Andrews House Station, leave the car-park and turn right on to a bridleway, crossing the railway bridge. At the second gate turn sharp left then right and follow the fence downhill. Cross a small bridge. To detour to Causey Arch (half a mile/800m) turn right for 50yds (46m) then left signed public footpath and Causey Arch. Return along the same path to rejoin the main route and turn left on to the road. Go uphill, cross the railway line and the road ahead, and pass the Causey Arch Inn. Turn right at the Beamish Park Hotel, then just before the bridge at the bottom of a steep hill turn left for Beamish Hall. Follow this road back to Beamish Museum and the car-park.

SPORTS ACTIVITIES IN NORTHUMBERLAND

Fishing

There are seven lakes and reservoirs in Northumberland which offer day-tickets to casual visitors. The 23-mile (37-km) shoreline of Kielder Water has three fishing lodges.

Horse-riding

Saddle up and take to the network of old lanes and tracks west of Morpeth, the taxing hill routes of the Cheviots or the beaches of the Heritage Coast.

Golf

For pure scenic splendour, the coastal links courses at Alnmouth, Warkworth, Dunstanburgh Castle, Bamburgh Castle and Berwick are simply unbeatable. Or head for Slaley Hall, 5 miles (8km) south of Hexham, which is of international championship standard.

Sailing

With its long coastline and the largest man-made lake in Western Europe, there are excellent facilities for sailing in Northumberland. The main watersports centre in Kielder is at the Leaplish Waterside Park.

Windsurfing

Tuition and board hire are available at Kielder and Seahouses. Popular beaches with good roadside access include Blyth South Beach, Beadnell Bay and Spittal Beach, Berwick.

THE BORDER HILLS & NORTHEAST COAST

Turbulent history and a sense of remoteness set the hills of Northumberland apart. These high, windswept moors and deep valleys were once bitterly fought over by the English and Scots. Now much of the area is protected as a National Park.

Bellingham makes an excellent base for exploring the National Park and the Kielder area. About 7 miles (11km) northwest of Bellingham, remote in the Tarset Burn valley, is Black Middens Bastle, a 16th-century defensive stone house in which livestock occupied the ground floor and the farmer and his family reached the upper floor by a removable ladder. The narrow Breamish Valley is one of the joys of the National Park. There is excellent walking from the village of Ingram right up to the Scottish border, taking in Iron-Age hillforts and deserted medieval villages.

Rothbury's attractive stone buildings spread outwards from an irregularly shaped green and a medieval bridge over the River Coquet. East of Rothbury, Cragside, set in 900 acres (365ha) of country park, is a cross between an English manor house and a Bavarian castle. The first house in the world to be illuminated entirely by electric light, you can see the ingenious timber flume, canal and pipeway that fed the hydroelectric plant.

From historic Berwick-upon-Tweed the golden Northumberland coast sweeps south, with a chain of strong castles and the heartland of

ISLAND WILDLIFE

For many visitors the attraction of the **Farne Islands** is their wildlife, especially the birds and the seals. Seventeen different species of sea birds and a large colony of grey seals have made these treeless islands a remarkable wildlife sanctuary. This is the only place in Great Britain where the light-bellied type of Brent geese overwinter, and there are many other species to be seen. The delightful little puffins are always favourites, but you may also see oystercatchers, wigeon, fulmars, petrels, razorbills, rock pipits, curlews, godwits, dunlins, turnstones and knots. Permits to land on Inner Farne and Staple Island are restricted during the breeding season, from May to July. The boat trips usually pass near enough to see the nesting sites, and on Staple and Inner Farne you can walk – with care – among the nests.

Looking inland from Alnmouth, situated on the Northumberland Heritage Coast

Berwick-upon-Tweed Drive

DRIVE

Northumberland's Coast and Hills

START/FINISH: Berwick-upon-Tweed. Off the A1 29 miles (47.5km) north of Alnwick

DISTANCE: 75 miles (120.5km); 85 miles (137km) if visiting Holy Island

Castles, spectacular views of the Cheviots, wild moorland and the islands off the beautiful Northumberland coast are among the highlights of this drive from England's most northerly town.

1 Berwick-upon-Tweed is an outstanding example of a fortified town and features Britain's oldest surviving purpose-built barracks (1721), now a local history museum. From the town centre go over Royal Tweed Bridge, signed Newcastle, A1, and turn right, signed Coldstream. Go right at the first roundabout and straight on at the second, following Coldstream signs. After 3 miles (5km), turn right along an unclassified road signed Norham Castle. In 2 miles (3km) pass the ruins of 12th-century Norham Castle and enter Norham. At the T-junction turn left on the B6470 and shortly turn right along an unclassified road, signed Norham Station, Cornhill. At the T-junction turn left on the A698, signed Berwick, then immediately right on to an unclassified road. Follow this winding road for 4 miles (6.5km), following signs for Etal and Ford, to reach the B6354, where you turn right.

2 Follow the road for 3 miles (5km) through Etal, and past restored 19th-century Heatherslaw Corn Mill, to Ford. Don't miss the murals of favourite Bible stories at Lady Waterford Hall. Just before Ford church turn right, signed Kimmerston, then turn right at the T-junction, signed Milfield. Go over Milfield Bridge and continue to the A697. Turn left towards Wooler. Follow the main road through Akeld. Turn right at a junction to Humbleton and continue into Wooler, known as the 'Gateway to the Cheviots'. Turn left by the church then cross the main road on to the B6348, signed Chatton. After 2.5 miles (4km), beyond a sharp right-hand bend at the top of a hill, follow the main road to Chatton. Turn right at the Chillingham, Alnwick, sign. Follow the road past the entrance to the Wild Cattle Park and the 800-year-old castle and at the brow of the hill turn left, signed Hepburn Wood Walks.

3 Go through Hepburn, then uphill past Ros Castle, an ancient hillfort commanding great views. Follow this narrow moorland road for 7 miles

Lighthouse keeper's daughter Grace Darling

ancient Christianity at Holy Island. Amid all this history are nature reserves and rocks sheltering birds, quiet country roads winding through gentle hills, and a wonderful sense of freedom under a spacious northern sky.

Berwick-upon-Tweed is a fascinating town, of unexpected levels and grey-stone houses. Its unique Elizabethan ramparts, 22-ft (6.7-m) high stone-faced walls topped with grassed mounds, provide a wonderful view over the muddle of streets below.

At Bamburgh, the castle dominates the village and the sandy beach. Grace Darling, the 19th-century heroine who rescued the survivors of the *Forfarshire*, is buried in the churchyard. The golf course at Budle Point has spectacular views to Holy Island.

PEDAL POWER

Even the least adventurous can enjoy cycling at **Kielder**. Bring your own bike or hire one, either from the north end of the dam at Leaplish Waterside Park or from Kielder Castle. From the dam, a popular route, suitable for families with children from about eight years upwards, is along the North Haul Road to Kielder Castle. Setting out from the castle, you can follow the old road and the former railway track to Deadwater Station, on the Scottish border, or for a little more adventure, have a go at cycle orienteering on the Archercleugh Trail Quest.

Lindisfarne, or Holy Island, seems ideal for the monastic life – windswept and flat, surrounded by sands which are covered by tides twice a day. The pilgrims' route is marked by posts leading to the village.

Further down the coast, Craster was a fishing haven in the 17th century. A dramatic but not too strenuous walk from the village leads to the ruins of Dunstanburgh Castle. Howick Gardens, a mile (1.5km) south of Craster, has fine woodland with a network of paths and glades where rare plants and shrubs thrive.

Alnmouth, where the River Aln meets the North Sea, was a busy 18th-century shipbuilding and grain port. Now the granaries, converted into houses, jostle for room with shops and ancient inns in the narrow streets. The sands, part of the 56-mile (90-km) Northumbrian Heritage Coast, stretch as far as the eye can see. Nearby Alnwick's cobbled market-place bustles with life, with plenty of shops selling local produce, crafts and antiques, and the road from Alnwick to Warkworth affords a sequence of stunning views.

(11.5km) and descend into North Charlton. At the A1 turn left and after a mile (1.5km), turn right, signed Preston Tower. After 2 miles (3km) turn left, signed Beadnell, at the T-junction just beyond Preston Tower. Continue for 3.5 miles (5.5km) past Beadnell and along the B1340 (views of the Farne Islands), into Seahouses. At the roundabout turn right and down the main street go left, following the Coastal Route to Bamburgh. Pass Bamburgh Castle. Go round Budle Bay and turn left in Waren Mill, signed Belford. Turn right on the A1 and then left into Belford.

4 Turn left on the B6349 signed Wooler. After 2.5 miles (4km), turn right along a narrow unclassified road signed Hazelrigg, Lowick. There are spectacular views of the Cheviots from this road. Turn right at a T-junction, signed Holburn, Berwick. A little way along the road is the track to St Cuthbert's Cave. After 5 miles (8km) cross the B6353, then turn right, signed Kentstone. Cross the A1 if you wish to visit Holy Island (check the tides); otherwise, turn left towards Berwick, passing Haggerston Castle. In 4.5 miles (7km) turn right at the roundabout along the A1167 and return to Berwick.

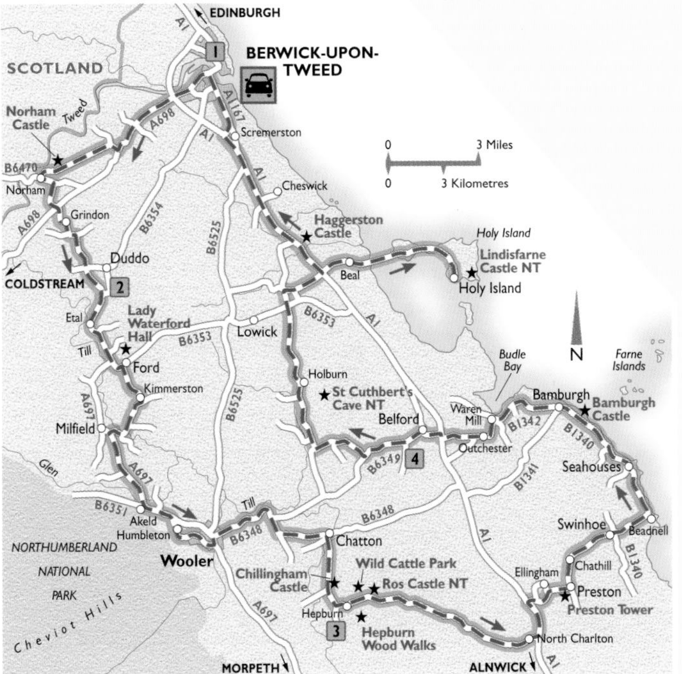

The romantic castle of Lindisfarne on Holy Island, only accessible at low tide

EXPLORING THE NATIONAL PARKS

If you want to really get away from it all amid glorious scenery, there's nowhere better in Britain than the 11 National Parks of England and Wales. Fifty years ago when they were established, they were seen by the government as offering the opportunity for the booming urban populations to escape into the clean, fresh air of the mountains.

All the first ten parks – the Peak District, Lake District, Dartmoor, Exmoor, Yorkshire Dales, North York Moors, Pembrokeshire Coast, Brecon Beacons, Northumberland and Snowdonia – are in the mountainous north and west of the country. The addition of the Broads of Norfolk and Suffolk in 1989 created the first lowland park, to be followed by the proposed New Forest and South Downs National Parks, and the first ever in Scotland at Loch Lomond and the Trossachs, and the Cairngorms.

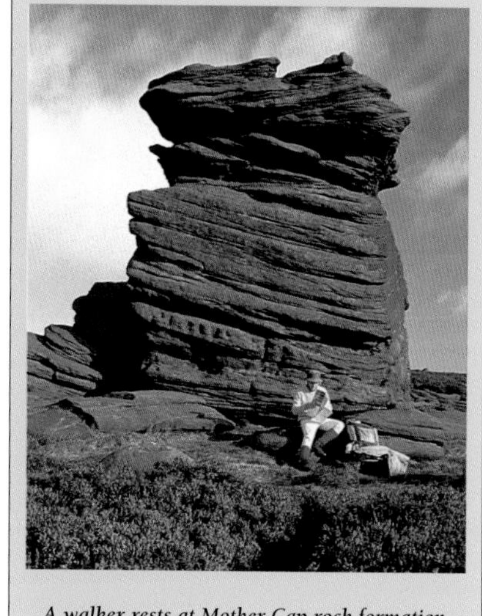

A walker rests at Mother Cap rock formation in the Peak District National Park

Of course, walking is the number one outdoor activity in the National Parks. All have extensive networks of waymarked rights-of-way and most run guided walks for less-experienced visitors. All parks also have horse-riding and pony-trekking centres where day hire is available, and most have cycle-hire facilities too. The parks provide excellent mountain-biking terrain, with their many miles of bridleways, from the former pack-horse routes of the Peak and Dales to the forestry trails of Northumberland.

But the parks are not just the place to go for some of the finest walking and riding in Britain, they are also in the vanguard of some of the newer and more unusual outdoor sports.

There are fewer more peaceful ways to admire some of the finest landscapes in Britain than by floating serenely in a hot-air balloon. All the parks have centres where you can hitch a ride in a balloon, but usually only in anticyclonic (high pressure) and windless weather conditions. And remember, you are never quite sure where you might land! Microlighting is a popular alternative, and there are gliding clubs at places like Hasty Bank in the North York Moors and Hucklow Edge in the Peak District, where you can have a day's trial flight.

Many of the rock-climbing meccas of the Peak District edges, Lake District and Yorkshire Dales fells, and Snowdonia and Brecon Beacon summits, are eminently suited to hang-gliding and parascending. And the great joy of these sports – as with sailing on the lakes or reservoirs at places like Ullswater and Derwent Water in the Lakes, Bala Lake in Snowdonia and Wimbleball Reservoir in Exmoor – is that they double up as relaxing spectator sports.

The relatively new sport of 'coasteering' (traversing along coastal cliff faces rather than climbing up them) is popular on the steep cliffs of the Pembrokeshire Coast and Exmoor, but it is an activity which should only be attempted in the company of experts, knowledgeable in both climbing and the local tidal ranges.

The Pembrokeshire Coast National Park is also a surfing hotspot, where beaches like Freshwater East and West and Manorbier are renowned for their consistently good waves. There is also some surfing in the Bristol Channel off Exmoor's rocky coast, and in Cardigan Bay off Snowdonia. And where there's surfing there's also usually windsurfing; even diving is catered for in the marine nature reserve off the Pembrokeshire Coast.

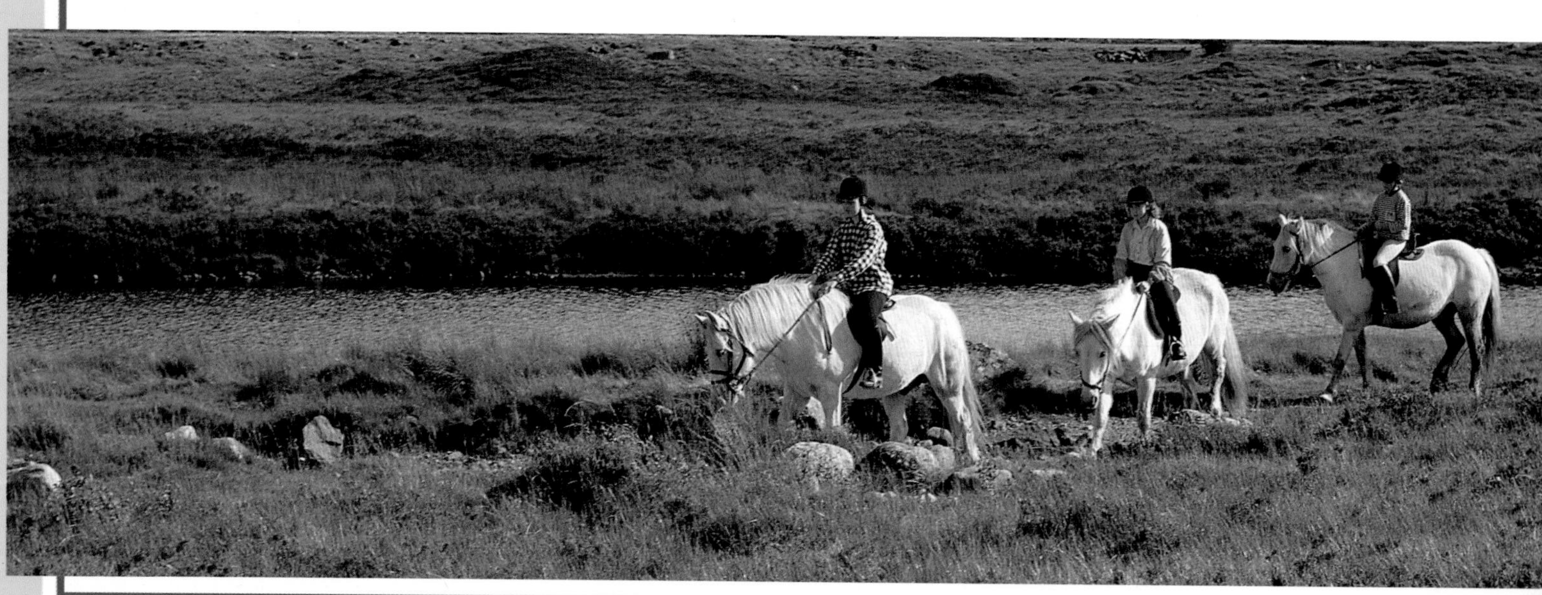

LETTERBOXING

One of the more unusual walking traditions established on Dartmoor is the pastime of 'letterboxing'. It began in 1854 when James Perrott, a Chagford guide, left a small box at remote Cranmere Pool where visitors could leave their calling cards and sign a visitors' book. Today, there are over 500 letterboxes scattered across the moor, avidly sought out by walkers.

Derwent Water in the Lake District, one of the most popular parks

Pony-trekking along bridleways and trails can be enjoyed at all the parks

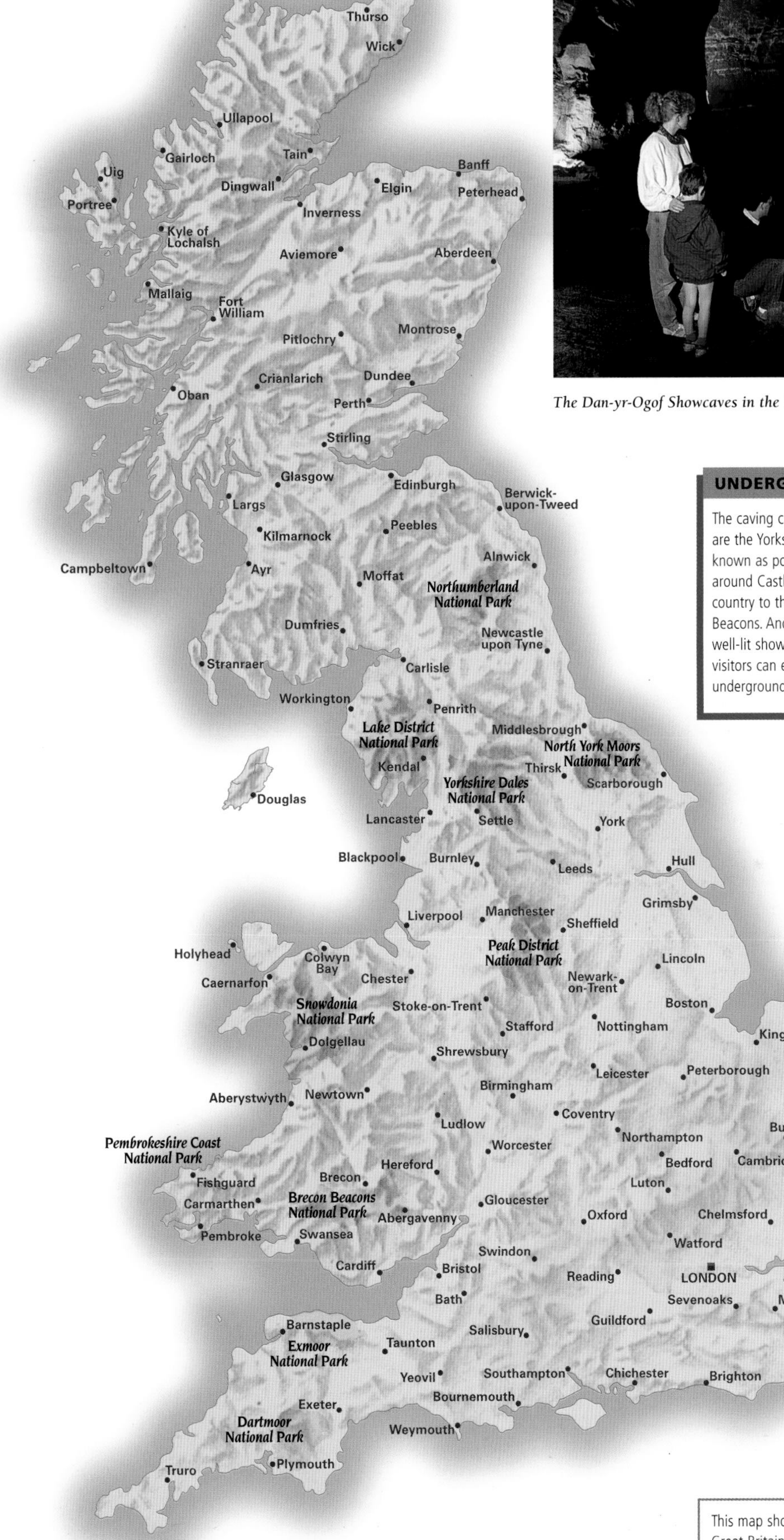

The Dan-yr-Ogof Showcaves in the Brecon Beacons

UNDERGROUND WONDERS

The caving capitals of the National Parks are the Yorkshire Dales (where it's known as pot-holing), the Peak District around Castleton, and the limestone country to the south of the Brecon Beacons. And all these places also have well-lit showcaves where less intrepid visitors can explore the usually unseen, underground wonders of the landscape.

This map shows the 11 National Parks of Great Britain.

SCOTLAND

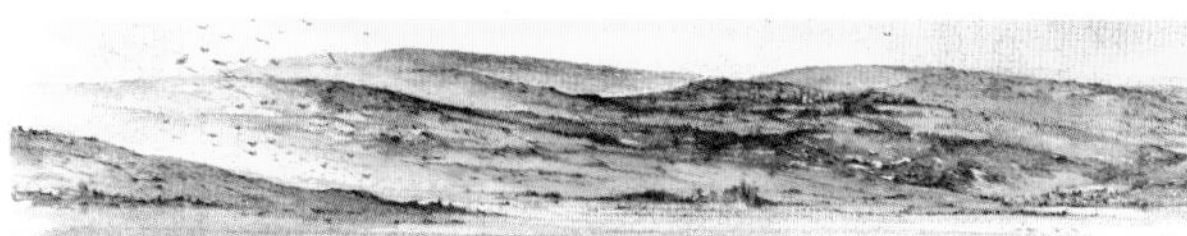

Glen Coe, Argyll & Bute

THE BORDERS, DUMFRIES & GALLOWAY

Around AD 122 the Roman Emperor Hadrian built a great wall from coast to coast to keep out the barbarians of the north. The border between Scotland and England is now further north, but the Scottish determination to retain a separate identity remains strong. Tall defensive towers hidden among the trees are reminders of later border skirmishes. Tales of robbers and pirates still colour the Galloway coastline, immortalised in the novels of Sir Walter Scott and others. Once the scene of constant border warfare between the Scots and the English, it is now a haven of peace and tranquillity, with quiet roads, lush pastures, hills and woodlands.

Caerlaverock
This 13th-century fortification is the only triangular castle in Scotland, with a double-towered gatehouse and huge ramparts. Besieged and rebuilt by Scottish and English alike, it has changed hands many times over the centuries.

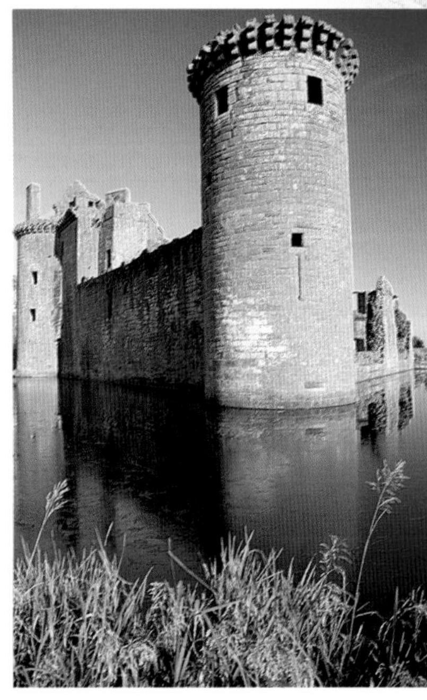

Glenkiln's Statues
At Glenkiln Reservoir near Shawhead in Dumfriesshire, a collection of sculptures by Henry Moore, Jacob Epstein and August Rodin is displayed in the sweeping pastoral landscape. Enjoyment of these works is enhanced by the setting and the experience is ever changing with the weather and light. 'The King and Queen', on the hillside overlooking the reservoir has, more than any other piece, become the symbol of Glenkiln.

DRUMLANRIG CASTLE

The seat of the Dukes of Queensberry and Buccleuch, near Thornhill, is an elaborate turreted confection standing imposingly at the end of a long drive. The castle is well worth a tour for its art and furniture collection, as well as for the building itself. In the grounds are beautiful formal gardens, waymarked forest paths, an adventure playground and birds of prey. There are also craft workshops, a cycling museum and cycle hire.

Kirkcudbright

The former county town of the Stewartry of Kirkcudbright, with its picturesque harbour next to the town square, has always attracted artists to set up home. It was the setting for the Dorothy L Sayers novel Five Red Herrings, *which featured some of the artists who lived there, including the painter Edward Hornel and his home. Hornel's Georgian mansion is now a museum to his life and work.*

MAP AND KEY

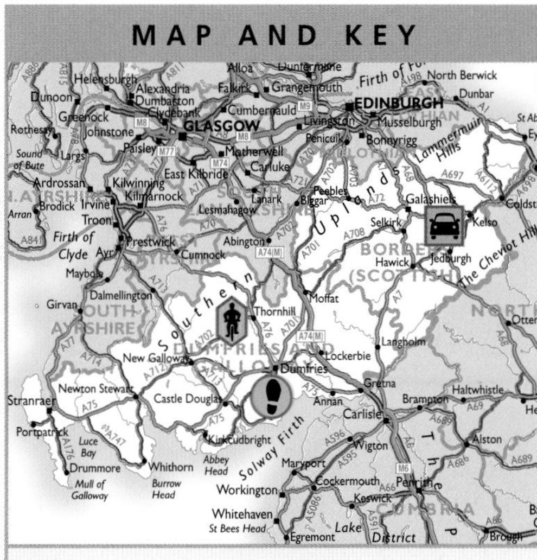

Sweetheart Abbey Walk

Thornhill Cycle Ride

Kelso Drive

Jedburgh Abbey

If you can only see one of the great medieval abbeys of the Borders, this is the one to see. In the quaint little town of Jedburgh stands the immense, graceful ruin of Jedburgh Abbey, founded in 1138. It gives the most complete impression of all the Border abbeys of these great monastic institutions, as if its medieval inhabitants might return next week to repair the roof.

LOCH TROOL

The Galloway Forest Park, centred around lovely Loch Trool and the Galloway Hills, is an Area of Outstanding Natural Beauty. Hill-walking in this empty wilderness is rewarded by stunning views over lochs, rivers and coastline. Less strenuous is a stroll or cycle ride through the myriad forest paths or a drive along the Queen's Way to the pretty village of New Galloway. There are plenty of cafés and tearooms in villages and towns throughout the park.

GALLOWAY & THE SOLWAY FIRTH

Galloway and the Solway Coast are Scotland's best-kept secret. There are endless miles of deserted sandy beaches, rocky coves and clifftop paths. In the Galloway Hills there is wilderness walking to match the Lake District or the Highlands but without the crowds. Cycling along the narrow winding roads, which meander through forest, hills and pastoral landscapes, is a delight to the senses. Stop to listen and all you will hear are the sounds of farming or wildlife. You will strain your ears in vain for the distant roar of traffic beyond the chugging tractor and the buzzing bees. The many lochs, rivers and the extensive coastline provide opportunities for a wide variety of watersports from fishing in the salmon-rich rivers to sailing in the challenging currents of the Irish Sea. Bird-watching on coast, in moorland or in forest will be rewarded by sightings of innumerable species of birds, particularly sea birds and raptors.

ORIENTEERING

Galloway is the most densely forested area in Britain. Orienteers map their way round the forest parks every weekend. Events are organised for all ages and levels of experience from family fun circuits on safe paths to serious cross-country competitions. It is a wonderful way to get exercise and fresh air, while developing your navigational skills. The **Galloway Forest Park** (260sq miles/670sq km) includes the Galloway Hills and Glen Trool, open moorland, vast tracts of forest, wilderness and picnic spots.

Historic remains abound, reminding us of times when the Scottish wars of independence raged back and forth to the border, fortified towers dotted the landscape and religious benefactors raised the magnificent abbeys of Sweetheart and Dundrennan. Much 13th- and 14th-century building work survives among Sweetheart Abbey's ruins, including the 90-ft (27-m) high central tower and parts of the nave and transepts. The New Abbey Corn Mill, dating

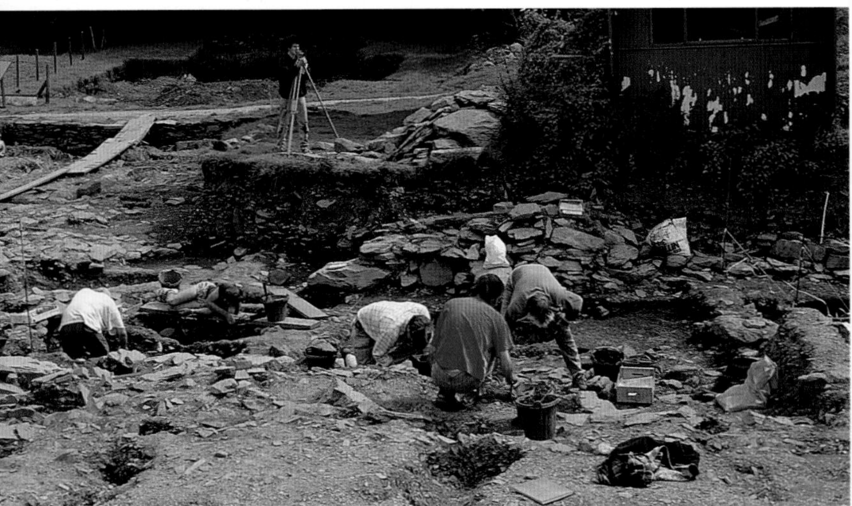

An excavation at Whithorn, where medieval and Viking remains have been unearthed

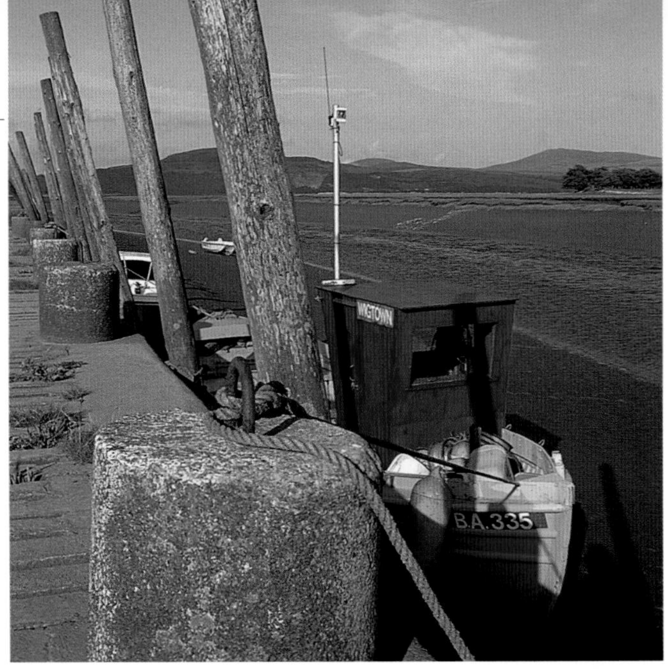

Small fishing vessels moored alongside Wigtown harbour, on the River Bladnoch

Sweetheart Abbey Walk

WALK

Four Kingdoms from Criffell

START/FINISH: New Abbey. On the A710 6 miles (10km) south of Dumfries
DISTANCE: 9 miles (14.5km)
ASCENT/GRADIENT: 1,867ft (569m); very steep up Criffell
TERRAIN/PATHS: road, fields, woodland, moorland, farm tracks; good paths; very boggy in winter and in wet weather
PARKING: Sweetheart Abbey car-park off A710 in New Abbey

England, Ireland, Scotland and the Isle of Man are all visible from this looming moorland eminence above the Solway Firth.

1 Sweetheart Abbey was built by Devorgilla, founder of Balliol College, Oxford and the mother of John Balliol, who became King of Scotland. It was a memorial to her husband, and she left instructions that their hearts were to be buried together at the abbey. From the car-park at Sweetheart Abbey, turn left on to the main road. Leave the village past the petrol station and over a bridge. Pass the farm roads for Lochhill and Ingleston Ford and later a bright bus shelter. As you leave the abbey, Criffell and Knockendoch rise from the fields, forming an impressive backdrop to the lush pastures enclosed by dry-stone walls.

2 300yds (274m) beyond the bus shelter, turn right at the signpost for Ardwall and Ardwall Mains to the parking area for Criffell. You could start and finish your walk here, but you would miss the walk down the far side of Knockendoch. Follow the sign – Criffell Walk 2 miles.

3 Go through the metal gate on the left, walk for 70yds (64m) on a farm track, turn right, following the track between two dry-stone walls to the foot of the hill. At the end, pass beside a gate across the track.

4 The forestry road curves to your left but take a rough trodden path to the right marked Criffell Walk. The path up through the woods is rough, uneven and narrow, with lots of large boulders to clamber over, but plainly visible and easy to follow.

5 Mostly the path follows the course of a stream uphill. Cross two forestry roads. At the top of the treeline there is a fence and a stile leading on to the hillside. To your right is Knockendoch; to the left, Criffell.

BIRD-WATCHING

The Wildlife and Wetlands Trust's reserve at **Caerlaverock** on the Solway encompasses 1,500 acres (607ha) of saltwater marsh. It has hide and observation facilities, giving impressive views of the large numbers of wildfowl that overwinter here, including barnacle geese, pink-footed and greylag geese, waders, whooper swans and many varieties of duck. Caerlaverock is also home to the most northerly colony of natterjack toads. There are plenty of other activities from bat-watching evenings to pond-dipping.

from the 18th century, has been restored and still grinds oatmeal on traditional stone.

Continuing along the coast to the far west you will reach the Isle of Whithorn, where Saint Ninian brought Christianity to Scotland in AD 397. For hundreds of years this was a destination for pilgrims, including kings such as Robert the Bruce and James V, until pilgrimage was banned during the Reformation. The Pilgrim's Way, a waymarked path from New Luce to Whithorn, now re-creates the route taken by those ancient travellers. Much of medieval Whithorn remains and at the Whithorn Dig, even earlier settlements are being excavated.

ARTS AND CRAFTS

Numerous artisans and artists have chosen to live and work in this area.

Clogs
Godfrey, from the tiny hamlet of Balmaclellan, makes clogs – from sandals to boots – following traditional methods. You can buy brightly coloured footware off the shelf or made to measure.

Hand-blown glass
Ed Iglehart philosophises as he demonstrates glass-blowing in his workshop at Palnackie. His idiosyncratic lamps, candle holders and dishes are for sale in a converted shed next door.

Stoves and art
Steve Dowling at Bladnoch makes virtually indestructible multi-fuel stoves from ½-in (1.3-cm) thick sheet steel. Above his workshop there is an art gallery selling pictures and sculptures by local artists.

Wood-carving
Fiona Allardyce Lewis at Kirkland near Moniaive specialises in wood-carving. Her hand-painted wooden artefacts, from small mirrors to furniture, are not cheap but her style is unmistakable and very collectable.

Art Garden at Moniaive
Much of the art and craft work here can be found nowhere else. Prices start at a couple of pounds up to hundreds. The wares range from oils, watercolours and prints, to reclaimed wooden sculptures, beadwork and colourful woven wall hangings.

Travelling through this countryside you will come across picturesque villages of low stone-built cottages, old-fashioned country towns such as Wigtown, its broad main street now deserted, and small fishing ports such as Kirkcudbright. Before the local government re-organisation of 1975, Wigtown was the county town of Wigtownshire. Its past civic pride is mocked by the magnificent French-styled town hall, which is gradually disintegrating. However, a new prosperity is growing since it became Scotland's Book Town, where another bookshop is tucked away around every corner. Whether you are looking simply for a good read to pass the evening or for some rare and particular treasure, this is the place to search.

This unspoiled area with its clear waters and unpolluted air is an oasis of tranquillity. Abundant wildlife thrives amid a rich historic heritage and those visitors to Scotland who turn left at the border, will be well rewarded.

6 Follow the path to Criffell summit, with its trig point and cairn. From here you can look into four kingdoms. The peaks of the Lake District, beyond the Solway, to the west lies the Isle of Man; turning further west and north the coast of Antrim is visible, while all around is Scotland. From the cairn, head (northwest then north) across rough ground for the wide ridge which runs from Criffell to Knockendoch, until you intersect a narrow path leading down, then back up to Knockendoch summit.

7 Descend Knockendoch via the path which continues from the summit in the direction you have been travelling. Cross the stile where a fence meets a dry-stone wall part-way down. Continue with the wall on your right and later, near a plantation of larches, veer to the left to a forestry track and turn right.

8 Go through several gates, cross a burn, bear right until the track joins the drive to Barbeth Farm. This leads into the village. Follow a road to the main road, emerging at the petrol station. Turn left and follow the road to the car-park at Sweetheart Abbey.

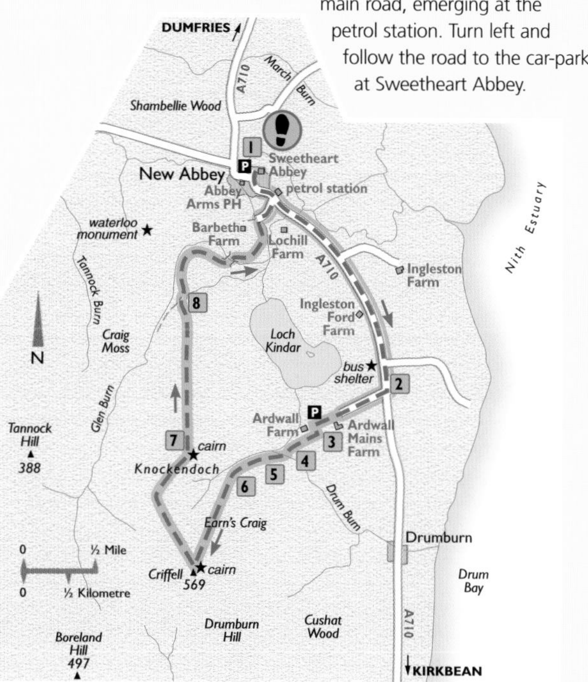

TOP FIVE GARDENS

Threave Garden
A wonderfully varied garden at every season, particularly famed for its spring daffodils. It is the National Trust for Scotland's horticultural training school.

Broughton House, Kirkcudbright
The Japanese garden here was designed by the painter Edward Hornel. It is not large, but it is exquisite and atmospheric.

Castle Kennedy Gardens
These gardens with monkey puzzle trees and azaleas in abundance surround the remains of a medieval castle set between two lochs.

Logan Botanic Garden
Next to Port Logan, in the Mull of Galloway, this is part of the Royal Botanic Garden based in Edinburgh. The Gulf Stream, which bathes the west coast of Scotland with warm waters from the Gulf of Mexico, sustains a range of unlikely plants at this latitude.

Arbigland Gardens
As well as extensive gardens overlooking the Solway Firth, the estate here includes the cottage of John Paul Jones, the founder of the American Navy.

The water garden at Logan Botanic Garden

DUMFRIES & THE TWEEDSMUIR HILLS

The countryside flanking the M74 as you head north changes gradually from fertile meadows, supporting large numbers of beef and dairy herds, to the massive green humps of the Lowther and Tweedsmuir Hills. These are part of the Southern Uplands, the range of hills stretching from east to west across Southern Scotland. The Southern Upland Way, cutting across the grain of the country from Portpatrick in Galloway to Cockburnspath in the Borders is one of the most challenging long-distance footpaths in Scotland.

The celebrated Scottish poet Robert Burns (1759–1796)

The peaceful lowland farmland of Dumfriesshire was a violent world in the middle ages. In 1306, in Greyfriars Abbey, in Dumfries, Robert the Bruce stabbed Sir John Comyn, and began Scotland's quest for nationhood. An outlaw on the run and in despair, legend has it that the Bruce spent three months in a cave and was inspired by the unrelenting web-spinning efforts of a spider. The cave at Kirkpatrick Fleming, on an open cliff face, is thought to be megalithic. Until recently it could only be reached by a rope descent, but there is now a footpath. At Ruthwell stands one of Europe's finest early Christian stone crosses, dating from the 7th century and carved with runic and Latin inscriptions around biblical scenes.

Looking across the River Nith to the Robert Burns Centre in Dumfries

Dumfries is the largest centre of population in the southwest. The idyllic setting, on the broad tree-lined banks of the River Nith, is subject to flooding whenever high tides and weather combine against it. The 18th-century water mill on the west bank houses the Robert Burns Centre, commemorating Scotland's national bard. From his farm at Ellisland, 6 miles (10km) north of the town, he wrote 'Tam O'Shanter' and collected 'Auld Lang Syne'. The Globe Inn, close to Burns' house in Dumfries, was one of his regular haunts for drinking and socialising. The landlady's niece, Anna Park, bore him a daughter in 1791. Visitors today can sit in the poet's chair, view the room where he engaged in his amorous adventures and read the poem he scratched in the window with a diamond. The Dumfries Museum has a camera obscura of 1836 on the top floor, giving a panoramic view of the town and surrounding countryside. Among the exhibits

Thornhill Cycle Ride

CYCLE RIDE

Highlights of Cycling History by Thornhill

START/FINISH:	Thornhill. On the A76 Dumfries to Kilmarnock road, 14 miles (22.5km) north of Dumfries
DISTANCE:	20 miles (32km), with 2 miles (3km) off-road
GRADIENT:	undulating; three significant hills
ROADS:	quiet roads
PARKING:	street parking in the village

This ride passes through beautiful mid-Nithsdale and is mainly on very quiet, well-surfaced roads. It takes in the place where the world's first pedal bicycle was conceived, as well as the Scottish Museum of Cycling and two splendid castles.

1 From the mercat cross, go north and turn left into New Street. Descend steeply and go straight ahead at the crossroads at the bottom. Continue over the bridge across the River Nith and turn first left. In 1.5 miles (2.5km), after the metal bridge and short uphill stretch, stop at the first houses of Keir Mill and walk along the path on the left to the cemetery. At the bottom of the cemetery is the grey-painted gravestone of Kirkpatrick McMillan, the 'Father of the Bicycle'. Return to the road.

2 Continue through Keir, and at the T-junction turn right. Shortly, pass Courthill Smithy. Kirkpatrick McMillan built the world's first pedal bicycle in this smithy in 1839. Continue to Penpont, and turn right at the crossroads. At Burnhead, take the left fork (30mph zone), and continue straight on for nearly 2 miles (3km) to cross a cattle grid. Shortly, bear left (cyclists ignore the 'No entry' signs) up a steep hill, passing on your left the flat area, next to the adventure playground, that was a Roman camp and where the KM Cycle Rally is held, to 17th-century Drumlanrig Castle. The castle houses treasures of the Dukes of Buccleuch and the Scottish Museum of Cycling.Trails are laid out through the parkland.

3 Leave Drumlanrig along the straight lime avenue, and continue downhill into the Nith gorge. Turn left over the bridge, continue up the hill to fork right, and cross the A76, signed to Durisdeer. To see a grove of the massive Wellingtonia trees, take the second track on your left just before the cottages, climbing steeply at first; fork right once and left twice and return. Otherwise, continue to a staggered crossroads at the

TYING THE KNOT

Gretna Green is still a popular romantic wedding spot for hundreds of couples every year. It owes its fame or notoriety to the fact that, after marriage by declaration was banned in England in 1754, it was the nearest point for runaway couples to secure a legitimate marriage under the laxer Scottish law. The blacksmith, popularly known as 'the anvil priest', would, in front of witnesses, hear the declaration of elopers' willingness to marry. After 1856 it became necessary for one of the parties to have been resident in Scotland for 21 days prior to the ceremony, but marriage by declaration was not prohibited until 1940. The anvil can still be seen in the Old Blacksmith's Shop Museum.

is 'Rekolections of a Schoolmaster', the childhood scribblings of J M Barrie, the author of *Peter Pan*. Barrie confessed in later life that 'Never Never Land' originated in a garden behind Dumfries Academy, where he and his school friends pursued marauding pirates, and that the pirate chief was none other than his maths master at the Academy, Mr Neilson!

CRICHOPE LINN

This tiny gorge encapsulates great natural wonders and waterfalls on a miniature scale. If you are following the **Thornhill Cycle Route**, it is well worth a detour to take in this little gem. On the return to Thornhill at the T-junction before the telephone box, turn left to Gatelawbridge. At the end of the road turn right and a mile or so along you will find Crichope Linn, signed to the left. You will have to explore it on foot and the pathway to the waterfall can be slippy. Returning to your bike continue down the road to Cample where you can rejoin the route.

From these lowland literary and historic sites, head east into the hills of Eskdalemuir, to find the last thing you would expect in this remote and lonely corner of Dumfriesshire. A Buddhist monastery, with elaborate oriental buildings in bright red and gold, sits high up in the Southern Uplands with the delicate sounds of wind chimes filling the air. Tibetan monks built Samye Ling and it is home to a community of Buddhists. Visitors are always welcome.

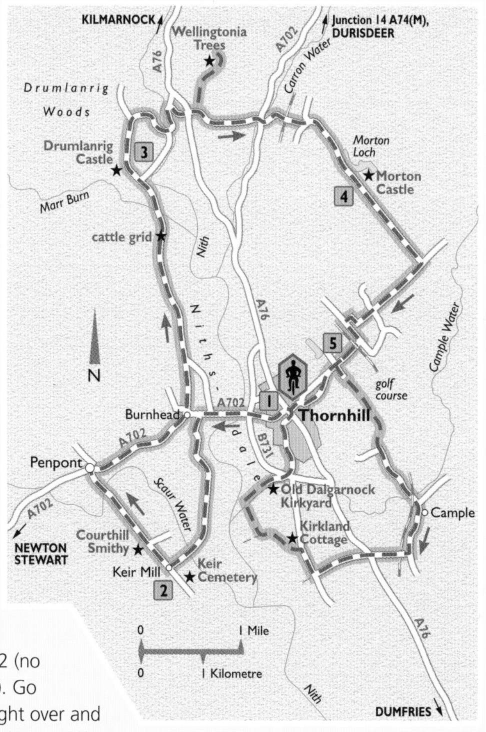

A702 (no sign). Go straight over and straight on at the next crossroads (no sign). In nearly 1 mile (1.5km) Morton Loch the substantial, picturesque ruin of Morton Castle are on your left.

4 Continue to the T-junction. Turn right, descending the biggest downhill of the route. Keep straight on past a phone box and at the next junction turn very sharp left. In half a mile (800m) turn sharply right, down under the railway. (For a short cut, continue straight along this road to return to the centre of Thornhill.)

5 After the railway turn left on to the road then track through the golf course. At the public road, go straight on to Cample and turn right just after the railway bridge. Turn next right, cross the A76 and at the next junction turn right. Soon turn left at Kirkland Cottage on to a track, continue down past a cemetery (Old Dalgarnock Covenanters' Memorial) to the road, and continue across a staggered junction to Thornhill.

Fishing

Salmon and trout fishing are popular on rivers such as the Nith and the Cairn. Day tickets are available from local angling clubs, councils and estates.

Shooting

The grouse shooting seasons starts on 'the glorious 12th', of August. There are shoots on many of the large estates, but it is an expensive activity. However, local gun clubs provide clay-pigeon shoots all year round at more reasonable rates.

Sheepdog trials

This is very competitive and obviously a specialised skill. A day out watching shepherds and their dogs is a magical experience as signals and whistles undetectable to the uninitiated send the dogs scurrying to nip the sheep into line.

Quad-biking

Shepherds used to walk miles every day over the hills to 'look' the sheep. But nowadays they can check their flocks by quad-bike. It is an exhilarating experience to head up the hills, over mud, rough terrain and a few rocks, in one of these sturdy four-wheeled buggies. You can take an outing on the hills in a quad-bike for a modest charge, which includes training and safety gear.

Gold-panning

This esoteric activity is demonstrated at the Leadhills mining museum. You can arrange to go out gold-panning in the river with an instructor. It is great fun paddling about in the river with your frying pan and a real thrill when you spot that glimmering fleck of gold!

THE VALLEY OF THE TWEED & THE SOUTHERN UPLANDS

This eastern part of the borderlands is characterised by rolling hills, the meandering Tweed and the North Sea coast. Inland, medieval abbeys, stately homes and small stone-built towns are tucked into the folds of the hills. The traditional wool-based industries of textiles and knitwear still survive in the mill towns of Hawick and Galashiels and nowadays many independent spinners, weavers, knitwear designers and tapestry makers are working in wool in this sleepy backwater where the calendar seems permanently stuck at around 1950.

The Border Abbey Cycle Route is an ideal way to take in the picturesque abbey towns of Jedburgh, Kelso and Melrose. As well as

Looking south from the ancient Eildon Hills over a patchwork of fields

The Italian-style gardens at Mellerstain give splendid views of the Cheviot Hills

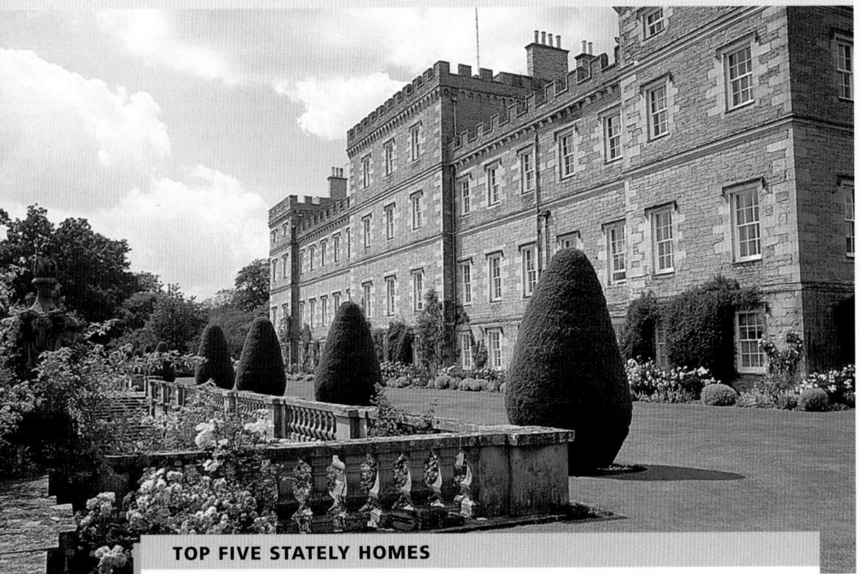

TOP FIVE STATELY HOMES

Traquair House

Dating from the early 12th century, Traquair is the oldest continually inhabited house in Scotland. The famous Bear Gates have never been opened since Prince Charles Edward Stuart rode through them in 1745. The Earl of Traquair swore that they would remain sealed until a Stuart returned to the throne of Scotland. In summer the estate is host to craft workshops and Traquair ale is brewed in the old brewhouse and fermented in the original 200-year-old oak casks.

Abbotsford

Sir Walter Scott designed Abbotsford in the Scots Baronial style, with medieval towers and turrets. The spacious library, housing Scott's huge collection of rare books, also displays his accumulation of bizarre Scottish memorabilia from Prince Charlie's hair to the crucifix carried by Mary, Queen of Scots when she was beheaded.

Mellerstain

Mellerstain (above) is possibly the finest Georgian mansion in Scotland, retaining its original Adam colours in the interior paintwork. Allow half a day to take in the superb collection of paintings, period furniture and terraced gardens.

Floors Castle

Floors Castle, a mile from Kelso along the Cobby riverside walk, is a huge early 18th-century mansion designed by William Adam and still home to the Duke of Roxburgh.

Lennoxlove

Just beyond Haddington, Lennoxlove is set in 600 acres (243ha) of verdant woodlands. It appears to have grown in an endearing mixture of styles around a medieval tower and has an impressive collection of fine furniture, paintings and mementoes of Mary, Queen of Scots, including her eerie death mask.

Kelso Drive

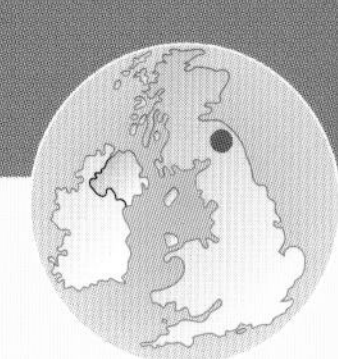

DRIVE

Discovering the Borders

START/FINISH: Kelso. Market town on the A698 20 miles (32km) southwest of Berwick-upon-Tweed

DISTANCE: 78 miles (126km)

Pleasant river valleys, rich farmland and green hillsides always in view make this a peaceful scene; but it was devastated by recurring Border wars. Four great abbeys were destroyed, although their stately ruins remain.

1 Kelso is a bustling Border town on the River Tweed. It has a preserved Georgian square and the largest and most splendid of all the Border abbey ruins, founded by David I in 1128. Leave Kelso on the A698 towards Hawick. Keep forward on the B6352 for Yetholm, then in 1.5 miles (2km) join the B6436 towards Morebattle. Keep to this road and take the second minor road right (not signed) to the B6401.

2 Turn right then left, signed to Cessford, and 1.5 miles (2.5km) further turn left then right. Keep forward, signed to Jedburgh, go over the crossroads, then in just over 2 miles (3km) bear right for Jedburgh. At the A68 turn right, then shortly left for Jedburgh town centre.

3 Leave by turning left on to the B6358 for Hawick. In 4 miles (6.5km), at the river bridge, go forward on the A698. At Denholm turn right on to the B6405 towards Hassendean. Turn left across the river bridge, then in 2 miles (3km) turn right on to the B6359 for Melrose. At the edge of Lilliesleaf, turn left on to the B6400. Cross a river bridge and, in a mile (1.5km), turn right along a minor road, signed to Selkirk. Turn right on reaching the A7 and continue to Selkirk, a former textile town with an excellent local museum at Halliwell's House.

4 Follow signs right towards Galashiels, then turn right on to the B6360 for Abbotsford. Sir Walter Scott invested most of his literary earnings in Abbotsford House, and his historical collections and library are on display. At the roundabout, take the A6091 for Jedburgh then, at the next roundabout, take the second exit for Melrose. The most mellow of the Border towns, Melrose lies between the lofty Eildon Hills and the meadows of the Tweed. Visit the Cistercian abbey and its museum, and the adjacent Priorwood Gardens which recreate the monastic orchards.

the best-preserved abbey, Jedburgh has a fascinating warren of medieval streets and a pleasant 16th-century tower house and garden, known as Mary, Queen of Scots' House. The centre of Kelso is Georgian, with a cluster of houses surrounding a vast cobbled square. The abbey here suffered badly at the hands of Henry VIII and little remains. Nestling in the Eildon Hills is Melrose, where the heart of Robert the Bruce is buried. Like most of these small border towns, Melrose has a fascinating collection of craft, antiques and specialist shops including the delightful Teddy Melrose, crammed full of cuddly bears, and The Hobby House, a real old-fashioned haberdashers.

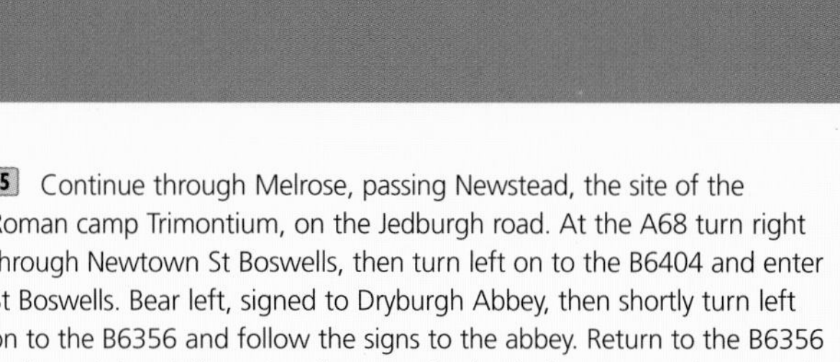

BIRDS OF PREY

There are a number of centres in the Borders where you can watch demonstrations of birds of prey, but at the **Scottish Academy of Falconry** in **Hawick** you can get tuition in flying the birds yourself. You can even fly falcons on horseback and imagine yourself a medieval lord or lady riding out to hunt!

To the north, the historic town of Haddington is an architectural delight, with its broad tree-lined streets and medieval street plan. Around the corner is Haddington House, complete with re-created 17th-century garden. Further on, a tranquil riverside walk leads to St Mary's Collegiate Church, where the marks of Henry VIII's bombardment are still visible on the stone work.

A fishing trawler enters the harbour at the coastal village of St Abbs

OUT AND ABOUT

With so much open countryside and coastline, and countless rivers and streams, there is no shortage of facilities in the Borders for activities out of doors. The **Active Sports Centre** in **Melrose** provides a huge variety of programmes based on the three elements of water, land and air. The activities include archery, canoeing, hang-gliding, paragliding, quad-biking, rafting, shooting, windsurfing, skiing on a dry-ski slope and more. **Scottish Border Trails** in **Peebles** will organise an individual multi-activity holiday around the Borders, which can include cycling, hill-walking, horse-riding, fishing or visits to historic houses and castles.

On the coast, the sandy beaches to the south give way to rugged cliffs and the endless miles of the North Sea. St Abbs is a working fishing village, with creels for the crab fishing piled around the little harbour. You can take a boat trip to get a closer look at the guillemots, kittiwakes, fulmars and razorbills which sweep and squeal around the rocks and cliffs. Diving is also available to view the spectacular underwater scenery and sea life in the clear waters. The nature reserve, close to the village, offers rock-pool rambles or you can follow the footpath to the lighthouse to appreciate the wonderful coastline and bird life.

5 Continue through Melrose, passing Newstead, the site of the Roman camp Trimontium, on the Jedburgh road. At the A68 turn right through Newtown St Boswells, then turn left on to the B6404 and enter St Boswells. Bear left, signed to Dryburgh Abbey, then shortly turn left on to the B6356 and follow the signs to the abbey. Return to the B6356 and turn left to follow signs for 1.5 miles (2.5km) to Scott's View. On the way pass a car-park where a walk leads to the Wallace Monument.

6 Soon bear right (no signs), then right at a trunk road (no signs), then left for Earlston. Turn right on to the A6105 and soon bear left towards Berwick-upon-Tweed. Continue forward, passing Greenknowe Tower and, at Gordon turn right on to the A6089 for Kelso. In 2 miles (3km) turn right, signed Mellerstain. Turn left on to the B6397 (signed Kelso), and turn left then right, through Smailholm (detour here to visit Smailholm Tower). Turn left then right, signed Kelso, past Floors Castle, and turn right on reaching the A6089. At the mini-roundabout, take the third exit back into Kelso.

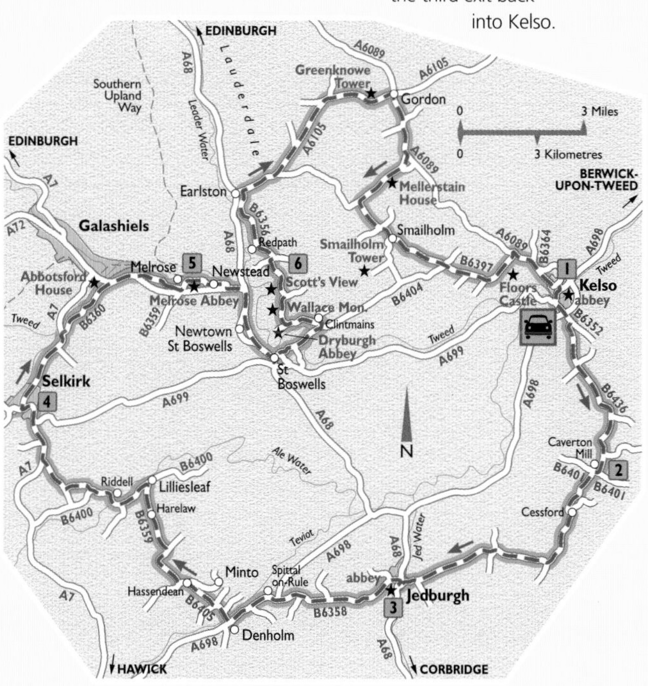

DID YOU KNOW?

Weaving wool into cloth is a long tradition in this sheep-rearing country. At first the rough homespun cloth was for domestic use, until Sir Walter Scott astounded London society in the 1820s with his checked trousers derived from the plaids of the Peeblesshire shepherds. When it was taken up by Prince Albert and Queen Victoria it became the standard and fashionable country clothing for the aristocracy. Today, Border mills and designers supply the high fashion houses of the world, and the Scottish College of Textiles in Galashiels has established itself as an internationally known centre, with the emphasis on quality, design and sophisticated colouring.

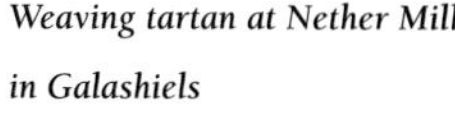

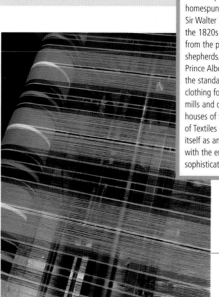

Weaving tartan at Nether Mill in Galashiels

GLASGOW, THE CLYDE & ARGYLL & BUTE

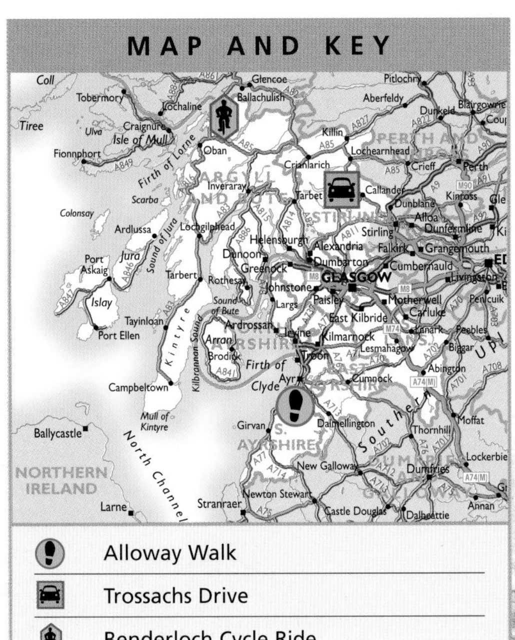

Glasgow is a confident city which has re-invented itself many times from Victorian Glasgow, with Templeton's carpet factory and the marbled halls of the City Chambers, through the arid sixties' and seventies' developments, to the daring modern buildings, reflecting Glasgow's ability to be bold and witty. Part of its charm is that the hills, forests and open countryside around Loch Lomond and the Trossachs and the resorts and islands of the Firth of Clyde are so accessible. From anywhere on the River Clyde you can sail off to a hundred islands.

ARRAN

Reached by CalMac Ferry from Gourock, the Island of Arran is a delight. The main town of Brodick with its castle and gardens can be explored in a day-trip. But a few days are necessary to visit the standing stones on Machrie Moor, climb Goatfell or watch the sunset over Ailsa Craig from the south coast. Pottery, paintings, textiles, basketwork and glass, as well as cheese and whisky, are produced locally.

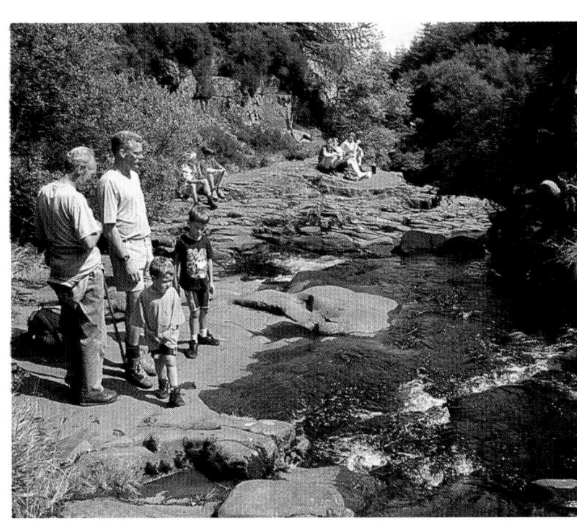

With so much natural beauty on one island, Arran is seen as a microcosm of the Highlands

HILL HOUSE

Hill House, designed by Charles Rennie Mackintosh for the publisher Walter Blackie, is in the attractive Georgian town of Helensburgh. Mackintosh designed the house, its interior and all its furnishings. The exterior echoes a traditional tower, with its irregular windows, its round turret and solid expanses of wall. Inside, it is light and elegant with perfect proportions and delightful glimpses of the adjoining spaces as you move through it.

Glasgow School of Art
Charles Rennie Mackintosh won the competition to design the new school in 1896. It is the earliest example in the UK of a complete art-nouveau building, including furnishings and fittings. The bold design, the delicate detail, the swirling natural lines and the harmony of wood, glass, stone and metal are breathtaking. Students today still remove books from Mackintosh bookcases and sit on priceless Mackintosh chairs to study them.

Kelvingrove Museum and Art Gallery
This elaborate mansion (above) houses works by Botticelli, the Pre-Raphaelites, the Impressionists and David Hockney. The museum has collections ranging from Egyptology to shipbuilding.

A pleasure cruise on the Lomond Mist is one of the ways to see the loch

BURNS COUNTRY – FROM THE CLYDE TO THE AYR

The castle at Brodick Country Park

This stretch of coastline used to be the playground for Glasgow and industrial southwest Scotland with the resorts of Ayr, Troon and Girvan attracting thousands of summer holiday-makers. Nowadays they are more likely to head to overseas. However the sandy beaches, first-class golf courses and noble castles in this undulating landscape still draw many visitors.

Ayr has a broad beach, lovely gardens and two golf courses, as well as Scotland's leading racecourse, with both flat and national hunt meetings. The dignified town of Troon, with its distinctive turreted and towered homes, is almost surrounded by its five golf courses. Royal Troon is the most prestigious, famed for the short par-3 hole known as the 'Postage Stamp'. The championship golf course of Turnberry at Girvan has the most breathtaking view, over the great volcanic lump of Ailsa Craig and to the Mull of Kintyre and Ireland beyond. It is impossible to exaggerate the beauty of the islands off the

Brodick Golf Course on the Isle of Arran

CULZEAN CASTLE AND COUNTRY PARK

Perched on a clifftop near Ayr, overlooking the Firth of Clyde, Culzean was built for the 10th Earl of Cassilis by the architect Robert Adam. The neo-Gothic towers and turrets on the outside belie the classical design of the inside, dominated by the majestic oval staircase. During his lifetime the former US President Dwight D Eisenhower had the use of the top floor where his life and work is commemorated in a permanent display. The castle is set in an extensive country park (below) with gardens, seashore, wooded walks and a small lake.

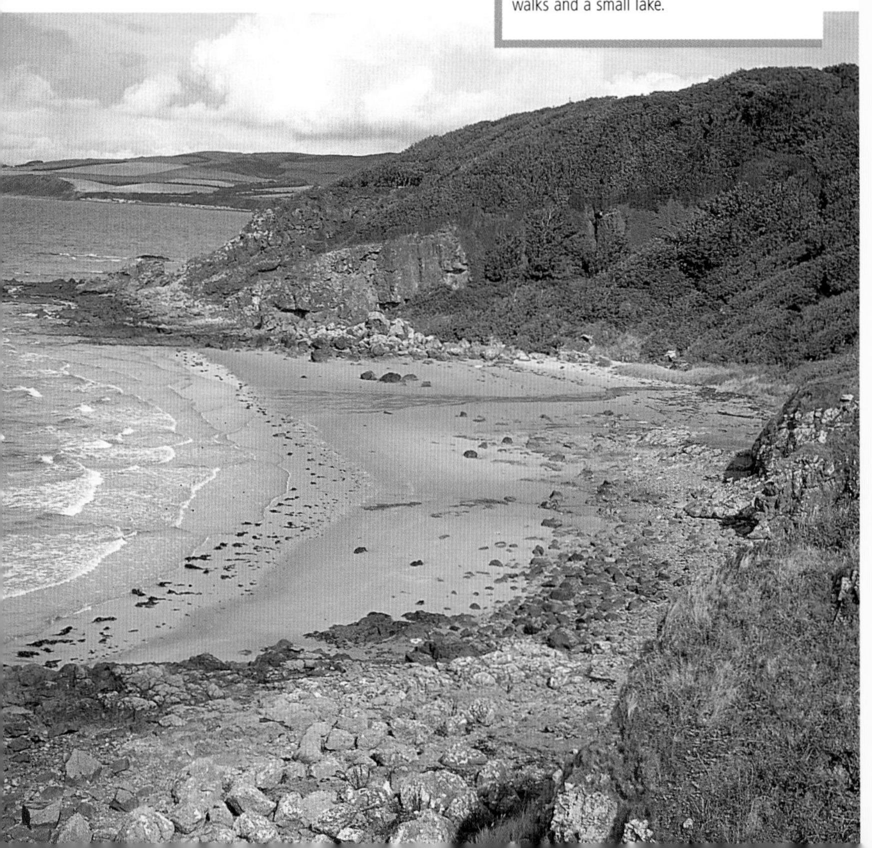

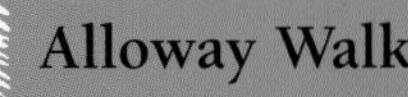

Alloway Walk

WALK

Burns' Alloway and the Brig O'Doon

START/FINISH: Alloway. On the B7024 3 miles (5km) south of Ayr

DISTANCE: 7 miles (11km)

ASCENT/GRADIENT: negligible; some steps

TERRAIN/PATHS: old railway, fields, beach, golf course and woodland; good path; can be muddy

PARKING: Tam O'Shanter Experience car-park

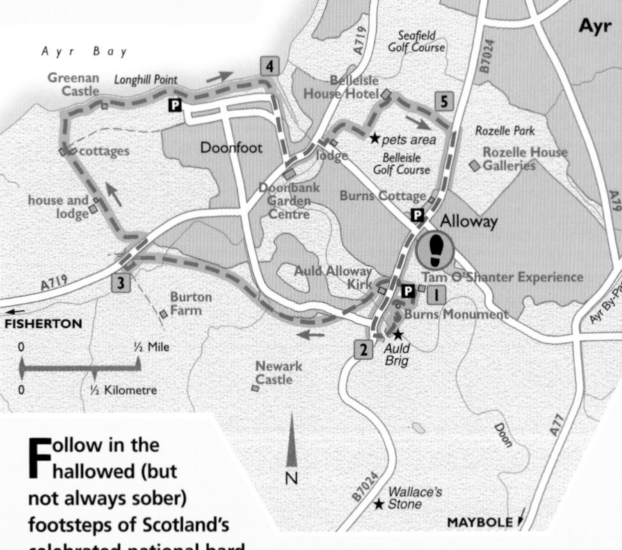

Follow in the hallowed (but not always sober) footsteps of Scotland's celebrated national bard.

1 The old church at Alloway is the setting for 'Tam O'Shanter', Robert Burns' atmospheric narrative poem of witches discovered by the drunken Tam in the Alloway churchyard, dancing to the frenzied piping of Satan himself. From the Tam O'Shanter Experience, which gives a potted introduction to the life of Robert Burns, walk to the end of the car-park, furthest from the entry road. Go right down the path into Burns Monument Gardens. Follow the path anticlockwise around the monument then towards Auld Brig (Brig O'Doon) ahead. Visit Statues

CURLING STONES

At one time all of the heavy round stones used in the Olympic sport of curling were made from **Ailsa Craig** granite. Nowadays, with the growing popularity of curling and the inaccessibility of Ailsa Craig, Welsh granite is more commonly used but all stones are still soled with Ailsa Craig granite. It is the hardest and smoothest granite in the world for sliding swiftly along the ice.

You can take a boat trip from **Girvan** to Ailsa Craig, where you can walk along to the quarry and collect some granite fragments for yourself, while you watch for seals and basking sharks in the surrounding waters.

Ayrshire coast and the best way to see them is by boat. The *Waverley*, the last ocean-going paddle steamer, sails from Glasgow and you can enjoy a magical evening dining on the boat, watching the sun set over the Firth of Clyde. Other historic vessels, including the world's oldest clipper, the *Carrick*, are berthed at the Scottish Maritime Museum in Irvine.

During the summer, the *Waverley* offers popular excursions from Ayr to the island of Arran, sometimes known as 'Scotland in miniature'. The main town of Brodick is set in a wide bay, with Brodick Castle rising from the trees on the lower slopes. The Arran glens, some small and mysterious, others grand and dramatic, attract climbers, walkers and picnickers. Glen Rosa, running inland from Brodick, is a wide and peaceful valley, ideal for a gentle walk. Glen Sannox is sharper, and awe-inspiring in stormy weather. Lochranza in the north is dominated by the 13th- or 14th-century ruined castle on a promontory in the bay. The walk from Lochranza to the Cock of Arran by the coast takes in a marvellous viewpoint overlooking the Sound of Bute. In summer, bird-watching tours offer the chance to see a golden eagle soaring above the granite cliffs, while by the shore colonies of sea birds swoop and dive. Shelduck, eider, mallard, shags, cormorants and herons are a common sight.

The pastoral farmland of Ayrshire, the rugged peaks of Arran, the deserted beaches, and the historical remains from standing stones to castles, are all within easy reach of the central belt of Scotland.

IN SEARCH OF ROBBIE BURNS

Alloway (below) is where Robert Burns, Scotland's national poet, was born on 25 January 1759. Near by are a cluster of Burns 'sites', including the Auld Brig O'Doon, and the Auld Kirk of Alloway where his parents are buried.

Kilmarnock, 17 miles (27km) to the north, is where John Wilson published the famous Kilmarnock first edition of Burns' poetry.

Mauchline, 8 miles (13km) south of Kilmarnock, overlooks Mossgiel Farm, once tended by Burns, and where many of his most significant works were written. At first glance signposts for the Burns Heritage Trail seem to outnumber the houses. They point out the Burns Museum in Castle Street, the house he took when he married Jean Armour in 1788, the Burns Memorial Tower of 1896, Mauchline Castle and Poosie Nansie's Tavern, where you can still take a dram.

Five miles (8km) to the west is the thatched cottage in **Tarbolton** where Burns founded the Bachelors' Club debating society.

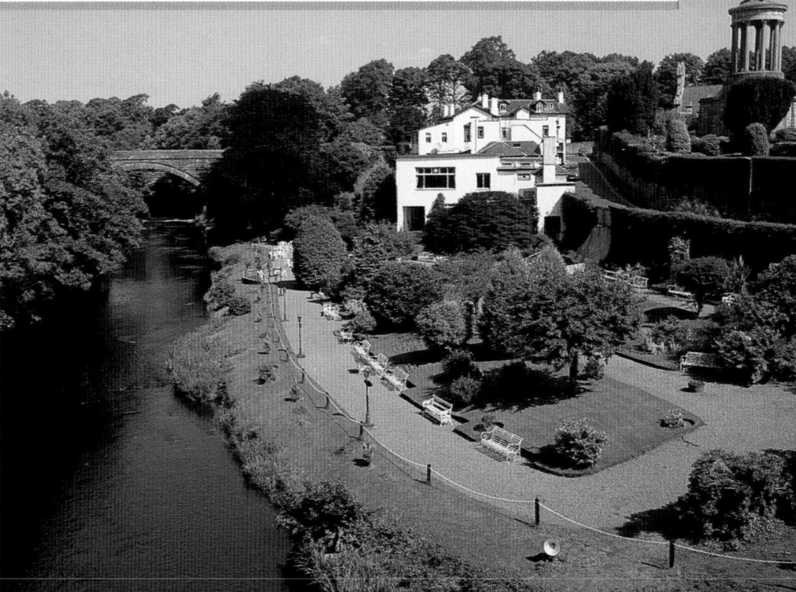

House, then continue to the top of the steps and down to the right. Descend to the road, turn right and cross over. Just short of a large white hotel, go down the steps on the left into Riverside Gardens. Walk around the gardens by the river towards the Auld Brig. Leave by the steps back up to the road, turn right and cross Auld Brig. Continue up the path, under old the railway bridge to the top, swinging right on to the main road.

2 Turn right and follow the main road back over the river. Just over the newer bridge, cross over and turn left, up steps, into Auld Alloway Kirkyard (opposite the parish church) to Burns' parents' graves. Leaving the kirkyard by the steps, turn left and go along the road until level with the Tam O'Shanter Experience. Cross right into Murdoch's Lone and go left immediately beyond a low white pumping station, steeply down to old railway line. Turn left through two tunnels and beyond.

3 Eventually, emerge on the main road at Burton Farm road end. Turn right and follow the road over the old railway, then turn left on the other side into a lane, turning back on itself before swinging right towards the sea. Continue past the estate house on the left to the cottages at the end of the track. Go between the cottages and leave the lane as it swings right, going through a gate and down a field, through a gate to the beach. Turn right along the beach past Greenan Castle and car-park to the river mouth. The path up to the 16th-century castle on Greenan Hill is steep on both sides, and the ruin itself is bricked up. The best view is from the beach.

4 Turn right up the road with the river to the left, to a T-junction, opposite a garden centre. Turn left over the river bridge and cross the road, turning right into Greenfield Avenue. As Greenfield Avenue curves, go left through gates by a lodge into Belleisle Park. Continue with the golf course on the right, through trees and then curve off right to a pets area. Just before this, turn left into a walled garden and carry on into a second garden with a large greenhouse. Leave by a path from the far left corner, up to the rear of Belleisle House Hotel. In the main entrance of the hotel there are magnificent carvings of the Tam O'Shanter story and other works of Burns. Pass in front of a golf shop and in 150yds (136m) turn right across the golf course, following signs to Practice Area.

5 At the path's end, go through green gates to the main road and turn right. Follow past Rozelle Park on the left and Northpark House Hotel on the right, until the road curves right into Alloway. In middle of the village, pass Burns Cottage on the right, where Robert Burns was born in 1759, and continue on the main road (B7024) past the cricket ground to return to Tam O'Shanter Experience on the left.

PREHISTORIC ARRAN

Arran is famed for its prehistoric stones. The most impressive are those on **Machrie Moor** – visible from a great distance in their isolated moorland setting. The site is signed just south of Machrie on the A841, from where the standing stones are reached via an ancient track.

Carn Ban, probably the highest prehistoric site in Arran, is surrounded by conifer plantations, though because it stands high there are views over some of the trees. It is reached by a long and sometimes muddy walk from the A841.

One very large stone circle is **Kilpatrick Dun**, thought to have been a defended farmstead about 1,800 years ago. The quiet and open position and the beautiful view north to the cliffs and fort of Drumadoon combine to make this great ring of stones and turf dike an awe-inspiring place. It is reached by a rough cart-track which starts just outside the farmyard at Kilpatrick Farm.

GLASGOW & LOCH LOMOND

Always famed for its friendliness, Glasgow has become known for its first-class shopping and superb museums and galleries. Shipbuilding, steam locomotive works and other heavy engineering have given way to a vibrant arts and entertainments scene. Exploring the city on foot is the best way to experience the real energy of the place and to appreciate some of the finest Victorian architecture in Britain. The Glasgow School of Art, designed by famous art-nouveau architect Charles Rennie

A walker rests to take in the still beauty of Loch Katrine, looking west towards Loch Arklet

Mackintosh, should not be missed – nor his Willow Tearooms where you can still take afternoon tea. Visitors to Glasgow are often surprised at the number of lovely parks and gardens, including the Botanic Gardens, Bellahouston Park and Pollock Country Park, where the magnificent and eclectic Burrell Collection is housed in a remarkable purpose-built gallery.

In the sprawling Glasgow conurbation you are never more than half an hour away from the countryside. Heading north through Milngavie will take you on a scenic route into the Trossachs, through Aberfoyle, over Dukes Pass, between Lochs Achray and Katrine. The spectacular 10-mile (16-km) long Loch Katrine is evocative of Sir Walter Scott's

The colourful tartan dress of traditional Highland dancers

Visitors crowd the bow of the Sir Walter Scott, *for a trip on Loch Katrine*

Trossachs Drive

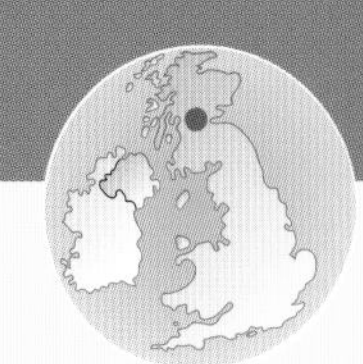

DRIVE

The Trossachs and Loch Lomond

START/FINISH: Callander. On the A84 14 miles (22.5km) northwest of Stirling

DISTANCE: 98 miles (157.5km)

Close to the Lowland cities, here is a stirring Highland landscape of lochs, mountains and forests in the homeland of Rob Roy MacGregor and the characters of Sir Walter Scott, in whose footsteps the first tourists enthusiastically came.

1 Parkland and lush, green meadows border the River Teith in Callander, an ideal tourist centre for the Trossachs. Surrounded by beautiful mountains, lochs and forests, the town is fortunate in having several beauty spots within walking distance, such as the Falls of Bracklinn, the Pass of Leny, and Ben Ledi. Leave Callander on the A84 towards Crianlarich. Continue through the Pass of Leny, through Strathyre and forwards. Due west of Kingshouse Hotel a striking valley leads to the tiny village of Balquhidder and the churchyard where you will find the grave of Rob Roy MacGregor, who died in 1734. At Lochearnhead keep forward on the A85 for Crianlarich.

2 Turn left on to the A82, signed to Glasgow. Continue through Inverarnan to Ardlui at the head of Loch Lomond, then make a 20-mile (32-km) run along its entire western side. Turn off the A82 for Luss, a most attractive lochside village at the mouth of Glen Luss with Victorian sandstone cottages lining the road to the pier. Rejoin the A82 after 2 miles (3km) and in a further 2 miles (3km) pass Duck Bay. At the roundabout, take the A811, signed to Stirling, to reach the edge of Balloch on the banks of Loch Lomond.

3 At the next two roundabouts follow signs for A811 Stirling (second exits) and then pass the turning for Balloch Castle Country Park, an extensive area beside the loch encompassing varying habitats, a walled garden, and lawns for picnics giving wonderful views. A visitor centre gives an insight into the local history and wildlife. Continue on the A811 to Gartocharn, then after 3 miles (5km), at the T-junction, turn left to pass Drymen. Four miles (6.5km) on bear left to join the A81 towards Aberfoyle. In 6 miles (10km) bear left on to the A821 and enter the village of Aberfoyle.

THE WEST HIGHLAND WAY

The 95-mile (153-km) West Highland Way, Scotland's first long-distance footpath, makes the transition from easy lowland walking to the more rugged terrain of the Highlands, on the shores of Loch Lomond.

Starting from Milngavie on the outskirts of Glasgow, the route makes its way north to Fort William, often using ancient and historic routes – drove roads used by cattle dealers to reach market (such as the Devil's Staircase out of Glen Coe), military roads instituted by General Wade to aid in suppressing the clans, old coaching roads and even disused railway lines. Walk all the way – experts recommend going south to north, to build up stamina for the hills – or take a short walk along the route; there is no shortage of spectacular sections, and you may see red deer and, just possibly, golden eagles on the way.

ballad, *The Lady of the Lake* and his novel *Rob Roy*. At the northwest end of the loch in Stronachlar is the graveyard of the Clan MacGregor, not far from Glengyle House, the birthplace of Rob Roy. A short but strenuous hike from the west bank of Loch Achray to the summit of Ben An offers a wonderful view southwards across Loch Katrine and the Trossachs.

Loch Lomond, to the west of the Trossachs, is another popular recreation centre within easy reach of Glasgow. Balloch, with its modern castle, country park and opportunities for boat cruises, sits astride the only natural outlet from the loch. Up the west side is the picturesque village of Luss, while Lomond's east side is quieter, and provides greater opportunities for walking and outdoor pursuits.

The peninsulas and islands of Argyll spill west and south from the Clyde. Rothesay, on the island of Bute, reached by ferry from Wemyss Bay, has a turn-of-the-century atmosphere created by its Victorian houses and decorative Winter Gardens. From Largs you can visit Millport on tiny Great Cumbrae and ferries from Gourock and Ardrossan will take you to Dunoon and the Cowal Peninsula.

CHIC SHOPS IN GLASGOW

There can be few cities in the UK outside London with such a wealth of exclusive shops, designer labels and sheer variety of retail outlets.

Merchant City
Intersperses classy wine bars, abundant restaurants and stockbrokers with exclusive clothes shops such as the Italian Centre, stocking designer labels seen nowhere else in the UK.

Princes Square
Award-winning loggia where Lacoste and Calvin Klein rub shoulders with exclusive leather and jewellery designers, while style-conscious Glaswegians sip cappuccino or cool white wine and watch the world go by.

Buchanan Galleries
The latest addition to the Glasgow shopping experience is this mall attached to the Royal Concert Hall. As well as the usual chain stores and John Lewis, there is Ottokar's bookshop with comfy sofas and a coffee shop to linger for a while.

Glasgow's 'Golden Z'
The three famous shopping streets of Argyle Street, Buchanan Street and Sauchiehall Street, where chain stores and specialist shops continue to multiply.

ARGYLL FOREST PARK

The towering, pine-clad mountains, deep valleys and narrow lochs of the Argyll Forest Park, established more than 60 years ago, are a perfect introduction to the area. You can reach the heart of the park up **Glen Croe**, with the 'Arrocher Alps' to the north, of which Ben Arthur, 'The Cobbler', is the most distinctive peak. From Rest and be Thankful an exciting single-track road descends Hell's Glen to Lochgoilhead, from where there are waymarked walks, including one to the legendary **Rob Roy's Cave**.

Mountain-bikers should head for **Ardgartan** and **Glenbranter**, where they will find signed mountain-bike trails. The latter is also the start point of the delightful **Lauder Forest Walks**, which go through old oak woodland and rare rhododendrons to a series of waterfalls. The best-known of the trails is **Puck's Glen**, crossing many bridges through a steep, tree-lined gorge on paths that zigzag up the mountainside to spectacular viewpoints.

The 53,630 acres (21,705ha) of the park are home to varied wildlife. Only the luckiest visitor will see a golden eagle or a wild cat, but buzzards and sparrowhawks are easier to spot, and you may get a glimpse of deer, foxes or even the rare red squirrel.

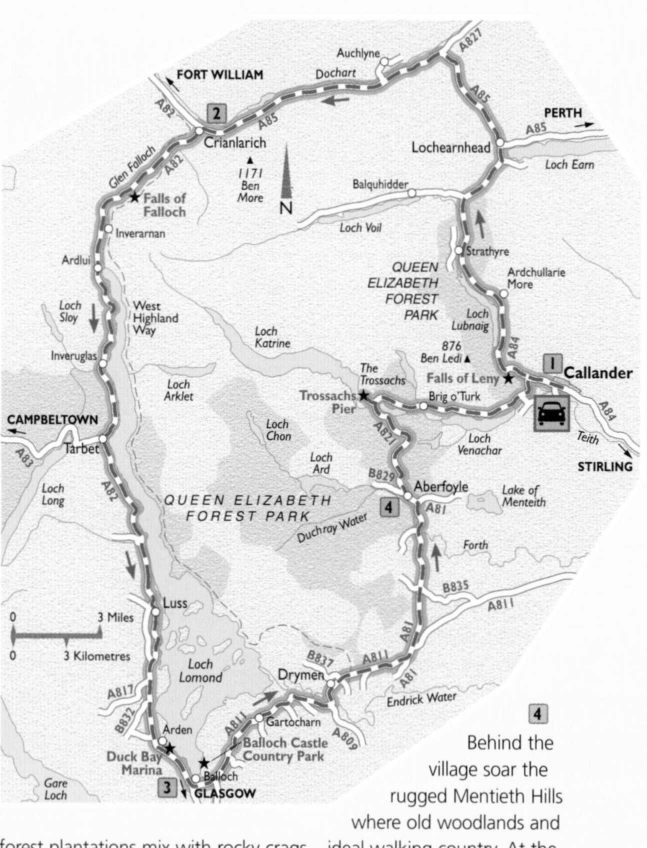

4 Behind the village soar the rugged Mentieth Hills where old woodlands and forest plantations mix with rocky crags – ideal walking country. At the end of the village stay on the A821 signed Trossachs and Callander, to take The Duke's Pass Road, a 5.5 mile (9km) long route through grand Highland scenery: mountains, forests and chattering burns, and shortly pass the entrance to the Queen Elizabeth Forest Park Visitor Centre with its network of walks. In 4 miles (6.5km) turn left for Loch Katrine. There are no public roads to disturb the peace of lovely Loch Katrine, but the elegant little 1900 steamer *Sir Walter Scott* (summer only) cruises from Trossachs Pier and gives visitors an appreciation of some of the Trossach's most secret and beautiful places. Return along the same road and keep forward with the A821 towards Callander. Pass Brig o'Turk and then cross the River Leny and turn right on to the A84, to return to Callander.

The view across Loch Katrine and the Trossachs from the summit of Ben An

THE MULL OF KINTYRE TO FORT WILLIAM

Tarbert, with its colour-washed houses, sits on the narrow neck of land joining the Kintyre peninsula to the mainland. Take the road down the wind-swept west fringe of Kintyre, with wide views over to Jura and Islay to the handsome port of Campbeltown, with the late 15th-century Campbeltown Cross and the unexpected 1913 art-deco front of the 256-seat Picture House.

To the north of Kintyre, Inveraray, on the shores of Loch Fyne, is a fine example of town planning, created by the 3rd Duke of Argyll in the 1740s. The little town is stylish, with a wide main street of white-painted houses running up to the classical kirk (church). In days gone by the harbour bustled with steam puffers shuttling cargo from Inveraray and Loch Fyne via the Crinan Canal to and from the islands. The canal ends at the picturesque Crinan Harbour, with views over the Sound of Jura and a cluster of islands.

Jura is dominated by the three peaks – the Paps of Jura. Neolithic standing stones and cairns here date back to 7000 BC. Islay is famed for the distinctive peaty flavour its water imparts to Islay whisky and for the abundance of birds, including the rare native chough. Gigha, east of Islay, is the home of the Ogham Stone, with its indecipherable inscription. Scarba, remote and

FERRIES AND BOAT TRIPS

You can't get far in Western Scotland without needing to catch a ferry, especially to its 130 or so inhabited islands. Many of the shorter routes are operated by local owners and provide an excellent service.

Caledonian MacBrayne – CalMac – is the name you will come across most. The company was formed in 1973 when MacBraynes, operators of shipping services mostly to the Western Isles since 1851, joined forces with the Clyde-based Caledonian Steam Packet Company. CalMac sails to 23 islands and operates more than 30 ferries in a huge range of sizes, from the largest vessel on the Ullapool to Stornoway route to the tiny four-car ferry that plies between Tarbert and Portavadie.

Look for signs on the harbour fronts of the countless boat trips around the islands organised by local operators. The cathedral-like interior of **Fingal's Cave** on **Staffa**, immortalised in music by Mendelssohn, is just one of the attractions which can be visited on a boat trip, weather permitting.

The Ullapool to Stornoway ferry

Kilchurn Castle, built in 1440, perched on the banks of Loch Awe

Benderloch Cycle Ride

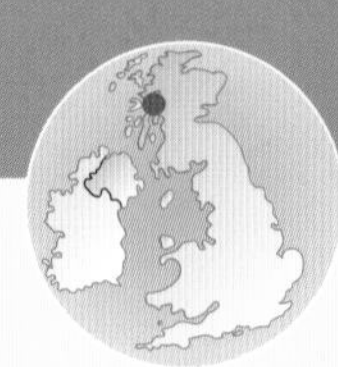

CYCLE RIDE

Benderloch, Loch Creran and Loch Etive

START/FINISH: Benderloch. 7 miles (11km) north of Oban
DISTANCE: 17 miles (27.5km)
GRADIENT: gently undulating
PARKING: car-park on the A828, at the phone box opposite the petrol station

This is a ride to give you a taste of the Scottish west coast and sea loch scenery, and is almost entirely on well-surfaced minor roads. The route is mainly gently undulating except for a short climb through the forest; but the rewards for that are superb views of Loch Etive plus a fine descent. You might even glimpse a golden eagle in this area.

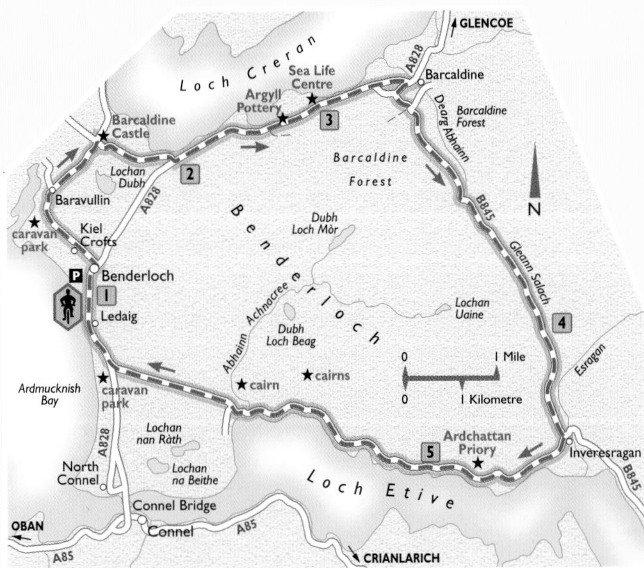

MOUNTAIN POWER

Ben Cruachan holds a secret – Scotland's first big pump storage power station. The visitor centre explains how water from an artificial loch high up on the mountain is fed down through the rock to turbines within the mountain. Off-peak power is used to pump the water back up to the reservoir. The highlight of a visit is a ride down tunnels to the huge turbine hall. The plants you'll see along the way are tropical species, which thrive happily in the artificial light, heat and humidity of the tunnels.

uninhabited, is separated from Jura by the treacherous whirlpool of Corrievreckan. The flood tide rushes through the narrow sound at speeds of up to 8.5 knots before reaching a great pyramidal rock rising from the sea-bed 719ft (219m) below to a depth of only 95ft (29m), forming the great whirlpool. The sound of its raw natural power can be heard over 10 miles (16km) away.

Kilmartin village, at the foot of Loch Awe, overlooks a remarkable prehistoric site. There are cup-and-ring marked rocks, tall, flat-faced standing stones, burial cairns and a crescent of boulders with carvings of axeheads and, possibly, a boat's keel. Glacial action reversed the waters of Loch Awe, the longest loch in Scotland, to flow through the dramatic Pass of Brander instead of through Kilmartin Glen. You can take a steamboat trip from Lochawe village which includes the impressive ruins of Kilchurn Castle. Nearby Inverliever Forest offers walks and spectacular high viewpoints over the loch.

At Fort William, look out for 'Neptune's Staircase' on the Caledonian Canal. It is a magnificent series of eight linked locks, at Banavie, designed by the great engineer Thomas Telford. Fort William is on the edge of the Highlands and most visitors head for the mountains, either on foot or, more easily, by the cable cars that climb the Nevis range to the north of the town or you can take the scenic West Highland Railway to Mallaig.

1 Turn left out the car-park, heading north, and in half a mile (800m) bear left on to a minor road signed to South Shian. Follow this road, passing Tralee Bay Caravan Site and Kintaline Craft Centre, then keep right to reach a crossroads in a mile (1.5km). Turn right, go uphill, and Barcaldine Castle is on your left. The 16th-century home of the Campbells of Barcaldine on the shore of Loch Creran, this restored castle was the last of seven castles built by Black Duncan to be held in Campbell hands, and to be associated with the Appin Murder and Glen Coe Massacre. Continue, to meet the A828.

2 Turn left and continue for 2.5 miles (4km), to pass the Argyll Pottery (potters at work). Shortly, reach the Sea Life Centre. In a beautiful location on the sea loch, this is a marvellous place to view the underwater life of Britain's coastline – without getting your feet wet. There is a touch tank, and in summer you may see young seals awaiting release back into the wild. There is always something going on with daily talks and feeding demonstrations.

3 Continue on the A828 to a main junction in Barcaldine. Turn right on to the B845, signed to Bonawe. This is a narrow road with passing places, which climbs steadily through Barcaldine Forest, offering plenty of picnic sites beside the burn.

4 The descent from here is steep, with superb views of Loch Etive and the adjoining hills. Look out for the cattle grid at the bottom of the slope. Where the main road leads sharply left, turn right, signed to North Connel. Continue along Loch Etiveside to reach Ardchattan Priory. The entrance to the priory is at the far end of the wall, to the right. The old granite house of Ardchattan began its existence in the 13th century, when a priory and church were built here for the French Valliscaulian order. Significantly enlarged at the end of the 15th century, the priory later changed hands and part of the house became a family residence. Ancient carved tombstones can still be seen in the remains of the choir and transepts. The attractive gardens here are well worth visiting (by appointment only).

5 Continue along the road which hugs the shore of the loch, until you climb gently away from the water and reach a junction. Look out for the chambered cairns on the slopes to your right, evidence that this part of Argyll has been occupied since earliest times. Keep straight on (do not go to North Connel) along this minor road for 1.5 miles (2.5km) to reach the A828. Turn right and continue to Benderloch, to return to the car-park.

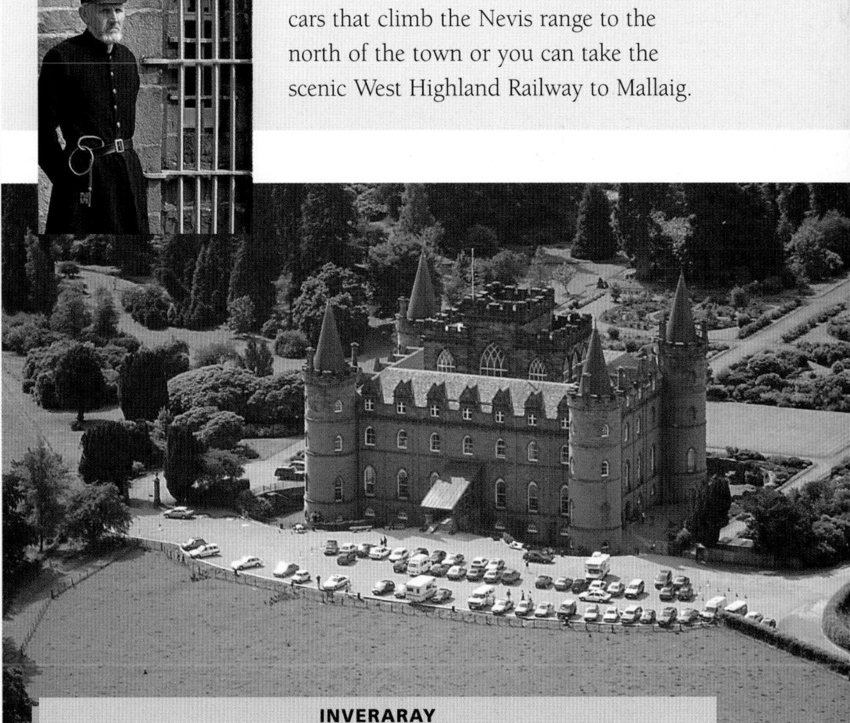

INVERARAY

Inveraray Castle, now home to the 12th Duke and his family, is a neo-Gothic building with pointed sash windows and slatey-blue pepperpot towers. Inside, its most spectacular feature is the Armoury Hall, the tallest room in Scotland, which is dramatically adorned with pikes, axes, swords and muskets. The castle includes splendid state rooms with ornate gilded plasterwork, fine furniture and Campbell family portraits. Moored on the loch side is the three-masted vessel *Arctic Penguin*, upon which you can take a turn at steering, ring the ship's telegraph, visit the engine room and watch archive film of old sailing and steam ships.

Inveraray Jail, near the kirk, has thrown open its doors to more willing visitors. In the semicircular courtroom you can be part of the crowd hearing a trial, and in the 19th-century cells you can try out canvas hammocks and turn the crank machine.

EDINBURGH & THE EASTERN LOWLANDS

MAP AND KEY

Edinburgh Walk

Fife Cycle Ride

Strathmore Drive

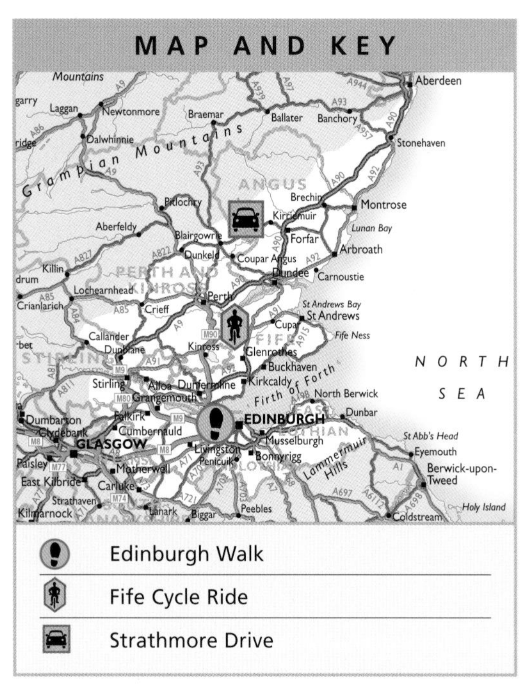

At the very heart of Scotland, this area includes three ancient capitals, two great rivers and hundreds of burns, and two royal residences. This is a land of battles and medieval splendour, of intellectual sophistication in the old universities of St Andrews and Edinburgh, of ancient trade routes from the port of Leith and the Tay, of fishing and farming. The architecture ranges from rugged castles on rocky strongholds to picturesque fishing villages, from the 19th-century industrial tenements of Dundee to the Georgian terraces of Edinburgh. With the re-establishment of the Scottish Parliament, this has once more become the political centre of Scotland.

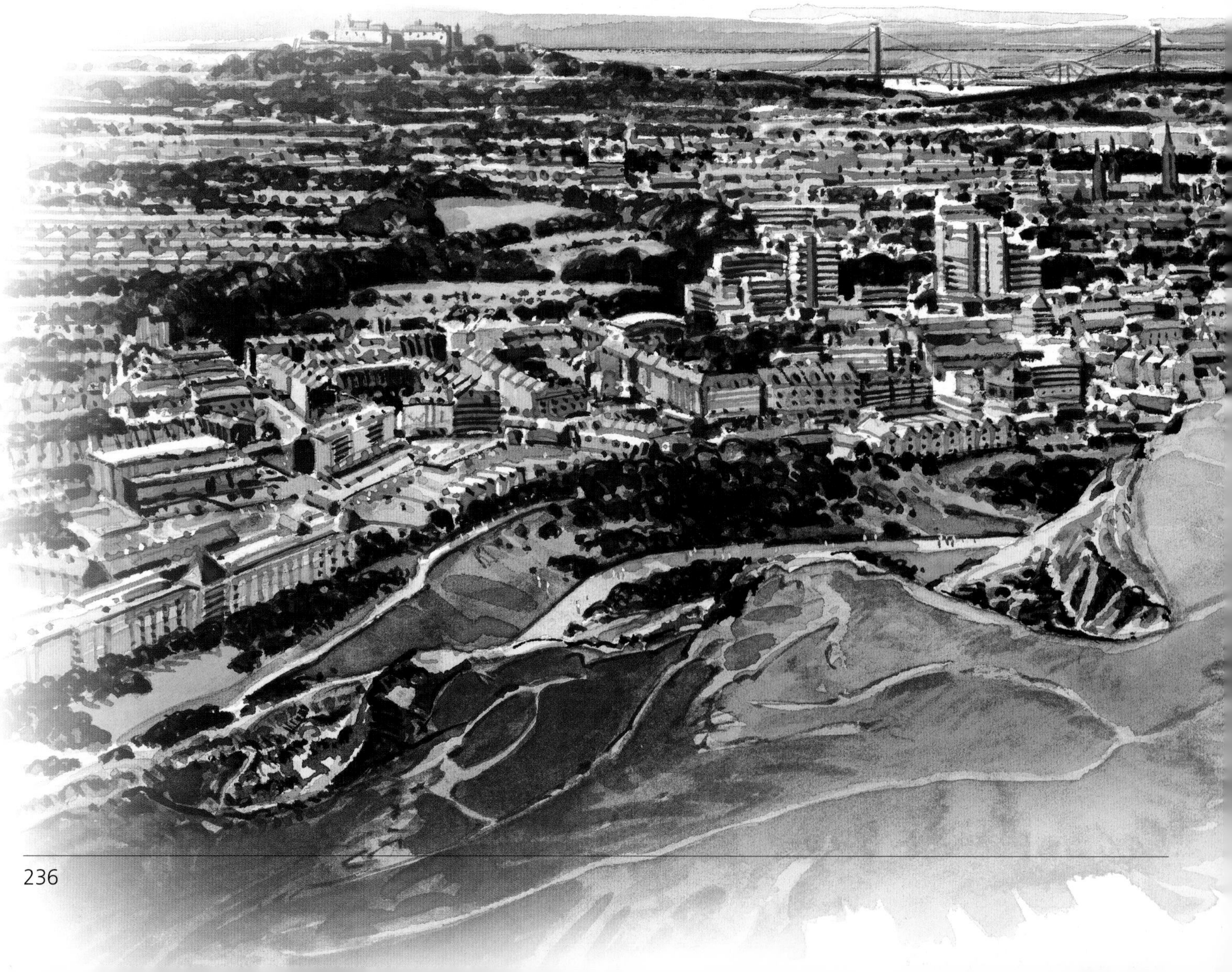

KILLIECRANKIE

The narrow, heavily wooded Pass of Killiecrankie, near Pitlochry, was the site of the last victory of the Jacobite Highlanders before their final defeat at Dunkeld. Under the leadership of Bonnie Dundee, the Highlanders routed the English, leaving the pass a bloody and terrifying scene. One Highlander escaped pursuing Redcoats in a spectacular jump from Soldier's Leap. The visitor centre describes the battle in detail and introduces the varied wildlife of the pass.

Fishing at Soldier's Leap, Killiecrankie

EDINBURGH CASTLE

Home to monarchs, scene of banquets and siege, this ancient rock is at the heart not only of Scotland's capital but of its history, and the Great Hall is still used for receptions by the Scottish First Minister. The ancient Honours of Scotland, held in the Crown Room, are the oldest crown jewels in Europe.

RRS *DISCOVERY*, DUNDEE

The pride of the Panmuir yard, where she was built in 1901 for the polar expeditions of Captain Robert Falcon Scott, the Royal Research Ship *Discovery* lay for years rotting on the Thames Embankment in London. She was finally returned to her birthplace, restored and housed at the purpose-built Discovery Point, and is now a major tourist attraction.

Angus Glens

Of the five glorious Glens of Angus to the north of Dundee, Glen Clova is probably the most picturesque. Jock's Road, leading through the mountains to Braemar, is spectacular. The path clings, precariously at times, to the edge of the hill, the water runs far below, and as you climb, the view of the glen falls away below you.

THE FIRTH OF FORTH & EDINBURGH

Edinburgh, Scotland's historic capital, is a city built on hills, and from its high crests and ridges you can overlook its steeples, twisting medieval wynds and the neat symmetry of its delightful Georgian crescents and squares. The Old Town brims with curiosity and history among the tall tenements and public buildings set in cobbled streets, while the New Town is an architectural delight of Georgian town houses among courtyards and crescents. Princes Street and its spacious gardens can be considered a demarcation line between old and new.

Edinburgh Castle dominates the city from every angle and over a million people visit it every year. At the bottom of the spine of volcanic rock known as the Royal Mile sits Holyrood Palace, home of Scottish monarchs since the 16th century. It is the Queen's official residence in Scotland and the state and historic apartments are open to the public. Beyond the palace, Holyrood Park, dominated by the great volcanic plug of Arthur's Seat, is an incredible open space to find in the centre of a city. There are paths for walking or cycling, rock-climbers and abseilers can practise their skills on Salisbury Crags, while the less energetic can watch the swans on the pond.

The Queen's former official residence at sea is now berthed at the Port of Leith. Visitors to *Britannia* can peep into the Queen's bedroom and other private rooms as well as the crew's quarters, the public rooms, the bridge and the engine room. To the west along the Forth, South Queensferry, with its 12th-century abbey, sits below the

BO'NESS AND KINNEIL RAILWAY

This is one of the best of the small independent railway lines. Situated in the town of Bo'ness on the Forth, it is the largest centre for vintage trains in Scotland. Three miles (5km) of track lead to Birkhill, where you can visit the **Birkhill Clay Mine** or stroll in the Avon Gorge before the old steam train departs for the return journey.

THE FORTH BRIDGES

Opened in 1890 at a cost of £3,177,000, the Forth railway bridge was considered the 'Eighth Wonder of the World'. Construction began in 1882 under Sir John Fowler and Benjamin Baker, and at its height it employed 4,600 men. The viaduct, standing 157ft (48m) above the water, is 8,296ft (2,528m) long, comprising 53,000 tons of steel that require 7,000 gallons (32,000 litres) of paint. It featured in an exciting episode of John Buchan's classic novel *The Thirty-Nine Steps*. The 1.5-mile (2.4-km) long suspension bridge for motor traffic was opened in 1964. The magnificent scale of the Forth road and rail bridges can best be appreciated from the foreshore at South Queensferry.

Edinburgh Walk

WALK

Edinburgh's Literary Past

START/FINISH: Edinburgh. Waverley railway station
DISTANCE: 5 miles (8km)
GRADIENT: a few short, steep sections
TERRAIN/PATHS: city streets; pavements throughout
PARKING: Waverley Station

A walk through the medieval closes and Georgian terraces of Scotland's capital reveals a world-class literary heritage.

1 From Waverley Station, turn right, then left into Princes Street. Walk down to the Scott Monument, cross, continue down Princes Street, then right into Frederick Street. Take the second turning on your left, George Street, then next left into Castle Street.

2 New Town's literary associations are numerous. No. 30 Castle Street was the birthplace of Kenneth Grahame, author of *The Wind in the Willows*, and No. 39 the home of Sir Walter Scott. Walk down, cross, turning right into Rose Street, and continue to the end. Turn right and right again, into George Street. Cross, turn left down North Castle Street to Queen Street. Cross, turn left, then right down Wemyss Place and right into Heriot Row. No. 17 was the home of Robert Louis Stevenson.

3 Walk down Heriot Row to Dundas Street, turn left, cross, then turn right into Great King Street. Cross at the end, then turn sharp right into Nelson Street, then left into Drummond Place. Follow Drummond Place into London Street, then turn right, up Broughton Street. Keep on to the main road junction at the top of the hill, then turn left into Picardy Place.

4 Cross the road opposite the Playhouse, turn left, then right at the roundabout with the clock and immediately right up Blenheim Place. Take the path on the right by Greenside Church, climbing up to Calton Hill. Taking the left-hand path, walk across towards the Edinburgh Experience and descend by the path leading to Waterloo Place and the closes of the Old Town. Here is Canongate Kirk, where Robert Burns' love, 'Clarinda', is buried, and a spot outside St Giles Cathedral marking the site of the prison which gave its name to Scott's novel, *The Heart of Midlothian*.

5 Turn right, cross, turn left at the Balmoral Hotel and up North Bridge.

TOP FIVE CASTLES

Edinburgh Castle

There has been a fortification on this great volcanic rock since Celtic times and the tiny Norman St Margaret's Chapel, the oldest building in Edinburgh, has stood intact for more than 900 years. In the castle's cellar is the colossal cannon Mons Meg, which fired its massive stone cannonballs at the Battle of Flodden. The magnificent Great Hall is still used for receptions by the Scottish First Minister.

Stirling Castle

Stirling Castle, 'the key to Scotland', has an equally formidable setting, on a great rock overlooking a wide plain where many battles, including Bannockburn in 1314, were fought. Most of the present buildings are late medieval, and Mary, Queen of Scots was crowned here in 1543.

Doune Castle

This awe-inspiring 14th- to 15th-century castle, seat of the Earls of Moray, is situated between the rivers Teith and Ardoch. The present Earl has an unrivalled collection of vintage cars at Doune Motor Museum.

Glamis Castle

The childhood home of Queen Elizabeth, the Queen Mother, and the legendary setting of Shakespeare's tragic tale of *Macbeth*, Glamis Castle has been a royal residence since 1372.

Balmoral

By the mid-19th century the 'Scottish Baronial' style was all the rage among the landed gentry. Most famous of all is Queen Victoria's Balmoral, a huge square keep with a comfortable country house attached.

Balmoral Castle, summer retreat of the Queen and the Duke of Edinburgh

Forth bridges. Queensferry was the ferry point on the Forth from 1169 until the opening of the road bridge in 1964. The Scottish Mining Museum at Prestongrange is at the oldest documented coal-mining site in Britain, which has been worked for some 800 years. Follow the coal trail to the Lady Victoria Colliery at Newtongrange to complete the story.

Close to Newtongrange is Rosslyn Chapel, a tiny and atmospheric medieval chapel perched above wooded Rosslyn Glen. There are many fine walks in the glen below, between the half-ruined Rosslyn Castle at one end and the cairn marking the site of the Battle of Roslin at the other.

West of Edinburgh, walk, cycle or take a slow boat along the Union Canal, the scenic route from Fountainbridge to Falkirk. Linlithgow has a canal museum and lots of cruising information. Linlithgow Palace, where Mary, Queen of Scots was born, was destroyed by fire in 1746, but the roofless ruin still has spiral staircases, stately rooms, the Great Hall and a brewery.

From ancient geological sites, medieval churches and castles to the industrial heritage of coal mining and canals, the mark of time is deeply ingrained on this part of Scotland.

THE EDINBURGH FESTIVAL

Founded in 1947, the three-week festival for the visual and performing arts transforms Edinburgh in August and September. There are two distinct sides. The 'official', with set programmes for opera, ballet, dance and theatre, and the 'fringe', informal music, theatre, dance and comedy in venues of all sorts from clubs to shops to the great outdoors. The city buzzes with street theatre, buskers, traders and cosmopolitan crowds at pavement cafés.

The Castle Esplanade is the venue for the world-famous Edinburgh Military Tattoo, a dramatic, floodlit programme of music, marching and historical re-enactments. The Tattoo and the final night open-air concert and firework display are sold out early, so make sure you book in plenty of time.

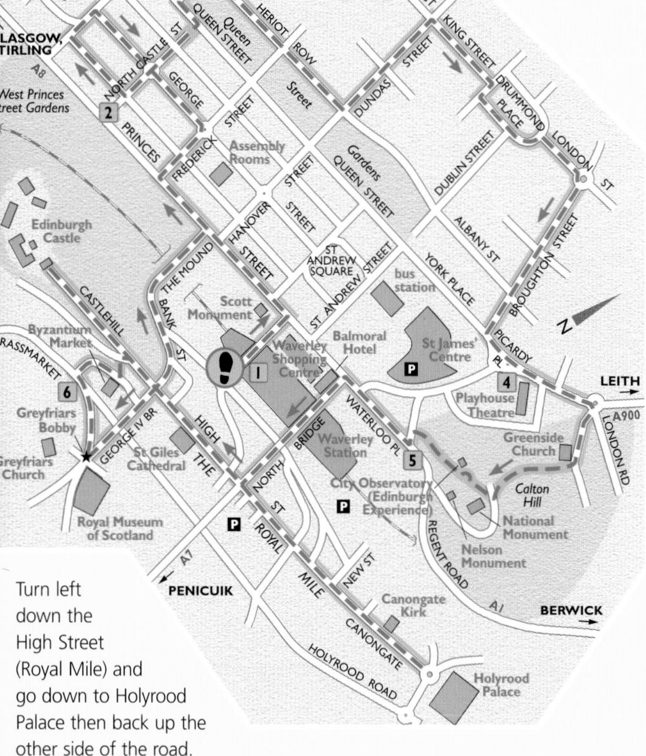

Turn left down the High Street (Royal Mile) and go down to Holyrood Palace then back up the other side of the road. Going back down the Royal Mile there is James' Court, where Dr Johnson stayed with James Boswell, Lady Stair's Close, where Robert Burns stayed, and Brodie's Close, named after Deacon Brodie who inspired Stevenson's *The Strange Case of Dr Jekyll and Mr Hyde*. Turn left along Melbourne Place (George IV Bridge). Cross and walk to the statue of Greyfriars Bobby. Sharp right down Candlemaker Row, and left into Grassmarket.

6 Go right up West Bow into Victoria Street. Opposite Byzantium Market, go up the steps leading to Castlehill and the castle. Walk up to the Castle Esplanade, then return down the hill of Lawnmarket to Bank Street on the left. Turn left, following the road down to Princes Street. Turn right and walk back to Waverley Station.

Crowds gather on Fringe Sunday at Holyrood Park, during the Edinburgh Festival

STIRLING & THE KINGDOM OF FIFE

Loch Leven by Kinross, an ideal spot for fishing, bird-watching or a quiet cycle ride

This area stretches from the major battlegrounds of Scotland's history, on the wide plain below the ramparts of Stirling Castle, to the fishing villages of the East Neuk of Fife and the ancient university town of St Andrews. The Lomond Hills at the centre provide a superb vantage point over the patchwork landscape of Fife.

Once the lowest bridging point on the River Forth, Stirling was for centuries the capital of Scotland. In past times the narrow bridge was a strategic gateway between North and South. Stirling Castle, like Edinburgh, is perched atop the plug of an extinct volcano. The castle-cum-royal palace, with embellished façades in the French style, was much favoured by the Stuart monarchs, and Mary, Queen of Scots was crowned here in 1543.

Until the Reformation, the small town of Dunblane was a city of power and influence with a cathedral. Restored in the late 19th century, its origins go back to 1240. The caves on the riverside walk to the Bridge of Allan are said to be where Robert Louis Stevenson sought inspiration for his books.

Kinross on the banks of Loch Leven is surrounded by rich farmland and hills. Loch Leven is world renowned for its fishing, and the RSPB reserve at Vane Farm on the south side of the loch has hides for observing migrant geese and duck. Close to the centre of the town, Kinross House is a Palladian-style mansion built in 1690 and noted for its formal gardens and yew hedges.

Tucked beneath the Lomond Hills, the tiny Royal Burgh of Falkland has over a hundred listed buildings, with twisting wynds and courtyards between the cottages and sandstone town houses of the 17th to 19th centuries. Its fame and influence were at their height in the 16th and 17th centuries, when the turreted, Renaissance-style Falkland Palace was the favourite hunting lodge of the Stuart monarchs. Royal monograms decorate the King's

FIGHTING FOR FREEDOM

William Wallace was a resistance fighter and appointed Guardian of Scotland. However, his great victory in the Battle of Stirling Bridge in 1297 was short-lived. He was later captured and executed in London in 1305. The **National Wallace Monument** (above) was built in 1860. The 246-step climb to the top is rewarded with panoramic views to the Ochill Hills and across seven battlefields. In the tower, Wallace's massive double-handed broadsword is a prized possession.

Robert the Bruce, born in 1274 of Norman ancestry, with lands in England, declared himself for Scotland and was crowned king in 1306. Even though defeated, excommunicated and outlawed, his guerrilla warfare campaign over many years culminated in victory at Bannockburn in 1314, despite the fact that Edward II's army was ten times larger than the Scots' force. The **Bannockburn Heritage Centre** includes an exhibition on the battle, outlining the confusion in the English army in the marshlands. The victory resulted in the surrender of Stirling Castle and recognition by the pope of Robert the Bruce's kingship, culminating in Scottish independence in 1328.

Fife Cycle Ride

CYCLE RIDE

Tannochbrae Trail

START/FINISH: Falkland. Small town on the A912, 4 miles (6km) north of Glenrothes

DISTANCE: 15 miles (24km)

GRADIENT: mainly level

ROADS: mostly country roads, following the Kingdom of Fife Millennium Cycle Way

PARKING: parking signed from South Street

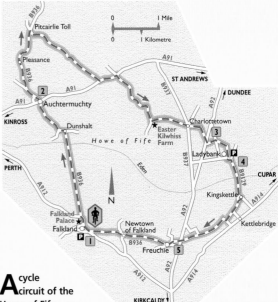

0 1 Mile
0 1 Kilometre
Pitcairlie Toll
Pleasance
2 Auchtermuchty
KINROSS
Dunshalt
PERTH
ST ANDREWS
DUNDEE
Easter Kilwhiss Farm
Howe of Fife
Charlottetown 3
Ladybank 4
CUPAR
Kingskettle
Kettlebridge
Eden
N
Falkland Palace
Falkland 1
Newtown of Falkland
Freuchie 5
KIRKCALDY
A91 A92 A912 A914 B936 B937 B9129

A cycle circuit of the Howe of Fife – a patchwork of fields, meadows, tiny farms and villages forming the fertile farming area of central Fife – on the trail of Dr Findlay, Mary, Queen of Scots and the Singing Kettle.

1 Falkland became an important place in the 14th century when the Stuart monarchy acquired Falkland Palace and transformed it into one of the finest Renaissance buildings in Britain. The beautiful Chapel Royal

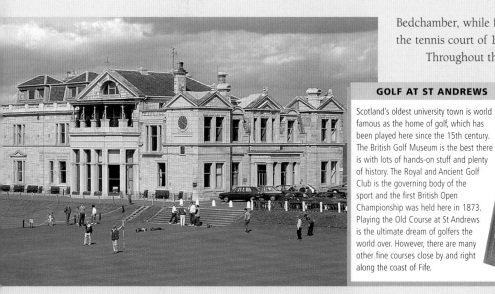

Bedchamber, while fine Flemish tapestries hang in the chapel and the tennis court of 1439 is the oldest in Britain.

Throughout the Middle Ages, St Andrews was the spiritual capital and became Scotland's seat of learning, with the nation's first university. It is best known today for golf. However, if golf is not your scene, take a walk around the historic streets to the great cathedral, once the largest in Scotland. It is an impressive ruin, particularly beautiful at twilight in half silhouette.

Contrasting with sophisticated St Andrews, the coastline of the East Neuk of Fife is dotted with a string of little fishing villages. Quaint cottages with red-tiled roofs and crow-stepped cables perch around secluded harbours. Crail is without a doubt the prettiest, while Anstruther and Pittenweem are still regular working ports. Anstruther is home to the Scottish Fisheries Museum, where the entire history of fishing in Scotland unfolds.

Political power, royal patronage, religious and cultural supremacy, rich farmland and fishing made the area around Scotland's ancient capital prosperous and influential. This legacy is evident in the countryside and buildings of Stirling and Fife.

GOLF AT ST ANDREWS

Scotland's oldest university town is world famous as the home of golf, which has been played here since the 15th century. The British Golf Museum is the best there is with lots of hands-on stuff and plenty of history. The Royal and Ancient Golf Club is the governing body of the sport and the first British Open Championship was held here in 1873. Playing the Old Course at St Andrews is the ultimate dream of golfers the world over. However, there are many other fine courses close by and right along the coast of Fife.

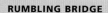

RUMBLING BRIDGE

This wayside site, some 7 miles (11km) west of Kinross, is a long-time favourite, especially after heavy rains. The River Devon dashes over waterfalls through a deep cleft beneath the bridge, which curiously has been built over an earlier crossing, and there are footpaths and walkways along the side of the ravine. The strange 'rumbles' emanating from 'the Devil's Mill' are caused by stones rubbing together in the depths of the gorge.

and King's Bedchamber are its most notable features, and it is also home to the oldest royal tennis court in the country (1539). Splendid gardens surround the palace. From the car-park, make your way back to South Street, and then the A912. Turn left down the A912, heading north on New Road until you turn right on to the B936 for Auchtermuchty. Go through the linear village of Dunshalt and at Auchtermuchty turn left onto the A91 at a T-junction. Shortly, turn right, uphill, following the Tannochbrae Tea Room sign. Auchtermuchty, originally a small agricultural community, was given a Royal Charter in 1517 due to its proximity to Falkland Palace, which allowed it to hold a weekly market and trade in commodities, including wine, cloth and candlewax. The town is also the location of fictional Tannochbrae from the television series *Dr Findlay's Case Book*. You will find the Flying Dutchman pub from the series, it's actually the village post office, and the tearoom is just past it on the left.

2 Return to the A91, turn left and left again, following signs for Newburgh, on to the B936. Climb, relatively steeply, to Pitcairlie Toll and turn right on to a single-track road. Continue climbing for fine views of the Howe of Fife. Cycle downhill through woodland to the T-junction with the busy A91. Turn left here for about half a mile (800m), before turning right on to the road signed Charlottetown. Follow the road left at Easter Kilwhiss Farm, keep ahead at the crossroads in Charlottetown and soon reach the T-junction with the A92.

3 Take care crossing this road then follow the cycle/footpath sign into a housing estate and on to a road. Turn right at the T-junction and follow the road to Ladybank station.

4 Go under the rail bridge and follow the Kingdom of Fife Millennium Cycle Way signs. After nearly 1 mile (1.5km) reach Kingskettle. Turn right into Main Street before the church, past the Singing Kettle shop and right again at the T-junction. Kingskettle seems an unlikely tourist village, yet every year people come here to visit the Singing Kettle shop in Main Street where the children's television favourites are based. On leaving Kingskettle, turn right at the next T-junction, under the rail bridge.

5 At the crossroads, outside Freuchie, take care crossing the busy main road (A92) into the village. At the junction near the Albert Tavern, turn right and follow the signs for Falkland. Pass the Lomond Hills Hotel on the left and continue through farmland to Newton of Falkland, and on to Falkland itself to return to the car-park.

Freshly caught crab and lobster can be bought at the harbour in the coastal town of Crail

THE FIRTH OF TAY TO THE MOUTH OF THE DEE

Rising in the Hills of Breadalbane, the River Tay dominates this area, moving more water than the Severn and Thames combined. It is world famous for salmon and the coveted wild pearls from the freshwater mussel.

At Aberfeldy the Tay is crossed by the handsome Wade's Bridge, with its four obelisks, begun by General Wade in 1733. To the west of the town, a water-driven mill is open to visitors, while to the north a nature trail along the banks of the Urlar Burn to the Falls of Moness passes through a rare example of native Scottish birch woodland, the Birks of Aberfeldy, celebrated in a poem by Burns.

Dunkeld, a few miles downriver, was an ancient cathedral city on the edge of the Highlands. It is now a well-preserved historic village at the centre of a network of riverside and woodland walks, harbouring many rare species, including red squirrel and capercaillie. Seek out Ossian's Hall, a tiny classical folly overlooking a waterfall, and Ossian's Cave, a roofed cell, ingeniously built on natural rock.

CAITHNESS GLASS

Since it was founded in 1961 in Wick, the world has taken to the hand-made paperweights of Caithness Glass and the company now has a second factory and visitor centre 2 miles (3km) north of the centre of Perth. It incorporates a popular viewing gallery, where visitors can watch the famous paperweights being made by craftsmen in abstract and modern designs, based on millefiori. The visitor centre tells the story of the coloured and engraved glassware, including jewellery made from intricate multicoloured glass canes.

Just before the estuary, the city of Perth maintains the atmosphere of a county town. Kinnoull Hill, overlooking the 'Fair City' offers spectacular views to the Highlands, and across the two green parks beside the river. Bells Cherrybank Gardens, covering 18 acres (7ha), incorporates the National Heather Collection, while Branklyn Garden, on the eastern side of the town, is noted for its rhododendrons and alpines. Just 2 miles (3km) north of Perth, Scone Palace is an imposing neo-Gothic fortified palace, splendidly furnished with exquisite collections, which include porcelain, china, ivory, clocks and needlework. Nearby Moot Hill is where the Scottish

FORFAR BRIDIES

The town of Forfar is famed for the bridie, a huge pasty made of flaky pastry, amply filled with a tasty meat and onion mixture. Like its close cousin the Cornish pasty, it originally served as a substantial midday meal to carry out to the fields. Buy them in bakers' and butchers' shops where they make their own, but avoid the limp mass-produced version.

Distant views reward a walk up Kinnoull Hill to the stone table

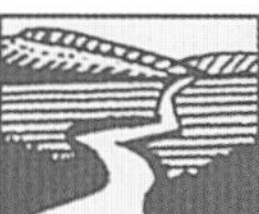

Strathmore Drive

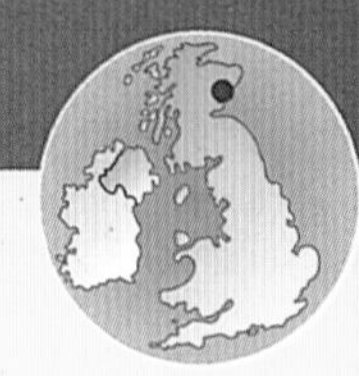

DRIVE

Strathmore and the Glens of Angus

START/FINISH: Kirriemuir. On the A926 between Forfar and Blairgowrie

DISTANCE: 68 miles (109km)

The lowlands meet the Highlands here, where the rich arable farms of Strathmore look north to the hills and forests of the Angus Glens. In this land of contrasts, one of Scotland's grandest castles is near tiny hamlets which the casual tourist never sees.

1 The creator of Peter Pan, Sir James Barrie, was born in Kirriemuir, a textile town of warm red sandstone buildings, in 1860. His boyhood home, 9 Brechin Road, is a fascinating museum containing manuscripts, mementoes and some of the original furnishings. A hilltop park in the town features one of only three camera obscuras in the whole of Scotland and offers superb panoramic views. Leave Kirriemuir on the B955, signed to Blairgowrie, Glen Cova and Glen Prosen, to reach Dykehead. Turn left on to a minor road towards Prosen. In 1 mile (1.5km) pass the memorial to the South Polar explorers, Captain Scott and Edward Wilson, who planned their tragic final expedition here, and enter Glen Prosen.

2 One of the quietest of the Angus Glens, Prosen has steeply sloping fields, forests and heather grouse moors. After 4.5 miles (7km) turn left towards Kirriemuir and cross the river bridge, then turn left to follow the west bank of Prosen Water. In 5miles (8km), at the crossroads, turn right for Glenisla, and in 1 mile (1.5km) turn right again. Continue through Balintore, one of the highest points in the Angus foothills with views to Strathmore and the faraway Sidlaw Hills, and, at the T-junction, turn right on to the B951.

3 Pass through Kirkton of Glenisla and in 4 miles (6.5km) veer left, signed Glenshee and Braemar. Ascend 1,200ft to enter Glen Shee then, at Cray, bear right to cross Shee Water. Shortly, turn left on to the A93 Perth road, continue forward for 8 miles (13km) then turn left at Bridge of Cally on to a minor road, signed to Drimmie. Re-cross the river to pass through Netherton, a riverside hamlet with a churchyard overlooking the

DID YOU KNOW?

D C Thomson, publisher of the *Beano*, the *Dandy*, *The People's Friend*, *The Scots Magazine* and *The Sunday Post*, is based in Dundee. The popular comic character Dennis the Menace actually originated from a music hall song:

Dennis the Menace from Venice,
He's a gay gondolier
Wears gold rings in his ears …

After the editor of the *Beano* got a hold of it, all that remained was the name, attached to the red-and black-striped sweater of Britain's favourite rascal.

kings were crowned on the Stone of Scone from the 9th century until its removal to London by Edward I in 1297.

Dundee, at the mouth of the estuary, straggles untidily along the river, its two distinctive bridges reaching out over the broad stretch of water to Fife. In the surrounding countryside, the berry fields, which used to supply the jam factories, now allow you to pick your own fruit. The Verdant Works, a jute mill which once employed 50,000 people, has been restored and reconstructed as a museum. In Victoria Dock, HMS *Unicorn*, a wooden frigate built in 1824 and now a floating museum, is anchored close to Captain Scott's *Discovery*, which was built here in 1901. To the east is Broughty Ferry, once a separate village, and now a popular suburb with an eclectic mix of restaurants, pubs and shops and a sandy beach. The museum in 15th-century Broughty Castle tells the story of Broughty Ferry and the whaling industry. The unassuming friendliness of the people, together with the unpretentious cultural life, make Dundee an agreeable base for touring the area.

Leaving the Tay, the Glens of Angus fan out inland to the north of Dundee, rich in wildlife and a botanist's paradise. Look out for red deer and arctic plants.

WATERSPORTS

The rivers and lochs in this area are well used for canoeing and boating. The length of the River Tay provides a wide variety of watersports from salmon fishing on the wide calm stretches at **Dunkeld** to white-water rafting down the waterfalls around **Aberfeldy**. The outdoor pursuits centre in **Kenmore**, on the banks of Loch Tay, offers water-skiing, rafting, fishing and much more on the river and the loch. **Lochearnhead** offers similar opportunities on Loch Earn and the River Earn. Although not strictly a watersport, the power station at **Pitlochry** is worth a visit to watch from the viewing gallery as salmon leap up the salmon ladder.

MONTROSE BASIN WILDLIFE CENTRE

The basin is a huge tidal lagoon of mud that is a rich habitat for all manner of wildlife. To the geese, waders and swans that frequent the basin, grubbing in the smelly mud is a gourmet experience! Telescopes, binoculars and video cameras are strategically placed to enable visitors to watch without disturbing the birds. There is a regular series of guided walks led by the resident ranger.

rapids on the Black Water, then bear right and ascend the valley. Shortly, turn right, then in 2 miles (3km) turn left towards Alyth.

4 After 3 miles (5km), at the T-junction, turn right and continue to Alyth, a one-time handloom weavers' town with a preserved packhorse bridge and a local folk museum. Leave Alyth on the B952 Dundee road and, at the end of the town, turn left. At the roundabout, take the B954, and in 2.5 miles (4km) turn left on to the A94 into Meigle. The glory of this village is its museum of Pictish sculptured stones.

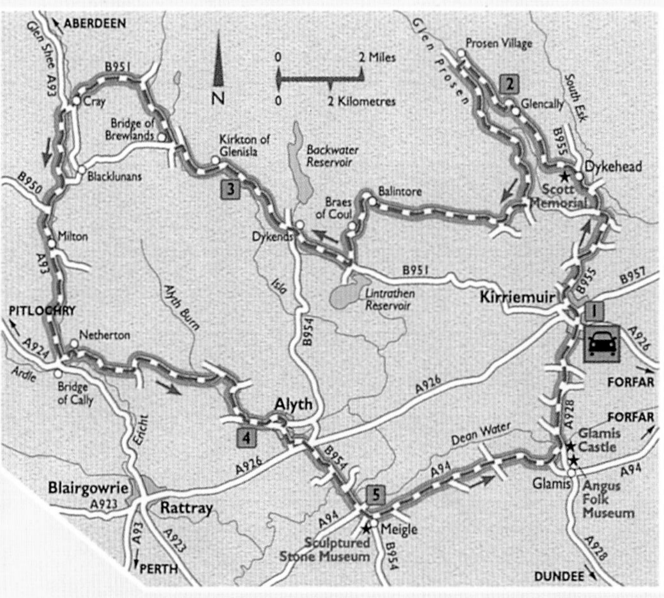

Bear left on to the A94 Aberdeen road and, in 6 miles (10km), turn left along a minor road to reach the edge of Glamis. Off the pleasant square is a row of stone-roofed, late 18th-century cottages which house the Angus Folk Museum, featuring collections of domestic equipment and cottage furniture. Shortly reach the T-junction opposite the gates of Glamis Castle. This splendid, turreted and battlemented castle was the childhood home of the Queen Mother, and contains royal apartments as well as a richly decorated chapel, portraits, tapestries and silver. Turn left on to the A928 for the return to Kirriemuir.

Boating across the mirrored surface of Loch Faskally at Pitlochry

NORTHEASTERN HIGHLANDS

The Highland Line, the divide between the smooth Lowlands and the sudden lifting of the mountains, runs from the south end of Loch Lomond towards Aberdeen and around to Inverness. Across it you are in what many people regard as 'real' Scotland. Here narrow roads twist through mountain passes and beside the lochs, and towering summits rear overhead. The Great Glen, the dramatic fault which slices Scotland in two, is part of a landscape which can be rugged and uncompromising, but never fails to impress. A land of extremes, it holds Britain's deepest area of fresh water, the highest mountain and the most Arctic environment – on the Cairngorm plateau around Ben Macdhui.

Rothiemurchus

In the lovely woodlands here there's access to a superb mountain-bike track and miles of footpaths through forests, over heather moorlands and by lochs and rivers. There's a nature trail around Loch an Eilein and other activities include clay-pigeon shooting and fishing on the Spey.

Glen Coe

There is an eerie stillness about this majestic mountain pass, which even the crowds of visitors, walkers and climbers never disturb. At the foot of the massive mountains, swathed in swirling cloud, the gloom can be oppressive. Under clear blue skies, the smooth green mountains, the wide floor of the glen and the distant mountain tops beyond have attracted countless film-makers. Braveheart, Restless Natives, Highlander *and many others were filmed in the Glen.*

MAP AND KEY

- Rothiemurchus Walk
- Banchory Cycle Ride
- Loch Ness Drive

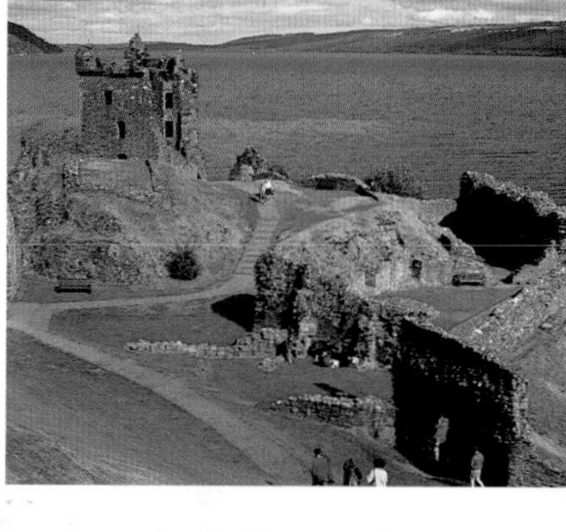

Loch Ness and Urquhart Castle

Urquhart Castle is the best monster-spotting site where most of the Nessie photographs have been taken. It is the only spot with a panoramic view of the entire length of Loch Ness. The ruins of the 14th-century castle, perched atop a rocky cliff, are spectacularly floodlit at night.

WHISKY DISTILLERY

The pure clear waters of the River Spey are at the heart of Scotland's whisky trade, with more distilleries in Speyside than any other area. You won't travel far without spotting their distinctive pointed chimney-caps. The grand malt whisky names, The Macallan, Glenfiddich, Glenlivet and many more, dot the Whisky Trail all the way to the sea.

THE CAIRNGORMS & GLEN COE

The Highlands are famous for their dramatic and colourful landscape – the splendid Cairngorms, the stunning beauty of the road to Kinlochleven, the grim reminders of the massacre at Glen Coe, and towering Ben Nevis. Rannoch Moor, best approached by car along Loch Rannoch, is a vast expanse of peat bog, which is treacherous even in the driest season. In places you will come across the blackened stumps of ancient trees protruding from the peat, evidence that this forlorn place was at one time covered in forest.

From Rannoch Moor to Glencoe village, the majestic mountain pass of Glen Coe, with the rocky summits of the Three Sisters, is one of the most spectacular sights in Scotland, familiar from hundreds of calendars and postcards. In summer a trip up the ski-lift to the 2,400-ft (731-m) summit of Meal a Bhuiridh will be rewarded by spectacular views over Rannoch Moor and the surrounding mountains. You can find out about the many exhilarating and challenging walks and climbs from the visitor centre.

Beyond Glencoe, the roads along the banks of Loch Leven provide some of the area's finest views of water and rugged hills. To the north, Ben Nevis, Britain's highest mountain, at 4,406ft (1,343m), dominates the scene. From its summit, on a clear day, the views are spectacular – the line of the Great Glen, the distant Cuillins on Skye and, very occasionally, the coast of Ireland. A drive into Glen Nevis ends by a waterslide. From here you can follow a rocky path through a dramatic ravine to a secret valley with a minimalist suspension bridge to the foot of Coire Dubh an Steill.

THE PARALLEL ROADS

In a quiet valley 18 miles (30km) northeast of Fort William, by **Roy Bridge**, is a geological phenomenon unique in Britain. **Glen Roy** and its side valleys are marked by three strange parallel lines known as the 'Parallel Roads', not roads at all, but the shorelines of an ancient glacial loch. Towards the end of the last Ice Age, the valley was dammed with ice that melted in three stages, leaving these horizontal ridges along the valley slopes. The Nature Conservancy Council explains it all on an interpretative board above the car-park.

The River Bà, running through the untouched landscape of Rannoch Moor

Rothiemurchus Walk

WALK

Heart of the Caledonian Forest

START/FINISH: Coylumbridge. On the B970, 2 miles (3km) southeast of Aviemore

DISTANCE: 5.5 miles (9km) or 8 miles (13km) if walking back from Loch Morlich

ASCENT/GRADIENT: 510ft (155m); gradual ascents

TERRAIN/PATHS: pine forest, heather moorland; mostly good, level tracks; wet in places after rain

PARKING: by roadside, just west of entrance to Rothiemurchus Camp and Caravan Park

A fragment of the past, these ancient woods harbour the very essence of Scotland's natural history.

1 Start on the footpath immediately to the right of the Rothiemurchus Camp and Caravan Park entrance, signed Public Path to Braemar by the Lairig Ghru. Walk south along the track into the forest, then on through a gate by Lairig Ghru Cottage.

In the forest, beautiful birch trees grow side by side with the old majestic pines, and there are excellent opportunities for observing rare Scottish birds, including crested tits, crossbills and the elusive capercaillie, a large species of grouse. Where the track divides take the right fork, signed Gleann Einich, passing a large cairn on the left. Soon after, go over a stile at the cattle grid. The track then rises to more open country.

3 Having gained about the highest point along the track, you are rewarded by a fantastic view. Turn sharp right for another track leading up over the heather. Reach a tarmac lane by a cattle grid, turn left and continue to where the lane terminates at Whitewell Croft. The true extent of the Cairngorm National Nature Reserve is seen to best effect from here. Bear left down a path for Rothiemurchus footpath. A short deviation leads first to a large memorial cairn on the left.

4 Walk down from the cairn and, on regaining the track for Gleann Einich, turn right for 700 yds (637m) to arrive at a major crossroads of estate tracks. There are fire beaters and signposts here. Follow the Lairig Ghru track to the left, passing Lochan Deo and walking beyond where the other path from Coylumbridge joins from the left. Soon after, reach

THE WHISKY TRAIL

The broad **Spey Valley** is renowned for the quality of its malt whisky, and there are more than 30 distilleries along the river and its tributaries. The pure Highland water of the region is the basic ingredient, together with malted barley – as well as much time and care. Eight distilleries and a cooperage, where barrels are prepared, are open to visitors and linked by the Whisky Trail, a signed route of around 70 miles (112km). You can see the great copper stills and learn about whisky production from start to finish. Nearly all offer a 'wee dram' of their product.

Further north, the little town of Kingussie is home to the Highland Folk Museum, with its reconstructed Hebridean mill, salmon smokehouse and primitive black house from Lewis. Near by, the ruins of Ruthven Barracks, built in 1718 to help subdue the Highlands, stand proud and roofless against the skyline. From Ruthven you can walk a surviving stretch of General Wade's military road, crossing a perfectly preserved example of a Wade Bridge near Dalwhinnie. The adjacent Insch Marshes Reserve (RSPB) has bird hides and nature trails.

In the Cairngorm mountains, outdoor enthusiasts can find skiing, canoeing, mountaineering, cycling and walking. The 25 miles (40km) of the Lairig Ghru, through a majestic mountain pass from Aviemore to Braemar, is reputed to be the best walk in Scotland, although its unpredictable weather and biting cold can test the endurance of the most experienced walker. The dramatic mountain scenery can be viewed from the comfort of the Strathspey Steam Railway, which runs for 5 miles (8km) from Aviemore to picturesque Boat of Garten. Aviemore village is ideal for exploring the area and its numerous shops sell and rent sporting equipment. Nearby Loch Morlich Watersports provide facilities and training.

Runners compete at the annual Ben Nevis Race, heading out from Fort William

THE MASSACRE OF GLEN COE

The peace of Glen Coe was rudely shattered on the winter morning of 13 February 1692, when the Campbell clan, under orders from the Crown, violated the sacred bond of hospitality after staying with the MacDonalds for several days. Throughout the glen, the Campbells dragged MacDonald men from their beds and murdered them, burning houses as they went. Their homes ablaze, their men folk dead, women of all ages, some carrying infants, fled into the mountains in a piercing snowstorm, many perishing miserably. The National Trust for Scotland's Visitor Centre tells the story graphically.

the Cairngorm Club footbridge over the Allt na Bheinn Mhor.

5 Go over the bridge and turn right on a rough track heading upstream of the river. From where the waters of the Am Beanaidh and the Allt Druidh join forces, veer southeast, passing close to a ruined house on the left before rising gently up to Piccadilly. East of Lochan Deo the forest has a more open aspect.

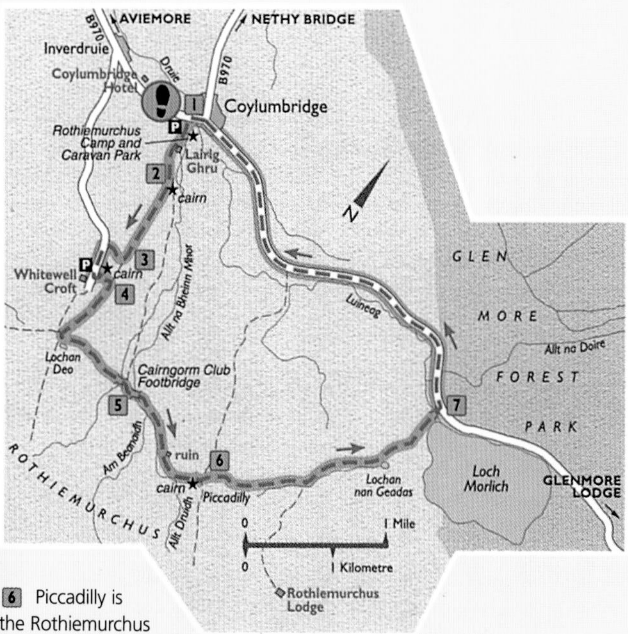

6 Piccadilly is the Rothiemurchus Estate name for this other major junction of tracks, marked by a large cairn. Walk northeast from here, following the Loch Morlich track. Shortly after passing through a stile at Tilhill, turn left joining the track from Rothiemurchus Lodge to Loch Morlich and continue through a further 2 miles (3km) of pine forest.

7 Join the road to Glen More and the ski centre by the western shore of Loch Morlich. At certain times of the year the road is served by buses connecting with Aviemore, offering a convenient return; otherwise, it is a further hour of walking by the roadside to return to Coylumbridge.

TOP FIVE SKIING AREAS

Glen Coe

From White Corries at the top of the glen, a chairlift takes skiers high into the mountains. There are 15 runs catering for all levels of ability. The Glen Coe area also offers cross-country skiing, ski mountaineering, speed skating, snowboarding and paragliding.

Cairngorms

Aviemore provides all the necessary facilities for skiers in the Cairngorms, including equipment rental, tuition and buses to the ski area. The Scottish National Sports Council's Glenmore Lodge provides an excellent introduction to a whole range of winter sports.

Glen Shee

Above the dramatic Cairnwell Pass the ski slopes of Glen Shee provide a gentle introduction for beginners with the more challenging Tiger run for experienced skiers. Tuition and equipment hire are available from Cairnwell Mountain Sports at Spittal of Glenshee.

The Lecht

Between Cockbridge and Tomintoul, the Lecht has dry-slope skiing all year round as well as snow-making equipment to extend the winter season. Ideal for the beginner, there is little here to challenge the experienced skier. Tuition and equipment hire are available from the base station.

The Nevis Range

To the north of Ben Nevis, the Nevis Range Gondola is a popular tourist attraction all year round, rising 2,130ft (650m) to exhilarating walking, mountain biking and spectacular views, as well as to the ski area at Aonach Mhor. There is also a dry-ski slope, equipment hire and tuition.

ABERDEEN & THE NORTH SEA COAST

Fish, oil and granite are, for many, words that sum up Aberdeen. Fishing remains a major industry, as an early morning visit to the fish auctions will confirm. Oil, too, makes its presence felt in the lights twinkling far out to sea in the dusk. Grey granite buildings dominate the city centre – most spectacular are the spiky towers of ancient Marischal College, founded in 1593. For a city so much associated with grey granite, the flowers of Aberdeen come as a surprise. The city blazes with colour everywhere; main roads are bordered with blooms, roundabouts become luxurious gardens and streets are festooned with tubs and baskets. Aberdeen has won the 'Britain in Bloom' contest so often that it has had to retire to give others a chance!

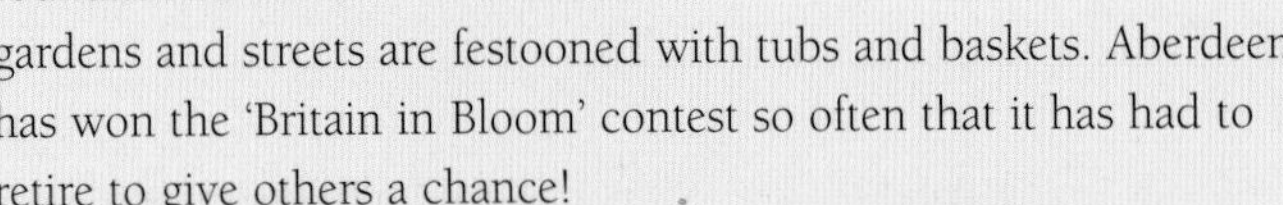

FINDHORN FOUNDATION

The Findhorn Foundation was founded in 1962 by Peter and Eileen Caddy and Dorothy Maclean. It is a major centre of adult education where sustainable ways of living for the world of today and tomorrow are developed through experimentation, practice and demonstration. The eco-village develops innovative ecological housing, the use of renewable energy systems and community-based recycling schemes. The Foundation offers a wide variety of workshops and programmes for 4,000 residential visitors each year.

The homes of two 16th-century Provosts of Aberdeen still survive – Provost Skene's, in Broad Street, which illustrates city life in a series of period rooms, and Provost Ross's in Shiprow, housing the fascinating Maritime Museum. There are no fewer than three cathedrals – St Mary's, St Andrew's and the oldest, the granite St Machar's, with its splendid heraldic ceiling. Near by is King's College, founded in 1495 and now part of Aberdeen University. The Mercat Cross in Castlegate, at the heart of the city, has portraits of the ten Stuart monarchs of Scotland. To complete the city's attractions, 2 miles (3km) of sandy beach stretch northward from the pier, backed by a wide promenade, and there is a wide choice of sporting and leisure activities, too, including Scotland's largest amusement park.

The boatyard at Fraserburgh, where you can take fishing trips from the harbour

Flowering Union Terrace Gardens bring colour to granite-grey Aberdeen

To the west of Aberdeen, between the Don and the Dee valleys, in the former province of Mar, are the Castles of Mar, each characterised by a plain lower storey, bursting into a riot of corbelled-out towers and gables. This fairy-tale style was developed

Banchory Cycle Ride

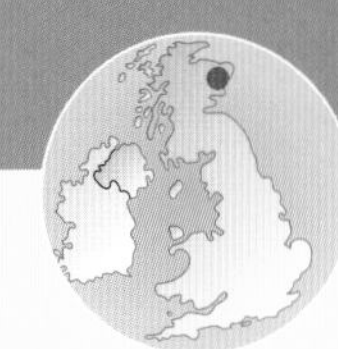

CYCLE RIDE

Along the River Dee

START/FINISH: Banchory. 18 miles (29km) west of Aberdeen, on the A93

DISTANCE: 25 miles (40km), with 3 miles (5km) off-road

GRADIENT: undulating

ROADS: B-roads in the Dee Valley; country lanes; former railway track

PARKING: Bellfield car-park (free) on the east side of the B974, close to the junction with the A93

This scenic route follows the Dee, one of the world's most famous salmon rivers, and calls in at the fine castles of Drum and Crathes. To avoid the hills, sections of the route are on main roads which may be busy at peak times; a quieter stretch runs along the line of a dismantled railway.

1 Banchory is a small town in the lower valley of the River Dee with a sunny aspect and a fine golf course beside the river. The great composer for the fiddle, James Scott Skinner was born here in 1843, and a memorial to 'the Strathspey King' stands on the High Street. From the car-park turn left on to the B974, cross the River Dee and shortly turn left, signed Durris. Cross the Bridge of Feugh, and proceed for 3.5 miles (5.5km) along the south side of the Dee valley to reach the A957. In spring and summer look for salmon leaping the falls in Water of Feugh.

2 Turn right and immediately left and stay on the B9077 for a further 3.5 miles (5.5km), passing through Kirkton of Durris. At the crossroads turn left, signed Park. Cross the River Dee by Park Bridge, the original toll bridge built to bring customers from the south side of the river to the railway, and continue to the A93. Turn right, signed Aberdeen. After 1.5 miles (2.5km) turn left, signed Drum Castle, and then take the first turning left into the Drum Castle estate. The magnificent castle of Drum combines a 13th-century square tower with a Jacobean mansion house, with fine furniture and paintings. Now in the care of the National Trust for Scotland, it has a walled garden with a collection of historic roses.

3 Return to the public road and turn left by a notice pointing to Cullerlie Stone Circle. After half a mile (800m) turn left and after a

ISLAND WILDLIFE

The northern islands are a wildlife paradise. The cliffs, maritime heaths, moorlands, freshwater lochs, beaches and sea are home to a range of birds. The elusive corncrake can still be heard, if not seen, on **Papa Westray**, and many other birds visit in the summer to breed, including red-throated divers, Arctic terns, Arctic skuas, great skuas, fulmars, kittiwakes and various auks. The maritime heath supports a rich flora, including heath spotted orchid, spring squill, primrose and Scottish primrose, *Primula scotica*. The seashores around the islands support a wide range of wildlife. Common and grey seals can be seen, and otters frequent the shore, but they are more wary of human company and often difficult to see.

after the union of the crowns of England and Scotland in the 17th century, to meet the demand for increasing comfort, without altogether abandoning a defensive role.

The rugged northern coastline from Aberdeen is the centre of the fishing industry, from busy fishing ports such as Peterhead and Fraserburgh. Duff House, in the charming Georgian town of Banff, is a restored Adam mansion now housing part of the collection of the National Gallery of Scotland. Burghead on the Moray Firth was an ancient Pictish settlement where the remains of six Pictish bull carvings on stones can still be seen.

SPECIALITY KNITWEAR

Almost anywhere in Shetland you will find workshops where you can buy a woollen garment made up in your own choice of pattern and colour, straight from the needles of traditional knitters. **Fair Isle**, between Shetland and Orkney, differs in that its brightly coloured and highly patterned knitwear is made from very fine wool.

Beyond in the North Sea, Orkney, Shetland and the oil rigs are the last outposts of Scotland. The islands of Orkney are like a handful of emeralds cast on the waters, their gentle, green, undulating landscape in sharp contrast to the rugged scenery of the north mainland of Scotland. The islands of Shetland are slashed by the sea into thousands of inlets, the rocky land backed by huge, ever-changing skies. The most northerly scrap of the UK is Out Stack just beyond Muckle Flugga.

further half mile (800m) keep left (both junctions are without signposts). Continue for 2 miles (3km) and at the Rashenlochy notice, turn right. Shortly turn left, signed Hirn, and keep straight on for 2.5 miles (4km) to Hirn and keep left twice. Follow the signs to Crathes, turning sharply left and then right, and go straight on at a minor crossroads to eventually reach the A93.

4 Turn right (no signpost) heading west, then in half a mile (800m) turn right into Crathes Castle estate. Crathes Castle is a splendid, turreted 16th-century castle in a beautiful garden setting. The ancestral home of the Burnetts of Leys, it has several features of particular note, including its famous painted ceilings (which were rediscovered in 1877),

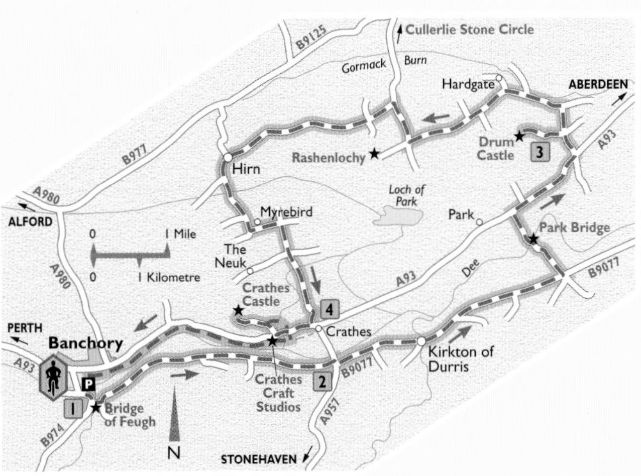

a finely carved long gallery, and a unique family treasure, the 'Horn of Leys', an ancient ivory horn presented by Robert the Bruce. Return down the estate road. Immediately before the A93, turn left on an unsurfaced track. Pass under the main road and turn immediately right on the path which leads up to the old railway line. Continue on this track for 3 miles (5km) into Banchory. Reach a tarred path, and go forward through the park keeping the houses on your right. Turn left to pass under the old railway bridge, and continue through Bellfield Park to return to the car-park.

TOP FIVE CASTLES OF MAR

Craigievar Castle

Among the best of the Castles of Mar, this has remained unaltered since it was completed in 1626. Built of pink stone, the top storeys are festooned with towers and balustrades.

Glamis Castle

Childhood home of the Queen Mother, Glamis Castle has fine collections of china, tapestries and paintings, a chilling selection of ghosts and a roofline stiff with cone-topped towerlets.

Castle Fraser

This castle has an usual feature, the 'Laird's Lug', a tiny room high above the impressive Great Hall, from where the Fraser family could listen to their guests' conversations!

Crathes Castle

This romantic tower house of turrets (below) is famed for its painted ceilings, swirling with leaves and flowers. The walled garden has massive 18th-century yews, where beautifully planned spaces offer tranquil corners and wonderful contrasts of shape and colour.

Drum Castle

Drum presents two faces – a gaunt, battlemented tower built in 1296 and a Jacobean mansion – which were joined in the 19th century. The walled gardens have a fine collection of historic roses.

THE GREAT GLEN & INVERNESS

IN SEARCH OF THE MONSTER

It would be difficult for anyone but the most hardened sceptic to gaze out over the waters of Loch Ness without just the small hope of a 'sighting'. St Columba is the first person reported to have met a monster in Loch Ness – he prevented it from eating his servant by making the sign of the cross. Quiescent for more than a millennium thereafter, 'Nessie' attracted public attention again while the main A82 road along the north side of the loch was being constructed in the 1930s. Photographs of varying authenticity, as well as inconclusive scientific research, have added to its fame. Yet still the loch keeps its secret, aided by its 24-mile (38-km) length and a depth in places of 900ft (274m). The **Loch Ness Lodge Visitor Centre** has a large-screen cinema, exhibition and sonar scanning cruises; the **Official Loch Ness 2000 Centre** in Drumnadrochit has audio-visuals and a 'life-size' model of Nessie; and the **Original Loch Ness Visitor Centre** offers films and boat trips.

This is quintessential Scotland – the sea, the lochs and the mountains – all converging on a congenial city, beautifully set beside the Moray Firth. Inverness, the 'Capital of the Highlands' sits at the northeastern extremity of the Great Glen on the banks of the River Ness. Southwest from Inverness the dark waters of Loch Ness refuse to yield up their secrets; to the east, the desolation of Culloden tells of the crushing of the clans; to the west, Beauly has links with Mary, Queen of Scots.

Culloden remains a sad and moving place. On this bleak, mournful moorland the hopes of the Royal House of Stuart to regain the throne of Scotland were forever dashed. The entrenched guns of the government's artillery laid waste the Highland ranks, and the wounded survivors were slaughtered where they lay. Flags mark the disposition of the armies, and the large cairn built during the 19th century commemorates the dead.

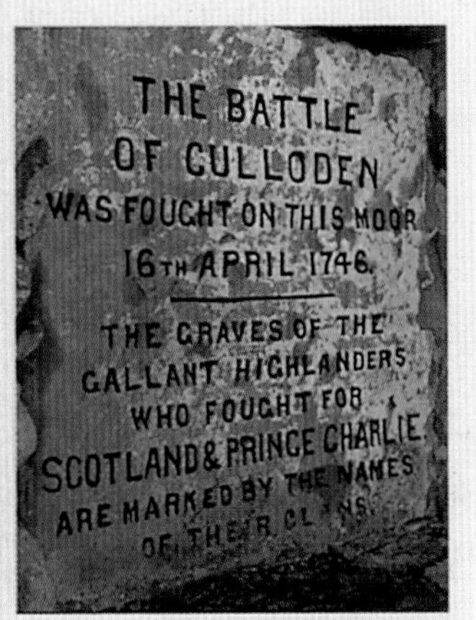

An emotive memorial to the Battle of Culloden

After the rout of Bonnie Prince Charlie's Highland army, the Hanoverians, intent on subduing 'rebellious Scots', constructed massive Fort George on a spit running into the Moray Firth. It continues as an army barracks to this day and is the home of the Regimental Museum of the Queen's Own Highlanders.

Nearby Cawdor Castle was made infamous by Shakespeare's chilling tale of the 12th-century murder of King Duncan by Macbeth. In fact the Cawdor family, who still live here, did not build this fairy-tale castle until the 14th century. According to legend the castle was built around a thorn tree, still on view in the Thorn Room. The extensive grounds are delightful, including nature walks, a walled garden and the winding Cawdor Burn.

Further back in the mists of time, the three Clava Cairns near Culloden, each surrounded by a circle of standing stones, were built

A bridge from Inverness to North Kessock, where forest walks allow views of the firth

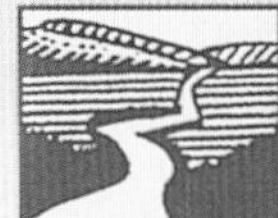

Loch Ness Drive

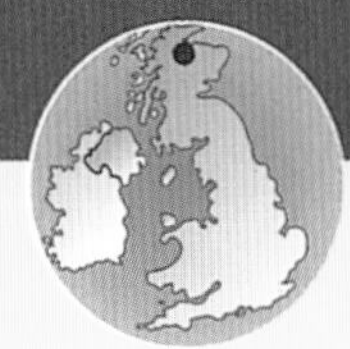

DRIVE

Around the Shores of Loch Ness

START/FINISH: Inverness. Off the A9
DISTANCE: 91 miles (146.5km)

Two narrow valleys, Strathglass and Glen Urquhart, slice through forested and deer-stalking hills to arrive at the dark waters of Loch Ness, a place of mystery and the longest waterway in the Great Glen.

1 The most attractive parts of the Highland capital are on its southwest side, where footpaths follow both banks of the fast-flowing River Ness and link up with wooded islands in mid-stream. Buildings of interest include 19th-century St Andrew's Cathedral, the early Victorian castle commanding a fine position overlooking the river, and Dunbar's Hospital, an almshouse of 1668. Leave Inverness on the A862 towards Beauly. After 11 miles (18km), passing the turning for Moniack Castle Winery along the way, cross the River Beauly and branch left on to the A831 for Cannich.

2 Continue through Kilmorack and pass the House of Aigas (not open), former home of Lord Lovat in 1697 and Victorian prime minister Robert Peel, into Struy. Cross the river and continue to Cannich, a charming stone-built Highland village near the head of Strathglass. Leave on the Drumnadrochit road and follow the River Enrick into Glen Urquhart passing Lochs Meiklie and Milton to reach Drumnadrochit. Situated on the west side of Loch Ness, this village is home to the Official Loch Ness 2000 Centre, a fascinating multimedia experience tracing the legend from its beginnings in Highland folklore to recent scientific investigations.

3 Turn right on to the A82, signed Fort William, and after Lewiston, join the western shoreline of Loch Ness at Urquhart Castle. Once Scotland's biggest castle, this ruined 13th-century stronghold stands on high ground overlooking Loch Ness. Continue to Invermoriston and turn left with the A82 to reach Fort Augustus. Situated in wooded hill country on the Caledonian Canal at the foot of Loch Ness, this pretty hamlet takes its name from a Hanoverian outpost that was built against the Jacobite Highlanders after the first rising in 1715.

between about 2000 and 1500 BC. The two outer ones have stone-lined passages to the centre. The central cairn has no passage, but, uniquely, odd rough pavements radiate from it. This group is the most important of a series of such cairns around the Moray Firth.

The Great Glen is the spectacular geological fault running from the Firth of Lorne to the Moray Firth, cutting Scotland in two. It has provided a way through the mountains for centuries of travellers. Loch Ness forms a major part of the Caledonian Canal, which follows the line of the Great Glen. The loch contains more water than all the lakes and reservoirs in England and Wales put together. It is 24 miles (38km) long, one mile (1.5km) wide and 750ft (228m) deep. The ruins of medieval Urquhart Castle, once captured by Edward I and then held by Robert the Bruce, are worth a visit. Perched atop a rocky promontory it was of strategic importance in guarding the Great Glen.

THE CALEDONIAN CANAL

One of Thomas Telford's greatest engineering achievements was the Caledonian Canal, linking Lochs Ness, Oich, Lochy and Linnhe from **Inverness** in the east to **Fort William** in the west. The north coast of Scotland had often proved hazardous to small boats, so the idea of avoiding that journey by constructing a canal along the Great Glen appealed to late 18th-century minds. Begun in 1803, the work raised the level of Loch Ness by 6ft (1.8m). When the canal was opened in 1822 it was not deep enough; after further work it was finally completed in 1847. Between the natural lochs on the 60-mile (96-km) route from Loch Linnhe to the Moray Firth are 22 miles (35km) of canal, rising through 29 locks. A slow boat through the **Great Glen**, watching the reflection of forest greenery, is a tranquil and awesome experience.

ANNUAL EVENTS AND CUSTOMS

Drumnadrochit – Glenurquhart Highland Gathering and Games, late August.

Inverness – Folk Festival, Easter weekend. Inverness Highland Games, late July. Inverness Tattoo, late July.

Kingussie – Badenoch & Strathspey Music Festival, late March. Shinty (Camanachd Cup Final), first Saturday in June.

HORSE-RIDING

Horse-riding is a popular way to explore the countryside and there are countless riding schools, stables and trekking centres in the area. Riding on old drove roads, disused railway lines, beaches and heather-clad moorland will give you access to more of this lovely land than any other way. There is a growing network of horse-and-rider bed and breakfasts where you can stay with your horse. Whether you are a novice content with pony-trekking on a docile beast, or an experienced rider looking for some adventurous trail riding, there are stables at **Aviemore**, **Carrbridge**, **Drumnadrochit**, **Fort Augustus**, **Grantown-on-Spey** and **Kingussie**, which will cater to your needs.

SEE CONTACTS SECTION FOR ADDITIONAL INFORMATION

Enjoying the scenery from the saddle

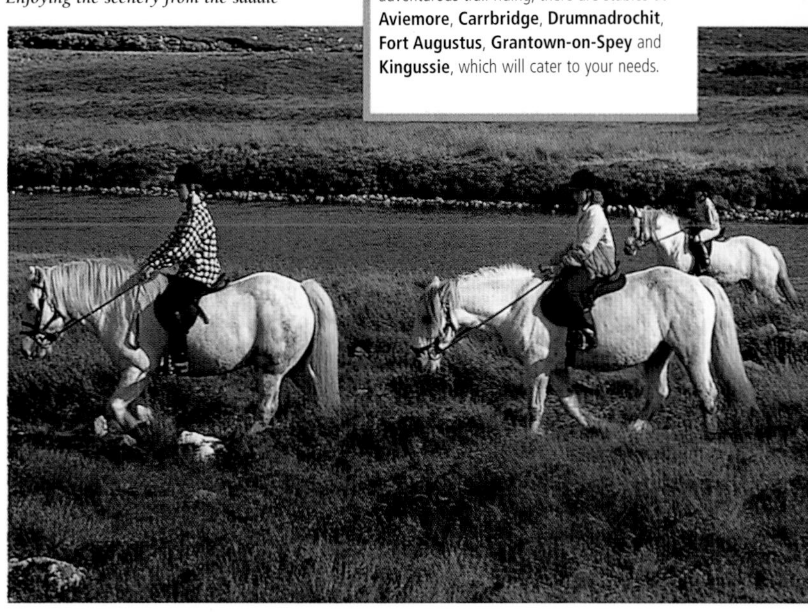

4 At the far end of the village turn left on to the single track B862 towards Whitebridge and Dores. Continue forward until 1 mile (1.5km) beyond Whitebridge, then turn left on to the B852, signed Foyers. Continue beside the shores of Loch Ness to reach Foyers, best known for the Falls of Foyers which descend a precipitous wooded gorge. This is the site of the first hydroelectric power-station in Britain, which was built in 1896, and is an ideal stopping place for refreshments and a variety walks. After viewing the falls continue through Inverfarigaig, where there is a permanent Forestry Commission display and waymarked trails that lead up to magnificent viewpoints over Loch Ness. Remain on the B852 and continue to Dores. Here rejoin the B862 and return to Inverness and the start of the drive.

THE WESTERN HIGHLANDS & ISLANDS

From space, Scotland north of the Forth and Clyde looks like a loosely woven cloth – an ancient tartan perhaps – ragged at its western edge and crumpled in a series of irregular folds with loose scraps and threads around its fringes. These are the Highlands and the Islands, where high mountains and deep glens, tumbling seas and shimmering lochs, open moorland and spreading forests lure the visitor to one of the most fascinating areas in Europe. This is the Scotland of literature, romance and the movies. It is a vast area, where nature and its ancient inhabitants have left dramatic and enduring marks on the land.

DUNROBIN CASTLE

On a raised beach overlooking the Dornoch Firth, Dunrobin Castle has been elaborately extended over the centuries, with later additions completely concealing the original 13th-century sandstone keep at its heart. Its spectacular turreted appearance today is largely the work of the renowned 19th-century architect Charles Barry. Inside, the castle is equally lavish, displaying the furniture, paintings and trophies of generations of wealth.

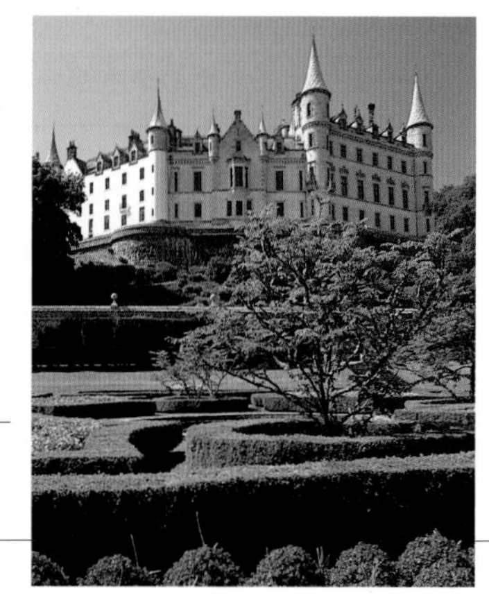

Ullapool

Ullapool, at the head of Loch Broom, was built as a planned fishing village in 1788 by the British Fisheries Society. Today it is still a bustling fishing port and the ferry terminal for the Western Isles, with a lively cultural centre at The Ceilidh Place, where people can enjoy the outdoors by day and sample live traditional music and dancing in the evening.

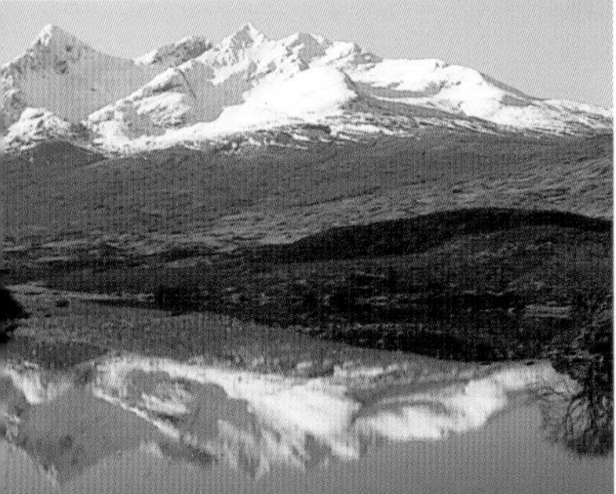

THE CUILLINS OF SKYE

Skye, the most famous of the Inner Hebrides, is dominated from every view by the high peaks of the Cuillins. The jagged gabbro of the Black Cuillins and the pink, scree-covered granite of the Red Cuillins have proved an irresistible challenge for mountaineers, and the most inaccessible peaks were only conquered at the end of the 19th century.

rsely populated, it teems with wildlife from red deer, wild cats
' otters to an astonishing variety of bird life. Scattered ruined
ages remain, testimony to a more populous past before the
arances, when the landlords drove the people from the land in
)ur of more profitable sheep.

MAP AND KEY

Northwest Scotland Drive

Dornoch Drive

Cuillins Walk

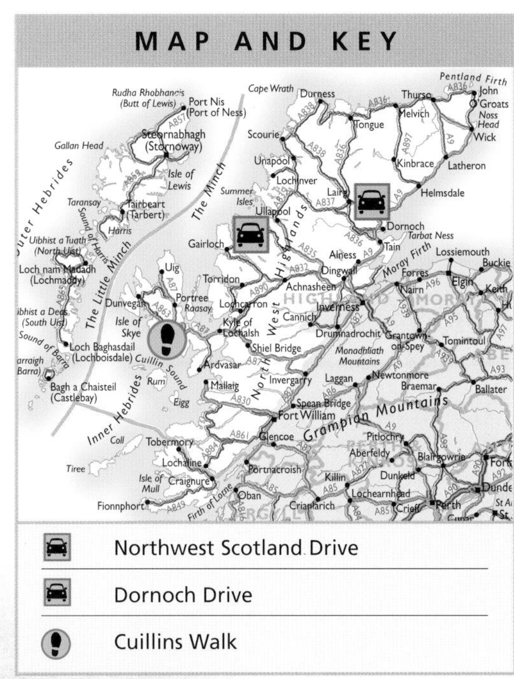

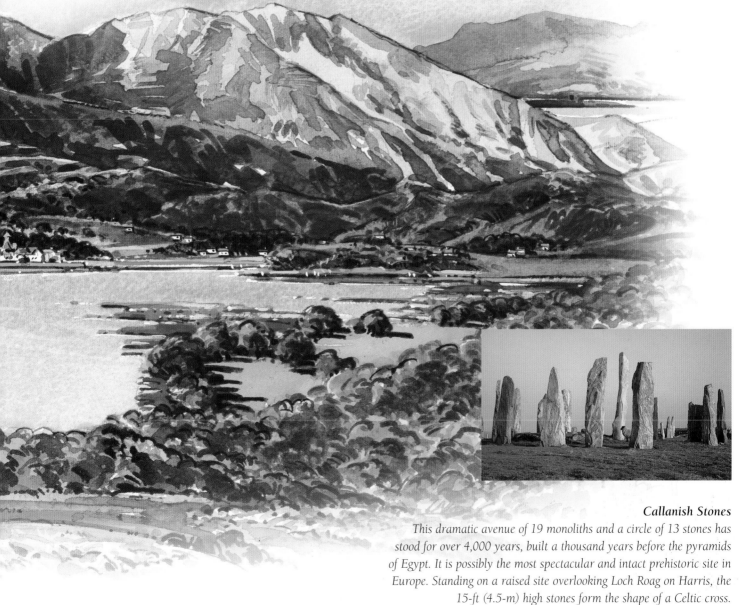

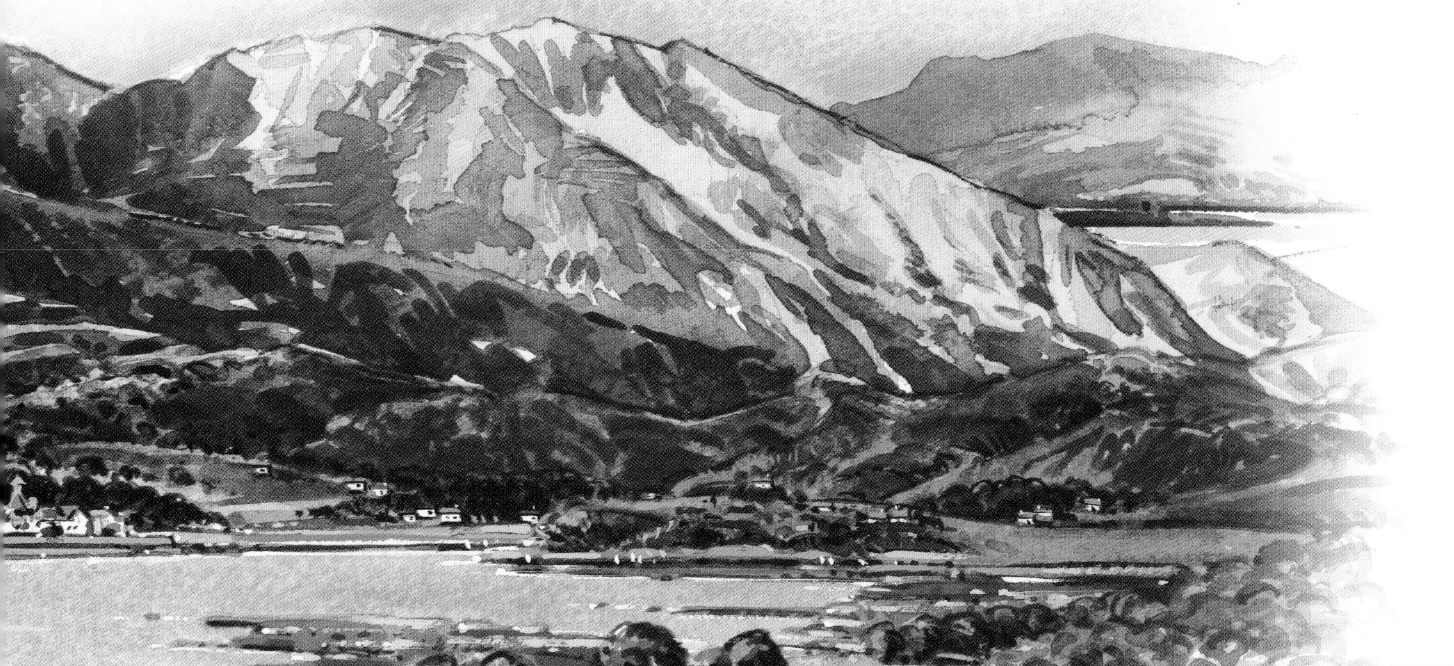

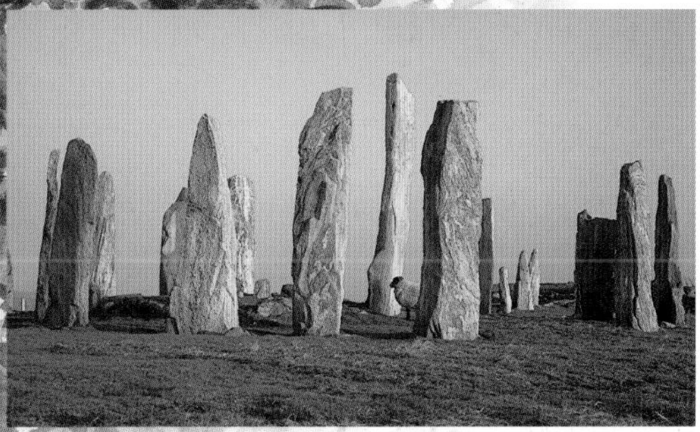

Callanish Stones

This dramatic avenue of 19 monoliths and a circle of 13 stones has stood for over 4,000 years, built a thousand years before the pyramids of Egypt. It is possibly the most spectacular and intact prehistoric site in Europe. Standing on a raised site overlooking Loch Roag on Harris, the 15-ft (4.5-m) high stones form the shape of a Celtic cross.

THE LAND OF THE LOCHS

The coastline of Scotland from Mull to Loch Broom breaks down into a succession of sea-girt promontories and long sea lochs each with its own character and secrets, and inland there's a hinterland of mountains, moorland, miles of wilderness, waterfalls, lochs and scenic glens.

You can go no further west on mainland Britain than Ardnamurchan Point, with spectacular views over to Mull, Coll and Tiree. The whole peninsula, with its rocky hills and desolate moorland, gale-blown trees and heather-capped promontories, has an 'end-of-the-world' feeling. Morvern, across Loch Sunart, is a rugged land with gentler green glens. Lochaline, a popular yachting haven, is reached either by road along Glen Gleann, or by ferry from Mull.

It's not all about walking and fishing: Gairloch sees some fast-paced powerboat racing

At the top of Loch Shiel, dividing Moidart from Sunart, is Glenfinnan, where Bonnie Prince Charlie unfurled his father's white-and-red silk banner to mark the start of the ill-fated '45 Rebellion. The figure of a Highlander is most romantically set at the head of Loch Shiel, overlooking the wooded Eilean Glean Fhianin and the mountains of Sunart and Moidart.

The 'Road to the Isles' ends at the busy fishing harbour and ferry terminal at Mallaig, which is also the terminus of the West Highland Line, one of Britain's most scenic railway routes. Knoydart, across Loch Nevis, accessible only by sea, provides wild and wonderful walking country.

From the picture-postcard village of Plockton look north to the rugged hills of the Applecross peninsula. The breathtakingly spectacular Bealach-na-Ba, the road to Applecross, reaches some 2,050ft (625m).

The road east from Shieldaig on Loch Torridon gives views over Upper Loch Torridon to the huge mountain mass dominated by Ben Liathach (3,339ft/1,024m). The road north of Loch Torridon, with wonderful views over to the Applecross peninsula, passes through several crofting settlements to end at Lower Diabaig, from where you can walk to Redpoint, far out on the coast of Wester Ross. Further north around the village of Gairloch, the road winds around

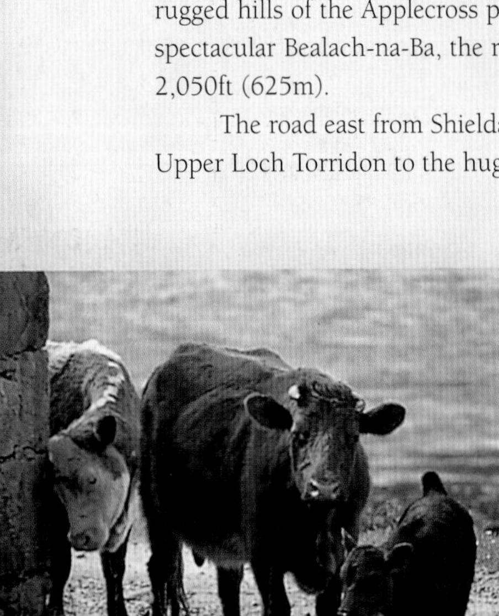

Inquisitive brown cows and a young calf at Applecross

The remote drama of the Highlands, looking north towards Liathach and Torridon

DRIVE

Northwest Scotland Drive

Gairloch to Ullapool

START: Gairloch. Village on the A382, 5 miles (8km) southwest of Poolewe

FINISH: Ullapool

DISTANCE: 50 miles (80km)

This is a magnificent linear drive, along the superb mountainous coastline of northwest Scotland, with plenty of viewpoints along the route.

1 The drive starts at Gairloch Heritage Museum, a converted farmstead which depicts the way of life in this West Highland parish, from Stone-Age times to the present day. It includes a Pictish inscribed stone, a reconstructed croft house room, and geology, archaeology, agriculture and fishing sections. From the museum take the A832 towards Poolewe. Pass Loch Tollaidh to reach the magnificent freshwater Loch Maree. Pull in at the unmarked viewpoint on the left to admire the scenery.

2 Continue through Poolewe and proceed to Inverewe Gardens. Owned by the National Trust for Scotland, these unique gardens were created over a century ago by Osgood Mackenzie, and his daughter, Mairi Sawyer, continued the work. Originally a windswept rocky and peaty moorland, with only two small trees, it is now one of Europe's most exotic visual extravaganzas. Taking advantage of its shoreline position and of the Gulf Stream climate, it now has over 2,500 species, including Himalayan lilies, Japanese hydrangeas, New Zealand shrubs and giant South Pacific forget-me-nots. Continue on the A832, passing on the left a viewpoint from which you can see the Isle of Ewe, and later pass the minor road to the old crofting townships of Aultbea and Mellon Charles. Continue to Laide.

3 Turn left before the garage to the ruined chapel, believed to have been founded by Columba's monks, and a viewpoint (not signed). From here there are magnificent views across Gruinard Bay to Gruinard Island. Return to the main road and continue on the A832 around the bay and over the headland to the viewpoint just before Badcaul, from where there are views over Little Loch Broom to Beinn Ghobhlach, and, to the right, the mountain of Sàil Mhór.

THE WEST HIGHLAND RAILWAY

The construction of this rail line was no easy task – the peat bogs of Rannoch Moor were traversed with a floating bed of brushwood, beneath tons of ash and earth; the rocky heights of Glenfinnan and the deeply indented coastline had to be crossed. Contractor Robert MacAlpine pioneered the structural use of concrete, building the high viaducts which give such magnificent views. Sit on the left for the outward journey (reserve a seat at peak times). Curving over 1,000ft (305m) over the River Finnan, the 21 concrete arches of Glenfinnan Viaduct (right) are up to 100ft (30m) high. It is said that buried within the viaduct are a horse and cart that fell into the concrete before it set.

TORRIDON ESTATE

Ben Liathach, 750 million years old and 3,339ft (1,024m) high, has a row of seven peaks topped with shining white quartzite from 150 million years later. Composed of red Torridonian sandstone, it forms part of the National Trust for Scotland's 16,100-acre (6,515-ha) Torridon Estate.

The Trust's Countryside Centre in Torridon village can advise visitors on the best routes through the mountains, but guided walks are recommended if you want to tackle the 5-mile (8-km) ridge between Liathach's peaks. The **Deer Museum** near by has a herd of wild red deer, and lots of information about their life on the hills. Further on, **Beinn Eighe** presents a forbidding face to the traveller, but like the other mountains has impressive corries to the north. It is also part of Britain's first national nature reserve.

4 Follow the road along Little Loch Broom, passing rectangular mussel rafts and later fish cages before you reach Ardessie. The square and circular cages are the salt-water stage of the salmon-farming process. Continue, passing the war memorial, to Dundonnell Hotel from where you can see the magnificent tidal flats exposed at low water, where wildfowl often feed. The road follows the Dundonnell River and a series of lovely waterfalls. On the bend near Sidhean na Sròine pull in to a view of Loch Broom, reputedly one of the most spectacular roadside views in Scotland. A little further on, at Corrieshalloch Gorge, walk down to the suspension bridge to view the gorge. This is one of the most magnificent sights in the northwest; the gorge is a mile (1.5km) long and 200ft (60m) wide, and has an unusual box canyon. The Falls of Measach here are 150ft (46m) high.

5 Continue on the A832 to a T-junction. Turn left on to the A835 towards Ullapool. Pass Lael Forest Garden on your right, descending towards the lush pasture land. Continue with Loch Broom on the left into Ullapool, the main ferry link to Stornoway and the Outer Hebrides.

the bay and eventually turns into a track, leading to the former lighthouse at Rubha Reidh. To the south of the bay there are intriguing woody inlets, perfect for exploring in a small boat.

Inland, the scenery of this area is equally spectacular – southwest of Inverness, the broad Strath Glass leads to the village of Cannich where four valleys meet. Eastwards, down Glen Urquhart, is the prehistoric Corrimony Cairn, with its stone roof and 11 standing stones. Glen Cannich is entered by a winding road between bare mountain tops, with groves of birch and alder. South along Loch Beinn a'Mheadhoin are parking places, many with fine walks from them. Across the loch is a rare remnant of the ancient Caledonian Pine Forest. Beyond the loch you can walk on to Loch Affric – a magical scene of clustered hills and pine forest. In the autumn there is dazzling colour and the hint of snow on the peaks. Follow the old track through the mountains to Sheil Bridge in Kintail and you're nearly at the coast again.

TOP FIVE GARDENS

LeckMelm Shrubbery and Arboretum

Three miles (5km) from Ullapool on Loch Broom is LeckMelm Shrubbery and Arboretum, dating from the 1870s. It is renowned for rare trees and plants including rhododendrons and azaleas.

Inverewe Gardens

Surrounded by barren peatbogs, rocks and water, Inverewe (below) is one of Britain's most remarkable gardens and a mecca for plant-lovers from all over the world. Rhododendrons provide one of the most spectacular attractions in the early summer.

Achiltibuie Hydroponicum

At Achiltibuie, 26 miles (42km) northwest of Ullapool, the Hydroponicum is an experimental garden and a scientific delight, where bananas and other exotic plants thrive without the benefit of soil.

Clan Donald Centre

Surrounded by lovely woodland gardens, this centre near Armadale is well worth a visit. There is an excellent museum, exhibitions, genealogical research facilities, guided walks and much more.

Dunrobin Castle Gardens

The gardens here, modelled on Versailles, were laid out in the 19th century. The formal gardens, paths and fountains in front of the extravagant turreted castle are set within a large park with extensive woodland walks.

FROM ULLAPOOL TO JOHN O'GROATS

On the mainland of Scotland, treeless and often windswept Caithness and Sutherland are at the northern extremity. The main towns of Wick and Thurso are good bases for exploration.

After travelling across the vast empty expanse of Sutherland it is somehow surprising to arrive at the thriving little town of Thurso, where a good salmon river pours through a long, narrow harbour and into the bay. Orkney, glimpsed across the stormy waters of the Pentland Firth, is reached by ferry from nearby Scrabster. The curing yard and old photographs at the heritage centre recall Wick's heyday, when the harbour bristled with fishing boats.

Tour buses bring droves of visitors into the village at John O'Groats – popularly considered the top of Scotland, though Dunnet Head projects further north – and takes them away again, laden with souvenirs. Dutchman Jan de Groot, who operated the ferry to South Ronaldsay at the end of the 15th century gave his name to the settlement.

SMOO CAVE

Between Durness and the inlet of Loch Eriboll is Smoo Cave, reached by a steep path down to the cavern, where the high arched mouth opens into three great chambers. The largest is 200ft (60m) deep and 110ft (33m) wide. There are watery pools within the cave, and dripping limestone has created a Gothic collection of stalactites and stalagmites.

Westwards is the Flow Country, Europe's most important and fragile area of blanket bog. This is a unique natural resource of global importance – a complex mosaic of peat bog and dark pools. Its barren appearance is deceptive; sphagnum moss forms the living skin of the bog, dotted with sundews, sweet-scented bog myrtle, heaths and heather.

Northwards, the coast is quiet and largely unvisited, with wonderful beaches and rocky inlets. Golfers can enjoy a game on the mainland's remotest golf course at Balnakeil, but most visitors are drawn by Cape Wrath where chill winds and the roar of the pounding waves remind you that there are only the Faroe Islands between you and the Arctic.

Turning south, the area becomes more mountainous as the road wanders beside sea or across boggy land. The port of

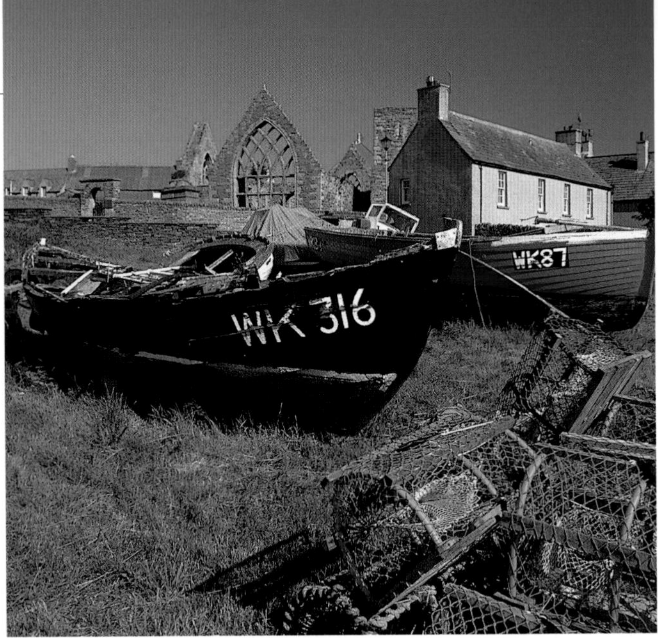

Looking across to the ruins of 13th-century Church of St Peter at Thurso

Dornoch Drive

DRIVE

Southeast Sutherland

START/FINISH: Dornoch. Small town on the A949 12 miles (19km) east of Bonar Bridge

DISTANCE: 69 miles (110.5km)

Here, Sutherland is a county of contrasts. Sandy beaches separate holiday resorts on the coast. Inland there are huge areas of sheep farms and deer forests. Two vastly wealthy men – a duke and an industrialist – cast very different shadows.

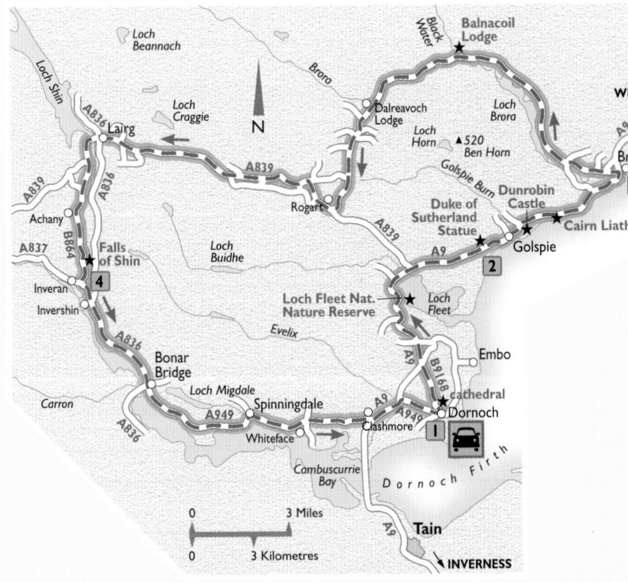

1 Some of Scotland's finest beaches follow the coast along the Dornoch Firth and sweep away to the north. Dornoch, Golspie and Brora revel in fine sands and top-class golf links on the springy turf,

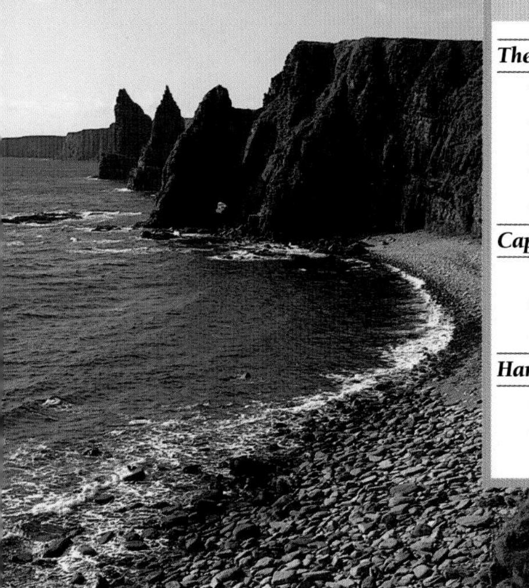

The pointed rocky formations known as Duncansby Stacks

TOP FIVE PLACES FOR BIRD-WATCHING

The Flow Country

This area supports around 70 per cent of Europe's breeding population of greenshanks, together with 20 per cent of the black-throated divers and others such as dunlin and golden plovers.

Cape Wrath

Britain's highest cliffs, at Clo Mor (918ft/280m), and offshore stacks support a famous colony of gannets.

Handa Island

Birds reign supreme on the cliffs – thousands of wheeling gulls, guillemots, kittiwakes, puffins and razorbills. The island can be reached by boat from Tarbet.

Duncansby Head

To the east of John O'Groats, the tall stacks of rock just offshore are home to thousands of noisy sea birds, including puffins and cormorants.

The Beauly Firth

The mud-flats at Beauly Firth attract large numbers of birds. Overwintering greylag and pink-footed geese graze the surrounding fields, and a variety of sea-ducks, including goldeneye and scoter, may be seen near the Kessock Bridge.

Ullapool is a bustling fishing centre, with the great hulks of factory ships from eastern Europe anchored in Loch Broom. It is the ferry terminal for the Western Isles and an excellent base for exploring Wester Ross. In summer you can take a boat to the Summer Isles where you can watch sea birds, seals, dolphins and porpoises.

On the opposite coast, from Wick to the Dornoch Firth, is the quiet, mild landscape of Easter Ross. The Dukes of Sutherland, responsible for much rural depopulation during the Clearances of the 19th century, have their ancestral home at Dunrobin Castle near Golspie. Golspie and Brora, midway between Inverness and Wick, offer lovely sandy beaches and facilities for sailing, golf and other holiday pastimes. The dignified town of Dornoch has a world-class golf course with stunning views across the Dornoch Firth.

The Black Isle, between the Cromarty and Beauly Firths, is actually a peninsula of fertile farmland. Cromarty, at its tip, is a delightful 18th-century town, an important centre of fishing and commerce until the 19th century, when it was bypassed by the railways.

INVERPOLLY NATIONAL NATURE RESERVE

The Inverpolly National Nature Reserve offers access to this fine, dramatic countryside in all its glory, and the visitor centre at **Knockan** is a good place to start. The diversity of habitats in the region is revealed, including bogs, lochs and patches of ancient woodland, with a corresponding diversity of flora. A geology trail here illuminates the formation of the Assynt area, and part of the 'Moine Thrust', a huge slab of land that was shifted many miles westwards, can be seen in the rocks of **Knockan Cliff**. There are excellent views from the top of the mountains of **Coigach**. Of these, **Stac Pollaidh** (2,008ft/612m) is the most popular. Look out for deer and birds of prey, and you may even see signs of wild cats in the area.

ANCIENT FORTS

Vitrified Iron-Age hillforts are found throughout Scotland, Ireland and continental Europe. Vitrification occurred when the wooden beams used in the construction of stone ramparts were set on fire by an attacking enemy. The intense heat could cause certain softer rocks to melt and re-fuse in great lumps on cooling. **Knock Farril** (below), above Strathpeffer, is a particularly good example; another is **Craig Phadrig**, set on a prominent hilltop to the west of Inverness.

SEE CONTACTS SECTION FOR ADDITIONAL INFORMATION

Royal Dornoch being rated among the top 12 courses in the world. Dornoch itself has a fine cathedral (now heavily restored) that was first used for worship in 1239. The Witch's Stone commemorates the last witch-burning in 1722. Leave Dornoch on the A949 Castle Street, and at the war memorial turn right on to the B9168 for Wick. On reaching the A9 turn right. Continue forward and cross the head of Loch Fleet by a causeway, The Mound, built by Thomas Telford in 1816. Continue ahead on the A9.

2 Pass a statue of the first Duke of Sutherland and continue into Golspie. Created from a few fishing huts to house victims of the Sutherland Clearances, Golspie is now a comfortable town with a long beach and magnificent walks around the waterfalls in Dunrobin Glen. Continue on the A9 past Dunrobin Castle. This splendid, gleaming, turreted mansion, originally a 13th-century keep and extensively rebuilt in 1856, contains paintings, furniture, and family heirlooms of the Dukes of Sutherland, and enjoys fine views out to the North Sea. Pass Cairn Liath Broch, a fortress-like building, dating from between 100 BC and AD 100, from where you can enjoy excellent views of the statue and Dunrobin Castle from the car-park. Continue on along the coast road to Brora.

3 In Brora pass the clock tower, then cross the river bridge and turn left on to a minor road, signed to Balnacoil. Continue as the road becomes a single track for some 18 miles (29km) to the A839. Pass through Rogart, a scattered crofting village above the upper valley of the River Fleet, ignoring all minor roads left and right and soon turn right on to the A839 towards Lairg. In Lairg follow the Lochinver signs and turn right across the River Shin to leave by the A839. Shortly, branch left on to the B864, signed Invershin (7 miles/11.5km), and follow a single-track road through Achany Glen and past the Falls of Shin. In June or early July you may see salmon leaping up the falls, especially if the river is in spate.

4 Continue on the B864, and turn left on to the A837 towards Bonar Bridge and re-cross the River Shin. Join the A836 at Invershin and continue for 5 miles (8km) to Bonar Bridge. Here turn left on to the A949, signed Spinningdale and Dornoch, passing by Spinningdale to reach Clashmore. In 1792 David Dale, one of the great Lowland cotton magnates, joined forces with a local laird to build the first northern mill at Spinningdale. It was burned out in 1806 and now only its jagged ruins remain. In 1.5 miles (2km) turn right on to the A949 for the return to Dornoch.

THE WESTERN ISLANDS

The group of islands off the ragged west coast of Scotland is steeped in the history and legends of the land. Skye, accessible by the road bridge from Kyle of Lochalsh, is the largest of the Inner Hebrides, characterised by the high peaks of the Cuillins. Portree, with its colour-washed houses round the harbour and delightful miniature square, is the island's capital. On the Trotternish peninsula, look for the distinctive column of the Old Man of Storr and the dramatic waterfall at the Kilt Rock. Waternish juts towards the Outer Hebrides, sheltering Dunvegan Castle, home of the chiefs of the clan MacLeod. Broadford, the main centre for exploring the south of the island, is the place to find good-quality souvenirs.

Coll and Tiree are low-lying and fertile. The low island of Coll is made up of Lewisian gneiss, the oldest rock in Europe, which can be seen in the rocky approach to the harbour at Arinagour. Inland, peat bogs dotted with lochans (small lakes) give way in the west to silvery beaches, with huge sand dunes. Tiree is somewhat windswept, but this is a positive attraction for windsurfers.

SKYE MUSEUM OF ISLAND LIFE

This 'living museum' is a series of seven thatched black houses, reconstructed to form an ancient island township. The original black house on the site is much as it was when it was last inhabited in the late 1950s. Here locals re-create the crofting way of life as it was a century ago.

Rum is a National Nature Reserve; Eigg has its 'singing sands' of quartzite and much of geological interest; Muck supports a small community, run as a model island unit by its paternalistic laird; and Canna, the most westerly of this island group, has northern cliffs noisy with sea birds.

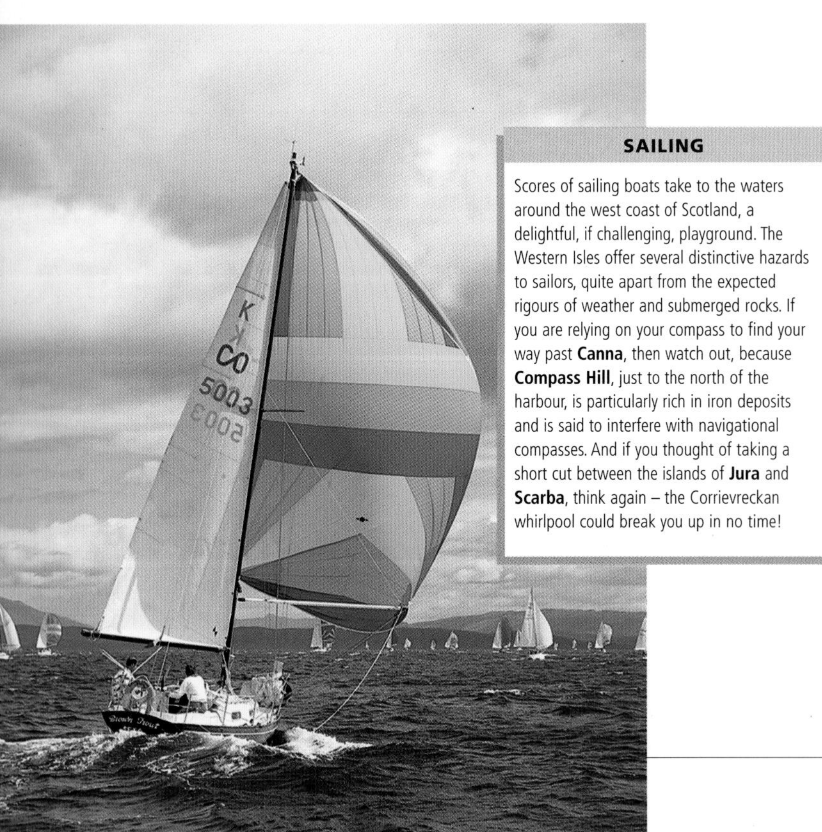

SAILING

Scores of sailing boats take to the waters around the west coast of Scotland, a delightful, if challenging, playground. The Western Isles offer several distinctive hazards to sailors, quite apart from the expected rigours of weather and submerged rocks. If you are relying on your compass to find your way past **Canna**, then watch out, because **Compass Hill**, just to the north of the harbour, is particularly rich in iron deposits and is said to interfere with navigational compasses. And if you thought of taking a short cut between the islands of **Jura** and **Scarba**, think again – the Corrievreckan whirlpool could break you up in no time!

Colourful cottages and small hotels line the harbour at Portree on the Isle of Skye

Cuillins Walk

WALK

In the Executioner's Shadow

START/FINISH: Sligachan Hotel, at the junction of the A87 and A863, Isle of Skye
DISTANCE: 5.5 miles (9km)
ASCENT/GRADIENT: 1,850ft (564m); gradual; optional extension very steep and strenuous
TERRAIN/PATHS: open moorland beneath high mountains; good paths; optional extension very rough
PARKING: car-park at Sligachan Hotel

Climbing in these rugged mountains is not for the inexperienced, but a walk on the lower slopes rewards the effort with dramatic views.

1 The sharp, distinctive profiles of Sgurr nan Gillean and Am Bàsteir – 'the Executioner' – represent the northernmost Munros (mountains over 3,000ft/914m) on the most magnificent mountain range in the British Isles, the Cuillin. As with the other 30 or so peaks strung out along this 8 mile (13km) arc of bare rock, their summits are mostly out of bounds to all but the most capable scramblers and climbers. However, much of their rugged grandeur can still be enjoyed at close quarters if you explore the more accessible corries of the range. From the Sligachan Hotel, walk along the A863 for about 200yds (182m). Take one of the paths on the left, opposite the top of a slip road to the hotel. Most lead across boggy ground to cross the Allt Dearg Mor at the footbridge. Walk south on the gently rising footpath towards Sgurr nan Gillean, the easternmost peak of the mountains seen clearly on the skyline ahead.

2 Do not cross the second footbridge, this time over the Allt Dearg Beag, but instead continue along the right bank of this river. There are many picturesque pools and waterfalls here and, higher up, the path traverses rock slabs and a few intervening burns, which can be forded easily.

3 The path fades away in the scree below the entrance to the Bhasteir Gorge. Most will be content with the breathtaking views from the mouth of the gorge, both ahead to the towering heights of Am Bàsteir and Sgurr nan Gillean and behind to the wide views of northern

Beyond Skye, across the sometimes treacherous waters of the Little Minch, lie the Western Isles (Outer Hebrides). Lewis and Harris, North and South Uist, Benbecula and Barra are linked by a series of causeways and ferry crossings. Almost treeless, the Outer Hebrides have attractive Atlantic beaches backed by fertile coastal plains known as 'machair'. Everywhere are reminders of the past – cairns and tombs, forts and churches. Barra sums up the whole chain, with empty silver beaches backed by flower meadows, stretches of peat bog and small crofts.

South Uist is dotted with lochans, many of them home to a wide variety of birds. Most of North Uist is shattered into fragments by lochs and inlets, and it is sometimes possible to glimpse precipitous St Kilda, 45 miles (72km) out in the Atlantic.

HARRIS TWEED

Harris Tweed is one of the mainstays of the local economy in the **Outer Hebrides** and is still woven by hand. The Harris Tweed Authority states that 'Harris tweed must be made from 100 per cent pure virgin wool, dyed, spun and finished in the Outer Hebrides and hand woven by the islanders in their own homes.' Always check for the famous Orb mark, the proof that a piece of cloth is authentic. The only place in the islands where the entire production process can be seen is the **Lewis Loom Centre** in **Stornoway**, where Ronnie Mackenzie has set up a small museum and exhibition centre. The centre gives regular demonstrations of carding, spinning, warping and weaving, explaining the use of natural and synthetic dyes. The Lewis Loom shop stocks a wide variety of Harris Tweed clothing.

Benbecula, often described as a stepping stone between the Uists, has a causeway that spans the mesmerising mosaic of freshwater lochs, sea lochs and sandbanks. This is a beautiful place for bird-watching and fishing. From a cave here, Bonnie Prince Charlie travelled to Rossinish Point and made his famous escape 'over the sea to Skye'.

Largest of the Outer Hebrides is the island that comprises Harris and Lewis. Harris is mountainous, with long empty beaches and wonderful views, while Lewis has great undulating blanket peat moors and hundreds of lochs. The capital, Stornoway, is a lively town and centre of the prestigious Harris Tweed industry. Away to the west is one of Scotland's most enduring and important monuments, Callanish Stone Circle, comparable to Stonehenge.

RAASAY OUTDOOR CENTRE

This is the place for anyone looking for an adventure holiday. The centre provides equipment and instruction for a range of exhilarating activities including sailing, water-skiing, sailboarding, mountain biking, walking and climbing. Accommodation is provided in the house where the 18th-century English writer Dr Johnson and his biographer, Boswell, lodged during their tour of the Hebrides. The activities are open to day visitors too.

OTTERS

Many people hope to spot wild otters around the shores and lochs of Scotland, and, given a bit of luck, a good pair of binoculars and some local guidance, there is every chance of doing so. Places to try include:

Kylerhea Otter Sanctuary on Skye

Loch Sunart on the southern coast of the Ardnamurchan peninsula

Loch Spelve in Mull

Loch Eynort in South Uist.

Skye. In dry conditions it is worth taking time to view the gorge itself by descending carefully to the bottom of the ravine. The passage up the gorge, however, is soon blocked by deep pools and precipitous waterfalls. Return to Sligachan by retracing your footsteps back down the upward path.

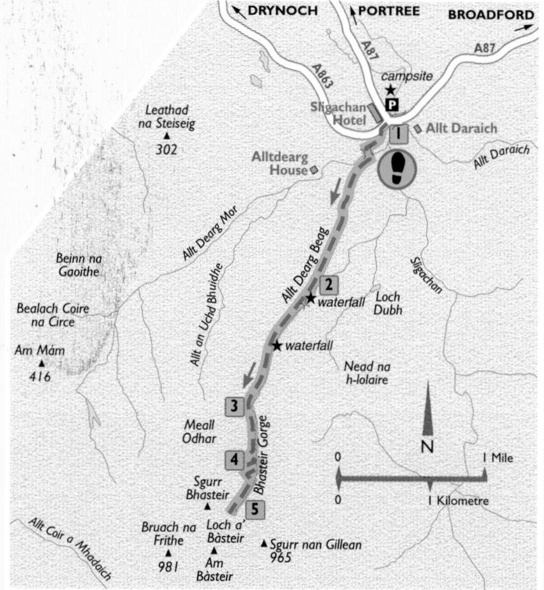

4 Experienced walkers may continue up to the corrie above the gorge by the rough path rising to the right of the gorge in steep zigzags over scree. Stay almost directly above the vertiginous sides of the gorge and the stream on the left; do not drift too far to the right. The clambering is quite hard going but on approaching a small cave, there is a less steep, better defined path for a while. Beyond the cave, continue the ascent over very rugged terrain, rejoining the uppermost reaches of the Allt Dearg Beag. Follow the stream up to its obvious source in the corrie.

5 The path ends at Loch a' Bhàsteir from where you can retrace your steps back to Sligachan – a wild and remote place surrounded by rugged peaks. **This upper leg of the walk should only be attempted by those with experience of mountain walking.**

DISCOVERING FARM & COUNTRY PARKS

Nearly everyone in Britain has a country park close to where they live. They are often situated quite close to the towns and cities which now provide the home of four out of five Britons. And they are purposely designed for use by urban-based people as a little bit of managed countryside, literally on the doorstep.

A country park is not a large wild and remote area like a national park. Although some, like the ancient rocks of Bradgate Park in Leicestershire, Tegg's Nose on the edge of the Cheshire Pennines, or the chalk cliffs of the Seven Sisters in East Sussex, are based on outstanding physical features, few can provide the challenge of the Snowdonia or Lake District peaks, for instance.

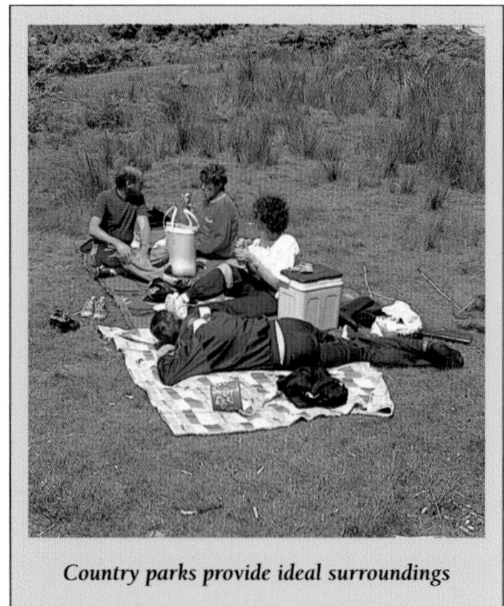

Country parks provide ideal surroundings for a relaxing family picnic

Most of the 250 country parks in Britain provide relatively small, secluded areas of woodland or open grassland where families or individuals can relax, picnic, watch the wildlife, or simply absorb the peace and beauty of the countryside.

But in nearly all cases, especially in the larger country parks, they provide excellent opportunities for formal or informal recreation, whether it is walking, cycling (several have cycle-hire centres), horse-riding, or sailing or fishing in the water-based parks, like Fritton Lake in Norfolk. More adventurous sports such as mountain biking, hang-gliding or paragliding can be enjoyed in the larger country parks, such as the forest parks of the Borders in Northumberland and Galloway, or the Queen Elizabeth Country Park on the rolling South Downs of Hampshire.

Country parks were both a response to and a product of the great exodus to the countryside of the 1960s, which was described by Michael Dower, son of National Parks founder John Dower, as 'the fourth wave'. He foresaw people swarming 'like ants' out of cities by car or public transport and effectively ruining the countryside they came to enjoy. The fuel crisis of the 1970s put a temporary brake on this leisure explosion, but it has boomed again in the affluent 1990s, and now a day out in the country, usually involving a short walk or some other kind of exercise, is by far the most popular form of outdoor recreation, easily beating watching football or angling.

Country parks are generally administered by local authorities, usually county councils, which were given the power to do so under the 1968 Countryside Act. But others have been set up by district councils, or private trusts or charities, such as the National Trust at Cragside in Northumberland or the fascinating Cregneash Story, an open-air museum near the southern tip of the Isle of Man.

Farm parks were originally set up, with encouragement from the Countryside Commission (now the Countryside Agency) in an effort to interpret farming to largely urban visitors. At places like Easton Farm Park in Suffolk and the Acton Scott Working Farm beneath the Shropshire Hills, young visitors are encouraged to touch and feed young farm animals, breaking down the barriers between town and country.

Other farm parks, like the Appleby Castle Conservation Centre in Cumbria and the Cotswold Farm Park in Gloucestershire, are also managed as specialist rare-breed survival centres, where the rarer and older breeds of farm livestock are bred for possible future genetic requirements.

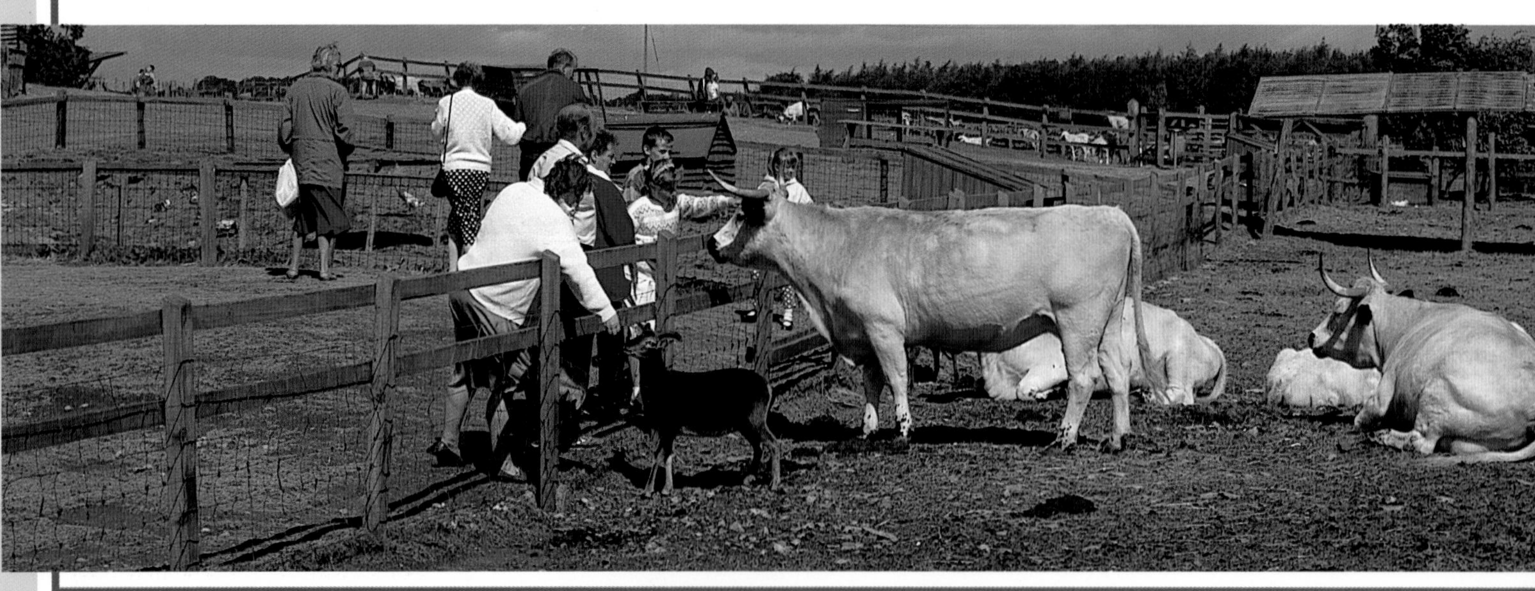

CATHEDRAL IN THE HILLS

Burton Dassett Country Park, near Kineton in Warwickshire, is not only one of the finest viewpoints in the Midlands, it also has a fascinating history. This little range of grassy ironstone hills – ideal for kite-flying – was once the centre of a thriving village, depopulated in the Middle Ages, leaving only a beacon tower overlooking Edge Hill, and the lovely parish church which is known as 'the cathedral in the hills'.

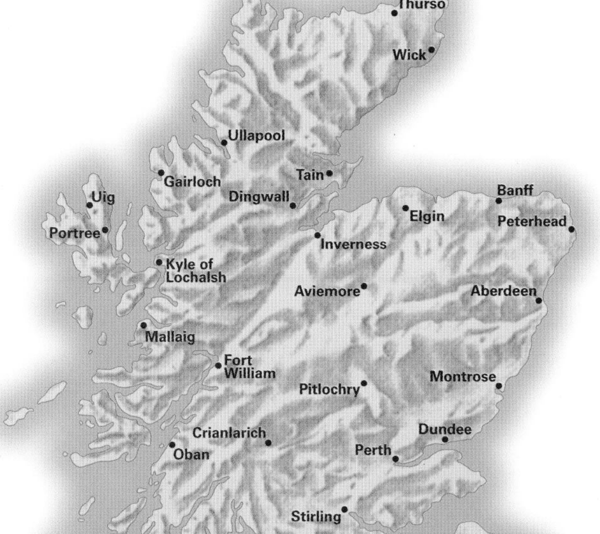

The coastal beauty of the Seven Sisters Country Park

BIKING THROUGH THE FOREST

Mountain biking on the numerous wooded rides through the extensive Border Forest Park of Northumberland is one of the finest ways to explore this challenging and historic countryside. Cycles can be hired from the Kielder Castle Visitor Centre or from Kielder Water, the huge man-made lake at the heart of the forest.

Many of the larger parks have easy traffic-free cycling routes

Getting acquainted with the cattle at the Cotswold Farm Park

Farm and country parks shown on the map have been chosen for their particular interest or attraction and to give a good geographical spread. It is not possible to show every one on the map.

WALES

View from Castell Dinas Bran, Powys

THE BRECON BEACONS & SOUTH WALES

The Brecon Beacons National Park, straddling the borders of Powys, Dyfed, Gwent and Mid Glamorgan, takes its name from and is centred on the triple peaks of the Beacons themselves, which rise above the lush valley of the River Usk. These sandstone mountains stand like a petrified wave about to break over the ancient county town of Brecon. To the west lies the wild expanse of Fforest Fawr and the Black Mountain, while to the east on the border with England are the Black Mountains. South of the National Park, the South Wales valleys, no longer grimy with coal dust but green with the shoots of regeneration, reach northwards from Glamorgan's largely undiscovered Heritage Coast, the Vale of Usk, and the exciting new regional capital of Cardiff.

PORTH-YR-OGOF

Porth-yr-Ogof is the most impressive cave entrance in the Brecon Beacons National Park, swallowing the infant River Mellte as it enters its underground course. This is a favourite spot for cavers, but with at least 14 entrances, only the most experienced should consider entering far from the gaping mouth of this impressive cave. Others should be content with the Dan-yr-Ogof Showcaves system, in the Tawe Valley north of Abercraf, claimed to be the largest showcave in western Europe, and with the largest chamber in any British showcave.

WATERFALL COUNTRY

South of the tiny hamlet of Ystradfellte, the Rivers Mellte and Pyrddin, tributaries of the Neath, flow through what has become known as the Brecon Beacons 'Waterfall Country'. As the rivers enter beautifully wooded valleys, a series of spectacular waterfalls, including Sgwd yr Eira (Falls of Snow), Sgwd Clun-gwyn (White Meadow Fall), Sgwd Isaf Clun-gwyn (Lower White Meadow Fall), and Sgwd Gwladys (Lady's Fall), tumble over 'steps' of limestone as the rivers leave the sandstones of their sources high on the Beacons.

MAP AND KEY

- Raglan Walk
- Caerphilly Drive
- Brecon Drive

CARDIFF CASTLE

The original Cardiff Castle was a Norman building begun in 1093, and its circular keep stands on the site of an even earlier Roman fort. The present extravagant, 19th-century Gothic-revival building is full of romantic medievalism and is the jewel at the heart of Cardiff's Civic Centre. The exotic building came about as a collaboration between the 3rd Marquess of Bute and the Victorian architect William Burges.

CARDIFF & THE VALE OF USK

The great city of Cardiff, capital of Wales, lies at the mouth of the Severn, with the Vale of Usk and Monmouth beyond. It is the natural focal point of the coastal plain, the southern gateway to Wales ever since the Romans and Normans built their fortifications at places such as Caerleon, Cardiff, Monmouth and Raglan.

Surprisingly, Cardiff has been the capital of Wales only since 1955, but it has quickly developed into a truly international city of culture and commerce. As devolution became a reality, it was chosen as the site for the new National Assembly of Wales. The city, once just a coal port, grew mainly due to the efforts of successive Marquesses of Bute, who were also responsible for restoring the castle. In 1898 the walls of an extensive Roman fort were discovered and restored, and its history had to be rewritten. The remains of the handsome circular Norman keep stand beside the romantic medievalism of the ornate 19th-century Gothic living quarters. Buildings of note include the splendid City Hall and Law Courts, the National Museum of Wales in Cathays Park and the University College. The National Stadium is the home of Welsh rugby football.

North of the centre is the leafy suburb of Llandaff, where the city's cathedral, Bishop's House and Deanery are overlooked by Joseph Epstein's soaring central arch depicting Christ in Majesty.

St Fagans is a small village of thatched cottages to the west of Cardiff which draws visitors to the Museum of Welsh Life, housed in the grounds of St Fagans Castle.

Just 2 miles (3km) south of Cardiff is Penarth, a popular seaside resort which came to prominence in Victorian times. The old harbour retains its charm, although sailing and water-skiing are

TOURING THE CASTLES

Three Castles Walk – takes in Skenfrith, White and Grosmont castles over a total distance of 18 miles (29km).

Four Castles Cycle Route – adds Abergavenny Castle to the above circuit for keen cyclists who like a glimpse of history from the saddle.

THE WIDE BLUE YONDER

South Wales has always been a magnet for keen paragliders, due to the fact that its hills and coastline providing plenty of ideal sites. Most activity centres around **Crickhowell** in the Usk Valley, an area affectionately known amongst the fraternity as the 'Crickhowell Triangle'. **Axis Paragliding and Hang-gliding Centre** at **Abergavenny** provides fun days and tandem flights for beginners, and also caters for the more experienced pilot.

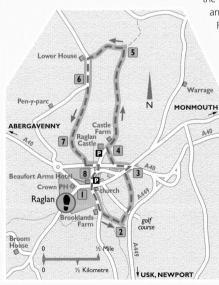

CAERLEON

Caerleon was an important Roman military base which accommodated thousands of men. The foundations of the barrack lines and parts of the ramparts can be seen, with remains of the cookhouse, latrines and baths. Most impressive is the great amphitheatre built around AD 80, which could seat 6,000 people – the most complete excavated Roman amphitheatre in Britain.

Raglan Walk

WALK

Raglan's Civil War Fortress

START/FINISH: Raglan. Off the A40 7 miles (11km) southwest of Monmouth

DISTANCE: 5 miles (8km)

ASCENT/GRADIENT: 250ft (76m); few gradual ascents

TERRAIN/PATHS: fields, enclosed bridleway; good paths; can be muddy after rain

PARKING: Castle Street, Raglan or by Raglan Castle

During the Civil War Charles I retreated to this imposing castle, built by the Marcher lords, in the beautiful Welsh Marches, and famously besieged in 1646. The walk circles this fine castle and explores the fertile land that the Marcher lords coveted.

1 From Castle Street, take the Chepstow road, past St Cadoc's Church, towards Chepstow. Ignore the footpath on the left after the school and health centre. Ahead, stay on the left-hand side of the road and, opposite Brooklands Farm B&B sign, enter a gate with the path leading towards the sewage works to the right. Before the sewage works continue over a concrete bridge, go straight across the field and cross the next field diagonally to the far left corner. Cross a stile and sleeper bridge and bear slightly left, following the edge of a sports field to a gate on to a lane.

Night falls on the Welsh capital, looking over the redeveloped area of Cardiff Bay

2 Cross the lane, go through a gate and bear left, uphill, towards a stile behind a railway wagon shed. Cross to a lane and go over a stile opposite into a cattle field. Follow a hedge to the right and cross a stile into another field. Keep to the right of a field to reach a stile on to a road. Turn right and walk towards the A40.

3 Turn left and cross to the far side of the A40. Walk along the verge to steps down to a signed footpath and a stile into a field. Cross the field uphill to reach a gate on to a lane leading to Raglan Castle car-park. On 14 June 1645 the Royalists were defeated at Naseby and Charles I rode west to stay at Raglan. The following year, a Parliamentarian army beseiged the castle and tunnelled beneath the walls. Their collapse brought down the outer walls, creating the imposing ruins we see today.

4 Turn right towards Castle Farm. Where the lane bears left cross the stile on the right and with the field edge on your left walk to another stile. Cross and follow the left edge, crossing the stile in it and bearing right to a stile. Cross and turn left through a gate. Cross a track, go over a stile and turn half-right across the field beyond, passing a small hillock. At the bottom of the field cross a stile and turn right, leaving the hedge to go through a left-hand gate ahead. Follow the hedge on the right, maintaining direction when it bears away. Cross a ditch and continue to a stile. Follow the hedge on the right, crossing a stile over it and turn left uphill. Where the field widens, turn left to a cross stile.

5 Turn left along an enclosed bridleway. Follow this downhill, then uphill, to reach a road opposite Lower House. Turn left.

6 When the road turns sharp right, cross a stile on the left into a field and walk to the right, round the edge of the field to a stile in a wire fence. Cross the field, bearing left but aiming well to the right of the castle and church tower. Cross a stile in a far hedge and bear left, aiming for the large hedge gap.

7 Go through the gap and bear away from the left field edge to reach a hedge elbow across the field. Bear left to walk with the hedge to a stile on to the A40. Cross and turn left along the verge about 330yds (300m), to reach a gap in the stone wall on the right.

8 Go through and turn right, crossing the bridge into Castle Street.

ROUND WALES IN A DAY

The **Museum of Welsh Life** at **St Fagans** allows visitors to travel round the whole of Wales – all in a day. You can also travel back in time to the days before modern technology and transport made many villages and homes the same as anywhere else in Britain. Farmhouses, workshops, a village school, chapel, bakehouse, mill and village shop are included in the many buildings which have been re-erected stone-by-stone, all in the beautiful parkland setting of St Fagans Castle.

now the most common activities. The Turner House Art Gallery, part of the National Museum of Wales, is one of the best in the country. Further south along the coast, beyond Lower Penarth, is Lavernock and the Cosmeston Lake Country Park and Medieval Village.

Barry was once one of the biggest ports in the world, serving the nearby coalfield. Today holiday-makers flock to the enormous amusement park, the beaches at Whitmore Bay and the Porthkerry Country Park. The Welsh Hawking Centre has over 2,000 birds of prey, while steam buffs gravitate to Woodham Brothers' scrapyard, renowned for its steam locomotives.

Home of the 2nd Augustan Legion for 300 years, the Roman fort of *Isca Silurum*, as Caerleon was known, was one of their most important fortresses in Wales, and is the most complete survivor.

Newport is a busy industrial town, standing where the River Usk flows into the Bristol Channel. The town's cathedral, St Woolos, has Norman arches and a medieval tower, plus a modern window designed by John Piper. Near by is the fine 18th-century mansion of Tredegar House, its grounds now a country park. Monnow Bridge in Monmouth is reckoned to be the only fortified Norman bridge left in Britain, and it stands at the entrance to this charming Tudor and Georgian market town. A pleasant walk to the southeast of the town takes in 800-ft (243-m) Kymin Hill, with its splendid views over the Monnow and Wye Valleys.

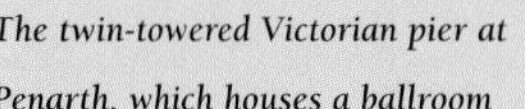

The twin-towered Victorian pier at Penarth, which houses a ballroom

GLAMORGAN HERITAGE COAST & THE VALLEYS

Once one of the powerhouses of the British Empire, the valleys of South Wales, with their abundant supplies of high-quality coal and iron were ravaged and blackened by the Industrial Revolution. It has been estimated that as much as a third of the wealth created during the Industrial Revolution was produced in the coal mines and iron and steel works of the South Wales valleys. But today, the valleys have largely reverted to their original green peacefulness. The only reminders of that grim industrial past are in museums such as the Big Pit Mining Museum at Blaenafon, where visitors can descend the 300-ft (90-m) shaft to find out what life was like for generations of miners, and at the Rhondda Heritage Park at Trehafod, Pontypridd, is a unique Living History attraction, based at the Lewis Merthyr Colliery, which provides a fun and interesting day out.

The former colliery at Rhondda Heritage Park, a memorial to the Welsh coal-mining tradition

The transformation of the valleys is typified by the inauguration of cycle trails through over 200 miles (320km) of some of the finest forest, valley and mountain scenery in South Wales, and leisure drives such as the Cwmcarn Forest Drive, at Crosskeys near Caerphilly, which leads through the conifers below the summit of Twm Barlwm mountain, where Druids once worshipped.

WELSH WALLS

Clawdd field walls – traditionally Welsh, these walls seem to grow naturally from the landscape. They are in-filled with compacted earth or rubble, and built up from large, flat foundation stones with the facing stones set vertically on edge, the length of the stones running into the wall. The courses are more or less even, with the height gradually diminishing with each one, and the capping is topped with turf.

Slab walls – sometimes known as 'tombstone walls', these can be found anywhere there are abundant supplies of slabby slate or sandstone. They are most common in Wales, and consist simply of large, thick slabs of stone set vertically upright, with about a third of the stone in the ground, sometimes topped by wire.

Slate fences – similar to slab walls, these slim, single-stone walls or fences are found especially around the blue-slate quarries of Blaenau Ffestiniog in Snowdonia. They can also be topped by a line of wire to make them more stockproof.

The squat towers and massive water defences of 13th-century Caerphilly Castle

Caerphilly Drive

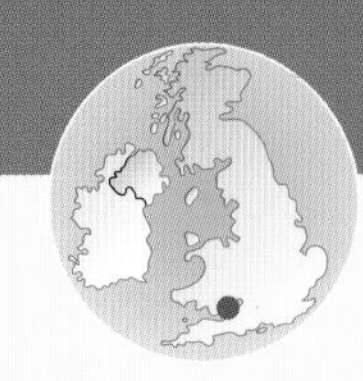

DRIVE

A Castle Beyond the Garden of Wales

START/FINISH: Caerphilly. On the A469 7 miles (11.5km) north of Cardiff

DISTANCE: 78 miles (126km)

Hilly coal-bearing country is the backdrop for one of the finest castles in Britain. Southward is the fertile Vale of Glamorgan, its rolling green farmlands forming the Garden of Wales.

1 Take the B4600, then the A468, Merthyr Tydfil road, then turn left on to the A470. Turn left and right along the Radyr road, then right to reach Pentyrch in 2.5 miles (4km). Turn right at the T-junction, then right again. After approximately 200yds (183m) take a sharp left turn.

2 Turn left then right and right again to Rhiwsaeson; then follow the signs to Llantrisant and the town centre. A path leads to Caerau Hillfort, an Iron-Age fortification, from the narrow lane leading straight ahead from the road junction in Rhiwsaeson. Llantrisant is the home of the Royal Mint. For the Royal Mint, turn right on to the A4119 for 1.5 miles (2.5km), then take the third exit at the roundabout and then immediately left. From the Royal Mint, return along the A4119, going straight through major traffic lights in Llantrisant, to turn right along the B4264 to Miskin. Turn right on to the minor road, under the M4, and right at the T-junction to Clawdd-côch. Turn right to Tre-Dodridge, then left and continue to the A48.

3 Turn right on the A48, then left through St Hilary towards St Athan. Old Beaupre Castle stands south of St Hilary, a pretty village of immaculate stone dwellings, and is more a manor house than a military fortress, dating as it does from Elizabethan times. Turn sharp right to Cowbridge. A handsome, prosperous old town, Cowbridge is known as the capital of the Vale of Glamorgan. Remnants of the medieval walled town remain. Take the minor road to Llanblethian, then turn right to the telephone box uphill to the B4270 and turn left. Turn right and follow signs to Marcross. For Nash Point proceed straight ahead (staggered junction). The limestone cliffs at Nash Point are striking and from the cliff-top car-park there are views across to Exmoor. Return and turn right to Llantwit Major. Along the way you pass St Donat's Castle, now a

South of the Valleys is the beautiful Vale of Glamorgan, an area steeped in ancient Celtic, Roman and Norman history. Caerphilly, best known for its tasty, white, crumbly cheese, boasts one of the largest and best-preserved castles in Britain. With its massive gatehouse, extensive land and water defences, and concentric lines of defence, it represents a high point of medieval military architecture. A unique feature is the ruined tower – the victim of subsidence – which manages to out-lean even the tower of Pisa!

The many rivers of the South Wales valleys, such as the Taff, the Ebbw, the Rhymney and the Neath run down to the coast on the shores of the Bristol Channel. Much of the coastline, with its dramatic cliffs and fine beaches, has been designated Glamorgan Heritage Coast. The seaside resorts of Barry Island and Porthcawl are among the most popular in Wales with their sweeping sandy beaches and lively amusement parks. Barry had only 85 inhabitants in 1880 but expanded at a furious rate when it became a major exporting point for coal from the Valleys during the early 20th century.

In the far west of the area is the ancient town of Neath. It has largely recovered from the worst of its industrial legacy and has rediscovered its past with the remains of a Roman fort, Norman castle, and a Cistercian abbey founded in 1130 by Richard de Grainville. Active explorers will want to venture northeast up the Vale of Neath to visit the lovely 80-ft (24-m) Melin Court waterfall towards the true 'Waterfall Country' around Pontneddfechan, on the edge of the Brecon Beacons.

SEASIDE RESORTS

On clear days, the coastline and tors of Exmoor can be seen all the way across the Bristol Channel from **Porthcawl**'s airy promenade. The resort has two fine beaches and a large and famous amusement park at Coney Beach.

Barry Island, linked to the mainland by a causeway, boasts one of the largest amusement parks in Britain (right), and is a popular weekend getaway for the citizens of nearby Cardiff. There is a fine sandy beach, perfect for all kinds of watersports. Don't forget your bucket and spade!

ON YOUR BIKE

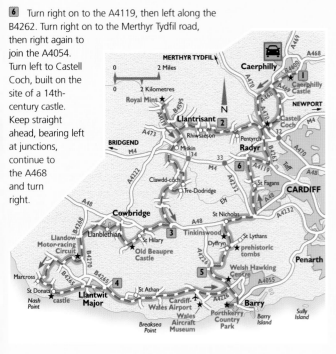

Celtic Trail – part of the 220-mile (354km) National Cycle Network, which runs from the Severn Bridge west to the Pembrokeshire Coast National Park.

Taff Trail Cycle Path – runs north–south through the South Wales valleys from Cardiff to Merthyr Tydfil and beyond, linking with the Celtic Trail.

Easy cycle routes – take the route through the Sirhowy Country Park from the 14 Locks Visitor Centre, the Ogmore Valley, Bedford Park or Margam Park. Easy for the inexperienced cyclist.

Mountain-biking routes – try the 25-mile (40-km) High Level route, which climbs up from Pontypridd to a height of over 1,960ft (600m) on Rhigos mountain, before dropping down to the Neath Valley.

college, which, although dating from 1300, was considerably restored in the early 19th century. Llantwit Major is full of character, with attractive old stone and whitewashed buildings.

4 Turn right on to the B4265. Turn right to pass the aircraft museum, then turn left to the A4226 and turn right. To visit Porthkerry Country Park, a long swathe of lush grassland, a pebble beach and towering cliffs, with picnic sites and nature trails, turn right on to the B4266 and follow signs. Return and proceed ahead on the A4226.

5 Turn right along the minor road towards St Lythans, then turn left to St Nicholas. Just north of Barry is the Welsh Hawking Centre and Wildlife Park. Here you can view a wide variety of birds, including buzzards, eagles and owls. South of St Nicholas stand a pair of megalithic tombs. St Lythans is the more accessible but Tinkinswood is more impressive. Turn right on to the A48. Take the Cardiff West road at the roundabout then turn left through St Fagans, home of the Museum of Welsh Life.

6 Turn right on to the A4119, then left along the B4262. Turn right on to the Merthyr Tydfil road, then right again to join the A4054. Turn left to Castell Coch, built on the site of a 14th-century castle. Keep straight ahead, bearing left at junctions, continue to the A468 and turn right.

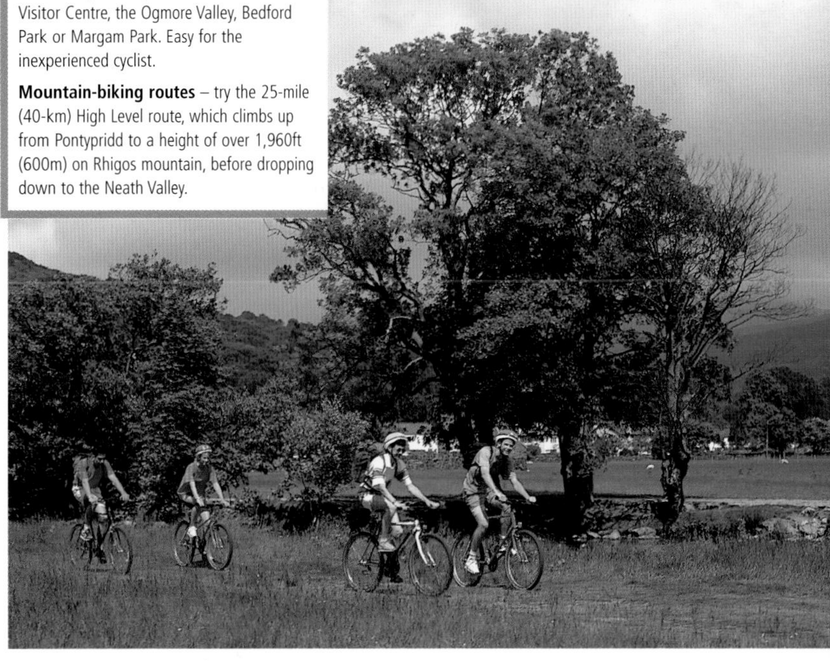

BRECON & THE BEACONS

There is much more to the 519-sq mile (1,343-sq km) Brecon Beacons National Park, established in 1957, than the north-facing scarps of the Beacons themselves, which are centred on 2,907-ft (886-m) Pen-y-Fan. The easiest ascent of Pen-y-Fan is from Storey Arms on the A470, on a largely paved track.

Two other quite distinct mountain masses make up the area, both of which confusingly carry the name 'Black'. The Black Mountains are a range of sandstone hills running north–south between Hay-on-Wye and Abergavenny. Offa's Dyke, the 8th-century boundary embankment and ditch that separated England and Wales, runs along their crest and makes a fine walk which is now a designated National Trail.

The Black Mountain is a far wilder, less-visited area, lying to the west of the A406 Sennybridge to Ystradgynlais road. It is centred on the sweeping crest of Carmarthen Fan, at 2,631ft (802m) the highest point, with the mysterious little glacial lake of Llyn y Fan Fach at its feet.

A leisurely way to enjoy the scenery, on the Brecon Mountain Railway

There is yet another landscape which is prevalent in the south of the Park. The area of Carboniferous rocks which stretches across the southern boundary has created a wonderland of tumbling waterfalls, huge caves and potholes, and beautiful woodlands, which are a major attraction to visitors and easily accessible from the valleys of South Wales. A pleasant way to view

The Norman remains of the circular keep at Tretower Castle

PUSHING THE BOAT OUT

A popular and more leisurely way to see the Beacons is to cruise in a narrow boat along the **Monmouthshire and Brecon Canal**, built between 1797 and 1812 to link Brecon with Newport and the Severn. After restoration it was re-opened in 1970 and is now exclusively used for leisure traffic.

Brecon Drive

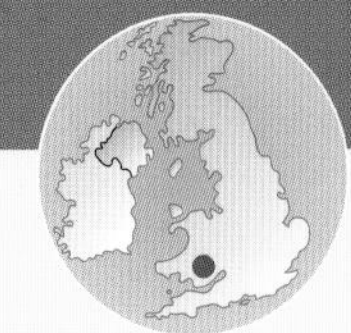

DRIVE

The Central Beacons

START/FINISH: Brecon. Town on the A470, 14 miles (23km) north of Merthyr Tydfil

DISTANCE: 68 miles (109.5m)

The Brecon Beacons is made up of four mountain ranges and takes its name from its central uplands, a mountain block sandwiched between the two very different towns of Brecon and Merthyr Tydfil. This tour takes in the magnificent scenery, including views of Pen-y-Fan, huge reservoirs, a restored canal and ruined castles in the peaceful Usk Valley.

1 Leave Brecon on the B4601, signed Cardiff A470, and at the roundabout, take the second exit (A470) to Libanus. In the village turn right and follow signs to the Brecon Beacons National Park Visitor Centre. Magnificent views can be enjoyed from the terrace, across the valley to Pen-y-Fan and its neighbouring peaks, and the centre has a good café and information centre. Return to the trunk road and turn right to cross Mynydd Illtud Common.

2 Turn left at the trunk road and soon turn left on to the A4215 (no sign). In half a mile (800m) turn left, signed Merthyr Tydfil, continue to the A470 and turn right. Continue forward for some time, until signs direct you to turn left on to a minor road to Cefn coed y cymmer. Soon turn left on to a minor road towards Trefechan. In 2 miles (3km) bear left and soon descend (1-in-9) to Pontsticill. Pass the road to the Brecon Mountain Railway Centre, a narrow-gauge railway that starts at Pant Station and continues for 3.5 miles (5.5km) through beautiful scenery to the Taf Fechan reservoir, and bear left. Pass the Pontsticill Reservoir car-park and in 1 mile (1.5km) turn left.

3 Turn right in a further mile (1.5km) and descend to cross the river bridge, then make an ascent, and another descent (1-in-5) to Talybont Reservoir dam. This large and attractive reservoir has become an important refuge for birdlife, especially winter wildfowl. Shortly, bear right, cross the Monmouth and Brecon Canal and turn right on to the B4558 (no sign) into Talybont-on-Usk.

4 Keep forward, signed Crickhowell, and in 3 miles (5km) bear right into Llangynidr. Shortly, turn right on to the B4560 for Beaufort. In 3 miles (5km) pass the quarry then turn left on to a minor road towards

Walkers approaching Pen-y-Fan on the 'Gap' Roman road

WALKING IN THE BEACONS

Walking is the most popular outdoor activity in the Brecon Beacons, and with over 620 miles (1,000km) of public rights of way, there's plenty of choice for the keen rambler. The most popular walks include:

Pen-y-Fan – the ascent from Storey Arms (the most popular route) or by the 'Gap' route north of the Neuadd Reservoirs.

Fforest Fawr – along sections of the Roman Road of Sarn Helen and through the forest.

Grwyne Fawr trackway – on to the Black Mountains east of Talgarth.

An extensive programme of guided walks leaves from the **National Park Mountain Centre**, signed off the A470 on Mynydd Illtud Common, near **Libanus**. The centre can also give essential advice about equipment and weather conditions.

the scenery is on the Brecon Mountain Railway from Pant Station, north of Merthyr Tydfil.

The Mellte and Hepste valleys, between Ystradfellte and Pontneddfechan, are at the heart of the Beacons caving country. The Dan-yr-Ogof Showcaves are now part of a large tourist complex with a number of attractions aimed at children, including a dinosaur park.

The Romans had a fort at Y Gaer, just outside the bustling old market town of Brecon, which provides an ideal starting point for exploration of the National Park. Near by at Libanus is the National Park's excellent Mountain Centre, which gives useful advice on walking and weather conditions and is the base for a number of expertly guided walks during the season.

RIDING THE RANGE

Mountain biking has become increasingly popular in the Beacons, and among the best-known routes are the **'Gap' bridleway** via Bwlch ar y Fan and down the slopes of Bryn Teg to Bailiea and Brecon, or the longer **Brecon to Llandovery route** over the Black Mountain, via Trecastle and the Usk Reservoir.

Pony-trekking is very popular, with over 1,000 ponies – usually the sturdy little Welsh cobs – available at trekking centres throughout the park, but especially in the **Black Mountains**, which are crisscrossed by a number of popular bridleways.

Watersports are well catered for at Llangorse Lake, near Crickhowell, the largest natural lake in the National Park. Although there has been some concern at the effect of powerboats on the lake, yachting and windsurfing provide more sustainable recreation for the watersports enthusiast. From Crickhowell, a pleasant, mainly Georgian village in the valley of the Usk, you can venture into the Black Mountains, and there are a number of pony-trekking establishments in the area.

The ruined 12th-century castle at Tretower, north of Crickhowell, is unusual because its cylindrical keep is enclosed inside the remains of an earlier, square structure. Further west, near the boundary of the National Park, remote Carreg Cennen Castle has one of the most spectacular situations of any castle in Wales, standing high on a limestone crag 3 miles (5km) southeast of Llandeilo.

DAN-YR-OGOF SHOWCAVES

The Dan-yr-Ogof Showcaves system, in the Tawe Valley north of Abercraf, has the largest chamber in any British showcave, and in the Bone Cave, evidence has been found of human occupation from 3,000 years ago. The caves were discovered in 1912 by the Morgan brothers and further explored in the 1930s. In addition to the vast 'cathedral', there are underground lakes, stone bridges and elaborate stalactites and stalagmites.

SEE CONTACTS SECTION FOR ADDITIONAL INFORMATION

Crickhowell. Keep to this road, cross a bridge and turn left to Llangattock. Turn left on to the A4077 (no sign), then at the traffic signals, turn right and cross the River Usk via a magnificent 13-arched bridge. Keep left, signed Brecon A40, to the edge of Crickhowell.

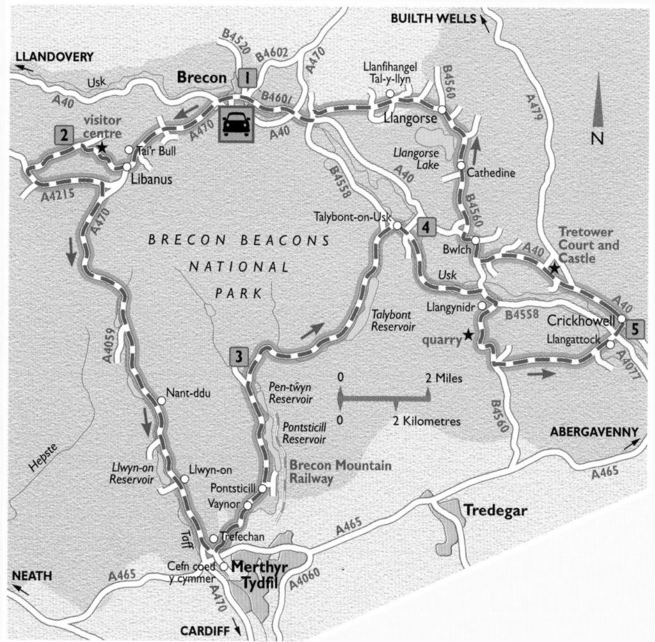

5 Turn left on to the A40, pass Tretower Court and Castle on the right and continue to Bwlch. Tretower Castle is a substantial ruin of an 11th-century motte and bailey, and nearby Tretower Court is a fortified manor house. Turn right on to the B4560 towards Llangorse, pass Cathedine church on the left and enter Llangorse. Bear right and soon turn left on to a minor road for Brecon. In 1 mile (1.5km) keep left and shortly bear left into Llanfihangel Tal-y-llyn. Keep right, then in 2 miles (3km), at the trunk road, turn left. Pass under the bridge and turn right to join the A40. At the roundabout, take the second exit (B4601) to re-enter Brecon.

PEMBROKESHIRE & THE SOUTHWEST

MAP AND KEY

Rhossili Walk

Carmarthen Drive

Tenby Cycle Ride

The rocky fingers of the glorious Pembrokeshire Coast stretch out into the blue waters of the Irish Sea, island-dotted and haunted by flocks of sea birds. The cliff-hemmed sandy bays of the coasts are perfect for watersports and one of the finest places in Britain for surfing, while botanists and bird-watchers are spoilt by

the 240-sq mile (620-sq km) Pembrokeshire Coast National Park. To the east, the gentler countryside of Carmarthen is a place beloved by anglers, who find fine fishing on the Rivers Teifi and Towy. It also gave the poet Dylan Thomas his inspiration. The gorse-studded peninsula of Gower, with its 14 miles (22km) of beaches, coves and charming fishing villages, has long been the playground of the industrial cities of South Wales.

PEMBROKESHIRE COAST PATH

The Pembrokeshire Coast National Trail (above and left) offers a crash-course in geology, for the route shows at a glance the story of the formation of the earth from the earliest pre-Cambrian rocks around the tiny cathedral city of St David's to the Ordovician volcanic structure of the north.

SURFING

Pembrokeshire is the British equivalent of California in the colourful world of surfing. Beaches such as those at Manorbier (below), Freshwater West and Newgale offer some of the best conditions for surfing in the whole of Britain, as huge rollers crash in from the blue Atlantic. Many *aficionados* of the sport 'hang out' here for the whole of the summer season, and these beaches are often the venue of the national surfing championships.

SWANSEA & THE GOWER

Between the industrial towns of Swansea Bay and the great sweep of Carmarthen Bay are some startling contrasts in landscape. The long limestone finger of the Gower Peninsula pokes out into the Bristol Channel, while on either side the industry-ravaged towns of the valleys are slowly recovering from generations of dereliction and decay.

'Golden Gower' is often dubbed the 'lung' of Swansea, but this peninsula is really a place apart from the rest of South Wales. It is also a place of great scenic beauty and contrast, designated Britain's first Area of Outstanding Natural Beauty (AONB) in 1956. Gower's south coast is more akin to southwestern Wales, with superb beetling cliffs of limestone on whose rocks many ships have foundered, terminating at the weird Worms Head. The northern coast consists of broad sand and mud-flats leading down to the Burry Estuary, while the interior is pastoral and scattered with pretty villages.

At the westernmost extremity of Gower is the spectacular headland of Worms Head. Rhossili stands at the southern end of the superb beach of Rhossili Bay, one of the finest stretches of flat sand in Wales. The church here contains a memorial to Edgar Evans who went with Scott to the South Pole. The village is backed by the open downland of Rhossili Down, a veritable treasure-house of prehistory which rises to The Beacon at 632ft (192m). On the bracing downs are 14 Bronze-Age burial mounds, and at Sweyne's Howes, just north of the Beacon, are a pair of neolithic burial chambers. Rhossili Downs are very popular with the hang-gliding fraternity, and are now owned by the National Trust.

Paragliding at Rhossili allows a bird's-eye view across the sweeping sands of the bay

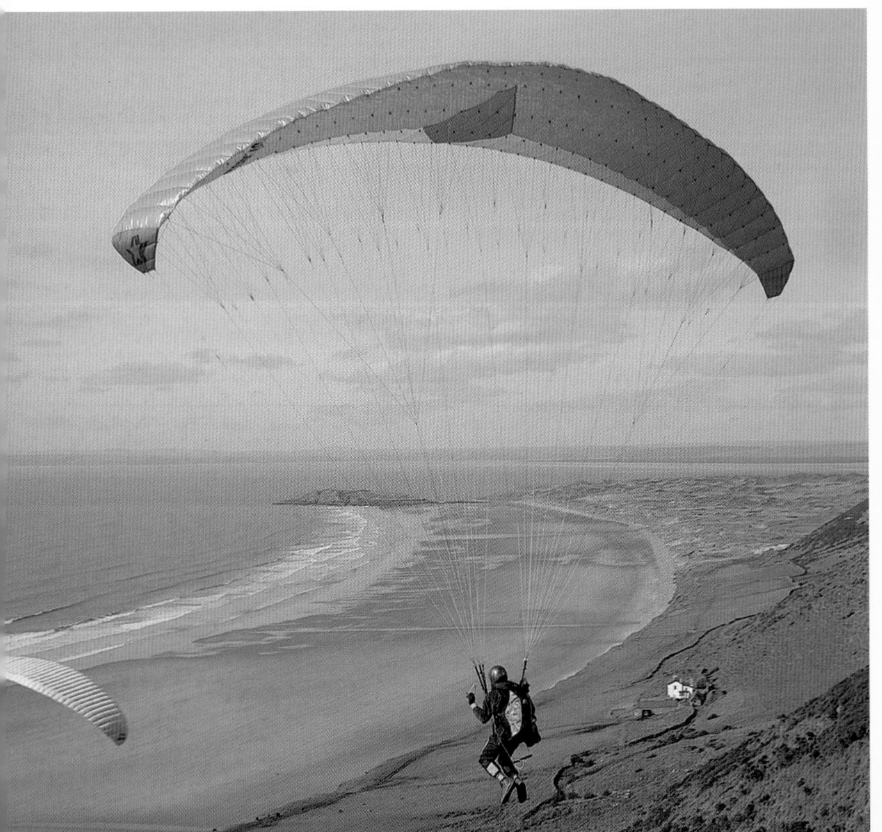

Swansea's renovated docklands are now home to shops and pleasure boats

Rhossili Walk

WALK

Rhossili Coastal Trail

START/FINISH: Rhossili. Village at the west end of the Gower Peninsula, on the B4247 (off A4118) 16 miles (26km) west of Swansea

DISTANCE: 6 miles (9.5km)

ASCENT/GRADIENT: 89.5ft (28m); a few steep climbs but mostly moderate

TERRAIN/PATHS: dirt tracks, farm tracks, green lanes, coast path and roads; good paths – can be muddy

PARKING: car-park at Rhossili

Rugged coastal scenery, peaceful meadows and secluded woodland lanes on the Gower Peninsula.

1 The Gower Peninsula has one of the most richly varied environments in Wales. Marshes, dunes and sandy beaches, lowland heaths and woodland combine to make it an area of great biodiversity. Humans first came here in prehistoric times and evidence of their settlements can be traced through the ages by the countless neolithic and Bronze-Age features that have survived. From the car-park go past the visitor centre and take the coastal path west. When the path turns left, head over the grass towards the coast keeping the old coastguard lookout on your left.

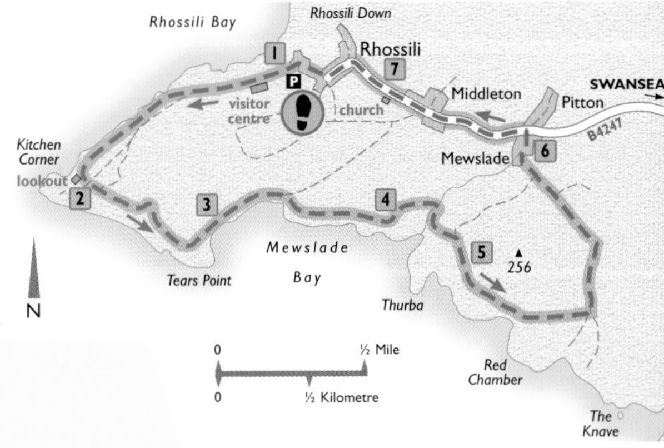

GETTING ABOUT ROUND SWANSEA BAY

The newly inaugurated **Festival of Walks**, held annually in October on the Gower, aims to highlight the fact that the peninsula offers some of the finest coast and countryside walking in the UK, with many prehistoric remains scattered around, as well as unusual flora and fauna.

Another great way to explore the Swansea Bay area is to get on your bike. There are a number of good cycle paths and the area forms part of the **Celtic Trail**, a long-distance cycle route covering the length of South Wales. Routes are available for all levels of fitness, from **The Mumbles** (right) into **Swansea's Marine Quarter**, taking in the broad sweep of Swansea Bay, or the more strenuous routes which go into the hills of the **Neath** and **Afan Valleys**.

Situated at the western end of the sweeping sands of Oxwich Bay, the charming little village of Oxwich, with its Devon-style thatched and whitewashed cottages, has been important since the Norman de la Mare family built a castle here in 1541. Their tombs can be seen in the lovely 12th-century church of St Illtyd, which stands deep in woodland at the edge of the bay, some way from the village. Oxwich Burrows is an important National Nature Reserve with walking trails.

At the very centre of Gower, Reynoldston stands on the west flank of the central Cefn Bryn ridge, on which visitors can enjoy fine walks with views across the entire peninsula.

Many of the finest prehistoric remains from the caves and burial mounds of Gower are to be found in the Royal Institution of South Wales in Swansea.

The southernmost headland of Swansea Bay is known as The Mumbles, and there are fine views from the summit of Mumbles Head. The modern resort of Mumbles, with its all-weather attraction of Mumbles Pier and its 600-berth marina, owes its existence to the first and one of the longest-running railway passenger services in the world, opened in 1807 between here and Swansea, using horses as the motive power. The railway closed in 1960.

GARDENS OF SWANSEA BAY

Swansea Bay is home to some of the finest gardens and parks in Wales, including:

Margam, with its Orangery and Gothic mansion;

Afan Forest Park, 8,030 acres (3,250ha) of forested hillside in the Vale of Neath;

The Gnoll Estate, based on 18th-century landscaped gardens;

Clyne Park, Swansea, famous for its rhododendrons and azaleas;

Singleton Botantical Gardens, Swansea;

Brynmill, Swansea, with its friendly ducks;

Cwmdonkin, with Dylan Thomas connections;

Plantasia, tropical glasshouse gardens in the city centre.

Enjoy boating on the lake or feeding the swans and ducks at Margam Park

2 Turn left at the lookout visitor centre and take the green track back to the coastal path. Follow this to the end of the wall in the next bay. Turn left and follow the path to a fork. An area of medieval open-field farming has survived on the peninsula. Known as The Vile, a name derived from the old English for field, it is unique in Wales and is best viewed from the coastguard lookout.

3 Take the left fork (the right fork is unsafe), follow the yellow waymarkers and the path round the coast, keeping the wall on your left, eventually reaching a stile and the South Gower Nature Reserve. Ignore this stile and continue to a small valley.

4 Descend down the valley, cross over a stile and head down the valley towards the coast. Shortly, take the small path to the left to ascend the valley quite steeply.

5 Continue around the coast and descend into a smaller valley. Cross the stile and head north (uphill) for 200yds (180m), ignoring the stile on the left-hand side. Continue through two gates and keep following the farm track. Cross over a stile and after approximately 150yds (135m) go through another gate into a farmyard, then past a barn on the left.

6 Continue through the farmyard, then turn left on to the main road. Continue past Rhossili parish church on your left-hand side.

7 Remain on the main road into Rhossili and back to the car-park.

SEE CONTACTS SECTION FOR ADDITIONAL INFORMATION

TOP TEN TWITCHERS' LIST

Look out for these birds on Gower's rocky coasts and fields:

- Stonechat
- Whitethroat
- Rock pipit
- Eider duck
- Oystercatcher
- Lesser black-backed gull
- Chough
- Jackdaw
- Raven
- Peregrine falcon

A male stonechat

CARMARTHEN & THE RIVER TOWY

Carmarthenshire offers a wealth of opportunities for the outdoor enthusiast – from walking along the beautiful 56-mile (90-km) Carmarthen Bay Coast Walk, which links to the Pembrokeshire Coast Path, to pony-trekking in the foothills of the Black Mountain or surfing and windsurfing on the golden sands of Cefn Sidan Beach at Pembrey, one of Europe's finest beaches.

The Rivers Towy, Teifi and Cothi are among the best in Wales for their salmon, trout and sea trout – or sewin – fishing, and there's sea-fishing and boating from coastal villages such as Ferryside and Llansteffan on the Towy estuary.

DID YOU KNOW?

The **Museum of Speed** at **Pendine** celebrates the many world-record speed attempts which were made on the famous 5-mile (8-km) long firm, flat sands of Pendine Bay. Sir Malcolm Campbell set the world land-speed record (146mph) here in 1924.

The Welsh name for Carmarthen is 'Caerfyrddin', which means 'Merlin's City', and King Arthur's legendary wizard is alleged to have been born in this pleasant town on a bluff above the River Towy. You can still see the remains of Merlin's Oak in Priory Street, embedded in concrete and wrapped in iron bands, for legend has it that when Merlin's Oak falls, so will Carmarthen itself. The town is noted for its ruined Norman castle, and its famous indoor and outdoor market. Near by is the exciting new attraction of the National Botanic Garden of Wales. Set in the estate of the former Middleton Hall, its centre-piece is the Great Glasshouse, the largest single-span glasshouse in the world, surrounded by lakes,

GOLD IN THEM THAR HILLS

The ancient rocks in the wooded hills above the beautiful **Cothi Valley** at Dolaucothi near Pumsaint, were first exploited for their reserves of gold by the Romans, 2,000 years ago. Mining resumed in the 19th century and reached a peak around 1938. Now visitors can take guided tours through some of the Roman workings – and even pan for gold themselves at this site, which is in the care of the National Trust.

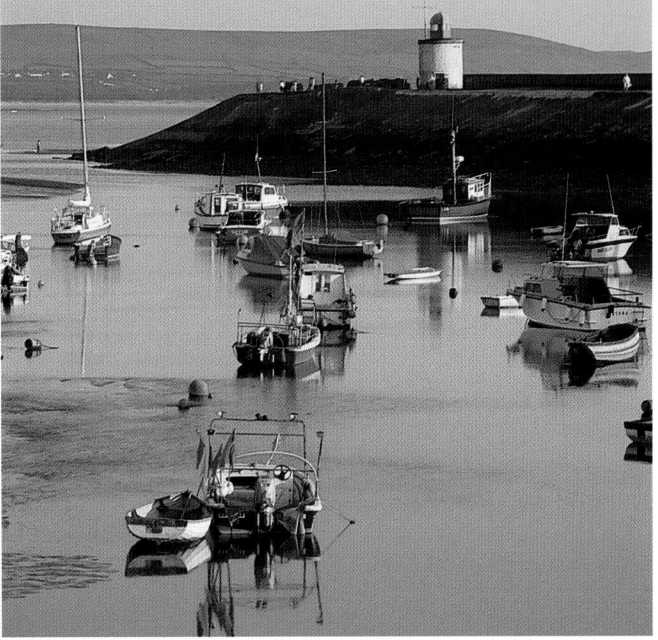

Boats moored in the still waters of Burry Port harbour, in Carmarthen Bay

Carmarthen Drive

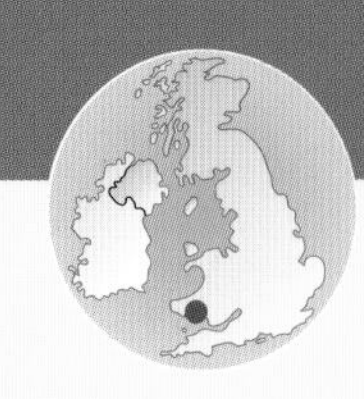

DRIVE

Merlin's Town and Carmarthen Bay

START/FINISH: Carmarthen. On the A48 22 miles (36km) northwest of Swansea

DISTANCE: 72 miles (115km)

Coastal roads offer spectacular seascapes along sandy estuaries, backed by gentle farmlands. There is one of the best-preserved castles in Wales, a country park and a folly to visit along the way.

1 Carmarthen is thought to be the oldest town in Wales. You will find a medieval gatehouse, a remnant of Carmarthen's 11th-century castle, and a narrow lane leading down to the Towy river. From the town centre take the A484, Llanelli road.

2 Turn right through Ferryside. This small, peaceful coastal settlement spreads along the banks of the Towy, which flows through sandbanks and cockle and mussel beds into the vast Carmarthen Bay. Views from the beach are captivating. Continue along the coastal route to Kidwelly and rejoin the A484. At Kidwelly a castle, church and tall chimneystack stand out on the horizon. The castle was built in the late 13th century and is remarkable for its state of preservation. For Kidwelly Industrial Museum, turn left on to the B4308 and keep ahead on to the minor road, then left before Gwenllian Court Hotel. This museum has original tinplate working buildings and there's a display of coal mining with pithead gear and a winding engine.

3 Leave Kidwelly on the A484 southbound. For Pembrey Country Park turn right. Situated at the end of a long straight road across a flat landscape, this country park features open grassland, dense conifer forest, and a magnificent stretch of beach, unbroken for 7 miles (11.5km).

4 Turn left up a steep hill at The Talbot pub at Pwll, then left on to the B4308 (Heol Trimsaran Road) and right at the crossroads to Five Roads. Turn right on to the B4309, then after 1 mile (1.5km) turn left and left again to reach the Upper and Lower Cwm Lliedi Reservoirs. Ivy-covered woodland leads down to the banks of the reservoir and a scenic footpath runs round the shore.

5 Bear right uphill then left on the A476. Remain on the A476,

cascades and woodlands.

Llandeilo, a market and fishing centre on the north bank of the Towy, retains its medieval character with narrow streets and historic buildings. Not far away is Dinefwr Castle and its park, held by the same family since the 9th century. Although the present castle dates from the 17th century, the ruined keep of the original can still be seen on a cliff above the river.

One of the newest attractions in the area is at Aberglasney in the valley of the Towy, where a garden constructed during the 16th and 17th centuries has been lovingly restored as 'a garden lost in time'. The yew tunnel is thought to be one of the oldest living garden features in the whole of Europe, and other attractions include the Cloister Garden, the Walled Garden, and the Kitchen Garden which leads to the Pool Garden.

Beautifully situated on a peninsula between the Taf and Towy is the pretty village of Llansteffan, from where you can hire a boat to reach Ferryside, near Kidwelly, with its immense castle dating from the 13th and 14th centuries.

Burry Port's picturesque harbour and squat white-painted lighthouse are very popular with yachtsmen and anglers alike, and although South Wales never receives much snow, even in the worst of winters, snowsport enthusiasts are catered for in the nearby village of Pembrey. Ski Pembrey, with its 425-ft (130-m) dry-ski slope, and 'The Cobra' – Wales's longest toboggan run – are both at the Pembrey Country Park. The beautiful beach at Cefn Sidan, near Pembrey, has been nominated as one of Europe's finest beaches.

Saundersfoot is a tiny hamlet whose popularity as a holiday resort is due to its development as a harbour to export high-quality coal (anthracite) in the early 19th century. Today its golden beaches and fine little harbour with broad quays and safe anchorages reflect nothing of its industrial past, and it has become one of the most popular resorts on this coast, and one of the finest yachting centres in the whole of Wales.

The Great Glasshouse at the National Botanic Garden of Wales, near Llanarthne

DYLAN'S LAST LAUGH

The tiny fishing village of **Laugharne** (pronounced 'Larne') on the Taf estuary was the home of poet Dylan Thomas for many years. He lived at the boathouse in Cliff Walk (his writing shed, right), now a heritage centre, which has been restored to the way it was when Thomas lived there, and has become a place of pilgrimage to many of his followers. His most famous work perhaps was the radio play *Under Milk Wood*, which traced a day in the life of the people, such as Captain Cat, Polly Garter and Mrs Ogmore-Pritchard, who lived in the fictional fishing village of Llaregub. Many people have equated Llaregub with Laugharne, and it is now the name of the local theatre group. You can get some idea of Thomas's sense of humour if you just reverse the spelling of the name of the fictional village!

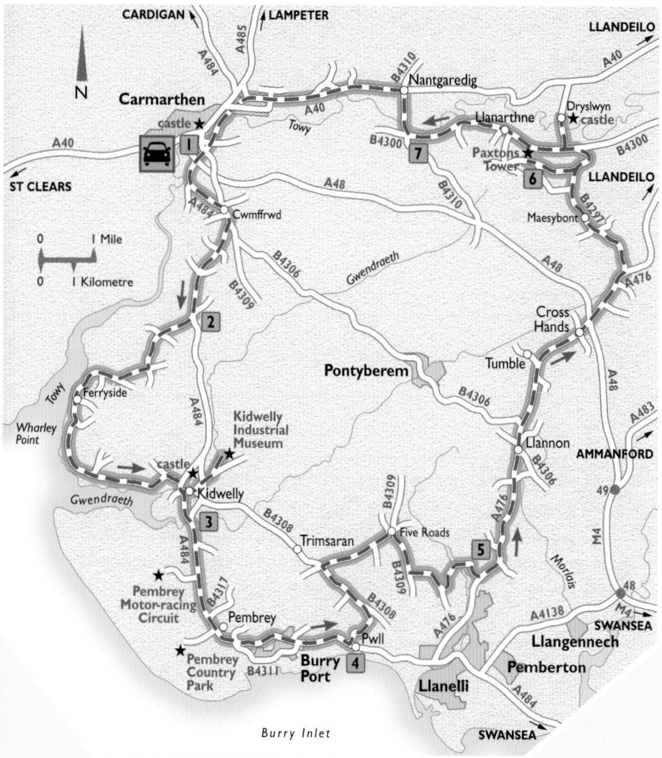

eventually crossing over the A48. Shortly, turn left on to the B4297. Continue for approximately 3 miles (5km), then turn left on to a minor road, signed Paxtons Tower.

6 A local landowner, Sir William Paxton, erected the tower in 1811 as a memorial to Lord Nelson. Triangular in plan with a tower at each corner, it offers a breathtaking view of the Towy valley. On leaving the tower, turn left to return down the same minor road, continuing to turn left on to the B4300 (next right to visit Dryslwyn Castle, a ruined 13th-century castle of the native Welsh).

7 After approximately 3 miles (5km), turn right to Nantgaredig, then left on to the A40 and return to Carmarthen.

PREHISTORIC BOATS

The circular coracles, which are still occasionally used for salmon fishing on the Rivers Towy, Teifi and Taf, are based on a boat design which has scarcely changed for 2,000 years – since the Iron Age. They are made from intertwined laths of willow and hazel, covered with fabric and finally waterproofed with pitch. The only major difference between them and the modern coracles, as seen at the **National Coracle Centre** at **Cenarth**, is that the ancient makers used animal skins for the fabric of their boats.

It takes many years of practice to confidently handle one of these inherently unstable craft with their single wooden oar, especially in the turbulent waters of the fast-flowing Carmarthenshire rivers.

ST DAVID'S & THE PEMBROKESHIRE COAST

The Pembrokeshire Coast National Park – at 240sq miles (620sq km), one of the smallest British National Parks – is the only one which is largely coastal. The Preseli Hills in the north are a self-contained moorland block of Ordovician rocks rising to 1,759ft (536m) at Foel Cwm Cerwym south of Bryberian. The hills are the source of the blue stones which were somehow transported to Wiltshire for Stonehenge's inner circle.

Britain's smallest cathedral city, St David's clusters in a hollow around the mainly 12th-century cathedral, dedicated to Wales's patron saint. South of St David's are several wonderful surfing beaches and bays, including St Non's Bay (named after St David's mother), Caerbwdi Bay and Caerfai Bay. From the high point of Carnllidi (595ft/181m) on the rocky headland of St David's Head, Ireland can be seen on a clear day.

Tenby, the largest town within the National Park, retains its medieval charm and character despite the annual influx of thousands of tourists. Regular boat trips from Tenby take visitors to Caldey Island, the only Pembrokeshire island which is permanently occupied. The inhabitants are the monks of the modern Cistercian priory, who make sweet-smelling perfume. The remains of a 12th-century Benedictine monastery survives, and the ancient priory church contains a stone with inscriptions in Latin and 5th-century Ogham script.

The ancient county town of Pembroke lies on a low ridge of limestone, where its impressive castle was built in the late 11th century. The circular vaulted keep is 75ft (23m) high with walls 7ft (2m) thick, and a subterranean cavern

PEMBROKESHIRE COAST NATIONAL TRAIL

Officially opened in 1970, the Pembrokeshire Coast National Trail has its northern terminus at **St Dogmaels**. It runs its roller-coaster route around the rugged coastline of Pembrokeshire, with only a slight hiatus at **Milford Haven**, to **Amroth**, beyond Tenby. It was surveyed by the distinguished local naturalist Ronald Lockley in the early 1950s, so it is appropriate that among its greatest attractions is the wildlife which walkers can see along the way, from the wheeling sea bird colonies on the cliffs to the glorious carpet of wild-flowers, especially in early summer.

A carpet of white lilies in flower on the lakes of Bosherston

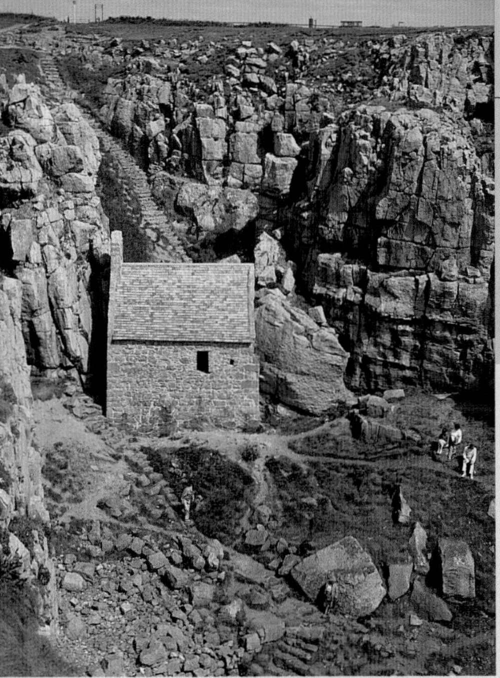

Tiny St Govan's Chapel and holy well, nestled in the Pembrokeshire cliffs

Tenby Cycle Ride

CYCLE RIDE

From Tenby to Pembroke

START/FINISH: Tenby. Located 4 miles (6.5km) south of the A477 Carmarthen to Pembroke road, 16 miles (25.5km) southwest of Carmarthen

DISTANCE: 26 miles (42km)

GRADIENT: undulating; steep half mile (800m) section after Manorbier

ROADS: mostly quiet, though Pembroke and Tenby can be busy

PARKING: car-park near the railway station

The coastline between Saundersfoot and Pembroke is one of the most beautiful in Britain. Although the route rarely keeps close company with the cliffs and beaches, it does often turn towards the coastline. The views from the high ground are extensive, more than justifying the occasional climbs. Along the way are two impressive castles – at Manorbier and Pembroke – and there are many picturesque corners to explore.

1 Tenby, in a beautiful location on the west side of Carmarthen Bay, is one of the most delightful coastal resorts in the UK. There are three sandy beaches, two of them divided by the headland on which stand the remains of a 13th-century castle. The narrow, quaint streets of the old town are enclosed by 14th-century walls. In Tudor Square stands the 15th-century Tudor Merchant's House (NT). Leave Tenby by the A4139 towards Pembroke. Turn right, signed Penally and Golf Course, to go through Penally and after 1 mile (1.5km) rejoin the main road. Continue for 2.5 miles (4km) into Lydstep.

2 For a panoramic viewpoint from Lydstep Haven, turn left and take a by-road down to the entrance of Lydstep Haven Estate. Retrace the route to Lydstep village and turn left. In half a mile (800m) turn left on to the B4585, signed Manorbier. In the centre of Manorbier, fork left and descend below the Norman castle walls to the beach. From the car-park, a footpath across the hillside leads to King's Quoit, the standing stones of a prehistoric burial chamber, with a 15-ft (4.5-m) capstone. Climb steeply and turn left at the crossroads. At the junction

BIRDS OF DYFED

One of the great joys of walking the 181-mile (292-km) Pembrokeshire Coast National Trail is the variety of bird life. The steep cliffs and sea stacks, such as those found around **Govan's Head** and **Castlemartin**, are home to the rare red-beaked chough, surely the most acrobatic of the crow family, as well as kittiwakes, guillemots and razorbills, the plump, penguin-like emblem of the National Park. Comical puffins and the rare Manx shearwaters nest in burrows on the islands of **Skomer**, a National Nature Reserve, and **Skokholm**, while **Grassholm**, an RSPB Reserve, is the site of the largest gannetry in England and Wales.

known as the Wogan leads out to the harbour. Pembroke has a pleasing High Street with some Tudor façades, and retains parts of its original town wall and water defences, including the attractive Mill Pond to the north. Pembroke Dock is a creation of the 19th century where around 240 men-of-war were built, and was an important flying-boat base during World War II.

The picturesque village of Bosherston is known for its lily ponds. These were formed by the Stackpole Estate in three narrow limestone valleys in the late 18th and early 19th centuries, and are now nationally important examples of calcareous marl lakes, protected as a National Nature Reserve. They are reached by raised causeways which cross the water. Southeast of Bosherston is a wonderful secluded beach at Barafundle Bay.

St Govan's Chapel is one of the real gems of the Pembrokeshire coast, approached by a steep flight of steps down through the cliffs near Bosherston. West along the Coast Path are the Huntsman's Leap, a giddy gash in the cliffs; the equally spectacular Elegug Stacks, two massive pillars of limestone standing out from the cliffs; and the huge natural arch known as the Green Bridge of Wales.

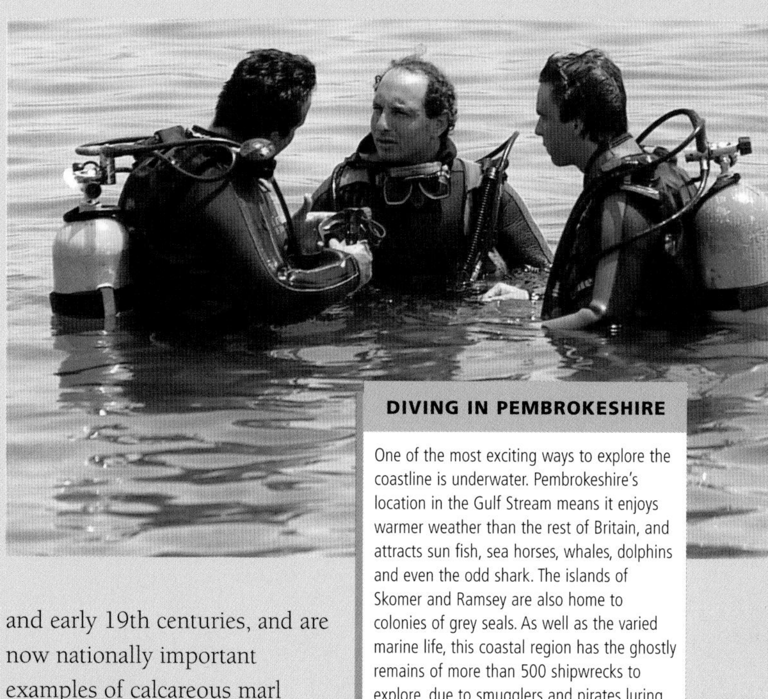

DIVING IN PEMBROKESHIRE

One of the most exciting ways to explore the coastline is underwater. Pembrokeshire's location in the Gulf Stream means it enjoys warmer weather than the rest of Britain, and attracts sun fish, sea horses, whales, dolphins and even the odd shark. The islands of Skomer and Ramsey are also home to colonies of grey seals. As well as the varied marine life, this coastal region has the ghostly remains of more than 500 shipwrecks to explore, due to smugglers and pirates luring boats on to the rocks. The most popular dive site is the *Lucy*, an almost intact vessel off Skomer Island.

with the A4139, turn left then immediately left again along a narrow road which climbs for 1 mile (1.5km).

3 Enter Freshwater East. At the crossroads in the village centre you can descend to the lovely beach and its fine view across to Caldey Island by turning left. Retrace your route to the crossroads and turn left on to the B4584. Enter Lamphey and, at the junction with the A4139, turn left.

4 Continue, and shortly after passing Pembroke railway station on the right, turn left and follow the one-way system around the town. At the castle entrance, turn right along Main Street and continue out of town on the A4139. The castle, built in 1207, stands upon a rocky spur above the Pembroke River, which is a creek off Milford Haven; Henry VII was born here in 1457. In 2 miles (3km) at Lamphey fork left on a by-road. Pass Bishop's Palace on the left as you climb for 2 miles (3km), continuing along The Ridgeway. After 3 miles (5km) turn left at a crossroads for St Florence. (For an alternative and more direct route back to Tenby, continue ahead and descend to Penally and then retrace the outward route.) Descend steeply into St Florence.

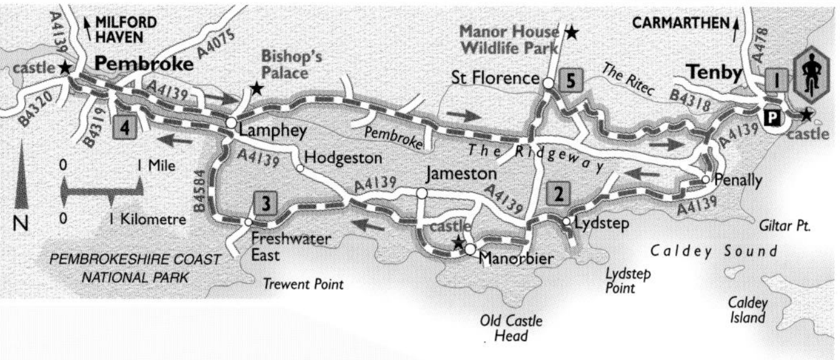

5 St Florence, once a port, has some old houses with Flemish chimneys, and the church contains several interesting monuments. At the crossroads by the church turn right and follow a narrow lane through the Ritec Valley for 3 miles (5km) to reach the old road to Penally. Retrace the outward route back into Tenby.

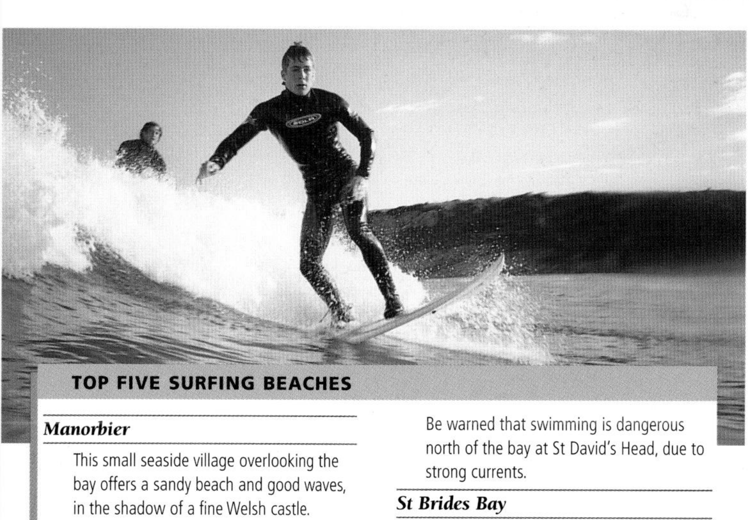

TOP FIVE SURFING BEACHES

Manorbier

This small seaside village overlooking the bay offers a sandy beach and good waves, in the shadow of a fine Welsh castle.

Freshwater West

Pembroke's most popular break is flanked by redstone cliffs, but avoid it when the red flags are flying as it is on an MoD firing range.

Whitesand Bay

Another popular break, this is one of the finest surfing beaches on the Welsh coast, with the added attraction of seals. Be warned that swimming is dangerous north of the bay at St David's Head, due to strong currents.

St Brides Bay

Take your pick from Newgale, Druidston or Broad Haven along this coast. The bay has several stretches of impressive cliff scenery and at low tide the sands reveal traces of a prehistoric forest.

Abereiddy

A good break in a beautiful setting. The dark-grey sands of the beach have been made from particles of slate.

MID WALES

MAP AND KEY

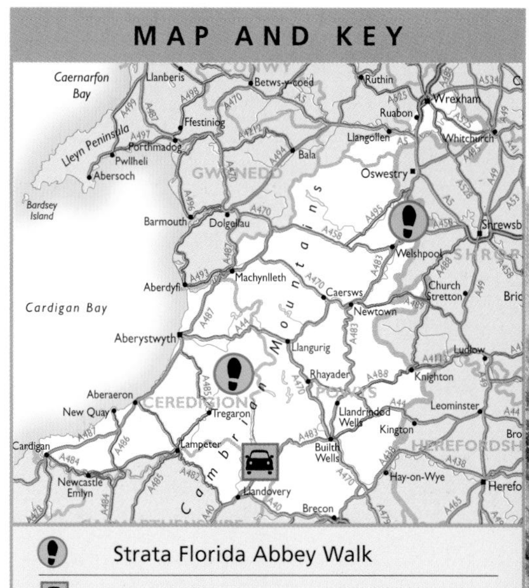

Walk	Strata Florida Abbey Walk
Drive	Llandovery Drive
Walk	Breidden Hills Walk

This area is the least-known and least-visited part of Wales. Yet it contains the source of both the mighty Severn and the Wye; the Welsh 'Lake District', the huge

Canoeing

Canoeing is one of the most popular activities in mid Wales, especially on the fast-flowing 'white-water' rivers of the upper Wye and Severn, where specialist activity centres can offer tuition in this invigorating sport. Both kayaks and Canadian-type canoes are used, and there are few finer ways to appreciate the beauty of the Welsh rivers.

LAKE VYRNWY

Lake Vyrnwy – 5 miles (8m) long and nearly a mile (1.5km) wide – was one of the earliest incursions of the English to export pure Welsh water. It was constructed in 1881 to slake the ever-increasing thirst of the industrial cities of Liverpool and the northwest of England, and its unusual Gothic-turreted dam has now weathered into the landscape quite harmoniously.

plex of reservoirs of the Vyrnwy, Elan and Clywedog Valleys; some of the finest unspoiled stretches of coastline, along ligan Bay. This natural beauty can be enjoyed on the fast-ing rivers of the interior, so beloved of canoeists, and the wide spaces of the Berwyn and southern Cambrian Mountains, re you can walk, ride or cycle and not see another soul.

PISTYLL RHAEADR

Pistyll Rhaeadr, about 4 miles (6.5km) above Llanraeadr ym Mochnant, is the highest waterfall in Wales. The waterfall plunges 240ft (73m) through a beautiful wooded gorge, and was traditionally named as one of the 'Wonders of Wales'. Both parts of the Welsh name actually mean a waterfall or spout.

Offa's Dyke Path

Offa's Dyke is a 177-mile (284-km) National Trail which follows the late 8th-century earthwork constructed by King Offa of the Mercians as a boundary between his kingdom and the Welsh. It runs along the border from Chepstow in the south to Prestatyn on the Irish Sea coast in the north, and its challenging route is marked by acorn symbols.

ABERYSTWYTH

Aberystwyth combines seaside attractions with a history that goes back to the Iron Age. The hillfort of Pen Dinas overlooks The Bar to the south of the town, and the ruins of one of many castles built in Wales by Edward I is perched on a headland. There is a Victorian pier, a small harbour and a beach of shingle and sand, where donkey rides are still given, to the delight of children.

CARDIGAN BAY

The 50-mile (80-km) sweep of Cardigan Bay was Britain's first Marine Heritage Coast, and its beaches regularly top the UK list of seaside award-winners, yet this undiscovered corner of mid Wales is another backwater on the normal tourist trail, and is all the more enjoyable for it. The university town of Aberystwyth, the ancient market town of Cardigan and the resort of Aberaeron all remain unspoiled, looking out on to the broad expanse of Cardigan Bay with the impressive backdrop of the mountains of Central Wales. These unfrequented hills give rise to the River Rheidol, which dashes down over wild waterfalls to enter the Irish Sea at Aberystwyth.

An old boat left high and dry alongside the River Teifi at Cardigan

TREGARON BOG NATIONAL NATURE RESERVE

The largest peat bog in Wales, properly known as Cors Caron, covers some 1,900 acres (770ha). This is a classic, rain-fed raised bog, cut in two by the River Teifi, where sphagnum moss and insect-eating sundews grow. There is a nature trail which follows the line of an old railway track, from which visitors can spot rarities such as golden plover, whooper swan, hen harrier, merlin and the occasional visiting red kite.

Aberystwyth, the largest resort on Cardigan Bay, is home to the first university to be established in Wales, in 1872. 'The college by the sea' – University College of Wales – occupies a splendid position in a former hotel on the sea-front near the pier; the rest of the campus is on the hills behind at Penglais, where the National Library of Wales houses some of the great literary treasures of the Welsh nation. A Victorian funicular railway at the north end of the promenade gives panoramic views from its 430-ft (131-m) summit to Snowdonia in the north and the Preseli Hills to the south.

Twelve miles (19km) inland along the narrow valley of the Rheidol is one of the great scenic highlights of Wales – the dramatic

VALE OF RHEIDOL RAILWAY

Running for 12 miles (19km) through the valley of the Rheidol between Aberystwyth and Devil's Bridge, the railway is the only narrow-gauge line still using steam locomotives operated by Regional Railways. Originally opened in 1902 to carry lead ore down to the coast from the mines in the mountains, the railway is now maintained just for tourists. It is a popular and attractive way to reach the graceful waterfalls of Mynach and Devil's Bridge from the coastal resorts of Cardigan Bay.

Strata Florida Abbey Walk

WALK

Abbey in the Wilderness

START/FINISH: Pontrhydfendigaid. On the B4343 between Tregaron and Devil's Bridge
DISTANCE: 5.5 miles (9km)
ASCENT/GRADIENT: 500ft (152m); gradual ascents
TERRAIN/PATHS: fields, country lanes and forestry; mainly obvious paths and lanes
PARKING: on main street or lay-by at southern end of village

Explore the ruins of Strata Florida, a once rich and powerful abbey set in a remote valley in mid Wales.

1 From lay-by at south end of village, continue south along road towards Tregaron, going gently uphill to stile and ancient wooden footpath sign on left. Before reaching the abbey itself, the route crosses peaceful hillsides where the monks once farmed their sheep. Cross stile and follow track beyond towards caravans. Go on to caravan site road and bear left, between vans. As road bears right, bear left past last caravan to stile in corner.

2 Cross, and follow fence on left, going through gate and across field towards ruin in trees to left. There, bear right, going through opening and heading diagonally right uphill, then turning right and following fence at top of field to cross stile, to right of woodland edge. Follow fence on left to another stile, ignoring gate, then go diagonally right across field to reach gate in top right corner. Go through and turn left immediately through another gate. Go diagonally right towards barn.

3 Go through gate beside barn and along farm lane opposite. Beyond first farm, lane degenerates to track, but remains obvious. Beyond farmyard keep to left of hut and take lower, right-hand track into trees. Ford stream, go through gate and follow track uphill to second farm. Go, through gate and ahead along farm lane to road.

4 Turn left. When road ends, go through gate and follow lane beyond. As farm comes into view about 450yds (400m) ahead, take lane coming in from left, following it uphill. Approaching barn, go through gate on left and turn right along fence to gate into forest. Follow bridleway through forest to forestry road. After 50yds (46m), as it goes

CILGERRAN CASTLE

The pretty village of Cilgerran contains the ruins of an early 13th-century castle perched high on a crag overlooking the River Teifi, which makes a splendid backdrop. It was built by William Marshall, Earl of Pembroke, shortly after he captured this strategic site, on a promontory between the Teifi and the Plysgog, from the Welsh. The gatehouse and the two great circular towers are the most impressive remaining features.

wooded gorge of Devil's Bridge. The River Mynach meets the Rheidol here in a series of spectacular waterfalls, the highest of which is about 300ft (91m) high.

Strata Florida Abbey was once one of the major cultural centres of Wales and governed a large part of mid Wales. The community of Cistercian monks, founded by Prince Rhys ap Gruffydd in 1184, administered huge sheep ranches over the surrounding Cambrian Mountains. Now, all that remains are romantic, though sparse, ruins – a soaring western doorway, foundations laid out in the grass, and some lovely medieval floor tiles.

WELSH CRAFT

Woodcarving and weaving are two ancient crafts which are still practised in many parts of mid Wales. The intricate love-spoons, traditionally carved from a single piece of wood, were made by young men as gifts for the girls they were courting. In some places, the tradition still lives on, although today most spoons are made as tourist souvenirs.

The same story is true of weaving, where specialist factories have largely taken over from the traditional hand-weaving which was a cottage industry in most villages. But even today's machine-woven wool blankets pay tribute to the past, following traditional designs and dyes which have been used for generations, to create a fair replica of the old craft. This important aspect of the area's industrial heritage is highlighted in the **Museum of the Welsh Woollen Industry** at **Derfach Felindre** near Llandysul.

On the River Teifi at Cardigan, coracles, the ancient handmade small Welsh craft, can still be seen fishing for salmon and sea trout and there is an annual coracle 'regatta' where local fishermen compete against each other in various contests of skill. In medieval days before the harbour silted up, this was an important seaport, giving its name to the whole sweep of Cardigan Bay. A weekly market is still held beneath the arches of the guildhall. The bustling little market town of Newcastle Emlyn, also on the Teifi, gets its name from the castle, which was 'new' in the 15th century – its builders wanted to distinguish it from the older Cilgerran Castle downstream. The town was the site of the first printing press in Wales, set up in 1718, and was also a centre of the 'Rebecca Riots' of the mid-19th century, in which men, dressed as women, protested against road tolls.

DEVIL'S BRIDGE

Devil's Bridge is in fact three bridges, built one on top of the other over the River Mynach in a sequence covering seven centuries. The first (lowest) bridge was built in the 12th century by the monks of nearby Strata Florida Abbey, and was succeeded by another stone bridge and lastly by a modern steel structure.

sharp right between trees, bear left along another bridleway. Follow to path coming down from right. Bear left with waymarker.

5 Follow track to gate and continue along lane beyond to ruin (Talwrn). Go left along ruin's top, near wall, to follow another lane to end. Go through gate and turn right, following stream. Soon bear left to gate, bearing right beyond to regain stream.

6 An indistinct path follows stream down, crossing it once, to footbridge. Cross and follow stream bank to gate. Keep ahead along road beyond. Strata Florida car-park is to left, ruins and church to right.

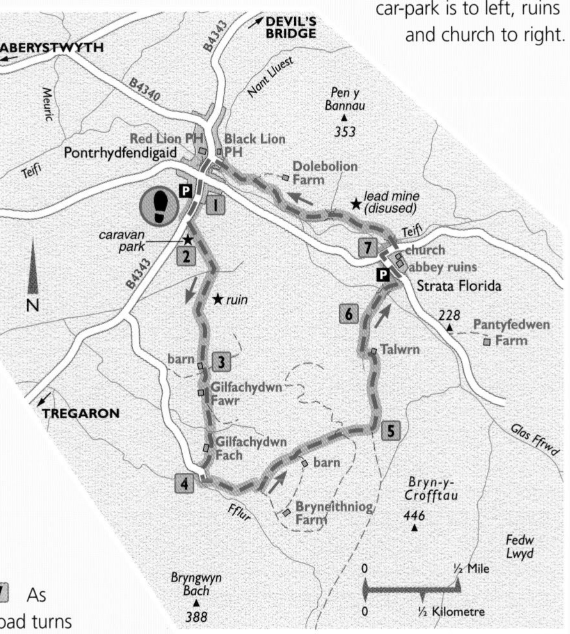

7 As road turns sharp left, go right past telephone box and, soon, cross waymarked stile on left. Cross footbridge and bear left towards waymarked stile by gate. The path now follows River Teifi (left) all the way to Pontrhydfendigaid, with occasional waymarkers, stiles and gates. At farm lane bear left to road. Turn left, crossing hump-backed bridge and passing road, on left, for Strata Florida, to return to start.

THE SOUTHERN CAMBRIAN MOUNTAINS

The insatiable thirst of the booming industrial cities of the West Midlands in the late 19th and early 20th centuries turned the attentions of the water engineers to the isolated, steep-sided valleys of the River Elan and its tributaries in the southern part of the Cambrian Mountains of mid Wales, sometimes known as the Welsh 'Lake District'.

The Elan's clean, unpolluted water and the comparative ease of providing gravity-fed pipelines to the Midlands made it an ideal choice, and the Craig Goch, Penygarreg, Garreg-ddu, Caban-coch and finally the Caerwen reservoirs followed. They now supply Birmingham and district with 75 million gallons (338 million litres) of Welsh water every day. The sheer scale of the engineering and the imposing architecture of the dams make a visit worth while and the area offers plenty of activities for outdoor enthusiasts, including walking, cycling and mountain biking, pony-trekking, bird-watching and angling.

The rural market town of Knighton

Rhododendrons flower on the banks of the Caban-coch Reservoir

The Cambrian Mountains provide rugged terrain for mountain biking

Llandovery Drive

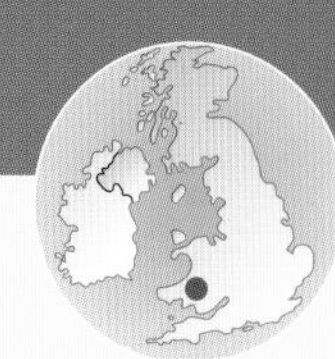

DRIVE

Wild Wales

START/FINISH: Llandovery. Market town on the A40 21 miles (34km) west of Brecon

DISTANCE: 63 miles (101km)

The 19th-century traveller and writer George Borrow called one of his books *Wild Wales*. This title also applies to this tour. The remote hills, known as the Cambrian Mountains, between Llandovery and Tregaron are still a true wilderness, infiltrated by few roads and populated by many more sheep than people.

1 At the confluence of the Rivers Brian, Gwydderig and Towy, Llandovery has been a place of significance at least since Roman times, a fact highlighted by the siting of a church within the ramparts of a hilltop Roman fort just outside the town. The centre of the town, with its cobbled square, covered market-place and clock tower, has changed little since the 19th-century. Leave Llandovery on a minor road, signed Llyn Brianne, and pass through the valley of the Towy. After 7.5 miles (12km) continue through Rhandirmwyn, a sleepy village beautifully located in the countryside of the upper Towy Valley, then in 4.5 miles (7km) pass, on the left, the turning to Llyn Brianne reservoir.

2 Bear right along a scenic road around the east side of Llyn Brianne, a vast, man-made reservoir that supplies Swansea with its water, and, after 7 miles (11km), turn left towards Tregaron and cross the river bridge. At the T-junction, turn right for Tregaron, the road in 3 miles (5km) narrowing to a single track. Continue for a further mile (1.5km) and, near the telephone kiosk, keep left to join the Abergwesyn Pass drove road. The memorable mountain road, once a famous drovers' route along which Welsh farmers led their sheep and cattle to markets in England, traverses a desolately beautiful high plateau, known as the 'roof of Wales'.

3 Later, make a gradual descent to Tregaron, a staunchly Welsh place that is still much involved with buying and selling sheep. Keep forward, then turn left on to the A485, signed to Lampeter. Continue through Llangybi and Bettws Bledrws then, in 3 miles (5km) turn left to enter Lampeter. After the emptiness of Abergwesyn, Lampeter, a busy university town with old coaching inns and Georgian and Victorian

KITE COUNTRY

The Southern Cambrian Mountains are the stronghold of the red kite, recently voted Britain's Bird of the Century by leading ornithologists. Down to just two breeding pairs in the whole of Wales in the 1930s, a vigorous and highly successful protection and breeding programme, centred on these mountains, has led to a remarkable recovery in numbers. And there is a special **Kite Country Centre and Museum** at Tregaron in Ceredigion.

You can watch red kites at close quarters at special feeding stations at the **Gigrin Farm Nature Trail**, near Rhayader; the **Nant-yr-Arian Forest Visitor Centre**, near Ponterwyd; and **Penlan House** at Talsarn, near Tregaron.

The area also contains one of the three great mountains of Wales, Pumlumon Fawr (2,467ft/752m). Although it may lack the imposing appearance of Snowdon and Cadair Idris because it rises from almost uniformly high ground, its significance as a physical feature cannot be denied. It is the source of three mighty rivers, the Severn, the Wye and the Rheidol, and its boggy and mainly featureless slopes also show signs of previous industry in the remains of former lead and silver mines. The easiest approach for walkers to the summit is from Eisteddfa Gurig Farm on the A44 between Ponterwyd and Llangurig.

Rhayader is the natural starting point for exploring the Elan Valley dams and reservoirs, standing at the junction of several roads. It has become popular for angling, pony-trekking and walking, and its shops offer many local products, from Welsh dressers to pottery and locally produced food.

Llandrindod Wells, standing high on a plateau overlooking the River Ithon, was once the largest and most popular of the Welsh spas. A mile (1.6km) north of the town stand the well-preserved ruins of the Roman fort of Castell Collen.

Although Llandrindod is the administrative capital, Builth Wells to the south is the ancient market centre for this part of mid Wales. Home of the Royal Welsh Show each July, Builth also has a weekly farm market. From here you can venture into the upper Wye Valley, whose rushing waters are turned into exciting white-water rapids for experienced canoeists at Aberedw, just downstream.

Travelling northeast will bring you to Knighton, a small town in the valley of the River Teme on the English border. The Welsh name for the town, Tref-y-Clawdd, gives away its history – it means 'the town on the dike' – and some of the best-preserved stretches of 8th-century Offa's Dyke are found near to the town.

FESTIVAL OF THE COUNTRYSIDE

A new and 'green' addition to the events list for get-up-and-go visitors to mid Wales is the annual Festival of the Countryside, based at **Newtown** in Powys. The festival promotes sustainable tourism by encouraging awareness and enjoyment of the countryside in ways which do it no harm. This partnership between the Countryside Council for Wales, the Wales Tourist Board, National Parks, local authorities and water companies promotes environmentally sensitive tourism through the production of two magazines a year, giving details of 'sustainable' events and attractions throughout the area. Among the events covered are country rides and walks, arts and crafts, natural history and gardens, and a useful calendar gives daily details of where and when you can join in.

WELSH SPA

Llandrindod Wells first became popular in the reign of Charles II and by Victorian times it was drawing up to 80,000 visitors a year. The 19th-century passion for 'taking the waters', combined with the arrival of the railway in 1865, resulted in a sudden spate of building. The town has managed to preserve much of its dignified past, including the original Pump Room, restored to some of its former glory. Although few of today's many visitors miss the opportunity to sample a glass of the famous waters, they are mainly attracted by the beautiful scenery, and outdoor activities such as golf and fishing.

architecture, seems a large place. The University College of St David's, founded in 1822, is the third oldest university in Britain after Oxford and Cambridge.

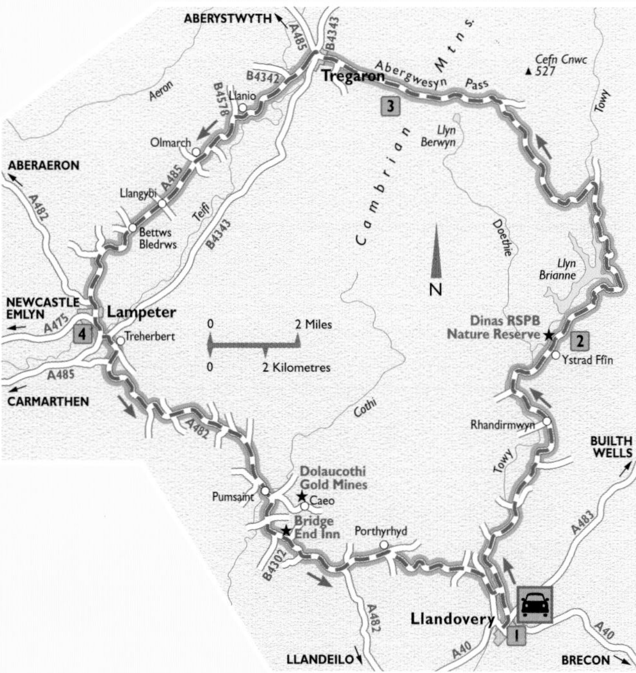

4 At the T-junction turn left and at the far end of the town take the A482 towards Llanwrda, and ascend through Treherbert. Descend to Pumsaint. Here, you will find the Dolaucothi Gold Mines (NT), established in AD 75 by the Romans and operational for around 100 years. A waymarked walk explores the site and a guided tour includes some of the underground workings. Remain on the A482, pass the Bridge End Inn, then in 2.5 miles (4km) turn left on to a minor road towards Porthyrhyd. Pass through Porthyrhyd, bear right for Llandovery and follow the signs, to re-enter Llandovery.

LAKE VYRNWY & THE BERWYN MOUNTAINS

The Berwyn Mountains of the northernmost part of mid Wales are one of the most extensive stretches of mountain and moorland in the whole of Wales, yet they remain among the quietest hills in the country. The highest point of the Berwyns is the 2,713-ft (827-m) summit of Moel Sych, on the old county boundary between Montgomery and Denbigh, one of three Berwyn summits which top 2,500ft (762m). Situated as they are, halfway between the ranges of Snowdonia and the Shropshire hills, one of the finest aspects of the Berwyns is the view which can be enjoyed across the two countries from their heathery summits.

The range is split on the east by the deep river valleys of the Ceiriog and the Tanat, which reach out of England and into Wales, and at Pistyll Rhaeadr, the highest waterfall in England and Wales, where the River Disgynfa cascades down through a natural arch into a deep pool below.

The deeper glaciated valley of Afon Vyrnwy was flooded and dammed in the late 19th century to create Lake Vyrnwy – the largest man-made lake in the whole of Wales. It would be difficult to imagine the valley of the upper Vyrnwy without the dam, and it now attracts a range of outdoor activities, including walking, cycling, watersports, bird-watching and trout fishing. There is also a visitor centre, craft shops and a sculpture trail, run by Severn Trent Water.

FOOD FOR THOUGHT

Locally reared, succulent **Welsh lamb** is a firm favourite in mid Wales and nowadays it is served not only as a traditional dish, but in the modern, lighter, nouvelle-cuisine style. **Fresh salmon** and **sewin** – the local name for sea-trout – are also popular local dishes which are on offer at bistros as well as some top restaurants.

Increasingly you will find fresh, tasty wholefoods and organically grown produce at your dinner table, and **Welsh farmhouse cheese** is enjoying something of a revival. For tea, why not try some of the delicious traditional **Welsh oatcakes** or **bara brith**, a locally baked type of fruit loaf.

Wrexham's pedestrianised town centre is a busy draw for shoppers

The tranquil beauty of Lake Vyrnwy, which is home to two bird reserves

Breidden Hills Walk

WALK

The Gateway to Wales

START/FINISH: Middletown. Located on A458 between Shrewsbury and Welshpool
DISTANCE: 6 miles (10km)
ASCENT/GRADIENT: 2,150ft (655m); steep gradients
TERRAIN/PATHS: woodland, upland pasture; good paths; steep and slippery on Moel y Golfa; some quiet lanes
PARKING: car-park in Middletown

Long famed for their extensive views, the Breidden Hills hint at the great mountains beyond.

1 The ancient settlements in these hills, on Middletown Hill, Breidden Hill and in the forests of New Pieces, were probably occupied until the Roman invasion in AD 57. From the car-park, walk up the lane opposite Breidden Hotel. Ignore the footpath left and follow the lane towards Middleton Quarry. Fork right at the junction, soon turning left on to the path uphill through gorse and bracken. Keep climbing through all path junctions to the ridge at the top. Turn right on the wide track to Middletown Hill.

2 Middletown Hill is the least wooded of the hills, and as such has uninterrupted views on the climb. Walk along the ridge to the summit then down to the saddle. Descend left to a lane and turn right. Pass Belleisle Farm and carry on to a track on the left, taking you past another farm, into pastureland. Maintain direction through the first field, then follow the left-hand hedge to the woods. Cross a stream and follow the waymarked bridleway rising through the woods. It crosses a flinty forestry road then continues to climb up to Rodney's Pillar, taking two left forks along the way. Beyond a stile in the fence, the path traverses open hillside to another stile preceding a steep climb to Rodney's Pillar.

3 From the summit, head along the ridge (southwest) to the edge of a wood, then turn sharp left to double-back down the hillside and through sparse woodland to an open area. From beneath Rodney's Pillar you can see the River Severn slithering like a serpent past the buildings of Welshpool, and on through the lowland plain etched with a web of hedgerow and forest, and framed by the Welsh foothills. Go through the gate and follow the grassy bridleway to cross a forestry track before climbing through the conifers of New Pieces. At a junction, ignore the

Although the collieries and steelworks on which Wrexham prospered are now largely things of the past, this bustling town is still the largest in mid Wales. A weekly cattle market still provides leather for tanning, one of the oldest traditional industries in the area. The church of St Giles is the chief architectural attraction, with its elegant 135-ft (41-m) steeple, dating from the 14th century. A copy of the church tower was built on the campus of Yale University in the 1920s in memory of Elihu Yale, the Pilgrim Father buried in the churchyard here, who gave his name to the distinguished American university.

Welshpool is a lively Georgian market town in the Severn Valley and a natural gateway into Wales. The red sandstone walls of Powis Castle on the outskirts are probably its chief claim to fame. Now in the hands of the National Trust, Powis was originally a 13th-century Welsh castle, but has been embellished by successive generations of the families of the Herberts and Clives, and now contains one of the finest collections of works of art in Wales. Its Italian- and French-style terraced gardens are internationally renowned.

Of the few other settlements in the area, Llanfyllin, which derives its name from Myllin, a 7th-century Celtic saint, provides a good base for walkers or drivers who want to explore Lake Vyrnwy to the west or the Berwyns to the north, and 18th-century Llanfair Caereinion, on the River Banwy, is the western terminus of the Welshpool and Llanfair Light Railway, one of the 'Great Little Trains of Wales'.

GLYNDWR'S WAY

This newest Welsh walking route threads through this part of mid Wales on its 128-mile (206-km) route between **Welshpool**, **Machynlleth** and **Knighton**. It is named after the supposed route taken by Owain Glyndwr, the 15th-century Welsh freedom fighter, as he gathered his army in readiness for battle against English and Flemish forces. Between 1400 and 1410, Glyndwr, a Welsh gentleman and lawyer, waged a guerilla campaign against the army of Henry IV. Although his uprising eventually subsided, he was never captured, leaving behind a legacy of national identity. He remains a hero for Welsh nationalists everywhere.

BERWYN BAGGING

A determined rambler could walk for almost 30 miles (48km) northeastwards traversing the Berwyns from **Bwlch Sirddyn** to the final flourish of **Moel Fferna** and its satellites above **Llangollen**, and nowhere drop below 1,500ft (460m). You would cross only one minor road, the unfenced B4391 route between **Llangynog** and **Bala** at the 1,595-ft (486-m) pass of **Milltir Gerrig**, on your high-level traverse of the range.

SEE CONTACTS SECTION FOR ADDITIONAL INFORMATION

grassy track descending southwest, but double-back left uphill to a vehicle turning-circle. Descend (southwest) to the forest edge. Go through a gate and past a cottage to a farm track leading to a narrow lane. Turn right for three-quarters of a mile (1km).

4 Turn left along a drive at Bescot to a stile, beyond which the path traverses the afforested western slopes of Moel y Golfa.

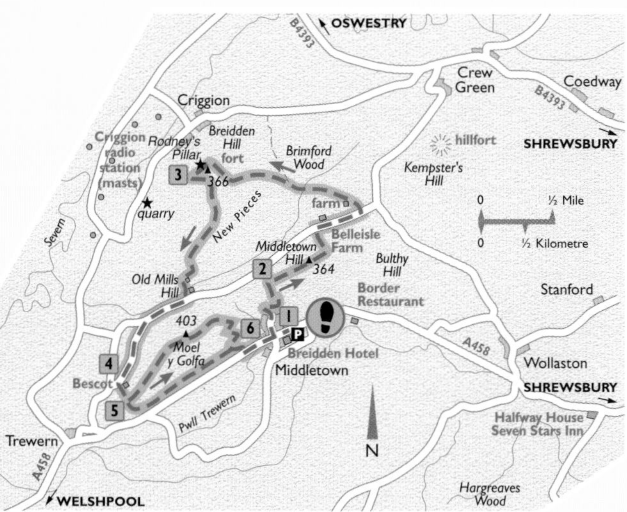

5 A signpost marks the diversion of a steep path to the top of Moel y Golfa. Tired walkers can continue on the lower path, tracing the woodland edge to meet the hill route, close to Middletown. A waymarked, winding hill route climbs through woods and up crags to the summit monument. From here, a narrow path continues along the crest to a gate at the edge of the woods. Turn right and follow the zigzagging path down towards Middletown.

6 At a signpost by the fence corner, near the lower edge of the wood, turn right. Two routes meet up by the stile at the edge of wood. Turn sharp left if you have just descended from the higher route. Another stile leads to a field. Turn left along its edge, past a pig enclosure to the farm track. Turn right to the road, a little way out of Middletown, and follow it left, back into the village.

Echoes of Wrexham's industrial past at the deserted Minera Lead Mines

SNOWDONIA, ANGLESEY & NORTH WALES

Medieval English sailors crossing the Irish Sea first gave Snowdonia its name – the wild, rocky landscape beyond Anglesey always seemed to be brushed with snow. To the Welsh, though, this mountainous region was known as Eryri, the 'abode of eagles', and in 1951, 827sq miles (2,142sq km) of Snowdonia were designated as one of the first and largest of Britain's National Parks. Snowdon, at 3,560ft (1,085m), is the highest peak in Britain south of Scotland, and the natural magnet for the peak-bagger. The rocky, westward-pointing finger of the Lleyn Peninsula, crowned by the twin peaks of Yr Eifl, has some of the finest beaches in North Wales. The ancient landscape of Anglesey is surrounded by rugged sea cliffs, which provide excellent sites for bird-watching and rock-climbing, while the resorts of the north coast and Vales of Conwy and Clwyd show an altogether gentler aspect of North Wales.

PARC CENEDLAETHOL ERYRI
SNOWDONIA NATIONAL PARK

Town of the Giants
Lleyn was one of the first inhabited parts of Wales, and the easternmost peak of the twin-peaked Yr Eifl – which literally means 'the forks' – is crowned by the Iron-Age hillfort of Treir Ceiri, known as the Town of the Giants. This is one of the most impressive of all British hillforts, with substantial remains of 15ft (4.5m) thick walls and gateways, and over 150 hut circles – plus magnificent views towards the hills of Snowdonia.

CAERNARFON CASTLE

Caernarfon Castle is perhaps the most impressive of Edward I's series of castles built during the late 13th century to subdue the Welsh. It was begun in 1283 but was never finished because of Welsh attacks. The sophisticated defences were built on the model of the walls of Constantinople, which Edward had seen while he was on the Seventh Crusade.

Bird-watching in Anglesey

Among the birds you may see from Anglesey's steep and rocky cliffs are thousands of guillemots, razorbills and kittiwakes, as well as puffins. Rarities include a few breeding pairs of the red-legged chough and the dashing peregrine falcons, which prey on the other sea birds from their secret eyries.

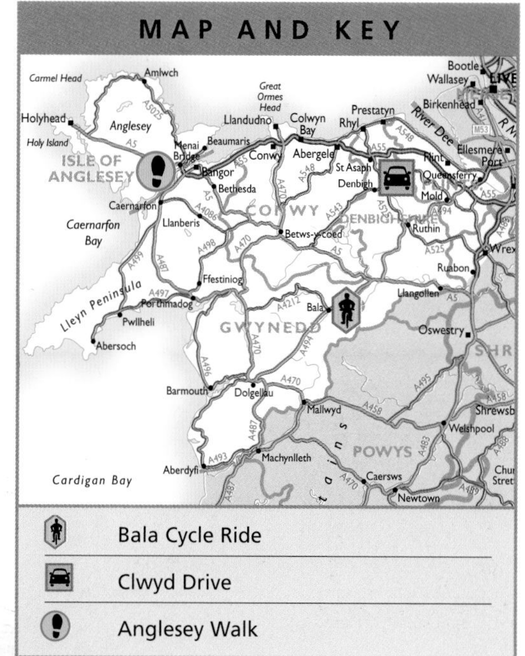

Rock-climbing

For rock-climbers, Snowdonia is a mecca with some of the most well-known climbing crags in the country, such as on Cenotaph Corner in the Llanberis Pass and on Clogwyn duír Arddu on Snowdon, where British 'tigers' have tested their skills before going on to conquer Himalayan giants. The first successful British Everest expedition trained here, based at the Pen y Gwryd Hotel, before their conquest of the peak in 1953.

SNOWDON

Snowdon, or more correctly Yr Wyddfa, is one of the most regularly climbed mountain peaks in Britain, with an estimated 500,000 walkers visiting its summit every year. This has necessitated extensive restoration work on the more popular paths, such as the Pyg Track and the Watkin Path.

SNOWDONIA & THE LLEYN PENINSULA

At 3,560ft (1,085m), Snowdon, or Yr Wydffa, is the highest point of the Snowdonia National Park, and in the whole of England and Wales. The other mountain ranges of the National Park also offer challenging hill-walking, riding and cycling for the well prepared and equipped. To the west, the rocky peninsula of Lleyn leads out to Bardsey Island past the prominent hillfort-crowned peaks of Yr Eifl.

Snowdonia National Park covers 827sq miles (2,142sq km) and is the second largest in Britain after the Lake District. It is shaped like a large diamond split into three facets by valleys which run northeast to southwest, separating the main mountain groups of Snowdon, the Glyders and Carneddau in the north; the rugged Rhinogs and Arenig in the centre; and Cadair Idris and the Arans to the south. Snowdonia is a great place for hill-walking with routes of varying difficulties, from gentle strolls in the valleys to much harder and more demanding routes on the tops.

Slate and forestry have always been the traditional industries of Snowdonia, but tourism is now as important. Slate predominates in the grey little town of Llanberis, at the foot of the precipitous Llanberis Pass. Just across the waters of Llyn Padarn are the terraced shelves of the Dinorwic Slate Quarry, in its time one of the biggest in the world. It is now the site of the Welsh Slate Museum, and one of the most advanced underground hydroelectric schemes in the country. Today, Llanberis is a tourist centre and the starting point of two of the easiest ways to the summit of Snowdon. One is the Llanberis Path, which winds up the southern slopes, and the other is the famous Snowdon Mountain Railway, operating on the rack-and-pinion principle since 1896. Between the lakes of Llyn Padarn and Llyn Peris is the circular 13th-century keep of Dolbadarn Castle.

The still waters of Llyn Idwal, Snowdonia

WELSH SLATE MUSEUM

Until its closure in 1969, the Dinorwic Quarry was one of the largest in Britain, employing over 3,000 men in its heyday. The workshops, most of the machinery and the plant have been preserved, including the foundry and the Dinorwic water wheel. The museum which was subsequently founded on the site includes displays and audio-visual presentations depicting life here, and much of the original atmosphere still prevails. Near by is a group of workshops and a woodcraft centre where visitors can watch craftspeople demonstrating their skills.

Capel Curig is very much a mountain village, with numerous climbing and outdoor shops and the presence of the national mountaineering centre of Plas y Brenin, on its outskirts.

The new marina at the seaside town of Pwllheli, on the Lleyn Peninsula

Betws-y-Coed (meaning 'sanctuary in the wood') sits in the densely wooded hills of the Gwydyr Forest, now almost completely covered in Forestry Commission plantations. Tracks through the forest

Bala Cycle Ride

CYCLE RIDE

Bala and the Dee Valley

START/FINISH: Bala. Situated on the A494 between Dolgellau and Ruthin, on the eastern rim of the Snowdonia National Park

DISTANCE: 19 miles (31km)

GRADIENT: gently undulating

ROADS: mostly single-track and B-roads

PARKING: pay-and-display car-park under the town bridge

A lovely ride through one of the most scenically beautiful areas of Britain, this route takes in some hilly sections as well as flatter valley roads. Although using predominantly minor roads, you will encounter very little traffic, for this area is one of the quietest in the country.

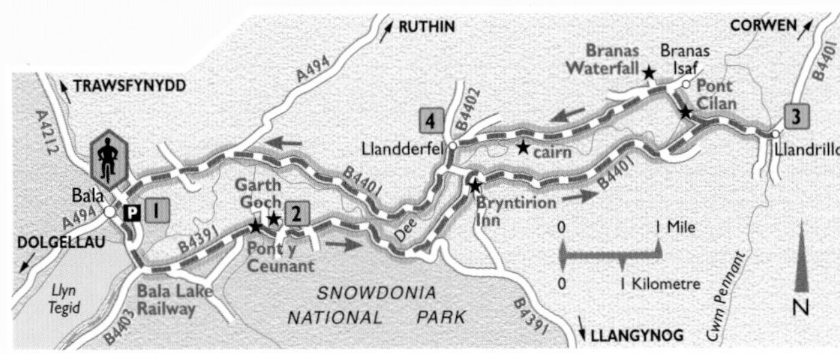

1 An old market town with many interesting pubs and buildings, Bala is situated on Llyn Tegid, the largest stretch of natural water in Wales, over 4 miles (6.5km) long. The Bala Lake Railway operates along the south side of the lake in summer using steam engines from former Welsh slate quarries. Turn right out of the car-park, then left into Bala High Street. At the pelican crossing, turn left into Heol Tegid Street and follow this road across the top of the lake to a T-junction. Turn right on to the B4391, cross the River Dee and follow signs for Llangynog. After 2.5 miles (4km) reach Pont y Ceunant (not signed). About 330yds (300m) after the bridge, on the left is the beauty spot of Garth Goch.

WAYS TO THE TOP

The seven most popular ascents to the summit of Snowdon, all possible in good weather conditions for reasonably fit and well-equipped people, are:

The Miners' Track, from Pen y Pass

The Pyg Track, also from Pen y Pass

Crib Goch, a high-level route requiring a good head for heights and the use of hands

The Llanberis route, following the line of the mountain railway

The Snowdon Ranger, from Llyn Cwellyn

The Rhyd-ddu or Beddgelert route

The Watkin Path, from Nant Gwynant.

Much more challenging is the 8-mile (13-km) **Snowdon Horseshoe**, which takes in the peaks of Crib Goch, Crib y Ddysgl, Yr Wydffa and Lliwedd.

are a regular haunt of walkers and mountain bikers, and there are several well-marked trails to follow through the blanket of trees. Nearby sights include the Swallow Falls, the Fairy Glen and the Conwy Falls.

Blaenau Ffestiniog is the 'ugly duckling' of Snowdonia, excluded from the National Park by reason of its enclosing mountains of slate waste which bear testimony to the hard labour of generations of workers. Visitors can now experience the awesome wonder of the man-made caverns at the Llechwedd Quarries, or discover the modern wonders of hydroelectricity at the Edison Mission Energy's Ffestiniog Visitor Centre.

The landscape of the Lleyn Peninsula is quite unlike the rest of North Wales – distant horizons broken by dramatic mountains falling sheer into the sea, rocky coves, wide bays and enticing beaches. The 112 miles (180km) of coastline is dotted with picturesque white-washed villages such as Abersoch, Aberdaron and Llanbedrog, and at Pwllheli there is a modern, 420-berth boating marina.

SEE CONTACTS SECTION FOR ADDITIONAL INFORMATION

SNOWDON MOUNTAIN RAILWAY

The Snowdon Mountain Railway is Britain's only public rack-and-pinion railway. It is operated by seven vintage steam and four modern diesel locomotives, and a three-car diesel electric railcar set. The leisurely journey of just over 4.5 miles (7km) takes passengers through pleasant rural and woodland scenery more than 3,000ft (915m) up to the summit of Snowdon. Breathtaking views at the top include, on a clear day, the Isle of Man and the Wicklow Mountains in Ireland.

FISHING IN THE MOUNTAINS

The llyns (lakes) and rivers of Snowdonia offer excellent fishing amid magnificent mountain scenery.

Llyn Padarn, at the entrance to the Llanberis Pass, gives great sport with brown trout and alpine char, and **Llyn Cwellyn** has outstanding brown trout. **Afon** (River) **Seiont** is a superb salmon river, **Afon Gwyrfai** has sea trout and salmon, and **Afon Llyfni** gives excellent sea-trout fishing.

Looking across the waters of Llyn Tegid to Bala

2 Continue along the B4391 for 2 miles (3km) and turn left at the red telephone box on the left, signed Corwen (B4402). Descend to reach a T-junction by Bryntirion Inn. Turn right and follow the Dee Valley eastwards. Pass the Crogen Estate (private), site of an ancient battle, where Henry II was defeated in 1165 by the Welsh prince Owain Gwynedd, and continue straight on to the village of Llandrillo. Follow the road through the village, and as you cross the river bridge, turn immediately left to find an ideal picnic site near the old bridge.

3 Retrace your route back through Llandrillo on the B4401. After half a mile (800m) turn right, signed Branas Isaf Development Centre, and cross the River Dee at Pont Cilan. Continue to a T-junction and turn left on to an unclassified road (can be muddy and wet). After a short distance, the Branas Waterfall can be seen to the right, by a house. (To visit the top of the fall, turn right past the house and take a steep path. There is no access to the falls. Return to the main road.) Stay on this road, passing a chambered cairn on the left, to reach Llandderfel village.

4 Turn left at a T-junction, and proceed to the war memorial and turn right, signed Bala. Follow the route along the River Dee for 3 miles (5km) to meet the A494. Turn left and after 1 mile (1.5km) reach Bala. The car-park is on the left as you cross the bridge into the town.

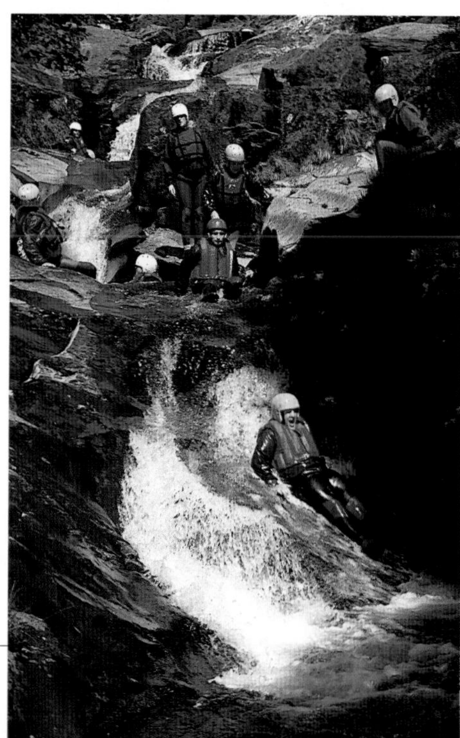

Organised watersports at Beddgelert are an exhilarating way to experience Snowdonia's fast-flowing waters

THE NORTH COAST & VALE OF CONWY

The imposing entrance to Conwy Castle, at the centre of this fortified town

One of the most pleasant and refined of the North Wales coastal resorts, Llandudno shelters between the great twin limestone headlands of the Great Orme and Little Orme, west of Colwyn Bay. Further east, the attractions of Rhyl and Prestatyn beckon the candy floss and kiss-me-quick holiday-maker. To the west lies Conwy, guarded by its splendid medieval castle, one of the finest in Wales, and inland are the fertile Vales of Conwy and Clwyd, where small, hedged fields sweep gently up to the Clwydian Hills Area of Outstanding Natural Beauty.

Abergele is an ancient market town which is now also a busy resort, with the caravan-besieged suburb of Pensarn on the coast at the centre of 5 miles (8km) of sand and shingle beaches, where windsurfing is sometimes possible.

A quayside cottage in Conwy which is said to be the smallest house in Britain

Colwyn Bay is a charming traditional Victorian resort, with some fine architecture and a wonderful promenade, unfortunately shared by the parallel railway line. Colwyn stretches round its east-facing bay from Old Colwyn to Rhos-on-Sea, and is home to the Eirias Park Dinosaur World and the Welsh Mountain Zoo, located 500ft (150m) above sea-level. A little way south on the A470 is Felin Isaf, a working flour mill on the River Conwy.

The eight drum towers of Edward I's superb 13th-century castle at Conwy have protected this pleasant little town at the mouth

Llandudno's spacious promenade, surrounded by elegant Victorian town houses

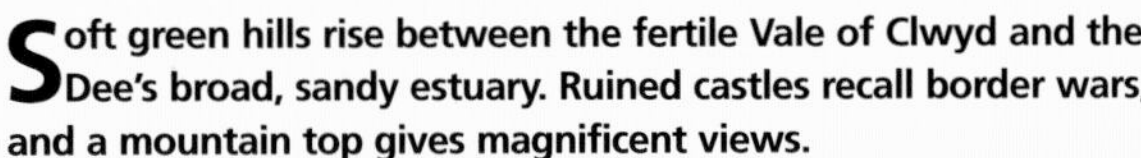

Clwyd Drive

DRIVE

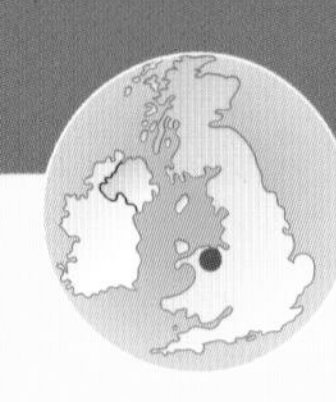

Castles Guarding Clwyd's Hills

START/FINISH: Denbigh. On the A543/A525 10 miles (16km) south of Rhyl

DISTANCE: 70 miles (122km)

Soft green hills rise between the fertile Vale of Clwyd and the Dee's broad, sandy estuary. Ruined castles recall border wars, and a mountain top gives magnificent views.

1 Overlooking Denbigh's attractive streets are the ruins of Edward I's 13th-century castle. On leaving the town take the A525 Rhyl road to reach St Asaph. St Asaph is technically a city containing Britain's smallest cathedral – founded in AD 560 by St Kentigern. The present building dates from the 13th century and contains a copy of the first Welsh bible, published in 1588. Turn left on to the A55, Conwy road.

2 Turn left off the A55 at Bodelwyddan. On the left at the roundabout is restored Bodelwyddan Castle, an imposing Victorian house set in rolling parkland. Turn right at the roundabout over the A55 to Bodelwyddan village. Continue through the village, after a mile (1.5km) turn left on to the A525. At the roundabout turn right to Rhuddlan. Ruined Rhuddlan Castle was begun in 1277 and became Edward I's headquarters whilst conducting the campaign to conquer Wales. Turn right on to the A5151 soon to pass Bodryhddan Hall on the left. This handsome red-brick mansion has ornamented gardens dating from the 1700s. In Dyserth turn left, signed Prestatyn (A547), then turn right to join the A547. For Graig Fawr, a craggy limestone peak with magnificent views along the coast to Great Orme whose cliffs tower above Llandudno, turn right on to the single-track Gwaenysgor road.

3 At Prestatyn follow signs for Flint A548 eventually turning right along the coast road (A548). Remain on this road for 9 miles (14.5km) to the village of Greenfield.

4 Turn right on to the B5121 to Holywell. On the left is a car-park for Greenfield Valley Heritage Park, with a farm museum and buildings rescued from their original sites. There is also the remains of a Cistercian abbey (Basingwerk Abbey). Approaching Holywell on the left is

TOURING HORSESHOE PASS

Motorists using the precipitous 1,299-ft (396-m) Horseshoe Pass between **Llangollen** and **Ruthin** get an intimate view of the Llangollen Hills. Passing **Eliseg's Pillar**, a 9th-century monument to a Welsh prince, and the lovely ruins of **Valle Crucis Abbey**, the A542 heads towards Pentredwr with tremendous views of the sweeping limestone escarpments of the **Eglwyseg Rocks** to the north, where the northern summit is known as **World's End** (1,614 ft/492m). These terraced hills of white limestone scars and scree are said to take their alternative name of Church Rocks from the abbey in the valley below. From Pentredwr, the road climbs relentlessly between Llantysilio and the Cyrn-y-Brain Mountains, with a bird's-eye view of the Vale of Clwyd below, before dropping down to the valley.

of the River Conwy. Three bridges span the river beside the castle – a modern road bridge, Stephenson's tubular railway bridge of 1848 and Thomas Telford's suspension bridge of 1826, which has 'medieval' towers to match those of the castle and is now in the care of the National Trust.

A century ago, Llandudno was just a sleepy fishing village, but today it is the largest resort on this coast and justly favoured by holiday-makers. The architect of this transformation was Owen Williams, who laid out the sweeping promenade, Marine Drive and the spacious streets. The limestone bulk of the Great Orme can be reached by foot, Victorian tramway, cabin lift or cable car.

Rhuddlan Castle, guarding the mouth of the River Clwyd and the coastal route into North Wales, is a good example of how a castle developed over the centuries. Just to the southeast are the earthworks of a much earlier motte-and-bailey castle, built in 1073 in the first phase of the English invasion.

Rhyl developed into a successful resort in Victorian days. 'Sunny Rhyl' now offers visitors all that a modern seaside town should, including the multi-million pound Sun Centre, which provides year-round amusements, recreation and protection from the unpredictable Welsh weather – although one of the more bizarre attractions is a 'tropical rainstorm'!

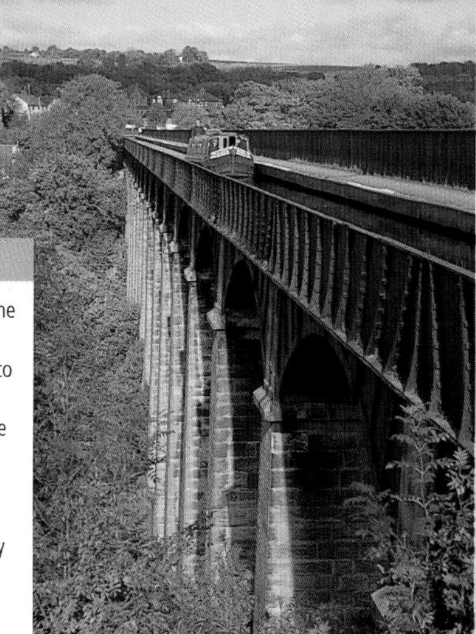

CANAL IN THE CLOUDS

The **Pontcysyllte Aqueduct** was one of the wonders of Britain when it was built by Thomas Telford as a revolutionary solution to the question of how to carry the Ellesmere Canal across the valley of the River Dee. The aqueduct takes the canal over 19 arches, in an iron trough more than 1,000ft (305m) long, 120ft (37m) above the valley of the Dee. Technology may have come a long way since Telford's day, but this is still a breathtaking piece of engineering.

Once the county town for this part of Wales, Flint has always occupied a strategic position on the western shore of the Dee Estuary. Flint Castle was the first of Edward I's chain of castles to control the Welsh, built between 1277 and 1284 at the then huge cost of £7,000.

Llangollen, sheltered in its green vale, has played host to the annual International Musical Eisteddfod since 1947. During this summertime festival of song and dance, the streets are colourful with folk costumes and music. But Llangollen has other gems, including the 14th-century bridge over the Dee – one of the 'Wonders of Wales' – and Plas Newydd, a black and white, timber-framed house on the edge of the town, which was the home of the hospitable 'Ladies of Llangollen'.

BODNANT GARDEN

Bodnant Garden, 8 miles (13km) south of Llandudno, is one of the finest gardens in the world, consisting of 80 acres (32ha) of formal, Italian-style terraces, a pinetum and a wild garden, all laid out in 1875. It shelters in the valley of the River Hiraethlyn, a tributary of the Conwy. Bodnant is especially noted for its rhododendrons, azaleas and camellias, and for its magnificent laburnum arch and walk.

St Winefride's Well. At the T-junction turn left and follow signs for Chester to join the A55 eastbound.

5 Turn left along the Northop Hall road, then immediately turn right to Ewloe. Standing in a deep, secluded wooded valley are the remains of 13th-century Ewloe Castle. In Ewloe turn left at the T-junction and at the roundabout take the A494 around Mold towards Ruthin and pass Loggerheads Country Park. Bordering the Afon Alun, its most dramatic feature is a lofty limestone plateau which forms part of a nature trail and has fine views of the Clwydian Hills.

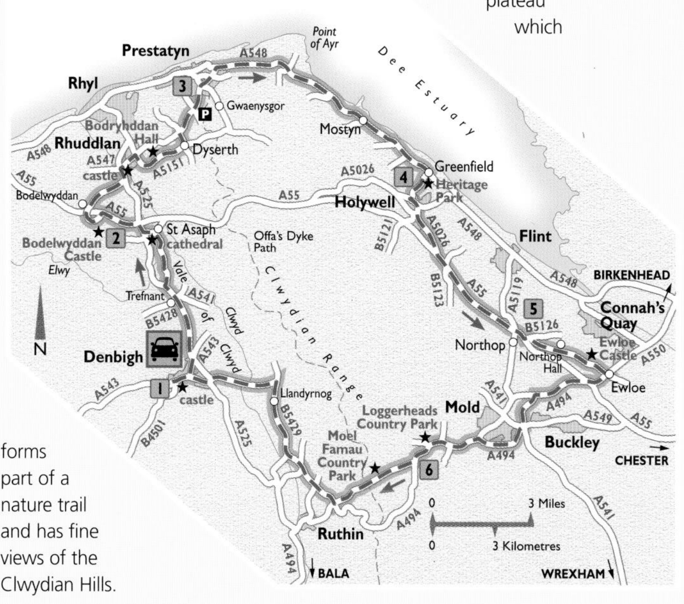

6 In half a mile (800m) fork right on to the Moel Famau road and pass Moel Famau Country Park close to the Offa's Dyke Path. The summit of Moel Famau (1817ft/555m) is reached by a footpath through woodland. Views from the top range from Snowdonia to the Isle of Man and the Pennines. Turn right on to the A494, then right again along the B5429 to Llandyrnog. Passing through Llandyrnog turn left at the roundabout to retun to Denbigh.

ANGLESEY & THE MENAI STRAIT

The Menai Strait, between the castle-crowned towns of Beaumaris and Caernarfon, has always made ancient Anglesey a place set apart from the rest of Wales. Its dolmen-dotted interior is fringed by a beautiful coastline of steep cliffs and sandy bays. Over on the mainland, the narrow coastal plain rears up to the cloud-capped foothills of Snowdonia.

Anglesey is linked to the mainland by two feats of civil engineering, constructed at the Victorian town of Menai Bridge. Thomas Telford's suspension bridge, which originally took mail coaches 100ft (30m) above the Menai Strait, was the longest single-span bridge in the world when it was built in 1826. Today it carries the A5, bound for the Holyhead ferries and Ireland. Near by is George Stephenson's tubular iron Britannia Bridge, built in 1850 to carry the railway but since adapted to carry both road and rail traffic.

The colony of sea birds at South Stack can be spotted from coastal walks

Holyhead Mountain (719ft/219m) is one of the best viewpoints in Anglesey, taking in the distant coast of Ireland to the west, the Isle of Man to the north, and the jagged peaks of Snowdonia to the southeast. Nearer to hand are a wealth of prehistoric remains and the rocky little island of South Stack, with its gleaming white lighthouse serving as a beacon to the ferries which scuttle in and out of this busy port. Holyhead is the biggest town on Anglesey, and its 13th-century church of St Cybil is built on the site of a Roman fort.

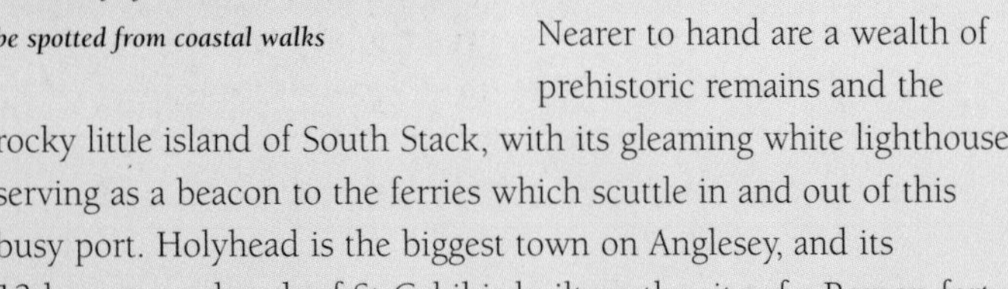

Plas Newydd, now in the care of the National Trust, was designed by James Wyatt for the Marquess of Anglesey in the late 18th century, and contains a military museum with a collection of uniforms and relics of the Battle of Waterloo, where the 1st Marquess lost his leg. There are magnificent views across the Menai

Hydrangeas blossom in the mild climate at Plas Newydd, on the banks of the Menai Strait

Thomas Telford's graceful suspension bridge, linking Anglesey with Wales

Anglesey Walk

WALK

Groves and Graves in Anglesey

START/FINISH: Moel-y-don peninsula, south of the A4080 near Menai Bridge
DISTANCE: 8 miles (13km)
ASCENT/GRADIENT: 280ft (85m); slight gradients
TERRAIN/PATHS: undulating farmland, some woodland; mostly tracks and field paths
PARKING: end of the Moel-y-don peninsula

This once-ritual region, now overlain with farmland and smallholdings, is crisscrossed by ancient tracks that are deeply scarred into the landscape.

1 Walk up the road away from the Strait. Turn left by the post box, along the lane and right at the T-junction, to a farm. Before the pond, turn left on to a track, going left where it swings to join another. At the end of the wood go right over a stone stile and across the field to a track between hedges. At the top, swing right, through a kissing-gate, between farm buildings, through another kissing-gate, between more buildings to the road. Cross the road, going right into a lay-by, then through Gwydryn Bach cottage gates. Keep to this track, through a gate and ahead to a gateway just before farm buildings.

2 Go right of farm buildings, through two gates. With your back to the second gate, go ahead (uphill) to keep right of a hedge, then cross an awkward gate. Go ahead, crossing two fields, keeping right of a cottage ahead, to reach a track. Turn left (downhill) and follow this track left around farm buildings to a stile. Go ahead, directly downhill, keeping right of a hedge to a footbridge. Cross this and head diagonally right uphill to a ladder stile. Follow the track ahead to the road. Turn right and walk through Llanddaniel Fab, straight ahead.

3 Before the speed de-restriction sign turn right to Tyddyn-Adda. As the track curves left, go right of the breeze-block building to a stile. Cross the field diagonally left to a gate near the corner, then again diagonally left to a stile in this second field corner. Cross the ditch and climb a stile over a wall. Go straight ahead for 150yds (137m). At a crossing wall, go right through a gateway, then eleven o'clock left across two fields to a stile near the corner. Follow the hedge and stream to a

ISLAND WILDLIFE

The cliffs of **Holyhead Mountain** and **South Stack** are a haven for flocks of wheeling sea birds, which include herring gulls, guillemots, skuas and gannets, while dolphins and grey seals can often be seen in calm weather in the sea below. The cliffs also attract rock climbers to some of the most severe coastal cliff-climbing in the whole of Britain.

A more gentle wildlife habitat can be found at **Newborough Warren**, a National Nature Reserve covering 1,500 acres (607ha) of shifting sand dunes and forest plantations on the southwestern tip of Anglesey. Here there are waymarked nature trails enabling visitors to enjoy the famous birdlife of the reserve, which includes curlews, godwits, sandpipers and oystercatchers.

Strait to Snowdonia from the mansion's park, which also has two fine prehistoric dolmens.

Dotted along the coast of the mainland and guarding the interior is the string of Edward I's defensive castles. Of these, Caernarfon was the most ambitious, intended to be not only a fortress but also the seat of government and the monarch's official residence. The banded walls and angled towers were built over a period of 44 years and completed in 1327. The old town is still ringed by the almost intact town walls built on the order of Edward I, and the even earlier foundations of the Roman fort of *Segontium* can still be seen a few hundred yards from the castle.

The elegant town of Beaumaris has kept its former gaol and courthouse, where visitors can see the treadmill, grim cells and 19th-century courtroom. The Museum of Childhood has nine rooms of exhibits reflecting 150 years of dolls, toys, games and other related items.

Bangor is a university and cathedral city which boasts the oldest bishopric in Britain. The University College of North Wales occupies modern buildings in Upper Bangor. In contrast, Old Bangor is a delightful maze of streets leading down to the sea. Three miles (5km) east is splendid Penrhyn Castle, with all the appearance of an authentic Norman fortress, including a cavernous Great Hall and staircase, but actually built in the early 19th century as a sumptuous family home.

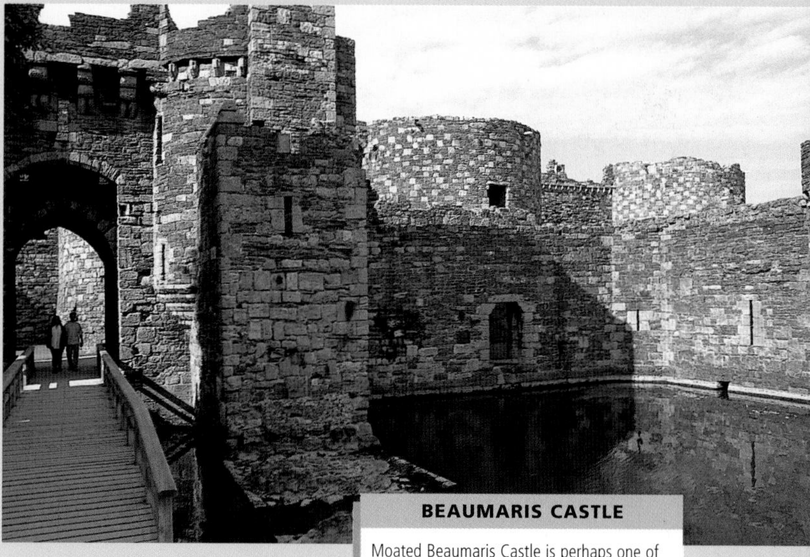

BEAUMARIS CASTLE

Moated Beaumaris Castle is perhaps one of the most beautiful of Edward I's castles, built in the late 13th century to guard the approaches to the Menai Strait. The concentric walls with their circular towers were never completed to their full height, and the castle never saw military action. The Great Hall and chapel in the central tower are particularly memorable.

gate, then follow the track to a ladder stile on to a major track. Turn left along this towards a farm. The entrance to Bryn Celli Ddu, a late Stone-Age burial chamber, is opposite the farm.

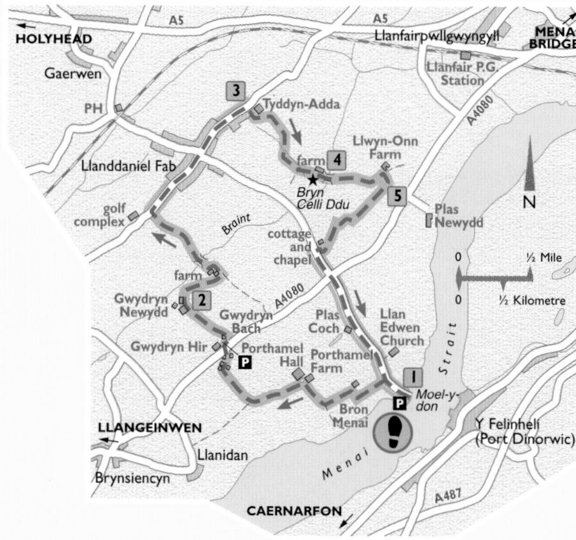

4 Beyond the farmhouse, go over a ladder stile then keep alongside the wall on your left and over a footbridge. Take the path eleven o'clock left ahead (passing a mound of rocks) to a stile. Head one o'clock right to the top corner of the field and a ladder stile by a gate. Go left, alongside the wall on your left, but immediately before the farmhouse go right to a stile by a gate. Don't go down the farm drive.

5 50yds (46m) beyond the gate turn right along a track. After the second stile, go right of a brick building, then diagonally left towards a rhododendron thicket, going right of it to a stile into woodland. Follow the track through the wood, keeping the wall to your left. At the gate, go across the field to a waymarker, then turn right towards the cottage and chapel. Immediately before the cottage, go left through its grounds to the road. Turn left, cross the main road and follow the road signed Moel-y-don for a mile (1.5km) back to the car.

PREHISTORIC ANGLESEY

The distinguished archaeologist Jacquetta Hawkes said that there was no better place than Anglesey to combine a seaside holiday with painless archaeology. Certainly, this small, ancient island, known to the Romans as *Mona*, is a treasure-house of prehistoric remains, and the fabled home of the mysterious priesthood known as the Druids, who caused the conqueror of Britain, Julius Caesar, so much anguish.

Among the most impressive sites are the neolithic chambered barrows of **Barclodiad y Gawres** near Llangwfan and **Bryn Celli Ddu** near Llanddaniel Fab, both unequalled outside Ireland, along with the various dolmens (prehistoric stone tables) at **Lligwy** (below), near Amlwch and Trefignath, just south of Holyhead. These are now known to be the exposed remains of other neolithic tombs and barrows.

SOUTHWEST ENGLAND

CORNWALL & THE ISLES OF SCILLY

TOURIST INFORMATION

Cornwall Tourist Board
Pydar House, Pydar Street, Truro, Cornwall TR1 1EA
Tel: 01872 322900
www.cornwall-online.co.uk

Isles of Scilly TIC
Wesleyan Chapel, Well Lane,
St Mary's, Isles of Scilly TR21 0JD
Tel: 01720 422536

ACTIVITIES

Adventure Sports
Carnkie, Cornwall
Tel: 01209 218962
www.adventure-sports.co.uk
Multi-activity residential holidays.

Adventureline Walking Holidays
Redruth, Cornwall
Tel/fax: 01209 820847
www.chycor.co.uk/adventureline

Alternative Cornish Holidays
Karensa Cottage, St Issey, Cornwall
Tel: 01841 540383
Coastal walking holidays.

Buccabu Hire
Porthcressa, St Mary's, Isles of Scilly
Tel/fax: 01720 422289
Bicycle hire (with rescue service).

Chichester Interest Holidays
Newquay, Cornwall
Tel/fax: 01637 874216
www.smoothhound.co.uk/hotels/chichest
Walking and special interest holidays.

Coast & Countryside Walking & Cycling
Poughill, Cornwall
Tel: 01288 352350
www.coast-countryside.co.uk
Southwest walking and cycling routes.

Cornwall Outdoor Education Centres
Truro, Cornwall
Tel: 01872 322448
Year-round multi-activity holidays.

Cornwall Walking Holidays
Pool, Cornwall
Tel/fax: 01209 715358

Footpath Holidays
Warminster, Wiltshire
Tel: 01985 840049
Guided walking holidays of Cornwall.

Gooseham Barton Riding Stables
Morwenstow, Cornwall
Tel: 01288 331204
Riding stables with accommodation.

TM International School of Horsemanship
Sunrising Riding Centre, Henwood, Cornwall
Tel/fax: 01579 362895
Moorland hacks and riding holidays.

WalKernow
Helston, Cornwall
Tel: 01326 572037
www.praze.org.uk/walkernow
Cornish cliff-walking.

Watergate Bay Hotel
Watergate Bay, Cornwall
Tel: 01637 860543
www.watergate.co.uk
Surfing and canoeing tuition, power kites and buggies.

Windsport International
Mylor Yacht Harbour, Falmouth, Cornwall
Tel: 01326 376191
www.windsport-int.com
Sailing instruction.

LEISURE

Bodmin & Wenford Railway
Bodmin General Station, Cornwall
Tel: 01208 73666
Steam railway from Bodmin General to Bodmin Parkway (Etr–Oct).

Flambards Village
Culdrose Manor, Helston, Cornwall
Tel: 01326 573404
www.flambards.co.uk
Re-created Victorian village and Britain in the Blitz street.

Hayle Estuary RSPB Reserve
Hayle, Cornwall
Tel: 01736 810783
Estuary with wildfowl and waders.

Heritage Tours
Santamana, St Mary's, Isles of Scilly
Tel: 01720 422387
Tours of St Mary's aboard a 1948 bus.

Isles of Scilly Travel
Tel: 0845 710 5555
www.islesofscilly-travel.co.uk
Flights and ferries to the Isles of Scilly.

Land's End Visitor Centre & Conservation Site
Sennen, Cornwall
Tel: 01736 871501
www.landsend-landmark.co.uk

Launceston Steam Railway
Launceston, Cornwall
Tel: 01566 775665
Narrow-gauge steam railway; Launceston to New Mills.

Marazion Marsh RSPB Reserve
St Michael's Mount, Cornwall
Tel: 01736 810783
Spotted crakes and aquatic warblers.

Neddi Donkey Sanctuary
St Kew, Cornwall
Tel: 01208 841242
www.neddi.org
Help groom rescued donkeys.

Scotia Helicopter Services
Heliport, Penzance, Cornwall
Tel: 01736 363871
www.helicopter-scilly.co.uk
Helicopter service to Isles of Scilly.

Tamar Otter Sanctuary
North Petherwin, Cornwall
Tel: 01566 785646
Otters bred for re-introduction.

SHOPPING

Cornish Goldsmiths
Tolgus Mill, Portreath, Cornwall
Tel: 01209 218198
Large selection of gold jewellery.

Cornwall Pearl
Quintrell Downs, Cornwall
Tel: 01637 872991
Pearls and pearl jewellery.

Kernow Mill
Trerulefoot, Cornwall
Tel: 01752 851898
Traditional Cornish products.

Merlin Glass
Liskeard, Cornwall
Tel: 01579 342399
Hand-made glass from workshop.

Phoenix Stained Glass Art & Craft Studio
St Mary's, Isles of Scilly
Tel: 01720 422900
Stained glass; watch, buy or learn.

St Neot Pottery
St Neot, Cornwall
Tel: 01579 320216
Hand-decorated earthenware pottery.

Waterloo Books
St Mary's, Isles of Scilly
Tel: 01720 422509
Antiquarian and second-hand books.

DEVON & DARTMOOR

TOURIST INFORMATION

Dartmoor Tourist Association
The Duchy Building, Tavistock Road, Princetown, Yelverton, Devon PL20 6QF
Tel: 01822 890567
www.dartmoor-guide.co.uk

English Riviera Tourist Board
Vaughan Parade, Torquay, Devon TQ2 5JG
Tel/fax: 01803 214885
www.theenglishriviera.co.uk

North Devon Marketing Bureau
1st Floor, Rolle Quay House, Barnstaple, North Devon EX31 1JE
Tel: 01271 323030
www.northdevon.co.uk

West Country Tourist Board
PO Box 57, Exeter, Devon EX4 4YH
Tel: 0870 442 0880
www.westcountryholidays.com

ACTIVITIES

Bideford Bicycle Hire
Bideford, Devon
Tel: 01579 350254
Bikes, tandems, trikes and trailers.

Bideford Bike & Canoe Hire
Bideford, Devon
Tel: 01237 424123
Bike and canoe hire on River Torridge.

Distin Boat Hire
Dartmouth, Devon
Tel: 01803 835034
Traditional wooden-launch hire.

Lydford Gorge (NT)
Lydford, Devon
Tel: 01822 820320 or 820441
Woodland walk along gorge.

North Devon Karting Centre
Barnstaple, Devon
Tel: 01271 328460
Go-karting; 200m and 400m circuits.

South West Water Leisure Services
Roadford Lake, Lewdown, Devon
Tel: 01837 871565
Watersports, fishing, bird-watching and walking.

Surf South West
Croyde, Devon
Tel: 01271 890400
www.surfsouthwest.com
Surf school, beginners to intermediate.

Tarka Trail Cycle Hire
Railway Station, Barnstaple, Devon
Tel: 01271 324202
Cycle hire; route following former railway line.

LEISURE

Grand Western Horseboat Co
Tiverton, Devon
Tel: 01884 253345
Canal trips on horse-drawn barge.

Kents Cavern
Torquay, Devon
Tel: 01803 215136
www.kents-cavern.co.uk
Chambers and passages.

MS *Oldenburg*
The Quay, Bideford, Devon
Tel: 01237 470422
www.lundyisland.co.uk
Sailings to Lundy Island from Bideford, Ilfracombe and Clovelly.

Paignton & Dartmouth Steam Railway
Paignton, Devon
Tel: 01803 555872
Steam train from Paignton to Dartmouth.

River Link
Dartmouth, Devon
Tel: 01803 862735 or 834488 (recorded info)
www.riverlink.co.uk
River Dart cruises; wildlife cruises.

Seaton Tramway
Seaton, Devon
Tel: 01297 20375
www.tram.co.uk
Open-top tramcar rides.

Tarka Cruises
Appledore, Devon
Tel: 01237 476191
River cruise, Appledore to Bideford.

Tarka Line
Exeter to Barnstaple, Devon
Tel: 08457 484950
Scenic railway through Devon.

SHOPPING

Appledore, Devon
Art galleries displaying local work.

Brannams Pottery
Barnstaple, Devon
Tel: 01271 343035
Pottery tours and shop.

Butchers' Row
Barnstaple, Devon
Traditional butchers, fishmongers, greengrocers and bakers.

Canvas Factory
Dartmouth, Devon
Tel/fax: 01803 832186
Traditional sailcloth and canvas bags.

D'art Gallery
Dartmouth, Devon
Tel: 01803 834923
www.lineone.net/~dart.gallery
Contemporary art for sale.

Dartington Crystal
Torrington, Devon
Tel: 01805 626266
Factory tours and shop.

Dartmouth Pottery
Dartmouth, Devon
Tel: 01803 832258
Decorative Dartmouth pottery.

Devon Guild of Craftsmen
Bovey Tracey, Devon
Tel: 01626 832223
www.crafts.org.uk
Contemporary furniture, sculpture, ceramics, prints, jewellery and more.

Hancock's Devon Cider
South Molton, Devon
Tel: 01769 572678
Traditional Devon scrumpy.

Lee Mill
Lee Mill, Devon
Tel: 01752 691100
Quality clothing, gifts and souvenirs.

Pavilion
Torquay, Devon
Boutiques and specialist shops in former Edwardian theatre.

South Molton, Devon
Antiques, fine art and craft shops.

Victoria Lace
Barnstaple, Devon
Tel: 01271 375524
Fine, hand-made lace.

Victorian Pannier Market
Barnstaple, Devon
Local produce, crafts, fashion, bric-à-brac and antiques.

Yelverton Paperweight Centre
Yelverton, Devon
Tel/fax: 01822 854250
www.paperweightcentre.co.uk
Paperweights from famous-name glass studios including Caithness.

EXMOOR & THE SOMERSET LEVELS

TOURIST INFORMATION

Exmoor National Park, Exmoor House, Dulverton, Somerset TA22 9HL
Tel: 01398 323665
www.exmoor-nationalpark.gov.uk

Exmoor Tourism
1 Upcott Avenue, Barnstaple, Devon EX31 1HN
Tel: 01271 336063
www.exmoortourism.org

Somerset County Council
County Hall, Taunton, Somerset TA1 4DY
Tel: 01934 750833
www.somerset.gov.uk

ACTIVITIES

Bike Park
Taunton, Somerset
Tel: 01823 252499
Bicycle parking, hire, repairs, changing facilities and showers.

Bridgwater Camel Co
Over Stowey, Somerset
Tel: 01278 733186
Camel treks across Bridgwater Bay.

Cloud Farm
Oare, Somerset
Tel/fax: 01598 741278
Riding and walking holidays on Exmoor.

Exmoor Holiday Group
Dulverton, Somerset
Tel/fax: 01398 323722
www.exmoor-holidays.co.uk
Walking, riding and fishing holidays.

Glen Lyn Gorge
Lynmouth, Devon
Woodland walks through gorge.

Holnicote Estate (NT)
Minehead, Somerset
Tel: 01643 862452
Walking, pony-trekking, sea-fishing, camping and minibus tours.

Mill on the Brue Outdoor Pursuits Centre
Bruton, Somerset
Tel: 01749 812307
Climbing, abseiling, canoeing, grass-skiing and tobogganing, archery, assault course and more.

LEISURE

Exmoor Coast Boat Trips
Lynmouth, Devon
Trips to highest cliffs in England, sea-bird sanctuary and Valley of the Rocks.

Exmoor Steam Railway
On A399, between Blackmoor Gate and Brayford, Devon
Tel: 01598 710711
Narrow-gauge steam railway.

Lynton & Lynmouth Lift Co Cliff Railway
Lynmouth, Devon
Tel: 01598 753486
Victorian water-powered cliff railway.

Secret World Badger & Wildlife Rescue Centre
East Huntspill, Somerset
Tel: 01278 783250
Badger observation sett plus other wild and farm animals.

West Sedgemoor RSPB Reserve
West Sedgemoor, Somerset
Tel: 01458 252805
Wet meadow attracting waders; one of the UK's largest heronies.

West Somerset Railway
Minehead, Somerset
Tel: 01643 704996 or 707650 (talking timetable)
www.west-somerset-railway.co.uk
Steam train from Minehead to Bishops Lydeard (near Taunton).

SHOPPING

Clarks Village
Street, Somerset
Tel: 01458 840064
Famous brands, not just Clarks shoes, at factory prices.

Exmoor Producers Association
Free leaflet Craft Tracker Guide, listing craft outlets all over Exmoor, available from local TICs or tel 01398 324383.

Morlands Factory Shop
A39 (Glastonbury to Street road), Somerset
Tel: 01458 835042
Sheepskin products.

DORSET & SALISBURY PLAIN

TOURIST INFORMATION

Bournemouth Tourism
Westover Road, Bournemouth, Dorset BH1 2BU
Tel: 0906 802 0234
www.bournemouth.co.uk

Dorset Tourism
Dorchester County Council, County Hall, Dorchester, Dorset DT1 1XJ
Tel: 01305 221001
www.dorset-cc.gov.uk

Salisbury TIC
Fish Row, Salisbury, Wilts SP1 1EJ
Tel: 01722 334956
www.salisbury.gov.uk/tourism

Wiltshire Tourism
Trinity House, Bryer-Ash Business Park, Trowbridge, Wilts BA14 8HE
Tel: 01225 712313
www.wiltshiretourism.co.uk

ACTIVITIES

Avago Karting & Laser Shooting
West Dean, Wilts
Tel: 01794 884693
Grass-karting; junior, adult and senior.

Brit Valley Llamas
Beaminster, Dorset
Tel: 01308 868674
Llama-trekking in rural Dorset.

Hayball Cycle Centre
Salisbury, Wilts
Tel: 01722 411378
Cycle hire.

Henley Hillbillies
Buckland Newton, Dorset
Tel/fax: 01300 345293
Quad bikes and mini mavriks by day; badger-watching after dusk.

Old Sarum Flying Club
Salisbury, Wilts
Tel: 01722 322525
www.old-sarum-flying.demon.co.uk
Flying lessons; microlights to light aircraft.

Ottons Land Rover
Salisbury, Wilts
Tel: 01722 414400
www.ottons.co.uk
Off-road driving instruction.

Rockley Watersports
Hamworthy, Dorset
Tel: 01202 677272
www.rockleywatersports.com
Watersports holidays and tuition.

Sea Fishing Poole
Poole, Dorset
Tel: 01202 679666
Fishing trips.

Tidworth Polo Club
Tidworth, Wilts
Tel: 01980 846705
Learn to play polo in three days.

Wiltshire Cycleway and Off-road Cycling in Wiltshire
Both leaflets available from TICs.

Yellow Penguin
Poole, Dorset
Tel: 01202 710448
Self-drive motorboats for hire.

LEISURE

Blue Line Cruises
Poole, Dorset
Tel: 01202 467882 or 0802 435654 (recorded info)
www.bluelinecruises.cwc.net
Circular cruises; Poole to Brownsea Island, Studland Bay and Old Harry Rocks.

Brownsea Island (NT)
Off coast at Poole, Dorset
Tel: 01202 707744
www.nationaltrust.org.uk
Island rich in wildlife; boats from Poole, Sandbanks and Bournemouth.

Cameron Balloon Flights Southern
Pewsey, Wilts
Tel: 01672 562277
www.cameron-flights.co.uk
Balloon flights over Salisbury, Stonehenge and the Wylye Valley.

Discover Dorset
Dorchester, Dorset
Tel: 01305 261135
www.discover-dorset.mcmail.com
Guided 'thrill'-themed tours by Dorchester's town crier.

Poole Cockle Trail
Poole, Dorset
Self-guided walking tour; leaflet from TIC.

Swanage Railway
Swanage, Dorset
Tel: 01929 425800
www.swanrail.demon.co.uk
Steam train from Swanage to Norden.

Vistarama Balloon
Bournemouth, Dorset
Tel: 01202 399939
www.vistarama.co.uk
Tethered balloon flights; views up to 20 miles (32km).

Wee Painted Wagon
East Knighton, Dorset
Tel: 01305 853873
Horse-drawn carriage rides.

SHOPPING

Brewers Quay
Weymouth, Dorset
Tel: 01305 777622
Victorian brewery with over 15 specialist shops and a craft centre.

Courtyard Craft Centre
Lytchett Minster, Dorset
Tel: 01202 623423
Crafts in 17th-century farm courtyard.

McArthurGlen Designer Outlet Great Western
Jct 16, M4; Swindon, Wilts
Tel: 01793 507600
Designer-name shopping outlet.

Owl Pottery
Swanage, Dorset
Tel: 01929 425850
Hand-made pottery and artwork.

Poole Pottery
Poole, Dorset
Tel: 01202 666200
www.poolepottery.co.uk
Factory shop with Poole Pottery and other brands at discount prices.

The Shambles, Bradford-on-Avon and Silver Street, Warminster, Wilts
Galleries, art, craft and antiques shops.

Wilton Shopping Village
Wilton, Wilts
Tel: 01722 741211
www.wsv.co.uk
Famous Wilton Carpets and other goods at factory prices.

THE MENDIPS, BATH & BRISTOL

TOURIST INFORMATION

Bath Tourism Bureau
Abbey Chambers, Abbey Church Yard, Bath BA1 1LY
Tel: 01225 477228/9
www.visitbath.co.uk

Bristol Tourism and Conference Bureau
St Nicholas Church, St Nicholas Street, Bristol BS1 1UE
Tel: 0117 946 2207
www.tourism.bristol.gov.uk

Mendip Tourism
Mendip District Council, Cannards Grave Road, Shepton Mallet, Somerset BA4 5BT
Tel: 01749 343399

ACTIVITIES

Bath Boating Station
Bath, Avon
Tel: 01225 466407
Boat hire; rowing, punting and canoeing up the Avon Valley.

Bath and Dundas Canal Co
Monkton Combe, Avon
Tel: 01225 722292
Electric-powered boat hire on Kennet and Avon Canal, self-drive or skippered.

Bath Skyline (NT)
Bath, Avon
Tel: 01985 843600
A 6-mile (10-km) circular walking route on the outskirts of Bath.

Castle Combe Racing Circuit
Castle Combe, Wilts
Tel: 01249 783010
www.combe-events.co.uk
Kart track, skid pan and four-wheel-drive course.

Country Wide Weekends
Cheddar, Somerset
Tel: 01934 743775
Climbing, abseiling, caving, mountain biking, off-roading, kayaking, archery and air-rifle practice.

Frome Valley Walkway, Monarch's Way, Avon Walkway, Severn Way and Cotswold Way
Long-distance footpaths. Information from TICs.

Mendip Walks, Village Trail and Mendip Cycle Routes
Information available from Mendip Tourism.

Southwest Karting
Cheddar, Somerset
Tel: 07000 616161
Grand prix karting; indoor and outdoor tracks.

West Country Water Park
Winterbourne, Avon
Tel: 01454 773599
www.king-creation.co.uk/westcountrywaterpark
Windsurfing, dinghy sailing, jet-skiing, surf-biking, water-skiing, canoeing, rowing and fishing.

LEISURE

Avon Valley Railway
Willsbridge, Avon
Tel: 0117 932 5538
Steam-train ride through Avon Valley.

Bath City Open Top Bus Tour
Bath, Avon
Tel: 01225 424157 or 859200

Bristol Balloons
Bristol, Avon
Tel: 0117 963 7858
www.bristolballoons.co.uk
Champagne balloon flights from Bristol and Bath.

Bristol City Open Top Guided Bus Tour
Bristol, Avon
Tel: 0805 715827

Bristol Ferry Boat Company
Bristol, Avon
Tel: 0117 927 3416
www.bristolferryboat.co.uk
Waterbus service around Bristol's harbour.

Bristol's High Point
Bristol, Avon
Tel: 0117 922 7075
www.a-highpoint.com
Tethered balloon rising 500ft (152m).

Cheddar Caves & Gorge
Cheddar, Somerset
Tel: 01934 742343
Gorge with clifftop walk and showcaves.

Wookey Hole Caves
Wookey Hole, Somerset
Tel: 01749 672243
www.wookey.co.uk
Britain's most spectacular showcaves.

SHOPPING

Black Swan Guild
Frome, Somerset
Tel: 01373 473980
Mendip's leading centre for fine arts and contemporary crafts.

Clifton Village
Bristol, Avon
Fashion, art and antiques.

Harveys Wine Cellars
Bristol, Avon
Tel: 0117 927 5036
www.harveysbc.com

Milsom Street
Bath, Avon
Speciality food and exclusive shops.

St Nicholas Markets
Bristol, Avon
West Country's largest indoor market.

Thatchers Cider
Sandford, Avon
Tel: 01934 822862
Cider-makers since 1904.

Upper Street
Bath, Avon
Antiques, antiquarian books and prints; antiques market (Wed).

Walcot
Bath, Avon
A browser's paradise.

West End
Bristol, Avon
Wares from all over the world.

THE SEVERN VALLEY & THE FOREST OF DEAN

TOURIST INFORMATION

Forest Enterprise (for Forest of Dean)
Bank House, Coleford, Glos GL16 8BA
Tel: 01594 833057

Gloucestershire Tourism
Shire Hall, Gloucester GL1 2TH
Tel: 01452 425673
www.visit-glos.org.uk

Wye Valley Tourism
The Old Station, Tintern, Chepstow, Monmouth NP16 7NX
Tel/fax: 01291 689566

ACTIVITIES

Chepstow Quad Trekking Centre
Sedbury, Monmouth
Tel/fax: 01291 629901
www.members.farmline.com/ chepstow-quad
Quad-biking on purpose-built trail.

Forest Adventure
Christchurch, Glos
Tel/fax: 01594 834661
Rock-climbing, abseiling, caving, mountain biking, canoeing, kayaking and archery.

Forest Cycle Centre
Coleford, Glos
Tel: 01594 832121
Mountain bikes, buggies and trailers for hire.

Littledean Riding Centre
Littledean, Glos
Tel: 01594 823955
Forest trails and hacks.

Pedalabikeaway Cycle Centre
Cannop Valley, Glos
Tel: 01594 860065
www.btinternet.co/~pedal/abikeaway
Bikes for hire; waymarked trail.

Whitecliff Off-road Driving Centre
Clearwell, Glos
Tel: 01594 834666
www.datasphere.ltd.uk/whitecliff
4x4 driving; hovercraft and military vehicles.

Wye Pursuits
Kerne Bridge, Glos
Tel: 01600 891199
Climbing, abseiling, caving, mountain biking, orienteering, canoeing, kayaking and rafting.

Wyedean Canoe & Adventure Centre
Symonds Yat, Glos
Tel/fax: 01594 833238
www.wyedean.co.uk
Canoeing, kayaking, climbing, abseiling, caving, archery and more.

LEISURE

Clearwell Caves
Clearwell, Glos
Tel: 01594 832535
Ancient iron mines.

Dean Forest Railway
Lydney, Glos
Tel: 01594 845840 or 843423 (recorded info)
Steam and heritage diesel trains, Lydney Junction to Norchard Railway Centre.

Hopewell Colliery
Cannop Hill, Glos
Tel: 01594 810706
Mine dating back to 1820s.

Kingfisher Cruises
Symonds Yat East, Glos
Tel: 01600 891063
River trip through Symonds Yat.

National Waterways Museum
Gloucester, Glos
Tel: 01452 318054
www.nwm.org.uk
Historic craft and boat trips.

Perrygrove Railway
Coleford, Glos
Tel: 01594 834991
Narrow-gauge steam train, Forest of Dean.

Slimbridge Wildfowl and Wetlands Trust
Slimbridge, Glos
Tel: 01453 890333
World's largest collection of wildfowl.

Symonds Yat Rock
Symonds Yat, Glos
Tel: 01594 834479
Viewpoint above River Wye. Site of Iron-Age fort; walking trails.

SHOPPING

Harts Barn Craft Centre
Longhope, Glos
Tel: 01452 830954
Working craft centre.

Ruardean Garden Pottery
Ruardean, Glos
Tel: 01594 543577
Specialist terracotta flowerpots.

Taurus Crafts
Lydney, Glos
Tel: 01594 844841
Pottery, stained glass, art and crafts.

Wye Valley Centre
Tintern, Monmouth
Tel: 01291 689228
Wye Valley Craft Association shops.

SOUTHEAST ENGLAND

FROM ISLAND TO FOREST & DOWNLAND

TOURIST INFORMATION

Isle of Wight Tourism
Westridge Centre, Brading Road, Ryde, IOW PO33 1QS
Tel: 01983 813813
www.islandbreaks.co.uk

New Forest District Council
Leisure Services, Appletree Court, Lyndhurst, Hants SO43 7PA
Tel: 01703 285102
www.thenewforest.co.uk

Southern Tourist Board
40 Chamberlayne Road, Eastleigh, Hants SO5 5JH
Tel: 01703 620006

Winchester TIC
Guildhall, The Broadway, Winchester, Hants S023 9LJ
Tel: 01962 840500
www.winchester.gov.uk

ACTIVITIES

Basingstoke Canal, Visitor Centre
Mytchett, Surrey
Tel: 01252 370073
Fishing, boating, canal trips and walks.

Burley Villa Equestrian Centre
New Milton, Hants
Tel: 01425 610278
www.users.globalnet.co.uk/~burleyv
Wild West-style horse-riding in the New Forest.

Camouflage Outdoor Activities
Privett, Hants
Tel: 01730 828292
Adventure activities including paintballing and off-road driving.

Carill Aviation
Southampton International Airport, Hants
Tel/fax: 023 8064 3528
Flying lessons or scenic flights over the Solent.

Gleneagles Equestrian Centre
West End, Hants
Tel: 023 8047 3164
Hacking, riding and jumping.

Gunwharf Quays
Portsmouth, Hants
Tel: 023 9275 5940
Outdoor ice rink and bowling complex.

Hampshire Borders Cycle Trails
Hampshire Borders Tourism, Basingstoke, Hants
Tel: 01256 811667
Cycle trails through north Hampshire.

Lasham Gliding Society
Lasham, Hants
Tel: 01256 384900
www.lasham.org.uk
Europe's premier gliding centre.

Marwell Activity Centre
Fishers Pond, Hants
Tel: 01962 777547
Horse-riding, mini motorbiking, archery, clay-pigeon shooting, .22 shooting, abseiling, climbing and assault course.

New Forest Cycle Experience
Brockenhurst, Hants
Tel/fax: 01590 624204
www.bikeshop.demon.co.uk
Cycle hire in the New Forest.

Quad Off-road Centre
Andover, Hants
Tel: 01264 771321
Off-road driving; quad bikes, mini-bikes, 4x4 jeeps and Honda Pilots, plus paintball, archery and airgun practice.

Queen Elizabeth Country Park
Waterlooville, Hants
Tel: 023 9259 5040
Trails for walking, orienteering, horse-riding and off-road cycling, plus areas for kites, model gliders, hang-gliding and paragliding.

Royal Yachting Association
Eastleigh, Hants
Tel: 023 8062 7400
Sailing, yachting and cruising courses on the Hamble.

Shalbourne Soaring Society
Marlborough, Wilts
Tel: 01264 731204
www.arsharpe.demon.co.uk/sss
Trial gliding lessons.

Southampton Waterborne Activities Centre
Southampton, Hants
Tel: 023 8022 5525
Windsurfing and sailing.

Tennyson Trail
National Trust, Newport, IOW
Tel: 01903 741020
www.nationaltrust.org.uk/regions/southern
Walking trail from Freshwater Bay to The Needles.

Winchester Walks
Self-guided walks around Winchester. Information from Winchester TIC.

LEISURE

Adventure Balloons
Tel: 01252 844222 or 020 8840 0108
www.adventureballoons.co.uk
Balloon flights over Berks, Hants, Herts, Oxon, Surrey and London.

Blue Boat Trips
Portsmouth, Hants
Tel: 023 9282 0564
Guided boat trip of Portsmouth Harbour; departs Clarence Esplanade, Southsea.

Blue Star Boats
Hamble, Hants
Tel: 023 8045 3542
Boat excursions on River Hamble.

Eastleigh Lakeside Railway
Eastleigh, Hants
Tel: 023 8063 6612
www.steamtrain.co.uk
Lakeside miniature passenger railway.

Kennet and Avon Canal boat trips
Newbury, Berks
Tel: 01635 44154
Horse-drawn barge trips from Kintbury; motor barge from Newbury Wharf.

Milestones
Basingstoke, Hants
Tel: 01256 845384
www.basingstoke.gov.uk
Nineteenth and 20th-century street re-creations with original transport.

New Forest Badger Watch
Ringwood, Hants
Tel/fax: 01425 403412
www.hants.gov.uk/leisure/natfarm/nfbadg
Badger watching nightly Mar–Oct.

New Forest Nature Quest
Ashurst, Hants
Tel: 023 8029 2166/2408
www.hants.gov.uk/leisuire/natfarm/natquest
Britain's largest native wildlife collection in re-created habitats.

Royal Victoria Railway
Royal Victoria Country Park, Southampton, Hants
Tel: 023 8045 6246
Miniature steam railway with views across Southampton Harbour.

Vintage Bus Tours and Wagon Rides
New Forest VIC, Lymington, Hants
Tel: 01590 689000.
www.thenewforest.co.uk
Open-top vintage buses from Hythe Ferry and Brockenhurst railway station; hop-on hop-off service to New Forest villages, connecting with walking routes and cycle tracks. Also, horse-drawn wagon rides from Brockenhurst or Burley.

Walks Talks
Tel: 023 9283 8382
www.infocentre.com/portsmouth
Guided walks of Portsmouth; information from Portsmouth VIC.

The Watercress Line
Alresford, Hants
Tel: 01962 733810; 01962 734866 (talking timetable)
www.watercressline.co.uk
Steam railway from Alresford to Alton.

SHOPPING

Antiquarian bookshops; antiques shops
Numerous in Winchester; lists available from Winchester TIC.

Gunwharf Quays
Portsmouth, Hants
Tel: 023 9275 5940
Waterfront shopping and leisure complex.

Hungerford Arcade
Hungerford, Berks
Tel: 01488 683701
Seventy stalls selling antiques, curios and collectables.

Lyndhurst Antique Centre, Hants
Tel: 01703 284000
Antiques, stamps, fossils and collectables.

New Forest Cider Farm
Burley, Hants
Tel: 01425 403589
Draught cider.

Marks & Spencer and Sainsbury's
Hedge End, Hants
Europe's largest combined Marks & Spencer and Sainsbury's.

Ocean Village
Southampton, Hants
Tel: 023 8022 8353
Waterfront shopping and leisure complex.

Port Solent Marina
Portsmouth, Hants
Tel: 023 9221 0765
Boardwalk shopping and entertainment area.

Whitchurch Silk Mill, Hants
Tel: 01256 892065
Working silk-weaving mill; shop sells range of silk products.

THE WEALD & SOUTH COAST

TOURIST INFORMATION

Brighton & Hove VIC
10 Bartholomew Square, Brighton,
W Sussex BN1 1JS
Tel: 0906 7112255
www.brighton.co.uk/tourist

Eastbourne Tourism, Leisure & Amenities
Eastbourne Borough Council, College Road,
Eastbourne, E Sussex BN21 4JJ
Tel: 01323 415400
www.eastbourne.org

West Sussex Tourism
The Grange, Tower Street, Chichester,
W Sussex PO19 1RL
Tel: 01243 777488
www.westsussex.gov.uk

ACTIVITIES

Bedgebury Riding Centre
Goudhurst, Kent
Tel: 01580 211602
Lessons, hacking and holiday courses.

Bewl Water
Lamberhurst, Kent
Tel: 01892 890661
www.bewl.co.uk
Fly-fishing, watersports, boating, cycling and walking.

Brighton Marina
Brighton, E Sussex
Tel: 01273 559583
Fishing and sightseeing boats from quayside; fishing from harbour wall.

Chichester Canal, W Sussex
Tel: 01243 771363 or 671051
Angling, canoeing and row-boating.

Christine Yacht Sailing Trips
Woodbridge, Suffolk
Tel: 01394 389089
www.christine.co.uk
Two-hour and full-day sailing trips from Brighton Marina.

Cowdray Park Golf Club
Midhurst, W Sussex
Tel: 01730 813599
18-hole golf course in parkland near ruins of Old Cowdray House.

Freewheelin' Trekking
Selsey, W Sussex
Tel: 01243 602725
Horse-trekking on Selsey Beach and the South Downs.

Hollingbury Park Golf Course
Brighton, E Sussex
Tel: 01273 500086
Downland course with sea views.

Hove Lagoon Watersports
Hove, E Sussex
Tel: 01273 424842
Windsurfing, sailing, canoeing and water-skiing.

King Alfred Leisure Centre
Hove, E Sussex
Tel: 01273 290290
Swimming pool in tropical-style surroundings.

Peter Ashley Activity Centre
Cosham, Hants
Tel: 023 9232 1223
Activity centre in fort with climbing wall and assault course.

Something Fishy Charters
East Wittering, W Sussex
Tel: 01243 671153
Sea-fishing trips; rods and bait supplied.

Southdown Gliding Club
Parham Airfield, Storrington, W Sussex
Tel: 01903 742137
Glider flights over the South Downs.

Southdown Llama Trekking
Newtimber, E Sussex
Tel: 01273 835656
Llama walks on the South Downs.

Stroll the South Downs
NT, Slindon, W Sussex
www.nationaltrust.org.uk/regions/southern
Eight self-guided countryside trails across the South Downs; walks pack available from National Trust shops, bookshops or by post from address above.

Waterhall Golf Course
Brighton, E Sussex
Tel: 01273 508658.
18-hole downland course next to the Devil's Dyke.

Willowbrook Riding Centre
Hambrook, W Sussex
Tel: 01243 572683
Horse-riding on the South Downs; 1–3-hour hacks, pub or day rides.

LEISURE

Amberley Museum
Arundel, W Sussex
Tel: 01798 831370
www.amberleymuseum.co.uk
Yester-year museum; vintage bus and narrow-gauge railway rides.

Biddenden Vineyards and Cider Works, Kent
Tel: 01580 291726
Kent's oldest commercial vineyard producing wine, cider and apple juice.

Bluebell Railway
Sheffield Park Station, E Sussex
Tel: 01825 723777 or 722370 (timetable)
www.rhbnc.ac.uk/~zhaa009/bb
Vintage steam-train ride through bluebell woods from Sheffield Park to Kingscote.

Brighton Fishing Museum
Brighton, E Sussex
Tel: 01273 723064
Museum of Brighton fishing industry and seafront; guided walks of Brighton's seafront and fishing quarter.

Chichester Harbour Water Tours
Chichester, W Sussex
Tel: 01243 786418
One-and-a-half-hour guided cruises of Chichester Harbour; depart Itchenor.

Guide Friday
Tel: 01273 746205
One-hour double-decker bus sightseeing trip of Brighton.

Kent and East Sussex Railway
Tenterden, Kent
Tel: 01580 765155
E-mail: kesroffice@aol.com
www.seetb.org.uk/kesr
The southeast's longest full-size steam railway.

Miniature Steam Railway Adventure Park
Eastbourne, E Sussex
Tel: 01323 520229
www.emsr.co.uk
Coal-fired miniature railway rides.

Nutbourne Vineyard
Nr Pulborough, W Sussex
Tel: 01798 815196
Award-winning wines.

Pulborough Brooks RSPB Nature Reserve
Wiggonholt, Pulborough, W Sussex
Tel: 01798 875851
Birds and other wildlife; nature trail.

Romney, Hythe and Dymchurch Railway
New Romney, Kent
Tel: 01797 362353
www.rhdr.demon.co.uk
The world's smallest public railway.

Seven Sisters Sheep Centre
Nr Eastbourne, E Sussex
Tel: 013323 423302
World's largest collection of breeds of sheep; shearing, sheep-milking and tractor rides.

Shoreham Airport
Shoreham, W Sussex
Tel: 01273 296900
Pleasure flights and flying lessons.

Sky Trek Ballooning
Hartley, Kent
Tel: 01474 702112
www.hotairballooning.co.uk
Balloon flights over Wealden countryside.

South of England Rare Breeds Centre
Woodchurch, Kent
Tel: 01233 861493
www.cot-rarebreeds.co.uk
Rare farm animals; trailer rides.

Sussex Falconry Centre
Birdham, W Sussex
Tel: 01243 512472
Birds of prey flying displays.

Tenterden Vineyard Park
Smallhythe, Kent
Tel: 01580 763033
www.chapeldownwines.co.uk
Wine shop, rural museum and herb garden; guided tours.

Volks Electric Railway
Brighton, E Sussex
Tel: 01273 292718
Electric seafront railway from Brighton's Palace Pier to the Marina.

Walking Tours of Brighton
Brighton VIC, E Sussex
Tel: 01273 292589 or 292599
www.tourism.brighton.co.uk
Original Brighton Cemetery Tour, Spooky Brighton, Brighton Sewer Tour, West Pier Tour and Brunswick Town Walk.

Weald and Downland Open-Air Museum
Singleton, W Sussex
Tel: 01243 811348
www.wealddown.co.uk
Over 40 relocated historic buildings demonstrating homes and workplaces of the past.

Wey and Arun Canal Trust
Loxwood, W Sussex
Tel: 01403 752403 or 753991
Narrow-boat cruise through restored section of canal.

Wildfowl and Wetlands Trust
Arundel, W Sussex
Tel: 01903 883355
Ducks, geese and swans.

SHOPPING

Antiques in Petworth
Petworth, W Sussex
Tel: 01798 343411
Brochure listing over 25 antiques shops.

Body Shop Tour
Littlehampton, W Sussex
Tel: 0800 960809 (freephone)
www.the-body-shop.com
Guided tour of the Body Shop factory; shop selling factory-priced products.

Brighton Flea Market
Kemptown, Brighton, E Sussex
Tel: 01273 624006
Daily indoor market with over 60 stalls; antiques and bric-à-brac.

Brighton Marina Village Factory Outlet Shops
Brighton, E Sussex
Tel: 01273 693636

Iden Croft Herbs
Staplehurst, Kent
Tel: 01580 891432
Herb gardens with shop.

McArthur Glen
Ashford, Kent
Tel: 01233 895900
Fashion and homeware designer outlet at Jct 10 off M20.

THE NORTH DOWNS & THE KENT COAST

TOURIST INFORMATION

Kent Tourism
Invicta House, County Hall, Maidstone, Kent ME14 1XX
Tel: 01622 691418
www.kenttourism.co.uk

South East England Tourist Board
The Old Brew House, Warwick Park, Tunbridge Wells, Kent TN2 5TU
Tel: 01892 540766
www.seetb.org.uk

Surrey Tourism
Guildford Borough Council, Millmead House, Millmead, Guildford, Surrey GU2 5BB
Tel: 01483 444338

ACTIVITIES

Buckmore Park Karting
Chatham, Kent
Tel: 01634 201562
www.buckmore.co.uk
Outdoor kart circuit.

Cobham Manor Riding Centre
Thurnham, Kent
Tel: 01622 738497 or 738871
www.cobham-manor.u-net.com
Indoor school and three floodlit-manèges.

Cycle Hire
Canterbury West Railway Station, Kent
Tel: 01227 479643

Downland Cycle Holidays
Denton, Kent
Tel/fax: 01303 844289
Self-led cycling holidays.

Guildford Boat House
Guildford, Surrey
Tel: 01483 504494
Narrow-boat and row-boat hire.

Manston Riding Stables
Manston, nr Ramsgate, Kent
Tel: 01843 823622
Riding lessons and hacks.

Medway Yachting Association
Tel: 01304 621002
Sailing on the Medway.

Orchard Trails
Horsmonden, Kent
Tel/fax: 01892 722680
Self-guided walking and cycling holidays in East Sussex.

Port Richborough Racing
Sandwich, Kent
Tel: 01304 621115
Super and grand prix go-kart track.

Revolution Skate Park
Broadstairs, Kent
Tel: 01843 866707
Rollerskating and rollerblading park.

Surrey Cycleway
Surrey Tourism, Kingston-upon-Thames, Surrey
Tel: 020 8541 8044
Cycle route through country lanes.

Thanet Flying Club
Manston Airport, nr Broadstairs, Kent
Tel: 01843 823520
Light aircraft flights and tuition.

LEISURE

Barnsole Vineyard
Staple, Kent
Tel: 01304 812530
Guided tours and wine tastings.

Birdworld
Holt Pound, Farnham, Surrey
Tel: 01420 22838 (24-hour info); 01320 22140 (enquiries)
Britain's largest bird park.

Brogdale
Faversham, Kent
Tel: 01795 535286
www.brogdale.org.uk
World's largest collection of fruit trees and plants; guided tours.

Canterbury Guild of Guides
Tel: 01227 459779
Guided walking tours of Canterbury.

East Kent Railway
Shepherdswell, Kent
Tel: 01304 832042
Former coal-carrying line from Shepherdswell to Eythorne.

Guide Friday
Tel: 01304 205108 (Dover); 01273 746205 (Medway)
Open-top double-decker bus tour of Dover and Medway.

Hop Farm Country Park
Paddock Wood, Kent
Tel: 01622 872068
Rural museum and hop exhibition.

MV *Princess Pocahontas*
Gravesend, Kent
Tel: 01732 353448 or 0831 300148
Cruises of Thames Estuary from Gravesend to London and Southend.

Museum of Kent Life
Sandling, Maidstone, Kent
Tel: 01622 763936
Open-air museum of Kent life.

Paddle Steamer *Kingswear Castle*
Chatham, Kent
Tel/fax: 01634 827648
Paddle-steamer cruises on the Medway from Rochester and Chatham.

River Wey Navigations
Guildford, Surrey
Tel: 01483 561389
River-boat launch from Town Wharf to Dapdune Wharf.

Samphire Hoe
Off A20 Dover to Folkstone
Formed from material dug to create the Channel Tunnel; self-guided and guided walks, bird-watching and sea angling.

Staple Vineyard
nr Wingham, Kent
Tel: 01304 812571
Walk the vineyard trail.

Stour River Bus
Sandwich, Kent
Tel: 0795 8376183 (mobile)
River cruise of Sandwich.

Theatrical Walks: Deal Trail of Blood, A Bite of Sandwich, Twilight Tours
Tel: 01304 369576
Guided tours through Deal, Sandwich or Dover Castle.

Topsail Charters
Maldon, Essex
Tel: 01621 857567
www.top-sail.co.uk
Day or weekend cruises on Thames sailing barge; trips from Rochester, Faversham, Southend, Maldon, Brightlingsea and Ipswich.

White Cliffs Boat Trip
Dover, Kent
Tel: 01303 271388
Boat cruise to Dover's White Cliffs.

World Naval Base
Chatham, Kent
Tel: 01634 823800
www.worldnavalbase.org.uk
World's most complete naval dockyard of the Age of Sail.

SHOPPING

Burgate Antiques
Canterbury, Kent
Tel: 01227 456500
Twelve dealers under one roof.

De Bradelei Wharf
Dover, Kent
Tel: 01304 226616
Factory shopping outlet; fashion and furnishings.

The Galleries
Aldershot, Hants
Tel: 01252 330667
UK's first in-town discount designer shopping centre.

Harbour Street
Whitstable, Kent
Craft shops on Whitstable's harbour.

Herne Bay Market, Kent
Second-hand and antiques market.

Longmarket
Canterbury, Kent
Area of specialist shops.

LONDON

TOURIST INFORMATION

London Tourist Board
Glen House, Stag Place, London SW1E 5LT
Tel: 09068 505440
www.londontown.com

ACTIVITIES

Beckton Alps Ski Slope
Beckton, E6
Tel: 020 7511 0351
A 656-ft (200-m) dry-ski slope.

Broadgate Ice Rink
Broadgate Estate, EC2
Tel: 020 7505 4068
London's only outdoor ice rink.

Bromley Ski Centre
St Paul's Cray, Kent
Tel: 01689 876812
Ski and snowboard instruction.

Docklands Equestrian Centre
Beckton, E6
Tel: 020 7473 4951
Horse-riding tuition.

Docklands Sailing & Watersports Centre
Millwall Docks, E14
Tel: 020 7537 2626
Dinghy sailing, dragonboat racing and rowing.

Docklands Watersports Club
Tereza-Joanne, King George V Dock, E16
Tel: 020 7511 7000
www.tereza-joanne.com
London's only jet-skiing venue.

Ealing Riding Centre
Ealing, W5
Tel: 020 8992 3808
Riding lessons; three floodlit arenas.

High Elms Golf Course
Down, Kent
Tel: 01689 853232
18-hole course with views over Lord Avery's former estate.

Hillingdon Ski Centre
Hillingdon, Middlesex
Tel: 01895 255183
Dry-ski slope.

Hyde Park Stables
Hyde Park, W2
Tel: 020 7723 2813
www.equiweb.co.uk/centres/hyde_park
Horse-riding in indoor arena or outdoors in Hyde Park.

Lee Valley Cycle Circuit
Stratford, E15
Tel: 020 8534 6085
A 1-mile (1.6km) cycle circuit and 2-mile (3.2km) cycle road.

Mile End Climbing Wall
Bow, E3
Tel: 020 8980 0289

Mount Mascal Stables
Bexley, Kent
Tel: 020 8300 3947
Riding lessons in woodland setting.

The Oasis
Covent Garden, WC2
Tel: 020 7831 1804
Fitness centre with indoor and outdoor swimming pools.

Original Bike Hire Company
Richmond, Surrey
Tel: 0800 013 8000

Paddington Recreation Ground
Paddington, W2
Tel: 020 7641 3642
Tennis courts, football and hockey pitches, cricket nets and athletics track.

Park Boats
Regent's Park Boating Lake, NW1
Tel: 020 7486 4759
Row boats for hire.

Parliament Hill Fields
Kentish Town, NW5
Tel: 020 7435 8998
Athletics track; open-air swimming lido available during summer months.

Peter Chilvers Windsurfing Centre
Royal Victoria Dock, Gate 5, E16
Tel: 020 7474 2500

Regent's Park Golf and Tennis School
Regent's Park, NW1
Tel: 020 7724 0643
Tennis courts and floodlit golf driving range.

Royal Victoria Dock Watersports Centre
Royal Victoria Dock, Gate 5, E16
Tel: 020 7511 2326
Dinghy sailing, canoeing and bell boating.

Scuba Training Ltd
Hammersmith, W6
Tel: 020 7381 5000

Shadwell Basin Outdoor Activity Centre
Shadwell, E1
Tel: 020 7481 4210
Sailing, canoeing, diving, angling, dragonboat racing and wall climbing.

Silver Blades
Streatham, SW16
Tel: 020 8769 7771
Well-established ice rink.

Slick Willies
Hyde Park, W2
Tel: 020 7937 3824
Rollerblade hire in Hyde Park.

Surrey Docks Watersports Centre
Greenland Dock, SE16
Tel: 020 7237 4009
Windsurfing, sailing, canoeing and powerboating.

Thames Young Mariners
Ham, Middlesex
Tel: 020 8940 5550
Children's courses in kayaking, canoeing, sailing, windsurfing and powerboating.

LEISURE

Big Bus Company
Westminster, SW1
Tel: 020 8944 7810
www.bigbus.co.uk
Hop-on, hop-off sightseeing tour of London by open-top double-decker bus.

British Airways London Eye
South Bank, SE1
Tel: 0870 500600
www.ba-londoneye.com
World's largest observation wheel; 1,443ft (35m) above the Thames.

Chelsea Physic Garden
Chelsea, SW3
Tel: 020 7352 5646
www.cpgarden.demon.co.uk
One of Europe's oldest botanic gardens.

City Cruises
Tel: 020 7936 2033 or 020 7839 4096
Circular, hop-on, hop-off, ferry service from/to Tower Pier via London Bridge City Pier, HMS *Belfast*, Butler's Wharf and St Katharine's Pier.

Jason's Trip
Tel: 020 7286 3428
www.jasons.co.uk
Trips on Regent's Canal.

London Loop
Tel: 020 7213 9714
Circular walking route from Erith Riverside to Old Bexley Village.

London River Services
Westminster, SW1
Tel: 020 7918 4753
www.londontransport.co.uk/info/river
Booklet listing passenger boat services and cruises on the Thames.

London Skyview Balloon
Vauxhall, SE11
Tel: 0345 023842 (24-hour info)
Views from the world's largest helium-filled tethered balloon.

Mudchute Park and Farm
Poplar, E14
Tel: 020 7515 5901; 020 7515 0749 (riding school)
England's largest city farm, also a riding school.

Original London Walks
Kilburn, NW6
Tel: 020 7624 3978
www.walks.com
Walking-tour company.

Royal Botanic Gardens
Kew, Surrey
Tel: 020 8332 5622; 020 8940 1171 (24-hour info)
www.rbgkew.org.uk
Guided tours year round.

Skyline Balloons
Tel: 020 7931 9707
www.skylineballoons.com
Views from tethered balloon.

Society of Voluntary Guides
Tel: 020 8977 2806 or 020 8894 2962
Guided walks of Richmond, Twickenham and Kew.

Stepping Out
Tel: 020 8881 2933
www.walklon.ndirect.co.uk
Themed guided walks in London.

Thames Path
Tel: 01865 810224 (general info)
www.nationaltrails.gov.uk
A 184-mile (294-km) path following the course of the Thames from the Cotswolds to the Thames Barrier.

Westminster Passenger Service Association
Tel: 020 7930 2062
www.londontransport.co.uk/info/river
Passenger boat service, central London to Kew.

SHOPPING

Bluewater
Greenhithe, Kent
Tel: 0845 602 1021
Europe's largest shopping centre; 320 fashion, homewear and lifestyle shops.

Burberry Factory Shop
Homerton, E9
Tel: 020 8985 3344
Famous-name raincoats at a fraction of the price.

Burlington Arcade
Mayfair, W1
Regency arcade with 38 specialist shops.

Camden High Street
Camden Town, NW1
Place for fashion trendsetters.

Charing Cross Road
Covent Garden, WC2
Antiquarian and second-hand books.

Covent Garden Market
Covent Garden, WC2
Tel: 020 7836 9136
Arts and crafts and special interest shops and stalls.

Greenwich Market
Greenwich, SE10
Tel: 020 8293 3110
Art, craft and antiques market.

Harrods
Knightsbridge, SW1
Tel: 020 7730 1234
www.harrods.com

Harvey Nichols
Knightsbridge, SW1
Tel: 020 7235 5000

Jermyn Street Association
Westminster, SW1
Tel: 020 7821 5230
www.jermynstreet.net
Some of London's oldest specialist menswear shops.

London Silver Vaults
Covent Garden, WC2
Underground arcade of over 30 shops with old and modern silver.

Neal Street
Covent Garden, WC2
The latest in style.

Nicole Farhi/French Connection
Bow, E3
Tel: 020 8980 2568
Samples, seconds and last season's designer clothes at bargain prices.

Scotch House
Knightsbridge, SW1
Tel: 020 7581 2151
Knitwear, tartans and kilts.

South Molton Street and St Christopher's Place
Mayfair, W1
Smart fashion and accessories.

Spitalfields Market
Mile End, E1
Tel: 020 7247 6590
Cosmopolitan shops, plus art and craft and antiques markets.

THE CHILTERNS & THE NORTHERN HOME COUNTIES

ACTIVITIES

Central Business Exchange (English Partnership)
Milton Keynes
Tel: 01908 692692
www.cnt.org.uk
A new £57 million leisure and retail complex including Sports Village with a 'real snow' indoor ski centre. (Not open at time of press. This is the present contact number; other numbers may become available as the Sports Village opens.)

Countryside Management Service
Tel: 01727 848168
Information on cycling, including Nicky Line Footpath and Cycle Way and Alban Way.

Hemel Ski Centre
Hemel Hempstead, Herts
Tel: 01442 241321
A 590-ft (180-m) main slope, wave run, training and nursery slopes.

Hitchin Swimming Centre
Hitchin, Herts
Tel: 01462 441646
A 25-m indoor pool and 50-m outdoor pool.

John Nike Leisuresport Complex
Bracknell, Berks
Tel: 01344 860033
Olympic-size ice rink, dry-ski slope and toboggan run.

Letchworth Open Air Pool
Letchworth, Herts
Tel: 01462 684673
Olympic-size heated outdoor pool.

London Gliding Club
Dunstable Downs, Beds
Tel: 01582 663419
www.powernet.co.uk.gliding
One of Britain's best-equipped gliding clubs.

Phasels Wood Climbing Complex
Kings Langley, Herts
Tel: 01442 252851
Outdoor climbing structure.

Wycombe Summit Ski Centre
High Wycombe, Bucks
Tel: 01494 4747111
Britain's longest dry-ski run; 984ft (300m).

LEISURE

British Waterways
Marsworth, Herts
Tel: 01442 825938
Angling, boating, walking and cycling on the Grand Union Canal and its towpath.

Courage Shire Horse Centre
Maidenhead, Berks
Tel: 01628 824848

French Brothers
Windsor, Berks
Tel: 01753 851933 or 862933
www.boat-trips.co.uk
Circular cruises from Windsor and Runnymede, plus scheduled service from Runnymede to Windsor and to Hampton Court.

Helicopter Services
Wycombe Air Park, Booker, Bucks
Tel: 01494 513166
E-mail: heliserve@aol.com
One-hour helicopter flights over central London.

Leighton Buzzard Railway
Leighton Buzzard, Beds
Tel: 01525 377814 (24-hour info)
www.btinternet.com/~buzzrail
Britain's largest collection of narrow-gauge locomotives; train rides.

Odds Farm Park
High Wycombe, Bucks
Tel: 01628 520188
www.btinternet.com/~oddsfarm.park
Rare breeds farm aimed at children.

Shuttleworth Collection
Old Warden Aerodrome, nr Biggleswade, Beds
Tel: 090 683 23310
One of the few remaining grass aerodromes; flying displays.

Thames Edwardian Boat Company
Tel: 01252 623313
Edwardian-style launch *Lollipop II*; pickup points at Reading and Henley.

SHOPPING

The Arcade
Letchworth, Herts
Restored 1922 arcade; specialist shops.

Architectural Antiques
Bedford, Beds
Tel: 01234 213131
Georgian, Victorian and Edwardian interior architectural artefacts.

Art and Crafts
Edlesborough, Beds
Tel: 01525 222268
Crafts and gifts from pottery to moccasins.

Bicester International Outlet Shopping Village
Bicester, Oxon
Tel: 01869 323200
60 shops, many belonging to the famous names of Bond Street and Knightsbridge; up to 60 per cent price reductions.

Boynett Fabrics
Bedford, Beds
Tel: 01234 217788
Curtain and upholstery fabrics; seconds and over-runs at discount prices.

Galleria Outlet Centre
Hatfield, Herts
Tel: 01707 278301
www.factory-outlets.co.uk
Retail outlet offering up to 60 per cent off high-street prices.

Goring Mill Gallery
Goring-on-Thames, Oxon
Tel: 01491 875030
Work by local artists and craftspeople.

Hoddesdon & Waltham Cross Street Markets
Hoddesdon and Waltham Cross, Herts
Tel: 01992 785577
Traditional markets (Wed and Fri).

Silver Editions
Chalfont St Giles, Bucks
Tel: 01753 888810
Sterling silver and silver plate at wholesale prices (mail order only).

St Andrew's Street
Hertford, Herts
Antiques shops.

The Soap Company
Windsor, Berks
Tel: 01753 868678
Over 100 different hand-made soaps.

Town Hall Antiques
Woburn, Beds
Tel: 01525 290950

EAST ANGLIA & CAMBRIDGE

TOURIST INFORMATION

East of England Tourist Board
Toppesfield Hall, Hadleigh, Suffolk
IP7 5DN
Tel: 01473 823063

Suffolk Coast & Countryside TIC
Station Buildings, Woodbridge, Suffolk
IP12 4AJ
Tel: 01394 382240

ACTIVITIES

Broads Bike Hire
Tel: 01603 782281
Network of Broads cycle-hire companies.

David Clarke Microlites
Worthing, Norfolk
Tel: 01362 637405
www.dcma.co.uk
Microlight tuition.

Essex Way, Stour Valley Path & Suffolk Way
Colchester Visitor Information Centre,
1 Queen Street, Colchester, Essex
Tel: 01206 282920
www.colchester.gov.uk/leisure
Details of three walking routes.

Gosfield Lake Resort
Gosfield, Essex
Tel: 01787 475043
Opportunities for waterskiing.

Grafham Water
Perry, Cambs
Tel: 01480 810521
E-mail: admin@gwsc.freeserve.co.uk
www.grafham.org.uk
Sailing and windsurfing.

Jesus Green Swimming Pool
Cambridge
Tel: 01223 213352 or 302579
One of the country's largest open-air pools.

Lakeside Lodge Golf & Bowling Centre
Pidley, Cambs
Tel: 01487 740540
An 18-hole and two 9-hole golf courses, plus ten-pin bowling and rally karting.

Mepal Outdoor Centre
Mepal, Cambs
Tel: 01354 692251
www.mepal.co.uk
Activity centre for watersports, rock-climbing and much more.

Norfolk Gliding Club
Tibenham Airfield, nr Diss, Norfolk
Tel: 01379 677207
www.ngcglide.freeserve.co.uk
Gliding tuition and pleasure flights.

Reepham Station
Reepham, Norfolk
Tel: 01603 871187
Cycling on former railway route.

Riverside Ice & Leisure
Chelmsford, Essex
Tel: 01245 615050
Ice rink plus an outdoor and two indoor swimming pools.

Rollerworld
Colchester, Essex
Tel: 01206 868868
www.rollerworld.co.uk
Rollerskating rink.

Suffolk Ski Centre
Ipswich, Suffolk
Tel: 01473 6022347
Ski tuition or open practice.

Ways Through Essex
TOPS Division, County Hall, Chelmsford, Essex
Tel: 01245 437647
Country Rides, a guide featuring six circular horse-riding routes.

Wildtracks Off-road Activity Park
Kennett, Suffolk
Tel: 01638 751918.
UK's leading off-road activity park with motorsport and military vehicles.

LEISURE

Abberton Reservoir Nature Reserve
Layer de la Haye, Essex
Tel: 01206 738172
Protected area for water birds.

Cambridge Chauffeur Punts
Cambridge
Tel: 01223 354164
Guided tours of Cambridge Backs.

Cambridge River Cruises
Cambridge
Tel: 01223 410100
90-minute circular cruise on River Cam.

Cawley's of Cambridge
Cambridge
Tel: 01223 572787
Guided tours of The Backs.

Granta Boat & Punt Company
Cambridge
Tel: 01223 301845
Punts and boats for hire, from Granta Inn.

Hickling Broad & Ranworth Broad
Norfolk Wildlife Trust, Norwich, Norfolk
Tel: 01603 625540; 01692 598276 (direct to Hickling); 01603 270479 (direct to Ranworth)
Nature trails around Hickling and Ranworth.

Lakeside Lodge Ballooning Rides
Lakeside Lodge Golf & Bowling Centre
Pidley, Cambs
Tel: 01487 740540
Hot-air balloon rides from sites around Huntingdon.

National Stud
Newmarket, Suffolk
Tel: 01638 663464 (general info); 01638 666789 (guided tours)
Guided tours of prestigious horse stud.

Skyride Balloons
Gooderstone, Norfolk
Tel/fax: 07000 110210
Balloon flights over Norfolk.

Tannington Hall
Tannington, Suffolk
Tel: 01728 628226
Horse-drawn carriage rides.

Wizard Balloons
Tel: 01379 898989
Balloon flights over East Anglia from launch sites close to Ipswich, Bury St Edmunds and Diss.

SHOPPING

Battlesbridge Antiques Centre
Battlesbridge, Essex
Tel: 01268 575000
Five old buildings housing 80 antiques dealers in riverside setting.

Cambridge University Press Bookshop
Cambridge
Tel: 01223 333333
www.cup.cam.ac.uk/bookshops/cambridge

Cat Pottery
North Walsham, Norfolk
Tel: 01692 402962
Life-size, lifelike pottery cats.

Clacton Common Factory Shopping Village
Clacton-on-Sea, Essex
Tel: 01255 479595
www.clactoncommon.co.uk
Save up to 60 per cent on top brand-names.

Coleman's Mustard Shop
Norwich, Norfolk
Tel: 01603 627889

Freeport Braintree Designer Outlet Village
Braintree, Essex
Tel: 01376 348867
Designer labels at up to half price.

Glendale Forge
Thaxted, Essex
Tel: 01371 830466
Hand-wrought ornamental ironwork.

Grove Farm Gallery
Catfield, Norfolk
Tel: 01692 670679
Oil and watercolour paintings of the Broads and Norfolk.

Henry Watson's Potteries
Wattisfield, Suffolk
Tel: 01359 251239
Factory shop sells seconds of Watson's distinctive Suffolk pottery.

Lakeside
Thurrock, Essex
Tel: 01708 869933
www.lakeside-shopping-centre.co.uk
Four department stores and 300 shops.

Norfolk Lavender
Heacham, Norfolk
Tel: 01485 570384
National collection of lavender; shop sells everything lavender.

Real Factory Shop
Holt, Norfolk
Tel: 01263 711447
End of run bargains.

Stokesby Candles
Stokesby, Norfolk
Tel: 01493 750242
England's largest variety of hand-crafted candles.

CENTRAL ENGLAND

THE COTSWOLDS & OXFORD

TOURIST INFORMATION

Gloucestershire Tourism
Shire Hall, Gloucester GL1 2TH
Tel: 01452 425673
www.visit-glos.org.uk

Shakespeare Country
South Warwickshire Tourism, Conco Centre, Warwick Technology Park, Gallows Hill, Warwick CV34 6DB
Tel:01926 404891
www.shakespeare-country.co.uk

ACTIVITIES

Cherwell Boathouse
Oxford, Oxon
Tel: 01865 515978
www.cherwellboathouse.co.uk
Punt, rowing boat and canoe hire.

Cotswold Country Cycles
Chipping Campden, Glos
Tel: 01386 438706
www.cotswoldcountrycycles.com
Cycling holidays in the Cotswolds.

Cotswold Gliding Club
Aston Down, Glos
Tel: 01285 760415
www.cotswoldgliding.co.uk
Gliding tuition; one lesson to five-day course.

Cotswold Trail Riding
Brookthorpe, Glos
Tel: 01452 813344 or 813447
The Cotswolds on horseback; guided rides and hacks.

Cotswold Walking Holidays
Cheltenham, Glos
Tel: 01242 254353
www.cotswoldwalks.co
Guided and self-guided walking holidays.

Cotswold Water Park
Shorncote, Glos
Tel: 01285 861459
Watersports, fishing, cycling and walking.

Cotswold Way
A 100-mile (161km) path from Chipping Campden (Glos) to Bath (Avon). Info from TICs.

Gloucestershire's Church Trail Scheme
Church Trail Secretary, c/o Church House, College Green, Gloucester GL1 2LY
Tel: 01452 410022
Walks connecting Gloucestershire's churches; leaflet from churches or address above.

Sanford Parks Lido
Cheltenham, Glos
Tel: 01242 524430
A 50-m outdoor swimming pool.

Stonehouse Accessories
Stonehouse, Glos
Tel: 01453 822881 or 0800 560249 (freephone)
Cycle hire and cycle trails.

Walking with the Cotswolds Wardens
Cheltenham Tourism, 77 Promenade, Cheltenham, Glos GL50 1PP
Tel: 01242 522878
www.cheltenham.gov.uk/tourism
Guided walking tours.

LEISURE

Adventure Balloons
Tel: 01252 844222
Hot-air balloon flights over Oxfordshire.

Avon Cruises
Stratford-upon-Avon, Warwicks
Tel: 01789 267073
Edwardian boat cruises from Stratford.

Birdland
Bourton-on-the-Water, Glos
Tel: 01451 820480
Over 500 birds in natural setting and in aviaries.

Cheltenham Balloon Flights
Woodmancote, Glos
Tel: 01242 675003
Balloon flights year round.

Cotswold Farm Park
Guiting Power, Glos
Tel: 01451 850307
Rare breeds conservation farm.

Folly Farm
Bourton-on-the-Water, Glos
Tel: 01451 820285
Europe's largest domestic waterfowl and wildlife conservation area, also lavender fields.

Gloucester–Warwickshire Railway
Toddington, Glos
Tel: 01242 621405
A 13-mile (21km) steam-train round-trip.

Guide Friday
Stratford-upon-Avon, Warwicks
Tel: 01789 294466
www.guidefriday.com
Open-top double-decker bus tour of Stratford.

Oxford Classic Tour
Didcot, Oxon
Tel: 01253 819393
Open-top double-decker bus tour.

Westonbirt Arboretum
Westonbirt, Glos
Tel: 01666 880220
One of the world's finest collections of temperate trees and shrubs.

SHOPPING

Aston Pottery
Witney, Oxon
Tel: 01993 852031
Working commercial pottery; chance to decorate your chosen piece.

Broad Street, Turl Street & High Street
Oxford, Oxon
Quality gifts, antiques, jewellery, books (old and new), rare maps and prints.

Cheltenham Antiques Centre
Cheltenham, Glos
Tel: 01242 573556
20 antiques dealers under one roof.

Cotswold Antique Dealers' Association
Shipston-on-Stour, Warwicks
Tel: 01608 661268
Antiques shops in Barnsley, Broadway, Burford, Chipping Norton, Cirencester, Fairford, Moreton-in-Marsh, Stow-on-the-Wold, Taddington, Tetbury, Winchcombe and Witney.

Country Artists
Stratford-upon-Avon, Warwicks
Tel: 01789 261283
Hand-painted wildlife sculptures.

Gloucester Green
Oxford, Oxon
Open-air market (Wed); antiques market (Thu).

The Green Shop
Bisley, Glos
Tel/fax: 01452 770629
www.greenshop.co.uk
Environment-friendly and energy-saving products.

Montpellier & Suffolk
Cheltenham, Glos
Areas of specialist boutiques and antiques dealers.

Oxford's Victorian Covered Market
Oxford, Oxon
Colourful stalls and small shops.

Prinknash Abbey & Pottery
Cranham, Glos
Tel: 01452 812066
Pottery, incense, rosaries, candles and cider.

Selsey Herb Farm
Selsey, Glos
Tel: 01453 766682
Up to 250 varieties of herbs and garden plants for sale.

Tetbury Antique Dealers Association
Tetbury, Glos
Tel: 01666 504043
Over 20 antiques shops centred on Long Street.

University of Oxford Shop
Oxford, Oxon
Tel: 01865 247414
www.oxlink.co.uk/oxford/oushop
Official sweatshirts, T-shirts and other gifts.

Winchcombe Pottery
Winchcombe, Glos
Tel: 01242 602462
Hand-thrown domestic pots.

HEREFORDSHIRE & SHROPSHIRE

TOURIST INFORMATION

Herefordshire Tourism
PO Box 44, Leominster, Herefordshire HR6 8ZD
Tel: 01432 260639

Malvern Hills District Council
Council House, Avenue Road, Malvern, Worcs WR14 3AF
Tel: 01684 862411
www.malvernhills.gov.uk

Shropshire Tourism
Craven Arms, Shropshire SY7 8DU
Tel: 01588 676166 (24 hours)
www.shropshiretourism.com

Worcester TIC
Guildhall, High Street, Worcester, Worcs
Tel: 01905 726311
www.cityofworcester.gov.uk

ACTIVITIES

Acorn Activities
Hereford, Herefordshire
Tel: 01432 830083
www.acornactivities.co.uk
Activity holiday company.

Angling (River Severn or Worcester–Birmingham Canal)
Worcester, Worcs
Tel: 01905 722312 for permits.

Berrow House Activity & Camp Centre
Ledbury, Herefordshire
Tel/fax: 01531 635845
Grass-sledging for young and old.

Border Kart Racing
Kinsham, Herefordshire
Tel: 01544 267006
Grand prix-style kart racing.

Elgar Bike Rides
Six cycle routes in the Malvern Hills area; details from Malvern Hills District Council.

Herefordshire Shooting School
Wellington, Herefordshire
Tel: 01885 490269 or 01432 830636
Clay-pigeon shooting.

Peddlers
Worcester, Worcs
Tel: 01905 24238
Bikes, tandems, tourers and mountain bikes for hire.

Sabre Air Sports Microlight Centre
Shobdon, Herefordshire
Tel: 01568 708168
www.kc3ltd.co.uk/local/sabre
Three-axis and flex-wing microlight flying.

Severn Way Walk
Riverside walk from Plynlimon to the sea at Bristol; details from TICs.

Sue Adams Riding School
Shobdon, Herefordshire
Tel: 01568 708973
Indoor school and cross-country course.

Walking in Worcestershire
Countryside Service, Worcestershire County Council, Worcester Countryside Centre, Wildwood Drive, Worcs WR5 2LG
Tel: 01905 766493
Gentle strolls to longer rambles.

Wheely Wonderful Cycling
Elton, Shrops
Tel/fax: 01568 770755
Hybrid, mountain, children's, trailer and tandem-bike hire; also cycling holidays.

Wyre Forest
Bewdley, Worcs (visitor centre)
Tel: 01299 266944
Waymarked walking and mountain-bike trails.

LEISURE

Acton Scott Historic Working Farm
Acton Scott, Shrops
Tel: 01694 781306 or 781307
Traditional (pre-mechanisation) farm; farming and craft demonstrations.

Astley Abbots Lavender Farm
Astley Abbots, Shrops
Tel: 01746 763122
Pick your own lavender, also garden with over 100 varieties of herb; lavender and bee products for sale (open Jul and Aug).

Bickerline
Worcester, Worcs
Tel: 01905 422499
River Severn boat excursions.

Bridgnorth Cliff Railway
Bridgnorth, Shrops
Victorian cliff railway.

Faithful City Guides
Worcester, Worcs
Tel: 01386 7540416 or 01905 24113
Worcester city tours; tickets from Worcester TIC.

Ironbridge Gorge Museum
Ironbridge, Shrops
Tel: 01952 432166 (24 hours) or 433522
www.ironbridge.org.uk
Birthplace of Industrial Revolution; nine museums (World Heritage Site).

The Pig Pen
Whitbourne, Worcs
Tel: 01866 884362
Guided tours of piggery.

The Pride of Avon
Tewkesbury, Glos
Tel: 01684 275906
Pleasure cruises on the River Avon.

Severn Valley Railway
Bewdley, Worcs
Tel: 01299 403816 or 0800 600900 (talking timetable; free)
www.svr.co.uk
Britain's premier steam railway; Kidderminster to Bridgnorth.

Shrewsbury Guided Tours
Shrewsbury, Shrops
Tel: 01743 350761
Tours of the town depart from The Square, Shrewsbury TIC.

SHOPPING

Brontë Porcelain
Malvern Link, Worcs
Tel: 01684 893999
Ceramic sculptures.

Bygones
Worcester, Worcs
Tel: 01905 23132 or 25388
Antiques; Worcester porcelain, silver, jewellery and curios.

Cider Museum & King Offa Distillery
Hereford, Herefordshire
Tel: 01432 354207
Distillery tour; cider brandy and liqueur for sale.

Gandolfi Dollshouse Emporium
Malvern Wells, Worcs
Tel: 01684 569747
Miniature houses and shops, ready-built or in kit form.

Hop Pocket Craft Centre
Bishop's Frome, Worcs
Tel: 01531 640323
Hop-based crafts.

Hopmarket (entrances: The Foregate and Sansome Street)
Worcester, Worcs
Specialist shops in historic courtyard.

Reindeer Court Shopping Centre
Worcester, Worcs
Specialist shops in 17th-century former coaching inn.

Royal Worcester
Worcester, Worcs
Tel: 01905 23221
Factory tours and shops.

Shrewsbury Antique Centres
Shrewsbury, Shrops
Tel: 01743 350761

Westons Cider
Much Marcle, Herefordshire
Tel: 01531 660233

THE MIDLANDS

TOURIST INFORMATION

Birmingham Convention & Visitor Bureau
2 City Arcade, Birmingham B2 4TX
Tel: 0121 643 2514
www.birmingham.org.uk

Coventry & Warwickshire Promotions
1 Castle Yard, off Hay Lane, Coventry CV1 5RF
Tel: 024 7683 4177
www.coventry.org.uk

Shakespeare Country
South Warwickshire Tourism, Conco Centre, Warwick Technology Park, Gallows Hill, Warwick CV34 6DB
Tel:01926 404891
www.shakespeare-country.co.uk

ACTIVITIES

Ashby Boat Co
Stoke Golding, Leics
Tel: 01455 212671
Narrow-boat hire on lock-free Ashby Canal.

Cannock Chase
SE of Stafford, Staffs
Wood and heathland with nature trails, forest walks and cycling.

Clumber Park
Worksop, Notts
Tel: 01909 476592
Nature walks, fishing and cycle hire.

Coombe Country Park
Binley, W Midlands
Tel: 01203 453720
Bird-watching, angling, and woodland and lakeside walks.

Heart of the National Forest Visitor Centre
Moira, Derbys
Tel: 01283 216633
Woodland walks and cycle hire.

International Warwick School of Riding
Warwick, Warwicks
Tel: 01926 494313
Horse-riding lessons, hacks and holidays.

The Open Road
Sherbourne, Warwicks
Tel: 01926 624891
Drive a classic British sports car on the open road.

Snowdome
Tamworth, Staffs
Tel: 08705 000011
www.snowdome.co.uk
Skiing, snowboarding and tobogganing on 'real' snow.

LEISURE

Ashby Trip
Sutton Cheney, Leics
Tel: 01455 213838
Narrow-boat and launch cruises on Ashby Canal.

Battlefield Line
Shackerstone, Leics
Tel: 01827 880754
Steam-hauled 10-mile (16km) trip, Shackerstone to Shenton.

Birmingham Ghost & Graveyard Trails
Birmingham, W Midlands
Tel: 0121 693 6300
www.guidefriday.com
Guided walking tours.

Birmingham Tour
Birmingham, W Midlands
Tel: 0121 693 6300
www.guidefriday.com
Open-top double-decker bus tour.

Dudley Canal Trust
Dudley, W Midlands
Tel: 01384 236275
Narrow-boat trip through underground canal.

Heart of England Balloons
Walcote, Warwicks
Tel: 01789 488219
Hot-air balloon flights.

Shakespeare Express
Birmingham, W Midlands/Stratford-upon-Avon, Warwicks
Tel: 0121 605 7000 or 01789 299866
www.vintagetrains.co.uk
England's fastest regular steam train; Brimingham to Stratford-upon-Avon.

Sherborne Wharf
Birmingham, W Midlands
Tel: 0121 455 6163
www.sherbornewharf.co.uk
Narrow-boat heritage tours of Birmingham's canals.

Sutton Park
Birmingham, W Midlands
Tel: 0121 355 6370
www.birmingham.gov.uk/parks
National nature reserve.

Virgin Skyride Black Country
Dudley, W Midlands
Tel: 01384 236777
Balloon flights over the Black Country.

SHOPPING

Burlington & Burlington Arcade
Birmingham, W Midlands
Stylish shops in Victorian building.

Great Western Arcade
Birmingham, W Midlands
Victorian enclosed shopping arcade.

Greenwood Bonsai Studio
Arnold, Notts
Tel: 0115 920 5757
www.bonsai.co.uk
Britain's most comprehensive range of bonsai trees and products.

Hatton Country World
Hatton, Warwicks
Tel: 01926 843411
Rural shopping 'village'; crafts, gifts, antiques and discount shops in Victorian farm buildings.

Hoar Park Craft Village & Antiques Centre
Ansley Common, Warwicks
Tel: 01203 394433
Crafts, antiques and farm shop.

Royal Brierley Crystal
Brierley Hill, W Midlands
Tel: 01384 70161
Factory shop.

Royal Doulton Crystal
Amblecote, W Midlands
Tel: 01384 552900
Hand-made English crystal.

NORTHAMPTONSHIRE & THE LINCOLNSHIRE WOLDS

TOURIST INFORMATION

Leicester County Council Tourism Unit
County Hall, Glenfield, Leicester LE3 8RJ
Tel: 0116 265 7039

Lincolnshire Tourism
Lincoln Castle, Lincoln LN1 3AA
Tel: 01522 526450
www.lincstourism.com

Nottinghamshire Tourism
Rufford Abbey, Ollerton, Newark NG22 9DF
Tel: 01623 822944
www.nottscc.gov.uk/tourism

Tourism & Conference Bureau
Northamptonshire Chamber, Royal Pavilion, Summerhouse Road, Moulton Park, Northampton NN3 6BJ
Tel: 01604 671200

ACTIVITIES

Billing Aquadrome
Great Billing, Northants
Tel: 01604 408181
Jet skiing and go-karts.

Bosworth Water Trust
Market Bosworth, Leics
Tel: 01455 291876
Lakes for dinghies, board-sailing and fishing.

Eyebrook Reservoir
Eyebrook, Leics
Tel: 01536 770264
Fishing from bank or boat.

Leicester Outdoor Pursuits Centre
Leicester, Leics
Tel: 0116 268 1426
Abseiling, orienteering, quad-biking, canoeing and archery.

National Ice Centre
Nottingham, Notts
Tel: 0115 989 5555
State-of-the-art ice-skating rink.

National Watersports Centre
Holme Pierrepont, Notts
Tel: 0115 982 1212
Rowing, canoeing, water-skiing and sailing.

Pitsford Water Cycles
Brixworth, Northants
Tel: 01604 881777
www.pitsfordcycles.co.uk
Bike hire for Pitsford Reservoir Trail and Brampton Valley Way.

Rockblok
Whitewell, Rutland
Tel/fax: 01780 460060
Outdoor climbing-practice block.

Sherwood Forest Country Park
Visitor Centre: Edwinstowe, Notts
Tel: 01623 823202
Waymarked forest trails.

Shire Cycle Treks
Great Dalby, Leics
Tel/fax: 01664 563919
www.shire-treks.demon.co.uk
Cycle holidays in the Heart of England.

Sileby Mill Boatyard
Sileby, Leics
Tel: 01509 813583
Narrow-boat hire for the day.

Silverstone Circuit
Silverstone, Northants
Tel: 01327 850205
www.silverstone-circuit.co.uk
Drive performance racing cars.

Wellow Park Stables and Saddlery
Wellow, Notts
Tel: 01623 861040
Dressage, show-jumping and cross-country riding; driving ponies also available.

Woodhall Spa Golf Club
Woodhall Spa, Lincs
Tel: 01526 352511
Hotchkin Golf Course, one of England's finest inland courses.

LEISURE

Batemans Brewery
Wainfleet, Lincs
Tel: 01754 882009
Brewery tour followed by sampling of Batemans Ales.

Blisworth Tunnel Boat
Blisworth, Northants
Tel: 01604 858868
Self-steer narrow boats on the Grand Union Canal.

Cresswell Crags Caves
Wellbeck, Notts
Tel: 01909 720378
Limestone gorge; guided tours of caves.

Farmworld
Oadby, Leics
Tel: 0116 271 0775
www.farmworld-stoughton.co.uk
Britain's largest farm park.

Gibraltar Point National Nature Reserve
Gibraltar Point, Lincs
Tel: 01754 762677
Bird reserve.

Great Central Railway
Loughborough, Leics
Tel: 01509 230726
www.gcrailway.co.uk
Britain's only main-line steam railway.

Great Northern & East Lincolnshire Railway
Ludborough, Lincs
Tel: 01507 363881
Lincolnshire's only full-size steam railway.

Lace Centre
Nottingham, Notts
Tel/fax: 0115 941 3539
Hand-made Nottingham Lace.

Lincoln Historic Cruise
Lincoln, Lincs
Tel/fax: 01522 881200
Cruises on River Witham.

Lincolnshire Road Car Co
Lincoln, Lincs
Tel: 01522 522255
Bus tour of Lincoln.

Naturescape Wild Flower Farm
Langar, Notts
Tel: 01949 860592 or 851045
www.naturescape.co.uk
Over 40 acres (16ha) of wild-flower fields; rare seeds and plants for sale.

Waterside Narrowboat Trips
Leicester, Leics
Tel: 0116 251 2334
Narrow-boat river trips.

SHOPPING

Hemswell Antique Centre
Hemswell, Lincs
Tel: 01427 668389
Period furniture, silver, jewellery, clocks, paintings, books and collectables at former RAF Hemswell.

Horncastle Antiques Centre
Horncastle, Lincs
Tel: 01507 527777
Over 40 dealers; period furniture, clocks, ceramics and collectables.

Junktion
New Bolingbroke, Lincs
Tel: 01205 480068 or 480087
Domestic bygones, toys, fairground amusement machines and advertising signs (Wed, Thu and Sat).

Leicester's Markets
Leicester, Leics
Tel: 0116 252 6776
Over 400 stalls; food, clothing jewellery and much more (Mon–Sat).

Long Clawson Dairy
Melton Mowbray, Leics
Tel: 01664 822332
Blue Stilton and other blue and speciality cheeses.

St Martins Square
Leicester, Leics
Tel: 0116 253 8247
Designer outlets and gift shops.

Station Pottery
Shenton, Leics
Tel: 0374 134458
Traditional country pottery at Shenton Station.

Whitemoors Antiques & Craft Centre
Shenton, Leics
Tel: 01455 212250
Antiques, fine art, bric-à-brac, books and curios.

Ye Olde Pork Pie Shoppe
Melton Mowbray, Leics
Tel: 01664 482068
Melton Mowbray's last remaining bakery producing authentic Melton pork pies.

THE PEAK DISTRICT

TOURIST INFORMATION

Ashbourne TIC
13 Market Place, Ashbourne, Derbys DE6 1EU
Tel: 01335 343666

Bakewell TIC
Old Market Hall, Bridge Street, Bakewell, Derbys DE45 1DS
Tel: 01629 813227
www.peakdistrict.org

Buxton TIC
The Crescent, Buxton, Derbys SK17 6BQ
Tel: 01298 25106
www.highpeak.gov.uk

Matlock TIC
Crown Square, Matlock, Derbys DE4 3AT
Tel: 01629 583388

ACTIVITIES

Derwent Pursuits
Cromford, Derbys
Tel: 01629 824179
Canoeing, caving, orienteering, climbing, abseiling and gorge scrambling.

Fishing
Most river fishing is private; some hotels offer day or week licences for guests. Day tickets are available for fly-fishing at Tittesworth, Rudyard, Carsington, Ladybower, Erwood and Combs Reservoirs.

Northfield Farm Riding & Trekking Centre
Flash, Derbys
Tel: 01298 22543
Rides along old packhorse trails.

Peak Cycle Hire
Bakewell, Derbys
Tel: 01629 816211
Cycle hire within Peak National Park.

Peak District Hang-gliding Centre
Leek, Staffs
Tel: 0700 426445
Britain's oldest BHPA-approved school.

Peak Practice Golf
Fairfield, Derbys
Tel: 01298 74444
www.peakpracticegolf.co.uk
A 300-m (330-yd) floodlit driving range and sand bunker.

Peakland Walking Holidays
Tideswell, Derbys
Tel: 01298 872801
www.walkingholidays.org.uk

Pennine Outdoor Pursuits
Midway, Derbys
Tel: 01283 210666
Multi-activity holidays in the Peak District.

LEISURE

Alton Towers
Alton, Staffs
Tel: 08705 204060
www.alton-towers.co.uk
Britain's premier theme park.

Barrow Hill Engine Shed
Barrow Hill, Derbys
Tel: 01246 854921
Britain's last working roundhouse; steam engines on display.

Castleton Caverns
Castleton, Derbys
Blue John Mine
Tel: 01433 620638
www.blue/johnenterprises.com
Peak Cavern
Tel: 01433 620285
www.peakcavern.co.uk
Speedwell Cavern
Tel: 01433 620512
www.speedwellcavern.co.uk
Treak Cliff Cavern
Tel: 01433 620571
www.bluejohnstone.com
Showcaves and the rare Blue John stone.

Chesterfield Canal Boat Trips
Tapton Lock, Derbys
Tel: 01246 274077
Boat trips on Chesterfield Canal.

Dragon Balloon Co
Nottingham, Notts
Tel: 0115 947 3778
www.dragonballoon.co.uk
Balloon flights in the Peak District, Derbyshire Dales and Amber Valley.

Heights of Abraham
Matlock Bath, Derbys
Tel: 01629 582365
www.heights-of-abraham.co.uk
Cable-car ride above gorge, plus show caverns.

National Tramway Museum
Crich, Derbys
Tel: 01773 852565
Rides on vintage trams.

Peak Rail
Matlock to Rowsley, Derbys
Tel: 01629 580381
www.peakrail.co.uk
Steam-train trips of the Derwent Valley.

Peak Safari
Buxton, Derbys
Tel: 01298 70524
Land Rover tours of Peak District National Park.

Poole's Cavern
Buxton, Derbys
Tel: 01298 26978
www.poolescavern.co.uk
Spectacular crystal formations; Derbyshire's longest stalactite.

Riber Castle & Wildlife Park
Matlock, Derbys
Tel: 01629 582073
Wildlife park around castle ruins.

SHOPPING

Ashbourne, Derbys
For gingerbread.

Bakewell, Derbys
For Bakewell pudding.

Castleton, Derbys
For semi-precious Blue John stone products.

Chesterfield Flea Market
Chesterfield, Derbys
Tel: 01246 345777 or 345778 (TIC)
One of the country's largest flea markets; antiques and memorabilia (Thu).

De Bradelei Mill Shop
Belper, Derbys
Tel: 01773 829830
Designer-label fashion at up to 70 per cent discount.

Denby Pottery Visitor Centre
Denby, Derbys
Tel: 01773 740799
Factory shop and tours.

Herb Garden
Hardstoft, Derbys
Tel: 01246 854268
One of the country's foremost herb gardens; herb plants for sale.

Individual Factory Shops Trail
Amber Valley, Derbys
Trail of around 30 factory shop outlets around Amber Valley.

Masson Mills
Matlock Bath, Derbys
Tel: 01629 760208
Shopping 'village' in converted textile mills; also a working textile museum.

McArthurGlen Outlet Store
M1 (Jct 28), Derbys
Tel: 01773 545000
End-of-season and excess-stock designer-name goods at 30–50 per cent discount.

Peak Village
Rowsley, Derbys
Tel: 01629 735326
Up to 70 per cent off brand names.

Ridgeway Craft Centre
Ridgeway, Derbys
Tel: 0114 251 3164
Traditional and modern crafts.

Royal Crown Derby Visitor Centre
Derby, Derbys
Tel: 01332 712841
Fine bone china from factory shop; also factory tours.

CHESTER & THE POTTERIES

TOURIST INFORMATION

Chester TIC
Town Hall, Northgate Street, Chester
CH1 2HJ
Tel: 01244 402111
www.chestercc.gov.uk

Shropshire Tourism
Craven Arms, Shropshire SY7 8DU
Tel: 01588 676166 (24 hours)
www.shropshiretourism.com

Staffordshire Tourism
Riverway, Stafford ST16 3TJ
Tel: 01785 277397
www.staffordshire.gov.uk/tourism

ACTIVITIES

Brown End Farm Cycle Hire
Waterhouses, Staffs
Tel: 01538 308313
Cycle hire for scenic Manifold Track.

Dearnford Hall Fly-Fishery
Whitchurch, Shrops
Tel: 01948 665914
Fly-fishing tuition and rod hire.

Llangollen Canal
Ellesmere, Shrops
Tel: 01691 622549
Boating, fishing, cycling and walking.

Maesbury Wharf Cruisers
Maesbury, Shrops
Tel: 01691 670826 or 670849
Boat and cruiser hire and fishing on Montgomery Canal.

Montgomery Canal
Oswestry, Shrops
Boating, angling and marked circular footpaths (info from Oswestry TIC).

Nantmawr Quarry
Oswestry, Shrops
Tel/fax: 01691 659358
Mountain-bike centre.

Penycoed Riding Stables
Llynclys Hill, Shrops
Tel: 01691 830608
Riding close to Welsh Border.

Racecourse Common
On B4580 Llansilin road, Shrops
Figure-of-eight walking circuit with fine views.

LEISURE

Bithells Boats River Dee
Chester, Cheshire
Tel: 01244 325394
Half-hour cruises on River Dee.

Boat Museum
Ellesmere Port, Cheshire
Tel: 0151 355 5017
Story of inland waterways; world's largest collection of traditional craft.

Chester Tour
Chester, Cheshire
Tel/fax: 01244 347457
Open-top double-decker bus tour.

Chester Zoo
Upton-by-Chester, Cheshire
Tel: 01244 380280
www.demon.co.uk/chesterzoo

Churnet Valley Railway
Cheddleton, Staffs
Tel: 01538 360522
Steam-train rides, Cheddleton to Consall Forge.

Churnet Valley Wildlife Sanctuary
Kingsley, Staffs
Tel: 01538 756702
Wildlife sanctuary and nature reserve.

Foxfield Steam Railway
Blythe Bridge, Staffs
Tel: 01782 396210
www.foxfieldrailway.co.uk
A 5-mile (8km) round trip through N Staffs countryside.

Froghall Wharf Boat Trips
Froghall Wharf, Staffs
Tel: 01538 266486
Narrow-boat dining on Caldon Canal.

Sow Valley Cruises
Great Haywood, Staffs
Tel/fax: 01785 663728
www.sowvalleycruises.co.uk
Narrow-boat trip of Sow Valley; Great Haywood Junction to Tixall Wide Lake.

SHOPPING

Aynsley China Visitor Centre
Longton, Staffs
Tel: 01782 593536
Factory tours and shop.

McArthurGlen Designer Outlet
Cheshire Oaks, Cheshire
Tel: 0151 348 5600
Europe's largest designer outlet shopping centre (160 stores).

Oswestry Market
Oswestry, Shrops
Shropshire's largest market; 120 stalls (Wed, also Sat in summer).

Royal Doulton Visitor Centre
Burslem, Staffs
Tel: 01782 292434
Shop for Royal Doulton figures.

Staffordshire Enamels
Longton, Staffs
Tel: 01782 596596
England's only enamel-maker open to the public.

Tutbury Crystal Glass
Tutbury, Staffs
Tel: 01283 813281
Factory shop with crystal-glass gifts.

World of Spode Visitor Centre
Stoke-on-Trent, Staffs
Tel: 01782 744011
www.spode.co.uk
England's oldest pottery on original site; factory tours and shop with slightly imperfect table and giftware.

NORTH ENGLAND

LANCASHIRE & LIVERPOOL

TOURIST INFORMATION

North West Tourist Board
Swan House, Swan Meadow Road, Wigan Pier, Wigan WN3 5BB
Tel: 01942 821222
www.visitbritain.com/uk/destinations/areas/nw-england/intro.htm

ACTIVITIES

Brian Seedle Helicopters
Blackpool Airport, Lancs
Tel: 01253 298802
Helicopter flying lessons and pleasure flights.

Liverpool Watersports Centre
Liverpool, Merseyside
Tel: 0151 708 9322
Sailing, canoeing and windsurfing in Queen's Dock.

Manchester Velodrome: The National Cycling Centre
Manchester, Lancs
Tel: 0161 223 2244
www.manchestervelodrome.com
Olympic indoor cycle track.

Ski Rossendale
Rawtenstall, Lancs
Tel: 01706 222426
The North's premier dry-ski centre.

Stanley Park
Blackpool, Lancs
Tel: 01253 25212
Park with boating lake and sports centre.

LEISURE

Blackpool Pleasure Beach
Blackpool, Lancs
Tel: 01253 341003
www.bpbltd.com
The world's biggest free-admission amusement park.

Blackpool Tower
Blackpool, Lancs
Tel: 01253 622242
Blackpool's most famous landmark; lifts to the top for superb views.

British Commercial Vehicle Museum
Leyland, Lancs
Tel: 01772 451011
Historic lorries and buses.

Castlefield Urban Heritage Park
Manchester, Lancs
Tel: 0161 834 4026
www.castlefield.org.uk
Restored canal basin; museums, towpath trail and walks plus boat trips.

East Lancashire Railway
Bury to Rawtenstall, Lancs
Tel: 0161 764 7790
Steam-train trip with views of West Pennine Moors.

Foulridge Canal Cruises
Foulridge, Lancs
Tel/fax: 01282 844033 or 870241 (talking timetable)
Canal-boat cruise through Pendle countryside.

Freshfield Red Squirrel Reserve
Formby, Lancs
Tel: 01704 878591

Knowsley Safari Park
Prescot, Merseyside
Tel: 0151 430 9009
www.knowsley.com
Britain's largest safari park; drive through wild animal reserves.

Manchester United Museum and Tour Centre
Manchester, Lancs
Tel: 0161 877 4002
www.manutd.com
Behind-the-scenes tour of one of the world's most famous football clubs.

Martin Mere Wetland Adventure
Martin Mere, Lancs
Tel: 01704 895181
Wildfowl and Wetlands Trust site; ducks, geese, swans and flamingoes.

Mersey Ferries
Seacombe, Merseyside
Tel: 0151 630 1030
Guided cruises of Liverpool's historic waterfront.

Port Sunlight Village
Port Sunlight, Cheshire
Tel: 0151 644 6466
19th-century garden village built for Lever's soap-factory workers.

SHOPPING

Barden Mill
Burnley, Lancs
Tel: 01282 420333
Chainstore brands at up to half price.

Botany Bay Villages
Chorley, Lancs
Tel: 01257 261220
Indoor shopping complex; five floors of unusual gifts.

Corgi Heritage Centre
Heywood, Lancs
Tel: 01706 365812
www.corgi-heritage.co.uk
Corgi model vehicles; shop and museum (Mon and Wed–Sat).

Freeport
Fleetwood, Lancs
Tel: 01253 877377
Designer products at up to 50 per cent off high-street prices.

Tommy Ball's Family Footwear
Blackburn, Lancs
Tel: 01254 261910
Thousands of shoes at reduced prices.

Trafford Centre
Manchester, Lancs
Tel: 0161 746 7777
www.traffordcentre.co.uk
One of Britain's largest shopping centres, with the only Selfridges outside London.

Willsmart Factory Shop
Salford, Lancs
Tel: 0161 737 9056
Bedding, curtains and towels direct from the mill; at least 50 per cent off.

Winfields
Haslingden, Lancs
Tel: 01706 831952
www.winfields.co.uk
Over 100,000 pairs of shoes, sportswear, clothing, toys, electrical goods and homeware items.

WEST YORKSHIRE & THE BRONTË COUNTRY

TOURIST INFORMATION

Gateway Yorkshire
Leeds Regional Travel and TIC, The Arcade, Leeds City Station, Leeds LS1 1PL
Tel: 0113 242 5242
www.leeds.gov.uk

ACTIVITIES

Doe Park Water Activities Centre
Denholme, W Yorks
Tel: 01274 833826

Ilkley Pool & Lido
Ilkley, W Yorks
Tel: 01943 600453

West Yorkshire Cycle Route
A 155-mile (250-km) route through the Pennines; details from TICs.

LEISURE

Apollo Canal Cruises
Shipley, W Yorks
Tel: 01274 595914
Lunch and dinner cruises of Leeds and Liverpool Canal; also waterbus service Shipley to Bingley.

Keighley & Worth Valley Railway
Haworth, W Yorks
Tel: 01535 645214 or 647777 (recorded info)
www.kwvr.co.uk
Britain's last remaining complete branch line; steam-train trips through Brontë Country.

Middleton Railway
Hunslet, W Yorks
Tel: 0113 271 0320
Steam- and diesel-train trips to Middleton Park (nature trails).

Shipley Glen Cable Tramway
Shipley, W Yorks
Tel: 01274 589010
Victorian cabled-hauled tramway through Walker Woods.

Tetley's Brewery Wharf
Leeds, W Yorks
Tel: 0113 324 0666
www.brewerywharf.co.uk
Tours of brewery; resident shire horses.

SHOPPING

Briggate
Leeds, W Yorks
Area of Victorian arcades (including Queen's and Thornton's Arcades); interesting small shops.

Corn Exchange
Leeds, W Yorks
Tel: 0113 234 0363
60 speciality shops.

Granary Wharf
Leeds, W Yorks
Tel: 0113 244 6570
International hand-crafted wares at affordable prices.

Kirkgate Market
Leeds, W Yorks
Tel: 0113 214 5162
Europe's largest indoor market.

Leeds Antique Centre
Leeds, W Yorks
Tel: 0113 242 3194
Affordable antiques and collectables; over 30 units in converted 19th-century warehouse.

Victoria Quarter
Leeds, W Yorks
Tel: 0113 245 5333
Fashion shops including the first Harvey Nichols outside London.

THE YORKSHIRE DALES

TOURIST INFORMATION

Yorkshire Dales TIC
4 Central Chambers, Railway Street, Leyburn, N Yorks DL8 5BB
Tel: 01969 623069
www.yorkshiredales.com

ACTIVITIES

Dales Mountain Bike Hire
Fremington, N Yorks
Tel: 01748 826960
Mountain-bike hire.

Grimwith Reservoir
Grimwith, N Yorks
Tel: 01943 874854
Sailboarding, dinghy sailing and canoeing.

Hawes Angling Association
Hawes, N Yorks
Tel: 01969 667362
Trout and grayling fishing; licences available.

Tracks 'n' Trails
Ripon, N Yorks
Tel: 01756 606686
www.bronco.co.uk/trails
Cycling and walking tours of Yorkshire Dales; bikes, routes and luggage transfer.

Wensleydale Golf
Wensleydale, N Yorks
Tel: 01677 450201
Pay-and-play at Akebar Park (9 and 18 holes).

Yorkshire Dales Guides
Horton-in-Ribblesdale, N Yorks
Tel: 01729 860357
Caving, climbling, fell-walking and orienteering.

Yorkshire Dales Trekking Centre
Malham, N Yorks
Tel: 01729 830352
Horse-trekking in the Dales.

LEISURE

Embsay–Bolton Abbey Steam Railway
Embsay, N Yorks
Tel: 01756 710614
www.yorkshirenet.com
Steam-train rides from Bolton Abbey to Embsay.

Ingleborough Cave
Clapham, N Yorks
Tel: 015242 51242
Prehistoric dry-stream passage.

Mother Shipton's Cave
Knaresborough, N Yorks
Tel: 01423 864000
www.mothershipton.co.uk

Pennine Boat Trips of Skipton
Skipton, N Yorks
Tel/fax: 01756 790829 or 701212 (talking timetable)
www.yorkshirenet.co.uk/pennineboats
Trip on Leeds and Liverpool Canal.

Stump Cross Caverns
Greenhow, N Yorks
Tel: 01756 752780
Large underground passages; stalactite and stalagmite formations.

White Scar Cave
Ingleton, N Yorks
Tel: 015242 41244
Britain's longest showcave; underground rivers and waterfalls.

Working Sheepdog Demonstration
Haylands, N Yorks
Tel: 01969 667431
Watch working sheepdogs.

SHOPPING

Brymor
Masham, N Yorks
Tel: 01677 460377
On-farm real dairy ice-cream parlour.

Dales Book Centre
Grassington, N Yorks
Tel: 01756 753373
Books, paintings and prints of the Dales.

Island Heritage
Healey, N Yorks
Tel: 01765 689651
Undyed woollen products from rare-breed sheep; working farm and shop.

Swaledale Woollens
Muker, N Yorks
Tel/fax: 01748 886251
Cottage shop; woollen sweaters, scarves, socks, hats, gloves, sheepskin rugs and more.

Teapottery
Leyburn, N Yorks
Tel/fax: 01969 623839
Unusual design hand-made teapots.

Watershed Mill
Settle, N Yorks
Tel: 01729 825539
Knitwear, co-ordinates and outdoor wear, plus crafts and fossils.

Wensleydale Creamery
Hawes, N Yorks
Tel: 01969 667664
www.wensleydale.co.uk
Home of Wensleydale cheese; viewing gallery, cheese tasting and shops.

White Rose Candle Workshop
Wensley, N Yorks
Tel: 01969 623544
Watch candles being made, then buy.

W R Outhwaite & Son
Hawes, N Yorks
Tel: 01969 667487
Ropemakers (est 1905); skipping ropes to church-bell ropes.

Yorkshire Flowerpots
Hawes, N Yorks
Tel: 01969 667464
Flowerpots made and sold on site.

YORK, NORTH YORK MOORS & EDEN VALLEY

TOURIST INFORMATION

East Riding of Yorkshire
Beverley TIC, 34 Butcher Row, Beverley, Humberside HU17 0AB
Tel: 01482 867430

York Tourism Bureau
20 George Hudson Street, York YO1 6WR
Tel: 01904 554488
www.york-tourism.co.uk

Yorkshire Tourist Board
312 Tadcaster Road, York YO24 1GS
Tel: 01904 707961
www.ytb.org.uk

ACTIVITIES

North Humberside Riding Centre
Easington, E Yorks
Tel: 01964 650250
www.spurnpoint.com/north_humberside_riding_centre
Rides along country lanes, byways, riverbanks and sandy beaches.

Pocklington Canal
Tel: 01904 623338
www.pocklington.gov.uk/pcas
Rural waterway popular with walkers, wildlife enthusiasts and anglers.

Royal Yorkshire Yacht Club
Bridlington, E Yorks
Tel/fax: 01262 678319
www.ryyc.org.uk/ryyc
Keelboat and dinghy racing.

Spurn Point
North entrance to River Humber, Humberside
www.spurnpoint.com
Bird-watching, sea-fishing, walking and fossil hunting.

Wolds Way
Filey, E Yorks to Hessle, Humberside
Tel: 01439 770657
www.woldsway.gov.uk
National Trail, 79 miles (127km) of chalk-hill walking.

Yorkshire Gliding Club
Sutton Bank, N Yorks
Tel: 01845 597237
www.ygc.co.uk
Gliders, hang-gliders and microlights.

LEISURE

Bempton Cliffs
Bempton, E Yorks
Tel: 01262 851179
www.rspb.org.uk/nature_res
Best place in England to see breeding sea birds (over 200,000).

Clifford's Tower
York, N Yorks
Tel: 01904 646940
Fine views of York from the tower.

National Railway Museum
York, N Yorks
Tel: 01904 621261
www.nrm.org.uk
World's largest railway museum.

North Yorkshire Moors Railway
Pickering, N Yorks
Tel: 01751 472508
www.nymr.demon.co.uk
18-mile (29-km) steam-train trip through North York Moors National Park.

Original Ghost Walk of York
York, N Yorks
Tel/fax: 01759 373090
Guided walk.

Trees to Treske
Thirsk, N Yorks
Tel: 01845 522770
www.yorkshirenet.co.uk/treske
Working furniture factory, plus visitor centre.

YorkBoat
York, N Yorks
Tel: 01904 623752
www.yorkboat.co.uk
River trips of York with commentary; evening cruise and ghost cruise.

York Tour (Guide Friday)
York, N Yorks
Tel: 01904 625618
Open-top double-decker bus tour.

Yorkwalk
York, N Yorks
Tel: 01904 622303
www.barstep.demon.co.uk
Guided, historical walks.

SHOPPING

McArthurGlen Designer Outlet
York, N Yorks
Tel: 01904 682700
E-mail: stuart.nanson@b-m-g.com
80 stores with designer-label items at 30 to 70 per cent discount.

Micklegate
York, N Yorks
Books and second-hand records.

Mulberry Hall
York, N Yorks
Tel: 01904 620736
One of the world's leading china and crystal specialists; 17 showrooms.

Red House Antiques Centre
York, N Yorks
Tel: 01904 637000
60 dealers in historic house.

Swinegate
York, N Yorks
Designer-fashion shops.

THE LAKE DISTRICT & EDEN VALLEY

TOURIST INFORMATION

Lake District Visitor Centre
Windermere, Cumbria LA23 1LJ
Tel: 015394 46601

ACTIVITIES

Armathwaite Hall Equestrian Centre
Keswick, Cumbria
Tel: 017687 76949
Escorted hacks around Skiddaw mountains and Bassenthwaite Lake.

Cold Keld Guided Walking Holidays
Ravenstonedale, Cumbria
Tel: 015396 23273

Cumbria Outdoors
Portinscale, Cumbria
Tel: 017687 72816
Inclusive activity holidays.

Low Wood Watersports & Activity Centre
Windermere, Cumbria
Tel: 015394 39441
Water-skiing, sailing, windsurfing, kayaking and boat hire.

Nenthead Mines Heritage Centre
Nenthead, Cumbria
Tel: 01434 382037
Lead panning in England's highest village; self-guided trails and archaeologist-led walks.

Pleasure in Leisure
Windermere, Cumbria
Tel: 015394 42324 or 88002
Mountaineering, caving, air sports, watersports and target sports.

Puddle Jumper
Windermere, Cumbria
Tel: 01539 821611
Mountain-bike hire and guided bike tours.

LEISURE

Lakeland Safari (Tours)
Ambleside, Cumbria
Tel: 015394 33904
Off-the-beaten-track full-day and half-day minibus tours.

Lakeside and Haverthwaite Railway
Haverthwaite to Lakeside, Cumbria
Tel/fax: 015395 31594
Steam-train journey through Leven Valley; connects with Windermere Lake Cruises at Lakeside.

Mountain Goat MiniCoach Tours
Windermere or Keswick, Cumbria
Tel: 015394 45161 (Windermere) or 017687 73962 (Keswick)
www.lakes-pages.co.uk
Mini coaches explore hidden valleys, lakes and passes.

Ravenglass & Eskdale Railway
Ravenglass, Cumbria
Tel: 01229 717171
England's oldest narrow-gauge steam railway from Ravenglass into Lakeland's mountains.

South Tynedale Railway
Alston, Cumbria
Tel: 01434 382828 or 381696
England's highest narrow-gauge railway line; steam and diesel engines.

Ullswater Steamers
Glenridding or Kendal, Cumbria
Tel: 017684 82229 (Glenridding) or 01539 721626 (Kendal)
Scenic cruise around Ullswater on 19th-century steam boat.

Windermere Lake Cruises
Lakeside, Cumbria
Tel: 015395 31188
www.marketsite.co.uk/lakes
Steamers and launches on Windermere connect Ambleside, Bowness and Lakeside.

SHOPPING

Cumberland Pencil Museum
Keswick, Cumbria
Tel: 017687 73626
World's largest pencil plus shop.

Eden Valley Woollen Mill
Armathwaite, Cumbria
Tel: 016974 72457
Tweed jackets and skirts, woollen rugs, hats, ties and scarves.

Gossipgate Gallery
Alston, Cumbria
Tel: 01434 381806
Quality regional art and craftwork.

K Village Factory Shopping
Kendal, Cumbria
Tel: 01539 732363
High-street brands of footwear, outdoor clothing and fashion.

Kirkstone Galleries
Skelwith Bridge, Cumbria
Tel: 015394 34002
Unusual home furnishings, plus Kirkstone, a volcanic sea-green stone.

Lakes Glass Centre
Ulverston, Cumbria
Tel: 01229 584400 or 581121
Full leaded crystal (Cumbria Crystal) and coloured art glass (Heron Glass).

Low Sizergh Barn Farm Shop
Low Sizergh, Cumbria
Tel: 01539 560426
Traditional cheese, local meats and home baking.

Slapestones Gallery
Grasmere, Cumbria
Tel: 015394 35252
Paintings and prints by local artists.

Wetheriggs Country Pottery
Clifton Dykes, Cumbria
Tel: 01768 892733
www.wetheriggs-pottery.co.uk
Steam-powered pottery; create or paint your own pot or buy from the shop.

NORTHUMBRIA & NEWCASTLE

TOURIST INFORMATION

Northumberland National Park
East Burn, South Park, Hexham, Northumberland NE46 1BS
Tel: 01434 605555

Northumbria Tourist Board
Aykley Heads, Durham DH1 5UX
Tel: 0191 375 3000
www.ntb.org.uk

ACTIVITIES

Alnwick Golf Club
Alnwick, Northumberland
Tel: 01665 620632
18-hole golf course (est 1907).

Consett to Sunderland Railway Path
Consett, Co Durham
Tel: 0117 929 0888
Cycle route along former railway line.

Deepdale Off-road 4x4 Driving Centre
Barnard Castle, Co Durham
Tel: 01833 630802
Off-road Land Rover driving courses.

East Durham Airfield
Shotton Colliery, Co Durham
Tel: 0191 517 1234
Light aircraft and parachuting.

Karting North East
Sunderland, Tyne and Wear
Tel: 0191 521 4050
Kart racing and quad-biking.

Kielder Bikes Cycle Centre
Kielder, Northumberland
Tel: 01434 250392
Cycles for exploring Kielder Water and Forest.

The Pursuit Centre, Slaley Hall
Hexham, Northumberland
Tel: 01434 673100
www.premier-leisure.org.uk
Off-road motorsports, paint-balling and shooting.

South Tyne Trail
Haltwhistle, Northumberland
Former railway line open to walkers.

Teesside White Water Course
Stockton-on-Tees, Tees Valley
Tel: 01642 678000
Purpose-built white-water canoeing course.

LEISURE

North of England Open-Air Museum
Beamish, Co Durham
Tel: 01207 231811
Re-creates 18th- and 19th-century life.

Billy Shiel's Farne Island Boat Trips
Seahouses, Northumberland
Tel: 01665 720308
Trips for bird- and seal-watching.

Cloud Nine Balloon Co
Ebchester, Co Durham
Tel: 01207 560304
Flights over Durham and Northumberland.

Dave Gray Boat Trips
Amble-by-the-Sea, Northumberland
Tel: 01665 711975
Trip around Coquet Islands to see puffins, terns, shags and seals.

Killhope Lead-Mining Centre
St John's Chapel, Co Durham
Tel: 01388 537505
Restored Victorian lead mine; tours.

Saltburn's Inclined Tramway
Saltburn-by-the-Sea, Cleveland
Tel: 0191 388 7545
Victorian inclined tramway linking Saltburn to lower promenade.

Tanfield Railway
Gateshead, Tyne and Wear
Tel: 01287 622528
World's oldest existing railway.

SHOPPING

Almost Unwearoutable Socks and Stockings
Seaton Burn, Tyne and Wear
Tel: 01670 789786
Walking socks, stockings, jerseys, garters, fingerless gloves.

Bargain Baggage Factory Shop
North Shields, Tyne and Wear
Tel: 0191 258 4451
Branded luggage well below high-street prices.

Barter Books
Alnwick, Northumberland
Tel: 01665 604888
www.barterbooks.co.uk
In restored Victorian railway station; one of the largest second-hand bookshops in Britain.

Lindisfarne Ltd
Holy Island, Northumberland
Tel: 01289 389230
Lindisfarne Mead and speciality food and drink.

MetroCentre
Gateshead, Tyne and Wear
Tel: 0191 460 5299
www.themetrocentre-gateshead.co.uk
Shopping complex and leisure centre; cinema, theme park, ten-pin bowling and laser game.

Morpeth Chantry
Morpeth, Northumberland
Tel: 01670 511217
Hand-made items from Northumbrian craftsmen.

Otterburn Mill
Otterburn, Tyne and Wear
Tel: 01830 520225
High-quality woollen tweed.

Royal Quays Outlet Shopping Centre
North Shields, Tyne and Wear
Tel: 0191 296 3743
Brand names and designer labels at bargain prices.

Simple Way
Prudhoe, Northumberland
Tel: 01661 830318
Shoe kits and ready-to-wear Northumberland-made shoes.

SCOTLAND

THE BORDERS, DUMFRIES & GALLOWAY

TOURIST INFORMATION

Dumfries & Galloway Tourist Board
64 Whitesands, Dumfries DG1 2RS
Tel: 01387 245550 and 253862
www.galloway.co.uk

Scottish Borders Tourist Board
TIC, Murray's Green, Jedburgh TD8 6BE
Tel: 0870 607 0250
www.scot-borders.co.uk

ACTIVITIES

Active Sports
Melrose, Borders
Tel: 01896 822452 (head office) or 01750 20118 (centre)
Outdoor activities on water, land and sea.

Annan Activities
Westlands, D & G
Tel: 01461 800274
Quad-biking, go-karting, paintballing, fishing and clay-pigeon shooting.

Barend Riding Centre
Barend, D & G
Tel: 01387 780533
Riding lessons, hacks and treks through forest.

Forest Park Cycles
Kirroughtree Visitor Centre, Palnure, D & G
Tel: 0798 931 8712
Cycle hire and guided rides of Galloway Forest Park.

Galloway Forest Park
N of Newtown Stewart, D & G
Tel: 01671 402420
Forest, moorland and lochs; opportunities for orienteering.

Galloway Sailing Centre
Parton, D & G
Tel: 01644 420626
www.freespace.virgin.net/galloway.sc
Sailing, windsurfing, canoeing, powerboating, improvised rafting, quad-biking and gorge scrambling.

Kirkpatrick McMillan Cycle Trail
Dumfries to Keir Mill, D & G
Signed cycle route dedicated to Kirkpatrick McMillan, the inventor of the pedal bike.

Scottish Border Trails
Peebles, Borders
Tel: 01721 720336
Multi-activity holidays in the Borders.

LEISURE

Logan Botanic Garden
Port Logan, D & G
Tel: 01776 860231
Scotland's most exotic garden; southern-hemisphere trees and plants.

Museum of Lead Mining
Wanlockhead, D & G
Tel: 01659 74387
Guided tour of underground lead mine, plus gold panning.

Open Road Classic Car Hire
Galashiels, Borders
Tel: 01896 751141
Classic car hire by the day or week.

Raiders Road
Nr New Galloway, D & G
Tel: 01671 402420
A 10-mile (16-km) timber road following a riverside cattle rustlers' route.

St Abbs Boat Charter
St Abbs, Borders
Tel: 01890 771681
Boat trips to view cliffs and birds around St Abbs Head.

Sanquhar: The Historic Walk
Sanquhar, D & G
Tel: 01659 50596
Self-guided walk through Sanquhar including the world's oldest working Post Office.

Scottish Academy of Falconry
Bonchester Bridge, Borders
Tel: 01450 860666
Tuition in flying birds of prey, including flying falcons from horseback.

Tweedhope Sheepdogs
Moffat, D & G
Tel: 01683 221471
Working sheepdog demonstrations.

Wildfowl and Wetlands Trust Reserve
Caerlaverock, D & G
Tel: 01387 770200
Saltwater marsh; wild waterfowl viewed from hides and observation towers.

SHOPPING

Art Garden
Moniaive, D & G
Tel: 01848 200466
High-quality and varied art and crafts.

Clog & Shoe Workshop
Balmaclellan, D & G
Tel: 01644 420465
Traditional clogs, from sandals to boots; 18 styles.

Gretna Gateway Outlet Village
Gretna, D & G
Tel: 01461 339028 or 339100
www.gretnagateway.com
Scotland's premier designer outlet centre; up to 50 per cent off.

Hobby House
Melrose, Borders
Tel: 01896 822222
Old-fashioned haberdashers.

North Glen Gallery
Palnackie, D & G
Tel: 01556 600200
Idiosyncratic hand-blown glass designs; visit the workshop for demonstrations.

Scotland's National Book Town
Wigtown, D & G
Tel: 01988 402036
www.wigtown-booktown.co.uk
The main centre for books in Scotland; 15 bookshops in all.

Teddy Melrose
Melrose, Borders
Tel: 01896 823854
Teddy bear museum and shop.

World Famous Old Blacksmith's Shop Centre
Gretna Green, D & G
Tel: 01461 338224 and 338441
www.gretnagreen.com
Knitwear, tartans, cashmere, crystal, luxury foods and gifts.

GLASGOW, THE CLYDE & ARGYLL & BUTE

TOURIST INFORMATION

Argyll, The Isles, Loch Lomond, Stirling and Trossachs Tourist Board
Dept SUK, 7 Alexandria Parade, Dunoon PA23 8AB
Tel: 01369 701000
www.scottish.heartlands.org

Ayrshire & Arran Tourist Board
Burns House, Burns Statue Square, Ayr KA7 1UP
Tel: 01292 288688
www.ayrshire-arran.com

Greater Glasgow & Clyde Valley Tourist Board
11 George Square, Glasgow G2 1DY
Tel: 0141 204 4400
www.seeglasgow.com

ACTIVITIES

Ardgowan Riding Centre
Inverkip, Renfrewshire
Tel: 01475 521390
Tuition, escorted hacks and evening pub rides.

Central Scotland Shooting School
Garbethill Muir, North Lanarkshire
Tel: 01324 851672
Clay-pigeon shooting complex; also lotrout fishery.

Gourock Outdoor Pool
Gourock, Renfrewshire
Tel: 01475 631561
Saltwater heated swimming pool.

Loch Lomond Water Ski Club
Balloch, West Dunbartonshire
Tel: 01389 753000
Water-ski lessons and banana rides.

Royal Troon
Troon, South Ayrshire
Tel: 01292 311555
One of Scotland's most demanding golf courses.

Scotkart Indoor Kart Racing
Cambuslang, Glasgow
Tel: 0141 641 0222
www.scotkart.co.uk
Indoor kart racing on Pro-Karts.

Turnberry
Girvan, South Ayrshire
Tel: 01655 331000
Coastal golf course with stunning views.

LEISURE

Alexander Thomson Society
Ascot Avenue, Glasgow
Tel: 0141 579 7976
Guided architectural and historical walks of Glasgow.

Caledonian MacBrayne Ferries
Gourock, Renfrewshire
Tel: 01475 650100 or 0990 65000 (car reservations)
www.calmac.co.uk
Sailings to 23 Scottish Islands across the Firth of Clyde.

Cruachan 'The Hollow Mountain' Power Station
Dalmally, Argyll
Tel: 01866 822618
World's first high head reversible pumped storage scheme; visit massive underground turbine chamber.

PS *Waverley*
Anderston Quay, Glasgow
Tel: 0141 221 8152
World's last sea-going paddle steamer; sailings on the Firth of Clyde.

Ruby Cruises
Ardfern, Argyll
Tel: 01852 500616
Three-hour sea cruise amongst the 12 Craignish islands and the Corrievreckan whirlpool.

SS *Sir Walter Scott*
Loch Katrine, Perthshire
Tel: 01877 376316
Trips around Loch Katrine on Scotland's only surviving screw steamer.

SHOPPING

Argyle Arcade
Off Buchanan Street/Argyle Street, Glasgow
Tel: 0141 248 5410
One of Britain's oldest covered shopping arcades; over 30 jewellers' shops.

Barras Market
Barras Centre, Glasgow
Tel: 0141 552 7258
Outdoor and indoor market; 100 stalls and 100 shops (Sat and Sun).

Buchanan Galleries
Buchanan Street, Glasgow
Tel: 0141 333 9898
Scotland's most prestigious shopping centre.

Freeport Outlet and Leisure Village
Westwood, West Lothian
Tel: 01501 763488
Designer outlets, high-street names and independent retailers.

Loch Lomond Factory Outlet
Alexandria, Dunbartonshire
Tel: 01389 710077
Over 20 outlets under one roof; save 30 to 80 per cent on designer brands.

Millshop Woollens
Lanark, South Lanarkshire
Tel: 01555 665966
Scottish knitwear at factory prices.

Princes Square
Buchanan Street, Glasgow
Tel: 0141 221 0324
Contemporary fashion, gifts, accessories, crafts and luxuries.

Q Mark
Giffnock, East Renfrewshire
Tel: 0141 633 3535
Scotland's largest factory outlet; clothes and household goods at up to 60 per cent off high-street prices.

EDINBURGH & THE EASTERN LOWLANDS

TOURIST INFORMATION

Angus and Dundee Tourist Board
7–21 Castle Street, Dundee DD1 3AA
Tel: 01382 527527
www.angusanddundee.co.uk

Edinburgh and Lothians Tourist Board
Edinburgh and Scotland TIC, 3 Princes Street, Edinburgh EH2 2QP
Tel: 0131 473 3800
www.edinburgh.org

Kingdom of Fife Tourist Board
St Andrews TIC, 70 Market Street, St Andrews KY16 9NU
Tel: 01334 472021
E-mail:info@kftb.ossian.net
www.standrews.co.uk

Perthshire Tourist Board
Lower City Mills, West Mill Street, Perth
PH1 5QP
Tel: 01738 627958 or 627959
www.perthshire.co.uk

ACTIVITIES

Bike Trax Cycle Hire
Tollcross, Lothian
Tel: 0131 228 6633
www.biketrax.co.uk
Scotland's best selection of bikes.

Lothians and Edinburgh Golf Pass
Tel: 0131 473 3838
www.edinburgh.org/golf
Allows discount on golf course fee.

Markle Fisheries
Markle, East Lothian
Tel: 01620 861213
Three lochs offering fly- and coarse-fishing.

Mavis Hall Park
Humbie, East Lothian
Tel: 01875 833733
Clay-pigeon shooting, 4x4 driving and quad-biking.

Midlothian Ski Centre
Hillend, Midlothian
Tel: 0131 445 4433
Europe's longest artificial ski slope; instruction and practice.

Pentland Hills Icelandics
Carlops, Midlothian
Tel: 01968 661095
Hill rides on rare Icelandic horses.

Port Edgar Sailing School
South Queensferry, West Lothian
Tel: 0131 331 3330
www.ccis.org.uk/pem/
Scotland's largest watersports centre; dinghy and catamaran sailing, cruising, powerboating and canoeing.

LEISURE

Auld Reekie Tours
Niddry Street, Edinburgh
Tel/fax: 0131 557 4700
Designed-to-terrify walking tours of Edinburgh's underground city, pagan temple and haunted vault.

Bo'ness & Kinneil Railway
Bo'ness, West Lothian
Tel: 01506 822298
Steam-train trip to the clay mine at Birkhill.

Guide Friday
Royal Mile, Edinburgh
Tel: 0131 556 2244
Open-top guided bus tours.

Linlithgow Union Canal Society
Linlithgow, West Lothian
Tel: 01506 671215
Boat trips to Avon aqueduct and half-hour cruises; also boats for hire.

Maid of the Forth
South Queensferry, West Lothian
Tel: 0131 331 4857
Cruises from under the Forth Rail Bridge to Incholme Island.

Nelson Monument
Calton Hill, Edinburgh
Tel: 0131 556 2716
Climb 143 steps for superb views.

SHOPPING

Carberry Candle Cottage
Carberry, East Lothian
Tel: 0131 665 5656
Candles made on site.
Edinburgh Bear Co
South Queensferry, West Lothian
Tel: 0131 331 4242
Collectors' and artists' teddy bears.

Edinburgh Crystal Visitor Centre
Eastfield, Midlothian
Tel: 01968 675128
www.edinburgh-crystal.co.uk
Edinburgh crystal from factory shop.

Kilberry Bagpipes
Gilmore Place, Edinburgh
Tel: 0131 221 9925
Manufacturer of bagpipes.

Macsween of Edinburgh
Loanhead, Lothian
Tel: 0131 440 2555
Haggis producers; buy direct from factory.

Q Mark
Stirling, Stirling
Tel: 0800 080080
Large factory outlet; discounted chainstore and designer-labels.

Tappit Hen
Royal Mile, Edinburgh
Tel: 0131 557 1852
Celtic and Scottish jewellery, pewter tankards, flasks and quaichs.

NORTHEASTERN HIGHLANDS

TOURIST INFORMATION

Aberdeen & Grampian Tourist Board
27 Albyn Place, Aberdeen AB10 1YL
Tel: 01224 632727
www.agtb.org

Highlands of Scotland Tourist Board
Peffery House, Strathpeffer, Highland
IV14 9HA
Tel: 0870 514 3070 (brochure hotline)
www.host.co.uk

Orkney Tourist Board
6 Broad Street, Kirwall, Orkney KW15 1NX
Tel: 01856 872856
www.orkney.com

Shetland Islands Tourism
Market Cross, Lerwick, Shetland ZE1 0LU
Tel: 01595 693434
www.shetland-tourism.co.uk

ACTIVITIES

Cairngorm Mountain Experience
Aviemore, Highland
Tel: 01479 861261
Skiing and snowboarding information; year-round chairlift.

Deeside Railway Line
Aberdeen to Peterculter, Aberdeenshire
Walkway from Duthie Park to Peterculter.

Gartly Ski Trail & Mountain Bike Route
Gartly, Aberdeenshire
Tel: 01466 794161
Forest ski trail and bike route.

Glencoe Mountain Sport
Ballachulish, Argyll & Bute
Tel/fax: 01855 811472
Highlands mountain activity holidays.

Glencoe Ski Centre
Glencoe, Argyll & Bute
Tel: 01855 851226
Popular skiing area.

Loch Inch Watersports & Skiing Centre
Kincraig, Highland
Tel: 01540 651272
Watersports and skiing centre.

Nevis Range
Torlundy, Highland
Tel: 01397 705825
www. sol.co.uk/nevisrange
Skiing, walking, cycling, mountain biking and gondola trips.

Tomintoul Riding Centre
Tomintoul, Moray
Tel: 01807 580210
Trekking, hacking and trail riding.

LEISURE

Glencoe Cruises
Glencoe, Argyll & Bute
Tel/fax: 01855 811658
Cruises on Loch Leven.

Glenfiddich Distillery
Dufftown, Moray
Tel: 01340 820373
Guided tours of whisky distillery.

Highland Wildlife Park
Kincraig, Highland
Tel: 01540 651270
www.kincraig.com/wildlife
Scottish wildlife.

Jacobite Cruises
Inverness, Highland
Tel: 01463 233999
Cruises on Caledonian Canal and Loch Ness.

Keith & Dufftown Railway
Dufftown, Moray
Tel: 01340 821181
Heritage railway; Keith to Dufftown.

P&O Scottish Ferries
Aberdeen, Aberdeenshire
Tel: 01224 572615
Ferries to Orkney and Shetland.

Strathspey Steam Railway
Aviemore to Boat of Garten, Highland
Tel: 01479 810725
5-mile (8-km) steam-train ride.

SHOPPING

Dean's of Huntly Factory Shop
Huntly, Aberdeenshire
Tel: 01466 792086
Shortbread and preserves.

Foggieley Sheepskin Rugs
Craigievar, Aberdeenshire
Tel: 013398 83317
Sheepskin rugs and clothing.

Just Scottish
Aberdeen, Aberdeenshire
Tel: 01224 621755
Ceramics, knitwear, textiles, silver and jewellery.

Paintings & Pullovers
Glenmuick, Aberdeenshire
Tel: 013397 55678
Original paintings and prints; hand-made knitwear.

Ugie Salmon Fisherings
Peterhead, Aberdeenshire
Tel: 01779 476209
Scotland's oldest fish house.

Walkers Shortbread
Aberlour-on-Spey, Moray
Tel: 01340 871555
Shortbread from factory shop.

The Whisky Shop
Dufftown, Moray
Tel: 01340 821097
Specialist whisky shop.

THE WESTERN HIGHLANDS & ISLANDS

TOURIST INFORMATION

Highlands of Scotland Tourist Board
Peffery House, Strathpeffer, Highland
IV14 9HA
Tel: 0870 514 3070 (brochure hotline)
www.host.co.uk

Western Isles Tourist Board
26 Cromwell Street, Stornoway, Isle of Lewis HS1 2DD
Tel: 01851 703088
www.witb.co.uk

ACTIVITIES

Fairwinds Bicycle Hire
Broadford, Isle of Skye, Highland
Tel/fax: 01471 822270
Cycle hire for island exploration.

Hebridean Exploration
Stornoway, Isle of Lewis, Western Isles
Tel: 01851 705655
www.hebex.co.uk
Guided sea-kayak tours.

Hebridean Surf Holidays
Stornoway, Isle of Lewis, Western Isles
Tel/fax: 01851 705862
Surfing holidays.

Ross Rentals
Strathcarron, Highland
Tel: 01520 722205
Car, bike, boat, canoe, fishing rod and equipment hire.

Rua Reidh Lighthouse Outdoor Centre
Melvaig, Highland
Tel: 01445 771263
Rock-climbing and abseiling instruction; also guided walks.

Uig Pony Trekking Centre
Uig, Isle of Skye, Highland
Tel: 01470 542205
Trekking in Fairy Glen.

Uist Outdoor Centre
Lochmaddy, Isle of North Uist,
Western Isles
Tel/fax: 01876 500480
Diving, watersports, climbing, field studies and wildlife watch.

LEISURE

Bella Jane Boat Trips
Elgol, Isle of Skye, Highland
Tel: 0800 731 3089 (freephone)
www.bellajane.demon.co.uk
Trips to Loch Coruisk and the Cuillins.

Glenfinnan Station Museum
Glenfinnan, Highland
Tel: 01397 722295
Restored railway station; museum for West Highland Railway.

Island Cruising
Uig, Isle of Lewis, Western Isles
Tel: 01851 672381
Wildlife, diving and bird-watching cruises around Western Isles.

Logan Air
Tel: 0345 222111
Air services to the Western Isles including Barra and its beach landing.

Scotpackers Bus Co
Ullapool, Highland
Tel: 01854 613126
Scenic guided minibus tours through the Highlands; also bike hire.

Summer Queen Cruises
Ullapool, Highland
Tel: 01854 612472
Cruises to the Summer Isles.

Trading Post Airboats
Bonar Bridge, Sutherland
Tel: 01863 766225
Sea-plane tours to areas not accessible by normal boat.

SHOPPING

Caithness Glass Factory & Visitor Centre
Wick, Caithness
Tel: 01955 602286
Factory tours and shop.

Cioch Direct Mountainsports & Leisurewear
Struan, Isle of Skye, Highland
Tel/fax: 01471 822270
Clothing for outdoor activities made on the premises.

Harris Tweed Authority
Stornoway, Isle of Lewis, Western Isles
Tel: 01851 702269
www.harristweed.org
Harris Tweed promotion.

Highland Stoneware
Lochinver, Sutherland
Tel: 01571 844376
Distinctive, high-quality hand-painted ceramics.

Lewis Loom Centre
Stornoway, Isle of Lewis, Western Isles
Tel: 01851 704500
Harris Tweed production demonstrated and items for sale.

Lochcarron Weavers
Lochcarron, Highland
Tel: 01520 722212
Manufacturers of world's largest range of pure wool tartans.

Orcadian Stone Co
Golspie, Sutherland
Tel: 01408 633483
Clocks, lamps and giftware made from local stone.

Skye Jewellery
Broadford, Isle of Skye, Highland
Tel/fax: 01471 822100
www.skyejewellery.co.uk
Gold and silver Celtic rings hand-crafted in own workshop.

Unlimited Colour Co
Ledmore, Sutherland
Tel/fax: 01854 666293
www.ullapool.co.uk/bothy
Hand-woven weavings, tapestries, scarves, throws, cushions, hats and wall hangings.

Stuart Crystal
Chepstow, Monmouthshire
Tel: 01291 620135
Quality cut-crystal from factory shop.

Welsh Porcelain Co
Maesteg, Neath Port Talbot
Tel: 01656 73499
Traditional Welsh pottery.

WALES

THE BRECON BEACONS & SOUTH WALES

TOURIST INFORMATION

Wales Tourist Board
Dept GE1, PO Box 1, Cardiff CF24 2XN
Tel: 029 2047 5226
www.visitwales.com

ACTIVITIES

Axis Paragliding & Hang-gliding Centre
Abergavenny, Monmouthshire
Tel: 01873 850910
www.paraglide.co.uk

Celtic Trail Cycle Route
Tel: 0800 243731 (info line)
Cycleway from Severn Bridge to Pembrokeshire Coast National Park.

Gwent Grass Ski Centre
Llanowell, Monmouthshire
Tel: 01291 672652
Grass-skiing and all-terrain boarding; equipment hire and tuition.

Llanthony Riding and Trekking
Llanthony, Monmouthshire
Tel: 01873 890359
www.llanthony.co.uk
Treks and hacks around Llanthony Priory.

Monmouth Canoe and Activity Centre
Monmouth, Monmouthshire
Tel/fax: 01600 713461
Canoeing on River Wye; also caving, rock-climbing and abseiling.

Monmouthshire and Brecon Canal
Goytre Wharf, Llanover, Monmouthshire
Tel/fax: 01873 881069
www.britishwaterways.co.uk
Boating, canoeing, fishing and walking.

Pedalabikeaway
Abergavenny, Monmouthshire
Tel/fax: 01873 830219
www.btinternet.com/~Pedal/abikeaway
Bike hire; bikes delivered.

LEISURE

Big Pit Mining Museum
Blaenafon, Torfaen
Tel: 01495 790311
www.citypages.co.ukwalesnpbigpit
Travel underground to a disused coal mine.

Brecon Mountain Railway
Pant, Merthyr Tydfil
Tel: 01685 722988
Narrow-gauge steam-train ride through Brecon Beacons.

Butetown History Tour
Cardiff
Tel: 029 2046 3833
Guided walking tour of Cardiff's historic waterfront.

Cwmcarn Forest Drive & Visitor Centre
Cwmcarn, Caerphilly
Tel: 01495 272001
Scenic drive, walking and cycling routes.

Museum of Welsh Life
St Fagans, Cardiff
Tel: 029 2057 3500
Open-air museum; over 40 re-erected buildings from all over Wales.

Rhondda Heritage Park
Trehafod, Pontypridd
Tel: 01443 682036
Ex-miners give guided tours of coal mines.

SHOPPING

Craft in the Bay
Cardiff
Tel: 029 2048 4611
Various crafts by members of the Makers Guild in Wales.

Festival Park Factory Shopping Village
Ebbw Vale, Blaenau Gwent
Tel: 01494 350010
38 shops with discounted brand-name and designer-label items.

Model House
Llantrisant, Pontypridd
Tel: 01443 237758
Traditional and modern Welsh crafts.

PEMBROKESHIRE & THE SOUTHWEST

TOURIST INFORMATION

Carmarthenshire County Council
Tourism and Countryside, Ty'r Nant, Trostre Business Park, Llanelli SA14 9UT
Tel: 01554 747508
www.carmarthenshire.gov.uk

Pembrokeshire Holidays
PO Box 103, Pembroke Dock SA72 6TQ
Tel: 01646 682278
www.pembrokeshire-holidays.com

Tourism South & West Wales
Charter Court, Enterprise House, Swansea SA7 9DB
Tel: 01792 781300

ACTIVITIES

Clyn Du Riding Centre
Burry Port, Pembrokeshire
Tel: 01554 832546 or 834084
Cross-country, dressage and show jumping.

Heatherton Country Sports Park
St Florence, Pembrokeshire
Tel: 01646 651025
www.heatherton2000.freeserve.co.uk
Country sports; boating, karting, horse-riding, golf and archery.

Pembrokeshire Walking Holidays
Haverfordwest, Pembrokeshire
Tel: 01437 766664
www.pembrokeshire-walking-holidays.co.uk
Tailor-made, self-guided walking holidays.

Pembrokeshire Watersports
East Llanion, Pembrokeshire
Tel: 01646 622013
Paddle, power and sail watersports.

Pembry Country Park
Burry Port, Carmarthenshire
Tel: 01554 833913 or 834443
Dry-ski slope, toboggan run, orienteering, horse-riding, pitch and putt and miniature railway.

West Wales Wind, Surf and Sailing
Dale, Pembrokeshire
Tel/fax: 01646 636642
www.heatherton2000.freeserve.co.uk
Watersports centre.

LEISURE

Gwili Steam Railway
Bronwydd Arms, Pembrokeshire
Tel: 01267 230666
Steam-train ride to wooded picnic area.

Kidwelly Industrial Museum
Kidwelly, Carmarthenshire
Tel: 01554 891078
Original tinplate works.

Millennium Coastal Park
Llanelli, Carmarthenshire
Tel: 01554 777744
Cycleway/footpath overlooking Burry Estuary.

National Botanic Garden of Wales
Llanarthne, Carmarthenshire
Tel: 01558 668768
www.gardenofwales.co.uk
Botanical science showcase; Great Glasshouse, gardens and lakes.

Skomer Island
Boat from Martin's Haven, Pembrokeshire
Tel: 01646 601636 (boat); 01437 765462 (accommodation)
National Nature Reserve, one of the best places in southern Britain to view sea birds and seals.

Wildfowl & Wetlands Trust Llanelli
Llanelli, Carmarthenshire
Tel: 01554 741087
Ducks, geese, swans and flamingoes on ponds, lakes and reed beds.

SHOPPING

Farmhouse Cheesemaking & Museum
Carmarthen, Carmarthenshire
Tel: 01267 237905
Caerphilly cheese made on the farm.

Gwili Pottery
Pontarsais, Pembrokeshire
Tel: 01267 253449
Hand-thrown, decorated ceramics.

Laugharne Glass
Laugharne, Carmarthenshire
Tel: 01994 427476
Hand-made glass; scent bottles, bowls and vases.

Pembrokeshire Art and Craft Trails
Tel: 0990 103103
Booklet (available from TICs) of centres and craftspeople in Pembrokeshire.

Pembrokeshire Craft Makers
Tel: 01559 362056
Leaflet (available from TICs) of craft specialists.

Trapp Art & Crafts Centre
Trapp, Pembrokeshire
Tel: 01269 850362
Welsh craft and works by local artists.

MID WALES

TOURIST INFORMATION

Mid Wales Tourism
Marketing Department, The Station, Machynlleth SY20 8TG
Tel: 0800 273747 (freephone)

ACTIVITIES

Cyclemart
Cilcennin, Ceredigion
Tel: 01570 470079
Mountain-bike hire, also BMX hire for use on adjoining track.

Lake Vyrnwy
West of Llanfyllin, Powys
Tel: 01691 870346
Walking, watersports, cycling, bird-watching and trout fishing.

Offa's Dyke Centre
Knighton, Powys
Tel: 01547 528753 or 529424
www.offa.demon.co.uk/offa
Information on the Offa's Dyke Path.

Rheidol Riding Centre
Capel Bangor, Ceredigion
Tel: 01970 880863
Riding on tracks, hills and in forests.

Wern Riding Centre
Crickhowell, Powys
Tel: 01873 810899 or 810152
Hacking, trekking and trail rides; panoramic views.

LEISURE

Aberystwyth Electric Cliff Railway
Aberystwyth, Ceredigion
Tel: 01970 617642
Britain's longest electric cliff railway.

Devil's Bridge Falls
Devil's Bridge, Ceredigion
Tel: 01970 890233
Wooded gorge and waterfalls.

Heart of Wales Line
Shrewsbury to Swansea
Tel: 0870 9000772
Passes through lovely countryside; many stations are the starting point of walks.

Kite Country Centre and Museum
Tregaron, Ceredigion
Tel: 01974 298977

Lywernog Silver-Lead Mine
Ponterwyd, Ceredigion
Tel: 01970 890620
Visit the mine dressed in mining gear and pan for fool's gold.

Vale of Rheidol Railway
Aberystwyth to Devil's Bridge, Ceredigion
Tel: 01970 625819
Narrow-gauge steam railway to the Devil's Bridge beauty spot (Apr–Oct).

SHOPPING

Museum of the Welsh Woollen Industry
Drefach Felindre, Carmarthenshire
Tel: 01559 370929
www.nmgw.ac.uk
Working woollen mill; traditional Welsh flannel, cloth and shawls.

New Quay Honey Farm
Cross Inn, Ceredigion
Tel: 01545 560822
Working honey farm; shop sells honey, mead, honey products, beeswax and bee-keeping equipment.

The Old Station
Welshpool, Powys
Tel: 01938 556622
Womens and menswear, outdoor wear, Welsh crafts, gifts and souvenirs.

Rhiannon Welsh Gold Centre
Tregaron, Ceredigion
Tel: 01974 298415
www.rhiannon.co.uk
Celtic-design silver, gold and Rhiannon Welsh gold jewellery.

Silver Scenes
Berriew, Powys
Tel: 01686 640695
Silver-plated gifts.

Welsh Royal Crystal
Rhayader, Powys
Tel: 01597 811005
Welsh crystal from factory shop.

SNOWDONIA, ANGLESEY & NORTH WALES

TOURIST INFORMATION

North Wales Tourism
77 Conwy Road, Colwyn Bay LL29 7LN
Tel: 01492 531731
www.nwt.co.uk

ACTIVITIES

Dolgellau Angling Association
Dolgellau, Gwynedd
Tel: 01341 422706
Salmon and sea-trout fishing.

Meifod-Isaf
Dyffryn Ardwy, Gwynedd
Tel: 01341 247651
Horse-riding and trekking centre.

Parc Glasfryn
Pwllheli, Gwynedd
Tel: 01766 810202
Go-karting or quad-trekking.

Rhiw Goch Ski and Mountain Bike Centre
Bronaber, Gwynedd
Tel: 01766 540578
Skiing, snowboarding and bike hire.

Snowdonia Llamas
Meet tour guides at start of trek by arrangement, Gwynedd
Tel: 01766 530444
www.llamas.co.uk
Llama treks through Snowdonia.

Tyddyn Philip Activity Centre/Bike Centre
Brynteg, Anglesey
Tel: 01248 853439
Canoeing, rock-climbing, abseiling, orienteering, archery, plus mountain-bike hire.

LEISURE

Ffestiniog Railway
Porthmadog to Blaenau Ffestiniog, Gwynedd
Tel: 01766 512340
E-mail: info@festrail.demon.co.uk
www.festrail.co.uk
Steam-train ride through Snowdonia.

Great Orme Tramway
Llandudno, Conwy
Tel: 01492 574237
Victorian tramway to the summit of Great Orme.

Llanberis Lake Railway
Llanberis, Gwynedd
Tel: 01286 870549
www.lake-railway.freeserve.co.uk
Lakeside steam-train ride.

Pontcysyllte Aqueduct and Horse-drawn Boat Trips
Llangollen, Denbighshire
Tel: 01978 860702
Narrow-boat trip to Pontcysyllte Aqueduct; horse-drawn narrow-boat trips.

Snowdon Mountain Railway
Llanberis, Gwynedd
Tel: 01286 870223
www.snowdonrailway.force9.co.uk
Britain's only public rack-and-pinion railway; views of Snowdon.

Sygun Copper Mine
Beddgelert, Gwynedd
Tel: 01766 510100 or 510101
Tour of 18th- and 19th-century copper mine; gold panning.

SHOPPING

Anglesey Pullover Co
Rhoscolyn, Anglesey
Tel/fax: 01407 860861
www.anglesey-pullover.co.uk
Original Welsh-wool Anglesey pullovers.

Bryn Melyn Studio Pottery
Llanelltyd, Gwynedd
Tel: 01341 430651
One of Wales' leading craft workshops; hand-made ceramics.

Corris Craft Centre
Corris, Gwynedd
Tel: 01654 761584
Wooden toys to candles.

James Pringle Weavers
Llanfairpwllgwyngyll, Anglesey
Tel: 01248 717171
Clothing, Welsh crafts, gifts and souvenirs.

Penmachno Woollen Mill
Penmachno, Gwynedd
Tel: 01690 710545
Penmachno rugs, knitwear and gifts.

St Asaph Tweedmill Factory Outlets
St Asaph, Denbighshire
Tel: 01745 730072
High-street fashions, luggage and gifts at factory prices.

INDEX

A

B

C

D

E

F

S

T

U

ACKNOWLEDGEMENTS

Contributors: Roly Smith, Hugh Taylor, Moira McCrossan, Des Hannigan, Nia Williams, Hilary Weston, Martin Dunning

Editorial: Suzanne Juby, Pam Stagg, Jo Sturges, David Hancock, Marie Lorimer, Maria Morgan, Colin Follett

Maps: Jenny Gill
Paste up: Kingfisher Design
Cover design: Andrew Milne Design
Illustrators: Ann Winterbotham, Peter Byatt, Brian Smith, Mark McLaughlin, Chris Orr Associates
Icon illustrations: Robin Lawrie

PICTURE CREDITS

The Automobile Association wishes to thank the following photographers and libraries for their assistance in the preparation of this book.

Action Plus 191b (Max Earey); **Cadbury World** 136c; **Bruce Coleman Collection** 172t, 259b, 275b, 285t; **Collections** 143t (Roy Stedall-Humphryes), 161c (Jonathan Hodson), 186c (Ashley Cooper), 190c (Roger Scruton); **Dartington Crystal** 27tl; **Dumfries & Galloway Tourist Board** 225b (Great Scot); **Gettyone/Stone** 8br, 46t, 55b, 58/9, 73t; **Robert Harding Picture Library** 14tr, 27tr, 35tl, 65b, 142tr, 144c, 159t, 193t, 197b; **International Photobank** 21, 30t, 31b, 32t, 41t, 47b, 63b, 64tr, 105tl, 186b, 204t, 273b, 274t; **Logan Botanic Gardens** 223b; **The Photolibrary Wales** 9br, 15b, 266tl, 267tc, 267tr, 269t, 271b, 274b, 275c, 276t, 276b, 277c, 277b, 279b, 284t, 286t, 287t, 289b, 291b; **Powerstock/Zefa** 35tr, 121b, 232b; **Rex Features Ltd** 57b, 90t, 122c, 225t; **Scotland In Focus** 8t (R Weir), 8bl (R Weir), 9bl (J MacPherson), 213b (A G Johnston), 248t (S J Whitehorne), 251b (R Weir), 254c (R Weir), 258b (R Weir); **Scottish Highland Photo-Library** 9tr, 225c; **Spectrum Colour Library** 40b, 49b, 50t, 51tr, 144t, 145b, 182bl, 182br, 196c; **Sutton Motorsport Images** 139b (Bearne); **Woburn Abbey** 97c; **Wookey Hole Caves** 39b; **World Pictures Ltd** 13b, 30c, 99b, 117tl, 146b.

The remaining photographs are held in the Association's own photo library (AA PHOTO LIBRARY) and were taken by the following photographers:

M Adelman 195t; **P Aithie** 279t, 288b, 295t; **M Alexander** 220, 221, 223t, 224t, 224c, 226t, 227t, 238c, 238b; **A Baker** 57tr, 108b, 120b, 186t, 229b, 241tr, 260/1; **J Baker** 46b; **P Baker** 13tr, 18b, 20t, 20b, 22t, 22b, 23t, 23b, 25b, 26b, 31tr, 44b, 45t, 48tr, 70t, 77tl, 79, 84t, 85t, 85b, 132, 134b, 136t, 136b, 138c, 141b, 142b, 145t, 148, 149l, 150t, 150b, 152t, 152b, 158b, 189t; **S Bates** 91t; **V Bates** 68t, 69b, 275; **J Beazley** 59tr, 153t, 157b, 162c, 174t, 201b, 208, 209t, 209b, 210b, 211, 212b, 214b, 216, 222t, 222b, 226b, 239t, 255b; **P Bennett** 193b, 194b; **A Besley** 10/1, 18t; **M Birkitt** 29, 97t, 97b, 100b, 102t, 102c, 102b, 103t, 109cl, 109cr, 110t, 111t, 111b, 138b, 142tl, 142c, 143b, 154b, 155b, 164/5, 261c; **E A Bowness** 201t, 203c, 205t, 206t, 206b, 207c; **P Brown** 71b, 76t, 77b, 146t; **D Burchill** 173tl; **I Burgum** 57c, 58t, 125t, 128c, 137b, 264, 265, 267b, 268t, 268c, 270c, 273t, 273c, 282t, 283b, 285b, 286b, 287b, 290t, 293b, 294b; **J Carnie** 230tl, 235c, 254b **C Coe** 110c, 110b, 261t; **D Corrance** 227b, 241tl, 294c; **J Cox** 106c (bird illustrations); **D Croucher** 2/3, 7, 9tl, 63t, 66b, 67t, 165r, 260t, 262/3, 269b, 281, 284b, 289t; **S Day** 28c, 36, 37bl, 37br, 39t, 40t, 41b, 42b, 43b, 49t, 51b, 56t, 101b, 112, 114/5, 118t, 118c, 118b, 119t, 119b, 120tr, 121tr, 122t, 160b, 165l, 166/7, 168, 169t, 169b, 170b, 173tr, 174c, 175t, 175b, 177t, 180c, 217l, 232t, 232c, 234t, 237tl, 240b, 242t, 243t, 243b, 245t, 246t, 246b, 247tr, 255t, 262/3; **R Eames** 161t, 291c; **E Ellington** 248b, 249tr, 250b, 256c, 256b; **R Elliot** 234b, 238t, 253b, 254t, 259t; **P Enticknap** 48b; **D Forss** 60/1, 64tl, 65tl, 72t, 72c, 73b, 74t, 74b, 75b, 78, 80t, 81b, 82t, 82b, 94t, 95b, 98t, 99t, 105tr, 106t, 113r, 214tr; **J Gravell** 277t, 278t, 278b; **V Greaves** 133b, 158c; **A Grierley** 295b; **S Gibson** 229t; **T Griffiths** 173b, 174b; **J Henderson** 112/3, 242c, 252, 256t, 257b; **A Hopkins** 64b, 113l, 150c, 151t, 152c, 153b, 154t, 154c, 155t, 282c, 290b; **C Jones** 50b, 51tl, 54b, 59tl, 59c, 96, 100t, 101t, 103b, 121tl, 126t, 126b, 127tl, 127tr, 127b, 130b, 147b, 157t, 163b, 266, 275t, 288t, 292t, 292c, 292b, 293t, 294t; **P Kenward** 88t, 89t; **A Lawson** 14b, 24c, 24b; **C Lees** 204b, 207b, 210t, 210c, 212tl, 212tr, 213t, 215tr; **S&O Matthews** 66t, 84b, 106b, 117tr, 156, 188b, 214tl, 215tl, 283t; **J McMillan** 86, 87t; **E Meacher** 42t, 44t, 57tl; **J Miller** 83t, 83b, 94b; **C Molyneux** 217r, 270t, 270b, 271t, 284t, 284c; **J Morrison** 187t, 187b, 188c, 190b, 198tl, 198tr, 198b, 199t, 199b; **R Mort** 90cl; **R Moss** 13tl, 15t, 16t, 16c, 16b, 17t, 17b, 18c, 19t, 19b, 26t, 33t, 34b; **J Mottishaw** 160t, 162b, 171b, 172b, 178c, 178b; **R Newton** 34t, 47t, 48tl, 53tl, 144b, 291t; **D Noble** 70b, 76c; **K Paterson** 228, 230tr, 230b, 235t, 235b, 237tr, 237bl, 239b, 240t, 250t, 258t; **A Perkins** 109b; **N Ray** 33b, 43t; **G Rowatt** 196b; **M Short** 55t, 56b, 123t, 123b, 130t, 130c; **P Short** 202t, 202b, 203b, 207t, 224b, 231, 251t; **B Smith** 92c; **T Souter** 65tr, 67c, 68b, 71t, 108t; **F Stephenson** 122b, 125b, 133t; **A Stonehouse** 14tl; **R Strange** 77tr, 88c, 88bl, 88br, 92t; **R Surman** 104, 205b; **D Tarn** 179t, 182t, 183t, 184, 185t, 185b, 188t, 189b, 190t, 191t; **M Taylor** 241b, 245b, 257t; **T Teegan** 30b; **J A Tims** 89b, 90cr, 91b, 92b, 95t; **M Trelawny** 75t; **A Trynor** 149r, 151b; **W Voysey** 25t, 31t, 32b, 43c, 67b, 69tl, 69tr, 69c, 72b, 74c, 76b, 80b, 81t, 81c, 87b, 94c, 107t, 116, 124, 128b, 131b; **R Weir** 233, 237br, 247b, 249tl, 249b, 250c, 253t; **L Wells** 98b; **J Welsh** 131t, 135t, 135b, 137t, 159b, 163t; **L Whitwam** 162t, 170tl, 170tr, 171t, 177b, 180t, 181b, 194t, 215b; **H Williams** 24t, 27b, 28t, 53tr, 53b, 54t, 107b, 128t, 129t, 129b, 218/9, 268b; **P Wilson** 178t, 180b, 181t, 182c, 183b, 196tl, 196tr; **G Wrona** 90b, 93t; **J Wyand** 38t, 117b, 123c, 134c, 139t, 158t, 160c.